PENGUIN BOOKS
INDIRA GANDHI

Pupul Jayakar was born in Etawah, Uttar Pradesh, in 1915. She was closely involved with the development of indigenous culture, handicrafts and textiles since the country achieved independence in 1947. She was the Chairman of the All India Handicrafts Board, Chairman of the Governing Body of the National Institute of Design, Chairman of the Handicraft and Handloom Exports Corporation of India, Chairman of the National Institute of Fashion Technology, Chairman of the Crafts Museum of India, Chairman of the Calico Museum of Textiles and Chairman of the Festival of India in Great Britain, France, USA and Japan, Chairman of the Indian National Trust for Art and Cultural Heritage (INTACH) and a member of the Krishnamurti Foundation India.

She was also Chairman of the Krishnamurti Foundation, India, and published a bestselling biography of Krishnamurti in 1986. She wrote several other books, including *The Earth Mother, The Children of Barren Women, The Buddha* and *God is Not a Full-Stop,* a volume of short stories.

Pupul Jayakar died in 1997 in Bombay.

D1121281

Books by the same author

- *God is not a Full-stop*
- *The Earthen Drum*
- *The Buddha*
- *J. Krishnamurti: A Biography*
- *The Earth Mother*
- *Indira Gandhi: A Biography (with Raghu Rai)*

PUPUL JAYAKAR

Indira Gandhi

A Biography

PENGUIN BOOKS

PENGUIN BOOKS

Published by the Penguin Group

Penguin Books India Pvt. Ltd, 11 Community Centre, Panchsheel Park,
New Delhi 110 017, India

Penguin Group (USA) Inc., 375 Hudson Street, New York, New York 10014,
USA

Penguin Group (Canada), 90 Eglinton Avenue East, Suite 700, Toronto, Ontario,
M4P 2Y3, Canada (a division of Pearson Penguin Canada Inc.)

Penguin Books Ltd, 80 Strand, London WC2R 0RL, England

Penguin Ireland, 25 St Stephen's Green, Dublin 2, Ireland (a division of Penguin
Books Ltd)

Penguin Group (Australia), 707 Collins Street, Melbourne, Victoria 3008, Australia
(a division of Pearson Australia Group Pty Ltd)

Penguin Group (NZ), 67 Apollo Drive, Rosedale, Auckland 0632,
New Zealand (a division of Pearson New Zealand Ltd)

Penguin Group (South Africa) (Pty) Ltd, Block D, Rosebank Office Park,
181 Jan Smuts Avenue, Parktown North, Johannesburg 2193, South Africa

Penguin Books Ltd, Registered Offices: 80 Strand, London WC2R 0RL, England

First published in Viking by Penguin Books India 1992
Reprinted in 1993
This revised edition published in Penguin Books 1995

Copyright © Pupul Jayakar 1988, 1992, 1995

All rights reserved

22 21 20 19 18 17 16

ISBN 9780140114621

For sale in India and Sri Lanka only

Typeset in Times Roman by dTech, New Delhi
Printed at Repro India Ltd., Navi Mumbai

How vast and interesting and how beautiful is our country.
How different is the climate, the scenery, how very different
the people and their customs in each part. Yet so few of us
have the time or the means to break through the narrow walls
of daily routine that enclose our lives, to get to know this
immense space of land that is India, to enjoy her loveliness
and to make friends with our fellow country-men who speak
a tongue and think thoughts that are not our own. How I wish
I were with you as you spread the magic message of freedom
from one distant corner to another.

— Indira Nehru (aged twenty) in a letter,
written from Oxford, to her father
Jawaharlal Nehru on 4 February 1938

Contents

Foreword

A serious biography is a dialogue between the author and the unfolding personality of the individual portrayed. The task becomes more complex when the life of the author is linked in several ways with the subject; for then the author has to measure her perceptions against a people's view of the individual and her actions.

This is not a political biography, but Indira Gandhi's life was part of the unfolding history of India, intricately woven with India's past and future. It becomes inevitable, therefore, that politics forms a backdrop to her public and often private actions. The book seeks clues to her life through access to the many personalities that lay hidden within her. And, if possible, to uncover and reveal Indira Gandhi's thoughts and feelings, her hates and prejudices, her insights and her ignorance, and her loves and the emotional entanglements that generated action. It is this alone that gives density to the material, enables Indira Gandhi to come alive. Unfortunately, we deify and worship our heroes and so destroy them.

It was in the 1970s that Prime Minister Indira Gandhi first asked me to write her biography. She was prepared not only to help me but to spend time with me—a Prime Minister's time—to enable me to understand the contradictions that made her life so complex and obscure. I had hesitated, telling her that to write a biography of a friend and Prime Minister was an impossibility and would lead inevitably to the loss of a friend. Years passed and a fortnight before her death, finding Indira Gandhi in a particularly mature and mellow mood, I suggested that I start an oral biography of her life. She was quick to respond, with a swiftness that took me by surprise.

Over the next four days, two interviews were arranged. Out of this came four hours of tape recording, in which she repeated many things she had already told me but also spoke of her more intimate relationships and hinted at her vision of the future. It was an ongoing story which was to continue over the next year. Her death brought this recording to an abrupt end. I had maintained, however, over the years, several handwritten notebooks of meetings and conversations with her; these I have re-created for the biography.

Although Indira Gandhi seldom discussed politics with me, she was eager to explore the Indian mind, its strengths and its weaknesses and she was frank and free in her views of political comrades and opponents. She had a sense of humour and, at times, enjoyed gossiping and hearing what people had to say of her and her government. During the years she was out of power, I spent much time with her. It was during this period that I came to understand, to an extent, the way her mind worked. She often spoke of a time when she loved with passion and hated with an equal energy, but she said that the hatred had, over the years, faded away.

During our talks she recalled some of her conversations with world leaders. Her observations were astute and detailed and she had an extraordinary skill of reaching what lay beyond the word. Her defeat in 1977 and the manner in which many of her associates had reacted left her with a deep sense of betrayal and sorrow. 'Sorrow comes in like a circle and cannot be rolled up as a mat,' she had commented on an occasion. She had an intense sensitivity to beauty: beauty healed some of her wounds.

Raj Mohan Gandhi, author and political pundit, grandson of the Mahatma, writing in *The Washington Post* of 1 November 1984, immediately after Indira Gandhi's assassination, comments:

> No unprejudiced chronicler will fail to note her ability to make the tough choice, take the hard gamble and stand unmoved before a hostile crowd. Her charm and astonishing stamina, her 1980 comeback, her fortitude when she tragically lost a son, Sanjay—these too will be recorded. And her independence. She was no one's and no superpower's stooge.

Indira Gandhi's life spanned over two-thirds of a century. It coincided with monumental happenings in India and the world. At the time of her birth, the rational and liberal world of the nineteenth and early twentieth century was fading away.

Luminous figures concerned with the sacred and its relevance to humanity and nature, were born, lived and taught in India. They were the prophets of a new age. Their teachings emphasized the perennial truth that India had sought to discover through millennia of search. Every age demanded a discovery of the truth, to meet the challenges of a changing world and of a disoriented humanity.

A vital political and economic force was rising in Europe. The outbreak of the Russian Revolution coincided with the month of Indira's birth. It was also during this period that strong and powerful figures emerged in India to fight the battle for freedom and independence. They emerged from all walks of life, for few shirked the terrors and the poverty the fight enjoined. Two great world wars were fought during her life. Their fallout generated explosions in science and technology. The concept of time, space and energy underwent immeasurable changes. A revolution in electronics and communications had invaded human consciousness. The human brain could no longer keep pace with the velocity of change or comprehend the interlinks between scientific discoveries, economic structures, religious frenzy and simple human values.

Commentators and critics have held Indira responsible for the breakdown of institutions and the distortions that entered the body politic. Unfortunately, they see the scenario as a static one where the old institutions could survive and continue at their own pace. But the world was in flux; the nuclear threat had reached its peak; whispers of doom from the ravaged environment were about to enter human consciousness; national frontiers were changing; human values were seeking new dimensions; the speed of events and a rapidly escalating population had brought an instability to the environment, to institutions and to the human psyche. Indira could at times sustain, could destroy, but she lacked the skill and the insights, in the midst of an earthquake, to structure the new or build institutions and relationships relevant to the future.

At the end of her life Indira Gandhi had one major concern: whether India could survive with its wisdom intact; for without this wisdom what was India? She died having posited the question but without finding an answer.

It was in 1986 that I decided to write the biography of Indira Gandhi. She was a controversial person and the controversies had not ended with her death. She was misunderstood and often misrepresented. I knew that I owed it to her to write and so I spoke to her son, the then Prime Minister, Rajiv Gandhi, and it was with his support that I commenced the story. In reply to a letter from me, he commented: 'You will recall that when you first told me about writing a book on my mother, I welcomed the idea. You knew her for so long and so well' He had promised to make available to me her correspondence with philosophers, scientists, artists, poets and others. He had also said that it would be possible to share some of her private papers with me. What was secret would of course not be available. Yet, in the three years after 1986 that he was the Prime Minister, no papers were forthcoming from Rajiv Gandhi or Sonia Gandhi, nor were they prepared to grant me an interview. This made my task more difficult as Rajiv Gandhi's perceptions of some of the actions of his mother would have been of great value. I had therefore to rely on my own observations, conversations, letters, diaries, newspapers and a number of interviews with her political colleagues and opponents, to tell her story.

I am deeply grateful to B.K. Nehru and Fori Nehru for making available to me their correspondence with Indira Gandhi, and to B.K. (Biju) for the time he spared for the interviews I held with him. Amongst the vast number of people who were prepared to meet and talk to me on tape, I would like to thank the late Vijayalakshmi Pandit, Atal Behari Vajpayeeji, the late Uma Shankar Dikshitji, the late Pandit Kamalapati Tripathi, C. Subramaniam, the late Achyut Patwardhan, Dev Kant Barooah, L.K. Jha, Dr P.C. Alexander, Dr P.N. Dhar, R.N. Kao, I.K. Gujral, Vasant Sathe, Dorothy Norman, N.K. Seshan, Professor Ravinder Kumar and H.Y. Sharada Prasad.

I am also grateful to Irma Oberdorf for showing me Indira Nehru's letters to Frank Oberdorf; to Helen Ciaoux and Arriene Mnouchkaine for so graciously sending me and allowing me to use the notes they had collected while in India, doing research on Indira Gandhi's life. I am deeply grateful to Dr Gisela Bonn for permission to use her photograph of Indira Gandhi, which forms the cover page, to Raghu Rai and T.S. Nagarajan for permission to use some of their photographs of Indira Gandhi, and to Dileep Padgaonkar of the *Times of India* for his support. My special thanks to Aroon Purie of *India Today* for permission to use the library which helped me greatly in locating various sources.

I would like to thank Sonia Gandhi for permission to publish letters from *Freedom's Daughter;* Dorothy Norman for extracts from her *Indira Gandhis—Letters to a Friend 1950–1984;* the Jawaharlal Nehru Memorial Fund for permitting extracts from the *Selected Works of*

Jawaharlal Nehru; the Indira Gandhi Memorial Trust for their support; the Publications Division, Ministry of Information and Broadcasting, Government of India, for permitting extracts from the *Collected Works of Mahatma Gandhi;* Cornelia Bessie of Harper & Row and later of Pantheon Books for help and advice; David Davidar of Penguin India who has provided support and advice; Allen Ginsberg for his kindness, and the many people who have helped me to write this book by granting permission to use extracts from their works. I also wish to thank Princeton University Press for permission to quote from "Winds" by St. John Perse. While every effort has been made to ensure that permission to reproduce copyright material included in the book was obtained, in the event of any inadvertant omission, the publishers should be notified and formal acknowledgements will be included in all future editions of this book.

The book would have been difficult to complete without the help of my daughter, Dr Radhika Herzberger, my niece, Tulsi Vatsal, and my granddaughters, Sunanda and Maya.

Bombay   *Pupul Jayakar*
July 1992

Prologue

MAGH MELA 1917

Allahabad, the ancient Prayag, is a city of pilgrimage. Situated at the confluence of three rivers, the Ganga, the Jamuna and the Saraswati, it forms part of the sacred landscape of India.

The descent of the Ganga from its source in the Himalayas is resonant with legend. Every curve of the river reveals a hamlet, temples and a site of pilgrimage. It flows through gorges turbulent with whirlpool and rapid, to reappear in dappled sunlight; at times flooding and ravaging in its fury field and city, at times gentle without a ripple; always with an immense dignity of depth and stately flow. It is the river of Shiva.

Through Prayag flows the Jamuna with its source in the Himalayas, with waters smoke-toned and quick. Regarded as the river of the netherworld, where Kalia the black, many-hooded cobra holds sway, it is a river playful, wayward, meandering, changing course; Krishna's river,.

Along these river banks, in 1917, the year of Indira Nehru Gandhi's birth, grew ancient shade-giving trees, the banyan and the peepal, heavy with leaf-cover; with leaves that absorbed the dust in summer, were washed clean in the monsoon rains; trees that gave shelter to the mendicant, the beggar, the weary pilgrim; to the parrot, the squirrel and the cobra.

The third river of Prayag is the subterranean Saraswati. The lost river of insight and intelligence; the river of the arts to be discovered in the inner spaces of humankind and in the dense recesses of the earth. Of the colour red.

Prayag is mentioned in the epic *Ramayana*. It was here that sage Bharadwaj established his ashram and brought to it trees, flowers and herbs from vast distances to provide groves with heavy leaf-cover and undergrowth where Sita with Rama and Lakshmana in exile from Ayodhya, could take shelter.

To the south-east of Prayag, the modern Allahabad, lie the Vindhya ranges, the highlands stretching across Central India to divide the north from the south. From these thickly forested hills of groves and wild grasses potent with seed, emerges the great mother, Vindhya Vasini Durga, the dark Goddess with hibiscus flowers woven in her hair. In these hills are found caves with prehistoric paintings; a bone icon of the mother goddess, carbon dated 18000 BC, established the antiquity of the settlements on the land and of the people.

On the day of the solar equinox, from the southernmost point of India, from the east, the west and the distant north, pilgrims gathered at Allahabad on 13 January to bathe at the meeting point of the sacred rivers to rendezvous with the sun.

Pilgrimage is discovery and adventure and has sacred sanction. Ancient Indian texts extol the culture of the pathways.

> *The feet of the wanderer are like a flower-*
> *The fortune of him who is sitting sits;*
> *it rises when he rises;*
> *it sleeps when he sleeps, it moves when he moves.*
> *Therefore wander!*
> *The wanderer finds honey and the sweet Adumbra fruit;*
> *behold the beauty of the sun, who is not wearied by his*
> *wanderings.*
> *Therefore, wander, wander!*[1]

A whole countryside moves. Along this road walk the wanderers; the barefooted pilgrims, the merchant and the shopkeeper who girdles the pilgrimage site with tiny bamboo booths decorated with brilliant coloured paper or cloth buntings or lithographs of the gods. Here are the sellers of burnt milk sweets, with a fine covering of hand-pounded silver foil; round balls of clarified butter and sugar; sweets coated with sesame seed and large iron cauldrons in which the syrup-filled *jalebis* are fried. The merchandise includes sun-dyed cloths, beads for human beings, camels and cattle; kites for the Uttarayana festival (the festival of kites) which follows the next day; brass or bell metal cooking utensils polished gold. For the child are paper toys, dolls, horse carts.

The photographer with a hooded camera, set on a tripod, stands at a prominent point; he has with him backdrops of cloth, painted with marble balustrades, swans, azure lakes and magenta lotus blossoms. He calls to passing family groups to come and get photographed, to take home mementoes of their sacred journey. 'The bird comes, the bird comes,' the photographer cries to keep the child still, open-mouthed with suspense.

Moving between the brilliantly-clad women and children, their province identified by the patterns on their clothes, and their eager talk, are the acrobat, the juggler, the picture showman, the monkeyman and the man with the performing bear. Parked in between the booths are the palmists and astrologers with their cloth-bound manuscripts, plotting the movements of the sun, the moon and the planets.

Within the stretching confines of the fair, sits the *katha vachak,* the storyteller, to recount tales from the Puranas or the myths associated with Prayag. Here are the Nautanki players, with their songs and drum beats, to enact through mime and theatre, episodes from the epics.

Here great abbots of religious sects establish themselves in clearly demarcated arenas. Here we find the shaman, the philosopher, the wiseman. Matted-haired sanyasis stand on their heads or sit on a bed of nails, while abandoned cows and bulls wander at will.

The swift flight of parrots to. their nesting in the great trees, announces the setting of the sun. At dusk and dawn, mists rise from the rivers to mingle with the fragrant smoke of wood fires; to catch the sounds of sacred chants of the Vedas or the religious bhajans (psalms) sung in praise of the Lord; resonances that in turn mingle with mist and smoke, to travel lightly to distant pilgrim sites. The cry of the jackal is the sound of the night.

It was to the Magh Mela, the festival of the solar equinox, that Indira came, from within a year of her birth, with her grandmother, Swaroop Rani, each year at dawn, to bathe at the confluence of the sacred rivers. She absorbed as a child, "through the pores of the skin", the intensity of the colours, strong and muted; the resonance of the chants and people's voices; the myths and their re-enactment; the swift movement of birds and the lazy walk of bulls. She saw the face of the peasant, gaunt and shrunk with ancient eyes, but with the strength and dignity that is part of sharing and belonging.

It is along these river banks that Indira came alive to the antiquity of the earth and the mystery of seasons. She learnt to observe nature's play; to see the colours of the earth change; the waters transformed by sun, cloud and rain; new shoots appear on the trees; and to identify the cry of birds. For many decades these intimations of her childhood were to remain as a dormant seed within her.

*

The room in the Naini jail was bare. Whitewashed walls exuded a winter damp. The pale sunlight filtered through the barred windows and intricately woven bamboo chicks hanging in the doorways. A row of chairs hastily arranged, faced a table and a straight-backed chair. On another chair, set apart, sat a fair-skinned man with a presence that filled the room. He was clothed immaculately in a white cotton, handspun dhoti and kurta, a fine Pashmina shawl draped like a toga around his shoulders. He had a strongly modelled face with a high-domed forehead, a slightly hooked nose, a pugnacious jaw and thin, finely drawn lips which were capable of expressing both an intense passion for life, as well as hauteur and swift anger. His eyes held a quizzical look as he gazed around the room; at times he turned to the magistrate who sat uncomfortably behind the desk or stroked the hair of the four-year-old child who sat upon his knee, open-eyed with curiosity. It was cold, but the child sat straight-backed, refusing to cuddle against his body for warmth.

Her grave and steady eyes were fixed on the Englishman who was one of the many she had seen laughing and drinking convivially at her grandfather's table. Why was he sitting grim and embarrassed in front of them? The girl listened intently to the endless drone of voices that spoke in words and phrases of matters she did not understand. Indira Priyadarshini Nehru observed every movement of the judge and the khaki-clad policemen who stood guard, red turbans tied to their heads and brightly polished buckles fastening their belts.

The small room was crowded; the chairs were occupied by Motilal Nehru's innumerable family members and friends. The unimaginable had happened. Motilal Nehru, one of the most affluent and respected lawyers of northern India, Motilal to his numerous British friends and admirers, and 'Panditji' to his Indian clients, relatives and colleagues had been arrested. He was being prosecuted by K.N. Knox, ICS, under Section 17 of the Criminal Amendment Act. His son, Jawaharlal Nehru, had also been arrested the previous evening. He was to be separated from his father, to be tried and sentenced in the prison at

Lucknow. The date was 7 December 1921.

Motilal Nehru called his trial a farce. The proud Kashmiri Brahmin had, with his son Jawaharlal, taken the first step on a journey of momentous consequences for him, for Jawaharlal, for his grand-daughter Indira Priyadarshini Nehru, and for India. Public Prosecutor Banerjee, deeply embarrassed and barely able to look into the eyes of the accused, his friend and senior at the Bar, had called as the sole witness an uneducated Brahmin—Kirpa Ram, who had caused much mirth amongst Motilal and the crowded courtroom by holding the paper upside down when asked to verify Motilal Nehru's signature in Hindi. The trial ended swiftly.

Motilal Nehru was sentenced to six months in prison and a fine of Rs 500. As the Magistrate left the room, the lawyer and accused rose from his chair, handed the little girl over to her mother and turned to walk out of the door. Indira watched, unable to understand why she could not accompany her much-loved grandfather.

The next day, 8 December 1921, Anand Bhawan, the gracious home of Motilal Nehru, was raided by the police. In lieu of the fine which remained unpaid, they started to remove furniture, carpets, some silver and Motilal's favourite guns and pistols. Kamala Nehru, Jawaharlal's wife stood gravely holding the hand of her little daughter while Dolamma, Indira's grandmother Swaroop Rani, stood with her widowed sister Bibi Amma, and her daughters, Vijayalakshmi and Krishna, holding back her tears. Instinctively, though not sure of what was happening, Indira broke away and charged like a tiger cub towards the police to avert what she thought was a robbery. She told them that she would not allow them to take away her Dadu's guns, the carpets and other objects, for they belonged to her family.

Fifty years later Indira said, 'From the age of three I felt responsible for myself. Whether I was or not, did not matter, I also felt fiercely responsible for my parents, for I thought they were defenceless and relations and friends took advantage of their goodness. I had a feeling of wanting to protect something very big. My earliest memories are of a feeling that there was a debt I owed; I could never explain to whom or for what; but it was a debt that I had to repay.'[2]

PART I

1919–1934

> *Circumstances have put you on the threshold of life and at every turn you will face a question mark. By the answers your future will be moulded. The answers will not be pleasant ones.*

–Jawaharlal Nehru to Indira Nehru[1]

ONE

The ancestors of Indira Nehru Gandhi came from a small village in the Kashmir valley, known as Bij Bihara, a corruption of the Sanskrit "Beej Vihara"—abode of the seed.

Legends coalesce in the hamlet. Traces of Buddhism and Shakti worship survive. The village was renowned throughout the valley for a rock that rose into the air when eleven men placed one finger beneath it and in one voice recited the seed sound of the goddess "Ka".

The local peasants had re-named the stone "Ka-Bal". An ancient chinar tree reputed to be the oldest in the valley gave the soil a sense of antiquity. In the 1930s, when Jawaharlal Nehru visited Bij Bihara, he stood in homage before the 400-year-old tree, the circumference of the tree was fifty-five feet. In time the majestic chinar tree came to symbolize, for Indira, the splendour, the strength and the energy of the Nehru lineage.

The original name of the Nehru family was "Kaula". In medieval Kashmiri texts and elsewhere in the Sanskrit tradition the word "Kaula" is used for a devotee of Shakti, the goddess as power and energy.

In the fourteenth century, a Kashmiri queen had as adviser and lover a resident of Ladakh, Rin-Chin. Confident of the strength of his position, the Ladakhi asked the Pandits of the valley to convert him to their faith. The Brahmins refused. The tough, unsophisticated barbarian swore revenge. He turned to a Muslim Sufi saint and asked to be converted to Islam. Soon the Ladakhi, now a Muslim, had engineered a revolt and taken power from the queen. Forcible conversions to Islam followed. Large numbers of Kashmiri Pandits who refused to be converted were massacred. It is said that only eleven families survived the holocaust. Others fled or were slaughtered. The survivors began migrating to the predominantly Hindu plains of India to seek their fortune. They settled in Lahore, Delhi, Lucknow, Agra and Allahabad. Here they encountered a rigid caste structure and clearly defined vocations into which they were both unwilling and unable to fuse. The struggle to hold on to their racial purity and the Kashmiri cultural identity brought to the surface a tenacity and a drive to succeed.

In the centuries that followed, Kashmiri poets, scholars and administrators sought service in the courts of the Mughal emperors and their viceroys. Where once they had been learned in Sanskrit, they how mastered Persian. Ambitious, with quick and supple minds, this migrant community became adept at statecraft. They rapidly learnt the nuances of court intrigue and the skills necessary for survival.

In the year 1760 the Mughal Emperor, Farrukh Siyar, on a visit to Kashmir came upon an eminent scholar, Pandit Raj Kaula, from Bij Bihara. Impressed by his learning, the Emperor invited the Pandit to visit Delhi, the imperial capital of the Mughal kings. The Kaulas were persuaded to settle there and were given a house situated on the canal. Raj Kaula's descendants assumed the surname of Nehru, after *nehr* or canal. The Emperor also gave gifts of villages and lands to the erudite Pandit. Unfortunately for this son of Kashmir, his patron did not live long, being murdered by his own advisers.

Deprived of their patron, Raj Kaula's family declined in importance. The wealth and lands slowly disappeared. By the middle of the nineteenth century, Gangadhar, a descendant of Raj Kaula, was reduced to the position of Kotwal, a senior police officer at the Mughal court. A miniature painting on ivory which has survived shows Gangadhar wearing an embroidered pointed cap and a muslin *choga*. Islamic culture and manners had influenced the habits of the Hindu courtiers and officials. They spoke and wrote in Persian, wore the dress prescribed by the court, patronized the arts of painting and calligraphy and were to be found at symposiums of poets and at musical soirées.

Although the Kashmiri Pandits had adopted the language, manners and dress of the Muslim courts, their women remained true to their heritage. They maintained the customs and rituals of their forefathers and preserved the separate Kashmiri identity and its links with their ancestral home in the high mountains. But inevitably they too were to change their dress—the long *firan* to a sari—and lose touch with the spoken Kashmiri language.

On 10 May 1857, the First War of Independence—the Indian Mutiny against the British—broke out. The intrigues and petty quarrels at the royal court of the Emperor Bahadur Shah Zafar led to disaster on the battlefield. British troops stormed Delhi in the summer of 1857 and the citizens of Delhi were massacred indiscriminately.

Gangadhar Kaul, his wife, Jeo Rani (also called Indirarani), and his two sons and daughters fled to Agra. Hunted along the way, they sought refuge in wayside shrines, reaching Agra with great difficulty.

Not long afterwards Gangadhar died suddenly at the age of thirty-two, leaving his wife and two sons, Bansidhar and Nandlal, in great financial difficulty. On 6 May 1861 Jeo Rani, a few days after her husband's death, gave birth to a son, Motilal.

It is fortunate that while living in Delhi Bansidhar and Nandlal had both learnt English. This enabled them to find jobs without much difficulty. Bansidhar got a job as a subordinate judge in the judicial service and Nandlal sought service in the Khetri Raja's establishment, first as a teacher, then as Private Secretary and later as Diwan. Motilal had the good fortune of studying under Qazi Sadruddin, the tutor of Raja Fateh Singh and soon became proficient in Arabic and Persian. He decided to join the local high school in Kanpur where his brother Bansidhar was posted as judge. The twelve-year-old Motilal wrote to H. Powell Esq., the headmaster:

> I respectfully beg to inform your honour that I am quite prepared for the examination of both classes i.e. 4th and 5th. Perhaps you know that when I informed to the Principal for my promotion in the 4th class, he refused and said "the other boys have also right as you have." Therefore now, I wish to be promoted in the 4th class by my own power.[2]

Highly intelligent, Motilal grew up a wild and wayward youth. He learnt English, but was not interested in his other studies and gave up the examination for a degree, after sitting for the first paper, in the mistaken belief that he had fared badly. He was one of the leaders of the rowdy element in the college at Kanpur:'. . .attracted to Western dress and other Western ways at a time when it was uncommon for Indians to take to them except in big cities like Calcutta and Bombay.'[3] Motilal now shifted to law and found a natural talent for it; he stood first in the Vakils' examination. In 1883 he started practising law at Kanpur.

Motilal married while still in his teens. His child-wife died while giving birth to their first son. The child did not survive. Shortly afterwards, Motilal married a girl from one of the original eleven families living in the Kashmir valley, Swaroop Rani Thussoo. She was small in stature, extremely fair, with gold brown eyes and nut brown hair. Her fine bones gave her a fragility much prized by the Kashmiri Pandits. Her beauty was enhanced by her exquisite hands and feet, features which her granddaughter Indira was to inherit and take much pride in.

*

Towards the middle of the nineteenth century, with British rule, Allahabad, the city of pilgrimage, was transformed into a centre of intellectual and political life; a university manned by British professors was established to provide an English education to its citizens and the High Court was shifted from Agra to Allahabad. The *Pioneer,* a major English daily, reflecting the views of the British government was published from Allahabad giving the city a flavour, that distinguished it from neighbouring towns.

With the shift of the High Court to Allahabad many provincial lawyers from smaller towns journeyed to the city to practise at its court. Among them were Nandlal and his family; Motilal followed in 1886. There was little money, so the Nehru family settled into a small house in the crowded part of the old city. Jawaharlal was born to Swaroop Rani and Motilal Nehru on 14 November 1889 at 11.30 a.m. There was great rejoicing on the birth of Jawaharlal.

In order to support their families, both Nandlal and Motilal started giving their total attention to the law courts. Unfortunately, before he could establish himself, Nandlal died at the age of forty-two leaving behind his wife, Nand Rani, two daughters and five sons. Motilal had not forgotten his brother's affection and support when the family was left defenceless after the death of their father. With a generosity of heart and mind Motilal adopted his brother's family. To the young children of the family he became "Dadaji", respected grandfather. The burden was heavy, but the pressure generated in Motilal a fierce energy, a distinguishing mark of the Nehru lineage. Motilal gave his total attention to the law and his work at the Bar. His rise was meteoric. He was an extremely astute and hard working advocate, fluent in speech and with a subtle mind that was razor-like in debate.

Handsome, with a disarming smile and grace, he dressed with meticulous care and elegance. His reputation soon spread over the United Provinces (now Uttar Pradesh). The feudal aristocracy, begums and nawabs, rajas and ranis and large zamindars sought his legal advice and engaged him as counsel to argue their cases. The most lucrative of these dealt with land disputes and with childless widowed women who sought advice on the laws on adoption.

With soaring prosperity, Motilal found his old house unsuitable. Jawaharlal was eleven years old when the family shifted to their new home, Anand Bhawan, a mansion with forty-two rooms. The house had been built to fit the needs of a joint family; it generated centrifugal energies that honed in on a central courtyard open to the skies where the family gathered on Sunday afternoons, on holidays in the winter, or at night in the summer.

Motilal ruled the household with an abundance of love but permitted no challenge to his authority. He brought to Anand Bhawan a British ambience and an altered way of life. Living habits changed dramatically. From living off the floor, eating and sitting and sleeping on wooden *takhts* covered with bolsters and mattresses, the family turned to sofas and four-poster beds (the linen used was imported from England), to a dining-table and liveried staff.

The house was divided into two distinct areas, a Western area (Motilal's) and an Indian area (Swaroop Rani's). At the front of the house was Motilal's office, bedroom, his sitting-room with its sofa and cabinets, carpets from Persia and Kashmir and a dining-room lined with Bohemian glass, silverware and Wedgewood china. Western cuisine and the choicest of wines appeared on Motilal's table. Much to the discomfiture of his nephews and their wives, Motilal issued instructions that English was the only language to be spoken in this part of the house.

Swaroop Rani, Motilal's wife, addressed by the family as "Huzoor Sahib", controlled the Indian side of the house. Imperious in manner and with an authority that was rarely questioned even by Motilal, she was the matriarch of the large extended family. Despite the delicate health that was a pre-requisite of the times for a woman in her position, she was a domineering woman whose outer fragile demeanour was at variance with her resilience and the authority she exercised over her household. To support and run her house, Swaroop

Rani had her elder sister, Bibi Amma, a child-widow who had come to live with her. Bibi Amma's life centred round gossip. She was forever carrying tales, real or imaginary, to Swaroop Rani. Tempers flared, small incidents were magnified out of all proportion, and there was little place in this part of the house for privacy.

Though Motilal was not religious and seldom participated in religious ceremonies, Swaroop Rani had a prayer room. She observed religious rituals, visited temples and shrines at dawn and participated in all the festivals.

By 1902, Motilal thought it necessary to employ Ferdinand Brooks, a talented tutor recommended by the Theosophist Dr Annie Besant, for his son who was now twelve. It was Brooks who instilled a love of reading in Jawaharlal and excited his interest in science, by means of a small laboratory established at Anand Bhawan. Motilal had instructed Brooks to prepare the boy for entry into England's most prestigious schools and colleges. The education of Motilal's daughters Vijayalakshmi and Krishna (also called Betty), the baby of the family, was entrusted to a British governess, Miss Hooper. In 1903, Motilal travelled with his fourteen-year-old son, his wife Swaroop Rani, and his three-year-old daughter Vijayalakshmi to Europe. Jawaharlal was admitted to Harrow and four years later to Trinity College, Cambridge.

Brij Kumar Nehru, Nandlal's grandson, later to join the Indian Civil Service and serve as Ambassador in Washington, recalled the feeling of inferiority he felt while living ill Anand Bhawan with his mother and father.

> My mother was not an anglicised woman and I started to feel an inferiority complex at not being a Sahib like the rest of them. My contemporary was Krishna (Hutheesing)—"Beti". We were about the same age. She had a Governess Miss Hooper, I had a munshi. Krishna could speak English, I could not. I started to resent their British ways. You must remember that at that time everything British was considered perfect. I began to feel that I was somehow inferior.[4]

Within a single decade, Motilal had transformed his image. His former life in the crowded lanes of the old city was forgotten, and a resplendent Motilal now held sway, surrounded by trappings to be found only in the palaces of maharajas. He made no efforts to husband his earnings; his income was astronomical; his expenditure, lavish.

British Commissioners and Chief Justices dined at his table as did the Gaekwad of Baroda and his Maharani. Sir Harcourt Butler, Governor of the United Provinces, became a close friend. This quick rise to affluence and splendour created some distance between Motilal and the local gentry. They gathered to greet him on festival days and partook of his bounties, but jealousy made them critical of his Western attitudes.

Yet the accent on things English did not alter the basic mores of Motilal Nehru. He remained inwardly a conservative Kashmiri Brahmin. His search for a bride for Jawahar started when his son was still at Trinity College, Cambridge.

Jawaharlal's response to his father's letters suggesting brides was a little supercilious, but he ultimately left the choice to Motilal. Motilal first saw Kamala, a daughter of the Atal Kaul family from Delhi, when she was twelve years old. She was fair, tall, slim with a translucent skin and liquid gentle eyes, a girl who smiled often. She was described as lively of spirit, a chirruping bulbul. She had received little formal education, knew only Hindi, and lacked the sophistication and social graces, wit and elegance so necessary for success in Motilal's Anglicized home. An apocryphal story maintains that Motilal finally chose Kamala because her horoscope predicted great glory for her future lineage.

In 1916, after his return from England, when Kamala was barely sixteen, Jawaharlal met her for the first time. He admired her beauty and grace and the marriage was arranged. Motilal suggested that she come to Allahabad and spend a few months at the home of a relative where Miss Hooper, Krishna's governess, could teach her table manners, deportment, the English language and the ways of a Western home. Kamala and Jawahar were permitted to go for drives, adequately chaperoned, in a phaeton drawn by two fine horses from Motilal's stable. Both shy, all the two young people did were exchange glances, make inane conversation.

The wedding took place on 8 February 1916, the day of the Basant

Panchami in Delhi and was celebrated with great pomp and ceremony. A special train decorated with flowers brought the bridegroom's party from Allahabad. A city of tents, that brought to mind the days of old Mughal glory, was erected on the outskirts of the old city. The tents were brilliantly lit with kerosene oil lamps, had wooden floors covered with Persian carpets and were furnished with Mughal-style wall hangings. There were separate bedrooms, a dining-room, drawing-room, and kitchen tents. A retinue of servants waited on the guests and there was even an orchestra to add to the gaiety. There were sumptuous banquets, musical soirées, and the beat of bands.

On his wedding day, the bridegroom wore a pink turban and arrived at the bride's home in an open carriage drawn by four horses. Every inch of the carriage was decorated with roses and sprays of jasmine. With Jawaharlal in the carriage were his two tiny nephews, Brij Kumar Nehru and Anand Kumar. They were the *Put Maharajas*. The tradition maintained that a wedding was a contract between two families, so in the event of the death of the bridegroom before the completion of the ceremony, the marriage was still celebrated with one of the *Put Maharajas* taking the role of the bridegroom. The contract once made had to be fulfilled.[5]

*

Kamala's entry into Motilal's household generated tensions within the family. The marriage was a traumatic experience for Vijayalakshmi, just one year younger than her sister-in-law. Vijayalakshmi, a lovely girl, was brought up as the little fairy princess and was admired by all who met her. She adored her handsome young brother; they had mutual interests, they rode together, recited poetry to each other, attended parties together. Suddenly Vijayalakshmi found that an awkward young girl had taken her place at her brother's side. For Vijayalakshmi, Kamala was an outsider; she lacked the graces and sophistication necessary to be the chatelaine of her father's home.

Kamala was aware she was marrying not only a man but a family. She had been trained to be a dutiful daughter-in-law and to accept her role without complaint. Swaroop Rani was a particularly difficult mother-in-law, and her anger, stoked by her husband Motilal's peccadilloes and by the intrigues indulged in by Bibi Amma and Vijayalakshmi, daunted the newly-wedded bride. Kamala wore no masks. She faced her mother-in-law with a child-like obstinacy. Unable to defend herself, the sixteen-year-old bride cried often, but asked for no favour. Indeed, to the dismay of Motilal, she did not even show an interest in rich clothes or expensive jewellery.

Her relationship with her twenty-seven-year-old husband was slow to mature. Jawaharlal, with the air of Harrow and Cambridge fresh upon him, did not quite know how to behave with his young wife, nurtured as she had been in an atmosphere so alien to his own. While getting to know her husband and exploring the many intimacies of a marriage, Kamala had also to build relationships with Motilal, with Swaroop Rani and her two daughters, Vijayalakshmi and Krishna, as well as with the vast number of relations living in Anand Bhawan. For a while, after Kamala's marriage, Jawaharlal and his sister continued to ride together in the mornings, returning for a late breakfast. They would share anecdotes, read poetry together. Kamala began to wilt under the pressure.

*

Indira Priyadarshini—dear to behold—was born at Allahabad on 19 November 1917. It was the year of the Russian Revolution.

Along the Gangetic plains of India, rural women, at the time of the birth of a child, paint on a red earthenware platter a labyrinth at the centre of which is the unborn babe. The coils of the labyrinth symbolize the dangerous path the baby travels from the womb to light and air. On the sixth day after childbirth, another labyrinth is drawn and placed before the eyes of the baby. For to be born into the world is to enter a labyrinth, to travel an unknown path, face obstacles, sorrow and pain, to find a way through all the vicissitudes of life.

No labyrinth was placed before Kamala's eyes in the sterile room in which Indira was born, but it may have hovered in the mind of the young woman, separated from her mother, but surrounded by nurses and doctors. Rightfully Indira's birth should have been in her parents' home and not on the ground floor of her husband's house, in a room that faced the inner courtyard.

Vijayalakshmi writes vividly of the birth.[6] Motilal Nehru, with an anxious Jawaharlal, Vijayalakshmi and possibly a host of uncles and cousins had gathered on the veranda to await the birth of the son they were certain would be born to Jawahar. When Swaroop Rani came out of the room, they turned to her eagerly. *'Hua,'* (it has happened) she said. There was some bewilderment. Motilal burst into laughter. No beating of the *thali* had sounded to announce the birth of a son and he was amused at Swaroop Rani's refusal to admit the fact. 'You mean a girl is born?' he asked. Jawaharlal, fresh from his days in Cambridge and determined not to show his excitement, refused to comment. The girl baby was named Indira after Motilal's mother Indirarani, a strong, stubborn and courageous woman.

TWO

Mahatma Gandhi returned to India in 1915. He was already a legendary figure. Reports of his indomitable courage and the strength of his passive resistance and non-violent struggle in South Africa had reached India, but the political leaders of the country considered Gandhi an unpredictable political entity. The Mahatma did not plunge into action immediately on his return. He was feeling his way into the situation in India, discovering the leaders and forces that were shaping political events in the country.

Motilal Nehru, at the height of his legal career, was a liberal and a member of the Indian National Congress; politics at the time was geared to pageantry and rhetoric, with little contact between the Congress and the peasantry, labour of the lower castes. Poverty and the massive oppression of the peasants were not subjects for deliberations by the Indian National Congress. Nor were they concerned that terrorism was on the increase and a number of activists sought exile from India.

In 1919, the Rowlatt Act was enacted to deal with criminal conspiracies connected with a revolutionary movement in India. The legislation provided for the suspension of ordinary laws safeguarding rights and liberties of the individual. The Rowlatt Act provided for special courts, quick trials and summary punishments. It became law on 21 March 1919. The Mahatma's response to the draconian act was the formation of the Satyagraha Sabhas. Satyagraha literally means "to hold to the truth". It was the approach Gandhi had evolved to fight white South African domination. An act of truth was a potent symbol in India; legend associated it with the power to make riverwaters flow back to their source. But Gandhi had still to work out the modalities of the action of satyagraha in India. On a visit to Madras, Gandhi fell seriously ill. He writes:

> That night I fell asleep while thinking over the question.
> Towards the small hours of the morning I woke up some-
> what earlier than usual. I was still in that twilight condition
> between sleep and consciousness when suddenly the idea
> broke upon me—it was as if in a dream.[1]

He decided to appeal to people all over the country to observe a day of prayer and fasting and stoppage of work to protest against the act and to purify themselves for the struggle that lay ahead. He placed his insights before the country. They were generally welcomed. It was decided to observe 30 March 1919, a date later postponed to 6 April, as the day when all business would be suspended and people would fast and pray.

Jawaharlal Nehru was restless. He had seen the Mahatma at the Lucknow Congress of 1916, but Gandhi's speeches made little impact on him at the meeting. On hearing the news of the satyagraha, he wanted to join the struggle immediately. 'I hardly thought of the consequences—law-breaking, gaol-going, etc.—and if I thought of them I did not care.'[2] He was determined to change his father's views from liberalism to a more direct confrontation against the British. Motilal was horrified. At first he argued with his son, but Jawaharlal was adamant. Strained nerves and violent outbursts of anger, punctuated the confrontation between father and son and rocked the house. The two-year-old Indira sensed the arhythmic pulse beat of Anand Bhawan. The charged atmosphere affected people's voices and the way they walked and talked. Indira was aware also of the hustle and bustle, comings and goings of strange people, of the grandmother's querulous behaviour and her mother's face aglow with pride. At the age of two it was unlikely that memories could survive but Indira, from childhood, had learnt, perhaps unconsciously, to superimpose her later memories on earlier events and so to create a palimpsest, through which fantasy and fact could interplay.

*

To find a way out of the tense situation in the household, Motilal invited the Mahatma to Anand Bhawan. Motilal and Gandhi had long talks and finally the Mahatma agreed to advise Jawaharlal not to take an immediate decision.

Protests against the Rowlatt Act were organized all over India; these had their tragic culmination on 13 April, with a massacre by General Dyer at Jallianwala Bagh in the Punjab. On the day of the spring festival of Baisakhi over ten thousand people had gathered in a walled garden at Jallianwala Bagh. There was only one entrance to the Bagh through a narrow lane. General Dyer, to teach the "natives" of the Punjab a lesson, stationed troops at the entrance and fired non-stop for ten minutes, killing 379 people and wounding over 200. Martial law was immediately declared in the Punjab and for hours the wounded lay without medical attention. Under the martial law provisions it became an offence for two Indians to walk together; Indians were forced to leave their carriages and salute any member of the British community they passed; Indians were forced to crawl on their bellies along a lane where a white woman had been attacked. The humiliation of Indians united political forces in India against the British. A furious Motilal cited some revealing statistics on the Punjab brutalities : one hundred and eight persons had been condemned to death, and the sentences of imprisonment passed out added upto a staggering 7,371 years. The figures for whippings, forfeiture and fines in villages were not available.

Any liberalism among the Indians vanished. Motilal gave up his legal practice, withdrew his daughter Krishna from the convent; made a bonfire of all his foreign clothes, including his Saville Row suits, and started wearing coarse khadi kurtas and dhotis. From a life of luxury, leisure and affluence father and son entered years of austerity that were to last a long time. Their decision would stretch the Nehru family to the limits of its endurance, make demands on its courage, and often end in solitude and death for its members. It was also to lead them to supreme heights of glory.

The Mahatma's decision to launch the Non-Cooperation Movement against British imperialism was taken at the Nagpur session of the Congress in the winter of 1920. An eleven-point programme was outlined at Nagpur. Among other things it instructed:

- titleholders to relinquish their titles;
- parents to withdraw their children from government-controlled schools;
- lawyers to give up their practice;
- businessmen to stop trading in foreign goods and council members to resign.

The Mahatma's call galvanized lawyers who left their lucrative practices, professors and landlords who joined the struggle to go to jail and a vast number of young students who flocked to the struggle. By the end of 1921, over 20,000 Indians, young and old, were behind bars. The call for a non-violent confrontation and boycott coincided with the visit of the Prince of Wales to India in November 1921. The boycott was total and the streets were deserted and shops closed. The British considered this an insult to the Prince and a vast number of political leaders were arrested all over India, including Motilal Nehru and his son Jawaharlal.

Some months later the Mahatma planned a major satyagraha movement at Bardoli in Gujarat. He wrote to the Viceroy Lord Reading to inform him of his decision. Three days before the Bardoli movement was to start, a police station was burnt down by angry mobs and twenty-two policemen killed at Chauri Chaura, a small village in UP. The final toll of the dead included the young son of a Sub-Inspector of Police. For the Mahatma this act of violence was a definite warning that the country was not ready for a non-violent struggle. He called off the civil disobedience movement and, as an act of purification and atonement, decided to fast for five days. Utterly disillusioned, a sense of betrayal replaced the high euphoria of the satyagrahis. A vast number of students returned to their colleges and lawyers went back to their practice at the law courts. The Mahatma turned away from political work to concentrate on his economic programmes. The Viceroy was jubilant. He felt that the struggle for independence had ended. He wrote to his son: 'Gandhi has pretty well run himself to the last ditch as a politician.'[3]

From 1921 to 1930, political activity in the country was at a low ebb. The Mahatma travelled the length and breadth of the country, listening to the voice of the people. He talked to peasants, women, Harijans, he came to understand the motivating force of religion and of the deep roots of culture that helped free people from the grinding burden of poverty. To launch any major non-cooperation programme, he now felt it was necessary to ascertain the capacity of the people to participate. Men and women had to be prepared for the struggle through *katha* readings and the deeper meaning of religious festivals. It was in these moments of cultural awakening that people were free of daily cares. Through this it was possible to bring about a social and cultural awareness and awaken a pride in Indian heritage. It was only when this was strengthened that the Mahatma felt a political struggle became possible.[4]

THREE

Motilal Nehru was freed from jail in June 1922. The Mahatma's withdrawal of the satyagraha movement had left Motilal angry and cynical. And though he returned to his practice—political events had irrevocably altered Motilal Nehru's outlook to British rule—he decided with his friend and colleague, Desh Bandhu Chittaranjan Das of Bengal, to launch the Swaraj Party. A brilliant lawyer from Calcutta, Chittaranjan Das was a mystic and a dreamer and Motilal's closest friend. He was elected President of the Congress party in 1922. He visited Motilal at Allahabad, his three-year-old grandson, Siddhartha Shankar Ray, accompanying him. Indira was with Motilal when they went to call on Das. Forgetting whether Das' grandchild was a boy or a girl, Motilal took a doll as a present for the child. Indira, then five years old, watched her grandfather, her Dadu, give the doll to the strange little boy.

Siddhartha Shankar Ray (now leader of the Opposition in West Bengal) in a conversation with the author recalled:

> The first thing Indira did was to snatch it away from me. My mother was to tell me, "Both of you struggled for possession of the doll—she took away the head, you were left with one of the legs—the body disappeared." That was our first encounter. What was evident from the beginning was Indira's determination. It was also indicative of her fierce possessiveness. She would fight like a tigress for what she thought was her's by right.[1]

A short while after this incident, Motilal presented Indira with a mini charkha, on which she learnt to spin. In one of the first of his letters to his daughter, Jawaharlal Nehru writes to her from jail on 17 October, 'Have you used the new spinning wheel which Dadu bought for you? Send me some of your yarn. Do you join your mother in prayers every day?' Soon Indira had organized a Bal Charkha Sangh where tiny children learnt to spin and weave.

Indira's childhood was not destined to provide the security a growing child needs; instead it had tremendous highs and lows,' depending on the time the adults in the household had at their disposal. Sometimes she was petted and spoilt, at other times she was neglected and on rare occasions she was forgotten. Adored by the grandfather and the grandmother, Indira was a boisterous playful child, delighting in pranks. She had the freedom of the house and the garden and would often rush through the house, peep into her grandfather's room, and finding him alone would climb on to his knee. He would send for pastries and she would eat them with relish, while arguing with him vehemently on every subject she could think of. On occasion, when secret meetings of the Congress Working Committee (CWC) were held in Anand Bhawan, she would refuse to accept the pleadings of the servants that her father and grandfather were busy, but would charge into the room shouting, 'No admission without permission,' and her grandfather would laugh, make her sit by him and hold her there while she listened seriously to talks of jail-going, lathi charges, and secret parleying. The atmosphere she found exciting, though what was said left few marks on her. Soon she would get bored, jump down from Motilal's knee and run into the garden to play around the swimming-pool. When Indira's pranks disturbed the harmony of the household, there would be stern rebukes from her father and even her mother; but the grandfather would intervene and the tears would be wiped away.

Motilal Nehru's practice at the Bar flourished between 1922 and 1929. Indira enjoyed meeting the more colourful of his clients, the begums and ranis who came to consult Motilal. Strict purdah was observed on these occasions. *Kanats* would be erected at the entrance and only women-attendants were present as the veiled women arrived in a curtained car or elaborate horse carriage, dismounted and entered the study to sit behind a screen, on the other side of which Motilal Nehru sat with his law books.

They were tough women who understood the nuances of property rights and adoption law and they would listen carefully to the legal advice of Motilal. Later, they often called on Swaroop Rani.

On these occasions men, both relations and servants, were forbidden entry into Swaroop Rani's rooms. The richly-dressed women, smelling heavily of rose-water and attar, would enter the room where Swaroop Rani held court. Delicate sweetmeats sprinkled with rose-water and covered with silver foil, were served on silver plates, sherbets in crystal glasses would appear and to end the visit paan-leaves covered with gold leaf, would be offered. Gold-embroidered fans with lacquered handles would be gently manipulated by women servants so as not to ruffle the hair or the harmony of the ladies visiting the house. At the time it was expected of aristocratic and rich ladies to be fragile in health. It was necessary to their station that they swoon easily, and be so well born and brought up that the slightest noise or disorder could destroy their delicate emotional balance. On one such occasion, Indira reminisced, she decided to storm in and break up the delicate talk. So she moved in with excited chatter. Swaroop Rani tried to stop her, but Indira had decided to be mischievous. The Begum, wilting under the noise, said, '*Nanni, itna gul na macha, main behosh ho jaongi. Mujhe ghabrahat hojati hai'* (Little one, don't make such a noise, I will faint. I feel very shaken). But said Indira, 'I refused to be quiet and continued to make a noise and waited to see whether the Begum would faint.'[2]

In those years, when her father was out of jail between 1923 and 1930, he, Kamala and Indira would, at times, have dinner together. Intent on instilling and developing courage in Indira, the parents would let her walk alone after dinner up the stairs and along a long veranda to her room. On the dimly lit stairs Indira would imagine shadows lurking in the garden, unspeakable things waiting. There would be no light in her room and she would stand on a stool to reach the light switch. It was a memory that she retained in later years. The terror of darkness and of mysterious presences never left her. She had not spoken of it to her parents, only acknowledged it many years later.

While Jawaharlal was at Anand Bhawan and not touring the villages around Allahabad, he taught Indira to walk and run. He would run with her on the lawns that surrounded Anand Bhawan, the wind blowing in their faces not fast, but with a certain elegance and grace. Unlike the Indian woman, who walks and runs with her weight thrown backwards, the heels pressing into the earth, Indira ran on her toes, with the weight of her body thrown forwards, running with long strides, her muscles perfectly coordinated, her breath in harmony with her body till 'I learnt to breathe with my heels.'[3]

*

With the Nehru family's entry into the political struggle, the gateways of Anand Bhawan were thrown open and privacy ended. At the time of the Ramlila or Kumbha Mela, vast crowds entered the gateways at all times of the day and sometimes till late at the night. They filled the veranda and the garden.

The slogans, 'became louder and louder, the verandas of the house were full of these visitors of ours, each door and window had a collection of prying eyes. . . . It was impossible not to feel humbled and awed by this abundance of affection and devotion.'[4]

As Indira grew older, she would seek to be alone, away from the din and turmoil, away from the crowded house. She would disappear into the garden, a thin, long-legged, gawky child, dressed like her father in a white hand-spun kurta and pyjama with a Gandhi cap worn at a slant; she was nimble of foot and could climb trees with ease. The thick foliage hid her from curious eyes. 'From childhood I looked upon trees as life giving and a refuge. I loved climbing and hiding there, in a little place which was my own.'[5] The sun filtered through to fall on leaf bud or on dark full-blown evergreen leaf.

Unconsciously she absorbed the green and sensed its capacity to renew energy. With passing clouds, shadows lengthened and she was plunged into worlds where mystery lurked; fantasy and reality, sun and shadow played hide-and-seek with Indira. At times she would seek a hollow within the tree she was on, where she would nestle and read *Alice in Wonderland,* tales of Hinduism, Bain's *Digit of the Moon,* fairy-tales, stories of Rajasthan's past. She would savour her fantasies, re-enact in her mind imagined adventures.

Servants called for her, but the sounds became distant filtered through thick foliage. She would pay them no heed. For she was watching birds settle on a branch or fly swiftly away, or a squirrel sitting alert with its ears cocked for the slightest sound. Butterflies, caterpillars and ants riveted her attention. She would descend from the tree only when she decided to do so, to the dismay of the servants and her mother who searched for her in the garden.

Within the house her room provided another retreat. The space was special, it belonged to her. It was here that she could bring her imaginary world to life, play with her dolls, re-enact stories of the freedom struggle; by turn her dolls became heroes and heroines, policemen and jail wardens. She loved to fantasize; to create a play and enact it, to design costumes and dress up. At times she became

Alice, the child who walks through the looking glass, dialogues with a grinning Cheshire cat. As Alice she defied the imperious queen of hearts, faced a trial where she saw the court collapse like a pack of cards. Yet again she would be Joan of Arc or the Rani of Jhansi leading her people to battle and death. She was always at the centre of the stage; all the action revolved around her.

It was in her own room that she learnt to interiorize her fears; and, as she grew older, it was here she read her father's letters written to her from prison. When she closed the doors to her room, she was able to escape the turmoil as well as the anxiety and tensions that lay dormant in the empty house when Jawaharlal and Motilal were away in prison.

Every summer the family went up to the Himalayan hill stations. Before joining the Mahatma, Motilal would travel with an army of horses and retainers bearing the choicest wines and other delicacies for the table. Even after he began going to jail, the sojourns continued. But now the horses had been sold, the number of servants brought down, and the wines and delicacies disappeared from the table:

*

In 1924, towards the third week of November, Kamala gave birth to a son. It was a premature birth and the baby lived only a few days. In the jail diaries of Jawaharlal and in the vast number of letters he wrote from prison, he makes no reference to the son who died. The only reference is a terse statement prefacing a telegram to Gandhiji: 'My wife gave birth to a baby son. He died within a week or so.' Gandhiji's telegram, dated 28 November 1924, says: 'Sorry about baby's death. God's will be done.'

A darkness engulfed Anand Bhawan; for Kamala the death of her son was a mortal blow. A traditional daughter-in-law, she remained an outsider with no real relationship with her mother-in-law and sisters-in-law. She had yet to develop, even after eight years of marriage, a close and direct connection with her husband. Distressed by the casualness of his affection, destroyed by his equally casual neglect, there was no one in Anand Bhawan with whom Kamala could share her unlimited grief. In the tradition of the Nehru family, Kamala could not permit herself to break down or find an outlet for her despair. Indira was only six years old then, but she could sense her mother's desperation, though the complexities of her mother's problems and the nature of the tangled relationship still eluded her. She had overheard "the mean remarks" of Bibi Amma and her aunt Vijayalakshmi. Defiant, Indira had at first rushed to her mother's defence. She had argued with her grandmother and grandaunt, spoken excitedly to her grandfather and father. Then, as she realized that her words had little effect on her grandmother and grandfather, and that the adored father was deaf to words he did not want to hear, she grew angry and turned away. It was at this time that Indira learned to cover up her emotions and to grow silent. She was growing aware that silence was a powerful weapon, to be used to help her mother; it could also, when it held strong emotions, exasperate her elders.

The seeds of a child's revolt were sown. She had begun to feel that there were two dark fairies whose acts thwarted harmony in the Motilal family. Indira identified them with her aunt Vijayalakshmi and her greataunt Bibi Amma. The old lady had a store of myths and old legends; she was familiar with the Nehru family's lineage and could relate stories of Indira's ancestors which delighted Indira although she hated Bibi Amma with a child's passion. At night Indira would take Bibi Amma to her room and ask her to tell her stories. 'I would screw up my eyes—listen, but would never look at her. I would fall asleep to her stories.'[6]

Kamala had suffered from minor ailments from the time of Indira's birth. She was a frail woman and her constant ill-health made it difficult for her to bear more children. Suppressed anguish led to a flare-up in her condition and she was removed to a hospital in Lucknow. Her illness was diagnosed as tuberculosis and she lay ill in hospital for several months.

Indira divided her days between Anand Bhawan in Allahabad and her maternal grandmother Rajpati's house in Lucknow, an Indian extended family home where uncles and aunts, cousins and a doting grandmother surrounded her. It was an old-fashioned house with a central courtyard and rooms around it. Indira was petted and spoilt.

> I had to be bribed to drink my milk in the morning and I was bribed with Delhi specialities, like very small puris and halva. They used to say: "If you drink up your milk, the

servant will go and bring you delicacies from the shop." That is how the day began. Then, since we were there on holidays, it was mostly meeting people—either their coming to the house or our going out. My mother's youngest brother was passionately keen on botany and zoology and finally took his degree in those subjects, and he was very keen on snakes. So anything you opened in the house you found a snake in it, much to my grandmother's horror. But it made me friendly with snakes and animals. I really lorded it over everybody there. I felt I was somebody.[7]

Indira returned to Allahabad in April, in time for Motilal's sixty-fourth birthday. She was seven years old.

Siddhartha Shankar Ray, rummaging amongst his grandfather's things in 1973, came upon an old heap of ancient papers, amongst which was an invitation:

To celebrate their father's 64th birthday, Jawaharlal Nehru, Vijay Lakshmi Pandit and Krishna Kumari Nehru would like you to join them at a Book Tea on Monday, April 20th at 5.30 p.m. You should represent a well known book in English, Hindi or Urdu, or any other book of international reputation. You will be required to guess the names of books represented by others. The highbrows who make the largest number of correct guesses will be installed in seats of honour and presented with souvenirs of the occasion.

There will be tea (or sherbat if you prefer it) with the usual eatables. If you stay long enough you may have ice cream and home-made lemonade also.

An answer conveying your acceptance of this invitation will be appreciated.

FOUR

Kamala Nehru did not respond to treatment in Lucknow and it was decided to take her to Switzerland for treatment. Since Jawaharlal Nehru's return from England, he had earned little money. With marriage and fatherhood, it was humiliating for him to have to draw on his father for all his family's expenditure, however frugal. Motilal Nehru was authoritarian, he gave generously, but he could at times exert pressure. Kamala by nature austere, cut her needs to the barest minimum. Jawaharlal's attempts to seek employment were not encouraged by his father who realized that in India to be a national hero, a political leader, like a sanyasi, could not take service or earn a livelihood. Motilal told Jawaharlal that what he could earn in a year, he, Motilal, could earn in a week. To assuage Jawaharlal's feelings, however, he arranged for him to prepare a law suit for which he was paid a fee of Rs 10,000, sufficient to cover the expenses of the journey and treatment of Kamala. The family, with Indira, left for Geneva in early March 1926.

Jawaharlal was returning to Europe after fourteen years. He was eager to observe and assess the rapidly changing world, to establish contact with the men and women responsible for its changing directions and to seek support for the Indian freedom struggle. The family took a flat at 46, Boulevarde de Tranche, and made Geneva their headquarters. Kamala commenced treatment at the local sanitarium and eight-and-a-half-year-old Indira joined the bilingual L'ecole Internationale. She had a flair for languages and was soon fluent in French. Jawaharlal would accompany her to school every morning, fetch her home at lunch time, take her back again to school after lunch and in the evening travel again to the school to bring her home. It was a tedious journey by train and by tram and the constant shuttling from the flat to the school took most of his day.

He soon decided to let Indira travel to school on her own. Kamala was anxious. Indira felt self-reliant and capable. 'I had this tremendous feeling of responsibility, I didn't think I had a dividing line. I felt I was looking after myself, and whether I was or wasn't, I thought I was looking after my parents.'[1] She had a toughness, lacking in most children her age. The educational standards at her school were high.

The school brought the children close to nature, helped them to cultivate the senses, encouraged observation. Project work was encouraged and Indira described spending hours collecting all the greens in nature from her surroundings.

She had started to dress like the other children in school: smartly-cut dresses, a ribbon tied in a bow in her short hair, white socks and black shoes with a strap.

She was present and acted as hostess when Albert Einstein called on Jawaharlal. She sat through the meeting, listening intently to what was being said, though she did not understand much of the conversation. Jawaharlal encouraged her to accompany him on his visits. She was with him when he went to call on Romain Rolland, the author and philosopher who lived at Ville neuve.

Krishna Hutheesing arrived in Geneva within a few months to take charge of the Nehru household. The family had expected that they would return to India within six months but there was little improvement in Kamala's health, and so they moved to Montana where Kamala was admitted to another sanitarium, Le Clinique Stephanie. Indira changed schools. She joined L'Ecole Nouvelle at Bex as a boarder. The head of the school was Mlle Hemmerline, an enlightened woman and a friend of Romain Rolland.

In the spring of 1927, Kamala's health improved. The family left Montana for London and Paris. They visited museums, art galleries and places of historical interest. They walked the streets, browsed in book-shops, went to the theatre. In Paris they saw *St. Joan* being performed on stage. Indira sat astride Jawaharlal's shoulders at Le Bourget airport to watch the triumphant arrival of Charles Lindbergh, the first man to fly solo across the Atlantic from New York to Paris. The spirit of adventure and the courage of the young American, exhilarated father and daughter. Jawaharlal's musings which he shared with Indira turned to the future of India; to the young men who would fly across Indian skies. Indira shared her father's excitement and his dreams.

The family was back in India by the end of 1927. Indira had returned from school in Bex argumentative, curious, stubborn and fearless. Jawaharlal found it impossible to answer all her questions. Any lack of attention or attempt to cover up a lack of knowledge, blocked channels of communication. So Jawaharlal started paying attention, sharing his books with her, stretching her mind to its limits, developing in her the capacity to pay attention. The books he gave her were often too difficult to understand for a child of her age.

> What I wanted to read at that young age, were fairy tales. I had to either read them in the bathroom or with a blanket over my head. My father disapproved strongly. He wanted me to read H.G. Wells. There were many words I didn't understand, many concepts I didn't understand. But he said, "It doesn't matter, you must read." So I read. And a long time afterwards, without re-reading it, I understood what it was about. I read about William Tell. True or not, I think it is a good story. Then Simon Bolivar, Mazzini, Garibaldi, I thought of them as real figures around me.

Indira had joined the Convent of Jesus and Mary in Allahabad but was often absent from school. She travelled with her grandfather wherever he went, and every summer spent months with her mother at a hill station in the Himalayas.

Kamala continued to be ill. The treatment was casual; Jawaharlal would suddenly grow aware of her condition and under the advice of Mahatma Gandhi or other friends start special treatments, but soon he would be back in the centre of political confrontations and Kamala's illness would be forgotten.

B.K. Nehru, a close relative of the family, was a student at Allahabad University and was staying at Anand Bhawan at the time. He recalls:

> I remember Allahabad and Anand Bhawan in 1928/29. Kamala was ill at the time. I do not remember her being well except sporadically. I used to go up (to see her) in the twilight. She would be lying down on the verandah outside her room and I read Turgenev to her. No one was with her—she was quite alone.
>
> I have no recollection of Indira at all. She must have been in the background, so insignificant that I cannot recall seeing her.

I found Kamala a very nice person. There was a deep bond
between us. We both seemed to be outsiders. Kamala was
an old-fashioned daughter-in-law who had been taught to
obey her mother-in-law. She must have had a miserable
life.[5]

In 1928 Indira and her mother went for the summer to Mussoorie.
Jawaharlal wrote a series of letters to Indira, answers to questions she,
had asked. They were Jawaharlal's first forays into writing. He was
learning the craft of writing even as he practised it. The letters were
concerned with beginnings. Jawaharlal explored the wonders of the
vast world and its mysteries. In those formative years, Indira's main
contact with her father were through his letters. They were to
strengthen her mind as her school in Allahabad, with its mediocre
teachers, could never do.

They helped me to see things in perspective and I never
saw an Indian problem merely as an Indian problem but
as an international one. These letters were to be published
under the title *Letters of a Father to a Daughter.* I don't
think he was consciously trying to form my mind, but he
was bubbling over with interest in things that it just spilt
out.[4]

In the mountains he taught her to look at rocks and stones and the
minerals locked in the rocks, and in this way transmitted to his eager
young daughter the wonder of the earth, nature and its transformations.

Motilal was elected President of the Indian National Congress for
the year 1928. Jawaharlal and his father had fierce battles on the
resolutions to be adopted at the session. The son was insistent on a
demand for complete independence, Motilal wanted Dominion
Status. Gandhi intervened. Ultimately it was decided that the demand
would be for Dominion Status to be granted within one year. If this
was not granted, the Congress would accept nothing short of full
independence. The plenary session was held in Calcutta. Father and
son travelled to Calcutta with Indira, now aged eleven. The organizers
had mounted a spectacular show with a procession of elephants and

a presidential carriage drawn by six horses. A vast crowd was present to receive Motilal. A special double-storeyed mansion had been requisitioned for his stay, with special cuisine, servants and butlers provided. The Congress session was held within a special marquee that was erected in the same compound.

Indira contacted her two cousins, Ballo Nehru and Nanne Madan who were in Calcutta. While the session debated vital issues, the three youngsters debated on their next prank. Once Madan challenged Indira as to who could eat the most bananas, Indira won the bet much to the envy of her cousins.

1929 was a year of hectic political activity. By the end of the year, Jawaharlal, who was barely forty years old, was elected President of the Indian National Congress at a session in Lahore. It was from a proud father that he received the Presidential mantle. Indira had travelled with Jawaharlal to Lahore and was staying in the Congress camp. It was bitterly cold and Indira remembered staying in tents. In the tradition of the Congress, a chariot drawn by bullocks had been suggested for the procession of the President-elect. Jawaharlal's response was one of anger. 'Do you expect me to go around Lahore in a bullock cart?' He wanted the organizers to cut out the procession, but they insisted and he finally agreed to ride on a thoroughbred white mare, to be followed by Congress volunteers on horseback. 1929 was a crucial year for the independence movement. The chief resolution on Purna Swaraj had been drafted by Indira's father. Indira Gandhi recalls this in *My Truth* (Vision Books, 1981):

> I remember when it was being typed by his Secretary. I was reading it aloud to my father who had drafted it. I mean, I was trying to read it. My father said: "Read it properly." So I read it out aloud and then he said: "Well, now that you have read it, you too are committed to it."
>
> I understood this much better than all the talk about Dominion Status and so on. This thing of being completely free made sense to me.

The family had gathered on the first floor of a house to witness the Presidential procession. There was wild acclaim when Jawaharlal rode past on his white mare. Indira remembered a band, part of the procession, playing the only tune they knew best "God save the King".

The past year had been one of preparation, of re-organization and a strengthening of the Congress organization. It was decided at the open session to launch a political and economic boycott of the British administration in India.

'We cannot command success,' Jawaharlal said in his Presidential address, 'but success often comes to those who dare and act; it seldom goes to the timid who are ever afraid of the consequences. We play for high stakes, and if we seek to achieve great things, it can only be through great dangers.'

The national flag was hoisted by Jawaharlal on 31 December 1929. It was a symbol of national independence and of the people's determination to claim freedom. Jawaharlal danced around the flag pole amidst a euphoric crowd of which Indira was part.

FIVE

On 26 January 1930, the country took the pledge of independence. Jawaharlal Nehru as President made an appeal for volunteers to join the coming civil disobedience struggle. Twelve-year-old Indira was the first to volunteer but was laughingly told that she was far too young.

The Congress leadership left it to Mahatma Gandhi to decide the modalities of the struggle. He had travelled extensively towards the end of 1929 through the villages of Bihar and the United Provinces and had been deeply wounded by the grinding poverty of the people. 'While travelling through the province, one does not come across a single light at night; one only hears the barking of dogs.'[1] He had met people in villages and cities to assess their commitment to non-violence and the extent to which they would journey with him; their capacity to face repression without reacting or breaking down. For the Mahatma this alone would determine the limits of the struggle he planned. He found the country seething with an under-current of anger and violence. Terrorism was on the increase; strikes were organized in Bombay and Calcutta. The Viceroy's train had been bombed though he had escaped unhurt. Mahatma found the country 'one vast prison house.' He saw that British rule had 'sapped the foundations of our culture and reduced us to political serfdom.'

The Mahatma brooded. 'I do not see any light coming out of the surrounding darkness.[2] Without insight he refused to commit himself to action. He sought in the laboratory of the self for an action so innocent, so clear, so universal that its very simplicity would disarm the government and release the energy essential to wipe away the lethargy of the peasant, the artisan and the labourer.

The Mahatma's truth when it was revealed, staggered his comrades as well as the British Government. The weapon he chose for the non-violent struggle was salt. He declared his intention to launch a salt satyagraha and to break the Salt Laws. There was a tax on salt. It cost the villager and the landless, five annas—thirty-three cents—per year. This sum was three days' wages to the poorest people of India. The Mahatma, looking at the tax from the poor man's standpoint, regarded it as the most iniquitous of levies. Consequently, he issued an ultimatum to the Viceroy, Lord Irwin, demanding among other issues, the repeal of the Salt Laws.

His letter at first drew the ridicule of the British Government. They were amazed at the idea that the King Emperor could be unseated by boiling sea water in a kettle. Even the Mahatma's comrades were cynical or bewildered. The Viceroy treated Gandhiji's letter with contempt, refusing to reply in person. A terse reply was received from the Viceroy's aide regretting Gandhiji's decision and pointing out that the Mahatma through the salt satyagraha was encouraging the breaking of the laws of the land. On receiving this letter, the Mahatma remarked: 'On bended knees I asked for bread and I have received stones instead.'

The salt satyagraha was launched early on the morning of 12 March 1930. After a bath and communal prayers, Gandhiji commenced his pilgrimage. Holding a staff in his hand, he left Sabarmati Ashram, clad only in a dhoti, and a handspun cloth draped over his shoulder. Following him were seventy-one satyagrahis who had taken vows of celibacy and non-violence. Their destination was Dandi, a tiny village on the sea, in the district of Surat. It was 385 kms from the Ashram. The Mahatma's call to his companions was: 'Salt in the hands of Satyagrahis, holders of truth, represents the honour of the nation. It cannot be yielded up except to force that will break the hand to pieces.'[3]

To the amazement of the Mahatma's comrades who, at first, had been unconvinced by the master's decision, the symbolic act touched the heart of the peasantry. Villagers gathered, travelling by foot or on bullock carts, to the roadside—peasants and artisans, men, women and children—to pay homage to the handful of rebels. They watered the dusty pathways with fresh water from their village wells and strewed mango leaves on the path so that the pilgrims' feet would tread softly. They offered them drinking water, food and their huts. They wept and laughed and joined the pilgrimage. They created songs, they sang them:

> Dandi *darya kinare*
> Mohan, *mithun banave.*[4]

Mohan, the first name of Gandhi, is one of the names of Krishna. These uneducated men and women of field and furrow, played on the name, likening the Mahatma's play with salt from the waters of the ocean, to Krishna's play on the flute on the waters of the Jamuna river. For the villagers of India, to re-create the dark cowherd lover in the bony, shaven-headed holy man, was appropriate. Of such is the raw material of myth.

Reports of Gandhiji's march and the unbelievable response of the people poured into Anand Bhawan. Indira, school forgotten, was at the centre of the excitement. 'Salt became a mysterious word, a word of power.'

Throughout the journey, a weary Mahatma would hold discussions with the headmen of the villages, and particularly with the women and the under-privileged. Late into the night he would deal with his correspondence; a vast number of letters awaited him at every halting place. He would write to the inmates of his Ashram, advise them on their health problems, on what they should eat, deal with the problems they faced in their observance of celibacy, enquire about the discipline in the Ashram, comment on the behaviour of a disturbed inmate. He fussed over them as if he were a mother. His puckish sense of humour was undiminished. To Abbas Tyabji, an old Muslim nationalist, he wrote:

> Dear Bhrr,
> Can't afford to think of you as an old man in spite of the whiteness of your ample beard. Mahadev tells me that you can dance. I feel like asking for short leave to come and see you dance, but that cannot be.[5]

Jawaharlal, with an ageing Motilal Nehru, was to meet the Mahatma at a village which lay beyond the Mahikantha river. The Mahatma did not interrupt the march to meet his famous friends but crossed the river at low tide. He had advised father and son that as they would reach the river at a most trying stage of high tide at 2.00 a.m., they should cross the river on the shoulders of fishermen. An exhausted and mud-splattered Mahatma sat on his bedroll to talk to an equally exhausted Motilal and Jawaharlal. It was a meeting of close and affectionate comrades. A sceptical Motilal had received early news of the salt march and had viewed Gandhi's weapon—salt—as another quirk, to be equated with the Mahatma's hand-spinning, fasting and chastity. Sitting beside him on the Mahikantha river bank, Motilal now saw an indomitable Gandhi prepared to stand alone, prepared to face ridicule from his friends and opponents.

Immeasurably moved, all scepticism washed away, Motilal on the instant decided to gift his old beloved Anand Bhawan, renamed Swaraj Bhawan, to the Congress party. By then Motilal had built a small luxurious building for himself and his immediate family. This building was now named Anand Bhawan.

Describing the revolutionary march in a letter to a twenty-nine-year-old friend, Padmaja Naidu, Jawaharlal wrote: 'The little man was going strong yesterday, trudging away staff in hand like Peter the Hermit, to the promised land where salt can be had for the picking up.'[6]

The women of Sabarmati Ashram had expressed their intention to join the salt march. Gandhiji had persuaded them to wait and look after the Ashram, for he was not yet clear about the role they would play. But events forestalled him. At Aat, four miles from Dandi, the police tried by force to snatch salt from the peaceful civil resisters. In the scuffle that followed, Ukabhai Rama of Bardoli was slightly injured.

The first drawing of blood, however little, brought practically the whole village to the scene.

> Men and women (some with babes in their arms), imme-
> diately they heard that salt was being forcibly seized and
> that one of the volunteers was injured, rushed out, and
> men on one side and women on the other descended to
> the channel and began to dig out the salt.[7]

The police arrested many of the more prominent satyagrahis. They were handcuffed, jailed and their heads shaved like common criminals. Gandhi was hurt by the police action to see human nature so debased.' But he told his fellow satyagrahis: 'The fist will acquire the strength of iron if you have faith in Satyagraha.'

On 30 March, an article by Gandhi appeared in *Nava-jeevan* (New Life), a magazine he edited, calling on the women of India to awake. 'If non-violence is the law of our being, the future is with women.' He asked women to come out of their homes to be unafraid and to take up two dangerous activities—picketing against the sale of liquor and the sale of foreign cloth. This would, he said, give them access to power and a self-confidence to which they had hitherto been strangers. The operation was to be initiated and controlled exclusively by women. Men were to step aside. He appealed to thousands of women, literate and illiterate, to take part in this agitation.

It was as if women had long awaited this moment. One by one girls, young women, mothers came out of their homes. In a mysterious mouth-to-ear communication, the word spread. Leaving their home fires untended and their babies in the care of husbands, mothers-in-law, neighbours, women, their oil-plastered hair tightly knotted, wearing handspun cloth saris draped over their heads, with a *tika* on their foreheads, walked alone or abreast with men—actors and comrades—not observers and dependants. The agitation was transformed into a revolution. The sweetness of women's voices had been added to the songs sung with triumph.

In the early mornings women walked the lanes singing songs of the rising dawn, *prabhat pheris.* They invoked the *Suras,* the heroic ancestors, to come out and join the battle unarmed and unafraid. It was a challenge to those who still sought security within their homes.

It was a dangerous assignment which Gandhiji had chosen for the sheltered women of India. Liquor shops were surrounded by violent men. The closure of foreign cloth shops meant serious damage to British economic interests. Gandhiji had warned the volunteer women that 'they may be insulted or even injured bodily.' But he said, 'who will cast an evil eye on you if you walk straight, with the name of god on your lips? Be convinced at heart that purity itself is a shield.'[8] Such was the moral authority generated that few cases were reported of women being assaulted by liquor shop-owners or their stooges, though the police were not so considerate.

Hundreds of women were arrested and sent to jail, to create chaos, for no facilities existed in prisons to house these delicately-reared women, many from well-known families. The conditions in the "female wards" were crude. Women prisoners were herded together; the toilets were primitive; the food inedible. However, to the bewilderment of the British, the women had savoured freedom, they were tough, and they took to the hardships with good cheer.

Gangaben Vaidya, who with her comrades was attacked by the

police, wrote to Gandhiji: 'Blood streamed out from a wound caused on my head, but I did not budge an inch, and asked the other sisters to sit down. It was at this moment that I understood somewhat the meaning of Ahimsa.'[9]

India was witness to a revolution. Women from all castes and creeds were out on the streets, a situation unheard of in India. This was a time when most of the women of the country, specially in urban India, were still secluded (in purdah). By a single call to action Gandhiji had freed women from their bondage, their social conditioning and their psychological fears. The future was still smoke-tinted, a long, hard struggle stretched ahead, but the shackles were broken. This freedom to suffer hardships, to conquer fear and to act, gave them inalienable rights; it made possible a woman Prime Minister, thirty-six years later.

In the early hours of 6 April 1930, Gandhiji walked into the sea, scooped up salt water with both his hands, placed water in a pan to be evaporated and so violated the Salt Law. The countryside awoke to a non-violent rebellion. Along the coast thousands marched to the sea to make contraband salt. Processions were held, the picketing of foreign cloth shops and of liquor parlours was organized.

On 14 April, Jawaharlal was arrested and sentenced to six months' imprisonment. He was followed by Gandhiji and other Congress leaders. The movement permeated to distant corners of the country. Rural India was awake. Frustrated young men, who had turned to acts of terrorism to express their passion and fierce anger, were suddenly offered the alternative of a non-violent protest. Many accepted the challenge. Vast numbers of young students left schools and universities to stoke the fires of a peaceful protest. It was the early 1930s and humanism and liberalism still had meaning. The jails were overflowing, the floggings increased, but Gandhiji's action halted the trend towards terrorism.

*

If the government was dazed by the revolutionary role of women, so was Motilal. In his own house, Kamala, Vijayalakshmi, Krishna and even Motilal's wife, Swaroop Rani, came out to picket, to face the police and lathi charges. The young women wore kurtas and pyjamas with white Gandhi caps on their heads. The women of the Nehru household had suddenly become orators, addressing public meetings at every street corner, moving from door to door persuading women who still observed purdah and were secluded within their homes to break free and to join them. Indira felt part of it all.

> It was not something happening which others were doing, but the nature of Indian family life is such and especially of our household—I was part of it. I was part of the processions and meetings and everything that took place; it was an extremely insecure childhood because we did not know from day to day, who would be alive, who would be in the house, what would happen next.[10]

Kamala astounded Motilal and the household by her energy and her capacity for organized action. In scorching heat she was in the forefront of the defiant crowds. It was as if an invisible power flowed through her. She was everywhere, addressing meetings, picketing, tending the injured knocked down by lathi blows of policemen, organizing voluntary services. From his jail cell, an astonished and proud Jawaharlal began to regard his wife anew.

Among the young men who gathered round the leadership of Kamala, was Feroze Gandhi, a Parsee youth, from a middle class family, staunch in its support of the British. Feroze was an observer, watching without participating in a demonstration headed by Kamala. The policemen lathi-charged, Kamala was in danger and Feroze jumped into the fray to save her. He was arrested and taken to police headquarters where he was severely beaten and only released on the intervention of his aunt, Dr Commissariat, a much respected physician in charge of the local hospital in Allahabad. The beating left deep scars and Feroze, in spite of his family's total disapproval, started visiting Anand Bhawan, fetching and carrying for Kamala, assisting her in every possible way.

As the lathi charges and police repression increased, students and Congressmen injured by the lathi blows were administered first-aid at Swaraj Bhawan. Indira was nurse and leader. She remembered in later life a boy with severe stomach injuries who was expected to die—she nursed him day and night, determined to see that he survived.

The atmosphere was taut with energy, heady wine for the twelve-year-old Indira. She started taking decisions on most matters concerning herself. As a mark of rebellion and as a gesture of participation with the marching pilgrims, she cut her hair straight to her earlobes, in a severe, no-nonsense style, she wore coarse khadi frocks which fell as a loose sack above her knees.

At the Jesus and Mary convent where she studied, the nuns were openly critical of her family's political views and the students were unfriendly and snide in their remarks about her family and her stark, unfashionable frocks. Indira told the nuns that she would not be returning to school after the holidays.

Restrained from accompanying her mother on political forays, in protest, she decided to go up to Nainital with her uncle Chand. While in Nainital, she learnt that an interview in jail with her father had been fixed for the family on 31 May. She was anxious to be present, but knew that it would be impossible for her to return alone. So she wrote to him. 'If our wishes could be realised, would we not have Swaraj immediately?' She also informed her father with pride that 'a crowd of ten CID men follow me.'

'Heigh ho,'[11] responded Jawaharlal.

On her return from Nainital she told Jawaharlal of her decision not to attend the convent school. Her father agreed and it was decided between them that her education would continue at home through tutors and pandits—learned Sanskrit scholars educated in the Indian tradition. Her involvement with the freedom struggle, her rebellious mood towards her school, her desire to take wings and fly to Dandi to be with the Mahatma at the centre of the excitement, made Jawaharlal realize that his daughter was entering a new phase of her life. She was growing up and he sent her a gift of Trevelyan's *Garibaldi*. She now added this hero from Italy to her pantheon of heroes and heroines which included William Tell, Joan of Arc, the Rani of Jhansi.

Eager to participate in the freedom struggle, Indira applied again for membership in the Congress but was again refused. Angry at being denied active participation, with vigour and determination she set about forming her own children's brigade, the Vanar Sena (army of monkeys).

The children of the brigade were between five and eighteen of age. Indira as General controlled the movement of her army from Anand

Bhawan. The little monkeys addressed envelopes, cooked meals, attended to wounded volunteers, sometimes acted as couriers carrying secret messages to hiding Congressmen.

Indira's diary, written neatly in a tiny scrap book, indicates her precise down-to-earth mind—adult in its planning and concerns, with an understanding that it is the little things that make great events possible, an astonishing state of mind for a twelve-year-old child.

6th September

Papu's interview at 10.00 A.M.

Meeting of the Students' Working Committee at 12.30.

Meet Gupta about Vanar Sena's work in different wards.

Katra Vanar Sena's meeting at Katra Ashram at 6.00 P.M. to 9.00 P.M.

Drill and meeting of Vanar Sena (monkey brigade) & Bal Sangh at Swaraj Bhawan at 5.00 P.M.

8th September

Boycott week Programme for Vanar Sena.

The whole week Prabhat Pheris—6–8 A.M.

Procession starting at Khadi Bhandar at 5.30 P.M.

Meeting at Purshottam Das Park.

9th September

Meet Gupta at Students' Association Office at 7.30 A.M.

To visit different wards about Vanar Sena.

Write to Bombay for material

Flag hoisting at *(illegible)*. Going to Congress Office at 8.00 A.M.

Meet Krishna Das and Gupta at Katra Ashram.

13th September

Strike in schools on behalf of Jatindra Das.

Procession and meeting.[2]

'Take care of yourself—little soldier boy,' wrote Jawaharlal from jail on 23 July 1930. 'We have many a fight ahead and no lack of high enterprise. India is today the land of adventure.' He also wrote, 'Indu dear, congratulations to the little monkey in enrolling fellow vanars in the vanar sena. Dadu suggested that you should run every morning. Also try to stand on your head. Nothing like it.' By now Motilal Nehru had joined his son in jail. Hearing about his granddaughter's monkey army he was amused and wrote to her. 'I suggest the wearing of a tail by every member, size of it should be in proportion to the rank of the warrior.'[13] Indira was not amused.

'I hope Indu is carrying on her studies regularly,' Jawaharlal wrote to Kamala on 2 September 1930. 'She is and I am glad of it—a high-spirited girl. I would rather have an ounce of spirit in her than a pound of learning. But learning and mind training is also necessary and so I do hope that she will pay attention to these.' Indira told her mother that she did not like the idea of learning Sanskrit as it was a dead language. She wanted to learn Urdu instead. From jail Jawaharlal wrote to Kamala, 'Certainly she should learn Urdu. But I should very much like her to learn Sanskrit in spite of it being "dead" '[14]

In spite of careful and devoted nursing by Jawaharlal, Motilal' health broke down in jail and he was soon desperately ill with asthma. The government ordered his release on 8 September 1930. He went to Mussoorie to rest. Indira was anxious to go to the Himalayas with her grandfather and Jawaharlal wrote to her. 'You are grown up enough to make up your mind for yourself. If you want, spend some time in Mussoorie. You should certainly go there.'[15]

Motilal's health continued to deteriorate and Jawaharlal was released on parole for ten days to be with his father. Kamala was in Anand Bhawan. They both went up to Mussoorie. Motilal's health improved, and Jawaharlal was able to relax with his daughter and his nieces. They would walk around the garden in single file, Jawaharlal leading, holding the Congress flag of independence, Indira trailing, the nieces in between; all the while, everyone would sing: "Let the flag of freedom fly high." Jawaharlal spent evenings with his daughter. She was eager to ask questions, many questions; he was the only person prepared to speak seriously to her, the others treated her as a child. She discussed with her father in their evening talks the vast world and the new energies that were transforming man and his environment, changing his ways of thinking. The unexplored had great fascination for both father and daughter.

Indira did not see much of her father. 'But when I did then the time was wholly mine. I mean when my father sat down with me, he was not disturbed by other things. That time was mine.'[16]

Jawaharlal went back to jail on 11 November. Indira wrote from Anand Bhawan, reminding him of his promises to answer any questions she sent him. 'Why do my toes bend downwards when we are walking? I have very often noticed this while walking with chappals on, and try as I would to keep them straight they somehow bend.'[17] She knew it was a question her father could not answer.

On Indira's thirteenth birthday, which fell on 26 October 1930, by the Indian calendar, Jawaharlal wrote to her the first of the letters, later to be published as *Glimpses of World History.*

> When in doubt, never do anything secret, which may bring discredit to one's cause or dishonour our people. Be brave and the rest will follow. Fear is a bad thing, never do anything secretly or furtively. If you do so, my dear, you will grow up a child of the light, unafraid, serene and unruffled whatever may happen. You are fortunate in being witness to this great struggle for freedom that is going on in this country. You are also very fortunate in having a very brave and wonderful woman for your Mummie, and if you are ever in doubt or trouble you cannot have a better friend.[18]

On New Year's eve, 1930 Indira was alone with her mother at Anand Bhawan. They were reading poetry—Tennyson's "In Memoriam"—when the telephone rang, a warning came through. Kamala was to be arrested the next day. Except for the mother and child there was no one else in the house. With her mother's arrest Indira would be alone but there was no time for anxiety or cogitation. Indira packed for her mother, while Kamala spent the night giving instructions to local Congress workers, planning future action as well as making arrangements for the running of Anand Bhawan. It was a supreme moment for Kamala. She had acted and redeemed herself. She realized that she could no longer be ignored or treated casually by Jawaharlal and his family. For Indira, too, her mother's triumphant entry into jail was a moment of victory. She sensed the change of relationship that was now inevitable.

Housed in Lucknow jail, Kamala wrote to Jawaharlal:

> When I was arrested, I was worried about Induji. I wondered what she would do by herself. But I now feel somewhat reassured about her being able to look after herself. She gave me her word that she would remain cheerful and take care of herself.[19]

Her letter to Indira was an anxious letter of a mother to a child who had just entered her teens:

> Please let me know your daily routine. Please send your teacher's fortnightly reports about your studies to your father. I hope you remember what I told you when I left home. Whenever I stroll outside the barrack, I think of you. You must also take a walk every day. When I am released, we shall go out for walks together. That will be six months away, but six months will pass without either of us feeling it.[20]

SIX

Motilal Nehru died in Lucknow in the early hours of 6 February 1930. His son Jawaharlal Nehru, released from jail a week earlier, in view of his father's deteriorating condition, had, in desperation, moved his father from Allahabad to Lucknow where the medical facilities were better. Motilal had been like an elder brother to Gandhiji and it was as part of the family that Gandhiji, released from detention by the British Government, hastened to see Motilal and accompanied him to Lucknow. He found Motilal's face swollen beyond recognition, his body racked by asthma and his kidneys failing. The old patriarch died cradled in the love of his family and friends. He remained a non-believer to the end of his life; scorning priests and the recitation of mantras, he had joked with Gandhiji, challenging him to a race to heaven. He said if they were to die at the same time, the Mahatma would probably walk alone across the river of death, while he, Motilal, would speed across it in a motor-boat and shoot past the gates of heaven. Whether he would be allowed into heaven or not was a totally different matter. In a more serious mood he told Gandhiji, 'I am going soon and I shall not be here to see Swaraj, but I know you have won it and will soon have it.'[1]

On the night of Motilal's death Jawaharlal was with him till midnight. Jawaharlal later told Gandhiji:

> A very strange thing happened to me. Papa told me last night that he had been taught the Gayatri Mantra in his childhood, but he never cared to repeat it and thought he had forgotten it completely long ago, but that night as he lay in bed it all came back to him and he found himself repeating it.[2]

Motilal's body, wrapped in the Congress flag, was brought from Lucknow to Anand Bhawan. He was cremated at the Sangam in Allahabad, at the point where the three rivers met. His ashes were cast into the rivers, to journey to the oceans. Vast mourning crowds accompanied the cortège. Gandhiji was present, so were Swaroop Rani, Vijayalakshmi, Krishna, Kamala and Indira.

Jawaharlal cried out in grief at the loss of his father, a mountain had crumbled; he was now head of the family, responsible for his mother and sisters. He resolved to make them feel that nothing had changed in the old home. The bond between father and son had matured beyond love into mutual respect and pride; a relationship that united them in a commonality of work though, perhaps, not of mind. Jawaharlal was in those early years an austere man of few needs, Motilal, a man whose laughter filled the vast house, who could gather his extended family and friends in his embrace, savour abundance and give with a generosity of heart. He had a razor-sharp intellect and a *joie de vivre* seldom seen amongst Indians in the third decade of the twentieth century.

Indira had loved her grandfather with the intensity of a child. He had protected her, come to her aid when her parents rebuked her, listened to her tiny problems and laughed them away. He was the anchor in her insecure, chaotic world; the foundation stone that was always there; a presence so total that there was no space left to be alone or insecure. Alone, almost forgotten in Anand Bhawan, Indira wept, hidden behind a pillar. It was her first introduction to sorrow; her body was racked by an emotion with which she was not familiar.

Referring to her grandfather Motilal five decades later, Indira said, 'With his death Anand Bhawan was silent. His resounding voice no longer echoed in the rooms or along the verandahs.' She described his warmth and his fierce short-lived anger. Smiling at her memories, she said:

> He always seemed to fill a room, although I now realize
> he wasn't really that tall, but at that time I thought he was
> very tall and broad . . . and when he laughed the whole
> house sort of shook and laughed with him. He was a
> biform human being, both man and woman, with strength,
> intellect and an abundance of feeling.[3]

With a twinkle in her eye she went on to say that she felt that she was like him.

Jawaharlal felt depleted. After his father's death, he felt the need to renew himself, to lay down the complex political problems that surrounded him, to relax, to look at trees, meet people, to have a holiday. So he sailed with Kamala and Indira on the *S.S. Cracovia* to

Ceylon (now Sri Lanka).

They spent two weeks in Ceylon in the mountains of Nuwara Eliya. With the pressures and burdens of his political work set aside, away from his possessive mother and sisters, Jawaharlal looked at thirty-year-old Kamala with fresh-washed eyes. He saw a woman, young and virginal. A spark was kindled. Kamala's eyes responded; she smiled. Suddenly youth was renewed in this stricken woman. Her face already tender, regained its delicate beauty.

With some pride Jawaharlal wrote to his sister Vijayalakshmi from Kandy on 25 April 1931 that Kamala had been mistaken for his daughter. 'Only Indu looks very ancient and very wise.'

Quick to respond to the historic past of Ceylon, the father, mother and daughter wandered the length of Ceylon, visited Anuradhapura and Buddhist viharas, where they met practising Buddhist monks, came together in the morning to recite the Gita or read the *Ramayana,* went for walks, met people, relaxed under the shade of towering trees.

As the holiday ended, they travelled along the Eastern Ghats of India to Cochin, where they visited the synagogue and the early Syrian Christian church. To Jawaharlal's astonishment they came upon a colony of Nestorian Christians, a sect which had disappeared from most other parts of the world.

Back in Allahabad, Jawaharlal reverted to his old life. The tenderness for Kamala that had surfaced during their holiday was trampled on and dissipated by the old relationships within the family. Political pressures were building up; Jawaharlal's work amongst the peasants of the United Provinces had intensified. He was soon travelling from district to district, addressing meetings of kisans; demanding from government relief for the peasant ground down by poverty.

At Anand Bhawan, the old tensions and jealousies long held at bay by Motilal's presence, re-surfaced. Those were dark days for Indira. A remark by Vijayalakshmi made casually and repeated 'She (Indira) is ugly, stupid,' was overheard by Indira. Anand Bhawan was a home of beautiful people, sophisticated and quick in intelligence. To be called ugly and stupid devastated the thirteen-year-old. As no one in the house cared to refute the remark, Indira started to see herself as an ugly duckling. She retreated, lost presence, and all her confidence dissolved. Overnight she changed from a boisterous child full of fun and mischief to a silent, withdrawn young girl, who rarely spoke, but listened with an intensity to every word spoken around her.

Indira never forgave her aunt for those annihilating words. They blighted her youth. She was to refer to the remark with an intense passion throughout the years I knew her. Fifty-three years later, a fortnight before her death, the remark remained fresh in her memory.

*

It was in that summer of 1931 that I first met Indira. My father, a senior member of the Indian Civil Service, was posted to Allahabad as Commissioner. He had known Motilal from his early years as the first Indian Joint Magistrate of Allahabad.

I look back through an amethystine mist to Allahabad, a city set in centuries, thickly wooded with huge, shade-giving trees. I remember early morning walks with my father along footpaths strewn with the fragrant white bell-shaped flowers of cork trees. With sunrise the walks ended, the relentless heat and scorching winds sent us back home, my father to his office, we to lazy afternoons spent before water-drenched *khas* grass screens, fragrant, moist, cool. I remember darknesses; savouring star-light; dreaming under the moon. I remember the scent of flowers and of fresh, wet grass; the sound of crickets, the croak of frogs, the cries of the koil bird heralding the monsoons. I remember the first rains, and the inhaling of rain on parched earth. We lived close to the earth, in a tranquillity and an easy flow of time which is the birthright of people who live on soil that has known millennia of civilization.

It was a moment in the 1930s when political turmoil was at an ebb; it awaited the next incoming tide.

I remember being invited to Anand Bhawan; the gracious house, the noble trees, the green lawns, the swimming-pool; lunch on *thalis* in the dining-room where Vijayalakshmi, on a visit, was hostess. Krishna, the younger sister, was present. Kamala was ill. Indira was introduced by her father. We looked at each other with the curious eyes of adolescence. I was outgoing; she fiercely shy and wary. Her personality had few accents. She merged into the background, became invisible, had to be specially drawn out. There is little I remember of her except her thin, lanky body and large questioning eyes. Was the inability to recall her with clarity due to Jawaharlal's presence? A presence that filled the room leaving no space for another. He was already a legend, with chiselled face, heroic ease and grace, quick turn of head, a shy, quizzical look, quick laughter, a lightness of body, an elegance of word and gesture, and we were enraptured. He turned to talk to us. My sisters were too shy to respond. I spoke.

My two younger sisters and I lit tiny fires in this ancient, sleepy, traditional town. We played tennis, wore roses in our hair; invited young professors, middle-aged lawyers, junior bureaucrats to our home; arranged boat rides on the river; treasure hunts in cars, where we raced through the town, to end with dinner at the house. We sang, told tales. We did not even hold hands, yet tradition-bound Allahabad was agog. Krishna often joined us. Indira did not.

My father would disappear to his room so that his presence did not inhibit our innocent festivities.

I had asked Indira, when she became a friend, why she had kept aloof. 'I was too shy; I felt unsure of myself; I felt I would say the wrong thing and people would laugh. I hesitated to come. It was a particularly difficult time.'[4]

Negotiations between the Mahatma and the British authorities had commenced on the ending of the salt satyagraha. The Salt Law had not been repealed but the power of a peaceful, non-violent revolt had introduced a new dimension to the freedom struggle and brought rebellion in India to the notice of the world.

Lord Irwin, the Viceroy, felt the need to meet the Mahatma and he was invited to talks with the Viceroy. Winston Churchill scoffed at the 'seditious fakir, striding half-naked up the steps of the Viceroy's palace, to negotiate with the representative of the King-Emperor.' But the Viceroy, Lord Irwin, has described the meeting as 'the most dramatic personal encounter between a Viceroy and an Indian leader.' When Gandhi was handed a cup of tea, he poured a bit of salt (tax-free) into it out of a small paper bag hidden in his shawl and remarked smilingly, 'to remind us of the famous Boston Tea Party.'[5]

At her next meeting with the Mahatma a thirteen-year-old Indira reacted strongly to his decision to participate in the Round Table Conference of 1931, called by the British Government in London to negotiate with all parties in India on India's future. She told the Mahatma that if her grandfather had been alive, he would not have permitted Gandhi to come to terms with the British.[6]

SEVEN

With the death of Motilal Nehru and Kamala's continued illness, Jawaharlal Nehru grew greatly concerned about Indira's future education. He sought the advice of Mahatma Gandhi who agreed that a fourteen-year-old Indira should no longer be left to determine her studies on her own. Jawaharlal's arrest was imminent. Without him there would be no one in Anand Bhawan who could influence or guide his self-willed daughter. Jawaharlal knew that Indira was a voracious reader. He was aware of her inner resilience and courage. He also knew she was obstinate. She needed a boarding-school with a routine and with companions of her own age. It was also thought very necessary to separate Indira from Kamala as the tuberculosis had flared up once again. 'Indu frequently kisses Kamala. This should be stopped, as according to the present theory, even perspiration carries the germs.'[1] Unfortunately, neither the Mahatma, nor Jawaharlal, nor Kamala talked over with Indira the reasons for their decision to send her to a boarding-school.

It was Gandhiji who suggested that Indira join the People's Own School in Poona (now Pune). A family school started by Jehangir Vakil and his wife Cooverbai, it attracted students from the homes of freedom fighters. Indira was to be amongst the first students. These were dark days for Indira. Overwhelmed by the events of the time, lonely, deeply wounded by her aunt, struggling to grow up, the decision to separate her from her mother and her mother's inability to do anything to prevent it, left Indira distraught. Without Indira, she knew that Kamala would have to cope on her own with the trivialities of house-keeping and the bickering that had started within the home and in local Allahabad politics. Once in Poona, it would be impossible for Indira to make frequent visits to see her mother or to visit her father in jail. Indira reacted. She started to interiorize her conflicts, to submerge them deeply so that her anxieties did not surface.

When she arrived in Poona, Indira found the few students at the school living with the Vakil family. The daytime classrooms were converted into dormitories at night. Students participated in all the daily chores; they scrubbed floors, washed clothes and, of course, made their own beds. Since a close relationship to nature was encouraged, classes were often held under shady trees and school tours were frequently arranged to the heavily forested Sahyadari hills and sometimes to nearby cities with historical monuments.

Indira's pride made any outer display of grief unthinkable; she took to hiding behind trees when the desire to cry became uncontrollable. The absence of a room of her own where she could cry, be alone, or silent, enhanced her loneliness. She was not used to communal living. Although she had grown up in an extended joint family, she had always had a room, some refuge and space of her own. She withdrew further into herself. Her letters to her father and mother became formal and model compositions, describing her school, the books she read, the excursions, and so on.

As the first shock of her parting from her mother began to wear off, she started to look around her. Poona was a haven for ancient trees, especially the banyan and the peepal. Indira discovered that in the green lush campus of the school she could slowly unwind. She ceased to brood. Her innate capacity for organization and for taking responsibility found an outlet in the way she took charge of the nursery children, amongst whom were her own cousins, Vijayalakshmi Pandit's children—Chandralekha, Nayantara and Rita. She organized a Children's Society with herself as the Mantri or the Minister of the Society.

Jawaharlal was arrested towards the end of December 1931. Indira in school felt depressed and lonely. Jawaharlal wrote to his daughter on 23 March 1932:

> . . .None of us, least of all you, has any business to be depressed and to look it. Sometimes you will feel a little lonely—we all do that—but we have to keep smiling through it. It is easy enough to smile when everything is right. But when everything is not all right? So, cara mia. . .[2]

Although she seldom wrote letters to her parents, a letter from Jawaharlal was a special event. Intensively possessive, Indira regarded these letters as personal property and was loathe to share her father's words with the other children. Any curiosity would lead to withdrawal, or when pushed, a display of anger. Her attitude to the letters was ambivalent. She would savour her father's words, be deeply influenced by them, but immediately something within her acted as a control. She was unwilling to trust anyone, even her own father. She was often critical of what her father said, but only she had the privilege of such criticism. She would not permit anyone else to say a word against her parents. She had inherited the fierce temper of the family but while in her grandfather and father it flared up violently only to disappear in a few moments, in Indira it went underground. On the surface she would return to calm, but she rarely forgot, and seldom forgave.

Ambiguities in her nature were surfacing. She would at times be shy, seemingly inaccessible; on other occasions, she would be aggressive. She. was very careful not to quote her father, but unconsciously, in later life, was to repeat many of his words. 'Indira was extremely proud of her father, perhaps fonder of him though more protective of her mother.'[3]

The Mahatma was held prisoner in Yeravada jail in Poona. Indira was permitted to visit him occasionally. He would converse with her, she would argue with him. As a sign of special affection, he would pull her ears. Indira regarded him as, 'an elder of the family to whom I went with difficulties and problems which he heard with the grave seriousness which was due to the large-eyed, solemn child I was.' Even as she argued with him, she was, 'amazed at his patience, his interest in and awareness of the minutest details, and the real pain he felt at any wrong doing.'[4]

The British Government, in a move to fragment the national movement, announced a separate electorate for the Harijans. The Mahatma, deeply concerned at this decision, decided to go on a fast-unto-death to protest against a divided franchise on the basis of caste. Indira felt supportive action by the school was necessary. She persuaded the Vakils to adopt a local Harijan colony, where the students started working. Two tiny Harijan girls in the neighbourhood were adopted by the school. One of the girls went back home. The other, named Urvashi by Indira, stayed on. Indira took charge of the child, bathed her, combed her hair, cut her nails and made sure that she started learning the alphabet.

The news of Gandhi's fast led to an upheaval, the like of which had seldom been seen. Temples were thrown open to the Harijans; meetings were held against untouchability; political leaders were at the vanguard of processions of Harijans who came to worship at the most sacred shrines. 'What a magician is this little man sitting in Yeravada jail and how well he knows how to pull the strings that move people's hearts!'[5] wrote Jawaharlal. Indira was observing Gandhi's shrewdness and his unerring sense of time; his insights and his capacity to tune into the hearts of the ordinary men and women of India, to be one with their rhythms. She was absorbing his capacity to concern himself with the seemingly trivial and the global. Human relationships were of vital importance to him. Right through his life, at moments of great challenge, he would continue to correspond with the inmates of his Ashram and to deal with their tiny personal problems; no letter remained unanswered.

On hearing the news of the Mahatma's fast, Kamala and Swaroop Rani hastened to Poona to be with the Mahatma. Gandhi's health deteriorated rapidly. Pressure was brought upon the Government of India to abandon the proposal for separate electorates. As the days passed the doctors grew anxious. No one knew what was going to happen. Rumours were prevalent that the government would yield. Rabindranath Tagore, who was in Poona at the time, was often by the Mahatma's bedside. On 27 September 1932, Indira wrote to her father:

> I stayed the whole day with Bapu and it was terrible to wait for the telegram to arrive, when the old man was getting weaker & weaker. At noon the Superintendent gave the good news that the tele, was on its way to Poona. Padmaja, Mummie and I rushed to the market and got the best oranges and other fruit that we could get. . .

> It was already nearly five o'clock and Bapu does not eat anything after six. So everybody, including Dr. Tagore and the jail authorities, persuaded him (Gandhiji) not to wait for Dr. Ambedkar. So immediately I prepared the juice of two oranges for him. Then Dr. Tagore sang a Bengali hymn and the Ashram people sang Bapu's favourite bhajan 'Vaishnav Jan'. Then Bapu drank the juice and everybody was given fruit and sweets as the prashad. Then we all went home—happy after an anxious day.[6]

The fast had made a great impression on Indira.

By November Kamala was back in Allahabad, seriously ill, with what the local doctors diagnosed as heart attacks and fainting fits. With no one to advise her, she decided to visit Calcutta to undergo treatment under Dr Bidhan Chandra Roy, an eminent doctor and a friend of the family. Jawaharlal was too busy with his own political life to pay more than cursory attention to Kamala; her illness continued to be treated as partly hysterical and was not considered serious.

Kamala awaited her daughter in Calcutta. A simple woman, filled with a growing morbidity, her resistance sapped by disease, Kamala had turned to religion. She desperately needed an anchor to survive. Her pride and an innate stubbornness made it impossible for her to confide in her husband and explore with him the growing darknesses which were overwhelming her. Before Indira's arrival, she had taken a sudden decision and with her mother's approval and accompanied by her, she visited the Ramakrishna Ashram and was initiated by the senior Swami Sivananda into the Ramakrishna order. Jawaharlal was not informed. Kamala asked Swami Abhayananda, a young disciple of Swami Sivananda, to keep her initiation secret; it was a personal affair 'which I want to, keep as a sacred treasure in the innermost recesses of my heart.'[7] By early March 1933, Kamala's health had improved and she travelled to Dehradun where she rented a house so that she could visit Jawaharlal whenever possible. Here she met Anand Mai Ma, the smiling woman-saint at her ashram.

Kamala had few friends and amongst them was Prabha, wife of Jayaprakash Narayan (popularly known as JP), a freedom fighter and a close friend of Jawaharlal; Prabha, sworn into celibacy by the Mahatma, spent most of her time at his Ashram. A correspondence between Kamala and Prabha commenced. Kamala wrote to Prabha: 'My visits to Mataji (Anand Mai Ma) give my Atma a great peace. If god so wishes, I will get what I desire. The question is how does one leave home? It is very difficult while staying at home.'[8] On 30 May, Anand Mai Ma left Dehradun. Kamala felt abandoned. Jawaharlal appeared unaware of her problems and did little to establish any deeper communion. Indira had returned to Poona, and seldom wrote. In another letter to Prabha, Kamala writes:

> In this world, it is your love which keeps me happy. But what will you gain by loving me? You should give your

affection to someone who can give you affection in return, for I am a stone image—I cannot even speak. Do not love me too much, sister, later you will regret it.[9]

The following summer, Indira spent her holidays with her mother in Dehradun, and often visited her father in jail. There was so much to say, so little time. Jawaharlal talked and talked and talked, 'like a tap left open.' When she returned to school, her repentant father wrote to her, 'Next time you will have to do the talking and I shall listen; and if I try to talk too much, stop me.'

Indira's grandmother, Swaroop Rani, in spite of changed circumstances, retained her imperious manner. She stayed with Kamala and Indira in Kamala's cottage. Stresses and strains were inevitable. An incident over a servant led to friction; Indira's temper flared up and there was a scene, reported in haste to Jawaharlal in jail. He wrote Indira a long letter urging her to go up to Mussoorie. Before his letter arrived, she had taken her own decision and had left for the Himalayan hill station. In his letter Jawaharlal said, 'to get hot and bothered was silly and looked ridiculous to others. To be excited or bothered is a sign of a crack in our education or harmony.' He referred to two kinds of children as problem children:

> One is the spoilt child who has been used at home to getting everything he or she wants without working for it or any other trouble. The other, the neglected child, whom people at home, usually in large families, where there are many children, ignore and who is thus not properly looked after.[10]

He further said that the spoilt child, when he goes out into the world, expects everyone to pat him on the back all the time as he was petted at home. The neglected child is not used to meeting people—so when he goes out into the world, he keeps apart from others and feels dissatisfied and angry and blames everybody.

Jawaharlal was outlining a portrait of his own daughter: spoilt and neglected. In her the two images fused.

Back in Poona, Indira sent him some limericks. 'They are not very brilliant,' he wrote back and in turn sent her amongst others, one from

Bishop Berkely's dialogues with God—remembered from his days at Trinity College, Cambridge:

> *There once was a man who said "God*
> *must think it exceedingly odd.*
> *If he finds that this tree continues to be*
> *when there is no one about in the Quad."*

> *The reply:*

> *Dear Sir, your astonishment's odd*
> *I am always about in the Quad.*
> *And that's why the tree will continue to be*
> *As observed by yours faithfully God.*[11]

EIGHT

Jawaharlal Nehru was released from prison on 31 August 1933, twelve days before the completion of his prison term. His mother lay ill in Lucknow. She had never recovered from the lathi blows she had suffered at the hands of the police, blows that had knocked her to the ground, a little over a year earlier. Her son hastened to her bedside. For the past few months, Kamala had travelled between Allahabad and Dehradun, nursing her mother-in-law and bringing some solace to her husband jailed at Dehradun. Later she took Swaroop Rani to Lucknow for medical treatment. While in Lucknow Kamala spent days nursing her mother-in-law, cooking for her and striving to please in spite of the old lady's temper. She had refused to acknowledge her own illness hoping that with the release of her husband a renewed relationship would emerge, a companionship necessary to heal her troubled mind and desperately ill body. Yet on his release, Jawaharlal immediately plunged into active politics. The little time he could spare, he spent with his mother. He had little time for Kamala.

Kamala had hesitatingly approached him to explain the events that had led to her taking initiation at the Ramakrishna Mission in Calcutta nearly a year earlier. He had been distracted and busy and had not listened. He was to admit later, when it was too late, that he had gradually grown aware of Kamala's religious inclinations but hadn't taken it seriously. At that time, he saw it as a form of hysteria and brushed it aside. 'It irritated me,' he confessed, partly because he found that her form of religion did not appeal to him and partly because,

> my vanity was hurt and I found I counted for less and less in her make-up. I seemed to be losing her. She was slipping away and I resented this and felt miserable. Many of our difficulties during the past two years were due to this background of conflict.[1]

The pressure of work or disinclination to deal with affairs that were distasteful made it impossible for him to give Kamala the attention and concern she expected. 'Indeed I tried to do nothing.' He told her that she had perfect freedom to think and act as she wanted to. 'I said so, but did not feel like it. If only I had known that those were the last days of our companionship.'

Staying with friends, nursing her mother-in-law, with a husband who showed little concern for her physical ill-health or her mental and emotional problems, and a daughter at war with the outer world, Kamala became a nervous and physical wreck. She wrote to Prabha, 'Why are you sad for me? I am not worthy of anyone's love. I have to suffer the fruits of my actions. I have sown seeds of Babul (the thorn tree) how can a mango tree sprout? . . . I am a burden in the world.'[2]

Indira, on holiday from her school in Poona, with her parents in Lucknow, sensed the ambiguity of her parents' relationship. They sapped each other's strength. Jawaharlal was neither in harmony with Kamala, nor free of her. Years later Indira was asked in what ways she was like her mother? It was suggested that they were both determined, had the same singleness of purpose, the same dedication. But perhaps Indira was more fitted for the world than Kamala. Indira replied: 'Yes, I think Kamala is responsible because I saw her being hurt and I was determined not to be hurt.'[3]

As his mother grew better Jawaharlal and his family returned to Allahabad. Having safely installed his mother at Anand Bhawan, Jawaharlal and Kamala took to the road. They travelled to Poona to see Gandhiji; they visited Indira in school; they went to Calcutta from where they travelled to Shantiniketan, the educational centre established by Rabindranath Tagore to explore India's traditions and its culture. A decision was taken in consultation with Indira that she would, on completing her matriculation examination, continue her studies at Tagore's unusual centre for the arts and learning.

As Kamala and Jawaharlal were about to return to Allahabad an earthquake devastated Bihar. The magnitude of the disaster came to light only on their return to Anand Bhawan. Relief work started—Kamala was closely involved. Soon both she and Jawaharlal embarked on a very strenuous visit to the worst-affected areas of the earthquake and were witness to the enormity of the havoc.

Jawaharlal was re-arrested five days after his return to Allahabad on 12 February, on the charge of an inflammatory speech he had delivered in Calcutta. He had been out of jail for a little over five months. His mother broke down on hearing the news. 'Kamala stood it well,'[4] but as they went upstairs to pack, she clung to him, desperate at his departure. He sent a telegram to Indira dated 12 February 1934: 'Back again to old home.' It was to reach her just before her examination.

The strain of Kamala's travels, the tragedies she had witnessed and the sheer fatigue of the journeys, particularly the very strenuous visit to the earthquake area in Bihar had accentuated her illness and soon she was confined to bed with breathlessness, pain and palpitations diagnosed as heart attacks. She was also prone to fainting spells. Emotionally she was shattered and often in tears. With Jawaharlal in jail and Indira in Poona, Kamala was totally alone and her disease struck again with fury.

By May, Jawaharlal was shifted from Alipore jail in Calcutta to Dehradun. Prison rules had become very strict. The ten-foot wall that surrounded his prison yard had been raised by four feet and he could no longer see the trees or the horizon. The starkness and loneliness of prison life closed in on him. The earlier years of euphoria were lost; Jawaharlal had left behind an ailing mother, a seriously ill wife and an empty home. His anxiety about Indira and her future clouded his mind.

Indira was tardy in writing letters and had lost contact with her father; she felt unable to cope with her mother's illness and growing morbidity. After Motilal's death there was no earning member in the Nehru family. Government fines had deprived the family of its silver, carpets, furniture and car, all confiscated and sold by the British authorities. Money was scarce. While Jawaharlal was out of jail, Kamala had sold her jewellery and part of the silver to form a trust for Indira out of the sale proceeds. Indira's grandmother constantly complained that there was no money. Indira grew acutely conscious of the fact that her father had never earned money and that they were living on the money left by her grandfather. She saw the frugal ways of Kamala; Indira grew austere and started to deny herself any luxuries. She was sixteen.

> It was in this period of my teens that I had the loneliness which people associate with the word. I felt I wanted to be more with my parents. I hated being left behind. I did not want to be with myself—it was a long period—now that I look back of my life.[5]

With her examinations over, Indira left school and joined her ailing mother at Allahabad. Kamala's illness made it impossible for her to rent a house in Dehradun as she had the previous year.

Helpless and frustrated, Jawaharlal wrote in his prison diary:

> I am definitely below par, physically and mentally. For many days I have been feeling very depressed and poorly. . . Kamala is again in the grip of her old disease and this news has oppressed me. Indu does not write to me and I get very angry. So during the last few days I have been full of irritation against Kamala and Indu and the world generally. Curious when one is in a bad mood, how one finds excuses for it and picks at otherwise trivial matters in the past.

Kamala and Indira came to see Jawaharlal on 30 June. Burdened by tensions and pressures within the family and in the outer world of politics, Kamala tried to share her anxieties with her husband. An irritated Jawaharlal asked her to keep out of it all and 'not to go to pieces at the slightest provocations.' After the meeting Jawaharlal's comments in his diary indicate the state of his mind. 'The future—the future—what is the future? It looks dark and ambivalent.'[6]

*

Kamala, from Indira's childhood, had dressed her in a kurta and pyjamas, and her thin, lanky body was often mistaken for that of a boy. But now, at sixteen, the first awareness of herself as woman arose; the coarse khadi dress gave place to coloured cotton saris.

While in Allahabad, she saw that Feroze Gandhi, whom she had first met in 1931, had become part of the household. She grew aware of the extent to which Kamala trusted him. 'He started to talk to me. I was not bothered. But I was terribly hesitant.'

With increasing ill-health, Kamala felt a growing apprehension about Indira's future. She was aware that her daughter had grown like a wayside plant, forcing its way through the soil with its own vitality. There was no one to watch over her, advise her, nurture her. Kamala had been too ill. Indira, from childhood, had begun to take her own decisions and to plan her own life, but now she was at a critical age; a dangerous age; she needed love, care and support. There was no one from amongst her family to whom Kamala could turn for advice. Swaroop Rani was old, her life centred around one obsession—her son—from whom she had been separated. Seeing Indira grown up, she suddenly came awake and started suggesting possible suitors for her granddaughter from within the Kashmiri community. Indira rebelled and turned to her mother, who stood firm and reassured her daughter that there was no question of her marrying at so early an age. But when Feroze Gandhi spoke to Kamala of his growing admiration for Indira and the hope that he could marry her, she listened. She had, over the years, developed a total trust in the young Feroze, who had befriended her when she was isolated and alone. He had fetched and carried for her; helped her with the household chores as in her political life. There was a squat earthiness in the youth, in his physical build, in his square, determined face that denoted strength. He had a drive and a latent aggression which he kept under control. She knew that he came from a strata of society far removed from the Nehru clan; she was aware of the Nehru family pride and knew that any thought of marriage between Jawaharlal's daughter and Feroze would be fiercely opposed. She mentioned Feroze's admiration to Indira but found that her daughter was not interested. Her answer to Feroze was that Indira was too young.

NINE

Shantiniketan was poet Rabindranath Tagore's response to the humiliation of a "British India." 'I said to myself that we should seek for our inheritance, and with it buy our true place in the world.'[1] The poet and philosopher in Tagore had no faith in the political struggle but instead sought a more profound basis for independence through education. He saw the civilization of the West, which had emerged from the refinement of city life, as a "brick and mortar affair". Indian civilization, on the other hand, had emerged out of forest hermitages, the ancient *tapovanam*. His school, Shantiniketan, an Abode of Peace, was located in the Bengal countryside.

A place that was wild and beautiful, with groves of *sal* and mango trees; trees that in the monsoons held the wild winds proudly, while thunder and lightning found echo in the drumbeats of the Santhals and brought peacocks out into the open as rain fell in torrents to enter and renew the rich, fertile soil of Bengal.

The poet's vision, and his search for the sources of India's heritage, brought to Shantiniketan and the school, to teach and to learn, the most sensitive minds from all over India.

Indira faced Shantiniketan with trepidation. The reputation built around the philosopher-poet Rabindranath Tagore and the awe and reverence evident amongst the people who surrounded him made her hesitant and shy. She was bewildered when on reaching Shantiniketan with her mother, she could find neither students nor teachers nor classrooms. Finally she discovered that the classes were being held beneath the trees. A life spent in the tumult and noise of political life had not prepared her for the world of art and poetry she now found herself in. 'My own home was so political and although my father had a very wide circle of friends, from intellectuals to peasants, and there were so many visitors to our house, there was not much art and music in our home.'[2]

At first Indira was lonely. A sudden vision of her father locked within a tiny jail cell in Dehradun, swept away the anger generated at her last meeting with him. 'I can never express myself well in letters,' she wrote 'but there is a strange pleasure in writing to you. I feel I am in another and a very happy world.'[3]

Her father had written to a friend and teacher in Shantiniketan to discuss Indira's courses of study. He and Kamala both felt that Indira's education should equip her for a future where she would be independent of her husband. He was aware that the academic standards were low at Shantiniketan and although he wanted Indira to study science (for without some scientific knowledge, he felt, it was hardly possible to understand the modern world), he realized that there was not much scope for that at Shantiniketan. Instead, he encouraged her to study languages and she wrote that she had taken courses in Hindi, Bengali, French and German.

Life in Shantiniketan was austere and the living conditions were primitive. The students cooked their own food, swept the floor, took cold water baths the year round. 'That itself freed me from the stresses of living in the atmosphere of my own home.' In some ways however she found the surroundings strange. 'I was never used to living amongst girls and their chit-chat. I had to get used to it.'[4]

For Indira, Shantiniketan was an interlude and an initiation. She joined the teachers and students in early morning chants, participated in the rites centred round seasons, planted saplings. 'I was in a quiet place for the first time in my life.'[5]

The presence on the campus of poets, painters, dancers and literary men from India and across the seas aroused Indira's latent artistic sensibilities. Every season had its festival, its colour, its music, its fruit, its changing sky. She learnt to tune in to seasons, to live in their flow and their flux, to savour colour, sound and touch. She relived in Shantiniketan many of the festivals she had celebrated with her grandmother when she was a child. Her favourite festival was Basant Panchami, the festival of spring; yellow was its colour; the mango blossom its flower; mating birds its resonance.

She started to walk barefoot in Shantiniketan. 'Gandhiji used to say walk barefoot because the poor man walks barefoot. But there is a walking barefoot to feel the touch of the earth, to feel its flow through the body.'[6] Although she walked barefoot in Shantiniketan her feet remained soft.

She listened to Rabindranath Tagore, fell under the spell of his personality, sensed the creative springs that flowed from the poet-philosopher. Asked by him whether she was afraid of him, she had hesitantly replied that she did not wish to disturb him. He persisted and after a time she would accompany the groups of students who sat under the flowering *mahua* tree outside Tagore's home while he painted or sang his songs.

In August Indira was urgently summoned to Allahabad where her mother was critically ill. Her father joined her, released from jail for a short period to be with Kamala. Jawaharlal found Indira weak physically; she could only do simple exercises. He chided her for allowing herself to grow limp and flabby. These were anxious days, but the crisis passed and Jawaharlal returned to jail. Before Jawaharlal's arrival, Kamala had poured out her hurt to her daughter. There was no one to attend to her needs; the servants did not come to her and Swaroop Rani and Bibi Amma did not care. An agitated Indira asked her father whether Madan Bhai, a cousin of Jawaharlal, could stay in the house and attend to Kamala's needs. Jawaharlal grew irritated, Indira tongue-tied was unable to explain the problem. Later, on her way back to Shantiniketan, her eyes bruised by pain, she wrote to her father from the waiting-room of Burdwan station:

> Do you know anything about what happens at home when you are absent? Do you know that when Mummie was in a very bad condition the house was full of people, but not one of them even went to see her or sit a while with her, that when she was in agony there was no one to help her? It was only when Madan Bhai came that she got a little comfort and with your release everything changed— people flocked from all directions, came to ask about her; sat with her—now that you have again gone and Madan Bhai cannot come as often as before, there is some danger of Mummie being left to herself as previously.[7]

Jawaharlal did not reply to his daughter's letter.

As Indira returned to Shantiniketan, leaving her desperately ill mother alone, it is possible that a feeling of guilt clouded her mind, but she cut it away with a ruthlessness surprising in a girl of her age. 'The reality of my life was so harsh that I needed to be free for my own survival.'[8]

On her return to Shantiniketan Indira had a dream. She was afloat in a vast sea. It was dark. She found she could not swim. As the waves closed over her, she awoke.

From jail her father wrote to her asking her what books he could send her—poetry, history, sociology? He suggested Plato and the Greek plays. ('Some of them so powerful that they make one shine almost.') She did not reply.

Silence and a refusal to be drawn into conflict were, Indira was to discover, formidable weapons; she learnt to disappear, to be silent.

A few days before her death I asked her what effect her Shantiniketan days had had on her life?

'I was away from myself. I do not know how to explain it. I was away from politics, noise,' she replied.

'Was it a refuge?' I asked.

'It was a refuge and a new world.'

In Shantiniketan Indira made friends. 'But I outgrew them.' She was hesitant. She spoke of one of her professors who admired her and told her that she was beautiful.

There was an elusive quality in her replies that intrigued me. She was at the threshold of a memory but shied away. I did not want to push her too far; time stretched ahead and there was no urgency to pursue the subject. I knew she would speak of it in her own time. Later the suddenness of her death left me still with the question. She had often hinted at close friendship, linking it always to her responsibilities to India and the limitations on her freedom.

A freak encounter gave me a clue to a relationship that brought, however briefly, incandescence to a hard and difficult life.

It was in Shantiniketan that she met Frank Oberdorf, a German who taught her French. He had met Rabindranath Tagore in South America in 1922 and, deeply interested in Indian culture, had come to Shantiniketan in 1933. Indira was sixteen, he thirty-four. Deeply attracted by Indira, he had no inhibitions in expressing his admiration. Indira reacted, angry at what she thought was an attempt to tease her. They quarrelled. She insisted that affairs in the country were too serious for frivolity; he persisted.

She continued to offer him friendship, he persisted in love and for a brief period they looked into each others' eyes. He was a stranger to her family. She could unburden herself, share with him many of her despairs and her loneliness. She could speak of her dearly loved ill mother and of her fears for the future.

He continued to call her beautiful, unique. She said she knew exactly what she looked like and what he or anyone else said made no difference to her.

As the intensity of the relationship increased, so did her withdrawal. She told him that there was nothing special in her; she was like any other girl. In one of her letters to Frank Oberdorf she insisted that she was an ordinary person. 'I say this is true, except for my birth, being the daughter of an extraordinary man and an exceptional woman.'

It was around the same time that Feroze Gandhi wrote to propose to her. Indira was sixteen and the admiration of men was an experience that found her vulnerable and insecure.

'I wept and wept because I was so terrified at the very idea of marriage.' Yet when Indira wrote back, her letter was free of emotion, she told Feroze that she had no intention of marrying him or anyone else. They were all involved in the freedom struggle and during a battle no serious person could think of such frivolities.

Indira, with her newly-awakened sensibilities, was eager to participate in activities where creative endeavour entered life. She joined Kala Bhavan and came under the influence of Nandlal Bose, a very well-known painter and a founder of the Shantiniketan school. Working with painters brought an intensity of seeing; Indira's eye came alive; she could touch colour directly. She was drawn towards dance and theatre. Tagore's play *Chitrangada* made a deep and lasting impact; she found the role of the woman particularly insightful. Adapted from the *Mahabharata,* the hero Arjun, while in exile, meets Chitrangada, the only child of a local king. Destined to lead her father's army into battle, she dresses and behaves like a man. Meeting Arjun, she falls in love, but he spurns her; he cannot find in her the frailty and attitudes he seeks in a woman, nor does she have a woman's wiles. Chitrangada prays to the goddess to grant her the boon of a woman's beauty and her graces. Arjun falls in love and they marry and have a son. When the time approaches for Arjun's departure Chitrangada reveals herself and proudly asks him to accept her as she is, not only as a wife, but as a companion and comrade. The story lingered in her mind. She often quoted it, in later years when speaking of the emancipation of women.

PART II

1935–1945

You educated my heart to liberty, to justice, to greatness, to beauty.

–Simon Bolivar to his tutor, Simon Rodrigues[1]

ONE

Prodded perhaps by Indira's anxieties about her mother, Jawaharlal Nehru decided, from the Allahabad jail, that Kamala should be moved to the Himalayan hill resort of Bhowali, to be in the vicinity of a TB sanitarium. Two cottages were rented for Kamala's use. Indira travelled with her mother to Bhowali from Allahabad with nurses and a doctor, Madan Atal, who was Kamala's nephew. Feroze Gandhi, Bul Naoroji and Jawaharlal's personal manservant, Hari Lal, made up the rest of the party. Up in the hills, far from the loneliness and neglect of her father's family, Indira felt that her mother was well on her way to recovery.

The Government of the United Provinces now offered to release Jawaharlal so that he could be with his wife. But the offer was conditional upon Jawaharlal's desisting from all political activity. This Jawaharlal was not willing to do, nor was Kamala willing to have her husband by her side on these terms. Later that year the government modified its stand, and in the third week of October Jawaharlal was transferred to a jail nearer Bhowali, in Almora; he was permitted to visit his wife once in three weeks.

In the Himalayas 'communing with the clouds and the sky,' Jawaharlal at first shared Indira's optimism about Kamala's recovery, even though Dr Kacker, a specialist from the sanitarium, had diagnosed an advanced case of tuberculosis. Very soon, however, optimism melted away, doubts arose.

> The brief visits I have paid her have been very precious to me and perhaps to her. We came nearer to each other than at any other time. We approach only to be parted and parted for good? The possibilities of her bright young life stare at me and mock at me.[2]

In his desolation at the prospect of losing Kamala all his earlier impatience with her dissolved; he drew close to her. After eighteen years of marriage, he again discovered the woman who was his wife. 'I was attracted by her and fascinated by the mental adventure.'

Jawaharlal's notebook entry on New Year's-day, 1935, after a two-day visit to Kamala, reveals his feelings:

> We talked and talked about the past, present & future
> and I think we succeeded in unravelling many a knot. I
> have left her today full of peace and goodwill for the
> future. And it really surprises me how attached we are to
> each other. How much she means to me and I to her.[3]

Jawaharlal's sense of exuberant rediscovery lasted only until the end of January, at which time an event occurred which brought all the incipient conflicts between husband and wife to the surface; it left Jawaharlal forlorn and resentful and was to cast a long, dark shadow across the lives of father and daughter. The prison notebook helps us reconstruct part of what occurred.

On 31 January, sitting at Kamala's bedside, Jawaharlal sensed a psychological change in her; Kamala was distant. He ignored her mood and began reading to her some of his recent writings and reciting her favourite poems. Suddenly she interrupted him to say that she wished to give away to charity part of the proceeds from the sale of her jewellery, which had been meant to be put away as an investment for Indira's future. Taken aback, Jawaharlal questioned "the objects of her charity" and asked her to reconsider the matter. Directly, and with great simplicity, Kamala told him what she had hinted at for three years but had never found the words to convey. She wanted to give herself to God. As a preparation for this, their relationship had to undergo some change. Wryly, he noted in his prison diary on 1 February 1935, 'Apparently I am not to come in the way of God.'

Jawaharlal spent the night in Bhowali at a complete loss. He had never had any sympathy for Kamala's religion; he thought it was a product of hysteria—the outcome of a diseased mind contributing its share to the disease of the body. As he wandered the hillside unable to sleep, he stumbled and groped his way in the darkness, gazing at the faint shapes of the mountains and the stars. 'How bright and changeless they were in a changing world.'

In the morning he was again at Kamala's bedside. He tried to reach her, to communicate his misery, but to no avail. They parted with brave efforts to smile; the sting remained with Jawaharlal. 'I seem to be losing her,' he wrote in his diary on 1 February. 'She seems to be slipping away and I resented this and feel miserable.'

Kamala's intuitive sense that Jawaharlal would not understand her need for religion was again justified at Bhowali. But she still had not developed any defences against this lack of understanding, and she wrote in despair to her friend Prabha, wife of Jayaprakash Narayan:

> He is angry with me. There is no one with me now except God. The world is a net and if one is entangled in it, there is sorrow and more sorrow. I made a big mistake by spending thirty-five years of my life as a housewife. If I had searched for God during that period, I would have found Him.[4]

Kamala was only thirty-five years old at the time and the detachment from life that she sought continued to elude her. For when Jawaharlal's whole family, his mother and sisters, came up to see her at Bhowali in mid-April and she saw Jawaharlal draw comfort and warmth in these old, familial relationships, she felt excluded: 'Who is mine and to whom do I belong? The world is an illusion, everything in it is a play of coming and going. If I were strong like Bapu (Gandhi), then while living in this world I would be out of it.'[5]

The illness accentuated Kamala's underlying religious fervour; contradiction and confusion filled her mind. She saw visions and felt exalted. She felt that the Lord Krishna had come to her. 'At times I feel that I am Krishna,' she wrote to Swami Abhayananda of the Ramakrishna Mission. As her physical condition deteriorated, Doctor Kacker advised a trip to Europe for further medical treatment.

Indira's short interlude at Shantiniketan came to an end in March 1936. Rabindranath Tagore received a letter from Jawaharlal to say that Indira was being withdrawn from Shantiniketan in order to accompany a seriously ill Kamala to Europe for medical treatment. Jawaharlal thanked the poet for everything he had done for Indira. When Indira saw Tagore before leaving Shantiniketan, he urged her to take a companion with her on the long journey to Bhowali, but she refused and by the middle of April was by her mother's bedside, alone.

Jawaharlal came to Bhowali on 1 May, and Indira observed the subtle change in her father's attitude to his ailing wife. He was formal towards Kamala and, in turn, Kamala's responses were ambivalent. Indira controlled her emotions but it tore her apart to see new divisive strains intrude upon her parents' relationship.

It had been decided that, besides Indira, Dr Madan Atal would accompany Kamala to Europe. They were to go via Allahabad to Bombay, and then proceed by an Italian liner to Genoa. Their eventual destination was Berlin where Kamala was to have an operation. It was also planned that Indira attend school in Switzerland during her mother's recovery period and eventually go on to university in Europe.

On the eve of her departure from Bhowali, Indira received a curiously ambivalent letter of farewell from her father. The letter reveals the growing strain between father and daughter and delineates the areas of conflict in the relationship between an Indian father and his only daughter. 'How far you will be from me then, moving rapidly across the Arabian Sea,' he wrote affectionately. 'And I wonder when and where I will see you again.' Nevertheless he recognized that it was neither the distance nor the high seas which really separated them. 'We create these distances in our minds, physically they are not really great.' He hinted that even when they were together there was a gulf. 'We met at Bhowali last week after nearly six months. And yet old habits and our early ideas persist . . .' He put the responsibility for the gulf between them on Indira's temper: she was too self-centred, brought up as she was in the hot-house atmosphere of Anand Bhawan. Towards the end of the letter he expressed the hope that she would change as she learnt the ways of cooperation in a larger world. 'Perhaps all this is for the good, good for you and good for me. You will have to shift for yourself and not rely on me.'[6]

Jawaharlal did not doubt his own love for Indira, nor his ability to break through the constricting prison walls and reach out to her. 'The mind cannot be enchained and I have developed the habit of undertaking great journeys mentally.' This was part of the self-image he shared with his father and his sister Vijayalakshmi—an open-hearted generosity, an expansiveness which encompassed the world. At another level, his own identification with his daughter was complete. 'I want you to be happy in your youth for so I renew my own youth and participate in your own joy.' And so he dwelt on the need for his daughter's mind to be as clear and unclouded as a mirror. Otherwise, 'one becomes self-centred and selfish, oblivious of one's own failings and always finding fault with others.' He told Indira that she must free herself from the traditions of her prominent family, be confident to do what she thought 'proper and right.' Then, he added:

> To some extent you cannot get rid of the family tradition, for it will pursue you and, whether you want to or not, it will give you a certain public position which you may have done nothing to deserve. That is unfortunate, but you will have to put up with it. After all it is not a bad thing to have a good family tradition. It helps us to keep looking up, it reminds us that we have to keep a torch burning and that we cannot cheapen ourselves or vulgarise ourselves.[7]

Towards the end of the long letter, Jawaharlal casually mentioned Allahabad, informing Indira of his decision to hand over Anand Bhawan to Vijayalakshmi and her husband, Ranjit Pandit. 'The whole house will be at their disposal.' He added that his and Kamala's rooms were to be kept unchanged, but that Indira's room was to be made available to the Pandits. 'If you want to put any of your personal effects apart, you may put them in my room.' He, however, was not very encouraging on this score. 'I do not want my room to be converted into a luggage room.'[8]

For Indira the letter marked the end of her childhood. Her room at Anand Bhawan was her refuge; it was a space of her own. It contained memories of her earliest years as she had always been a hoarder of little things: a ribbon, a pressed leaf, a schoolbook with notes and doodles, her dolls, a costume worn at a fancy dress party— for she loved dressing up—a birthday gift, however insignificant. These were her cherished treasures, her memories. With a single parental decision, taken without even a by-your-leave, the room and much of what it contained was to be handed over to a person who symbolized for her the darker moments of her childhood, the person she held most responsible for her mother's tears.

Jawaharlal's decision to hand over the family house to Vijayalakshmi inflicted a wound that never healed. Indira spoke of it half-a-century later when a wide grey streak like a bird's wing had entered her hair. At the time she did not protest her father's decision, but along with her room and her cherished belongings, her childhood was swept away. Indira did not forgive, however in 1970, Vijayalakshmi Pandit attended the ceremony marking the conversion of Anand Bhawan into a memorial, as a guest. Indira, then Prime Minister, denied her aunt's request that she be allowed to stay overnight at Anand Bhawan.[9]

The journey to Allahabad was very strenuous for Kamala and she arrived at Anand Bhawan on a stretcher. Feroze Gandhi accompanied the mother and daughter on the next lap of the journey. In Bombay they were met by many of Jawaharlal's friends and also by Mahatma Gandhi who sensed that Kamala would not return to India. Their meeting was marked by emotion on both sides. It is likely that Kamala sought Gandhi's help and advice on behalf of Feroze, the young man who had nursed her so devotedly during her illness. Feroze's aunt, Dr Commissariat, who was to sponsor his education in England had withdrawn her offer because she disapproved of Feroze's devotion to the Nehrus; Feroze's family was conservative and opposed to the Congress party. Gandhiji promised to help the young man.

Indira now took charge of her mother's life in her own practical and matter-of-fact manner. She saw herself as a young woman with a strong will, responsible for her mother, sure of herself and with the ability to determine the future course of her life. She told Jawaharlal not to worry, that she and, 'Mummie would manage things marvellously.' 'You have no business to do otherwise, for you have the family reputation to keep up,' came Jawaharlal's reply in a letter dated 26 May 1935.

As Jawaharlal's letters, illuminated with snatches of schoolboy Wordsworth and Byron, followed Indira's journey from Bombay to Berlin, it became transmuted in his romantic mind into a daughter's voyage of discovery—of a wider and more liberal world. He hoped that she would give up her adolescent, self-centred, "valetudinarian" attitudes and emerge as her father's and grandfather's daughter— open-hearted, generous and ready 'to make friends with life and to meet it with open arms and mind.'[10]

*

A group of Indian nationalists, including Subhas Chandra Bose, were present to receive Indira and her mother when they got off the *wagon lit* in Vienna on 4 June 1936. Their ship had docked the previous day, just as 40,000 Fascist troops were leaving for Abyssinia (modern Ethiopia). On 16 June they reached Berlin where Kamala was operated on by a Doctor Unverricht. Though the operation was declared a success, Kamala developed a very high fever soon afterwards. The doctor advised a period of complete rest in a sanitarium in Germany where he could keep in touch with his patient. A sanitarium in Badenweiller, a small town close to the Swiss border, was chosen. Dr Atal accompanied Kamala to the sanitarium.

Determined now to enlarge her world and, in her father's words, grow "out of her narrow national self", Indira wrote to Mile Hemmerlin, the lady in charge of the L'Ecole Nouvelle at Bex, Switzerland, about possible admission to the school. She planned eventually to enter the University at Zurich to study Economics and Sociology. She cut her hair short and noted defiantly that Subhas Bose and his friends thoroughly disapproved of an Indian woman with short hair. She also decided to discard her Indian saris in favour of dresses because she felt that everybody turned round to stare at her. In Berlin she went to a dressmaker and ordered several 'frocks'. When these were not ready in time for the planned departure to Badenweiller, Indira decided to postpone her departure.

Germany was preparing for war; there was the constant sound of low-flying aeroplanes, and the night sky was criss-crossed with searchlights. Despite the tension in the air, Indira enjoyed the three days she spent wandering the streets of Berlin by herself. She was neither nervous nor frightened, nor did she shut herself up in her room without eating, as Kamala had feared.

In Badenweiller, Indira found Kamala had settled comfortably into the sanitarium, looked after by nurses and doctors and watched over by a companion, the high-spirited Mrs Geissler, a lady who spoke perfect German, French and English. Dr Atal had taken rooms in a *pension* in town and was trying to lose the weight he had gained on board the Italian liner. However, on reaching Badenweiller, Indira herself fell ill. The doctors suspected appendicitis, but the tests did not reveal anything.

Indira's original plan had been to spend three days at Badenweiller and then go on to the school at Bex. But now that she had fallen ill, she allowed Mrs Geissler to convince her that the entrance tests to the University at Zurich were too demanding, and that she could not possibly get through the test in her present state of health and her less than adequate command of German.

Jawaharlal was more upset by her illness than by her change in plans; his deep fears that Indira had inherited her mother's morbidity surfaced. To Dr Atal he confided his worries: 'It is curious how nothing radically wrong has been found with Indu and yet she does not prosper.' To Indira he wrote gently of his dislike of her 'hob-nobbing too closely with a tribe of doctors,' and of his fears that she had no friends of her own age at Badenweiller. 'Companionship draws us out of ourselves and we forget our narrow selves in cooperative habits and wider questions.'[11]

As Kamala's health improved under Mrs Geissler's good-humoured care, Indira grew light-hearted in pine-scented Badenweiller. She made friends with Mrs Geissler, went bathing early in the morning in the famous springs. Basking in the soft sun she fed birds and protected the caterpillars on which the birds fed; she attended band-concerts at Kurpark. Soon she felt the need to put some distance between herself and Dr Atal and moved away from the, *pension* to live with Mrs Geissler and her sister. In a cheerful letter to her father, dated 5 July, Indira described Dr Atal's hapless attempts at learning German. 'He is now more keen on improving his figure. His tummy was large enough as it was, but he increased it by a good inch on board the *Conte Rossi.'*

Dr Unverricht had promised that Kamala would be cured within the month. So it was a cheerful and optimistic Indira who set out for Switzerland at the end of July to explore the possibilities of entering her old school at Bex. At Bex, she met her former teacher Mlle Hemmerlin and also Romain Rolland's sister. Travelling to Ascona, near Lake Lugano, Indira appears to have attended a conference on Eastern and Western thought, motored around a few villages around Lago Maggiore "with friends" who may have included Frank Ober-dorf, her admirer from Shantiniketan. There is no mention of this meeting in her letters to Oberdorf, with whom she carried on a regular correspondence, but a photograph found among Frank Oberdorf's papers, of a demurely radiant Indira, seated outdoors in an European café, survives as an emblem of the meeting. Frank Oberdorf continued to address ardent letters to her at Badenweiller; he talked about her beauty; and about the spirit that passed from her to him. Her replies were hedged in negatives. She thought he was flattering her—she did not like flattery; she was not beautiful; he had bad taste; nothing had passed between them. Moreover, she felt that it was intensely irritating to be called beautiful again and again.

Isolated in prison in Almora, several weeks behind in the news of his sick wife at Badenweiller, Jawaharlal pondered over Kamala's illness, the religious life that Kamala had taken refuge in, his own character and their relationship. He put these reflections in a letter on 19 July. The letter reached Kamala in August when she was in a particularly vulnerable state. Indira was away in Switzerland and the cheerful Mrs Geissler had decided to take a holiday. Parts of the letter were pointedly harsh:

> What is called the religious life is absolutely dangerous for it increases selfishness and suppresses the real matter of the spirit and secondly there is only one remedy for both the individual and for the country and that is right education.[12]

Indira returned to Badenweiller at the end of June, deeply tanned and looking healthy, to see her mother tired and very weak. In a letter to her father, dated 29 August 1935, she wrote, 'Mummie is very tired & exhausted because of the continuous high temperature and so she doesn't talk and hardly listens when anyone else talks.' The idyll of summer was not to last into the autumn. With the advent of autumn's chilly winds, once again Indira entered the emotional distress of her mother's world.

As the long summer days grew shorter Kamala's life began to ebb. Indira would visit her twice a day, in the morning and in the evening. As she returned home to her *pension* every evening from the sanitarium, she would feel the trees of the Black Forest closing in upon her. Memories of forgotten fairy-tales, of children lost in brooding forests, would come alive. The darkness pursued her; the branches of trees, distorted in the half light of mist and rain, reached out to hold her. There were sudden storms, lightning lit the sky and thunder struck, and the sounds of the wind tortured tree and leaf. Back in her room, Indira would sit alone with the curtains drawn. For her these dark forces of nature came to symbolize the furies pursuing her stricken mother, as defenseless against her incurable disease as she had been against her husband's domineering family. The storms' terror settled in Indira's heart.

Fifty years later, as I sat with her at her home in 1, Safdarjung Road, a violent storm broke. I had rarely seen Indira so agitated. She rang for the servants, asked them to close the doors, draw the curtains, all in a very agitated way. She was so unlike herself that I asked her what had happened. She turned to me and said: 'Ever since Badenweiller, I cannot bear thunder and lightning and the sound of high winds in the trees.' She spoke in broken sentences. 'I was alone in the Black Forest, my mother was dying and I cannot bear to hear the sound of the winds, particularly when it rises at night. I have never been able to free myself of this terror.'

On 1 September, Amiya Chakravarti, an old friend of the family, visited Badenweiller and was told by the doctors that Kamala's case was now hopeless and that she could die at any moment. Informed that her mother was now dying, Indira found it impossible to keep her composure. Dr Madan Atal was away in Austria, so she wrote to several of her father's friends. To Agatha Harrison, an old friend of Gandhi's and Nehru's, she said: 'Dr. Steffan has already cabled to Lord Zetland the Viceroy to India. He has also sent a telegram to my father, informing him of my mother's critical condition.'[13]

Jawaharlal was released from jail in Almora on 4 September; he took the first flight to Germany to be with his dying wife. Agatha Harrison arrived in Badenweiller to find Indira with Subhas Bose. In a letter to Gandhiji, she described Indira as a thin, desperate adolescent, with huge eyes burdened with sorrow—'a pathetic figure— though young in years—old beyond her years in experience and suffering.' She was at Badenweiller when Jawaharlal arrived and Amiya wrote to the Mahatma of the meeting between father and daughter:

> Nehru was standing in the sun talking to Dr Atal, Subhash and Indira. So strange to think a few days before, he was in prison in India—and now in the sun in the heart of the Black Forest—free. What touched and moved me most

was to watch this father and daughter. Indira was holding tight to his arm, every now and then rubbing her head against his shoulder and some of the "years" that I had noticed the day before seemed to have slipped away, and she was a different person.[14]

TWO

'The essential thing is to develop in oneself the thirst for learning and understanding which may always prod us on.' These words, written by Jawaharlal Nehru to Kamala Nehru on 19 July 1935 from the Almora jail, were, in the context, a form of rebuke, but they concealed as well Jawaharlal's anxieties about his daughter. Shortly after his arrrival in Badenweiller, and once the immediate crisis in Kamala's illness had passed, Jawaharlal began to plan Indira's future. Indira's education had so far been erratic. She had been to several schools in India, yet had not taken very much from them. She had managed to pass out from the school at Poona without really discovering where her interest and talents lay. Her sojourn at Shantiniketan was all too brief. She therefore found herself in Europe at the age of eighteen without any real academic focus.

Added to her lack of academic direction, there was her shy manner and her tendency to withdraw into brooding silences, a trait that even her father found unnerving. Jawaharlal was convinced that Indira had a good ear for languages, and so it was decided that she should spend a year at Mlle Hemmerlin's school at Bex learning German and building up a knowledge of French. Before sending her to join the Swiss school, Jawaharlal decided to travel to England with Indira, to find a publisher for the book he had been writing in the Almora jail, and to see whether Indira would be able to join Oxford University after leaving Bex.

On 29 October, with Dr Madan Atal watching over Kamala, Indira and Jawaharlal left for London. There they met V.K. Krishna Menon for the first time. Krishna Menon had by this time founded the India League and was to emerge later as a doughty critic of the British Government and its Indian policy. He and Nehru became good friends; Menon accepted the responsibility of arranging to publish Jawaharlal's autobiography. At Oxford, Indira was interviewed by Vera Farnell for entrance to Sommerville College, a women's college affiliated to Oxford University.

Two days before Indira and Jawaharlal returned from Europe another crisis brought Kamala to the edge of death. Kamala's face seemed to change from day to day; at times she looked young and beautiful, deluding Jawaharlal and Indira into imagining that she was better, the next day she would gasp for breath and they would feel that she was about to die. 'One finds it hard to hope,' wrote Jawaharlal to Ghosiben Captain (daughter of Dadabhai Naoroji) in a letter dated 28 December 1935 'and yet I must say that I am not hopeless. Both Kamala and I have a hard core which carries on and it is difficult for us to admit or imagine defeat.'[1] Indira was to inherit this 'hard core' in full measure.

Indira left Badenweiller for Bex at the end of November. She could not settle down there. Between the nagging anxiety about her mother's health, her inability to learn a language systematically through its grammar, her dislike of the German teacher, the fact that she was much older than the rest of the students, and the howling of the "föhn", Indira found schoollife oppressive. She fretted over the singing and dancing which took up much of her time and the walks which were compulsory.

It was only when the first snow arrived in December and the gymnastics teacher began ski lessons that her spirits lifted. She loved the sport and became so proficient at it that she planned a skiing holiday in Wengen with her cousin Vidya. Frank Oberdorf was in Wengen when they arrived (whether by chance or by design, is difficult to ascertain.) He was an expert skier and taught Indira to tackle the more difficult slopes. As full of admiration as ever, he showered her with compliments. Indira basked in his admiration but continued to fend off his ardent overtures.

Meanwhile, Feroze Gandhi's aunt, Dr Commissariat, who had up to that moment threatened to stop supporting Feroze Gandhi's education in England because of his links with radical Congress politics, relented. She agreed to finance his education at the London School of Economics (LSE). Feroze intended to stop at Badenweiller to see Kamala before going on to London. He arrived in Switzerland in late December. In the sanitarium he found Kamala with Jawaharlal by her side. He was told that Indira, who had spent Christmas with her parents, was now away on a skiing holiday in Wengen.

On 31 December, on the eve of the New Year, Feroze Gandhi travelled to Wengen to see Indira. He found Indira exhilarated, but preoccupied. For a while, they talked of Kamala's illness and of Indira's future plans. Indira was sure her mother would recover; she had left her looking young and beautiful. Hope surged within her, she felt everything was well, it could not be otherwise. Feroze, perhaps sensing her preoccupation, though it is not certain that he met Oberdorf, felt excluded, and left Wengen the same evening.

Feroze stayed with Kamala at Badenweiller while Jawaharlal went on a short visit to France and to London. Did Feroze communicate to Kamala his apprehensions of Indira's friendship with Oberdorf? Did they discuss Indira's future? Did Kamala make Feroze promise that he would protect Indira, marry her if possible? Kamala was aware of the circumstances that made it difficult for Jawaharlal to take care of an adolescent daughter, but she must have also been aware that a marriage between her daughter and Feroze would lead to explosions within the Nehru family. She also knew of her daughter's deep attachment to her father, and how painful it would be for Indira to cut herself off from her father, should he disapprove of the marriage.

Before returning to Bex from Wengen, Indira stopped at Badenweiller and spent long hours with her mother. In those last days, it is possible that Kamala spoke to her about Feroze's devotion and her absolute trust in his ability to protect Indira. She may even have suggested to her daughter that she would be able to die in peace, knowing that Indira would be taken care of by this strong and reliable young man.

Jawaharlal's visit to London and Paris was a great success. In Paris he met the intellectuals of the French Left, André Gide and André Malraux. In London he was surrounded by admirers who saw in Jawaharlal a heroic symbol of the struggle for independent India. In London he received a telegram informing him that the presidentship of the Indian National Congress had been conferred on him and that his presence was urgently required in India. The news was exhilarating. Returning to Badenweiller, though, doubts returned when he found Kamala deeply disturbed. A young Irishman she had befriended in the sanitarium had died, leaving her distraught. She pleaded with Jawaharlal to take her away from Badenweiller to a sanitarium in Switzerland. Jawaharlal agreed to do so, but soon after his attention slipped away to events in India.

Under pressure from his political colleagues in India to return and accept the presidentship of the Congress, he hesitated and finally booked his passage back to India by a KLM flight on 28 February. It is a matter of wonder how a man as sensitive as Jawaharlal, so awake to natural beauty, so concerned with poverty, so fired by the freedom struggle, could inflict a grievous hurt on his critically ill wife, and was unaware of the enormity of the responsibility he was about to place on his eighteen-year-old daughter's shoulders, that too in a foreign country. 'Think of me as I am,' he wrote once to Padmaja Naidu, 'full of conceit and full of myself, callously unaware of what I do to others. It is not a lovely picture but it is nearer the truth than the imaginary picture in most minds.'[2]

Dr Madan Atal made arrangements for moving Kamala from Badenweiller to the Clinique Sylvana near Lausanne. On 30 January, the day of the move, Jawaharlal was away in London where he was invited to address members of the House of Commons, and Indira was at Bex. Indira wrote to her father: 'The journey is going to be an awful strain and I should feel happier if you were accompanying her.' Jawaharlal did not return. It was Dr Atal, and not Jawaharlal, who finally accompanied Kamala to Lausanne. Indira's letter of 23 January is full of anxieties she could not name.

> I woke up on Sunday morning with a queer singing feeling in my heart. At first I was not quite sure whether it indicated sorrow or joy—later I decided . . . the feeling is one of joy. I lay in bed . . . thinking of . . . the past and what the years . . . would bring. I thought of you and Mummie. I felt curiously peaceful. Where and when had I felt like this before? . . . Since then, the feeling has remained. I love everything—the horrible south wind included—and I am feeling happy and frightfully optimistic about everything.[3]

When on the evening of 30 January no telegram of her mother's safe arrival reached her at Bex, she telephoned Dr Atal. She was at the clinic in Lausanne, the next day, with a bouquet of spring flowers, violets and primroses, for her mother. Indira stayed at Lausanne until Jawaharlal's return on 7 February. With the date of Jawaharlal's departure fixed for 28 February, Indira contemplated the prospects of the future that awaited her. 'I am afraid I have really got all the bad qualities of an only child and feel so dependent on you. I do not know what I am going to do when I shall be left alone.'[4]

As the day of Jawaharlal's departure approached, Kamala's condition deteriorated. Her temperature soared and in her delirium she began to see visions. 'Her body, after the terrible long fight it has put up seems to have exhausted all its strength and is deteriorating,' Jawaharlal wrote to Swami Abhayananda on 26 February from Lausanne. 'I was to have left day after tomorrow for India but now I have postponed the trip for ten or twelve days.'

Kamala was only thirty-seven years old when she died early on the morning on 28 February, the very day Jawaharlal was to have left for India. She faded away without losing any of her grace or beauty. Indira had spent many hours with her the previous day, and then gone out on a short walk. On her return, Kamala had asked her, 'Where have you been?' Those were her last words to Indira. Jawaharlal and Dr Atal were by Kamala's side when the end came, Indira was in an adjoining room.

Kamala was cremated at Lausanne in a small ceremony with very few people present. Jawaharlal and his eighteen-year-old daughter went to Montreaux to be alone together, to face and to share, if possible, the agony of Kamala's death. Indira's grief was silent, its depths could not be fathomed. She had loved her mother with a passion and a protective feeling that were instinctual. Unable to come to terms with her mother's life, in particular with the manner in which she had been treated by her father's family, and the neglect she had suffered from Jawaharlal, Indira withdrew from the situation to spin invisible threads that would enclose her pain and shield her from the world. Thirty-five years later, a woman journalist asked Indira whether it took her a long time to recover from Kamala's death. Indira replied: 'I don't know. I don't like the word "recover" because I think that a wound like this never heals. The scar and the effect of it are always there in some way. . . . I do think of her as if she were here quite often.'[5]

Jawaharlal, lost in regret, sought solace in nostalgia; and dedicated his autobiography, published by the Bodley Head, "To Kamala, who is no more". Returning to India, he was overwhelmed by the tributes to his late wife that flowed in from all sides. Among them was a letter from the Mahatma: 'So you leave Kamala forever in Europe and yet her spirit was never out of India and will always be your precious treasure as it will be of many of us. I shall never forget the last talk which melted our four eyes.'[6] He ended the letter with a hope that:

'Indu bore well the grief of Kamala's death and the almost immediate separation from you. What is her address?'

After Jawaharlal's departure, Indira went back to Bex and then accompanied her fellow-students on a tour of Italy. In Taormina for the first time she saw a Greek tragedy in an open air theatre, and felt her whole life reenacted on the stage. To discover life through an ancient art form provided a sense of release.

She returned to Bex lighter in spirit with fresh plans to transfer to the Badminton School in England. The school would prepare her for entrance to Oxford. A letter from the Mahatma reached her at the same time. It began with the traditional form of address:

*Chiranjeevi** Indu,

Kamala's passing away has added to your responsibilities but I have no misgivings about you. You have grown sufficiently wise to understand your *dharma* completely. Kamala possessed qualities rarely found in other women. I am hoping that all these qualities of Kamala will be manifest in you in equal measure. May God give long Life and strength to emulate her virtues.[7]

For five years after Kamala's death Indira found herself adrift in a world which had lost its old certainties. Anand Bhawan, the family home, which in her grandfather's time had seemed to be the hub of the universe, could no longer sustain her. Her grandfather and mother were dead, her great-grandmother Dolamma was old, almost a wraith, weary of life. Moreover, various compulsions in Jawaharlal's own life had brought him to a stage when he felt he was a 'homeless itinerant'. The way back to her father was for many years to remain blocked for Indira.

Jawaharlal's decision to leave the eighteen-year-old Indira behind in Europe after the tragedy of her mother's death, can be explained partially by his fear that as an only child she was spoiled in the family home, and that only the discipline of an European education would give her the strength and the independence of mind which were

---

* Meaning "Long Lived".

necessary in order to play a role in public life in India. In December 1938, at a moment of self-doubt, he had confessed in a letter to her:

> Many years ago I used to dream that when you grew up, you would play a brave part in what is called public life in India, to shoulder this heavy burden, to help in putting brick upon brick in the building of the India of our dreams. And I wanted you to train and fit yourself in body and mind for this engrossing task. But I am not sure that I desire you to do this now, and to experience the heartache and the crushing of spirit that this involves. Each one of us had enough burden to carry, so we do much good by shouldering the burden of others? Yet we may not and cannot escape from them. *But it is perhaps better for us to function in a limited sphere that we understand and to serve India in that restricted field, rather than presume to enter the wide expanse of Indian humanity.*[8]

This dream for his daughter, in keeping with his own expansive temper, occupied a large canvas—"not to serve India in a restricted field" but to "presume to enter the wide expanse of Indian humanity." This was the mystical tradition of the family to which Jawaharlal held the door open for his daughter to enter. This was the role for which he had prepared her since her childhood when he wrote the history of the world for her in letters from jail.

For the next five years Indira bent her will and her intellect to living out Jawaharlal's dream. And she took the first steps towards a good education by accepting a place at the Badminton School in Bristol, in preparation for Oxford. This too was part of her father's dream: the Western education which would free her from her narrow self.

Prior to entering school she spent several months in London sharing a flat, 24, Fairfax Avenue, with Shanta Gandhi, an old friend from Poona. It was at this stage that Feroze Gandhi entered Indira's life, to become the counterpoint to her father's world. He was everything that Indira was not: outgoing, exuberant, warm, public where she was inward-looking, secretive and private. He was the man Kamala had trusted. She invited Shanta to meet Feroze, calling him "a very special friend". Feroze took the two young women to a small café where they had supper together. This gesture touched Indira, for she knew that Feroze had very little money and worked at manual jobs to supplement his income.

Feroze introduced Indira to the world of classical music; taught her to attune her ear, to listen, to allow sound to fill her. This was a new experience for Indira. The Nehrus were not musical, they neither sang nor played any musical instrument, nor were there any musical soirées in their home in Allahabad, even in the old days of luxurious living.

The memory of Kamala was a bond between Indira and Feroze. Shanta remembers that both appeared resentful of Jawaharlal and of Vijayalakshmi Pandit's influence over him. They shared the feeling that Jawaharlal and his family had not understood Kamala's innocence and her simplicity.

In London, Shanta found Indira more self-assured, eager to meet her father's friends, to go out to lunch and to the theatre. Harold Laski and Agatha Harrison, Indira's guardians in England, spoiled her, invited her constantly to their homes.

When Frank Oberdorf came to visit her in London, he was as ardent as ever. Indira and he went for long walks in Regents Park. He told her again of his love and perhaps proposed marriage. Indira was not swept away by him; indeed she was not a woman to be swept away by any man's adorations. Her upbringing had left her with a certain primness and rectitude which she did not lose, and marriage to Frank Oberdorf in 1936 would certainly have entailed the betrayal of her father's dream. She told Frank that some things were impossible between them, not because of what people might say, but because of how she felt. Feroze was her refuge; Frank Oberdorf was a friend. Certainly her future did not lie in Europe.

Indira's letter to her father reflects her pleasure at being among friends in a large city:

> It is funny how living in a city by oneself one grows to love it. Such is my feeling for London. I got to love the grounds, the parks and everything . . . a tiny room to sleep in—the whole city to live in and no one to bother about you—to go and come whenever you want to. . . . If only one did not miss some people so much.[9]

And yet, beyond the powers of her cognition, and simultaneously with her outer life, the lean shadow of pain continued to hover over her heart and sometimes closed in. On 29 September 1936 the prospect of joining school allowed these feelings to surface. It was an anxiety which she could not name, recorded in a letter to her father:

I have begun to laugh (not giggle) rather a lot. That ought to be a good thing but I am not sure that it is—I never know whether I laugh because I am amused or to hide some other feeling or just like that for nothing. Some people remarked that I had become younger and gayer— but I don't know that I feel it. And that laughing business I do not like.[10]

'I do miss you terribly,' she continued, 'at times there is a terrible desire to fly to you.'

*

Indira was reluctant to leave the pleasant life she had built around herself in London to go to school in Bristol. It meant the loss of familiar friends and a return to rules and regulations and the anonymity of community life in an alien culture. She realized, how- ever, that she needed discipline and that she would not be able to prepare for her examinations in London, and so went to school in Bristol.

After Indira left London, Feroze began confiding in Shanta; he spoke with bitterness of Kamala's last days and of how she was neglected and hurt by the Nehru pride. He saw in Indira traces of this pride, which, he felt, occasionally affected their relationship. He told Shanta that the Nehru connection was fraught with many dangers. When Shanta asked him what he meant, he told her: 'If my relation- ship with Indira continues as at present, I see many difficulties ahead.' He did not have many illusions; they discussed Indira's incapacity to completely surrender herself to anyone. She could take but not give. She was not prepared, he thought, to merge or lose her separate identity, even for a moment.

School was not a happy experience for Indira, even though the

Badminton School was beautiful 'with terraces of roses, wistaria trailing over stone balustrates, green lawns and clipped yew hedges.' It was also progressive and left-wing; its principal, Beatrice May Baker, was involved with the women's movement for peace, and her anti-Fascist students felt passionately about the Spanish Civil War. But the cold together with the icy winds and the 'chatter of the girls' made a stronger impression on her than all the political discussions. 'I woke up this morning with a rather wretched feeling—a strange emptiness and desperate loneliness. . . . I attended a couple of lectures but don't know what they were about and it was impossible to read.'[11]

The students' reaction to King Edward VIII's abdication convinced Indira that imperialism lurked underneath the liberal socialist exterior of the students there, even though 'they hate to hear you say so, they worship the king.'

To Indira, writing nostalgically about her school days at Shantiniketan, Jawaharlal sent back the flattering letter he had received about her from Tagore: 'Indira is a charming child who has left behind a pleasant memory in the minds of her teachers and fellow students. She has your strength of character as well as your ideas.'

Iris Murdoch, the writer, who was at the same school, remembered Indira. 'She was frail and delicate, looking very shy and withdrawn. gentle and responsive and anxious to "fit in", but, not unnaturally aloof.'[12]

Indira wrote to her father:

> It is difficult to fit in with the usual British school girl. I have inherited a different life—an entirely different background. . . . I hate chatting unless I have something to say. I can get used to it, as one does to everything. Though having settled down in a regular school life I feel—dead (that is the only word which approaches the meaning I wish to convey.)[13]

Implicit in sorrow and death is the aftermath; two pathways lie open—one, a stepping forward, wherein loss is transmuted; the other a stepping backward into the intoxicating desire to follow death into remoter regions of the self. Across Indira's 'terrible desire to fly to her father' fell Kamala's shadow—young, beautiful, dead; and there-fore eternally pure. Indira's fascination with the thought of following her mother found expression in a letter to Frank Oberdorf:

> Do you know I would like to die like my mother. Not in pain like her for I have not the courage to bear it—but young and pure and loved. My mother was 35 years old when she died but she never looked a day over 22 and each day, lying in her bed, she looked beautiful. Today she lives in so many hearts (for whoever knew her loved her) as a beautiful picture of youth and purity and courage, a picture that will help and encourage them. Would it have been so if it had been an old wrinkled woman, however lovable? Age seems terrible. Each time I see an old person, almost unconsciously I think, "Oh God, don't let me ever be like that. . ."[14]

The correspondence between Indira and Oberdorf continued. Frank questioned her about her wanting to be a boy. Indira's response was that it was her mother who, in her father's orthodox household, was always trying to dress herself as a man and later saw to it that her daughter Indira as far as possible wore boy's clothes in the Nehru household.

Flying kites, climbing trees, playing marbles with her boy-cousins, Indira said she hardly knew the difference between a boy and a girl till the age of twelve. It was then that she realized that boys were arrogant and full of themselves; she hated that.

Invited by Frank Oberdorf to go with him to Germany, the im-perious streak dormant in the nineteen-year-old Indira surfaced. On 13 October 1936, she wrote to Frank Oberdorf that her going with him to Germany was out of the question, not because of public opinion but because she did not love him. Nor did she want to either, not if he was the last man on earth.

Frank did not give up but continued to write and sent her a large bouquet of flowers on her birthday, 19 November.

THREE

Soon after his wife's death in Switzerland, Jawaharlal Nehru returned to India in March 1936 to take over as President of the Congress party. The party was in upheaval; the British Government's offer to allow elections for the provincial assemblies had divided the party ranks. A breakaway group with a strong socialist base sought a separate identity within the Congress. Its adherents felt that an economic programme and models for the development for a free India were essential and needed to be worked out along with the struggle for independence, so that when freedom came it would have clear directions about the evolution of the nation. They were unwilling to participate in the elections or accept any palliatives offered by the foreign government. Equally determined conservative elements within the party had fiercely oppposed moves to establish a socialist base for an independent India; they were anxious to fight elections and to exercise power, however limited. Jawaharlal belonged to the former group; he and his young socialist friends were against any compromise, even though it was evident that there was a general groundswell of support for participating in the elections and holding office at the provincial level.

As was usually the case when difficulties arose, the groups within the party looked to Gandhiji to resolve their differences. The Mahatma, alert to the changing mood of the country and of the rising ambition of the party cadres to become part of the political process of government, had to use all his tact and his not inconsiderable influence on Jawaharlal and also appeal to the bonds of friendship which existed between them, to persuade him from bringing matters to breaking point. At the party session in Lucknow, over which he presided as President, Jawaharlal spoke with passion against the acceptance of office, emphasizing the revolutionary over the reformist approach to political change. However, when it came to action Jawaharlal did not support his own position. He set up a Working Committee in which the socialists had minimum representation. The resolutions passed at this meeting chose to tread the path of compromise; controversies were avoided and a split within the Congress party was averted. The socialists felt betrayed. And even though

Jawaharlal felt frustrated and unhappy about the compromise, he plunged into action to canvass on behalf of the candidates standing for the legislative assemblies.

Jawaharlal travelled the country by plane, car, bicycle, bullock cart, and boat; he travelled on horseback, elephant and camelback, and also on foot. Once he ran half-a-mile to reach the podium with a large crowd running after him. The adoration of his people rejuvenated Jawaharlal, a new influx of energy akin to intoxication filled him. He wrote to Padmaja Naidu: 'Half mad they were and their madness entered my mind.'[1]

Jawaharlal was a physically young forty-seven. He, who believed that human beings should constantly grow, was now filled with a renewed sense of himself; this gave him, as he self-deprecatingly said, 'a flair of youth in spite of my appearance.' Added to that were poise and a refinement of learning, the reward of many years spent in jail. 'Growth at 47,' he observed in a letter to Padmaja dated 26 March 1937 'is a curiously disturbing affair.'

It was Gandhiji, with his unerring sense of the right symbol and his home-spun rhetoric, who had in 1922 transformed a small intellectual and middle-class movement for freedom in India into a mass movement that united peasant and urban élite. He thus created a vast and many-layered dialogue between the peoples of India. The dialogue was conducted in a new language where politics and myth merged. Gandhi was transformed by the people into the great-souled one, the Mahatma, and the handsome, youthful Jawaharlal became a *vira,* the heroic ideal, heir to the *Ramarajya* which was soon to come.

The disturbance in Jawaharlal's life came in the form of Padmaja Naidu, Sarojini Naidu's vivacious daughter. 'No,' he wrote to Padmaja Naidu early in their evolving relationship, 'I have no desire to be desireless.' In the eleven months between 1936 and 1937, between their rare meetings in the midst of his vast journeys across India—from the Himalayas to Cape Comorin—he wrote her twenty-eight letters, sharing his experiences and his emotions. He bantered with her, called her an eighteen-year-old—she was thirty-six at the time. Compared to her years, he was 'old, immeasurably old.' Padmaja intruded on his mind, was present when he viewed the Taj by moonlight, addressed meetings and admired the temples at Bhubaneshwar. Their relationship can be read between the lines of these intimate letters that passed between them. He asks her: 'Will I ever know how much you love me?'

> No. I shall not, nor will you. Nobody knows, nobody can
> know, for it is changing variable stuff, mocking us and
> eluding us, self-willed and vagrant. How can one know or
> measure it? Was it a turn of head, touch of hand? Strange,
> this way love began, I as little understand love's decay.
> How foolish it is to talk of it even. When the apple reddens,
> never pry.[2]

A little over a year after her mother's death, Indira flew to India, eager to share with her father her confidences and the contradictions which she felt only he could help her to understand. Highly sensitized by her separation and sorrow, she needed her father's companionship and his total attention. But the man she had come to meet had undergone vast changes. Jawaharlal was preoccupied. A gesture, a word, a look revealed to Indira that her father's attention was fragmented.

Jawaharlal, Gandhiji said, had the transparency of a crystal. He could not conceal his emotional entanglements from his daughter. In the midst of a conversation Indira suddenly found that his mind had wandered. A new relationship filled Jawaharlal's consciousness. Indira was not prepared to share her father with another human being, and halted midway in her confidences. Another doorway had closed.

Journeying through the bazars of India, Jawaharlal Nehru had once come upon a photograph of himself with Kamala—with the caption "the perfect couple". The United Provinces was vibrant with the legend of Rama. Rama was regarded as the perfect warrior, virtuous in word and deed, the dutiful son, the constant husband, the good father, the protector and the saviour of his people. The people of the United Provinces re-lived this legend in Jawaharlal. His lonely years in prison became the fourteen years Rama spent in forest exile. Jawaharlal Nehru could neither betray the portrait nor that image He could not betray the people of India. How could he betray his daughter?

Half-a-century later, I asked Vijayalakshmi Pandit of Jawaharlal Nehru's relationship with Padmaja. 'Didn't you know, Pupul?' she replied. 'They lived together for years—for years.' Questioned further as to why he had not married Padmaja, Vijayalakshmi Pandit replied, 'He felt that Indu had been hurt enough. He did not want to hurt her further.'[3]

Wanting to get away from the national scene, Jawaharlal took Indira on a holiday; they travelled east by train to Burma (now Myanmar) and then to Malaya. The Tamils of South India would maintain that the journey commenced in "the hour of *Rahu*", the inauspicious hour. When they reached Calcutta by train, a young man eager to greet Jawaharlal slipped and fell between the platform and the running train and severed his foot. Blood flowed as he clung to his hero for support. Later, on board the ship which took them to Malaya, a man fell overboard and was lost at sea. Despite these bad omens, father and daughter travelled with zest across Burma meeting Indian traders, Burmese abbots, monks, and visiting pagodas and monasteries. On board ship they joined in the games on deck and dined at the Captain's table.

On the return journey, Indira suffered from a very severe attack of tonsilitis which lingered for too long, even after her return to Allahabad. It was decided that her tonsils be removed. The operation would be performed in Bombay and she would recuperate at her aunt, Krishna's home.

During Indira's absence in Burma, Frank Oberdorf had been to India, but had missed seeing her. From Allahabad, lying ill in bed, she wrote to Oberdorf expressing her disappointment at missing him. She felt that although she had a lot to do in Allahabad—swim, go for long drives and for walks along the shores of the Ganga in the setting sun—she would have liked to be in England.

On 1 September 1937, Indira travelled from India back to Oxford on the *SS Victoria*. Sharouk Sabavala, a fellow-student at Oxford, travelled on the same boat. He was asked by his uncle, Sir Cowasji Jehangir, to look after his friend's daughter on board ship. He recalls that Indira locked herself in her cabin for the first few days and refused to see anyone. She ate by herself, and did not appear in the lounge or on deck. When she finally emerged outside her cabin, she was extremely reserved, took solitary walks and hardly spoke to anyone. Sharouk Sabavala got the clear feeling that she wanted to be left alone. But Indira's letters to her father from on board ship were deceptively cheerful, filled with what she did and what she saw on board. There is a particularly vivid description of watching the explosions on the volcano Stromboli with Sir C.V. Raman, the physicist and Nobel laureate, who explained optical illusions to her.

After the ship docked at Venice, Indira proceeded to Paris where Feroze awaited her. And it was in Paris that she first began to think of marriage with Feroze as an alternative to the life offered by her father.

> Although Feroze had been proposing to me since the age of 16, it was on the steps of Sacre Coeur that we finally and definitely decided to marry. It was at the end of summer, Paris was bathed in a soft sunshine and her heart seemed young and gay—not only because we ourselves were young and in love, but because the whole city was swarming with people who were young at heart and in a holiday mood.[4]

Feroze and Indira strolled through the streets of Paris, browsed in book-shops, visited museums, went to the opera and ate at outdoor cafés; Paris was a relief after the tense summer of India. Significantly in her letters to her father, Indira does not mention her meeting Feroze in Paris.

*

Oxford was a daunting experience for Indira. With hardly any academic preparation to fall back on, she did not know whether to study History or Politics, Philosophy and Economics—a combination then offered at Oxford. A passing mark in Latin was essential at the time.

Indira was also young and self-consciously shy. It was not easy to separate the elements out of which her self-conscious diffidence was compounded. Certainly she did not find words easy and froze in the articulate and argumentative company of her fellow-students. But more than that as a young girl she and her mother had felt cruelly excluded by the brilliance and the good looks that set her father and Vijayalakshmi apart in the admiring glances of the people around her in Allahabad. She had been driven into herself by feelings of inferiority, feelings which remained with her all her life, and were very alive during the years at Oxford.

It was Feroze, warm-hearted and gregarious, who continued to draw her out of herself. And even though she had been receptive to Feroze's proposal of marriage, she continued to keep her commitment to Feroze from Jawaharlal; it remained something she held within her, perhaps because somewhere in her she hoped that as a result of Oxford she might succeed and so gain the approbation of her father.

On the eve of the Second World War, political ferment at Oxford had reached its peak. Two years before Indira's arrival, the Oxford Union had passed a resolution 'refusing to fight for king and country'. But now left-wing ideologies attracted young intellectuals deeply concerned about totalitarian trends in Europe. Members of the youth wing of the Communist Party dominated the Oxford Union. A radical student, who was Indira's contemporary at Oxford, remembered Indira as 'proud and unapproachable; a solemn young woman, touching the fringes of political ferment, but never permitting herself complete involvement.' Emotionally tied to the Indian world of politics, Indira did seek wider connections; she joined the Indian students' union called the Majlis and also the youth wing of the Labour Party. And yet her wider political identity remained part of the left-wing ideology she inherited from Jawaharlal.

During occasional visits to London, she helped out at the India League, sticking envelopes and mailing appeals, joined the Left Book Club and visited the homes of several of her father's friends—Aneurin Bevan and his wife Jennie Lee, Ellen Wilkenson and Agatha Harrison, John Strachey. At Oxford she was invited home by Professor Radhakrishnan and Julian Huxley and his wife. Here, too, her self-conscious shyness made her appear detached. Jawaharlal's impressive friends accepted her as his daughter but saw little in her to kindle their interest; they felt she had no political ideas of her own.

*

Feroze came up to Oxford to visit her from London on weekends. They would go for long walks and have lunch together. Sometimes they visited Satish Kalekar's room where radical Indian students gathered. And while Feroze joined vociferously in argument, Indira sat tongue-tied. Nikhil Chakravartti, the journalist, fellow-student, and friend of Feroze's, remembered Indira. 'She looked ill,' he said, 'and made very little impact on other students.' There was an intellectual snobbery amongst these Indian students at Oxford, and the unexpected lack of brilliance in Jawaharlal Nehru's daughter meant that she was judged and then ignored.

Feroze and Indira fell under the influence of V.K. Krishna Menon and the left-wing groups in London; they helped raise funds for the India-China League by selling tickets to a concert at which they persuaded Uday Shankar, the Indian dancer of international repute, to dance. As Jawaharlal Nehru's daughter, Krishna Menon nominated Indira to read out her father's message of solidarity with the Chinese people. She arrived at the meeting straight from the railway station and found to her chagrin that Menon also expected her to speak to the audience. She refused, but prevailed upon to say something, she rose and mumbled a few words. Menon tried to prompt her in whispers which confused her even further. She faltered but continued until a wit in the audience cried in a loud voice: 'She does not speak, she squeaks.' Indira swore to herself never to speak in public again. She was to repeat this story with a certain glee after she became Prime Minister.

Feroze was Indira's anchor. Shanta Gandhi in an interview with the author said: 'She clung to him as if she were drowning.' With him she did little things, joyful things, unnecessary things like standing before bus-driver's kiosks drinking tea and eating hot chestnuts; going for walks in the thick, late-night fog and emerging wraith-like into the light. She also attended lectures on Political Science at the London School of Economics (LSE) to hear Harold Laski. Laski was an eloquent speaker who had created a new vocabulary to describe the ruthless ideologies which at the time held Europe in their grip and in the process created a grammar of politics that was to become the Bible of the many young people who attended his lectures. London was to remain in her memory a place that she cherished, a place where freedom and companionship flowered for her. It is significant, however, that none of her letters to her father during this period contains a single reference to Feroze and her growing intimacy with him.

1938 began with the death of her old grandmother. Dolamma died on 11 January surrounded by her son and her daughters. Twenty-four hours later Bibi, Dolamma's sister, also died. Jawaharlal notes in his letters to Indira: 'One generation in our family has now gone completely, and I have become an elder . . .' Indira responded to the news wordlessly, 'I have never been able to speak or write when I feel deeply,' she wrote in a brief letter dated 12 January 1938. February found her again complaining about the 'cold and the the moaningly dark windy and dark' world, and the "monotony" of life at Oxford. The dreariness she felt lifted when she had news that Jawaharlal was planning a trip to Europe in the summer. 'Gosh! it's good to get a letter from you,' she exclaimed, in her letter to Jawaharlal, dated 8 February 1938, and then apologized for lapsing into Americanisms.

Between 1937 and 1938 the Indian national movement had gone into "reverse gear" as far as Jawaharlal was concerned. Tensions and struggles developing within the Congress, between the more conservative elements led by C. Rajagopalachari and Vallabhbhai Patel, and the left wing of the party with which he himself was identified, disheartened him. Open hostility had also erupted with M.A. Jinnah now head of an increasingly communal Muslim League. Far ahead of his colleagues, Jawaharlal had also begun to realize that India's freedom was inevitably tied to the world situation. Events were transforming the worldscape and would inevitably affect the Indian struggle. 'The frontiers of our struggle lie not only in our country but in Spain and China also.'[5]

Jawaharlal's earlier feelings for Padmaja Naidu were unravelling; and during his European visit he put in perspective a relationship into which he had ventured after his wife's death. 'Perhaps you have not understood me aright in spite of your deep insights into me. I have human feelings and emotions certainly, and they move me, but not for very long, for other impersonal feelings overwhelm me.'[6]

In Europe there were signs of war. Valencia was bombed, Anthony Eden resigned, students at Oxford tried to persuade department stores to boycott Japanese goods. In March 1938, with Adolf Hitler's move into Austria, Jawaharlal's anxieties mounted, as is evident in his letter dated 15 March 1938 to Indira. 'What will happen to you and me when the war comes?' And old fears about Indira's health resurfaced, to be expressed in terms of familiar dualites. 'Perhaps you have inherited this lack of resisting power from Mummy. . . . Do you know that my grandfather died probably of T.B. So also one of my aunts . . .' To counteract the fears he offered familiar advice, 'deal with the matter scientifically: Keep your bowels functioning and do not get constipated; accustom yourself to good breathing'—he meant the exercises prescribed in yoga. And he held up Motilal Nehru and himself as examples of people who, born with a weak constitution, mastered their weakness. It was a familiar theme between father and daughter: Indira did not have to succumb to tuberculosis, the dreaded disease which claimed Kamala; she was after all Motilal's granddaughter and Jawaharlal's daughter. But there were ominous portents that Indira would follow her mother's path into disease.

Indira failed her Latin examination; she was obliged to remain in Oxford until the third week of June, to take the test over again, and could not join Jawaharlal in Europe nor travel with him to Spain. Krishna Menon was in charge of planning Jawaharlal's European visit in concurrence with Indira. The plans included weekend visits to various country homes in England, to Beatrice and Sidney Webbs', to Sir Stafford Cripps', and to Lord Lothian's at Blicking Hall. Indira, with a young person's sense of what was politically correct, was dead set against the last visit. 'After all Lothian is against all you stand for and believe in—all the people you are likely to meet at his house, will be the same.'[7] Jawaharlal in reply reminded Indira that though he agreed with her about 'the Clivenden set and Lothian's pro-Fascist pro-Hitler activities,' he felt Lothian was something more than the leader of a prominent group. Jawaharlal had a special position in India and a certain special responsibility. He had to function as such whatever his likes and dislikes. Indira did accompany her father to Blicking Hall but, unlike her father, sat grim and silent when Lady Astor, who was also one of the guests on the occasion, started a tirade against socialism.[8]

The visit to the Webbs' country home was a great success. An eighty-year-old Beatrice Webb, still vital in mind and body, welcomed Jawaharlal and, as she noted in her diary, 'his lovely daughter' with genuine warmth. She took them for long walks over the meadows and presented Indira with her latest book.

After England, father and daughter proceeded to France to attend an international protest meeting against the bombing of civilian populations in Spain. Feroze Gandhi was also present when La Passionara, the woman revolutionary from Spain, was disbarred from addressing the conference by the anti-Communist organizers of the meeting. Indira was outraged and, joining forces with Feroze, moved behind the scenes to have the delegates reconvene unofficially and hear out the revolutionary woman. As La Passionara took the floor, two attendants seized her and carried her off the platform. Jawaharlal Nehru was furious and eloquently pleaded the cause of free speech on behalf of those who fought Fascism, but in vain. The assembled delegates, though moved by his dignity and the passion of his words, did not relent.

Feroze Gandhi returned to London and Indira travelled on with her father to Prague, then to Bratislava and Ziln. The Nazi invasion was imminent. Indira and Jawaharlal watched the bleak, fearful faces of the Czechs as large numbers of people including writers, philosophers and artists began to flee the country. This was Indira's first exposure to an exodus and the inhumanity of it left a powerful impression.

In Prague Indira caught a chill which she neglected. As her ill-health continued, she was examined by a doctor in Budapest. The doctor diagnosed pleurisy and advised hospitalization. She spent three weeks in a hospital in Budapest before being permitted to travel to England where she entered Middlesex Hospital. Her weight had dropped to eighty-five pounds, and she felt terribly tired.

In November of 1938, Indira was sufficiently recovered to travel back to India with Jawaharlal. The pleurisy had interrupted her education at Oxford; reluctantly she allowed Jawaharlal to persuade her to return to India in order to build up her health.

FOUR

For Indira it was a grim homecoming. With her grandmother dead—Anand Bhawan the residence of her aunt Vijayalakshmi, and her father engrossed in political work—the house ceased to provide a meaningful context for a sick young woman entering adulthood, without any sense of individual achievement. The family home under these conditions was intolerable and Indira decided instead to recuperate in Almora, a Himalayan hill station. At first she stayed with friends, and then her aunt Krishna Hutheesing set up house in a bungalow, Snow View, which, true to its name, commanded a magnificent view of Nanda Devi, Trisul and K2.

The five months that Indira spent in India, between November 1938 and April 1939, was not a happy time. The three surviving letters to her father from this period are desultory; she complains of the cold rooms in the house inadequately warmed by only one wood fire; describes a picnic to Shimtola, planned and then abandoned because she was not feeling "too bright"; and repeats her little cousins' daily enquiry: *'Kya ham aj Bombay jaenge?'*[1] (Will we be going to Bombay today?)

Jawaharlal Nehru was travelling widely, chairing the Planning Committee—consisting of economists, scientists and social workers—who were to plan the future of India. But, caught in a personal struggle, within the party against the right-wing, and outside it, with Mohammed Ali Jinnah, the leader of the Muslim League, Jawaharlal's dreams of India emerging as an independent, united and socialist country seemed forever out of reach. "The wide expanse of Indian humanity" into which Motilal Nehru and Jawaharlal submerged their individual destinies was a family achievement as well as a legacy which Jawaharlal had dreamed of bestowing some day on his daughter. It now seemed to Jawaharlal that the dream that Indira had been unconsciously absorbing, even in the nursery, was not worth the cost.

On 15 April 1939, Indira once again set sail for Europe with the intention of spending five months in a French or Swiss clinic and then entering Oxford in the autumn of 1939. Even with the shadow of war hanging over the world, Indira was determined to break out of the undefined situation she found herself in; the trust that her mother

99

had established for her perhaps gave her some financial self-reliance. Jawaharlal was reluctant to let her go; he saw her leave with sadness, and, as Indira put it, 'with something more than just sadness.' For it was beginning to dawn on him that his daughter had a tough will of her own and that he could no longer treat her as a child, to be dictated to, to be loved and admonished at the same time. 'Papu understood concepts; it was a long time before he could understand relationships.'[2] This was the way Indira remembered her father in later life.

On board the *S.S. Strathaird,* a longing to be back with her father swept over her. 'I did hate leaving you this time,' she wrote. 'It has left a strange sort of emptiness inside me and indeed the fault is entirely mine, for mine was the decision to leave.'[3]

Indira stopped in Paris *en route* to England. She loved the city, its refinement, its sophistication, its search for the creative at the frontiers of the mind. And it was Paris in spring that found its way in the letter she wrote to her father after seeing Claude Monet's *Nymphiades:* 'The fatigue fell off me like an unwanted cloak, my eyes felt as if I had just washed them in soothing cold lotion and I came out into the outside world fresh enough to do anything.'[4]

In England, London's Harley Street specialists found a shadow ("or some such thing") on the left side of her lung and advised her to spend the next few months in Switzerland resting. But before leaving England, she visited Oxford and arranged to enrol again as a student in September 1939. If Indira's lonely return to Switzerland in search of a cure from suspected tuberculosis held terrors for the young woman, whose mother had just recently and unsuccessfully travelled the very same path, she did not reveal these fears to her father. From Hotel Winkerlried Stansstad, she wrote to her father on 5 June 1939:

> Every morning after breakfast I take a small flat boat—you hire them for fifty centimes—take it out towards the middle of the lake and then let it drift while I stretch out in my bathing costume and sunbathe as well as do some reading. Already I have gone a deep sienna brown. It is very pleasant. I come back to the hotel after lunch—rest a bit and then go for a walk.[5]

The faithful Feroze Gandhi travelled fom London to Lucerne to see her in June, when the school year ended. He and Indira went on long walks together; one day they climbed up to Jock Pass, about 1,303 feet above the sea level, and then even higher to a peak above the pass called JockStockli. On the way she picked spring flowers for her father. But instead of the flowers she sent Jawaharlal photographs that Feroze had taken with his Leica. The letter also contained a response to a favourite sonnet that Jawaharlal had sent her recently. The sonnet was addressed to the contemplative Buddha and contained the following lines which cast a spell on Jawaharlal:

Nay, do not mock me with that ecstasy,
Born of peace abstracted from life's pain.

In response to the sonnet Indira wrote:

The *Sanyasi* (world renouncing) idea was bound to come to you—I suppose all people entertain it for a while. But it passes off. . . . I have strange moods and strange ideas come fleeting across my mind; for some time I am like one possessed, and always with disastrous results. But all this too is the outcome of being alone—for I am lonely too—terribly lonely and alone. So dependent on you.[6]

The words, which appear drawn out of Indira in a moment of anguished insight, express in traditionally dichotomous terms the character of father and daughter and their relationship at this stage in their lives—Jawaharlal, the visionary intellectual, involved in action but detached from it; and Indira, the woman driven by energies she did not understand; the father beckoning his daughter to enter into a larger vision of the family and of India; the daughter deeply attached to the aloof visionary, but unable to enter into the vision held out to her.

By the time Hitler invaded Poland in September 1939, and war was declared, Indira was back in England, still determined to return to Oxford. However, a week before the term was to begin, she caught a chill and it developed into pleurisy. She was admitted to Brentford Cottage Hospital in Middlesex, her weight down to seventy-seven pounds. She blamed herself for her illness and the shame and anguish of failure engulfed her once more.

Edward Thompson wrote a reassuring letter to Jawaharlal after seeing Indira in hospital. Though she was thin and what used to be called "delicate", Thompson felt sure that once she passed adolescence she would certainly gain strength. The doctors had suggested that Indira return to Switzerland and Thompson assured Jawaharlal that in case the war widened and Germany were to invade Switzerland they would 'see to her.'

Indira's aunt, Sheila Kaul, then in London, visited her regularly. She found Indira, as advised by doctors, lying on her stomach. Feroze was often there with gifts of fruit and honey. Sensing Indira's closeness to the Parsee youth, Sheila Kaul asked Indira whether she was in love with Feroze. Indira was quick to reply that they were only friends.

Travel was difficult. Agatha Harrison, Indira's guardian in England, arranged to accompany Indira after Christmas to the Clinique Frenes, a sanitarium nestling in the Rhine valley of Switzerland. The turmoil within Indira seemed to now sweep over her, and hesitatingly she conveyed to Agatha the conflicts that were tearing her apart. Agatha advised Indira not to allow her self to be submerged by her emotion, to let conflict lie fallow, as that was the best course to recovering her health. And on returning to England, Agatha hastened to inform Jawaharlal about Indira's state of mind. Jawaharlal wrote back:

> I quite agree with what you say about Indu. She is going through a difficult period of her life. None of us can be of very much help to her. She will have to find her way out herself. All we can do, and that is very little, is to enable her to find herself. I am terribly afraid of interfering in any way and thus add to the difficulties of the situation.[7]

Back in the dread but familiar world of grey-eyed doctors, nurses and an environment clouded with illness and death, Indira grew morbid. The Gothic darkness of the Black Forest, cold memories of Badenweiller and her mother's death swamped her mind. The doctors attempted to reassure her; they promised to bring her back to perfect health in three months, to make her into a Diana. Their words remained unheeded. Life in the sanitarium was deadly—the daily routine left no time or space for the unexpected. To become a victim and to die, the way her mother had done, seemed a seductive alternative.

*

Jawaharlal was in China, a guest of Chiang Kai-shek and his wife, old friends, when war was declared. Returning almost immediately to India, he was faced with a dilemma. His abhorrence for the Fascists was absolute, yet there was no way he could support Britain at this stage when Britain had already declared war against Germany and her Allies on behalf of India without the consent of the Indian people. The outbreak of the war hardened British attitudes, with the country at war there was no tolerance of dissent.

'There are elements of a Greek tragedy in the world situation today,' wrote Jawaharlal to the Viceroy Lord Linlithgow, after his return. 'And we seem to be pushed along inevitably to a predetermined end.' Jawaharlal demanded immediate independence. The Viceroy was not in a mood for political parleys in India at a time when Britain was fighting for its survival. Meanwhile Gandhiji was silent, conscious of the savage consequences that would follow any call for civil disobedience at this stage.

As a diversion from the pressures and stresses of political life, Jawaharlal undertook a slow train journey through the country, rediscovering India. The political despondency and confusion that filled his comrades seemed to lose their immediacy in an Ahir village where visitors had to wait before being offered water, for the first offering of water drawn from a well in leather containers (*masak*) by bullocks was to the *Kanhaiyaji* (Lord Krishna).

Jawaharlal's letters to Indira were her only contacts with the country she had left behind. In the intensely cold winter at Leysin, these letters brought her the warmth and the variety of Indian life; they offered the promise of sunshine and a sense of belonging.

Finding herself stranded mid-stream now, when swift currents threatened to wash away her footholds on life and she could not go forward to reach the other shore safely, she thought of returning to India, to the starting point of her journey. In her despair she wrote to Jawaharlal asking for advice. He replied:

I long to help you or do something for you, but I feel so helpless. Not only are you far away from me, with a major war coming, but otherwise too I am hardly capable of advising. . . . I wish that I could take the burden somewhat from you, but I have lost faith in myself in many ways.

Everything that I can possibly give you is yours for the asking, but do not seek advice from me for my mind is disturbed and lacks clarity.[8]

February came and Indira was still confined to bed. She developed a fearful cold and complained of a pain in the left side of her lungs. Her physician Dr Rollier told her that her lung capacity was small and had to become stronger. A shattered Jawaharlal tried to reassure her she was in good hands, the Swiss doctors were the best in the world.

In April, after receiving a tormented letter from Indira, Jawaharlal's impatience with her illness resurfaced: 'But you are wise enough to realise that health is not merely a physical condition. It is very much a mental affair. You complain of nerves, put worry and nerves on the shelf. It can be done, it has been done.'[9]

Jawaharlal's hard-heartedness, so apparent in the letter of 1 May, had its source in his deep conviction that it was necessary for Indira to become independent of him. He told her that her 'obsession,' with thoughts of 'return to India, to come to me. . .'was misplaced. 'I cannot help you, however I might try. I might make matters worse . . .' He further said: 'One may err, that cannot be helped. But always to be in doubt and not know what to do is a greater affliction. I want your love, not your duty or a feeling of responsibility which becomes a burden to you or to me.'[10]

Furthermore, Jawaharlal's conviction that the solution to Indira's problems lay in becoming emotionally independent of him, was also an acceptance of his own failings. Jawaharlal confessed to Indira earlier in March that the ease with which he related to crowds and the way they adulated him covered up a failure to understand individual human beings. 'The crowd ceased to fascinate me as it used to, and I found how utterly alone I was.' Perhaps such isolation was the lot of humankind:

You came very close to me or rather the image I made of

you became part of me, but then that was the creature of my thoughts; you were far away.

I do not know even how your mind works, though vaguely I might sometimes guess. You told me very rightly once how blind I was. That is perfectly true. I miss the most obvious things and so we have grown progressively more and more ignorant of each other, and even now our love of each other has not brought any understanding. You are such a stranger to me, and perhaps you do not know much about me.[11]

When Jawaharlal told Indira 'be mistress of your own life, your present, your future and go ahead, consult me certainly, but decide for yourself,' he did not anticipate the consequences.

FIVE

In the spring of 1940 when both Dr Bhandari, the doctor friend from London, and Dr Rollier felt that it was in Indira's interest to remain in the sanitarium until she was cured, she reluctantly agreed to remain in Switzerland, even though Jawaharlal Nehru's letter hinted at the financial difficulties he was now facing, because the war had put an end to the royalties from his books. 'I realised two days ago in Allahabad that it was not an easy matter to pay next month's servants' salaries,'[1] he wrote while continuing to assure her that she should not economize or take chances with her health.

By August the Maginot line was pierced, France and Holland were occupied by Germany. Contact between Europe and India was reduced; distances appeared to expand, "the waste land spread", letters trickled through, and gradually Indira's health began to improve.

As her health improved, she learned to cope with the routine of life at the sanitarium with a stoic demeanour, and with grace and repose. A sense of survival, germinating over many years, now surfaced.

> You know how the species have survived—by developing faculties which are needed at a particular stage. Each one of us also evolves the same way, by developing what is needed for survival in a particular period of life. The only way I can put it perhaps is to say that my life was so hard that something had to develop to help me to meet that hardship.[2]

The wild flower, she noticed as soon as she was well enough to be allowed to travel within Switzerland, 'blossomed on its own' in the most adverse circumstance, 'while there is a tremendous wind and the odds are against (life).'

In 1940, the Congress party in India was faced with a difficult choice: either it could revive the sagging momentum of the struggle for independence and call for massive disobedience to the authority of the Indian Government or it could call off the struggle in order to support Britain, now fighting almost single-handed against the Nazis, and so risk putting back freedom for an unspecified length of time. The problem was resolved by the Mahatma's decision to launch a civil disobedience movement in October 1940, but to make it a symbolic gesture; selected persons were to offer satyagraha on an individual basis against the government for having committed India to a war without the consent of her people. The first offerings were to be Vinoba Bhave's, the anchorite and spiritual disciple of Gandhiji's; the second was to be Jawaharlal's. The Government of India, totally preoccupied with the war, had no use for ritual gestures, and before Jawaharlal could offer resistance, he was arrested and taken to the Gorakhpur prison in the United Provinces. Here the magistrate sentenced him to four years at hard labour.

Even Winston Churchill, then Prime Minister of Britain, reacted to the severity of the sentence and sent a message to the Viceroy of India expressing the hope that the actual rigour of the sentence be modified, and that Jawaharlal not be treated like a common criminal. Learning in Switzerland of the savage sentence, Indira telegraphed from Bex on 11 November: 'Am well. Trying come India. Have enough money. Constant thoughts. Love to all' And Jawaharlal cabled back: 'Darling, your cable. Don't upset your programme because of conviction. Keep me informed of your movements. Love.'

Indira returned to India with Feroze Gandhi in April 1941, after travelling from Leysin to London, when the blitzkrieg was at its most devastating. The ship she and Feroze sailed in four months later was part of a convoy that went around the Cape of Good Hope. It was a dangerous journey with total blackouts at night, punctuated by the insistent whine of sirens calling passengers on deck for ship-wreck drill practice.

The ship berthed at Capetown. Indira and Feroze spent two days in the city. Here they saw apartheid in action, the humiliation of the coloured races, and the appalling living conditions of the blacks, She met members of the Indian community, but was angered by their incapacity to either fight for themselves or to make common cause with the blacks.

Arriving in Bombay, Indira spent a few days with her aunt Krishna and then went to pay her respects to the Mahatma at his retreat, Sevagram. She was no longer the awkward adolescent with short straight hair that the Mahatma had last seen accompanying her mother to Europe. She now wore silk; her hair was long and tied back to reveal her Nefertiti neck and lean face; she had on a trace of lipstick. The Mahatma disapproved; he felt disappointed that her years in Europe had radically changed her values. Indira was not afraid to argue with Gandhiji, to explain her views on life. It was a difficult meeting.

Her confrontation with Gandhiji angered Indira and she was in an abrasive mood when she reached Dehradun on 27 April to visit her father in jail. For the official in charge of the prison her arrival was an exciting event. He had consulted with Jawaharlal and arranged for a car to fetch her and was anxious that Indira have lunch with his wife.

Jawaharlal had aged in the two years he had been separated from Indira, a time which had been filled with the turmoil of war and with anxieties about Indira's health and the dangers of the journey. The prison official conspired to allow father and daughter to be together much longer than was permitted under the rules.

Father and daughter were shy and awkward with each other. Jawaharlal was alarmed to see how frail Indira had become. She told him that the journey had been hard; she had not been too well on board ship; and the tensions of living under the blitz in London had taken their toll. But it was not about her health that she was presently concerned. Decisions had to be taken about the future; she needed her father's support, but did not know quite how to ask for it.

Indira had begun to add up the cost to the family of her father's dedication to the larger cause. Throughout his younger days, she felt, Jawaharlal had found neither place nor time in his life for affection and care of Kamala; little time for the daughter who sought his confidence. She began to question the traditions of the family, to evaluate a dedication to larger causes against the love of home and family. Above all, she felt the need for someone who would cherish her, a close companion, a small home, children. During those hours with her father in the Dehradun jail, she spoke with as little emotion as possible of her decision to marry Feroze.

Jawaharlal was wise enough not to argue. Exercising considerable self-restraint, he reminded her that the doctors had warned her about the dangers of having children in her state of health. It was true that she was cured, but she was not strong. He spoke hesitantly and advised that before marrying she devote time to recovering her strength.

Indira did not yield: she told her father that she wanted anonymity and a life free of turmoil. She wanted to marry, have children, care for her children and her husband in a home filled with books, music and friends.

Jawaharlal was stunned. A fierce pride in the family tradition was integral to his being: 'Tradition as of great ability, great courage, great perseverance, great sacrifice, all directed to the service of India.'[3]

For his daughter to turn away from her obligations and lead a life filled with trivialities was totally unacceptable to him. In his diary Jawaharlal wrote: 'She is so—or it seems to me—immature, perhaps to take things superficially, yet she must have depth. She will reach them slowly. I hope the pressure is not too rigid or else there may be shocks.'[4]

The meeting in jail had not brought any real communication between father and daughter. Jawaharlal's next letter to her revealed his anguish. 'I do not know how to unlock the doors of my mind and heart, which burst with things to say. Nor do you I fancy, for you have found it even more difficult to do so even from outside jail.' From the solitude of the cell, he asked if words had any importance unless they unlocked doors of understanding. 'I wonder sometimes if my love for you has been so wanting in something to prevent those doors from opening.'[5]

Trying to ease the situation and to reassure Jawaharlal, Feroze Gandhi came to Dehradun jail. But the prison officials did not permit the interview to Jawaharlal's probable relief.

When Indira returned to Allahabad from Dehradun, Vijayalakshmi Pandit was still in occupation of the family house. It was the first summer after many years that Indira was spending on the plains, but she was determined to make her presence felt. 'I was determined to face the heat. To keep cool I sat in my room on a block of ice placed in a zinc tray filled with saw dust.'[6]

By mid-May the heat of Allahabad forced her to move to the Mussoorie hills. Her resentment was held in check, but the conflict with her father subtly showed through her letters in which she talked about Beethoven and asked whether Jawaharlal enjoyed music. Intended both to display the classical tastes of her future husband-to-be and also to exclude Jawaharlal, the barbed remark found its mark. 'I am very fond of Beethoven,' he replied, 'but my life has been spent far away from cultivation of graces and pleasures which sometimes accompany it. Happiness is rather a fleeting thing. A sense of fulfilment is far more abiding.' Jawaharlal was anxious to avoid a confrontation with his daughter, and so he advised her to remain in Mussoorie tending to her health. But he could not help adding, 'Rights carry obligations and duties with them and I have got rather entangled in this sense of obligations and duty.'[7]

Sensing the hinterland that lay behind Jawaharlal's emphasis on duty and obligations, Indira became angry. She replied reaffirming her determination to mould her own life, to marry, to have children and to lead a life of anonymity in a space of her own making. The letter was delivered to Jawaharlal in the Dehradun jail by Dr Madan Atal who had been to Mussoorie to see Indira. Jawaharlal realized that all his long letters and his indirect reminders of her obligations had not helped matters. 'So much for my insight into human beings and my general confidence,' he wrote in his diary on 29 May 1941.

With Jawaharlal advocating caution and her ill-health pursuing her, Indira's plans to marry Feroze stalled. Between June 1941 and July, father and daughter met twice in the Dehradun jail without resolving anything. Following the meeting in July, Jawaharlal, 'discovered with a little shock that her mind was elsewhere.' He tried to reach out to her the next day in a letter. 'Sometimes I felt and wished that you had told me frankly and directly that you distrusted me and imagined things about me which naturally made it very difficult for me to help you in any way.' He wanted to assure her that he did not want in any way to obstruct her plans, so there was no place for conflict between them. 'If you want to marry Feroze, then go and marry Feroze. Nobody will stop you.'[8]

And then he described the innumerable plans he had built around her: he had hoped that after finishing her education she would travel, visit Russia, learn many foreign languages. He wanted to help her discover India and wanted,

> gently, slowly but surely to train your mind in that wider understanding of life and events that is essential for any big work.

> In this task I wanted to help you personally and I expected

you to help me somewhat also. There are a few persons
in India, I think, who could give effective help not only in
public life but almost for any activity other than technical,
better than I could. Hundreds and thousands of young
men and girls had wanted to serve me as secretaries or in
some way to get this training. I have not encouraged
anyone and have shouldered my burden alone, for I have
always imagined you to occupy that niche. Till you come,
that niche had better be kept empty. No one can take your
place.[9]

Marriage, he suggested, was important, yet marriage was not the
whole of life. 'Life is a much bigger thing. It is difficult to understand
it. One has to try.' Her health was bad and she had to let the doctors
decide the timing of her marriage. 'There is an element of the absurd
in your returning from Europe in frail health and suddenly marrying.'
Emphasizing form over content, he told her that: 'How one does
something is as important as the thing itself.'

The attempt of this proud father to advise and support his daughter
ended up by exposing his own hurt and despair. Not only was Indira
discarding 'very precious traditions and heritage' as well as the future
he had dreamed for her, she was marrying into a family whose
traditions and upbringing were so far removed from his own. She must
give time and opportunity, he felt, to adjust to events and avoid
breaking old relationships.

You do not know what the new ones will be like and you
might well be landed high and dry. I am not referring to
Feroze but life's other contacts including Feroze's family.
Of course, one does not marry a family; yet one cannot
ignore it either and it can make itself pleasant or unp-
leasant. I know nothing about his family or other contacts.

Life does not give its gifts over and over again, and we kick
away the valuable gifts at some peril to our future.[10]

Shortly after this letter was written, Rajeshwari Kaul, Kamala's
mother, came up to Mussoorie to see her granddaughter with whom

she enjoyed a warm relationship. Indira spent many hours discussing with her, her decision to marry Feroze. Rajeshwari, aware that Feroze belonged to a very different background and class from Indira's, said, 'You have been brought up in luxury, in a large house with servants. Feroze has no money and we do not know how his family will view the marriage. Will it be possible for you to adjust to this entirely new situation?' Indira was quick to assure her that organized religion counted for little in both their lives. 'Like my mother I am an austere woman, very frugal and although I lived in Anand Bhawan I will be equally happy in a peasant's hut.' Her grandmother was reassured. 'How wonderful it is that you have been born at a time when you can do what you want to do.'[11]

SIX

Jawaharlal Nehru was released from prison on 4 December 1941. From behind bars he had watched the agony and sacrifices of the Allies fighting for freedom against a ruthless adversary. His sympathies were with the Allies and yet every fibre of his body rebelled against continued British rule.

> I am sick and utterly weary of British rule in India and I am not prepared to put up with it any longer. Whatever may happen I cannot cooperate with it or reconcile myself to it. I can only keep on rebelling against it. The British will go. They must and will have to.[1]

Three days after Jawaharlal's release, on 7 December 1941, Japan attacked Pearl Harbour and crippled the US Pacific Fleet. The United States declared war on the Axis powers. With the destruction of the US Navy, the Indian Ocean lay open. The Japanese advance was relentless. Bombay was in ferment. War was approaching India's frontiers. It was clear to Jawaharlal that the world was changing so swiftly that the human mind could not comprehend the nature of the global war or its consequences.

Indira was in Bombay and her father hurried to meet her. Major decisions awaited Jawaharlal. While in Bombay he introduced his daughter to his old comrades and senior Congress workers. 'She was shy, anxious to be liked, spoke sparingly and with hesitation.'[2]

Faced with a world on the edge of disaster, the members of the Congress Working Committee (CWC) were hesitant to launch a civil disobedience movement. Jawaharlal was quick to see that India was facing an Armageddon—the global holocaust could not be met by minds concerned only with national issues.

On the Eastern front Singapore fell in February 1942, to be followed by Malaya, Burma and the Andaman Islands. Colombo was bombed. By July, the Japanese forces were poised on the borders of India. Winston Churchill had warned King George of the possible loss of Burma, Ceylon, Calcutta and Madras.

In between the CWC meetings, Jawaharlal and Indira had talks with the Mahatma on India's future. She was tough and adamant in her decision to marry Feroze Gandhi. With no alternative, no options, Jawaharlal finally gave his permission.

Mahatma Gandhi in his many statements was prepared to fully support the war and the Allies against the totalitarian forces, but for him this could only be possible if India's birthright to freedom was recognized and interim arrangements were reached that were satisfactory to India. 'If lustre is to be put into the Indian people's eyes, freedom has to come not tomorrow but today.'

Britain with its back to the wall, fighting for life and liberty for itself and for occupied Europe, was not prepared to parley with India or concede the right to freedom and liberty for India even after the war. Franklin Roosevelt intervened. As a sop to the United States, Churchill sent Sir Stafford Cripps, a friend of Jawaharlal, to India with proposals endorsed by his Cabinet.

The Cripps Mission was doomed to failure. Stafford Cripps had little leeway to negotiate. Inbuilt into the proposals was the communal divide, the germ of partition and the break-up of India into three parts. Britain was not prepared, during the interim period, to hand over to India administrative control over her destiny, even though Jawaharlal and the Mahatma were prepared to leave the defence of the frontiers to a British Commander-in-Chief, on the condition that India was declared independent and the armies fought on behalf of a free India against the enemy. Jawaharlal and the CWC were not prepared for less. Meetings with Stafford Cripps took place in Delhi and Anand Bhawan in Allahabad. In between, family preparations for Indira's wedding went on. The Cripps Mission failed and Stafford Cripps returned to England, a defeated man. Jawaharlal and many members of the CWC, who were concerned with the outcome of the war, were desolate. They had reached an impasse. No further negotiations were possible.

In Burma, with the Japanese invasion, the British administration crumbled and the administrators fled, leaving the Indian refugees to their own devices. Many died on the long arduous trek back to India. The discrimination against the Indian residents of Burma aroused an intense anger in India. A sense of betrayal and helplessness swept the country.

With the fall of Burma, panic seized the port cities of Bombay,

Madras and Calcutta. An invasion appeared imminent. Air-raid sirens were installed, shelters built in gardens and open spaces. The stock exchange crashed. Property prices plummeted and those who could afford it retreated, as they had done for centuries when faced with invasion, into the vast Indian hinterland. The Indian people waited with bated breath; they had not faced an invasion for over 500 years.

The CWC met in Allahabad in May. The Mahatma was not present. Sardar Vallabhbhai Patel voiced the intensity of a people's anger when he said to the British, 'You have proved your utter incompetence. You cannot defend (the Government of India). We cannot defend it either because you won't let us do so. But if you withdraw, there is a chance for us.'

Jawaharlal, acutely aware of the peril India faced, endorsed the final resolution of the CWC demanding from the British an immediate withdrawal. "Quit India" became the call, for Indians were no longer prepared to live in slavery.

Turning to the Mahatma, the Congress leaders asked him to launch the final struggle for freedom.

SEVEN

Indira's wedding was to take place in 1942. She was to remain up in the hills at Mussoorie until November, then return to Allahabad where, courtesy demanded, her father said, that she talk over the arrangements for her wedding with her aunts, Vijayalakshmi and Krishna. She was then to go to Sevagram, where she must, he urged, have a long and frank talk with the Mahatma. 'He is one of the wisest men I know,' he told her. He stressed the Mahatma's long association with the family. Indira agreed to follow the course Jawaharlal Nehru had set out for her, to return to Allahabad, to talk with the Mahatma. However, she had made up her mind about marrying Feroze irrespective of what her father or the Mahatma had to say about the matter.

Indira kept her word to her father, even though she found returning to Allahabad in November to stay with her aunts at Anand Bhawan very difficult. 'Not Anand Bhawan anywhere but Anand Bhawan,'[1] she told her father. Stopping only sufficiently long in Allahabad to collect some clothes, she went on to Sevagram to see the Mahatma.

The Mahatma had already met Feroze Gandhi and had extracted a promise from him not to marry Indira without first obtaining Jawaharlal's formal consent. The Mahatma hoped to intervene and to dissuade Indira from going through with a marriage that would face fierce opposition, both from the country because of its inter-religious nature and within her family, but seeing her obdurate, Gandhiji did not persist.

Some of his own obsessions with celibacy must have surfaced on the occasion, for before she left Sevagram he asked her numerous questions about her relationship with Feroze. Indira was a woman of great reserve, and wary of Gandhiji's interest in this side of her personal life. She answered him frankly, but the questions stirred some resentment.

> Gandhiji had some peculiar views like asking newly married couples to be celibate. I told him, "You can ask a couple not to get married—that makes sense to me. But when they are just married, to ask them to live a life of

celibacy, makes no sense. It can result only in bitterness
and unhappiness."[2]

Indira discussed the wedding ceremony with Gandhiji. She wanted
a simple one. 'Neither of us likes pomp and show,' she told him. The
Mahatma, on the other hand, saw matters differently.

> There is going to be opposition to your marriage; if it is a
> quiet marriage, people will say that the family did not want
> it because you are marrying outside your religion. So,
> while there need not be pomp as such, there must be a
> party and you must invite people.[3]

It was only after she had received the Mahatma's consent to the
marriage that Indira returned to Allahabad to face her aunts with the
news of her decision to marry Feroze. The two ladies were horrified
that the young man who had cared for Kamala in the Thirties would
now want to become a son-in-law of the house. Indira listened without
reacting when Vijayalakshmi Pandit said to her, 'If you love him you
can live with him, but why marriage?'[4] She said very simply that she
wanted children and companionship. Krishna's initial opposition softened as her affection for her niece surfaced; they embraced and the
arguments ended.

'The whole nation was against my wedding,' Indira said with some
pride. There were scurrilous letters attacking the marriage; both
Gandhiji and Jawaharlal had to defend Indira's decision in public.
'When I was assured that Indira and Feroze wanted to marry one
another, I accepted willingly their decision and told them that it had
my blessings,'[5] Jawaharlal wrote. But even though he had given way
before Indira's determined stand, he was desperately unhappy. He
was liberal enough not to be worried that Indira should want to marry
a Parsee, but that this Parsee was not from the families of Jawaharlal's
high-placed Parsee friends in Bombay, but a young man from a totally
different stratum of society, was difficult for him to accept. Was this
defiant marriage to Feroze a chapter in her continuing dialogue
between father and daughter, a stormy dialogue which had begun
when she entered her teens? Was the final mark of that defiance, this
marriage? Relatives and close friends were aware of the opposition

to the marriage in the family and were not, until the invitations were finally sent out, quite sure whether or not the wedding would take place.

It was a wedding between two people who belonged to different religions, and should have been registered under the civil code, but this would have meant taking an oath that neither of them had any personal religious beliefs. This Indira was not prepared to do. So a carefully choreographed wedding ceremony had to be arranged. The Nehru clan gathered from various parts of the country, as did friends. There were lunches, dinners, and receptions with sweets covered in silver foil, savouries of various kinds, and cold drinks. While the preparations for the wedding were going on, Jawaharlal continued to hold meetings in his room with members of the All-India Congress Committee (AICC). Gandhiji was present in Allahabad, to give his blessings to the wedded pair, and also to attend the political meetings.

Indira was married on Ramnavami day, oh 16 March 1942, in a quiet moment amidst the excitement of Sir Stafford Cripps' visit and negotiations with the Congress. The ceremony was performed by enlightened pandits in the open *chabutra* outside Anand Bhawan Indira looked fragile, dressed in a cotton sari of the palest pink, the yarn for which had been woven by her father during long hours spent in jail. She wore no jewellery except for an armlet, glass bangles, and a garland of flowers round her neck. Her father sat beside her, dressed in a khadi kurta and a dhoti. Facing the father and daughter was the bridegroom—a fair, thick-set young man with a determined chin, dressed in a long achkan and churidar pyjamas. To the chanting of Sanskrit hymns, the couple circled the altar of fire, sacred to both the Vedic Aryans and to the ancient Zoroastrians, seven times, taking a vow at each turn. They pledged fidelity, love, and devotion. At the end of the ceremony all those who were gathered showered the couple with rose-petals.

An unexpected visitor to the wedding was Eve Curie, daughter of the famous physicist, Marie Curie. In Anand Bhawan she was witness to the hustle and bustle of large Indian households. She watched with fascination the colourful travelling peddlers announcing their wares with sing-song voices who came to the house: the people bringing fruit and vegetables, sweets and savouries; the man with dancing monkeys and bears; the sari peddlers with the bundles of cloth, woven, printed, of finest cotton and silk, multicoloured and pristine white, the dyers and cloth printers, the tailor who sat in the veranda all day sewing. She watched Indira buying bangles from a travelling bangle peddler. His baskets full of satin smooth glass delighted the young bride. The scene transported Eve Curie to classical times. 'She could well have been born in Greece, slender and pale with a pensive classical face.'[6]

Traditionally, India sees the departure of a daughter from her father's household to the unfamiliar house of the bridegroom's family, as fraught with anguish. Most brides weep and much sadness is felt by relatives and friends. Jawaharlal's eyes were moist. Indira did not weep.

The young couple moved into their own tiny rented home immediately after the ceremony. Indira had decorated the house with her usual austere sensibility and Feroze's skills in carpentry and cabinet making were evident in the handcrafted furniture.

Feroze joined the Congress office and began working at Swaraj Bhawan, the headquarters of the Congress. The Working Party of the Congress met there in early May, and Indira soon became engaged in preparations for the meetings.

It would appear that with marriage the walls which Indira had erected against her father broke down, for later in May she decided to leave Feroze in Allahabad and travel on a holiday to Manali, a Himalayan hill station in the Kulu valley, with Jawaharlal. Father and daughter stayed with the aged white Russian painter, Nicholas Roerich. Here, amid the mountain streams and the ancient deodars, Indira and Jawaharlal rediscovered the love they had for each other.

Jawaharlal returned to Allahabad, refreshed in spirit, and Indira joined Feroze at Lahore from where they travelled to the Kashmir valley on their honeymoon. Sheikh Abdullah, the freedom fighter who was also Jawaharlal's friend, was their host. He felt it was his duty to accompany the newly-married couple every where. Indira remembered the vast retinue that followed them to Kangan as they travelled to Sonemarg, a mountain retreat surrounded by glaciers and snowy peaks, which lay 8,000 feet above sea level on the tortuous road to Ladakh. She recounted with some mirth the early morning knock at the door, which announced that Sheikh Abdullah was ready for breakfast with a picnic lunch to follow. Behind him would be the inevitable large retinue of friends. It needed all her tact to convince the Sheikh that she and Feroze would prefer to travel alone.

Indira and Feroze spent more than two months in the mountains, away from the excitement of city life. They trekked to glaciers and camped alongside mountain streams; they talked with shepherds and did not read any newspapers. It was only on their return to Allahabad that they found Anand Bhawan in turmoil, preparing for the Congress Working Committee (CWC) meeting in Bombay on 7 and 8 August.

EIGHT

Mahatma Gandhi told the people of India:

> Here is a mantra. A short one that I give you, you may
> imprint it in your hearts and let every breath of yours give
> expression to it. The mantra is, "Do or Die". We shall
> either free India or die in the attempt. We shall not live to
> see the perpetuation of slavery.[1]

It was 8 August 1942. A fire raged in Gandhiji's heart. He had
watched the British retreat from Burma with anguish and anger. The
Japanese stood poised on the borders of India. At this critical point
in history, he asked the All-India Congress Committee (AICC):
'Where shall I go and where shall I take the forty crores of India?' His
eyes were hot, his words militant; his message was one of non-violence
and compassion.

Gandhiji was a friend of the Viceroy's and was anguished at the
bombing of Britain. His sympathies were with Chiang Kai-shek, but his
message was tough, and clear. India would fight the British. If invaded
by the Japanese, it would fight the Japanese. It would fight until the alien
presence in the country was ended or until he and vast numbers of Indians
were dead. But it would have to be a non-violent struggle.

The Mahatma was a master of the dramatic moment, he could
charge it with potency. His demand openly stated was—'I want
freedom immediately, this very night, before dawn if it can be had.'
He defiantly added, 'Nothing should be done secretly. This is an open
rebellion.'[2]

Gandhiji's decision was a controversial one. Jawaharlal Nehru, in
particular, was worried that any precipitous action would affect the
battle in Europe, Africa and Asia and open the flood gates to the
Fascist forces of Japan and Germany. Gandhiji had countered by
saying that the 'Quit India' resolution would not mean that the British
army would have to leave Indian shores, but it did mean the handing
over of political power to the Indian people so that it was they who
would decide whether to join the Allies in the war against Fascist
forces.

The 'Quit India' resolution was formally moved by Jawaharlal later that day and carried by the AICC meeting. The news was received with wild acclaim by the thousands of people who had gathered under the vast shamiana at Gowalia Tank in Bombay to listen to their leaders defy the might of the British Empire. They gathered from all over the vast hinterland of India. Congressmen, socialists, student leaders, businessmen, delegates, observers and invitees sat together. The Indian press was present as was the world press. The Government of India had its spies at the occasion as did the Japanese Government.

It was the middle of the monsoons. Thick angry clouds filled the sky; occasional thunder and lightning reflected the tension inside. There was no standing room in the vast tent lit by artificial light. The future was as opaque and threatening as the clouds overhead obscuring the sun.

Indira Gandhi, back from her long honeymoon in Kashmir, was present, with Feroze Gandhi, at the meeting. Her earlier resolve to withdraw from the noisy tumult of politics and take refuge in the nest she and Feroze were building was swept away. The needs of the moment brushing aside the ideal of a sanctuary of solitude and peace was something that was to recur throughout her life. A weary Jawaharlal returned to Krishna Hutheesing's flat past midnight that evening with Indira. They dined together and talked until early morning. Later that night Indira stood up to answer the ring at the door. She found a police contingent with a senior officer holding out a warrant for her father's arrest. It was a little past 5 a.m. She woke Jawaharlal with a familiar phrase 'The police are here.' He had been out of jail only eight months.

While Jawaharlal shaved, Indira packed his suitcase and bedding. She was with him as he entered the police car and waved to him as the car turned the corner.

Gandhiji and other members of the Congress Working Committee (CWC) were also arrested.

Jawaharlal was to unfurl the national flag at Gowalia Tank the morning of his arrest. News of his and of the Mahatma's arrest spread across the city, and huge crowds converged on Gowalia Tank, where the police had built barricades. Indira was there with Feroze and watched Aruna Asaf Ali as she slipped past the cordon erected by the police and unfurled the flag. The crowd went berserk as teargas shells were fired into the crowds by the police. Indira, caught in the frenzy, managed to escape unnoticed.

The arrest of the leaders of the Congress unleashed civil disobedience movements all over the country; there were public demonstrations, strikes as well as acts of sabotage—railway lines and bridges were blown up, students overturned buses and villagers courted arrest by the hundreds. The Government of India put down the movement with brutal force. On the very same day as Gandhi and Nehru moved the 'Quit India' resolution, the Viceroy, Linlithgow, had declared, 'I feel very strongly that the only possible answer to the "declaration of war" by any section of Congress in the present circumstances must be a declared determination to crush the organisation as a whole.' Mass arrests and fines were followed by police firing, the use of machine guns by low-flying aircraft, the whipping of suspects and the burning of villages.[3]

Indira had meanwhile returned to Allahabad to find Swaraj Bhawan occupied by armed police. Vijayalakshmi Pandit and her daughter, Chand, had been arrested the day before Indira's arrival. While Feroze, disguised as an Anglo-Indian, took refuge in a crowded section of the city, Indira, alone at Anand Bhawan now, maintained a low profile, meeting Congress workers in secret and arranging for the distribution of pamphlets and money. A senior Congress worker, Lal Bahadur Shastri, was hidden in Anand Bhawan nextdoor to the police. There was panic among the servants. When news of her imminent arrest reached her, Indira left Anand Bhawan to hide at a friend's house in the inner city of Allahabad. She was in a belligerent mood, determined to defy the police before being arrested.

On 10 September she addressed a meeting in the heart of the old city of Allahabad. Within minutes of the crowd's gathering, a large contingent of armed police formed a cordon around her. Feroze, who had been watching from a nearby house, and did not expect to be involved, saw what was happening. Indira recalled the event:

> At the sight of a gun barrel just a yard away from my head, excitement and anxiety got the better of him and he came charging down, yelling at the sergeant . . . The sergeant made the mistake of touching my arm to lead me to the prison van. It was like a signal. The crowd surged forward.

My other arm was seized by some Congresswomen and I
thought that I would be torn asunder. Somehow we all
survived. There was no firing though rifle butts were used
and many were hurt. A large number of us, men and
women, including my husband and me, were arrested.[4]

The policemen in the van were apologetic; in a gesture of atonement they laid their turbans at her feet.

Indira was jailed in the 'female ward' of the Naini jail where
Vijayalakshmi and Chand awaited her. Conditions in the prison were
grim, for the authorities were determined to break the rebel spirit of
the Nehru women. The prison cell was dirty with grey coloured walls
and floor; there was barred openings in the wall without shutters; the
beds were concrete and stone without blankets. If anything fell off the
structure, it was eaten by white ants. Two blankets were provided per
detenu, and Indira was allowed to keep the books she had brought
with her. All means of communicating with the external world were,
however, barred—no letters were permitted to be written or received,
interviews were prohibited, newspapers and magazines confiscated.
Everyone was locked into their cells at night.

The tough obstinate streak in the Nehru women asserted itself as
they devised strategies to deal with their confined environment. A
blanket was stretched between the living area and the toilet, and they
amused themselves inventing games, studying Hindi and Sanskrit.
Indira adopted a stray cat, called her Mirabelle, shared her meals with
her. When a fellow-convict's baby fell sick, Indira took over the care
of the baby, fed it, put it to sleep and even considered adopting the
child.

It was September and a lone peepal tree in the yard provided a
spot of green in the grey landscape. The changing tints of the peepal
leaves, sprouting in the autumn rains, growing dark green in the
winter, registered the seasons and their cyclic flow.

With winter, when the winds blew through the openings in the cell,
the evenings became long. It grew dark by six; there was no electricity
and tiny hurricane lamps provided a flickering light. It turned bitterly
cold, and Indira found it difficult to sleep, but finally when sleep came
she dreamt of the Himalayas and their snowy peaks. The heat began
in March; and by April the dust-storms. Relentlessly, like an incoming

tide, dust took over, it crept into crevices, covered books, papers, clothes, hands and faces. They tried to hang blankets over the barred windows, but were suffocated. A cobra in the cell brought excitement and relief from the monotony of life. An aeroplane crashed nearby with an Australian pilot on board; the jail was thick with rumour that the pilot was in love with the jail superintendent's daughter. The temperature soared to a 112 degrees Fahrenheit and the cell was resonant with mosquitoes.

By March, six months of brutal repression by the authorities found the rebellion in the country ebbing. Jawaharlal noted in his diary: 'We had hardly ever been quite so weak as we are now.'[5] Vijayalakshmi Pandit and her daughter were released from jail on parole. The rules were relaxed and Indira, alone in jail, was permitted to write one 500-word letter a month, and also to receive letters.

Jawaharlal, interned at the Ahmednagar Fort in Maharashtra, waited for news of Indira. The jail rules in Bombay Presidency were more lenient. He had been permitted to write letters, had written to Indira but when he received no reply from her, became anxious and restless. It was through the newspapers that he learnt of her arrest, and her internment at the Naini jail in Allahabad, and from his younger sister Krishna that Indira was not allowed to write.

In the Ahmednagar Fort, Jawaharlal was surrounded by friends of the CWC, amongst whom were some of the most learned minds of the country. There was Maulana Abul Kalam Azad, whose knowledge of Urdu, Arabic and Persian poetry brought luminosity to jail life. Jawaharlal spent long hours with him learning the verse of Mirza Ghalib and the songs of the fourteenth century Sufi, Amir Khusro. If he learnt Persian from the Maulana, it was to the Sanskrit savant, Acharya Narendra Dev, that he turned for the study of ancient Sanskrit and Buddhist texts. They read Kalidasa and Bana, and discussed the doctrines of the Buddha. Flanked by the Maulana and the Acharya, Nehru was rediscovering the poetry of India.

After seven long months father and daughter began writing again. For Jawaharlal the break in communication was hard: in his first letter to Indira, dated 5 March, he writes, 'Ever since you were a tiny tot and learnt laboriously to spell out your letters and write a fantastic hand, I do not think there has ever been such a lengthy period without my writing to you.' He wrote five more letters, and was overjoyed when he finally received her first letter to him from jail. It was a cheerful letter, despite this Jawaharlal's diary entry of 13 April, reveals his anxieties for her. Jawaharlal had confidence in Indira's courage, but he was worried about her health, especially during the summer months. He scanned the newspapers every day for temperatures in Allahabad.

Jawaharlal's response to Indira's letter is subdued: 'What shall I write to you, my dear?' He senses that she has matured, that jail which is 'a terrible narrowing of the world of experience and sensation' has helped her move out of narrow grooves and given her new poise. But he expresses this feeling indirectly, drawing a distinction between those human beings who go to pieces when confined and those who find through solitude a way to inner resources. He tells her that he himself matured slowly and late, and is apologetic for the implied comparison. 'Being your father, my mind immediately goes back to a similar period in my own growth.' Towards the end of the letter his thoughts are tinged with regret: 'I have few regrets. But one there is that in your childhood and early girlhood I saw so little of you.' In his diary he later notes:

> She writes long delightful letters and is much concerned
> with the changes she is discovering in herself. From the
> closed house that was herself, she is looking out more and
> more and finding a new interest & new excitement in the
> world.[6]

In her second letter from jail Indira asked her father to send her some Urdu poetry; Jawaharlal began to send her stanzas from the poetry of Ghalib, Mohammed Iqbal, Taba Tabai, Mir Taqi, Amir Khusro, among others, transcribed into Devnagari, sometimes with biographical and explanatory notes attached. And when she asked him whether the heroic Begum Somroo was a Kashmiri, he consulted the Maulana and sent her details of the life of the Mughal lady, 'endowed by nature with masculine intrepidity.'

Indira was discharged from prison on 15 May on account of her health. She was ill and the prison authorities did not want to be held responsible for her well-being. Emerging from the stark monotones of her prison surroundings she was plunged into the hard brilliance of the Allahabad landscape in summer. The experience now akin to a blind person recovering sight—the red heat of the gulmohur flowers in fierce bloom; the curve of the river Jamuna, half-remembered—filled her eyes. The temperature had risen to 117 degrees. Her body broke down; she was admitted to hospital with a high fever, a severe cough and pain in the chest.

When she recovered, she returned to Anand Bhawan; at this point the government asked for an undertaking from her and Vijayalakshmi that they would go to Khali in the Himalayas and live there, and remain there. In other words, they were to be placed in detention in more congenial surroundings. Indira and Vijayalakshmi both refused the offer. The government jailed Vijayalakshmi again in Allahabad and considered doing the same with Indira but soon released them both unconditionally.

She had spent eight months in prison. It had been a period of inner growth which she herself summed up in a matter of fact way afterwards: 'It all helped to strengthen your determination, and of course it helped to harden you physically and mentally, to put up with a lot of hardships.'[7]

Unable to bear the heat of Allahabad, Indira decided to spend the summer at Panchgani, a tiny hill resort south of Bombay. On her way there, she stopped in Bombay with her aunt Krishna Hutheesing. Krishna's house on Carmichael Road was a meeting point for the rich socialites, journalists, political analysts and foreigners living in the city. The conversation was vivacious even though the concerns of many present touched only the surface of the mind. Indira felt oppressed by the talk and the impact of the wealthy city unnerved her; her stark prison life and the simplicity of Allahabad were in sharp contrast to the glitter she saw here. She experienced a sense of complete dislocation. Challenged by her surroundings she withdrew into herself; the noise and the turmoil of the outer world became unreal. She wrote to her father about the strange manner in which her mind worked and her difficulties in finding anyone who would respond or try to understand her.

Jawaharlal was alarmed by the letters he received from her. He was worried that she might again cut herself away, withdraw into her old immature and childishly prejudiced self. It is a stern letter that he wrote back, warning her about the dangers of retreating into an ivory tower. He analysed her feelings:

> Almost every person, who thinks, imagines that he or she
> is a peculiar person, apart from the rest. And so of course
> every individual is. Then there is the feeling of lack of
> sympathy and understanding. True enough, again, for we
> are all again deep down strangers to each other and even
> to ourselves. But the doors and windows of sympathy and
> understanding do not open out of us of themselves: They
> await our initiative.[8]

Jawaharlal did not stop to wonder whether or not this withdrawal
into an interior space, to create a buffer state against the world, was
not regressive, but, for Indira, part of her strength.

Jawaharlal's fears about Indira retreating into her own world
turned out to have been unfounded—she had changed. Going to jail
had earned her a place in her father's world; the act had brought a
new focus and new meaning to her life; a new relationship between
father and daughter had been forged. She wrote frequently to her
father, who expressed his feelings in his diary: 'We are closer to each
other than ever before. Almost we might be friends rather than father
and daughter—how she reaches out to me.'[9]

The release from prison brought a void in her life which Feroze,
who had served out his jail sentence and was with her by the third
week in June, was not any more able to fill; they were together after
a separation of nearly ten months, they went for long walks, discussed
family matters. But a restlessness had taken hold of Indira; she now
decided to go back to the north, visit her grandmother and friends.
Feroze dissuaded her and she stayed in Panchgani until August,
becoming increasingly more depressed.

News of a devastating famine in Bengal began to appear in the
newspapers. The administration's callousness was nowhere more
apparent than in the following entry in the *C. & M. Gazetteer,* a
government newspaper: ' "Death by starvation" appears on none of
the legislative lists attached to the Government of India Act and is
therefore the concern neither of the Centre nor of the State.'

Indira was anxious to become involved in the famine relief work
and wrote to Swami Abhayananda of the Ramakrishna Mission asking

if she could come to Calcutta. The Swami told her that what he needed was money, food and clothes, not more workers.

The monsoon storms brought on 'a brooding sense of tragedy, as much personal as national' The future was so insecure. On 6 August 1943 she wrote to her father of her depression. A helpless Jawaharlal wrote back on 14 August: 'Everything changes. In the present lie the seeds of the future. Have the seeds been truly sown? Are they the seeds of noble and straight growing trees? If the proper seeds are there, the harvest is sure.' He sent her the words of Beethoven stricken by deafness:

> *I shall seize fate by the throat.*
> *It shall never wholly overcome me.* [10]

Indira and Feroze returned in the third week of August to Anand Bhawan in Allahabad. By now her fantasy of being a contented housewife had disappeared: the home that she had built with Feroze was wound up and the furniture was stored in the godowns of the large compound at Anand Bhawan.

Feroze was happy to be back in Allahabad; he had a large number of friends and was often out of the house. Indira, on the other hand, had few friends and little to do. She found Anand Bhawan a lonely place, abounding in memories, scarred with old conflicts. She wandered the empty corridors of Anand Bhawan, whispers of the past crowded her mind. She started to learn typing and bought a charkha to learn spinning. While in Europe she had allowed her hair to grow, tied it back to the nape of her neck; the hair-style suited her, softened her face. But back in Allahabad a new austerity, a sense of rebellion made her cut it back to 'a service bob'. She found solace in writing letters to her father; she raised philosophical questions with him; they conversed on man's relationship with nature—Indira felt that there was an organic connection, that the Indian peasant understood.

She told her father that she was keeping the door to his room closed. On hearing this Jawaharlal wrote that he had kept the door to her room open when she was away in Switzerland, and went in to say good-night to her every evening. In a letter dated 6 November 1943 he suggested that Anand Bhawan be redecorated. 'Like me it has developed a faded passé look.' Indira responded to this suggestion eagerly. She went to Bombay, bought cutlery, cloth for curtains, and gave the house a fresh, new look.

In mid-October, Indira wrote to Jawaharlal saying that Vijayalakshmi, who had made her home at Anand Bhawan since Kamala's departure in 1935, was leaving Anand Bhawan to set up a separate home on Mukerji Road in Allahabad. Jawaharlal was anguished at these signs of discord in the family; and even though as he learnt later, Indira had no part in her aunt's departure, Jawaharlal's letter to her is indicative of his feelings. Harmony in personal relationships is the key, he tells her, to the larger good of society. Ancient societies like India and China, he wrote, tended to concentrate on the cultivation of those virtues which made the individual less self-centred and willing to cooperate—tact, poise, balance were essential. 'There is an aristocracy and well-bredness about the Chinese which is impressive,' he wrote and ended his letter with an apt quotation from Hali:

> *Who has the right on the garden*
> *Both the cypress tree and the winged dove contend;*
> *Whose is it?*[11]

Ranjit Pandit, Vijayalakshmi's husband, died in Lucknow on 14 January; Indira and Feroze accompanied his body back from Lucknow to Anand Bhawan. It was Indira's third encounter with death and the shock was intense; she felt devastated, engulfed in darkness, and came close to a breakdown. She described her feelings to her father in Eugene O'Neill's words:

> *And day is night*
> *Is day again, and I have no pleasure*
> *In sun and stars, for all these were to me*
> *As nothing.*[12]

A doctor examined her and found her pregnant. Indira was joyous at the news, but her feelings were edged with the fear that her body would not be able to bear the strain of child-birth. When she married Feroze she had told him that in marriage she primarily sought children and companionship. So to be near the best doctors Indira went with

Feroze to Bombay to stay with her aunt Krishna. There she consulted
the eminent gynaecologist D.V. Shirodkar and was put under his care.
Feroze and she were happy; they lunched often with friends at
Bombelli's, met friends and argued over the name of the baby. They
were both certain that the baby would be male, and fancies of
becoming a home-maker once again revived in Indira.

Rajiv Ratna, named after his grandmother Kamala and his
grandfather Jawahar, was born on 20 August 1944, at ten-past-eight
in the morning. The birth was uncomplicated. Her aunt Krishna
offered prayers to Ganesha and to Hanuman, and her father was
anxious that the correct time of birth be noted, taking into account
the extra hour that had been added to extend daylight hours. He told
Krishna to arrange for an astrological chart to be drawn up and sent
on to him.

In October Indira returned to Allahabad with Feroze. They stayed
at Anand Bhawan once again. The war was drawing to an end.
Jawaharlal had been permitted interviews, but had little desire to see
Indira in the grey shadow of prison walls, even though he had not seen
her for almost two-and-a-half years. He wrote her a deeply tender
letter:

> When I meet you again, wherever that may be, I might
> remain silent for some time, just look at you and try to find
> out what you are now, how you have changed, what private
> universe you inhabit; or I might break out in unmeaning
> talk as a reaction from the long silence, a torrent of words
> trying to cover my own shyness and uneasiness, reaching
> out and seeking for something which eludes me. Gradually
> as we see more of each other, we shall adjust ourselves
> as we understand each other afresh—and so I feel it is
> better for me to avoid these jail interviews.[13]

Jawaharlal was released from jail on 15 June. The British Cabinet
Mission was in India. Jawaharlal's presence at the talks was necessary.
Indira was in Srinagar with the baby, staying at the home of her cousin,
Brij Lal Nehru who was the Maharaja of Kashmir's Financial Adviser.
Hearing of her father's likely release on the radio, she forgot the baby
Rajiv and rushed out to book seats on the fastest available transport

to Allahabad. Leaving the one-year-old child with Brij Lal Nehru's family, she returned to Anand Bhawan. She did not want her father to enter an empty home.

Father and daughter were seeing each other after a little over two-and-a-half years. They were both shy at the start, it was a new experience to meet in an atmosphere of freedom and leisure. Jawaharlal wanted her to accompany him to Bombay where the members of the Congress Working Committee awaited him. It was in the mid-monsoon season, the rains were relentless. Indira was caught in a shower, which led to a severe cold which soon developed into bronchitis. It was several weeks before she could return to Kashmir and Rajiv.

In time, Jawaharlal's presence was necessary in Simla for discussions with the Cabinet Mission. He wrote to his daughter and Sheikh Abdullah that he would be in Srinagar by 22 July 1945 and hoped that no programmes would be arranged which would keep him apart from his daughter. He arrived in Srinagar to see his year-old grandson Rajiv for the first time. The families travelled to Pahalgam from where they were to cross the mountains to Sonemarg. Indira left Rajiv with her aunt, Rameshwari Nehru, at Pahalgam and joined her father on the ten-day trek. They camped alongside mountain streams, watched pale flowers force their way from under boulders of icy streams, crossed mountain meadows of wild flowers, encircled by snow-filled ranges, bathed in the waters of Gangabal lake.

> We travelled about 100 miles at altitudes varying from 9000 ft. to 14000 ft., crossed a dangerous pass, seldom traversed, leading from one river valley to another. It was a tricky business involving a great deal of leg work and a false step would have sent us 400 ft. below. However, we survived and felt rather elated over it all.[14]

Indira, in spite of her recent illness, stood the trip well.

PART III
1946–1966

I have been in public service all my life. I have been travelling all my life. I have regarded the whole of India as my home all my life.

–Indira Gandhi[1]

ONE

On 4 April 1946, Jawaharlal Nehru wrote to Indira Gandhi: 'I have been thinking of you since my arrival here. I wanted you to be here with me to cheer me up. I have no idea as to how long I shall have to stay here, but it seems that these Cabinet Mission negotiations will continue till the end of this month.' The letter to Indira was sent along with a letter to Feroze Gandhi in which he sought an excuse for Feroze to accompany Indira to Delhi: 'If you have nothing particular to do,' he writes, 'you might be able to make yourself useful in a rather odd kind of way.' He suggested that Feroze could help in setting up a centre for the foreign correspondents who were in Delhi in large numbers but were wandering around helplessly as there was no one to take charge. 'I should like Indu to come here very much.'[2]

Indira's resolve to leave Anand Bhawan and Allahabad, to leave her husband and to respond to her father's need, was a momentous decision. She seldom acted in haste. Her sense of isolation and loneliness had been building up for some time. She discussed the situation with Feroze. He encouraged her to go. Tensions between Indira and Feroze had already started. In reply to a letter from Frank Oberdorf in early 1946, after a silence of nine years, she wrote:

> In March of 1942 I got married. Unlike you I have not been able to have any domestic life. Now I have a small son and he will soon be two years old . . .

> We are still leading very busy lives—with a great deal of travelling all over the country. All of us never seem to be in the same town at the same time.

> As you see from the above address, I am now living in my father's house.[3]

Indira went to Delhi with her little son Rajiv to act as her father's hostess; Jawaharlal, as interim Prime Minister, had an official residence at 17, York Road, in New Delhi. The niche which Jawaharlal Nehru had kept vacant, was now hers by right.

Indira from her childhood was used to a crowded house, people coming and going, the telephone constantly ringing, but now an official hostess she had to take upon herself arduous responsibilities. Her father Jawaharlal by now was a legendary figure. Presidents and prime ministers lunched and dined at his table. There was a constant stream of scientists, political activists, philosophers, poets who visited Nehru. They hardly noticed the daughter; shy and reserved, she was always seen two steps behind her father.

Indira was the product of many cultures. Her close association with the freedom struggle and the stalwarts of the independence movement had moulded her life. In many ways she was a reflection of her father's mind. Her years in England and her association with Feroze Gandhi's left-wing friends, journalists and political thinkers had given her a radical conditioning. She was a rebel, anti-traditional and anti-establishment but a natural cautiousness kept her far away from any major Left commitments. Astrology, prognostication, ritual, superstition had little place in her consciousness. Her early upbringing and her father's interests expressed with such limpidity in his letters to her, gave her a love of adventure, a fearlessness, an inbuilt sense of the secular; it also awakened a live curiosity and a constant search for new frontiers. From childhood she had an intimate feeling for nature. Her year alone in Leysin had encouraged her to observe, to be silent and let the seasons roll by. But in spite of her early exposure to intellectuals and powerful activists, she had lived within the confines of a society which hemmed her in, gave her little opportunity to reach out, meet people, and explore the arts or investigate a life of the mind.

She had her own refuges; her world of fantasy and an inner sanctuary where from childhood she could take shelter when threatened. Her early years in Allahabad, her sharing with her grandmother in seasonal festivals and her grandaunt's tales, exposed her to living myth and ritual, that quickened the ground of her mind, made it rich and potent, but the seeds of that living energy were still dormant. They awaited germination.

*

Meanwhile, Feroze moved to Lucknow to take charge of the *National Herald,* a daily founded by Jawaharlal in 1937. Feroze had a flair for journalism. Those who worked for him on the *National Herald* and later in Delhi, where he became an active journalist for the *Indian Express,* found him meticulous in his research and reporting. 'He could have risen to the top position in the newspaper world of this country.'[4]

Indira was aware of Feroze's roving eye. Faced with her father's strong disapproval when she sought to marry Feroze, Indira and Feroze had visited Bhupesh Gupta, a Marxist and a close friend, while they were together in London. When he heard of their intention to marry he turned to Feroze and asked him with the utmost gravity: 'Will you be faithful?' Feroze had laughed, gone down on his knees like a penitent, and in a mocking voice asked, 'Do you want me to take a vow?' Bhupesh Gupta did not answer Feroze, but turned to Indira: 'You really want to marry Feroze?' He knew she was obstinate and strong-willed and was not surprised to find her adamant in her resolve. He then advised them to seek the Mahatma's advice.[5]

In Lucknow, separated from Indira, Feroze soon became entangled with a woman from one of Lucknow's prominent Muslim landed families. Rumours of Feroze seeking solace elsewhere reached Indira while she was with her father. She was pregnant and awaiting the arrival of her baby, due in late December.

Feroze came to Delhi and was present when the family gathered at 17, York Road—Jawaharlal, Indira, Feroze, Krishna Hutheesing and her two sons—to await the new arrival.

The house was overcrowded and Feroze moved into a tent pitched in the garden. Indira had been feeling unwell, but on the request of Lady Cripps who was a house-guest, had accompanied her to buy a Kashmiri shawl. Late the same night Indira started premature labour pains and was admitted to a hospital where a British surgeon took charge. She suffered a massive haemorrhage and the doctors feared for her life. The Prime Minister was informed and he rushed to the hospital to find that the bleeding had been controlled. A male child, threatening the life of the mother, was born late in the night. Jawaharlal named the child Sanjay—after the visionary Brahmin who in the epic *Mahabharata* describes to Dhritarashtra, the blind King of Hastinapur, the battle on the fields of Kurukshetra.

*

India became independent on the midnight of 14 August 1947. The country was filled with a wild delight; a thousand Diwalis were celebrated that night. Darkness was banished, houses in cities were ablaze with light; oil lamps were lit in village homes. The million temple bells of India chimed in celebration. Women, men and children were out on the streets in the cities of Bombay, Delhi, Madras and Calcutta and in all the other small towns of the country, singing freedom songs, holding hands, dancing, creating poetry, reciting it; praying, weeping and laughing; waiting for that momentous hour to strike. The breeze of freedom had reached distant villages, however poor and cutaway from the mainstream. The word *azadi* (freedom) was sweet to the ear, sweet to the tongue. No one quite knew what it all meant, whether burdens would be lifted, or the hungry fed. But it seemed as if a massive boulder that had held India down for centuries had been lifted. The doorways to a new life lay open.

Indira was present in Parliament House when the clock struck the magic hour of midnight. Pandit Jawaharlal Nehru, the first Prime Minister of free India, rose to make a speech that lingered for decades in the ears and minds of the Indian people:

> Long years ago we made a tryst with destiny and now the time comes when we shall redeem our pledge, not wholly or in full measure but very substantially. At the stroke of the midnight hour when the world sleeps, India will awake to life and freedom.

Recalling the day, two decades later in an interview with Lord Chalfont of the British Broadcasting Corporation (BBC), Indira spoke of a feeling of numbness.

> It was impossible, to take in that after all these years something that we had thought of and dreamt of and worked for ever since I could remember, had happened. It was such a powerful experience that I think I was numb. You know when you go to an extreme of pleasure or pain there is numbness. Freedom was just so big a thing that it could not register, it seemed to fill all of you and all your world.[6]

At the glittering midnight function and the next morning when

Jawaharlal Nehru first unfurled the flag at the National Memorial at Rajpath and later from the ramparts of the Red Fort, Indira was hardly visible. But she was present, tucked away in a corner, observing the day's solemnity, a moment that would remain alive within her for the rest of her life.

If freedom brought a wild euphoria, it also brought devastation and massacre. A vast exodus of Hindus from Pakistan and Muslims from India took place. Massacres, rapes, brutalities convulsed the land and its people. Walking along the long roads, crossing rivers, travelling by trains, by car, fearful, laden with sorrow, leaving behind their relations and friends, their homes and their belongings, the two communities fled for refuge. Mahatma Gandhi was not present in Delhi when independence was declared. He was travelling in Noakhali, in what is now Bangladesh, where a massacre of a Hindu population by Muslims had devastated the villages which now needed the Mahatma's healing touch. He was totally unconcerned with his own security.

After independence Indira went to Mussoorie to look after her two young sons—the four-year-old Rajiv and the eight-month-old Sanjay. It was in Mussoorie that she first heard of the massacres. Disregarding the advice of Feroze she started the journey to Delhi with her two children. On her way down, the train was stopped by agitators at a midway station. The noise of voices raised in hatred, the shrieks of terror from the victims reached her as she was freshening up for her arrival in Delhi. She looked out of the window and saw the crowd attack a man they took to be a Muslim. 'I wrapped a towel around me, jumped out of the train and grabbed this person being attacked and took him into our compartment.'[7] The crowd, taken by surprise by this fearless act, turned in other directions. The train restarted and ultimately reached Delhi.

Devastated by what she had witnessed, Indira joined forces with Hannah Sen and Mrs John Mathai, social workers in charge of refugee work. While on their way to old Delhi they saw a Muslim being chased by a crowd. Indira asked the driver to stop the car. The driver hesitated. Indira jumped out, leaving behind her chappals in the car. She managed to get hold of the victim and repeatedly told him to get in the car. He was an oldish man, already hurt and bleeding. She then confronted the crowd.

Since I was a small girl I have always felt at home in crowds. Even if they are hostile it does not worry me. I think that I can calm them more than almost anybody I know. But this rioting—I had seen communal rioting before and I had seen people being killed in Allahabad, but here it was quite different. The common rioting erupts suddenly, there is a burst of hatred, there is killing and then it subsides. For the first time it was a cold-blooded thing.[8]

The Mahatma heard of Indira's work and sent for her to suggest that she work in the camps where Muslims were taking refuge. 'I am not feeling too well,' she responded, 'but if you want me to do it, I will. But who will go with me? It is many years since I have been to Delhi and even at that time I didn't know where the Muslims lived.' He said: 'My dear girl, if I had somebody else to go, I wouldn't ask you. I know you are not well. But you have to go and find whatever help you can.' The conditions in these refugee camps were desperate. Nothing had been cleaned for many days.

I used to go at 5.00 in the morning and come back long after dark. We got the streets cleaned. We went to the Town Hall, the ration shops. There was no conveyance. We had to bully and persuade people to lend us trucks to take the rations. The sweepers were not prepared to go because they said they would be killed. We had to provide two young men for each sweeper as a guard.[9]

When things were under control she went to Gandhiji and told him: 'I am sorry I could not come to see you earlier, but I thought you were too big a person to be disturbed.'[10] His comment was that he had misjudged her earlier and that exterior appearances did not matter. He then asked her to meet him every day. At times when she could not come he would send her a rose and a message. Her attitude to the Mahatma was never reverential. For her he was part of the family and she went to him with her woes, little and big. He would listen carefully to her and was rarely flippant though at times he could crack jokes and laugh merrily.

As a young person she felt many of his ideas were old and out of date. It was only later in life that she realized she did not see far enough to understand the reason why his actions and attitudes were not intellectual. 'He had to take the masses with him and he had to put everything in that idiom which they could understand.'[11]

She remembered vividly the day before Gandhi's assassination. She had gone to visit him, along with her aunt Krishna Hutheesing and her four-year-old son Rajiv. As she was leaving the Prime Minister's House the gardener brought her a little garland of jasmines. The Mahatma was in a jovial mood. They did not discuss politics, but films. 'While we were talking Rajiv had taken the flowers and was playing with the Mahatma's toes and entwining the garland around his foot.'[12]

She had intended to go to the prayer meeting the next day, but because of some engagements could not go. The news of Gandhiji's assassination 'came as a terrific shock.' But here again although the grief was personal—her earliest memories were linked with the Mahatma who was part of the family—she had confided in him, he had joked with her, quarrelled with her, shared her grief with her—yet now in his death there was no place for personal grief. A vast river of sorrow swept the nation. For Jawaharlal it was the death of a dearly loved human being, his mentor and teacher. For Indira, it was the sudden disappearance of an immovable rock, an anchor and a refuge. 'It was as if with his frail two hands, he lifted up a people.'[13]

TWO

The house at 17, York Road was inadequate for a prime minister's requirements. Shortly after independence, therefore, Jawaharlal Nehru moved with Indira Gandhi and her children to Teen Murti House, which became the official residence of the Prime Minister. It had previously been occupied by the British Commander-in-Chief. An aura of stiff formality still lingered in the place. It was a vast rambling building with formal sitting-rooms, dining-rooms, a ballroom, master bedrooms and tiny bedrooms, reception areas, offices and vast corridors. There was no space for privacy or lazy relaxation. Indira found it difficult to adjust. She removed the portraits of the Commanders-in-Chief from the walls, had the house painted an eggshell white. Although there were a number of rooms to choose from, she decided on a small bedroom for herself with a tiny room next to it for the children. She furnished her own room with frugality, with simple furnishings and very few artifacts. The ballroom was converted into a meeting room where she could receive visitors and her personal friends. In the early days, there was only one portrait of Nehru by Topolski that hung in the ballroom on a distant wall.

Feroze Gandhi lived in Lucknow, but between 1946 and 1952 husband and wife visited each other for short periods. Her father had sensed his daughter's growing unhappiness in the marriage but did not feel he had the right to probe; the daughter in turn did not permit any outward display of disagreement between her and Feroze. At first she was fully occupied in looking after her children and dealing with the human problems arising out of Partition. Many refugees with nowhere to go were living in the out-houses of the Prime Minister's mansion. A senior army officer, who was a young child at the time, remembers looking out of the barred windows of the servants' quarters on to the garden of Teen Murti House to watch the second birthday party of Sanjay. Indira noticed the little children's faces peeping out of the window and immediately asked the staff to invite them to join the party.

Her first visit abroad was in 1949 with her father, who was to pay an official visit to the United States. A short time before the trip Indira suffered a miscarriage in Allahabad and was desperately ill. Jawaharlal and Feroze were away, but rushed to her bedside on hearing news of her illness. The crisis passed, but the doctors advised rest. They told Indira not to accompany her father abroad as she was extremely weak. But Indira was desperately anxious to go. The Prime Minister supported her and insisted that he would take her, even if it was on a stretcher. Vijayalakshmi Pandit was the Indian Ambassador to the United States. Indira was very angry when, according to her, on the advice of her aunt, the Prime Minister did not include Indira's name in his party and she was therefore not treated as a State Guest; nor was she invited to any of the official functions held in honour of her father. It was Dr Homi Bhabha, the physicist and founder of the Tata Institute of Fundamental Research (TIFR) and later chief of the Atomic Energy Commission, who was in Washington at the time, who sensed the situation, and took her out for lunches and dinners. Otherwise she would have been left alone to have breakfast, lunch and dinner in her own room.

It was in New York, at the several receptions arranged for her father by the intellectual and business community, that Indira met Dorothy Norman, a sensitive, warm woman who had helped during India's struggle for independence by creating public opinion in support of India in the US. Dorothy was a writer, editor, photographer, a woman with a deep commitment to the arts and literature. A friendship developed between Indira and Dorothy that was to continue throughout her life. While Nehru was busy with official functions, Dorothy Norman introduced his young shy daughter to thinkers, authors, painters, musicians. A new life of the mind and sensibilities was opening for Indira. She visited museums and art galleries, went to the theatre, visited the opera and came back to India with the sense of having visited what was, for her, a new world.

On her return to India, Indira retreated into herself once again, but she was soon travelling with her father to distant parts of the country. In tribal areas and villages she witnessed the dances and the music of tribes and people from settled village societies. The Prime Minister and his daughter loved dressing up and they wore the local costumes as they danced to the sound of drumbeats, the circular dances of tribal India. Indira would laugh and say: 'I and my father never developed the muscles in our backsides to imitate the way the birds move.'[1]

After 1952, Indira was to organize in New Delhi performances of rural and tribal dances from all corners of India to coincide with the Republic Day celebrations. It was perhaps Indira's first contact with the vigour and virility of tribal culture, the infinite variety of costumes, the ancient recreation of myth through dance; it was a rich and rewarding experience. These dances became an yearly ritual. The day after Republic Day was celebrated, a reception would be held at Teen Murti House where the dancers would gather along with some of Indira's close friends. Father and daughter never ceased to participate in the dances, moving from group to group, laughing, joyous, entering into that spirit of delight, that innocence and direct contact with nature's abundance that characterizes the culture of tribal India. Even in the early 1960s, when Jawaharlal was over seventy and his energy was at a low ebb, the function continued to be held. The Prime Minister would become light of spirit, the pace and tempo of his life would change, his eyes would come alive and his grave, tired face would break into smiles as he entered the magic circle to join hands with these children of the 'leafdark earth.'

"Did the gods declare that just the young or just the old should danee."[2]

Indira's interest in children made her seek avenues of work where creativity could be brought to the poorest child. She was a Trustee of the Indian Council for Child Welfare and soon became its Chairman. She established Bal Bhavan, a centre for under-privileged children in New Delhi, where all the arts were taught, where there was living theatre, and science was taught as play; and Bal Sahyog where homeless waifs from off the streets of Delhi were provided security and taught a craft.

Feroze was elected to the Lok Sabha from Rae Bareilly in 1952. He came to stay in the Prime Minister's House in New Delhi. He found the atmosphere stifling. Security was lax, the house was always full of people yet there was no place in that vast house where Feroze could meet his friends. Shanta Gandhi, an old friend from the London days, visited Delhi in the early 1950s. She recollects Indira and Feroze coming to pick her up in a small car. 'We went for lunch to her house. Feroze seemed withdrawn. He took me to a window overlooking the vast spaces, now the Diplomatic Enclave, and said: "This whole place is going to become Chanakya Puri (town of intrigue)." ' Shanta had never seen him in such a mood. He had always been full of fun. The sneering tone in which he spoke, puzzled her. She asked him what had happened. He replied: 'That which was to happen, has happened.' She could tell that he resented having to stay in the Prime Minister's House. Feroze turned to Shanta and asked her what she felt about the whole house. She said: 'How can you live here? It is a museum, not a house to live in.' Indira was upset, spoke back sharply. 'Everyone is not as lucky as you are. You have to take things as they are.' There was an abruptness and sharpness in her voice. Shanta could tell that the relationship between Indira and Feroze was under severe strain.

Indira, as the First Lady, had pride of place at the Prime Minister's dinner table. Feroze was low in protocol and often found himself below the salt. Humiliated and angry, after a time he refused to attend any of the official functions and before long shifted to an official house as Member of Parliament where he cultivated roses and held his own "durbars". He had a vast number of friends in Parliament and in the newspaper world. In the morning he held a Diwan-e-Am (open audience) where journalists and radical young MPs would gather to discuss politics and events, to gossip, to intrigue and to laugh. In the evenings would be the Diwan-e-Khas (special audience) where Feroze met his special friends, amongst them a number of women. Gossip filled the coffee-houses and the drawing-rooms of Delhi that Feroze sought solace away from his wife. They were now rarely seen together.

Yet Feroze continued to lunch every day at Teen Murti House and always had time to play with his children. On weekends the boys would go over to their father. Indira had made great efforts to give her children the feeling of a home. The garden was full of pets—little tiger cubs, a tiny panda and all manner of animals were cared for by the boys. There were a number of dogs. Sanjay's favourite pet was a crocodile, which was finally sent to the zoo, after it almost bit off Indira's fingers. Rajiv and Sanjay grew to love animals and yet the Prime Minister's House had little space for children to run and play freely: there were no nooks and corners where they could play hide-and-seek with their friends or fill the house with laughter. It was a house for adults. The gravity of discussions in offices, in sitting-rooms and studies stilted the atmosphere. It is surprising that with a mother and a grandfather who loved books the children never developed a love for reading.

When they visited their father, Feroze gave them his total attention. He showed them how to pull apart and put together toy trains
and cars. He taught them how to plant and care for roses. Away from
the grim formality of the Prime Minister's House the boys found in
their father a figure with an overflowing capacity for fun. The feeling
that their father considered them of infinite importance left a deep
impact on the two sons. Sanjay Gandhi in an interview with *Surya* in
July 1979 said: 'What stood out in my mind is that he was a very
thorough person. If he took up something he always saw it through
to the last detail. I also remember him as being very outspoken, honest
and independent.'[3]

*

Indira found that her father's friends gave her scant attention. They
saw in her a lovely young woman, were polite, bantered with her, little
realizing that they were dealing with a woman who in her silence was
absorbing every nuance of conversation between them and the Prime
Minister. She was determined to seek friends outside her father's
ambience.

It was around this time that I started seeing her more often. I did
not form part of her father's circle of friends. I was an outsider in her
political world. We would meet, in the early 1950s, in the sparsely
furnished ballroom of the old Commander-in-Chief. The room had
no windows to overlook the garden. There was little to distract us. At
first I found her fiercely shy, wary, on the defensive. She saw me as
the friend of her aunt Krishna, a product of that sophisticated Bombay
society that could converse with ease, analyse, dissect, be brittle and
destructive. She was a natural observer with a rare capacity to listen
and absorb.

She knew of my closeness to J. Krishnamurti, my interest in craft
and handmade textiles, had read some of my short stories. At times,
during our meetings, she would carry a notepad with her to scribble
something that had come to her mind or to make a note of something
I had said. I noticed a precision and a sense of order in most things
she did. In the middle of our conversation she would get up to put a
flower vase straight without interrupting the flow of conversation. She

had a capacity for simultaneous action which intrigued me, as did her silences. I could sense that behind the shy quiet woman, behind her seeming naïveté, was an unexplored density, an ancient face.

As months passed, and I made no attempt to draw close, she started to relax in my presence. She would draw on memories of Anand Bhawan and the halcyon years of her childhood. She would speak of her closeness to nature and express haltingly her feeling for the earth, for trees and growing things. These journeys of discovery refreshed her, provided footnotes to her present.

With her children in boarding-school she had time on her hands and travelled extensively throughout the country. She visited small towns and villages by car, bullock cart and even on foot, to come in direct contact with the problems of village India. She met and came to recognize the faces of important people—social workers and political activists—visited their homes and ate at their tables. She had an uncanny memory for faces and names which proved to be a powerful skill when she became Prime Minister. She kept a low profile, but was seen physically by a vast number of people in the country.

As the 1957 elections drew near, she was appointed a member of the Central Election Committee (CEC) of the Indian National Congress. She refused a seat in Parliament for herself but worked incessantly for her father's constituency located in Allahabad. At first she drew very small crowds, but there was a doggedness in her, a refusal to let go, an energy that impelled her to make her presence felt. She recalls electioneering in a remote village in the Punjab. She found that there was a dais but no people to welcome her:

> It was a cold and misty January morning with a sharp breeze and at 6 a.m. still quite dark. Not a soul was in sight. All doors and windows seemed to be tightly secured. However, there was a takhat (platform) and a microphone and some durries (carpets), wet with the heavy dew. Hansrajji felt that we had done our duty by coming and we could now drive on to the regular programme with a clear conscience. However, much to his embarrassment, I insisted on giving a speech whether there was anybody to listen or not. Almost with my first word, windows started

banging open and tousled heads appeared. Immediately afterwards the entire village poured out from the warmth of their houses, wrapped in blankets and razais (quilts), some with datun sticks (twig of a neem tree, used to brush teeth) and some with tumblers of steaming tea. . .[4]

*

She accompanied her father on most of his trips abroad. In 1953, she had visited the Soviet Union on her own and had come back deeply impressed by the work the Soviets had accomplished for children. She was particularly taken with their organization of out-of-school activities. She was determined to set up similar institutions in India. She visited Soviet Russia again in 1955 when her father paid his official visit to the country. Nikita Khrushchev was then Prime Minister. Her father was shy when it came to asking for aid and the talks were going badly. Indira was deeply worried and recollects waiting in a sitting-room to join her father at an official lunch after the meeting. Suddenly Khrushchev came into the room and seeing her came up to her to tell her that the dialogue was blocked and there was little progress. Her response was instinctive. Knowing her father so intimately she could sense his difficulties. She knew that the Communist Party of India (CPI) had briefed the Soviet Government before her father's visit. She said to Prime Minister Khrushchev that the Soviet Government should remember that her father's voice was the voice of the people of India and that the CPI did not represent the Indian people. Khrushchev was taken aback, but responded warmly, went back to the meeting and solutions emerged.[5] Later, Prime Minister Khrushchev to express his deep gratitude to Indira, gave her as a gift a mink coat which figured prominently in attacks against her in later years when she became Prime Minister.

THREE

In 1956, after an absence of seven years, Indira Gandhi accompanied her father on an official visit to Washington and New York. The skyline of New York during the last decade had undergone major transformations. A young race of creators, a fusion of many cultures, children who had lived through the horrors and brutality of the world war of the 1940s, were creating a new pulsating world of the future. Architecture was the predominant art. Buildings emerged, escaping the gravity of the earth to reach out—the vertical taking the place of the horizontal, the opaqueness and density of concrete transformed by the transluscence of glass and the startling use of new materials like steel and aluminium. It was an exhilarating and inspiring experience.

While her father was busy with meetings, Indira with Dorothy Norman as her guide—she could not have found a more sensitive friend—explored New York. She visited the museums and saw vast treasures of art from all parts of the globe. At the Metropolitan Museum she stood silent before Richard Lippold's sculpture of the sun, a masterpiece of sacred art where thousands of gold wires, woven into mysterious forms hung in space, to move with the slightest breeze.

The United States was entering a period of enquiry into myth and symbol. Japan, Mexico, China, Africa, South America, India and the Island cultures were coming together to reveal through myth the racial unconscious of humankind. Indira savoured the myth of the hero and the early musings on the goddess, heard spellbound, Stella Kramrisch, read Mircea Eliade, met Joseph Campbell and listened to his encounters with myth. She was slowly awakening to the insight that all myth, however separated by space and time, had universal recurrent themes.

An anti-Communist wave was at its peak in the US. Eminent writers, actors and scientists were under surveillance and were summoned to face the Committee of Un-American Activities, to confess or to be fined, jailed or denied jobs and passports. But this appears to have left little impact on Indira nor is there in any of her speeches or writings mention of her meeting with any of the creative people in the US with even mild left-wing ideologies.

*

Indira returned to India light with the breadth of her discoveries, anxious to share her perceptions. It was a period which coincided with my own enquiry into myth and symbol, a journey of discovery that gave me new eyes. Our dialogues turned to the classical and rural myths of India and to the unexplored rural psyche which was the cradle of the mind of India's past. We shared experiences, insights, perceptions. She was eager to share, eager to learn and was enthralled with the journey. We spoke of the need for a flexible mind that could hold the strength and beauty of heritage yet would participate in the technological revolution. Was that possible? It was a question she was to ask again and yet again. But on other occasions we spoke of the hard realities of the weaver, the potter, the basket maker and the need for providing solutions to the problems of the rural poor, the skilled craftsmen; to find markets and services without which the way of life of rural India could wither away.

Charles Eames was invited by the Government of India to prepare a blueprint for a national design institute. Eames was one of the frontier minds, one of the new communicators who could comprehend the new sciences and their artifacts and had place in his vision for man, the machine, and for the seemingly non-essential, the fantasy. To him the contemporary approach was not a style but an insight. I met Eames in the United States in 1955 at the Museum of Modern Art where an exhibition on textiles and ornamental arts of India was presented for the first time. Integrated with it was the world premiére of Satyajit Ray's *Pather Panchali*. Shanta Rao, at the height of her magnificence, danced in the museum's auditorium and the New York audience heard for the first time maestro Ali Akbar Khan on the sarod.

Eames' visit to India was an aftermath of this encounter. He came to explore the actuality of India before preparing his blueprint. He and his wife Ray travelled through India visiting shoe factories and potters' huts, observing the landscape, the people—the hennaed foot of a woman riding a gaily decorated bullock cart—entered the magical village groves of magnificent clay horses and bulls, observed the way women and men worked in the fields—their economy of movement, their use of hands, the drape of a cloth, the rural capacity for attention, their skills and the intensity of their minds. He prepared out of this raw material his blueprint, an integral view of the Indian scene in which he quoted the Bhagavad Gita and eulogized the *lota* as amongst the most distinguished objects of design; functional, beautiful, multi-purpose and a perfect answer to human needs. I remember being present when his report was placed before Manubhai Shah, the then Minister for Commerce and Industry; a puzzled Douglas Ensminger, head of the Ford Foundation was also present, as was Gautam Sarabhai. The Minister could not understand what the Gita had to do with design—design to him meant drawing pictures. I tried in Gujarati to explain to Manubhai, a graduate of the Massachusetts Institute of Technology (MIT) that behind the philosophic introduction, Eames had a tough mind with a profound understanding of the new tech-nologies. Gautam and I waited with bated breath. The Minister was confused but trusted Sarabhai's acute business sense and was aware of my down-to-earth approach to development. Finally the report was accepted and the National Institute of Design (NID) came into being and was built in Ahmedabad on the banks of the river Sabarmati. Charles Eames' document on the National Institute of Design became a classic.

I repeated the story to Indira. Intrigued, she invited herself to dinner to meet Eames and his wife Ray at my home. Language was not Charles' strong point. He thought and communicated in visuals, but when he did speak, haltingly, with many pauses there was rarely a gap between the word and meaning. Indira was delighted. She arranged for Eames to show his films to the Prime Minister. Charles and Ray had brought two—one on tops and the other on toy trains—films that were exquisitely lucid and precise, making mystery and magic of everyday objects. They were shown to the Prime Minister in a small theatre within Rashtrapati Bhavan. Charles strode up and down the aisle, trying in broken sentences to explain the reason and the relevance of the films. A tired, bewildered Prime Minister, half asleep after a long day, could not understand what it was all about; what tops had to do with designing objects. Indira, sitting next to her father, kept assuring Eames that everything was crystal clear.

Buckminster Fuller followed a month later. Indira came to dinner to meet him. Unlike Charles he could talk for hours; most of what he said was technical, too mathematical for us to understand, but suddenly a word, a phrase would come through, evidence of a genius that was seeking to formulate through form, the geometry of the universe. He too was invited by Indira to her home to meet the Prime Minister, where Bucky spoke for five-and-a-half hours on higher mathematics. According to Indira his talk was, 'Quite exhausting, but so stimulating.'[1] Buckminster Fuller and Indira became friends. He was invited to the Prime Minister's House whenever he was in India. Nehru listened enthralled to Bucky speak with passion on his new architecture and the possibility of being able to design the needs of the globe, creating the maximum from minimum material.

In 1969, Bucky had suddenly arrived unannounced at Prime Minister Indira Gandhi's home to present her with his map of the universe, on which he wrote, what to her was one of the greatest compliments she had received. 'To Indira on whose integrity God is entrusting much of the evolutionary success of humanity and with utter safety.'[2]

FOUR

For the first few years Feroze Gandhi kept a low profile in the Lok Sabha. He was learning parliamentary procedures and preparing himself. He was observing the great parliamentarians of the day—Hiren Mukherjee, Bhupesh Gupta, Nath Pai and his own guru Keshav Dev Malviya. Feroze's maiden speech in the Lok Sabha in 1954 was a scathing attack against the nexus between insurance companies and the business community. His brief was meticulously prepared. It compelled the attention of his father-in-law, the Prime Minister; Ramakrishna Dalmia, the businessman concerned, was arrested and later jailed. Feroze soon emerged as a formidable parliamentarian and now he turned his full attention on those close to the Prime Minister. T.T. Krishnamachari (popularly known as TTK), one of the most competent ministers under Nehru, a man of long vision with a capacity for decisive action, was his next target. Feroze exposed, with full knowledge of facts and figures, the case that came to be known as the Mundhra Deal and forced the resignation of Krishnamachari and some senior, highly respected bureaucrats. Every blow he struck at the Prime Minister's government was deeply satisfying for him. He was at last able to respond in full measure to Jawaharlal Nehru's aloofness and disdain through the early years of his marriage to Indira Gandhi. Next to receive his attention was M.O. Matthai, Prime Minister Nehru's Special Assistant and confidant. Through a prodigious effort, he collected facts and verified enough gossip to prepare a dossier on the arrogant bureaucrat from Kerala. He released this to one of his journalist friends. When published, it led to an uproar and M.O. Matthai was called upon to resign. Jawaharlal Nehru was now totally isolated, save for his daughter whose anger against Feroze reached a peak during 1958–59.

While her husband was moving from triumph to triumph in Parliament, Indira was being inducted into the Congress party's higher councils. She was already a member of the Congress Working Committee (CWC). In 1957, her name was proposed for the Congress Central Election Committee (CCEC). In the elections that followed the membership she topped the list and emerged as a powerful figure on the Congress Parliamentary Board (CPB). As Indira's power and strength within the Congress increased, the relationship between Feroze and her grew steadily worse. By now Feroze, to humiliate her, was flaunting his relationship with other women openly.

Indira's deeper involvement in politics, her participating in social welfare work, her growing interest in arts and culture gave an intensity to her day, but her relationship with Feroze brought to the surface dark moods and depression. We had continued to meet over the years, in spite of the heavy burdens she now carried. Her management of time was prodigious. She would find time for long and leisurely meetings, but the topics of conversation underwent a change. I found that her mind was a labyrinth. All outlets led to a blind wall. There was a feeling within her of deep betrayal, an isolation and loneliness and a mounting fear of the future. Confused, unable to steer a course through the storms and contradictions that threatened to overwhelm her, she sought to discover herself, to find a way through the many personalities that kept asserting themselves within her.

One afternoon in September 1958, I remember paying her a visit. Rumours were current that her marriage to Feroze was on the rocks—various stories were doing the rounds that she was taking revenge on Feroze by having affairs with other men. She was outraged and angry. She told me, 'Before you hear from gossip circles in Delhi, let me tell you that I am divorcing Feroze.'

She felt an urgent necessity to discover herself. I could sense that she had seldom explored within, never faced the starkness and shadows that lurk in the unconscious and distort all straight seeing. Her brain crowded with thoughts, never still, eroded her strength. We spoke of opening the windows of the mind and letting life flow through. Of letting nature take over and do its spring cleaning. She did not quite understand. We then discussed the nature of thought and conflict, sorrow, hatred and fear. She was listening intently but kept on asking: 'How does one enquire, if the mind is so riddled with thought, each one battling against the other?' It was then that I described some personal experiences of mine when in a similar depressed mood I had decided to write out my mind by spending an hour every morning writing down every thought as it emerged in consciousness. It was an arduous discipline, a way of discovering the self through watching thought arise, watching it disappear, never attempting to change thought or stifle it. for you were the thought, you were not separate from thought.

'To record every movement of consciousness, attention has to move at the same speed as thought. Is this possible?' I enquired. 'At the end of the hour of observation and recording, consciousness is washed clean and there is a weightlessness to the brain.' Indira was interested, listened very carefully, continued to ask questions on observation and self-knowledge, spoke of the observer and the observed, then said: 'Is there not a need for a seeing eye to explore within?' 'Yes, it is a seeing into "what is" and moving with what is.' She was quiet at the end of the discussion, did not make any further comments.

Decades later, walking through the Indira Gandhi Memorial Museum, I saw framed and hung upon the wall a sheet of paper in her own handwriting, torn from a notepad with "Prime Minister's House" printed on it. Immediately my mind went back to the day of our discussion, for the words used in the short paragraph indicated a mind in torment:

> But your thoughts, they will not rest, They flutter like bats in ghostly confusion Round and round the exhausted brain. They gnaw and nibble their way like rats Through your leaden weariness.[1]

They were words which were applicable to any individual who with honesty observed the mind in moments of dark depression and for an instant saw thought engulf consciousness. Yet throughout this period when she was desperately hurt and angry, in deep conflict over her relationship with Feroze, no evidence of the storms raging within her ever surfaced. She was meeting artists, writers, visiting exhibitions and going to performances of music and dance. She was deeply involved in her social work and had been appointed on to the most important committees of the Congress party. Outwardly she appeared cool, composed and decisive in her planning and action.

FIVE

In September 1958, Indira Gandhi accompanied her father on a visit to the kingdom of Bhutan. There were no planes, no restorable roads and the prime minister's party had to travel on horseback along steep mountain paths. The air was exhilarating and Indira, after many years, was temporarily free from political and domestic turmoil. Half-way on their journey, an urgent message reached them that Feroze Gandhi had suffered a heart attack. By the time Indira returned to Delhi, her husband was already out of danger. There was a reconciliation, old memories that bound them close, were revived. They took the boys with them on a month's holiday and spent it on a houseboat in Nagin Bagh in Srinagar. Indira nursed her husband with care and affection but the sense of togetherness they discovered foundered when they returned to Delhi.

Indira's name was proposed as the new President of the Congress party. Feroze saw this as the final assault on their relationship. He gathered all his cronies around him, retreated to his home and stopped his visits to the Prime Minister's House. Indira Gandhi was unanimously elected President of the Indian National Congress on 2 February 1959. She was forty-one years old. She was the third Nehru to be elected to this supreme position. Rumours abounded that it was Jawaharlal Nehru who had manoeuvred to get his daughter elected, but from discussions I had with some of the senior members of the Congress, who were colleagues of Jawaharlal, it would appear that the father did little to ensure her election. C. Subramaniam, a minister in Tamil Nadu, where K. Kamaraj was Chief Minister, maintained that after U.N. Dhebar, the outgoing President (who was from Gujarat), it was suggested that a man from the south should be selected. Gobind Ballabh Pant had proposed Subramaniam's name. But Chief Minister Kamaraj refused to relieve him. Also, Subramaniam was not anxious to give up the work he was doing in Tamil Nadu and take up organizational work. Several names were suggested at the time and it was finally decided by the senior members of the Congress party that Indira would be the best candidate. She demurred, was nervous, but was ultimately persuaded to accept the Presidentship. In an interview Jawaharlal remarked: 'Normally speaking it is not a good thing for my

Kamala Nehru with Indira in 1918

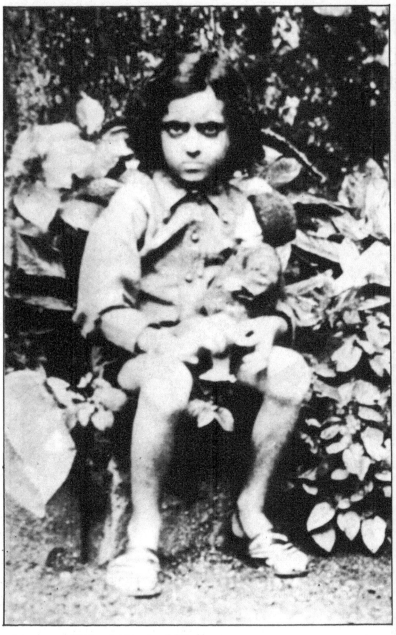

A two-year-old Indira clutching her doll in her arms

Indira in Geneva during her visit abroad with Jawaharlal Nehru and Kamala who was ill and needed medical treatment, 1925

Indira, her grandmother Swaroop Rani and mother Kamala at the time of the Salt Satyagraha, 1930. Anand Bhawan, Allahabad. Photograph by Jawaharlal Nehru

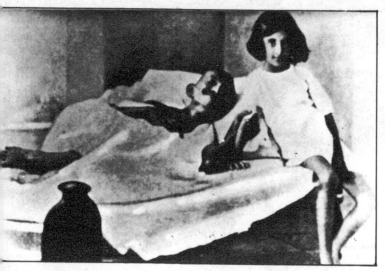

Indira with Mahatma Gandhi, when he was recovering from his fast in Delhi in September 1924

A determined Indira as head of the
Vanar Sena, Allahabad, 1930

Indira at Shantiniketan. Photograph
by Frank Oberdorf

Indira in Wengen, Switzerland, at the time of her mother's illness, 1935.
Photograph by Frank Oberdorf

Indira skiing in Wengen with Frank Oberdorf in 1935

Indira convalescing in a sanitarium in Leysin, Switzerland, 1940

Indira in Western clothes with her father in London, 1938

Indira Nehru. Photograph by Feroze Gandhi

Indira Nehru and Feroze Gandhi on board *S. S. Cracovia* on their return journey to India in 1941

Wedding of Indira Nehru and Feroze Gandhi, Basant Panchami; 1942, L to R: Jawaharlal Nehru, Vijayalakshmi Pandit, Feroze and Indira

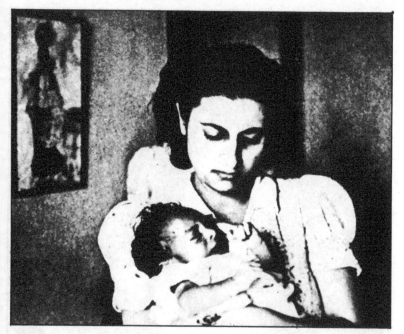

Indira Gandhi with Rajiv, Bombay, 1944

Indira with Jawaharlal Nehru, Teen Murti House, New Delhi, 1949

Feroze Gandhi with Sanjay, New Delhi

Indira with Nehru in Uzbek costume during state visit to the Soviet Union, 1955

Indira Gandhi, Congress President stands in front of her old family home, 1959

Indira Gandhi at Nigambodh Ghat, New Delhi, at the funeral of Feroze Gandhi on Thursday, 9 September 1960

Indira and her son at the funeral of Feroze Gandhi

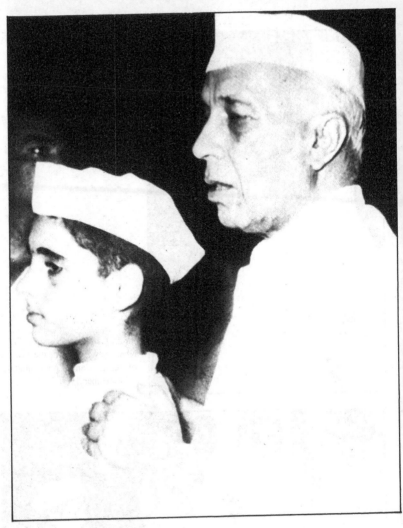

Jawaharlal Nehru with thirteen-year-old Sanjay at the funeral of Feroze Gandhi, Nigambodh Ghat, New Delhi

Jacqueline Kennedy and Indira Gandhi on a swing on the lawns of Teen Murti House, New Delhi, 1962

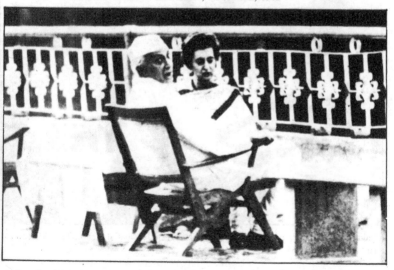

Indira Gandhi with Jawaharlal Nehru in Dehradun, 25 May 1964. The last photograph of father and daughter together

Indira Gandhi stands next to the body of her father, Jawaharlal Nehru, Teen Murti House, 27 May 1964

daughter to come in as Congress President when I am Prime Minister.'[1] He appeared, nonetheless, to have been proud of her and paid her a handsome tribute at a meeting of the Congress Parliamentary Party soon after her election:

> It is superfluous for me to say that Indira is my daughter and that I have love for her. I am proud of her good nature, proud of her energy and work, and proud of her integrity and truthfulness. What she has inherited from me I do not know. Maybe she has inherited these qualities from her mother.[2]

In the eleven months that Indira held office she revealed an immense energy within her seemingly fragile body. Her first act was to remove her father from membership of the Congress Working Committee (CWC), making him a permanent invitee instead. At a party meeting presided over by his daughter as President, Nehru remarked 'At first Indira Gandhi had been my friend and adviser, then she became my companion and now she is my leader.'[3]

Indira travelled relentlessly, visiting inaccessible parts of the country that had never before received a VIP. Wherever she went she would call upon the youth to come forward and bear the new burdens of developing a nation. She talked to women, asked about child health and welfare, enquired after the crafts of the region, listened to local legends and myths, met leaders of various communities and spoke at length with the old men and women of the area, for she realized that it was they who were the holders of heritage. Back in Delhi at her first press conference she spoke of the nation being in a hurry. Action to alleviate poverty was immediately called for.

In the early months of her Presidentship she fought a battle to eradicate corruption, taking on entrenched Congress leaders. Seeing their hesitation she had a stormy meeting with her father who listened quietly to what she had to say and then suggested that she discuss the matter with G.B. Pant, an elder statesman and an intimate friend of the family. He was then Home Minister in Nehru's government. Indira spoke to Pant in the strongest terms of cleaning the Augean stables. Pant, a tall and heavily built man, who had suffered permanent damage to his nervous system in a lathi charge during the freedom struggle, spoke to her with great gentleness. 'Beti, (daughter) you do not understand, you are too young. It is only when you grow older that you will realise that complex issues are involved.'[4] She was furious, for a moment, even threatened to resign, but the mood passed.

One of the first items on her agenda was the problem in Kerala. A Marxist government had come to power through democratic elections. In their attempt to strengthen their hold and capture the minds of the young, they introduced an Education Bill which would have seriously threatened many private educational institutions. Indira reacted strongly, particularly when she came to hear that the Communists had introduced in the curriculum of their schools, text books which carried the speeches of Mao Zedong. With the help of the local Kerala Congress and other parties who felt strongly about the strengthening Communist position, she organized a massive campaign against the bill and against what she claimed to be the authoritarian rule of the Communist Party. Her father, a true democrat, was deeply disturbed. He felt that nothing should be done to threaten a duly elected government. She disagreed and fought him on every platform. Indoctrination of the minds of the young, she felt, was the death of freedom and democracy. The threat had to be met, even confronted.

Feroze Gandhi, who counted many Marxists as personal friends, was appalled at the attempts by Indira to topple the Communist government in Kerala. Husband and wife had violent arguments, where Feroze expressed his anger against what she was attempting to do; but the same strength that she had shown against her father to marry Feroze now came into action and she was defiant with Feroze. She met the President and started a massive campaign to force her father's hand and declare President's rule in Kerala. A reluctant Nehru finally agreed. The storm over Kerala, which Feroze took as a personal confrontation, further threatened their married life. On 21 July she wrote to Dorothy Norman:

> A veritable sea of trouble is engulfing me. On the domestic front, Feroze has always resented my very existence, but since I have become President (of the Congress party) he exudes such hostility that it seems to poison the air.

Unfortunately he and his friends are friendly with some of our ministers and an impossible situation is being created.

The Kerala situation is worsening. The movement is not petering out as the Communists claim but gathering momentum. The women, whom I have been trying to organise for years, had always refused to come into politics. Now they are out in the field. Over 8,000 have been arrested. . . .[5]

But her battles with Feroze did not come in the way of her work as Congress President. A serious international problem had arisen when the Dalai Lama who had earlier visited India in 1954, fled Tibet in 1959 and sought asylum in India. Indira played a major role in persuading her father to agree to provide refuge for the fleeing monk-king and the vast number of monks who accompanied him from Tibet. Nehru hesitated. He knew the Chinese would view this as an unfriendly act. They had invaded Tibet and established their hegemony over the mountain kingdom which had, till 1959, enjoyed autonomy and for centuries was regarded as a mysterious and unattainable territory. Indira set up a Central Relief Committee for the Tibetan refugees and acted firmly though she continued to use very restricted language in dealing with the Sino-Tibet problem.

There were problems brewing in other areas as well. In the then Bombay Presidency, a decision was taken to bifurcate Gujarat from Maharashtra on a linguistic basis. The problem was Bombay city. A majority of the people spoke Marathi, but the city had been built with the initiative and monies of established Gujarati and Parsee industrial houses. An attempt was made to declare Bombay an independent city under Central rule. Maharashtra was not prepared to accept this and riots began all over the State. Indira visited Maharashtra and returned to Delhi to advise her father that Bombay should not remain independent, but should form part of the new State of Maharashtra. Morarji Desai, Chief Minister of the combined State of Gujarat and Maharashtra, was made Finance Minister in the Central Cabinet and ultimately Bombay was merged with the State of Maharashtra.

Indira Gandhi refused to continue as Congress President for a second year. She had developed severe pains in the abdomen, a result of her near-continuous journeying across India by car and bullock cart. Her ailment was diagnosed as a stone in the kidney and she was advised an early operation. Padmaja Naidu, who was in Delhi, insisted on giving a name to the kidney stone and it was christened "Jewel in the Lotus", shortened to "Jules". At first, it was suggested that she should have the operation abroad, but it did not appear possible and finally she was operated on in Bombay by Dr Shantilal Mehta, one of India's most eminent surgeons. Everything went well and Indira was soon her normal self. Feroze, in spite of the growing distance between his wife and himself, was with her at the time of the operation and also helped in the nursing, but the gossip in the cafés and homes of the Delhi élite, made any real reconciliation impossible.

Indira's views had prevailed with the Prime Minister and President's rule had been imposed in Kerala, to be followed by elections at a later date. Indira was jubilant when the Congress, with the aid of several other parties, finally won the Kerala elections, defeating the Communists. When she returned to Delhi, from a flying visit to Trivandrum (now called Tiruvananthapuram) to preside over a women's conference, she was told at the airport that Feroze had suffered a second heart attack and was in the hospital. She rushed to be by his side, but he died without regaining consciousness.

Jawaharlal Nehru, who over the years had not developed a close relationship with his son-in-law, was amazed to see the large number of people, from all walks of life, who came to pay homage to the young Member of Parliament. Feroze died four days short of his forty-eighth birthday. Indira blanked out. A great darkness descended on her, she felt totally disoriented.

She wrote to Dorothy Norman on 24 September:

> Isn't it strange, when you feel full, you are light as air but when you feel empty and hollow you feel an enormous weight crushing you down. Will I ever be free from the burden or be able to touch and see without feeling. The heartbreak in the heart of things?[6]

The death of Feroze awakened memories of her mother and of those early years when, with Feroze by her side, she learnt to face her mother's death. Through the years they had quarrelled fiercely, had separated, had fought on every issue, but had shared too many memories that returned, filling Indira's mind with dark depression.

She felt deeply indebted to Feroze. 'When my mother died and at all times of stress and difficulty, he was by my side even if he had to travel across continents to get there. I feel I am alone in the midst of the unending sandy water.'[8]

Indira could see that her father was ageing. The stress and strain of a Prime Minister's life had left its mark. He had lost his elan, his energy, his intuitive touch with the people of India. After him, deep within her she had always known that Feroze would be there. 'Upto now I had somebody to whom I could pour out my thoughts even if there was lack of attention and sympathy and with the removal of that outlet I have to look outwards.'[9]

There is no evidence of what the sons felt at the death of their dearly loved father. It was obvious that they resented their grandfather's antipathy towards Feroze. In the way children do, they had made up their minds on the rights and wrongs of the situation. Their mother, they felt, had neglected their father. So in the hour of their father's death, the sixteen-year-old Rajiv and fourteen-year-old Sanjay, young adolescents, had little solace to give their mother.

SIX

Before Feroze Gandhi's untimely death Indira Gandhi had planned to visit Africa, South America, Mexico, and the United States in the autumn of 1960. She cancelled her visit to Africa and South America but was persuaded to travel as planned to Mexico and the US. On the eve of her departure, she wrote to Dorothy Norman of the deep change she had undergone within herself: 'I am not the same person now; neither to look at nor deep down inside.'

Dorothy awaited her in New Mexico where they stayed in Santa Fe. Indira met the presiding genius of that area, Dorothy Brett, the painter who was well into her eighties, who told Indira that she longed to come to India to ride a large elephant under a huge umbrella and also to meet holy men. She was with them when Dorothy and Indira visited Taso Pubulo, an American-Indian reservation. Indira was deeply disturbed to witness the apathy of the American-Indians as well as the treatment meted out to them.

On her return journey she stopped in Paris to join the Indian delegation to UNESCO. Vice-President S. Radhakrishnan had proposed her name as a permanent member of the Executive Board and so she stayed on after the delegation left. She found Paris and the UNESCO conferences dull and had little interest in the day-long discussions, the lunches, dinners and receptions. She knew very few people in Paris; she was spending her birthday away from Delhi after many years and was miserable, homesick and lonely.

By December she felt a new awakening. 'The fits of dark dark despair and depression do come, but that is something I have always had—but on the whole I have got over that awful self-pity and preoccupation with my own sorrow.'[1] Feroze's name disappeared from her letters. She rarely referred to him when we were together alone, nor did she mention his name in later years when we dined together with the family. No photograph of Feroze appeared in her bedroom or study.

The year had transformed Indira, she was no longer the shy young woman who walked two steps behind her father, seemingly seeking his protection. Her year as President of the Congress and the way she had to face her loneliness after the death of Feroze had given her a silent, yet assured, confidence. She participated in conversations, with her father's friends, her insights were clear and unambiguous. Welles Hengen, a writer, who interviewed her for a book he was planning called *After Nehru Who?* found Indira an enigmatic figure.

> She is much more attractive than her sinister-looking newspaper pictures, but at first glance there is something forbiddingly regal about this child of the Indian Revolution. Her long, thin Roman features are severe in repose—she enters the little sitting room where visitors are received so swiftly and noiselessly that I am always startled and slightly flustered—but her imperial aura and my confusion vanish as she greets me in a voice so soft that I must strain to hear. Her smile is disarming, almost girlish.[2]

Tensions on the boundaries that separated India from China had been brewing for some years. Unconcerned with India's protests, China had gone ahead to build a road that linked Tibet with Sinkiang, through the Indian territory of the desert of Aksai Chin. India's giving asylum to the Dalai Lama in 1959 accentuated the tensions between the two countries. Ill-informed by his Defence Minister, V.K. Krishna Menon and his Generals on the preparedness of the Indian forces in the North-East, an ageing Jawaharlal Nehru ordered an aggressive military policy and an attack against positions that China had wrested from Indian control. The Chinese hit back with a massive assault on Indian territory in the North-East and in Ladakh. The morale of the Indian Army was low at this time; the soldiers were ill-equipped, with inadequate clothing to ward off the cold, and much of the military hardware was obsolete. In the face of a relentless Chinese attack, the Indian Army retreated from Bomdilla, the gateway to the plains of India. There was panic in Delhi, Assam and Calcutta. President Sarvepalli Radhakrishnan came out with an open attack against the Prime Minister for living in a make-believe world and for his credulity and negligence.

Speaking on All-India Radio (AIR) in tones that broke the country's heart, Prime Minister Nehru expressed his agony and sympathy for the people of Assam as if Assam was already lost and the

Chinese had over-run the territory. The Assamese reacted furiously to the speech of their Prime Minister and debated amongst themselves whether Assam was a part of India.

In Tezpur there was chaos. There were no military defences to guard the people; the District Commissioner had fled, leaving people to fend for themselves. In Teen Murti House, New Delhi, the Cabinet had gathered to review the situation. There was confusion everywhere. It was at this moment that Indira decided to visit Tezpur. The Prime Minister was horrified, for he feared that the Chinese would capture his daughter and hold her as hostage. A message reached me asking to come over to the Prime Minister's House. As I entered the building I found a shattered Prime Minister standing at the base of the stairs. 'You have come to see Indu,' he said. 'She is being very obstinate. Her visit is very dangerous, she should not go.' I mumbled something and walked upstairs to find Indira ready with an overnight bag. She was in a raging temper. I could hardly get a word in. The news that the district authorities had abandoned the people had outraged her. An instinctive response had awakened in her that the Assamese must be assured that someone cared. She refused to listen to her father, to the Army Chief or to her friends, but was determined to go; first by aircraft to Gauhati (now called Guwahati) and later by helicopter to Tezpur. Knowing her temperament I had brought along a Nikos Kazantzakis novel for her journey. She was delighted to take the book with her, wrote me a note from the helicopter that she was reading the little book, *God's Messenger.*

As she landed in Tezpur swarms of people surrounded her, begging her to help them to leave the city. The Chinese army was within thirty miles of Tezpur, the doorway to Assam; there was little food, few social workers, not a sign of a district official. The Assamese told Indira that they felt they had been betrayed by the Prime Minister. Indira maintained an extraordinary calm. She gave them solace, promised not to leave them till the crisis passed, arranged for emergency rations and saw that some of the administrators returned to duty. On the same day as she arrived in Tezpur, China decided to announce a unilateral ceasefire and started withdrawing its troops. A deeply humiliated Jawaharlal Nehru never recovered from the defeat.

Back in Delhi Indira found her father under severe attack by Parliament and by the media. The politicians who had fawned on him a few months earlier were the fiercest in their assault. V.K. Krishna Menon was forced to resign under pressure. Nehru was alone, no longer his old self. The shock and humiliation had destroyed something vulnerable and passionate in Jawaharlal; old age had suddenly descended on him, robbing him of energy and a zest for life. Indira refused to accept that time could touch her father. She prepared to do battle.

*

The last eighteen months of Nehru's life were a period of slow decline. Krishna Menon, Defence Minister and Nehru's friend and confidant of many years, was forced to resign and take responsibility for the China debacle. Reminiscing after the death of her brother, Vijayalakshmi Pandit said: 'Apart from declining health and vigour—his left foot dragging, a sign of things to come—he no longer had any zest for life.' When on occasion Vijayalakshmi Pandit tried to persuade her brother to rest, he replied, 'What for; to what end should I recover my strength?'[3] He was withdrawing almost totally from his surroundings during these months, rarely speaking to anyone; he was becoming totally alone.

J.B. Kripalani, Minoo Masani and Ram Manohar Lohia, the most virulent critics of Nehru, elected to the Lok Sabha through by-elections held in the spring of 1963, decided to launch a full-scale attack on Nehru soon after Parliament reopened, "to weaken, and if possible to dislodge him." It was clear to an agonized Indira that her father had neither the energy nor the will to confront his critics at their level. One by one Nehru's old colleagues had died. Indira considered the present leadership entrenched in the states and at the Centre 'small men of little stature. It was understandable that Nehru's *joie de vivre* should be dimmed.'[4]

On his part, the Prime Minister was turning to his daughter on virtually all the complex issues that were brought to him. Her years as Congress President had convinced him of her shrewd political sense, her passion, energy and determination. So in the summer of 1963 a move was started, supported by Indira, amongst the young ginger group in the Congress party, to revitalize and bring new blood into the party's working.

Shrouded in secrecy, the Kamaraj Plan was discussed by K. Kamaraj and Nehru in the first few days of August 1963 and endorsed by the Congress Working Committee (CWC) on 9 August on the basis of the slogan "Party before Post". It was a powerful cry for senior Congressmen who could do little to obstruct suggestions to re-mould the structure of the political leadership. The suggestion to the Working Committee was that some of the senior leaders should be asked to resign from chief ministerships and Central ministerships and work at the grassroots level to revitalize the party. To give credibility to the plan, Nehru pressed for his own resignation. But face to face, the very people who had started to whisper behind the Prime Minister's back were the first to suggest that he was indispensable. The decision as to who should be asked to quit was left to the Prime Minister. None of the senior leaders entrenched at the state and Central level appeared to have taken the matter seriously. Suddenly, on 25 August, the plan was announced. Six chief ministers, the strongest in the country, and six Cabinet ministers at the Centre, were asked to resign and take up Congress party work. Included in the list were Kamaraj, Morarji Desai, Lal Bahadur Shastri, Jagjivan Ram, Biju Patnaik of Orissa, S.K. Patil of Maharashtra and C.B. Gupta of Uttar Pradesh.

Taken by surprise, the eleven axed leaders were numb, the twelfth Kamaraj was elected President of the Congress soon after the plan came into effect. The plan was riddled with ambiguities. No agenda for coordinated action was devised. What were these sixty-year-old satraps, powerful leaders in their own right, masters of the art of political manoeuvre, to do at the level of village work? No one appeared to have an answer to this question. The whole operation had a rapier-like thrust which could not possibly have been the inspiration of a sick, weary Prime Minister; nor was it his style. It also lacked the down-to-earth homespun style of Kamaraj, a heavy-weight political strategist who trod cautiously, sought consensus, was adamant only when he was sure of his position. When asked as to who took the final decision to draw up the list and select the names of the ministers to be axed, both Nehru and Kamaraj denied responsibility. The strategy, the timing, the speed with which the whole operation was enacted, the lack of consultation with senior colleagues, suggests Indira's signature. The voice was the father's, but the strategy was the daughter's. She was, at the time, acting as her father's conscience, a guardian of his doorways. In retrospect, it hardly seems plausible that Jawaharlal Nehru had, on his own, suggested the names of the leaders to be asked to quit without consulting his daughter. Other aspects of the political situation at this time seem to underline the above contention.

Indira had been complaining to her friends of the attempts being made to destabilize her father's position and to dislodge him. Suspicious, unable to trust any of her father's colleagues, she had once again influenced her father to act with strength. At one stroke all the leaders inimical to Nehru were deprived of their power base and removed from positions from where they could step into the prime ministership. Weaker men were placed in charge of state governments while all power vested in the Centre. Perhaps this was the first move to centralize power and to deny any single person a claim to the prime ministership after Nehru.

What was Indira's purpose? To drain power from the political leadership in the states and concentrate it at the Centre in the hands of the Prime Minister; to clear the way for her own prime ministership? Her record as Congress President had brought her to the forefront of Congress politics, but she was aware that the Congress stalwarts underestimated her. They were so conditioned in their male chauvinism that they were not willing even to consider her as a possible claimant. No woman, they felt, could have the stamina, the drive and capacity to manage and manipulate men and situations, which a prime minister needed, to rule the country. But, unfortunately for Indira, the follow-up action necessary to create a new power structure, could not materialize, because of the sudden illness of her father, hardly four months after the Kamaraj Plan had gone into action.

Indira was in Africa in late December. On her return she found her father ill with kidney trouble. He was advised complete rest. The roles had been reversed and now it was her father who turned to her for succour and support. She was firm with him, nursed him as if he were a child and ensured that he did not tire himself. Nehru insisted that important files should be brought to him, but they were channelled through Indira. Nehru's illness once again brought to the surface Indira's feeling of insecurity. She was anxious for her sons, about her lack of a home; there was a shortage of money, the future haunted her. 'They will not let me survive when Papu is no more.'[5]

SEVEN

Indira Gandhi was by her father's side on 6 January 1964, when the Prime Minister suffered a sudden paralytic stroke at the 68th session of the Congress held at Bhubaneshwar. The Prime Minister had been ailing for some time, his step was heavy, his shoulders bent, there was a swelling on his face. Indira, who was sitting next to her father, noticed that something was wrong and immediately helped her father to his feet, shielding him from the crowd. The news could not be kept secret. Jawaharlal Nehru was taken by plane to Delhi and K. Kamaraj, in his position as President of the Congress, advised that Lal Bahadur Shastri be called back and the Prime Minister's work divided between Shastri and T.T. Krishnamachari.

Nehru was again told to rest, but insisted on attending to many papers. At times, Indira treated him as a child, kept him away from certain foods, saw to it that he took his medicine and cut his workday from eighteen hours to twelve hours. In addition, she acted as a conduit between the ministers and her father. 'People do not realise how much Papu depended on me during this period.'[1]

Vinoba Bhave, the anchorite, sent a message to the Prime Minister that when the body was ill, the Prime Minister should rest and give it a chance. He advised Jawaharlal to learn to play the flute. Nehru was indignant. 'Play the flute,' he said. 'What does he mean by asking me to play the flute?' Indira tried to explain that perhaps what Bhave had intended was that Nehru should relax and turn to activities other than his office work, to relieve his mind. A few days later, Nehru remarked to his daughter: 'Aristotle had also suggested that gentlemen learn to play the flute, but not too well.'[2]

As the Prime Minister appeared to be better, Indira left him to visit New York at the time of the opening of the New York World Fair. She was Chairman of the India Committee and had looked into every detail of the Indian pavilion. I was also a member of the Committee and was deeply involved in this first major exhibition being held abroad. The Indian pavilion was a success and Indira was glowing with pride when she returned to India.

At home there were rumblings within the party. It was obvious that Nehru's life was coming to an end and the old stalwarts of the

Congress party sought to position themselves as well as they could to make their bid for power. Indira, in a letter to B.K. Nehru, dated 17 May 1964, writes:

> Campaign against Papu is studied and well organised. Every effort is being made to fully exploit recent events to weaken, and if possible, to dislodge him. He is well and still tops and has been quite magnificent these days. But he is no longer his old self. One after the (other) old colleagues have gone. He is surrounded by people of such small stature, of little understanding and of no loyalty or sincerity or sense of purpose. Is it not understandable that *his joie de vivre* should be dimmed?[3]

On 22 May, Jawaharlal Nehru held a press conference. It was just after his illness. Nehru walked to the dais alone, but there were long silences between the questions put to him by the correspondents and his responses. He was asked whether in the interest of the country he should not settle the problem of succession during his lifetime. Nehru's answer was, 'My lifetime is not ending so very soon.' The cynical and hard-core members of the press were hushed by this response, but applause followed soon.

The father and daughter left for Dehradun where they were to spend a short holiday. Indira had never been closer to her father. She hovered over him, attended to his slightest needs, kept visitors away. The last photograph of Jawaharlal Nehru taken on 26 May shows the father sitting on an easy-chair, the daughter kneeling close by his side. There is a deep sorrow, a tenderness in Indira's face, a sense of grave concern and care and above all love. They returned to Delhi the same evening.

Krishna Hutheesing, Jawaharlal's youngest sister, was in Bombay when, on the morning of 27 May, a telephone message from Vijayalakshmi Pandit, then Governor of Maharashtra, informed her that she had just heard that 'Bhai (Jawaharlal) was rather unwell.' Krishna rang Delhi immediately. Indira came on the line at 8.15 a.m. She was hysterical on the phone and said, 'He is not rather unwell; he seems very very serious. Doctors are here, but don't seem to know what is wrong. I think he is collapsing.'[4] The doctors had hesitated but the daughter's instinct was unerring. Jawaharlal died that afternoon at 1.40 p.m.

Dressed in an immaculate white cotton handspun sari, and a long-sleeved blouse, her head covered, Indira sat beside her father's body as thousands of people, presidents and prime ministers, peasants and the poor, filed past his body. Many wept.

The question of succession came up immediately with Nehru's death. Kamaraj was in Delhi. Gulzari Lal Nanda, then Home Minister, had been sworn in as interim Prime Minister, and Lal Bahadur Shastri's name along with Gulzari Lal Nanda's were discussed as possible prime ministers. The "Syndicate"; a loose body of Congressmen made up of all shades of opinion, from all parts of the country, and critical of Nehru during his last days, chose Shastri as the next Prime Minister. As a gesture of courtesy, he met Indira and offered her the prime ministership. She refused without reflection. 'If I had become Prime Minister at that time, they would have destroyed me.'[5] Shastri urged her to accept a ministership. At first she was reluctant, but when he insisted and said that he felt he could not form a stable ministry unless she joined him, she agreed and chose to preside over the Ministry of Information and Broadcasting. Many of her friends and close advisers—D.P. Misra, Pitambar Pant—had advised her not to go into the wilderness, but to accept a ministership. They would ensure she made a success of her charge.

Dazed after her father's death Indira did not quite register the loss. She met a vast number of people who came to see her to share her sorrow. She responded with the right answers to presidents and prime ministers. It was as if she stood at a distance watching herself. Awakening one night she switched on the light to see a single white rose placed in a vase by her bedside. The beauty of the flower brought an intensity of physical pain and she woke to the reality of her father's loss. She would never see him again; his radiance and his warmth would never again cradle her. She wept ceaselessly for hours.

On 11 June, she wrote to Dorothy Norman: 'Personal grief is so minute a part of the void he left. He burnt like a gem-like flame. How can I believe that can go out? I feel his presence all around and pray that it may always be so.'[6]

Her sons had returned to England to continue their studies. Within ten days, the faceless bureaucracy commenced to shift from Teen

Murti House the furniture specially provided for the Prime Minister; the secretaries and a vast number of retainers left. Within three months Indira had shifted from Teen Murti House to a modest bungalow on 1, Safdarjung Road. She was desperately lonely. No. 1, Safdarjung Road was small but provided a privacy which she lacked in Teen Murti House. She started her morning 'durbars'. The gates were open for people to come and meet her in the garden. Peasants, artisans, students from afar, came to see Panditji's daughter.

Pitambar Pant and Romesh Thapar were her main advisers in the Ministry for Information and Broadcasting. She had brought into the Ministry consultants and specialists and saw to it that their advice was implemented. Her profile was low and very few people were aware of the major changes which took place in her Ministry during this period.

Indira Gandhi's political instincts were alive and active. Prime Minister Lal Bahadur Shastri sensing this prevented her access to his inner councils, although she was on all the political committees.

Trouble was brewing in the South on North India's attitude to Hindi, the official language. With the death of Nehru, the decision not to force Hindi on the South Indian population was in question. Riots broke out in South India and some young people set fire to themselves in protest. It was Indira who rushed to Madras on the first available plane and assured the leaders of the movement that she would not permit Hindi to be imposed on them. She knew that her visit would create flutters in the Prime Minister's Office, but she was determined to assert herself. She said that she did not look upon herself as a 'mere Minister for Information and Broadcasting' but as one of the leaders of the country. 'Do you think this government can survive if I resign today? I am telling you it won't. Yes, I have jumped over the Prime Minister's head and I would do it again whenever the need arises.'[7]

Indira's most immediate plan was to organize an exhibition on Nehru's life and work. She discussed it with passion with the people who were close to Nehru. She asked me to help and I suggested the possibility of Charles Eames coming back to India to plan the exhibition and work out the details with the National Institute of Design (NID) in Ahmedabad. Outlining her ideas she wrote to me of her fear that the policy of the Government of India would be to give a new interpretation to the cultural ethos of this country: 'The important point to stress about Papu is—what would India have been like without him.'

She then referred to the feeling she was sensing amongst her colleagues:

> Gandhism as understood and spoken of today has come to mean an utter joylessness—beauty and enjoyment, the arts, all forward thinking, all adventure and desire, all experimentation—these things could have been suppressed and we would be living in an atmosphere of dull Victorianism, which, contrary to all the evidence of our sculpture, painting and literature as well as the lives and habits of unsophisticated folk, is now accepted as our "way of life" and "ancient culture!" Just one small story by way of illustration. In Sevagram, the Aryanayakams built themselves a hut as simple as any other, made of mud and thatch but with lovely lines and a feeling of spaciousness because of the shape of the window and the position of the door—such small but terribly important details. It did not cost them a rupee more than the other huts and Gandhiji objected as did the other ashramites because it had taken thought and the stress was on beauty![8]

Charles Eames was invited by the Government of India and the exhibition took shape. It was to be inaugurated in the Union Carbide building in New York. Eames brilliantly culled together the essence of India in the Thirties and the Forties. The President's bodyguard was present; Kamala Nehru's wedding was shown with her wedding sari and the ritual utensils used in a Kashmiri wedding ceremony. Nehru's prison cell within Naini jail was reconstructed through enlarged photographs and his original prison diaries were on display. Handcrafted textiles, artifacts and museum pieces illumined the story of Nehru with all the glamour of the British Raj and the grim story of the freedom struggle. The exhibition was to travel to Soviet Russia and London and would be finally housed in New Delhi.

Indira was present at the opening and was later in London. I was a member of the committee and was also in London for the opening. We were both staying with the Indian High Commissioner Dr Jivraj

Mehta. The "Tribute to Nehru" was inaugurated by British Prime Minister Harold Wilson with a host of distinguished guests in attendance.

Indira came with me the next day to a poetry reading at Albert Hall. A vast number of poets of the Beat generation had gathered from all over the world. The central figure was Allen Ginsberg, a major poetic voice and a founder of the Beat movement. We were late and went up to sit in an overcrowded gallery. Allen spotted us. I knew him well from the early Fifties; he came up and insisted that we join the poets on the podium. To a tough woman, unused to the culture of these rebel poets, the scene was bizarre, magical and exhilarating. With power, grace and fervour, passionate words were scattered like rose-petals by the poets across the hall. Four-letter words were used freely. Queen Victoria's consort, Prince Albert, would not have been amused.

Allen, who had just returned from India, was playing his harmonium as he walked around reciting mantras. 'I've made it, I've made it' he sang to me as he brought a young girl and introduced her to Indira and me. I was happy for Allen, embraced him and the girl. Indira did not quite understand what was happening. She broke into Hindi to ask what it meant. I tried to explain the intricacies of Allen's love life—she suddenly caught on and was quick to join the conversation.

The poets danced, sang, recited poetry, or just sat together. There was warmth, friendship and freedom in the atmosphere. Indira was a woman enchanted, watching closely, speaking with zest to the poets who came up to her; alert, enjoying herself; laughing. It was past 1 o' clock when a starry-eyed Indira agreed to leave.

We were both hungry and walked through a sleeping London. A few restaurants were still open and we finally chose a small Spanish restaurant where we ate omelettes and watched flamenco dancing. We returned to 9, Kensington Palace Gardens, at three in the morning to find Dr Jivraj Mehta in a state of panic and about to ring the police.

It was on this trip that Indira learnt of Rajiv Gandhi's determination to marry Sonia Maino, an Italian studying languages at Cambridge. Rajiv had asked his mother to meet his young love in London and she had set aside a day for them.

The meeting with Sonia was a happy one. Indira found her gentle, soft-voiced and liked her. Their personalities did not clash, but it was to be four years before the wedding took place on Sunday, 25 February 1968, at 6 p.m. at 1, Safdarjung Road, New Delhi. By then, Rajiv had joined Indian Airlines, the domestic carrier, as a pilot. The wedding ceremony was attended by the Prime Minister's extended family and her close friends. Rajiv and Sonia exchanged garlands and rings while a magistrate was present to register the wedding. Sonia, a tall, slim, good-looking girl, wearing a very pale pink khadi sari, appeared in control of her emotions, although, seeing so many new faces, she kept turning to Rajiv for support. The young couple were beautiful and deeply in love with each other. The wedding was followed by a dinner at Hyderabad House where the invitees sat on the floor and ate a Kashmiri vegetarian meal. The budget was low. There were no excessive lights, no special music, but the food was excellent. A reception was held the next day at Hyderabad House where politicians, friends and acquaintances were present. After the wedding, Sonia disappeared into 1, Safdarjung Road. Rajiv and Sonia had their own circle of friends and led very private lives. They were rarely seen with Indira on any formal occasion.

A son, Rahul, was born to Sonia in the summer of 1970 and a daughter, Priyanka, followed a year later. Indira was transformed. She loved children, and Rahul and Priyanka brought her great delight.

She was now determined to find a beautiful Kashmiri bride for her younger son, but Sanjay Gandhi had other intentions. It came as a shock to the Prime Minister when, in 1974, he informed her that he wanted to marry Maneka Anand, the daughter of a Sikh Colonel in the Army.

Sanjay's wedding was even more private than his brother's. Indira Gandhi wrote letters to close friends and relations announcing the wedding and asking for their good wishes and blessings for the bridal couple. The wedding took place in the home of Mohammed Yunus Khan (who had known Sanjay from his boyhood), now a member of the Rajya Sabha, in the presence of a few relations and Sanjay's close friends.

A seventeen-year-old Maneka entered the Prime Minister's House with some trepidation. She was young, gay, full of energy, demanding attention and excitement. Sanjay's room was located in the front of the house—next door to the main sitting-room. The atmosphere in

174

that area of the house was formal and protocol prevailed. It was clear that even a very pre-occupied Prime Minister could not maintain harmony in a small house, with two daughters-in-law reared in totally different cultures and with opposite interests. I tried to speak to Indira of the difficulty she was likely to face, but she was distressed at the thought of one of her sons setting up house away from her; she wanted her children, her grandchildren, around her when she came home from her office. Before the family could adjust to the changed situation with its undercurrents of stresses and strains, the growling voice of the people's discontent had reached the Prime Minister.

*

But let me return to the chronological sequence of events. In August 1965, Indira was in Srinagar when Pakistani forces invaded the Kashmir valley. She refused to return to Delhi, but stayed on till the situation stabilized. She visited troops on the borders, helped maintain the morale of the civilian population and even insisted on going by helicopter to the Haji Pir Pass, one of the most dangerous spots of the war. The Pass had been taken by Indian forces after heavy fighting. The troops were amazed to see her and hailed her with cheers. She returned to Delhi to advise the Prime Minister, much to his chagrin, on how she thought the war in Kashmir should be run. International powers eventually intervened to end the conflict and a summit was called at Tashkent in Soviet Central Asia with the Russians acting as mediators between Lal Bahadur Shastri and President Ayub Khan.

EIGHT

The Tashkent Agreement was signed by President Ayub Khan and Prime Minister Lal Bahadur Shastri in the presence of the Soviet Prime Minister Aleksei Kosygin on 10 January 1966. India had agreed to give back to Pakistan the Haji Pir Pass. Shastri was aware that this clause in the agreement could cause turmoil amongst the Indian people and that they would hold him responsible. However, he did not have to face the people's opprobrium because by midnight he suffered a severe heart attack and died soon after.

Indira Gandhi had come to learn the details of the treaty a day before and realized that Shastri had been pressured into the return of Haji Pir Pass. She expressed her unhappiness to Romesh Thapar, by now a close friend. 'The country will never take it.' The news of Shastri's death reached her at 2 a.m. Her personal advisers within the party were called in immediately.

Romesh Thapar recollected a telephone call from V.K. Krishna Menon asking him to come at once to his own house. He found Krishna Menon stalking about the room, dressed in his long Johns. 'Lal Bahadur Shastri is dead,' he told Thapar. 'He had a massive heart attack in Tashkent.' Romesh Thapar was shocked as he had listened in to the radio and heard Shastri speak the night before. Krishna Menon turned to him, 'To whom should I go? To Nanda or that friend of yours, that chit of a girl, Indira.' 'Go to Mrs. Shastri,' said Romesh. 'Yes,' said Krishna Menon, put on his trousers and shirt, took his walking-stick and walked out.[1]

R. Venkataraman, Industry Minister in Tamil Nadu, who would become President of India two decades later, travelled with K. Kamaraj in a special plane to New Delhi, on hearing the news that Prime Minister Lal Bahadur Shastri had died in Tashkent. Kamaraj was worried and deeply concerned as to who could be the next prime minister. He was certain that Morarji Desai would contest the election and he could not think of any candidate who could defeat Desai. He went to sleep mulling over the problem. Shortly before they arrived in Delhi, Kamaraj woke up, turned to Venkataraman, and said, 'We will have Indira as Prime Minister.' Venkataraman was taken aback. Kamaraj further said:

She knows all the world leaders, has travelled widely with her father, has grown up amongst the great men of the freedom movement, has a rational and modern mind, is totally free of any parochialism—state, caste or religion. She has possibly inherited her father's scientific temper and above all in 1967 election she can win the election.[2]

On reaching Delhi Kamaraj realized that the right-wing of the Congress—Atulya Ghosh, Neelam Sanjiva Reddy, Morarji Desai and S.K. Patil—would not accept Indira's candidature easily, especially as she was known to hold leftist views. The names of Morarji Desai and Y.B. Chavan were already being discussed as potential prime ministers, even before Prime Minister Shastri's body returned to Delhi. Gulzari Lal Nanda who had been sworn in to officiate as Prime Minister after the death of Nehru had put forward his claim and early on the morning of 11 January was at Indira's house to ask for her support.

Kamaraj visited President Sarvepalli Radhakrishnan; they were friends and the possibility of Indira being chosen as Prime Minister was discussed. The President thought Indira an ingénue. He thought little of her intellectual activities, was condescending, but realized that she had the outer facade necessary for a prime minister of India. Indira's main adviser and supporter was D.P. Misra, then Chief Minister of Madhya Pradesh. A wily Brahmin, he instinctively knew the moves necessary to ensure success. No. 1, Safdarjung Road buzzed with activity when I went to see Indira that morning. I could tell that she was holding her excitement in check. Outwardly she appeared calm and controlled, but instinctively she knew that her moment had come. She spoke of Nanda's visit. She said she had kept quiet and was discreet. Then, in a flash of supreme confidence, she said, 'No one can be Prime Minister without my support.'[3]

Immediately on his arrival, Kamaraj and Indira had met and he had promised her his full support. She was too shrewd not to see the reason why this wily man of the soil from the south was backing her to be prime minister: not because he thought she was the most competent candidate, but because he saw in her shy exterior and reticence a prime minister who could be manipulated. Neither the President of India, nor the President of the Congress were aware that behind her silent demeanour there was a formidable capacity to assess people and act swiftly and with precision. She had tenacity and a fierce courage; she had an alert mind, she could listen; learn swiftly; in retrospect it is easy to see she had seen through the stratagems of both these great men. She needed Kamaraj's support and therefore assumed the role of a pupil, agreeing to every move suggested by him.

Four days later, Morarji Desai, Y.B. Chavan, G.L. Nanda and Indira Gandhi had emerged as major candidates in the prime ministerial sweepstakes. D.P. Misra knew that power lay in the hands of the chief ministers and started sounding them out. She was assured of the support of most of the country's chief ministers, with the exception of Uttar Pradesh where Sucheta Kripalani was head of the State and owed allegiance to Morarji Desai. Here, too, Indira knew that given her popularity amongst the people of Uttar Pradesh, the members of the Congress Parliamentary Party from Uttar Pradesh, given the choice, would support her.

A message reached her, from D.P. Misra, that the chief ministers had met and their support was hers, still she hesitated. The aftermath of the Indo-Pak war and the drought that had hit the country had led to rising prices and grave hardships amongst the people. It would mean her taking over a very difficult economic situation.

She was at breakfast when I saw her the morning the news of the chief ministers' support for her appeared in the press. By now she was unable to contain her joy and confidence of one who sees her destiny fulfilled. It struck me how soon a Prime Minister loses innocence. She was already withdrawn, her mind busy working on several permutations and combinations; individuals had become expendable.

She had met L.K. Jha, then Principal Secretary to Lal Bahadur Shastri, several times at my house, had liked him, but remarked: 'It is a pity that L.K. is so associated with the USA and the West, in the public mind. If we have to take aid, which we will be forced to do, we have to play our dependence down. The weaker we are, the more strength we have to show.'[4]

The day before the meeting of the Congress Parliamentary Party to elect its leader I suddenly got a phone call from her. I found her very excited and disturbed. It appeared that the officiating Prime Minister, Gulzari Lal Nanda, had called the Border Security Force (BSF) to Delhi. She saw in it an attempt at a possible coup. I said,

'Nanda! How is that possible?'

'You don't know how ambitious he is. And his astrologers have been feeding his ambition.'

Later, she was to comment that when challenged Nanda had said that he had sent for the BSF to guard against a possible military coup. Indira Gandhi was not convinced and felt that in his weak way he had thought that he could still stay in power.

On 15 January only two contestants remained—Indira Gandhi and Morarji Desai, the ascetic, proud, strong-willed leader of Gujarat who had been axed during the Kamaraj Plan. He told Kamaraj that he would not submit to a consensus, as he had when Lal Bahadur Shastri was elected Prime Minister. An election became inevitable and intense canvassing commenced. The Congress Parliamentary Party was to meet on 19 January to elect its leader. Indira continued to maintain a low profile, but announced her availability. As the date of the election approached, Vijayalakshmi Pandit came out with a statement in support of her niece: 'It is a certainty that Indira Gandhi will be India's next Prime Minister. We Nehrus are very proud of our family. When a Nehru is chosen as Prime Minister, the people will rejoice.' She could not however avoid a sting in the last part of the statement. 'Mrs Gandhi has the qualities, now she needs experience. With a little experience she will make a fine Prime Minister—as fine that we could wish for. She is in very frail health, but with the help of her colleagues she will manage.'[5]

On the eve of her election, Indira Gandhi wrote to her son Rajiv Gandhi in London, quoting a poem from Robert Frost:

How hard it is to keep from being king
When it is in you and the situation.

Indira Gandhi had at last found her true vocation.[6]

On 19 January, the day of the Congress Parliamentary Party meeting, she visited Rajghat early in the morning and stood silent before the Mahatma's samadhi. Her next visit was to Teen Murti House. It was inevitable that she would feel the need to be close to her father at such a time; his presence was at her side as she stood before his portrait. She was stepping over the threshold, entering, even taking possession of that "wide expanse of Indian humanity" for which her father had prepared her from her childhood. Jawaharlal's presence was with her as she entered Parliament House. No speeches were made. When the ballot papers were counted, Indira had won by 355 votes to the 169 which went to Morarji Desai. Indira thanked Morarji Desai for his offer of cooperation. She expressed her gratitude to K. Kamaraj and all the other members who had displayed their trust in her by voting for her. She referred to herself as a *Desh sevika* (servant of the nation). 'I hope it will be possible for me to fulfil the trust that you have reposed in me.' She came out of Parliament House to be faced by a vast crowd that had gone delirious with joy. With garlands of jasmine around her neck, she ultimately found her way to her car and was driven to Rashtrapati Bhavan where the President awaited her, to invite her formally, as leader of the largest party in Parliament, to form the new government.

PART IV
1966–1971

In the juice of the egg of a peacock are the many wondrous colours of its tail.

–Maxim from Kashmiri Shaivism[1]

ONE

On 24 January 1966, Indira Gandhi was sworn in as Prime Minister by President S. Radhakrishnan in the Ashoka Hall of Rashtrapati Bhavan where her father had taken the oath of office as Prime Minister nineteen years earlier. Her sons were away in England but the galleries were crowded by personal friends and relations and Members of Parliament. She took the oath of office, solemnly affirming her allegiance to the Constitution rather than swearing in the name of God. Facing her was a towering red sandstone sculpture of a fifth century Buddha, with the hand raised in the *Abhaya Dan* mudra—Be Without Fear.

Interviewed later on her religious beliefs, she clarified that she was not an agnostic. 'Religion is understood by most people as a crutch. I don't need that kind of crutch, yet I have faith.' She quoted the Bhagavad Gita: 'I am the beauty in beautiful things; I am the evil in sin. This is what I believe that each person has god within himself.'[2]

On the day of her swearing in, an Air-India flight from Bombay to Geneva crashed on Mont Blanc in Switzerland. On board was Dr Homi Bhabha, India's top physicist and head of India's atomic research programme. It was a critical blow; Bhabha was the driving force behind India's scientific development. Possessed of a renaissance mind, he was a musician, an art-lover, and had nurtured the development of the contemporary art movement in Bombay. He had also been a friend of the new Prime Minister.

Indira Gandhi had joined the Congress party in 1938 and from 1953 onwards had led an active political life in her father's household. Her several attempts to escape from politics remained a fantasy till at last she recognized that politics was her heritage and could not be denied. But she had her own definition of what politics was all about. 'I was brought up to believe that politics is not a career, it is not a job. Politics is certain world trends, where humanity is going, what it is doing. That is what interests me, for politics is the centre of everything.'[3]

She had throughout her life maintained a low profile. Now the world and India turned to discover the reality of the woman. To see how a woman prime minister with a little known capacity for administrative skills, would handle the immensity of the problems that awaited her. The politician watched her every move waiting for her to stumble. The bureaucrat was cynical yet wary, concerned with guarding his own position and assessing the extent to which he could take advantage of the Prime Minister's inexperience to exercise greater power in decision making.

It was towards the end of her father's lifetime that Indira commenced moving away from strong ideological commitments. While Congress President, and as her father's confidante, she had soon realized that what was wrong with India was not the absence of socialist thought but an inelastic administrative structure, geared to maintaining law and order—a structure which needed to be transformed into a vital-instrument for creative change. In one of her early speeches, after her election as Prime Minister, she called for an administrative revolution. However tentative her approach, she was clear on certain basic issues. The old order was over. The country was changing with a rapidity beyond measure. The leaders of the Congress party, who had hitherto dominated state politics were prisoners of their own narrow beliefs. The fight that lay ahead was between old men, entrenched traditionalists, and young minds teeming with ideas.

Indira had little room to manoeuvre or bring about changes in her Cabinet; K. Kamaraj had insisted on her retaining most of the ministers of the Shastri period. She was anxious to drop Gulzari Lal Nanda but under pressure was forced to retain him as the Home Minister. The only new faces she could draw in were that of Ashoka Mehta, an intellectual and socialist, who became Vice-Chairman of the Planning Commission, and Fakhruddin Ali Ahmed of Assam. Dinesh Singh, an MP from Uttar Pradesh, joined the Prime Minister's Office as Parliamentary Secretary. He was to emerge as the centre of the coterie that formed around the Prime Minister in her early years in office.

*

On 20 January, the forty-seven-year-old Indira—slim, delicate and appearing far younger than her years—entered the Prime Minister's Office, to be greeted by her senior administrators—many of whom she had known during her father's time and also when she was Minister for Information and Broadcasting.

The country was in ferment—a severe drought, famine and acute food shortages cast shadows over the country. Rice riots were reported in Kerala; in the North-East, the Mizo tribes were in revolt; the demand for a separate state for the Punjabi-speaking population in Punjab had gained momentum. Fateh Singh, a Sikh leader, was threatening to immolate himself unless it was granted. The sadhus and sanyasis had come out on the streets of Delhi demanding an end to cow slaughter.

Faced with mounting problems, Indira realized that a pragmatic response was needed, a will to act that was free of all theories and paradigms. Indira had courage, determination, ruthlessness, but that was not enough for her to be a successful prime minister. New skills were necessary; to keep her opponents guessing.

For the time being, the need to discover herself, to listen to the intimations from her racial unconscious, to contact and absorb the immensity of the mind of the past, to uncover and discover, was set aside.

Her instinct for survival enabled her to chart a new course through the intrigues and attempts at domination.

She kept a watchful eye on the manoeuvrings of the stalwarts within the Congress while the Opposition members and their strategies remained under constant scrutiny. During her father's Prime Ministership and as Congress President, she had carefully observed the strongmen of the party and carried in her mind a dossier of their strengths and weaknesses. However complex the situation, she realized she could not afford to lose her nerve or her contact with the voice of the people. Over the years her constant travelling to distant parts of the country had given her insights into the symbols that moved the people of India. She had learnt from the Mahatma that no approach to the people could be an intellectual one, an idiom had to be found that they understood and responded to; logic and rational arguments had a limited place.

She started seeing, every morning, before she went to office, a vast number of people from all over the country. She would go round, meet people individually, listen to their sorrows and troubles, accept petitions, ask her secretary to take notes and take follow up action to provide relief, wherever possible. There was no letter that remained unanswered. On any single day she would meet between 200 to 500 people.

L.K. Jha, Principal Secretary to Lal Bahadur Shastri, had offered his resignation immediately after she took over as Prime Minister. She had asked him to stay on till the next elections. Many names of administrators close to her had filtered through her mind as possible replacements for Jha, but with her need for someone to galvanize the bureaucracy, Jha seemed most suitable. Jha found that the Prime Minister kept her political life and her administrative one totally apart. She trusted no one.

To renew herself, in between the most tempestuous meetings, she would find time for artists, painters and dancers. Her management of her eighteen-hour weeklong day was admirable. She was available, punctual, and could switch from political problems to administration, with its entangled decision taking, to scientists, to her chiefs of staff, and to a visitor from abroad, an architect or a poet.

One of her first acts as Prime Minister was to agree to the separation of the Punjabi-speaking areas of Punjab from the Hindi-speaking villages. A new State, Haryana, was carved out. The Sikhs were joyous; the Hindi-speaking population revolted. Riots broke out and Indira Gandhi rushed to the disturbed areas and stormed at the local people. 'There are no tears in my eyes. There is anger in my heart. Is all the suffering and martyrdom of thousands during the freedom struggle to end in this?'[4]

The two main priorities on her agenda were the immediate task of finding grain for a drought-riven country so that starvation deaths did not occur and to harness the forces of intellectuals and youth for the eradication of poverty. The US administration had stopped aid to India and Pakistan during the 1965 war between the two countries; Indira knew she would have to accept in the near future the pressing invitation from President Lyndon Johnson to visit the US. L.K. Jha's rapport with the US administration could be of immense help in crossing the first hurdle. But the visit still lay ahead, the problems within the country needed her full attention.

An All-India Congress Committee (AICC) meeting was scheduled to take place in Jaipur within three weeks of her taking over as Prime Minister. A great deal of heat had been generated amongst Congress chief ministers over a food distribution system Indira had inherited from Shastri's time. The country was divided into food zones; under the prevailing system foodgrains from a surplus state could not leave the state without the state government's instructions. The deficit in foodgrains demanded an end to this zonal system.

Indira was aware of the contradictory forces that could devastate the meeting. She needed alternative proposals. She had sat with her Food Minister, C. Subramaniam, and prepared her brief with great care so that she would be able to answer any questions that arose. Subramaniam was working on proposals for foreign collaborations to establish fertilizer factories and the introduction of new methods of agriculture. He believed that without a better management of the agricultural sector, it would be difficult to ensure increased grain yields.

The AICC meeting was, as expected, explosive. Voices were raised by the chief ministers of drought-affected states demanding an end to food zones. They were shouted down by chief ministers from surplus food producing areas. Subramaniam's strategy was also under serious attack and the Prime Minister was forced to the mike to defend and clarify her government's position. Her voice could hardly be heard. She forgot her carefully prepared brief, lost confidence and had to retreat. Kamaraj intervened and order was restored.

Back in Delhi, she sent for me. She was in bed, her back being massaged by a maidservant. Visibly shaken, her face was taut with fatigue. She said, 'There is so little maturity amongst the leadership.' Her lack of confidence at the Jaipur meeting had been clearly revealed. She was angry with herself. The shock to her self-image had devastated her. With hurt and bitterness, she began to speak of her aunt Vijayalakshmi Pandit. Indira held her responsible for her own lack of confidence. 'From my childhood,' said Indira, 'she did every-thing to destroy my confidence; she called me ugly, stupid. This shattered something within me. Faced with hostility, however well prepared I am, I get tongue-tied and withdraw.'[5]

When she had calmed down, I asked her what the three weeks of Prime Ministership had meant to her. 'Is it only three weeks?' she queried. Then she turned to me and said, 'You know, I am scared of the coming Parliament session. I have no friends in the Cabinet. Subramaniam and Ashoka Mehta would support me, but they have no political sense.' She was wary of Nanda who was in a thrall to his astrologers.

On 1 March, in reply to the President's address, refusing to be overwhelmed by the weight of her problems, or the storms brewing in her own party, her determination to save the country came through with a surging passion. 'India simply cannot fail. We are all in this together. It is not a question of this government or that government. We simply cannot fail.'[6] These words were to reverberate within her throughout her life.

L.K. Jha was to comment some years later:

> Initially Indira Gandhi was very diffident, almost incompetent as a Parliamentarian. She would have the prepared text, she would go through it carefully, study every word, but while she was speaking, someone would deliberately interrupt and ask her some side questions, to see whether she could revert to her text after interruption. This embarrassed her. Ram Manohar Lohia, one of her father's protégés and later his severest critic, referred to her incapacity for quick repartee. He called her a *"gungi gudia"*—a dumb doll.[7]

Over the months a relationship of confidence grew between her and L.K. Jha. 'At first she was a little uncertain. She did not know whether I would understand her political compulsions and be responsive to them.'

Immediately before she became Prime Minister, the US Vice-President Hubert Humphrey had come to India for Shastri's funeral. He was anxious that the new Prime Minister, Indira Gandhi, should not support North Vietnam and so weaken the US position. Jha was present at the meeting. 'I commented if we were to exercise a sobering effect on Ho Chi Minh, then it was only possible if he looked upon us as his friend and not as the friend of the US.' Jha emphasized that it was of utmost importance that India remain friendly with North Vietnam otherwise there would be an erosion of Ho Chi Minh's trust in India. Humphrey said: 'My God, am I to go back and say to the President that India feels closer to Vietnam than to the US.'

'I am glad you said it,' Indira commented later to Jha. 'It was in my mind, but if I had said it, it would have been misunderstood, but your interruption was very timely and very welcome.'[8]

*

President Lyndon Johnson had sent a message through Vice-President

Humphrey suggesting that the Prime Minister visit the United States as early as possible. Once the programme was settled, she prepared meticulously. Romesh Thapar, editor and friend, was helping her. Yet she called me in, we read out the speeches together, timed them, corrected wherever necessary. She had a little notebook of quotations which she would refer to. She was comfortable with simple sentences and avoided complex ideas. She was as meticulous about her clothes as with her speeches. Her sari, her blouse, her shoes, her bag were selected for every single function. She was anxious to appear at her best, had written to a few of her friends in the US to locate the latest makeup that would lessen the shadows under her eyes and make her long nose less prominent. The white streak in her hair over the years was carefully groomed to give her a touch of distinction. She was very much a woman.

Indira Gandhi was not familiar with the workings of the international financial institutions. Her economic advisers had briefed her on the pressures exerted from Shastri's times, by the World Bank and the International Monetary Fund (IMF), for a devaluation of the Indian currency. She sensed that devaluation would have political repercussions and so, before she left for the United States, she had consulted senior economists, including D.N. Gadgil, Vice-Chairman of the Planning Commission, a highly respected figure who had leftist leanings. He had agreed with her advisers that, with two wars, a severe drought and an empty treasury, there were no alternatives to devaluation; the value of the rupee had already been lowered by the various subsidies on exports. She realized that it was a political decision, but determined that there would be no starvation deaths and that she would pull India out of the morass into which it was sinking; whatever had to be done to ensure this would be done.

Before she left for the United States, towards the end of March, she spoke of the problems she would face in Washington. She was mortified at having to put out her hand for aid, yet she knew she had no options. She was determined, however, not to be a supplicant. 'The weaker your position, the stronger must be your stand. To appear to bend and accept is a sign of immense strength.'[9]

She stopped in Paris on her way to Washington, to hold talks with President Charles de Gaulle. He hosted a lunch for her. 'I could see that he was sizing her up,' said L.K. Jha. Prime Minister Gandhi spoke to President de Gaulle throughout lunch in fluent French. After lunch, for a few minutes L.K. Jha was alone with the President. 'He asked me,' Jha recollected, 'whether I was *Chef de Cabinet.'* I said 'Yes.' Charles de Gaulle was distrustful of women in politics. 'I don't think they have it in them, but your Prime Minister is a woman of amazing strength. She has something—she will make it.'[10]

André Malraux was to ask de Gaulle shortly before his death: 'What impression did Indira Gandhi make on you?'

'Those fragile shoulders on which the huge destiny of India rests—and they don't shrink from the burden,' was de Gaulle's response.[11]

President Johnson hoped to help strengthen India so that it could take its place along with Japan as a bulwark against Communist Chinese aggression in Asia.[12] He was anxious that the Prime Minister's visit was carefully planned by Washington; a White House 707 reached Paris for her flight across the Atlantic.

B.K. Nehru, then the Indian Ambassador to the US, recalled Indira Gandhi arriving in Washington, imperious and elegant. On the morning of her meeting with President Johnson, *Life* magazine had published an interview with Prime Minister Gandhi in which she was reported to have said that she did not like to be addressed as Madame Prime Minister. The President had sent a message to Ambassador Nehru asking what he should call her. Her answer was typical—she did not have the slightest objection to being called Madame Prime Minister—Prime Minister—Your Excellency or nothing at all. 'By the time I had reached the door,' writes Nehru, 'the mood of imperiousness had returned; she added: "And you can tell him that my Cabinet colleagues call me "Sir"." '[13]

At their first meeting on the White House lawns, the President called for 'frankness and candour and detail, that mark conversations between good friends.' Indira approved of the directness of his approach. She replied: 'India and the USA cannot and should not take each other for granted or allow their relations to drift.'[14]

The talks between the President and the Prime Minister were extremely cordial. The President spoke of the need for India to control its population growth, 'revamp its outmoded agricultural methods,' and make friends with Pakistan.[15] Indira discussed emergency food aid to face the acute drought in India and the resumption of US economic aid. The President was supportive, but it is possible that he hinted at a devaluation of the rupee.

Their tête-à-tête over, President Johnson and Prime Minister Gandhi came into the Cabinet room where the two delegations awaited them. The President said: 'Gentlemen, I have had a very good talk with the Prime Minister and I told her that, with regard to the economic policy, she could take stock with the World Bank and we will fully support the Bank's efforts.' It was a loaded remark; the main agenda for discussion with the financing agencies was the devaluation of the rupee. Without the Prime Minister agreeing to this, no food aid would be available. 'Johnson believed that India had to be pressurised for its own good, to make significant changes in her economic policy. He used pressure (to ensure this).'[16]

That evening the President held a banquet for the Prime Minister; later there was dancing. Indira was embarrassed as she knew that if she were to dance with the President, it would be completely misunderstood in India. So she made her excuses and left.

The next day Ambassador B.K. Nehru hosted a dinner for the Vice-President of the US, in honour of the Indian Prime Minister. However, shortly before the dinner, President Johnson made an unscheduled call on the Prime Minister at the Indian Embassy. He kept on talking, guests started to arrive. An embarrassed Fori Nehru asked the President, 'Mr. President, why don't you stay for dinner?' He said, 'Yes, I will.' That created a major crisis. Protocol demanded that the seating arrangements for dinner be changed and one person of the Indian delegation had to be dropped.

P.N. Haksar, then Deputy High Commissioner in London, had joined the Prime Minister during her visit to Washington. Two major agreements had to be reached on behalf of India. One was a continuance of food aid; all aid from the US had ceased to India and Pakistan during the 1965 war. The other, the setting up of an educational foundation to utilize the rupee funds accruing from the import of grains from the United States into India. The proposal for the establishment of an educational foundation had been approved by the Indian Cabinet. On the flight to the US, Haksar had warned Indira against permitting American academics to enter the educational system in India. The Prime Minister supported Haksar's view and the agreement was not signed. Johnson took it well and refused to make it an issue. The visit ended. The President walked with the Prime

Minister to Blair House where she was staying.

Later, she had a session with George Woods, President of the World Bank, and Schweitzer, head of the International Monetary Fund. She had little knowledge of international finance and the possible impact of devaluation on political equations in India. Both the Chairmen were considerate with the Prime Minister on devaluation. 'It is for you to choose the time,' they told her. 'We understand your political difficulty, but a consortium is coming up. It will be easy to give you several million dollars in aid.'[17]

Practically everywhere she went on her US visit, India's Prime Minister was greeted with roses—red roses, yellow roses, artificial roses—an impressionistic painting of a rose and a gilded rose from Tiffany's. 'All of them could serve well to symbolize the result of her five-day visit; a new flowering in the relations between the world's two largest democracies.'[18] Indira Gandhi had proved to be 'a very proud, gracious and able lady, but a fiercely independent ruler with a determination to equal his (the President's) own.'

Before she left the US, she spoke on the phone to the President to thank him for all his courtesies and be reassured by him that food aid would be given some urgency by his administration. She was polite, complimented the President and relayed all the courtesies demanded of her. As she put down the telephone, H.Y. Sharada Prasad, one of her trusted bureaucrats, who was present said she commented 'Never again will I permit myself to be put into this situation.'[19]

TWO

On Indira Gandhi's way back to India from the United States, she visited the Soviet Union accompanied by Dr I.G. Patel, her Secretary for Economic Affairs, and Pitambar Pant, a brilliant young economist in the Planning Commission. Aleksei Kosygin was Prime Minister of the USSR. T.N. Kaul, Indian Ambassador to the Soviet Union for some time before the Prime Minister's visit, was exerting pressure on the Soviets to fund a number of heavy industry projects in India. The Soviets were very unwilling to do so. During the discussions with Kosygin, I.G. Patel found the Prime Minister extremely shy, she hardly spoke. Prime Minister Kosygin vehemently told Indira Gandhi:

> Madam, your Ambassador, has been telling you, as he has been telling us, of the need to set up a new heavy industry plant, but neither of you know about machines. I do know something about it and I can tell you that you do not need a second Ranchi or another heavy electrical plant. What we have given you has not yet been fully utilised. You have a better infrastructure than we have here. I would strongly advise you that this is not the time for India to go in for another big dose of heavy industry.[1]

This was exactly the language which the World Bank had used. The discussions went on till 2.00 in the morning. I.G. Patel and Pitambar Pant were with the Prime Minister throughout the period. Indira Gandhi was listening carefully but made few comments. When they were about to leave the old man put his arms around her and said: 'Madam, Prime Minister, I am old enough to be your father. Can I tell you something?' She said, 'Yes.' He then said:

> Nothing is more difficult than being the Prime Minister of a country, to be Prime Minister of India is even more difficult. But, please believe me, no matter how hard your task is you take some time off, because if you do not take some time off you will make your task even more difficult and if you find that because of your political system you

cannot take time off in India, my permanent invitation to you is to take a plane and come to any part of Russia. We promise not to meet you during your holidays. Come even for a day or two and go back. I say this as a man who understands.[2]

*

Indira Gandhi was in bed, lying on her stomach, completely relaxed, when I went to see her on her return from the US. There were no papers, no phones surrounding her. The warmth and admiration showered on her in the US, had washed away all traces of nervousness and lack of confidence. She had blossomed. She had liked President Lyndon Johnson and found him warm and direct in his approach. She spoke of the dinners and her speeches and the appreciative response of the media, but the flattery and adulation had not erased her shrewdness, her capacity to see what lay behind words. With a whimsical smile she said: 'You know, Pupul, because I appeared young and spoke little, both Johnson and Kosygin felt I was a fledgling; they tried to teach me the direction in which to fly.' I smiled with her.

We had many mutual friends in the US, and she and I chatted and gossiped for an hour. Sometime later, I asked if she had met John Kenneth Galbraith in the States.

'Galbraith,' she queried. 'Why?'

'Well, Galbraith was Ambassador at a critical period during India's post-independence. He was a friend of your father's and must have lunched and dined at your table where you acted as hostess. On his return to the US, when he published his Ambassador's journal, he hardly mentions you. You were to become Prime Minister within two years of his departure. Did he not sense the role you would play in the years that lay ahead? Did he never have any serious conversations with you?'

'No. I have hardly spoken half a dozen sentences with him. He never ceases talking. He never listens. Do you think he listened to Kennedy? And in any case he is too tall and I do not like to look up to a person when I speak.' A little later she turned back to Galbraith. I could sense that he must have ignored her and that she had resented him.

'Do you consider Galbraith intelligent? I think he is very overrated. He thinks Jackie Kennedy beautiful and intelligent.'

'Jackie is very attractive and bright.' I said.

'Hmm. Biju (B.K. Nehru) also thinks so, but I don't,'[3] was Indira's comment.

The attacks against Indira Gandhi commenced soon after her return to India. V.K. Krishna Menon spoke sarcastically in the Lok Sabha of the Prime Minister's personal success in the US. 'But,' said Menon, 'personal success is not the same as policy.' He accused Indira Gandhi of coming under the influence of the United States. 'The empire comes in by the back door, front door and the side door.'[4] He felt that she had abandoned non-alignment.

With a new confidence, Indira had started meeting editors and columnists; she did not fight shy of being photographed, held press conferences once a month, and had started informal "Person to Person" talks on All-India Radio (AIR). Her reply to Menon was in her radio talk:

> This government is fully committed to the objectives of a socialistic and democratic society, but our socialism is related to the realities of the Indian situation. It is not wedded to any dogma. What we aim at is a better life, with more food, employment and opportunities. Let us not become prisoners of words.[5]

The stalwarts in the Congress party were disturbed by Indira's self-assurance and the confidence with which she had started tackling problems. They had elected her Prime Minister because they felt she had little independent judgement and could be replaced whenever they chose. A powerful attack was launched on her for what they considered a deviation from her father's policies. Gulzari Lal Nanda said openly that Indira would not be the Prime Minister after the next elections. It was Morarji Desai who sent Indira a message through me: 'She should realise that I have not done a single thing to shake her position or weaken her.' When I saw her, I spoke of what I had heard in Bombay: 'Dark clouds are gathering.'

'I know, but clouds pass.'

K. Kamaraj and Indira had drifted apart. According to Indira, he was doing everything possible to weaken those who supported her.

The friends of Kamaraj and Indira were making efforts to bring the two together; they considered a split very dangerous. Indira said: 'I have tried everything, including asking Kamaraj whether I have made any mistakes, but he is in no mood to listen or be open. The fact is he wants to be Prime Minister. He has always wanted to be Prime Minister.'[6]

As the velocity of the attacks increased, Indira, addressing a Congress workers' meeting in Poona, lashed out at her critics:

> Do not tell me I do not know Nehru's ideology. We worked together. I was intimately connected with all his thinking. In any case I do not see myself in the role of an imitation of Nehru. If I think it is necessary to depart from his policies in the interest of the country, I shall not hesitate to do so. Foreign aid is necessary to make us independent. I say this with firmness today; nobody outside or inside this country can ask me to deviate from my chosen path.[7]

And if they did not like her approach, challenged Indira, 'then remove me.' The speech flashed across India, even reached newspapers abroad, leaving the Congress leadership bewildered. It was clear that she would either be Prime Minister in her own right— or—one fact was clear: 'The lady is not for shelving.'[8]

The negotiations for the devaluation of the rupee were carried on in the utmost secrecy. On 6 June 1966 the Prime Minister announced the devaluation by 35.5 per cent. In a broadcast to the nation on 12 June 1966, she said:

> Let me be frank with you. The decision to devalue the rupee was not an easy one. It was taken after the most anxious and searching consideration. How much easier it would have been to have evaded a decision, to have drifted along—waiting, hoping! There are times in the history of every nation when its will is tested and its future depends on its capacity for resolute action and bold decision. This is such a time in India.[9]

It was shortly before she announced the devaluation of the rupee that she spoke to Kamaraj. He was very upset and angry, and felt that the Prime Minister should not have relied on bureaucrats and advisers like C. Subramaniam and Ashoka Mehta who had little understanding of the political scene. Speaking to a friend, Kamaraj commented on his great mistake in making Indira Prime Minister: 'A great man's daughter, a little man's great mistake.'

What made the devaluation even more critical for India was the fact that the monsoons failed once again and India faced a second year of drought. Despite all expectations to the contrary, President Johnson used food-aid as a lever to keep India under control. He demanded that all files regarding foodgrain shipments come to him for clearance. The situation became intolerable. Indira Gandhi had a map of India put up in her South Block office to trace the movement of every food ship. As a symbolic gesture, she gave up eating wheat or rice.

In the midst of the drought, the Prime Minister, with her Minister for Food, C. Subramaniam, launched a major programme for solving the food problem in India. Indira knew very little about agriculture, but it was decided, that she and her Minister would visit every state to discuss, in detail, the problems and find right solutions.

C. Subramaniam said:

> We used to travel by plane taking scientists, people in the production field, experts on marketing, with us. They would brief the Prime Minister in one or two hours with regard to the State which we were visiting. She would listen very carefully, ask questions which were relevant, understand the solutions offered by experts. By the time we reached our destination, she would initiate the discussion with the Chief Minister, the Agriculture Minister and the Secretaries of the State Government. It would appear as if she understood the problems faced by the State. The Chief Ministers would be very impressed.[10]

Decisions were taken on the spot and action initiated, collaborations with fertilizer firms finalized, improved seeds to revitalize agriculture in India introduced. In three years a Green Revolution was to make India self-sufficient in food.

THREE

On 15 August 1966, I listened in to Indira Gandhi's first Independence Day address to the nation. She sounded emotionally moved; the rostrum from where she spoke was directly in front of the Diwan-e-Am from where the Mughal Emperors had addressed the people of India. She knew her voice would reach far beyond the crowds that stood before her, to distant towns and large villages. A sense of history permeated her speech. She made a reference to the "tryst with destiny" speech of her father at midnight on 14 August 1947 when India attained freedom. As she spoke, her confidence returned; there was passion in her voice; her choice of Hindi words was eloquent; she spoke from unsuspected depths. As she appealed to the youth of India to come forward and share the responsibilities of building the nation, an earthquake struck. She felt that the iron railing against which she stood would collapse, but the shock passed, she did not falter and continued to speak.

The elections to the Lok Sabha were due in early 1967. By now the Congress leadership, which had made Indira Prime Minister, was convinced that, once the elections were over, she would have to be removed. Till then they did not want to attack as they knew that she was an asset in capturing votes. Despite this, a scurrilous series of posters began to appear on the walls and bus-stands of the capital. It is difficult to say who instigated the campaign; all the posters emphasized her inauspicious stars: an Air-India plane had crashed and Dr Homi Bhabha was killed on the day she was sworn in as Prime Minister; on her first Independence Day speech, an earthquake had struck Delhi, drought, floods and railway accidents were headlined in newspapers; she was a widow and widows in the minds of vast numbers of people in India were regarded as inauspicious.

Devaluation, a second year of drought, rising prices and a slackening of demand for consumer goods had hit the poor in distant parts of the country. Language riots had taken place. The cow-slaughter agitation had coloured the minds of the orthodox Hindu voters. Adding to her problems, several incidents of violence and the breakdown of law and order preceded the elections. K. Kamaraj and the state leadership had refused to allow Indira a voice in the selection of candidates. Indira Gandhi refused to be cowed down. She travelled incessantly, faced hostile crowds. In Orissa, a State which had a non-Congress government, she addressed a major public meeting. The organizers were afraid of violence erupting during the proceedings and had asked her not to speak but to sit at the rear of the platform. She refused. As she spoke to the crowds gathered to greet her, a stone thrown from the crowd hit her on the nose, fracturing the bone. Blood started pouring down her face, but she covered it with her sari and continued to address the audience. She told them that the attack on her 'was not an insult to her personally, but to the country because as Prime Minister I represent this country.' She returned to Delhi. Her upper lip was heavily swollen and her nose slightly crooked. An ice-pack on her face, she refused to complain of the pain. The nose was set under anaesthesia. When she came around, her major concern was whether there would be permanent damage to her face.

Though in pain, she was eager to know what people were saying in Madras, from where I had come. There was speculation in Madras, I said, on Kamaraj's break with her. The people were wondering whether without his support she could be the Prime Minister after the elections. She broke in: 'Kamaraj is manoeuvring to see that the struggle between Morarji Desai and me becomes so acute that Kamaraj could step in as the consensus candidate. He wants to be Prime Minister. Morarjibhai would then be offered Home Ministership.'

She had been told that a meeting was arranged between Morarji Desai and Kamaraj in Madras, but at the last minute Kamaraj thought better of it and cancelled the meeting. She was playing with the idea of offering the Presidentship of India to Morarji Desai but did not know whether he would accept it. 'The trouble is our "Netas" (leaders), are so busy dividing the spoils, they are unaware of the mood of the people.'[1]

When the results started coming in, the Congress faced a debacle. Although they retained a bare majority in the Lok Sabha, the senior leaders, the strongmen of the states were defeated. S.K. Patil in Maharashtra lost to George Fernandes, Atulya Ghosh was defeated in West Bengal, and Kamaraj, President of the Congress, was defeated by an unknown young man belonging to the new Dravida Munnetra

Kazagham (DMK) in Tamil Nadu. The strong conservative force which had ruled the country was in shambles. Indira had been re-elected with a vast majority. With the defeat of her opponents within the party, she emerged in a much stronger position.

She was in a sparkling mood when I met her a few days after the election results had come in. She told me that most of the leaders in the Congress had lost contact with the new emergent India. The young had exercised a great influence on the votes.

The contest for the leadership of the party, which would determine the prime ministership, lay ahead. Indira felt that the voting would go heavily in her favour, yet there was an undercurrent of anxiety. A defeated Kamaraj was trying to re-establish his central position. The business community, the princes and the press had backed the Opposition and, to hedge their bets, donated money to S.K. Patil before the elections and were doing so again to ensure the leadership of the party. As the day for the election of the leader came near, Indira organized her plans with meticulous care. The leadership issue was tangled, Kamaraj noncommittal; her senior bureaucrats and advisers had urged Indira to support Morarji and induct him into a very senior position in the Cabinet. I.G. Patel had called on Morarji Desai and pleaded with him to cooperate with Indira as the country was facing many challenges. He had listened, asked whether Indira knew of his visit and did not reveal his mind.[2] Pitambar Pant had strongly urged Indira to invite Morarji Desai to join her Cabinet. Her political advisers—Y.B. Chavan, Ashoka Mehta and Dinesh Singh—took the opposite view, they felt she should not placate Morarji Desai.[3] I had known Morarjibhai, for many years. I knew of his pride and, for the first time in my life, I made a political suggestion to Indira, that she should call on Morarji Desai and so disarm him. I suggested that flexibility was needed. If she refused, it was possible that, as the underdog, he might invite the sympathy of the voter. She agreed. She said she had felt that she should go but her political advisers were strongly against it and felt that a visit by her would be taken by the Members of Parliament as a sign of weakness. The next day the news was in the press that the Prime Minister had called on Morarji Desai. No one knows what took place at this meeting, but the situation was resolved. Morarji Desai accepted the Deputy Prime Ministership and with it the Finance portfolio.

Sworn in for a second time as Prime Minister, Indira shortly after gave a radio talk on 15 March, in which she thanked the people of India for reposing their trust in her and placed before the nation her priorities:

> A very difficult year for food (lies) ahead; the government would have to restrain the upward spiral of prices.

> What is needed was more production—agricultural and industrial. This calls for work. I know only one alternative to hard, unrelenting work. It is yet more work.

> We have to control our population before we are submerged by the sheer weight of numbers. Family planning is only one aspect of manpower planning. Education constitutes the other part. The year of student unrest has been a warning. The educational system (is) in urgent need for reform—we must act boldly and soon.

> We have to keep open and enlarge outlets for the creative talents of our people—intellectuals, scientists, writers, artists, artisans. They provide the aesthetic and inspirational force to uplift and sustain the Indian revolution.[4]

A search had started for a new home for the Prime Minister. No. 1, Safdarjung Road was totally inadequate for her needs. Her sons were to return from England and she needed space for her office and for meeting visitors. It was obvious that she would have liked to have gone back to Teen Murti House, which in Lal Bahadur Shastri's time had been earmarked for a Nehru Museum and Library. She did not want to suggest it herself, but would have liked public opinion to be created so that the Teen Murti House could be declared the official home of the Prime Minister. When rumours reached Padmaja Naidu, who was living on the Teen Murti campus, she reacted strongly and was not prepared to even consider the suggestion. Two large and commodious houses were available in the President's Estate and it was suggested that they could be converted into the Prime Minister's official residence and office. I mentioned it to her one evening. She was silent for a while. When she spoke, it was as if the past of India, of intrigue and betrayal, of emperors holding captive their sons and heirs, came to her mind. 'A time may come when the President could hold the Prime Minister prisoner.'[5]

Indira finally decided to stay on in 1, Safdarjung Road, the sitting-room was extended and furnished in muted tones of rose and moss green; a sliding glass door opened on to a landscape of huge trees, bushes, birds and butterflies. Later, the bungalow next to her's was converted into her private office.

*

President S. Radhakrishnan's term as President was coming to an end and the Congress party intended to nominate him for another term, but Indira demurred. From the first day of her assuming prime ministership, through her first year in power, whenever she went to him, he would rarely listen to what she had to say, but would instead lecture her on what she should do. She could not afford a President whose attitude to his Prime Minister 'was affectionate, supportive and non-serious.'[6] When the elections were over and she was re-elected Prime Minister, she was in a much stronger position and decided against giving another term to President Radhakrishnan. She opted instead for Vice-President Zakir Hussain, an educationist of renown, gentle, sensitive and a Muslim. There was strong opposition to her choice, but she refused to change her mind. The Opposition, sensing the conflict in the Congress party, had put up Subba Rao, Chief Justice of the Supreme Court who had resigned his Chief Justiceship shortly before nomination day, as their candidate for Presidentship. Indira knew that a defeat for Zakir Hussain would be a disaster for her, but she stood her ground and to her joy found that Zakir Hussain won with a comfortable majority. I met her shortly after. She was happy, relaxed, but intuitively felt that the "Syndicate" would not give up without a further struggle to destabilize her. They were only waiting for the right opportunity.

*

The relations between the Governments of the US and India were on the decline. India's support for the Arab powers and her criticism of Israel's attitude towards the Arab nations had angered America.

On the eve of the West Asian crisis, Indira's Foreign Minister, M.C. Chagla, delivered a very strong anti-Israel speech at the UN. I was in the US in May 1967. Many of Indira's friends in the US had reacted strongly; the newspaper reports were anti-India. On my return I met her and told her what I had heard. She said she had seen the report; Chagla had overreacted—he did not understand the reasons for India's position on the Arab Israel dispute. She and her father had admired what Israel had accomplished by turning a desert into fertile land. Her father, during Hitler's years, had tried his utmost to find a homeland for the German Jews, in India, but the British had refused. 'Why were the Jews in the USA so identified with Israel?' she asked. She too was angry with the US for not interfering to ease the situation in the Middle East and for encouraging Israel in its belligerent attitude.

'The USA was trying a pincer hold in Asia—Vietnam and Israel—India would be encircled.' Suddenly she got excited: 'It is better that we die than give in to the constant pressure from the USA. Chester Bowles had come to see me recently; he lectured me and did not give me a chance to say what was in my mind. He did not want to know. So I refused to speak, was cordial, wished him a pleasant trip, but kept silent—and that was that.'[7]

War between Israel and the United Arab Republics (UAR) broke out on 5 June 1967. Speaking to the Lok Sabha on 6 June the Prime Minister was in a sombre mood:

> The world faces a disastrous war in West Asia. The armed forces of Israel and those of U.A.R. and other Arab countries are locked in combat . . . if not stopped this war is likely to expand into a much wider one, drawing into its vortex other countries and developing perhaps into a world war. Our own national interests are bound up with peace and stability in West Asia.[8]

*

Indira Gandhi's silences had intrigued the international world of diplomacy and challenged her friends and her opponents. Apocryphal stories were current in India and abroad that when Chancellor

George Keisinger of West Germany was in India in November 1967 on an official visit, Prime Minister Indira Gandhi paid a courtesy call at Rashtrapati Bhavan. The Chancellor spoke for over an hour with the Prime Minister, requesting the Government of India to refrain from recognizing East Germany. Indira had listened with attention and respect to him. When he stopped speaking and waited for her response, the Prime Minister looked out of the window and spoke as if the future of the world depended on it: 'Oh dear, it has stopped raining.' The Chancellor was stunned. The German Ambassador's heart missed several beats. After the meeting, the Ambassador had rushed to P.N. Haksar, Prime Minister Indira Gandhi's *Chef de Cabinet,* who suggested that he request the Chancellor to wait. That night, at the banquet, she turned to the stiff-lipped German who sat beside her and said very sweetly that India would postpone her recognition of East Germany for six months.[9]

Vijayalakshmi Pandit, reminiscing on the old days, said: 'Malcolm McDonald, former British High Commissioner to India was on a mission to India with a letter from Harold MacMillan addressed to Indira Gandhi.' In a meeting with Vijayalakshmi Pandit, McDonald observed that 'Indira Gandhi's greatest weapon was her silence. He waited for an answer to his Prime Minister's letter from Indira Gandhi. Though Indira Gandhi saw him several times, she continued to keep silent.'[10]

The silences of Indira Gandhi became famous. Silences which could be opaque, would presage ruthless responses and silences that were limpid like clear, sweet lakewater, could assuage fears and welcome.

FOUR

The death by cardiac failure of President Zakir Hussain in April 1969 gave Prime Minister Indira Gandhi's critics within the Congress party, an opportunity to confront her and devise a strategy to ultimately replace her. K. Kamaraj and the "Syndicate" had never forgiven her for the independent stand she had taken on vital issues relating to the country. She was learning fast, and was emerging as a formidable force. They knew that her capacity for winning votes, would break their own power in the party if they did not act swiftly and in unison. The 1967 election results had left them helpless, but they now saw their opportunity.

A web of intrigue surrounded the preliminary moves to nominate the new President of India. Nijalingappa, then President of the Congress, had discussed the issue with the Prime Minister. She was deliberately vague, not prepared to express her choice, but suggested the name of Jagjivan Ram, a senior member of the Congress who belonged to the Scheduled Castes. This, she said, would create a new image for the Congress. Nijalingappa had not commented on her proposal, but later in meetings held with Kamaraj, Atulya Ghosh, S.K. Patil and Morarji Desai, it was decided to propose the name of Neelam Sanjiva Reddy, at one time Chief Minister of Andhra Pradesh, and a powerful figure in his own right.

The All-India Congress Committee (AICC) met in Bangalore between 10–33 July. According to Indira, Kamaraj and the "Syndicate" and her group were equal in strength, with the casting vote held by Y.B. Chavan. She had held discussions and talks with Y.B. Chavan before the AICC met and he had promised to support her candidate.

She had a very bad cold and was uncomfortable when I saw her on the evening before she left for Bangalore. As usual she had a little notepad by her side and at times took notes as we spoke. The coming session did not make her apprehensive. She said there would be no confrontation over the election and appeared to suggest that a compromise had been reached. She felt gravely concerned about the country. The Naxalites, the extreme left-wing Maoist group, committed to violence, were gaining strength in West Bengal. With growing unemployment, the youth of the country were in a desperate mood and turning to violence to express their sense of hopelessness. She felt that something had to be done urgently to restore their confidence.

She was not present on the first day of the meeting of the Congress Working Committee (CWC), but sent a message that she was unwell and would come the following day. Her emissary was Fakhruddin Ali Ahmed, one of her Cabinet colleagues. With him, she forwarded a short note on some stray thoughts on the economic strategy to be adopted by the Congress. The note included the nationalization of commercial banks—a subject that had been raised several times in the past by the young radical elements in her party. She suggested that the various points should be discussed on the first day of the meeting, expecting them to create a storm in the CWC, many of whose members were entrenched conservatives. However, the CWC paid scant attention to the economic suggestions made by her. Their response was to adopt the Prime Minister's stray thoughts, but suggested that as Prime Minister it was up to her to implement the follow-up action.

The crucial meeting of the Parliamentary Board to select a name for the future President of India was held the following day. The meeting started in a grim atmosphere; various names were proposed, discussed and finally it came to a choice between Sanjiva Reddy and Jagjivan Ram. When the votes were finally counted, Jagjivan Ram, who was Indira's candidate, lost by one vote. Y.B. Chavan, at the last moment, had deserted Indira and voted against her. Indira left the meeting in a very grave mood. The "Syndicate" was jubilant. With Sanjiva Reddy as President, a situation could be created whereby the President could ask for the Prime Minister's resignation and instal a new leader of the Congress party who, in turn, would assume the office of prime minister. To the press who awaited her reactions, Indira Gandhi made an ominous comment; she said that the senior members of the Congress who had voted for Sanjiva Reddy, would have to face the consequences of attempting to force a presidential candidate on the Prime Minister. 'It was,' she said, 'an assault on her office and attitudes.'

She returned to Delhi in a grim, defiant mood. I could feel the brooding. Her political advisers offered their suggestions, but she kept her options open and refused to reveal her mind.

There was something special in the manner in which Indira Gandhi confronted a major crisis. As the assault against her increased in velocity, she instinctively avoided any reflexive reaction or confrontation, waited till the energy of the attack had abated and her opponents felt a false sense of security, certain that they had outwitted the Prime Minister.

While she turned inward, her ear was open, tuned in to remarks which otherwise would have gone unnoticed. She observed people's faces, their glances, their gestures—out of this conservation of her resources, when the time was right, she struck when it was least expected. Her action flew straight as an arrow and was lethal.

Suddenly, one morning, the newspapers announced that Morarji Desai had been relieved of the Ministry of Finance though he was asked to continue as Deputy Prime Minister. Indira had decided to keep the Finance portfolio with herself. Deeply aggrieved, Morarji Desai refused to accept any other portfolio and sent in his resignation. Bank nationalization was announced within days of Morarji Desai's resignation. It was met by wide acclaim all over the country. Crowds gathered at the Prime Minister's House to hail her action.

When I saw Indira briefly at this time, she looked amazingly alive. 'They had driven me to the wall; some decisive action was necessary.' She appeared genuinely sorry about Morarji Desai. 'He had to be sacrificed. I could have done it over the business of his son (stories of corruption surrounding Morarjibhai's son were widely prevalent) but I did not want him to go out like that. It is really Chavan who should have gone. Morarji Desai is straight and direct and says what he feels; Chavan is devious.'[1] She spoke of Congress slogans on the removal of poverty.

> Poverty is not an abstraction. It means physical things—food, clothing, a roof over one's head. We have to get down to concrete action. Bank nationalisation was inevitable if Communism had to be stopped. The business community don't understand that there is no alternative, the extreme Right position has just no place in India. The whole mood of the country is Centre Left.[2]

For nearly two-and-a-half years Indira had awaited her opportunity, permitted the press and the public to feel that she had no will of her own, that she was being pushed around. Romesh Thapar, commenting in the *Economic and Political Weekly,* wrote:

> Everyone in the capital is asking the same question: What persuaded Indira Gandhi to choose this moment to launch her ferocious and sustained assault on the men who have been trying to hold her captive. The nationalisation of the leading banks of the country marks the opening of an entirely new phase in the country's development.[3]

I.G. Patel, who was then Secretary Economic Affairs, in the Finance Ministry, and was regarded as a Morarji Desai man, was very upset with the turn of events. The Prime Minister came to know of his feelings and he was called in to see her the next day. She asked whether he wished to leave the government. I.G. Patel replied: 'It is true, I am upset, but I have no intention of leaving the government unless my bona fides are doubted. In that case I have no place.' The Prime Minister replied: 'I have no reason to doubt you,' and asked him to stay on as Economic Affairs Secretary. Just as he was leaving, he asked her hesitantly how long she proposed to keep the Finance portfolio. He hoped she did not mind his asking her that question. She said, 'No, not at all,' but did not reveal her mind. A few days later she said to him:

> Morarji Desai knew something about Finance, I know nothing. I have taken this portfolio because the Prime Minister of India should understand the economic problems of the country and also know how to com-prehend the budget. So it is up to you to see how soon I can achieve this.

She asked him to send her the most detailed briefs.[4]

She had to answer questions in Parliament on Finance every Tuesday and Friday. She would send for her financial advisers, insist that they go to her at 9.00 a.m. and go over every question in detail. To meet the difficult economic situation prevalent, a tough Budget had to be presented in 1969. I.G. Patel wrote the speech she would have to deliver as Finance Minister. She did not change a word of it nor did she compromise or announce any concessions in spite of all kinds of pressures from Members of Parliament. It was clear by now that she was in complete control of the political situation in India.

FIVE

Indira Gandhi signed the nomination papers for Neelam Sanjiva Reddy. Vice-President V.V. Giri had also staked his claim for the Presidency as an independent candidate, and the Opposition parties had fielded C.D. Deshmukh, a former Finance Minister, as their candidate.

The election of the President was through an electoral college composed of Members of Parliament and Members of the State Legislative Assemblies. Aware that Indira Gandhi was mortified at the choice of a President without her consent, Nijalingappa, nervous of the outcome, made the fatal mistake of seeking support for Sanjiva Reddy from the Jana Sangh and the Swatantra Party, both right-wing parties of the Opposition. Indira seized the opportunity. She claimed that Nijalingappa's action was a betrayal of Congress policies and came out in favour of a free 'conscience vote'. Both sides realized that the point of crisis had come; they started assessing their strength. The old stalwarts, Morarji Desai, S.K. Patil, Atulya Ghosh and Nijalingappa, canvassed vigorously in favour of Sanjiva Reddy. D.P. Misra, Chief Minister of Madhya Pradesh, was on the side of the Prime Minister, so were the 'Young Turks' within the Congress party. The election was to be held on 20 August, her son Rajiv Gandhi's birthday. Wild rumours were spread all over the country that Giri would lose. When Indira heard of this, she said: 'That may be the end. I may have to go.'[1]

I met her on 14 August, on the eve of her Independence Day speech at the Red Fort. She had just returned from a stormy meeting of the Executive Board of the Congress Parliamentary Party. Tarkeshwari Sinha, one of Morarji Desai's staunchest supporters, launched a major attack against Indira in which she accused her of betraying the Congress party and demanded a change of leadership within the Lok Sabha. Voices were raised. Indira supporters refused to listen to Tarkeshwari and the buxom lady from Bihar was in tears. Indira seemed a little shaken and was not quite certain about the votes Giri would get in the Presidential election. We talked of her speech at the Red Fort the next morning. She said that she would like her speech to be a gentle one, avoiding any controversy and embracing all aspects of the country. It was an important moment and perhaps her father's speech at the moment of independence could be a central point. Romesh Thapar came in at this point. He was very confident and felt that Giri would win with a big majority. According to him 250 MPs had signed for the free vote, but she was cautious, said 'people are too optimistic; the figure is much less, the position is very fluid.'

The leaders of Indira's group were confident that Giri would win on the first count, but not so certain of victory if neither Sanjiva Reddy nor Giri got the required majority and a second count was to be held. The second preference votes of the third candidate, CD. Deshmukh, would be distributed between Reddy and Giri and it was likely that Reddy would get a majority.

I listened in on the radio as the results started coming in on the evening of 20 August. Giri had not won on the first count. There was wild rejoicing amongst K. Kamaraj's group; as they thought that victory was theirs. I got into the car and went to the Prime Minister's House. The second count had begun. Her staff were very depressed. I was about to return home when they asked me whether I would like to meet the Prime Minister. I had thought that she would be in Parliament, but she was in her room. I found her listening to Beethoven and eating an omelette. I was with her for half an hour. I said the second count would mean the defeat of Giri. She smiled and said, 'Probably. Don't be low, Pupul. It will mean a tough fight, but I am ready.'[2] I received a telephone call some time after midnight from one of her staff members to inform me that Giri had won the Presidential election. I was with her the next morning. She was anxious to play her victory in a low key, but could not suppress a smile. 'The old guard feels disinherited.' I joined her for breakfast, 'So far you have needed courage, now you will need great wisdom.' Her response was, 'The crisis has only now begun.'

The Congress party had come to a parting of the ways. The Congress structure had survived for nearly a hundred years, continually transforming itself as events and situations in the country changed, but this time around it hadn't proved nearly as flexible as the situation required. It was the first major break the Congress had faced.

Indira had learnt to position herself correctly. She was prepared to continually move, adjust, change her role. It was impossible for her to function in the country as Prime Minister and bring in the changes she intended without the support of the party. She was determined, therefore, to capture the organization. She began touring the states, spoke of change. A signature campaign had started to elect a new President of the Congress party in place of Nijalingappa who had, according to the dissidents, lost the trust of most Congressmen. Both sides were adamant. The vested interests in India who had seen bank nationalization as a major assault on their positions were convinced that her moves were directed to bring in a Communist ideology. They pointed to the fact that the Marxists were in power in West Bengal and Kerala and the Naxalites were spreading terror in West Bengal.

The confrontation between the Prime Minister and the strongmen of the Congress party had reached a point of no return. A split in the party had become inevitable and yet Indira hesitated. From 1966 she had observed the way political forces operated in the country. She had carefully assessed the strongmen within the Congress, and seen that in their thirst for power they had allowed their political antennae to grow blunted. Intuitively Indira Gandhi knew that, to establish her authority as Prime Minister, she could no longer compromise on any major issue. The confrontation between the Prime Minister's position and the Congress party and its President had to be resolved, but unity talks still continued.

In the midst of the talks a sudden demand was made by her supporters to requisition a special meeting of the All-India Congress Committee (AICC) to elect a new Congress President. Nijalingappa, shattered by the defeat of the Congress candidate in the Presidential election, wrote an open letter to the Prime Minister accusing her of plotting to destroy democracy within the Congress party. To place the Prime Minister at a disadvantage, he hit out at Indira by dismissing two of Indira's close associates—Fakhruddin Ali Ahmed and C. Subramaniam from the AICC. Indira's response was to refuse to attend the meeting called by Nijalingappa.

1 November 1969 saw two meetings of the Congress Working Committee (CWC) take place at the same time—one in the home of the Prime Minister and the other at the Congress office at Jantar Mantar Road. The Congress strongmen still felt that Indira Gandhi's power within the party was minimal and that strong action on their part would remove her from the political scene. After the meeting presided over by Nijalingappa, an announcement was made expelling Indira from the primary membership of the Congress on the ground

that she had revolted against the Congress party decision. The Resolution read:

> The Congress is regrettably obliged to remove Mrs. Gandhi from the primary membership of the Congress organisation for her deliberate action of defiance.

It went on to say that,

> with Mrs. Gandhi ceasing to be a member, Mrs. Gandhi ceases to be the leader of the Congress party in Parliament and the Working Committee directs the Congress party in Parliament to take necessary steps immediately to elect a new leader.

Indira Gandhi had joined the Congress in 1938. To face expulsion from the party was something which hurt her deeply. But she showed no emotion when the notice reached her. She was aware that if she and her colleagues accepted the expulsion, she would automatically cease to be leader of the Parliamentary Party and so cease to be Prime Minister. She was quick to react and immediately called a meeting of the Congress Members of Parliament. Both sides claimed that they were the authentic Congress. Throughout the night frantic efforts were made to contact and win the support of members of the Parliamentary Party. When the meetings took place, 310 out of 429 Congress members of both Houses of Parliament attended Indira's meeting. To maintain their separate identities, Indira's Congress came to be known as Congress (R) and Nijalingappa's Congress as Congress (O). After a hundred years the Congress party that had battled the British, won freedom, survived innumerable crises, continued to hold within its ambit members of totally opposed political and economic views, had split. The Congress would never be the same again.

With the split in the party, Indira had lost her majority in both Houses of Parliament. To maintain her prime ministership she sought support from a medley of parties which included the Communist Party of India (CPI), the Dravida Munnetra Kazhagam (DMK) of Tamil Nadu and various independent members. The Congress (O)'s attempt to bring a motion of no-confidence against her failed.

SIX

In the elections held in 1967, the Swatantra Party with members drawn from the princely community, industrialists and extreme right-wing activists, proved to be a powerful force. Some of the princes had stood for elections to the Lok Sabha and won many of the seats. The majority of the Congress in the Lok Sabha fell dramatically. In the state elections held at the same time, eight states were lost to the Congress.

With the split in the Congress in 1969, Indira Gandhi's minority government was under great pressure from the 'Young Turks', a ginger group within Indira's party, to take action against the princes by abolishing their privy purses and privileges. Indira knew she had to bend with the wind or break. Negotiations with the Concord of Princes, an organization set up by the princes two years earlier, to negotiate a settlement had reached an impasse. The chief spokesman on behalf of the princes was the Maharaja of Dhrangadhra, a suave, highly intelligent negotiator with skills of repartee that delighted the Prime Minister.

The abolition of the princes' privy purses would mean an amendment to the Constitution, for which Indira Gandhi needed a majority of two-thirds of the votes in both the Houses of the Parliament. The Bill to abolish the privileges of the former rulers was introduced in the Lok Sabha in August 1970. It was passed by a two-thirds majority on 2 September. But, when the bill went to the Rajya Sabha, the government lost the two-thirds majority by a single vote. The princes and the Opposition were jubilant. The same evening, after an emergency meeting of the Cabinet, Indira Gandhi got a Presidential proclamation issued, de-recognizing the princes; with this withdrawal of recognition, their claim to privy purses vanished into thin air.

On 30 December, the day before the administrative order depriving the princes of their privileges was issued, the Prime Minister met the Maharaja of Dhrangadhra. They were friends and there was nostalgia in the meeting. After a while, the Prime Minister asked:

Was this inevitable?'

'It is not for me to say. The answer is in your patch,' responded Dhrangadhra.

The Prime Minister smiled.

'So be it,' said the prince. 'Let us now change the conversation. Let us speak of cabbages if not kings.'[1]

The old Congress opposition which had joined hands with the conservative Swatantra Party and the right-wing Jana Sangh, had not given up its plans to remove Indira as Prime Minister. Large industrial business houses, right-wing politicians, princes, and that part of the media controlled by industrial barons claimed that Indira was intent on turning India into a Communist state. The banks had been nationalized, the princes' position was in danger. The Naxalite movement was gaining ascendancy. In West Bengal the law and order situation was causing deep concern. It was in this situation that Indira's Intelligence agencies reported the possibility of the army staging a coup. Gossip was rampant in Bombay, Delhi and Calcutta that such a coup was imminent. General S.H.F.J. Manekshaw, then Commander-in-Chief of the Indian Army, commented that everywhere he went, he was being asked, 'When are you taking over?' Among those asking the question were some of Indira Gandhi's ministers. One afternoon General Manekshaw got a telephone call. It was the Prime Minister on the line: she said, 'Sam, are you very busy?'

He was a friend and joked with her on the telephone. She asked him to go over and he did. 'I had known her for a very long time,' he said. 'She was a supreme actress. I could see that she had assumed a role to meet me. She was sitting at her kidney-shaped table, with her hands supporting her head. I asked:

"What is the problem, Prime Minister, you look very harassed?"

"I have so many problems," she replied.

"What are your problems?" I asked. "Why don't you cry on my shoulder and tell me?"

She looked straight into my eyes, "You are my problem."

"Oh," I said. "Now what have I done?"

"Are you trying to take over from me?" '

That shook Manekshaw for some seconds. Recovering, he walked across and faced her.

'What do you think?' he asked.

'You can't,' she said.

'Do you think I am so incompetent?'

'No, Sam. But you won't,' she replied.

Manekshaw then said:

'You know I have no political ambitions. My job is to command my army and see that it is kept as a first rate instrument. Your job is to look after the country.'

'My Ministers are saying that a military coup will take place.'

'You appointed Ministers. Get rid of them. You must have trust in me. If not, find someone else. I am not here to be bullied.'

'Who bullies you?' she asked.

'No one does, but . . .'

Manekshaw could see that she was very worried. 'She had so many political enemies. There were plots against her.'[2]

Hemmed in, she felt that the forces which had gathered together to destroy her could only gather strength in the future months and that a minority government, dependent solely on the support of the Left parties, would not survive. A mid-term election was inevitable. It was at this moment—aware that power and money lay in the hands of business houses and the right-wing elements within the political system—that she took a lonely decision to go over the heads of the entrenched political leadership and directly contact the people of the country. Intuitively she was aware that they would support her. On 27 December, she went to the President and asked him to dissolve the Lok Sabha and announce fresh elections to be held in February 1971.

Both sides knew that it would be a crucial election; the stakes were very high. The great powers were using the influence of money and men to determine the outcome of the elections. The Opposition had one election slogan throughout India: "Indira *Hatao*" (Remove Indira). They had made her removal the central issue. She refused to reduce the election to a personal matter and her response was the slogan: *"Garibi Hatao"* (Remove Poverty). In the forty-three days of her election tour she travelled over 36,000 miles and addressed over 300 meetings. About thirteen million people attended the meetings and another seven million lined the roads. At meeting after meeting Indira was hailed.

The voice of the Indian people raised in unison takes the place of the chorus in Greek tragedy. They see events unfold; foretell victory or defeat; record the blind movements of individuals thwarting the incoming tide and so being swept by forces beyond their control to their inevitable destiny. Indira Gandhi rarely ate, rarely slept. People flocked to her, grew aware of her determination, her courage, her sense of responsibility. They felt a sense of protectiveness in her presence. They were aware that she could fight like a tigress for the people and the country. Their eyes lit up when they saw her. It was a triumphant Indira who returned after the election campaign to await the results.

I was present at the Prime Minister's residence on the evening the election results started coming in. The house was ablaze with light. 150 million people had voted. The trend soon became clear. Indira's Congress was leading all over the country. Cars with visitors were driving in and out of the gate; flowers and sweets were everywhere. The Prime Minister was flitting in and out of the study where we were sitting. A small sitting-room, left of the entrance, was soon crowded with people. Telephones were ringing. Dogs walking in and out. Her sons were present and so were her two grandchildren, the baby, Priyanka, and Rahul. Indira tried her best to suppress her delight. She had triumphed, defeated her opponents; the Opposition was in a shambles. When the final results were declared, Indira had won by a two-thirds majority in the Lok Sabha.

PART V
1971–1974

In Sumerian, the word for ear and wisdom is the same. The ear, which is located mostly internally and is coiled like a spiral or labyrinth, takes in sounds and begins to transform the imperceptible into meaning.

–Inanna–Queen of Heaven and Earth[1]

If Sophia is generically what we mean by wisdom, it is also skill, craft, cleverness, know how and the specific craft of expedience.

–The Bacchae[2]

ONE

The partition of the Indian sub-continent in 1947 saw the nation state of Pakistan emerge fragmented into two distinct parts: to the west Punjab, Sind and Baluchistan, to the east the Muslim sector of East Bengal. In between them lay a thousand miles of India. Islam provided a common religion to Pakistan but the cultural background: heritage, language, poetry, songs, customs and the emotional and psychological ethos, lacked a warp thread to bind them into one. Communications between the twin sectors of Pakistan were difficult. With a military dictatorship centred in West Pakistan, power was frozen in the hands of the army chiefs, bureaucrats, businessmen and the landed gentry who ruled the country from the west, with little regard for their eastern compatriots.

In the Parliamentary elections held in India in February 1971, the Indira Gandhi-led Congress party was swept back to power with an overwhelming two-thirds majority. In the midst of the euphoria of her victory—the distribution of portfolios to her Cabinet, the drawing up of a new agenda for the country—the Prime Minister's attention was diverted from events at India's doorstep.

It was in December 1970, before India held elections, that Pakistan's President, Yahya Khan, surprised the world by calling for free and fair elections to the national assembly. The President appeared supremely unaware of the depth of resentment that the people of East Pakistan had against the arrogance and domination of the rulers of Pakistan. He expected to retain his own power through the inability of any other single party to obtain a clear majority. To his horror, the Awami League of East Pakistan, under the leadership of Sheikh Mujib-ur Rehman, won not only ninety-nine per cent of the seats in East Pakistan, but ended with an overall majority in the Pakistan national assembly. Sheikh Mujib-ur Rehman staked his claim for Prime Ministership. President Yahya Khan, the army and the bureaucracy refused to consider the democratic rights of their fellow Pakistanis. Zulfikar Ali Bhutto, leader of the Peoples Party of Pakistan (PPP), joined hands with the President to resist any move on the part of the Awami League to seize power.

The election and its results had unleashed forces that made a confrontation between East and West Pakistan imminent. Negotiations between the two dominions of Pakistan on the issue of autonomy to East Pakistan were still active, when on 25 March, swiftly, without warning, an army of 40,000 West Pakistani soldiers descended on East Pakistan.

A systematic reign of terror was unleashed, to quench all revolt. Hindu and Muslim writers, artists, philosophers, thinkers, student leaders and university teachers from both the left and the right were indiscriminately slaughtered. Mujib was arrested and airlifted to a jail in West Pakistan. Hindus were killed mercilessly. United States' estimates of the killings during this period range from 50,000 to three million. In spite of strict censorship, reports of inhuman brutality, rape, torture and murder appeared in the world press. Even 'children did not escape the horror: the lucky ones were killed with their parents; but many thousands of others must go through what life-remained for them with eyes gouged and limbs roughly amputated.'[3] This brutality was to continue relentlessly for over six months.

With the ruthless energy of an incoming tide, women, children and men, the aged and the very young, crossed the frontier to seek shelter in the Indian province of West Bengal. A massive wave of sympathy was generated in India for a ravaged people that less than twenty-five years ago were compatriots. Amongst the East Bengal refugees who escaped were political leaders who had worked under Mujib. The Awami leaders announced the formation of a government in exile in Calcutta with Tajuddin Ahmad as its head.

Indira Gandhi, with an instinct that rarely betrayed her in those early years, sensed that these developments would inevitably lead to war between India and Pakistan. There was a question whether the major powers would become involved. With her capacity to view events in perspective, linked with her meticulous planning skills, she summoned her advisers and laid out her priorities. The organizational structure for the refugee camps and the provision of primal necessities of food, shelter and clothing were entrusted to senior bureaucrats. She knew the volatile reactions of the Indian people and the danger of communal riots. To minimize these threats she made efforts through consultations with the Opposition, daily briefings of the press and contacts with chief ministers, to build an atmosphere in which the people of India would be prepared to view the refugee influx with sympathy and face a dangerous future with an open mind.

On 25 April, the Commander-in-Chief of the Indian Army, S.H.F.J. Manekshaw, was summoned to a Cabinet meeting. He found the Prime Minister in a rage.

'Do you know what is happening in East Pakistan?'

'Yes, there are killings,' Manekshaw replied.

'I have telegrams from the Chief Ministers of Tripura, Manipur, Assam, Bengal, refugees are pouring in. You must stop them. If necessary, move into East Pakistan but stop them.'

'You know that means war.'

'I don't mind if it is war,' said the Prime Minister.[4]

The General then explained the dangers. The monsoons were about to break—troop movements would be confined to roads; the rest of the land would be marshy, and the rivers would become like oceans. 'The Air Force will not be able to operate. I will be tied down.' He told the Prime Minister that in such a situation they could not win a war. Large contingents of troops were held in West Bengal, to check the Naxalites. It would take him one-and-a-half months to bring them together—they would have to be re-trained.

'Harvesting has started in Punjab and Haryana. If the country goes to war in harvest time, I will have to take over all the roads, all the horses, for troop movements. If food cannot be transported, there will be famine.' He then spoke of the danger China posed. The passes would open in the next few days. 'If the Chinese give us an ultimatum, what do we do?'

'The Prime Minister was getting redder and redder in the face. She postponed the meeting till 4 p.m., asked me (Manekshaw) to stay back.' He asked her whether, in the light of what he had said, she wanted his resignation. 'But I have to tell you the truth.'

'All right, Sam; go ahead—I trust you.'[5]

And from that time on, the Prime Minister and the Commander-in-Chief worked in the closest harmony. She did not allow anyone to interfere between them.

I.G. Patel, then Principal Secretary in the Finance Ministry, was summoned by the Prime Minister. She wanted to know 'whether we have the power of sustaining ourselves if the Americans go against us?' I.G. Patel replied, 'For the first time we have a thousand crores in foreign exchange reserves and foodgrains are in our granary. The country would not collapse if we have to sustain ourselves for the next five or six months.'[6]

Indira returned from a visit to the refugee camps in Assam, Tripura and Bengal to address the Lok Sabha, on 24 May. About three-and-a-half million refugees had crossed over to India in eight weeks. They belonged to every religion—Hindus, Buddhists, Muslims, Christians. They came from every social class and age-group. Indira said: 'So massive a migration in so short a time is unprecedented in recorded history. . . . They are not refugees— they are victims of war who have sought refuge from the military terror across the frontier.' Many of the refugees were badly wounded. Special teams of physicians, surgeons and nurses were deputed to the camps.

> Every available building, including schools and training institutions, have been requisitioned, thousands of tents have been pitched and temporary shelters constructed and 335 camps established so far.
>
> We have sought, to awaken the conscience of the world through our representatives abroad and the repre-sentatives of foreign governments in India. We have ap-pealed to the United Nations and at long last the true dimensions seem to be making themselves felt.[7]

The members of the Lok Sabha were united in their support for the East Bengal victims. They urged the Prime Minister to act swiftly.

Aware that unplanned, immediate action could lead to chaos, the Prime Minister remarked: 'To some members guts are equated with voice power and the use of passionate words. I wish life was so simple.'

She refused to accept the immediate demand for recognition of Bangladesh, the name the government-in-exile had given East Pakis-tan in the event of its becoming independent. She assured the House that every aspect of the situation, internal and external, was under constant review. She insisted that the problem of the refugees was an international one and the burden of their support should be borne by the international community. Some members of the Lok Sabha taunted her about reaching out to the nations of the world with a begging bowl. 'I am not in the habit of begging,' she responded, 'I have never begged. I have no intention of begging now.'

*

Prime Minister Indira Gandhi was fortunate in having strong, able advisers. D.P. Dhar was the head of the Policy Planning Committee and her main adviser, P.N. Haksar, her Principal Secretary. P.N. Dhar was next-in-command. T.N. Kaul was Foreign Secretary and L.K. Jha was India's Ambassador to the United States. A few months earlier the Prime Minister had approached Jha to accept the Ambassador-ship. He was hesitant as he was not a diplomat and his friends in the United States belonged to the Democratic Party which was out of power at that time. Indira responded: 'The fact is that you know the academics, business community, the media people; that is what is important and I want you to cultivate them. That is the surest way of strengthening Indo-US relations.'[8]

Jha found on his arrival in the United States that Henry Kissinger went out of his way to be friendly, possibly on the instructions of President Richard Nixon, despite Nixon's strong antipathy towards India. Jha's brief was to build bridges, but it soon became evident that the scales were sharply tilted against India, because of President Nixon's intense dislike for Indians and particularly for Indira Gandhi. President Nixon felt that Indian public opinion was pro-Kennedy and anti-Nixon. From his first meeting with Indira Gandhi in New Delhi, Nixon had returned to the United States angry. There was something in her manner, an austere distancing, that brought to the fore an-tagonistic feelings, a visceral feeling of dislike for India and its Prime Minister.

The tilt towards Pakistan was born of this strong emotion. It assumed the status of national policy when President Nixon achieved a breakthrough to China with Pakistan's help. Pakistan played a key role as the intermediary in softening China's attitude towards the US and it was Pakistan that was to act as the conduit for all future talks between the two powers. Close ties with Pakistan were integral to US policy in South-East Asia.

I visited the United States towards the end of May and went to see the Prime Minister before I left. She was troubled. 'The situation is very dangerous. You know a great many people in the U.S.A.—

writers, artists, thinkers—they are the decision makers. They will ask you what will happen to the refugee problem. I would like you to answer on the authority of the Prime Minister of India, that in one year there will not be a single refugee on Indian soil.'

Articles on the genocide, the tortures and the unspeakable horrors of happenings in East Bengal appeared in the world press. The response of the media and the public in the US was cataclysmic. Editorial comments were strong and critical of the US President's soft attitude to Pakistan and stressed the urgency of immediate diplomatic action to solve the crisis before it led to war. Writers, poets, musicians, philosophers and other members of the intelligentsia were united in their strong condemnation of Pakistan; schoolchildren came forward to offer their services and money to help the refugees. In France, André Malraux, who had fought in Spain during the Spanish Civil War, offered to take up arms to defend the cause of the Mukti Bahini, the guerrilla fighters in East Pakistan (which was increasingly being called Bangladesh by the international press). A huge concert with the Indian sitar maestro Ravi Shankar and former Beatle, George Harrison, was organized to raise funds for refugee relief. Allen Ginsberg, the premier poet of the Beat movement, who had visited India in the 1960s and had many friends in Bengal, captured a moment in "September on Jessore Road":

> *Millions of babies watching the skies*
> *Bellies swollen, with big round eyes*
> *on Jessore Road. . .*
> *Millions of fathers in rain*
> *Millions of mothers in pain*
> *Millions of brothers in woe*
> *Millions of sisters nowhere to go. . .*[9]

Jayaprakash Narayan, a fiery product of the freedom movement, hailed as a hero second only to Jawaharlal Nehru during the 'Quit India' movement of 1942, travelled to world capitals in order to awaken the people abroad to the atrocities being perpetrated in East Bengal. On his return he met Indira Gandhi and urged her to act immediately with strength and invade East Bengal. World opinion, he said, would support her. She listened silently but refused to respond or give any firm commitment. Jayaprakash Narayan organized a world conference in New Delhi to condemn the tortures and genocide continuing in East Bengal, but the Prime Minister instinctively felt that her party's participation in such a conference would narrow her options. She issued instructions to the Congress party to avoid attending the conference. Jayaprakash Narayan was livid. 'What does Indira think of herself? Does she think she can ignore me? I have seen her as a child in frocks.'[10] His outburst reached Indira and it became increasingly difficult for Narayan to get an appointment to see her. Indira did not want a confrontation with him. She was also not prepared to reveal her plans, nor was she willing to give Jayaprakash Narayan the central position as the spokesman for India on Bangladesh.

The late Ganga Saran Sinha, a close friend of both Jayaprakash and Indira said:

> I have always felt that from that time Jayaprakash and Indiraji did not trust each other politically. Whatever I said to Indiraji, she felt I was saying it on behalf of J.P. On the other hand, when I spoke to J.P., he felt I was voicing Indira's views. It was very unfortunate.[11]

*

Regiments of the East Bengal Rifles, the East Pakistan Army and the police, who had rebelled against the Pakistan Army were part of the exodus to India. Within days of their arrival on Indian soil they established camps and organized themselves into the Mukti Bahini. Volunteers were selected from amongst the refugee students and were trained by the East Bengal regiments. With the outbreak of the monsoons all paths in the area of hostilities were washed away and the fields became quagmires. Indira visited the refugee camps in pouring rain. She saw that the deluge of refugees continued; liquid-eyed, dark, starving women and men, children and babies, old women and men, carried on the backs of their sons, waded through flooded fields, crossed rivers and at times stood for hours in mud and slush as there was no dry ground on which they could sit.

News reached the Prime Minister on 9 August, that an increasingly beleaguered President Yahya Khan had decided to start a secret military trial of Sheikh Mujib-ur Rehman, without affording him independent legal assistance. The threat to Mujib's life was clear. Addressing a public rally at India Gate on the evening of 9 August, Indira Gandhi spoke with anguish and passion:

> The path ahead is steep and hard. We are a nation of poor, illiterate people, but we shall show the world that no power on earth can intimidate or subdue this country. We know it is only weak nations who are unsure of their own strength that resort to abuse and threat and demonstr-ation of military might.

The day President Nixon was to announce to the world that Secretary of State, Henry Kissinger, had visited China and established his first contact, Jha got a message from Kissinger. He was out at the time and a security guard who hardly knew any English informed Jha, 'Ambassador Sahib *Bahadur ke liye* Kishan Chanderji *ka* phone *aya tha.'* (A phone message came from Kishan Chanderji for the honourable Ambassador). Jha was puzzled, asked his Secretary to call the number left with the security guard. Kissinger (Kishan Chanderji) came on the line. He was in Los Angeles at the St. Clement White House. Kissinger asked, 'Where will you be at 8.30 tonight?' L.K. Jha said he would be out to dinner. Kissinger took the number and said that he would ring up at 8.30 that night. He would not say what it was about. Everything was very hush-hush. Jha himself answered the phone at 8.30. Kissinger was on the line: 'In half-an-hour the President is going to broadcast that I have been to China on the trip when I went to India and Pakistan. You will hear the details on the broadcast. The President wants you to convey the following message to your Prime Minister. Don't take it down—I will repeat it for you.'

The. message was that President Nixon was going to establish relations with China and if India opposed the move, he would deem it an unfriendly act. President Nixon had taken it for granted that India would oppose the move.[12]

Jha's report of the imminent China–US alignment and Pakistan's role as a conduit between the two nations had escalated the dangers for India. A belligerent US–Pakistan–China triangle could threaten

India's integrity. Swiftly, Indira Gandhi acted. Messengers were sent to the Soviets and the Indo-Soviet Treaty of Peace, Friendship and Cooperation, long on the anvil but held in abeyance, was signed by mid-August. It came as a bombshell to the US and confirmed President Nixon's obsessive belief that the Soviets were advising India to declare war, invade East Pakistan, liberate Bangladesh and destroy the Pakistan Army in the west. The President saw in the treaty a decision on Soviet Russia's part to humiliate China.

Meanwhile, secret reports of increasing unrest in the refugee camps, which could lead to insoluble law and order problems, were reaching Indira through her secret services. By September ten million refugees had arrived on Indian soil. Most of the refugee camps were within a few miles of Calcutta. The Naxalites were active in the refugee camps. So were subversives who had entered India with the refugees. 'The Naxalites saw in the situation the beginning of a revolution in India.' Gita Mehta, author and journalist, had visited the refugee camps in August and was told that the Naxalites were assaulting people who were distributing food and other amenities to the refugees. 'The intention appeared to be to force the ten million people to march on Calcutta. The Naxalites thought that the historical moment was right, it could be the beginning of the Long March. If Calcutta had to absorb ten million starving people, it would have unleashed an explosion.'[13]

On 2 September, the Prime Minister visited Moscow. She held long talks with President Aleksei Kosygin which continued till two in the morning. The Soviets were sympathetic and responsive. A joint statement was released, which emphasized the great economic and political burden India had to bear with the influx of the refugees.

The East Bengal forces were ready for action by the end of August and started to infiltrate back into East Bengal. Volunteers from amongst the Mukti Bahini, marine officers and other accomplished swimmers, were selected to enter the waters around the ports of Chittagong and Jalna and sow mines. Fifty thousand tonnes of Pakistan shipping were sunk at the ports. This ensured that Pakistan was unable to send any further forces and war supplies to East Bengal by sea.[14]

Even though they were disorganized, the Mukti Bahini set up cells in a vast number of villages. This led to an escalation of the assaults against the Pakistan Army. With the ports blockaded, it was becoming extremely difficult to bring in new troops or supplies to East Bengal. President Yahya Khan lost his nerve. He sent frantic messages to the US President, asking him to intervene and pressurize the United Nations to despatch observers to keep watch on both sides of the frontiers of India with East Bengal. This would divert attention from the refugees, make it impossible for the Mukti Bahini forces to start any major operation in East Bengal, increase India's already intolerable burdens and make the country vulnerable. What the President of Pakistan desired was to 'freeze the status quo.'

A decade later, in an interview for the *Washington Post,* Jonathan Power asked Indira Gandhi what had enabled her to withstand the pressures of the Indo-Pakistan war. Indira's response was that it was Hindu philosophy and a deep commitment to India.

Power: And what is this Hindu philosophy which outside is often regarded as passive and acquiescent?

Gandhi: No, it isn't. It just faces reality. It's something that gives you an inner strength. I don't get uptight, as the Americans would say. In a situation of war you must face the situation as it comes. You give it your all. You do your very best. That's all you can do. You can't do better than that, and then you shouldn't be bothered about the rest.

Power: You said when you were talking with Mr. Nixon you found small talk difficult.

Gandhi: I don't like small talk. There are a lot of interesting things happening in the world and this is not small talk. I did not know whether the President was interested in any of the things which were happening in India or what India is.

Power: I know that you have been racing around the country getting absolutely exhausted, and yet here you are the next day fresh as a daisy, totally relaxed.

Gandhi: Because I am an Indian, I think.

Power: I can see why you got on Nixon's nerves.

Indira Gandhi's response was typical.

> *Gandhi:* You know there was that Peter Sellers film, *The Party*? In that film Peter Sellers was an Indian. He was always putting his foot in it, extremely foolish but very lovable. It's all about film people. The director is saying to this poor girl, "If you go to bed with me I'll give you the part." Peter Sellers barges into the middle of this. The director grabs hold of him and says, "Who do you think you are?" Sellers replies, "Indians don't think. We know who we are."[15]

It was in this state of mind that Prime Minister Indira Gandhi visited the major capitals of Europe towards the end of October. Everywhere she went the Heads of Government expressed their great sympathy for the refugees and for the burdens India was called upon to bear. They promised financial help, but were unwilling to take any initiative against Pakistan. Kissinger's secret diplomacy had introduced more complexity into an already tangled situation. The international community advised India to be patient and suggested that she should accept UN observers and find a peaceful solution.

In her various interviews to the press, Indira Gandhi said, 'I think that the more serious problem is not the confrontation on the border—but this constant effort of people in other countries to divert attention from what is the basic question.'

'Naturally,' she said, 'India will have to take whatever steps are necessary for the protection of the security of our borders and for the maintenance of our integrity and stability. This does not depend on what other Governments do or say.' She expressed her dismay on the lack of support for the demand that talks should commence between Sheikh Mujib-ur Rehman and the Pakistan High Command. She insisted that that was the only way of finding a peaceful solution to the problem.

During this period Prime Minister Indira Gandhi was interviewed by one of the British Broadcasting Corporation's (BBC's) toughest interviewers, Michael Charleston. He asked her why India was not prepared to accept the proposal for posting UN observers on both sides of the border, to defuse the situation. It was suggested that India needed to be patient. Indira flared up. Years later, I watched the interview on television. She had lost weight and in her face one saw Motilal Nehru's pugnacious jaw; it was the face of a formidable Prime Minister, angry-eyed, imperious. There was tenseness in her neck, the veins showed clearly through her translucent skin. Indira was angry and hit out at world leaders:

> Would the massacre have stopped? Would the rape have stopped? Does your question mean that we allow massacres to continue? Do you support genocide? Does your question mean that? There has been the worst possible violence. When Hitler was on the rampage, did you keep quiet—let Jews die?

> How do you control an exodus? If the world community had woken to the situation, would it not have stopped?[16]

She returned to India convinced that war was inevitable. She felt, however, that a visit to the US to meet President Nixon was essential to prove that she was open-minded and prepared to listen to the President before the situation escalated into war. She also wanted to thank the people of America for their support to the Bangladesh cause. It was December before Indira Gandhi could visit Washington. Five years had passed since her last visit, when as a shy, young Prime Minister, she had been welcomed with roses, to symbolize the growing warmth in Indo-US relationship. Her visit in 1971 was of another order. She was stern, determined, "as formidable as she was condescending." She hardly smiled throughout her visit.

The aides who had accompanied her to Washington were aware of her rage and were apprehensive about the outcome of the meeting between the President and the Prime Minister. She was quick to sense a slight condescension in the President's opening speech of welcome. He had referred sympathetically to recent floods that had devastated parts of India, but was silent on the main purpose of her visit. She responded:

> To the national calamities of drought, flood and cyclone
> has been added a man-made tragedy of vast proportions.
> I am haunted by the tormented faces in our overcrowded
> refugee camps reflecting the grim events which have com-

pelled the exodus of these millions from East Bengal. I have come here looking for a deeper understanding of the situation in our part of the world, in search of some wise impulse. . .[17]

The President and the Prime Minister met in the White House. The President refused to recognize the dimensions of the human tragedy being enacted in East Pakistan. In an attempt to transform the human problem into a political abstraction, he spoke of time frames and peace initiatives which, by their very nature, would make solutions increasingly difficult. Indira's outward demeanour remained icy in its withdrawal. There was in her a fierce pride, the sense that she was the head of a democratic country with a vast population, a country of the poor, yet with a millennia of civilization.

Kissinger, waiting with P.N. Haksar in the outer room, suggested that it was dangerous to leave the two Heads of State alone for a long time. So they went in and sat through the meeting. The President spoke uninterruptedly of his assessment of the situation. Indira listened without a single comment, creating an impregnable space so that no real contact was possible. To ease the situation, Kissinger joined in the conversation, suggesting various options—the posting of UN observers; a meeting between Prime Minister Indira Gandhi and President Yahya Khan; mild pressure to be used by the US to defuse the imminent conflict. Towards the end of the meeting Indira said that she would give thought to the many suggestions made, and give her reply the next day.

On the second day of the visit, Nixon made his annoyance clear. 'What had been Nixon's visceral dislike of ascetic Indians had been elevated to a personal vendetta against Indira Gandhi.' According to Seymour M. Hersh, the President kept Indira waiting in the anteroom for forty-five minutes before he appeared. If this report is true, one can well understand Indira's fury when the President and the Prime Minister met. It was the turn of Indira to talk. She decided to deliberately ignore any questions relating to the Indo-Pak dispute or suggest any solution to the refugee problem. Instead she spoke of Vietnam, praised Nixon's role and asked questions on the general world situation.[18] Obviously her refusal to respond to Nixon's suggestions of the previous day was, for the President, unforgiveable.

TWO

On 4 December, with time running out and no room left to manoeuvre, Indira Gandhi issued secret orders to the Indian armed forces to launch an all-out attack to liberate East Bengal. On the previous night, hoping to take India by surprise and to gain advantage of the full moon, President Yahya Khan ordered Pakistani aeroplanes to strike at five of India's main airbases.

Indira was in Calcutta at the time. She had addressed a public meeting in the evening and was later present at a gathering of writers, artists and literary personalities. Frantic efforts were made to contact her. It took two hours to locate the Prime Minister and give her the message. Her demeanour did not alter and she did not immediately react or end the meeting. That night she flew back to Delhi. The Pakistan Air Force was airborne and there was danger to the Prime Minister's plane. If identified, the plane could have been shot down. On landing, she told P.N. Dhar, Secretary in the Prime Minister's Office, that she had not been sure whether she would reach Delhi. She rushed immediately to the maproom, and was briefed on the Indian military preparedness and the damage to the air-fields.

A short while later, she attended a meeting of the Opposition leaders. Atal Behari Vajpayee, now one of the seniormost members of the Bharatiya Janata Party (BJP) and a Rajya Sabha member, remembers her 'as a picture of worry and concern' as she shared the news of the attack with the Opposition and informed them that she had issued orders for the Indian Army to march into Bangladesh. After midnight she spoke to the nation on the radio. Pakistan had launched a full-scale war against India, she said, and warned of the great perils that faced the nation.

Indian troops advanced rapidly into East Bengal. The Mukti Bahini had infiltrated deep into the East Bengal countryside, its village cells creating chaos and confusion amidst the Pakistani armed forces. The Pakistani Army was demoralized as the local population hailed the Indian troops as saviours.

With the commencement of war, the Prime Minister insisted on being briefed every morning. General S.H.F.J. Manekshaw would breakfast with the Prime Minister and let off steam. She would listen, be supportive. On the sixth day of the war the army got bogged down. The Commander-in-Chief reported to the Prime Minister the exact position; the number of casualties and the number of planes shot down. She asked questions, was cool and positive in her approach. 'But Sam, you can't win every day,' she said. They came out onto the porch; there was not a shade of anxiety on Indira's face as she shook hands with her Army Chief and responded to the victory calls from the people. 'Her courage was an inspiration.' Manekshaw went back to command headquarters, took measures to reverse the slide and the crisis was resolved. He phoned Indira Gandhi. She was in a Cabinet meeting, but took the call, thanked him for the news and went back to the meeting. As soon as she was free, she phoned Manekshaw and asked him to come over. 'I was so nervous,' she told him.[1]

On 6 December 1971, as the Indian Army approached Dhaka, Indira made a statement in Parliament, recognizing the independence of East Bengal, now Bangladesh. She spoke of how the people of Bangladesh, battling for their existence and the people of India fighting to defeat aggression,

> now find themselves partisans in the same cause. Our thoughts at this moment are with the father of this new State—Sheikh Mujib-ur Rehman. I am sure that this House would wish me to carry to their Excellencies the Acting President of Bangladesh and the Prime Minister and to their colleagues, our greetings and warm felicitations.[2]

From all sides and all parties she received massive support. They expressed complete and unshakable unity under her leadership. 'If President Yahya Khan thought that he was a General, Indira Gandhi represented,' they said, 'not only the velvet in the nation but also the steel and the granite in it.' She was likened to Durga, the invincible goddess who had defeated the demons in battle, fighting as a General on the Indian side.

Within a week of the war, the Pakistan High Command in Dhaka was ready to lay down arms. It was at this moment that President Richard Nixon acted against the advice of the State Department, and flying in the face of media and public opinion in the US, planned moves which could have led to a world conflagration. He saw in Prime

Minister Indira Gandhi's actions a devious Soviet plan; after victory in the East the Indian Army would turn West, invade West Pakistan, annex Pakistan-occupied areas of Kashmir and destroy the Pakistani armed forces. Nothing could deter him from this belief. Misreading the signals sent from China, and expecting China to enter the war on the side of Pakistan even at this late hour, Nixon ordered the US Seventh Fleet to move from Sulva Bay in the Philippines, towards the waters of the Indian Ocean. He had completely misunderstood the situation and the Soviet role.

L.K. Jha in Washington was the first Indian to hear news of these developments through a leak in the State Department of the White House. At first, he asked himself whether the leak was deliberate. Was the news conveyed to him inadvertently or purposely with the aim of intimidating India? He realized that if the US intended to attack India, then secrecy would help, but if the intention was to wage a psychological war, then the leak could be understood. He informed the Prime Minister immediately. He did not believe that US forces would invade Bangladesh. 'They might however aim at some bombardment, some rescue operation to evacuate the top Pakistan army officers.' Jha called a press conference immediately after he heard the news. Questioned on the refugees, his response was: 'If you ask me is America being neutral in this, then I will give you an answer—but I will not volunteer any news otherwise.' So the reporters asked him whether the United States was neutral in the situation that was developing. 'I believed that they would be neutral. I was assured that they would be neutral, but what I have heard today has disturbed me: The Seventh Fleet is moving towards the Bay of Bengal' The pressmen said, 'You cannot be serious—the USA cannot open another front in Asia after what is happening in Vietnam.'

'That was my calculation when I heard this,' was Jha's response. 'I went to the Assistant Secretary of State, Mr. Sisco, for confirmation or denial. He said, "I can neither confirm nor deny."'[3]

The press was agog. The next morning American newspapers attacked the US President and the Administration. Jha was summoned to the State Department and a message was read out to him. Obviously, it had come from Nixon, via Kissinger: 'The US Government finds it intolerable the way the Indian Ambassador uses the American media to attack the Administration.'

Jha's reply was:

> Look, if I have made a mistake, then throw me out. But I
> did not volunteer any information—I repeated my faith in
> the fact that America would remain neutral as promised.
> I only said I could get no denial from the State Department
> officials on news which came from India. The rest are the
> (comments) of your Press.[4]

The instant she heard the Ambassador's report that the Seventh
Fleet was heading for the Bay of Bengal, Prime Minister Indira
Gandhi rushed to the naval headquarters. Every possibility was
discussed. Her advisers felt that a marine invasion was unlikely
because of that country's involvement in the Vietnam war. It was
possible, however, that the Fleet could break through the blockade
of Chittagong and Khulna and subsequently land troops or fly
helicopters to evacuate Pakistani officers from Dhaka. It was also
likely that the move was intended to put psychological pressure on
the Indian High Command, demoralize India and force her to the
negotiating table before the Pakistan Army surrendered.

Orders were issued to the Indian Army, moving in for their final
assault on Dhaka, to divert their forces to the port cities of Chittagong
and Khulna. The Seventh Fleet was thirty-six hours sailing time from
the Bay of Bengal. Pressure was now mounted on the Indian forces
to ensure the surrender of Pakistani forces before the Seventh Fleet
reached the Bay of Bengal. As the morale of the Pakistani troops at
the ports was low, the Indian forces occupied the ports with ease and
destroyed the installations.

On 12 December, as news of the Seventh Fleet moving towards
India broke in the national press, Prime Minister Indira Gandhi
addressed a public rally at the Ram Lila grounds in New Delhi. Indian
fighter planes circled overhead to ensure that a sudden attack by the
Pakistan Air Force from the west did not threaten the gathering. She
had been advised to speak over the air, but she was insistent on
appearing in public. I listened to the proceedings on the radio. The
Prime Minister put aside her carefully prepared speech. I have rarely
heard her speak with such passionate intensity. Her voice rose to a
crescendo as she turned to the people: 'We will not retreat. Not by a

single step will we move back.'[5]

If the presence of the Seventh Fleet was meant to unnerve Indira and the Indian people, the strategy failed. The country rallied behind Indira Gandhi. A great anger against the United States swept the nation. Not since the freedom struggle had such strength been demonstrated. The President of the United States and his advisers were taken by surprise; they had not expected this response. The press in the US accused the President of forcing India into the Soviet sphere of influence. Kissinger is reported to have told State Department officials: 'The President wants the tilt towards Pakistan and those of you who do not agree, go and ask the President, don't ask me and don't tell me that we are throwing India into the lap of the Soviets. The lady is too tough to become anyone's stooge.'[6]

Henry Kissinger was correct in his assessment. On 15 December 1971, at a time when one wrong move could have led to an all-out war between the US, China and Pakistan on one side, and India and the Soviet Union on the other, Prime Minister Indira Gandhi wrote an open letter to President Nixon:

> I am writing at a moment of deep anguish at the unhappy turn which the relations between our two countries have taken.

> I am setting aside all pride, prejudice and passion and (am) trying, as calmly as I can, to analyse once again the origins of the tragedy which is being enacted.

> The tragic war, which is continuing, could have been averted if, during the nine months prior to Pakistan's attack on us on December 3, the great leaders of the world had paid some attention to the fact of revolt, tried to see the reality of the situation and searched for a genuine basis for reconciliation.

Towards the end of the letter, she kept the door to the United States open. She reiterated her earnest and sincere hope that,

> with all the knowledge and deep understanding of human affairs you, as President of the United States and reflect-

ing the will, the aspirations and idealism of the great
American people, will at least let me know where precisely
we have gone wrong before your representatives or
spokesmen deal with us with such harshness of language.[7]

THREE

The Pakistani forces in East Bengal, commanded by General A.A.K. Niazi, surrendered in Dhaka to Lieutenant General Jagjit Singh Aurora of the Indian Army at 4.30 p.m. on 16 December 1971. By the time the Seventh Fleet entered Indian waters, the war was over.

Indira Gandhi and an anxious Parliament had waited since early in the morning of 16 December 1971 for news of the surrender. In spite of the tension, Indira refused to cancel an engagement with Swedish television. She was in the middle of the interview when her secret telephone rang. It was Commander-in-Chief S.H.FJ. Manek-shaw on the line to inform the Prime Minister of the Pakistani surrender. She answered him in monosyllables, without a change of expression on her face. She then turned to the Swedish team, asked them to wait for her return, and left her office.

I was in the galleries of the Lok Sabha as the Prime Minister ran into the House as if she was a nimble girl carrying good tidings. It was 5.30 p.m. when she reached her seat; and rose to address the House.

My Speaker, Sir, I have an announcement to make, which I think the House has been waiting for, for some time. The West Pakistan forces have unconditionally surrendered in Bangladesh. The instrument of surrender was signed by Lt. Gen. A.A.K. Niazi on behalf of the Pakistan Eastern Command. Lt. Gen. Jagjit Singh Aurora, GOC-in-C of the Indian and Bangladesh forces in the Eastern Theatre accepted the surrender. Dhaka is now the free capital of a free country.

This House and the entire nation rejoice at this historic event. We hail the people of Bangladesh in their hour of triumph. We hail the brave young men and boys of the Mukti Bahini for their valour and dedication. We are proud of our own Army, Navy, Air Force and the Border Security Force, who have so magnificently demonstrated their quality and capacity. Their discipline and devotion to duty are well known. India will remember with gratitude

the sacrifices of those who have laid down their lives and
our thoughts are with their families.

We hope and trust that the Father of this new nation,
Sheikh Mujib-ur Rehman, will take his rightful place
among his own people and lead Bangladesh to peace,
progress and prosperity. The time has come when they can
together look forward to a meaningful future in their
Sonar Bangla. They have our good wishes.[1]

She received a tumultuous standing ovation. For once no inhibitions held back the full-throated acclaim. They hailed the Prime
Minister as Durga the Invincible. Speeches were made by Opposition
leaders and by her own party members, hailing the victory.

As I left the galleries, I found the Prime Minister standing outside
her office room surrounded by Members of Parliament. She saw me
and came forward. There is little I remember of our thirty-second
meeting. She embraced me and I could notice the tears in her eyes.
As we parted, she said in a whisper: 'Will we win the peace?'[2]

That evening she was in the maproom with the army chiefs and her
advisers. Pressure had already mounted from the hawks within Parliament to send the victorious Indian Army into West Pakistan.
Discussions were held as to what would be the cost of taking one city
in Pakistan and how long such an operation would take. The reply
given to the Prime Minister was that the Pakistan Army was composed
of highly trained soldiers and the cost of taking one city would lead
to approximately 30,000 casualties. The Prime Minister sat silent for
some time.

Members of Parliament, the press and her most trusted advisers
were of the view that she should launch a major attack on West
Pakistan which was in a state of chaos. An uncanny instinct operated
in her, she sensed that any move towards West Pakistan would lead
to the entry of other powers and the situation would get out of control.
The Soviets wanted her to call a halt. The Chinese were restless; they
were friends of Pakistan. The American presence in the form of the
Seventh Fleet, led by a nuclear aircraft carrier, was close to West
Bengal. Like her grandfather she was as hard as jasper; she listened
carefully to her advisers, emotions playing little part in her decision.
Once taken, there was no flinching from the decision, no moving away,

whatever the circumstances. She decided to declare a unilateral ceasefire on the Western front and took all the major powers by surprise. As she left the room, she remarked that, if she had not decided then, it would have been too late: the euphoria generated by the victory would have led to pressures which would have made further military action inevitable. She congratulated the Chiefs of Staff on their victory. The Bangladesh war had ended as a clean and decisive operation.[3]

*

On 17 December 1971, at 12.29 p.m., the Prime Minister rose to make a statement in Parliament:

Mr. Speaker, Sir, on March 31, 1971, six days after the great upheaval in Bangladesh, I had the honour to move a Resolution in this House.

I said then that India's permanent interest in peace and our commitment to uphold and defend human rights demanded the immediate cessation of the use of force and of the massacre of defenceless people of Bangladesh. I had called upon all peoples and Governments to take urgent and constructive steps to prevail upon the Government of Pakistan to immediately end the systematic decimation of a people. I had concluded my statement by expressing the profound conviction of this House that the historic upsurge of the 75 million people of East Bengal would triumph. We also gave an assurance that their struggle and sacrifice would receive the wholehearted sympathy and support of the people of India.

Today, the pledge we then made together in this House and in the country stands redeemed. It is natural that the people of India should be elated. We can also understand the great rejoicing of the people of Bangladesh. I share the elation and the joy. But, as the Gita says, neither joy nor sorrow should tilt the balance of our equanimity or blur our vision of the future.

All those who have borne arms, all those who have been involved in the planning and direction of the operations, all the people of India who have responded so generously—these are to be thanked and congratulated.

It is a victory, but a victory not only of arms but of ideas. The Mukti Bahini could not have fought so daringly but for its passionate urge for freedom and the establishment of a special identity of Bangladesh. Our own forces would not have been so fearless and relentless had they not been convinced of our cause.

We should like to fashion our relations with the people of Pakistan on the basis of friendship and understanding. Let them live as masters in their own house and devote their energies to the removal of poverty and inequalities in their country.

It is this sincere desire which prompted us last evening to instruct our Army, Navy and Air Force to cease operations from 2,000 hours today on all fronts in the West.[4]

A shattered President Yahya Khan resigned after his failed military adventure and Zulfikar Ali Bhutto took over as Prime Minister of Pakistan. Sheikh Mujib-ur Rehman had been sentenced to death in the secret military trial held by the Pakistan Army. Waiting in his cell, he could hear the sound of a pit being dug; the warders told him that it was his grave. Prime Minister Bhutto realized the danger of carrying out the death sentence against Sheikh Mujib-ur Rehman. The Sheikh was released in early January. On his way back he halted in New Delhi. A tumultuous welcome awaited him. Indira, her Cabinet colleagues, Members of Parliament and the Chiefs of the armed forces were on the tarmac to receive the new President of Bangladesh. Later, the Sheikh and the Prime Minister addressed a massive meeting to celebrate the victory of their armies and the birth of Bangladesh.

On Republic Day, 26 January 1972, Prime Minister Indira Gandhi drove in an open jeep to the saluting base on Raj Path to receive the President of India. A vast sea of people had gathered to offer their salutations to their victorious Prime Minister. The earth reverberated with the roar of the crowd. Throughout the war Indira had drawn the country into herself, girdled it with protection. In her victory she had assumed a mythic role in this country of myths. The image which was projected that pale winter morning was of a woman who had stood alone, single-minded in her defiance. She had faced and emerged victorious against Pakistan. She had challenged the President of the United States and his wily aide, Henry Kissinger. She had kept them guessing, called their bluff, outmanoeuvred them. She had reached those heights which from childhood she had felt were her destiny. The debt she had kept referring to as her earliest memory stood repaid, for her the myth had become reality. Like Charles de Gaulle of France, she could well say: 'I am India.'

FOUR

In March 1972 I received a message from the Prime Minister's House saying Indira Gandhi would like to see me that evening. I found her in her study, curled up in her Eames chair. Her eyes had lost their melancholy and with it some of their mystery. The ancient look, a look that lurked and made its presence felt deep in her eyes was absent, as was the look of the child that had never grown up, and its impish humour.

Elegantly laid out trays of caviare, other delicacies and rare fruit were placed before us. Orchids filled the room. It was an occasion for rejoicing and she wished to share of herself. I was there as a friend and perhaps a scribe.

She spoke of the Bangladesh war and her meetings with President Richard Nixon. She had geared up her inner resources for the meetings. She had found in Nixon a condescension which had made her very angry. 'I refused to react,' she said, 'but let go. Right through those tense days I did not act, but something acted through me. I do not know what operated. I listened, saw all the facts and a solution emerged. I then examined the solution in the harsh light of reality.' The people around her were anxious and hesitant and as the pressure had mounted, the atmosphere had grown turgid. 'I never worried through the Bangladesh crisis about what were the personal consequences to me. When I have to do anything I think right, I do it without concerning myself with the consequences. I knew that the war had to come in Bangladesh. All my actions arose from that perception.' There was little hesitancy on her part. The days when she had spoken in half-finished sentences were long over. 'Throughout the war and even previous to it,' she said, 'I had strange experiences—an extended vision I had known at times in my youth. The colour red suffused me throughout the war. On occasions I found myself speaking, saw things behind me which I could never have seen. The intensity disappeared immediately after the war ended and so have the experiences.'

The war left its mark on others as well. Gita Mehta covering the war for the Western media was in Dhaka, ten hours after the surrender of the Pakistani forces. Amidst the wild rejoicing she found that she was the only woman present. 'The women had either fled to refugee camps or had been captured and kept prisoners in the trenches. I saw a fifteen year old child who must have been raped at least two hundred times in four months. She could not cry—the question of crying just did not arise. She was in a state of catatonic shock.'

When she came back to New Delhi, Mehta heard an Indian General say to D.P. Dhar, Indira Gandhi's Principal Adviser: 'I want my troops out in 48 hours.' 'Impossible,' was Dhar's reply. 'We have only twelve policemen left in Dhaka.' The General insisted: 'I want my army out in 48 hours—that is the time I give it: for young men who have just come out of a war and seen the horror of what is taking place with the women in the trenches, for the horror to become pornography, and my army to begin doing what the Pakistan army is doing. For them these girls have ceased to be human beings.'

A few days before the surrender of the Pakistan forces, Gita Mehta, waiting to enter Bangladesh, to be present at the moment of triumph, had shown the Prime Minister her film on the Bangladesh refugees. Sponsored by the National Broadcasting Corporation (NBC), the film had been shown on prime time television in the United States from coast to coast, a week before the war broke out. The NBC telephones were jammed for over four hours, with offers to help the Mukti Bahini forces. I was present with the Prime Minister, Rajiv and Sanjay Gandhi to see the film. The faces of the old and the young returning from hiding to their empty demolished homes, the barren scorched fields devastated us. Indira wept. Later, I asked her whether the war had hurt her. She said, 'As a woman and a mother, I know war is a deathly thing. I have grown older, suffered, have survived and matured.'[1]

There was little of that emotion that spring evening as she spoke of the many people who had tried to advise her, of Jayaprakash Narayan's insistence on an early attack on Pakistan and her refusal to consult him or reveal her state of mind. She had kept her plans to herself. 'It was necessary,' she said, 'to see that the situation did not get out of control.'

We talked of her relationship with Jayaprakash Narayan and many of her father's old comrades. 'Jayaprakash has never taken me seriously. He does not understand that, for action to be potent, time is of the essence. In a war it is not possible to vacillate or to be weak or to play the role of Hamlet. One has to be really ruthless if the need arises. I am ruthless for what I think right. The difficulty is I move. These people remain static and so relationships drop away. Circumstances, experiences challenge me and change me. I am no longer the same person.'[2]

Twilight turned to darkness, and I rose to leave. She commented: 'The present holds the past and one has to have the capacity to feel the present and place it in relation to the future. I move with the flow of events, that is why people are apt to misunderstand me.' I saw that all doubt, all enquiry had ceased. A euphoria filled her, leaving little space for any other emotion. It was a dangerous situation for a human being, more so for a Prime Minister. She had inherited a splendid legacy, to this she had brought the gift of her own carefully nurtured perceptions. This gave her an instinctive capacity to act in the present, to reach out and touch people. With victory and adulation, if this capacity was erased, the vulnerability corroded, the many strands of karma that lay entangled within her would surface with their contradictory pulls and pressures. How would they unravel? Karma is blind and has its own inevitability, its own ruthless energy and potency. Without sensitivity and awareness, contradictions could drive Indira to a self-destructive future. I feared for her. But I sensed that this was not the day when dialogue was possible.

*

On 14 June 1972, Indira Gandhi delivered the keynote address at the plenary session of the UN Conference on Human Environment at Stockholm. She was amongst the first of the world's Heads of States to view nature and the biosphere as a problem of singular global importance.

From her childhood on she had had a kinship with nature in all its manifestations and was anguished at the seeming inevitability of 'progress (becoming) synonymous with an assault on nature.' But she had also to take into account the misgivings of the developing nations who felt that an emphasis on environment and concern with growing population, were a ploy by the affluent nations to vitiate growth amongst the poorer countries. Indira was aware of the major responsibility of the industrialized countries in contributing to the ecological disaster the world faced. But she regarded conservation and a right approach to nature as of primary importance to the countries of the world, whether affluent or poor. She was firm in her support for any global action. 'This gathering represents man's earnest endeavour to understand his own condition and to protect his tenancy of the planet. Must there be conflict between technology and a truly better world or between enlightenment of the spirit and a higher standard of living?' She stressed the need for spirituality which, for her, meant the enrichment of the spirit, the ability to be still in the midst of activity and to be vibrantly alive in moments of calm; to separate the essence from circumstances; to accept joy and sorrow with the same equanimity. 'We must concern ourselves not only with the world we want, but also the kind of man who should inhabit it. We want thinking people capable of spontaneous self-directed activity, people involved and concerned with compassion and concern for others.' She ended her speech with a quotation from a hymn to the Earth, where the sages of the *Atharva Veda* chanted:

> *What of thee I dig out, let that quickly grow over,*
> *Let me not hit thy vitals, or thy heart.*[3]

FIVE

War between India and Pakistan had ended, but rumours of mounting discontent in West Pakistan threatened any lasting peace between the two countries. On 28 June 1972, a summit meeting was held at Simla, between Prime Minister Indira Gandhi and the President of Pakistan, Zulfikar Ali Bhutto. Indira Gandhi travelled a day earlier to Simla, inspected the arrangements made for Bhutto's stay, refused the furnishings provided by the Himachal Pradesh government; recollected hangings and furniture in the special suites of Rashtrapati Bhavan, New Delhi, and ensured that the rooms for the President of Pakistan and his daughter Benazir were decorated in impeccable taste. The programme for the President and his daughter was scrutinized and finalized by her. These were the little details which she felt were essential to ensure that the Pakistani President felt welcome. She was determined that nothing should disturb the atmosphere of peace at the meeting, especially as it was taking place at a time when 'it was for us to guide affairs.'

India held the upper hand. It had won the war, it held 93,000 prisoners of war, and 5,000 square miles of Pakistan territory. In addition, there was a demand for war trials for crimes against the people of Bangladesh. But Indira knew that even in defeat Bhutto was a formidable foe and that the eyes of the world were on Simla and the summit talks.

Benazir Bhutto who had accompanied her father to Simla remarks in her autobiography: 'How tiny she (Mrs. Gandhi) was, much smaller than she seemed in the countless photographs I had seen of her. And how elegant, even in the raincoat she wore over her sari under the threatening skies.'[1] While the President was busy in meetings, Benazir went shopping on the Mall, visited museums, factories and a handicrafts centre. She was her father's eyes and ears and was quick to sense the mood of the Indian people. Benazir was excited to find cheering crowds everywhere. Letters and telegrams piled up welcoming her to India. India had won the war, it had no place for small humiliations.

For five days no breakthrough in the talks seemed possible. Prime Minister Indira Gandhi insisted on a full settlement of all problems between India and Pakistan. President Bhutto was equally insistent that the Kashmir issue be kept out of the final settlement. 'The very first remark I made to Mr. Bhutto was that Pakistan and India have to decide whether the interests of our two countries are complementary or are they always going to be conflicting.' She had told the President that a hundred agreements would not bring peace unless this issue was decided. She said to him:

> We believe, as India has believed and India does believe today, that our interests are largely the same, that the major problems we face are the poverty of our people and the economic backwardness of our countries and the incessant efforts of foreign powers to pressurise us.[2]

The Indian Cabinet, which had accompanied the Prime Minister to Simla, met every evening to review the day's talks. The Prime Minister would ask for comments from her colleagues, but not a single member was prepared to express his view. In exasperation she is reported to have remarked: 'For God's sake, say something.' But the silence continued. It was left to P.N. Haksar, her Principal Secretary, to sum up issues and suggest points on which India should remain firm. Tensions grew between the two delegations as the last day for the talks approached. President Bhutto knew that he could not go back emptyhanded, nor could he agree to a permanent settlement of the Kashmir issue, if he desired to survive as President.

On the last day the Prime Minister and the President met for a tête-à-tête, after a dinner hosted by the President of Pakistan. No one knows what happened at this meeting. It is believed that some secret agreement was reached which was never made public; whatever the cause, the two Heads of State came out of the room with smiles on their faces. India had agreed to return 5,000 square miles of occupied Pakistani territory, save for some strategic points in Kashmir. India had also agreed to return the 93,000 Pakistani prisoners of war, but only with the approval of the Bangladesh Government. From India's viewpoint the most important clause in the agreement was that India and Pakistan would refrain in the future from use of force and that all issues between the two countries would be resolved bilaterally. The world hailed the outcome of the Simla Agreement. Indira had emerged as a statesman of stature and foresight.

At the next meeting of the Lok Sabha, Indira faced an onslaught from the Opposition on the concessions India had made to Pakistan. In her reply, on 31 July 1972, she said:

> All I know is that I must fight for peace and I must take those steps which will lead us to peace. If they do not work out, we are prepared. Had we stood up saying as when two children are quarrelling, "You have taken my toy: I must have it before I speak to you", or something like that, if we had that kind of attitude what would have happened? The time has come when Asia must wake up to its destiny, must wake up to the real needs of its people, must stop fighting amongst ourselves, no matter what our previous quarrels, no matter what the previous hatred and bitterness. The time has come today when we must bury the past.[3]

It was to take another year before Pakistan recognized Bangladesh. In turn, Bangladesh agreed not to hold war trials and the prisoners of war were sent back to Pakistan.

*

The monsoons were approaching and prayers were offered to the rain gods, for the refugee problem had left the grainbins of India empty and the treasury was at an all-time low. But the monsoons failed, prices rose and widespread economic discontent prevailed all over the country. Victory does not spare the victor. India was desperately wounded.

During the war in Bangladesh, Sanjay Gandhi was not permitted by his mother to make his presence felt on the Indian scene. With victory he suddenly appeared. He now had plans to convert his Maruti project, conceived and crafted in two garages, into a full-fledged factory. A Letter of Intent had been issued to Sanjay Gandhi before the Bangladesh war as had been a licence for the factory. Bansi Lal, Chief Minister of Haryana, helped the young man to acquire land in the State. The land was situated in a prohibited area, near a military base. The base was shifted, according to the Opposition and the media, in order to facilitate the location of the Maruti factory on this land. The Lok Sabha reacted strongly to what it considered blatant nepotism.

Indira had been warned by her Principal Secretary, P.N. Haksar, of the naïveté of Sanjay's plan and his lack of expertise to see through a major industrial project. He had told her that Sanjay's failure to produce a car would affect her political position. The Opposition parties were seeking a chink in her armour, Maruti would provide the opportunity. Sanjay had taken a strong dislike to Haksar and kept urging his mother to take action against him. All manner of rumour now began reaching the Prime Minister. It was said that Haksar had become very arrogant, that he was taking credit for the Bangladesh victory and the negotiations that followed, that he held court where a vast number of people gathered, where favours were asked for and granted. To this were added reports from senior administrators that Haksar was holding up files from various ministries. In her own inimitable way, the Prime Minister started to marginalize Haksar and turned to P.N. Dhar for advice and decision taking.

'The Prime Minister had become very very arrogant. She loved being called Durga. The Bangladesh victory was the turning point. Sanjay was the only person who had a total hold on her. She had no tolerance for any other person,'[4] commented her former Private Secretary N.K. Seshan.

The ineptitude of Sanjay soon became clear. Vast sums of money borrowed by him from Indian nationalized banks were used to poor effect. Sanjay in turn put the blame for his failure on the bureaucracy, and the red-tape he had to cut through to get the project moving. The Lok Sabha was becoming more strident and newspapers were openly calling the Maruti affair Indira's Watergate. Towards the end of 1973, an anxious Prime Minister asked C. Subramaniam, now Finance Minister in her Cabinet, to look into the Maruti affair. She was very worried. The company seemed to have run into all kinds of difficulties.

> An interview took place. Indira Gandhi was present. I asked Sanjay for the project report on Maruti. He replied that there cannot be a project report before the project starts. I tried to explain to him that this was very complicated, that he could

possibly design a car, but he had to have a project report
which goes into the manufacturing of every component
and the manner in which components would be produced.
The total picture was the project report.

Sanjay's reply was that those were all old methods of operating,
they were not necessary.[5] But Subramaniam had insisted. He later
told the Prime Minister that the young man, however dynamic, did
not know how to proceed with the setting up of a company. He
promised to help by inducting professionals. But Sanjay refused and
Subramaniam was forced to direct the Governor of the Reserve Bank
of India (RBI) to issue instructions to all the banks not to lend more
money to Maruti. This meant a confrontation between him and
Sanjay. 'It was a very unhappy experience.' He found Indira Gandhi
very upset about the whole affair. According to Subramaniam, 'She
even shed tears before me.'[6]

*

The monsoons failed again in 1973. International oil prices rose
sharply and inflation in India registered an all-time high of twenty per
cent. An immense unrest swept the country. There was massive labour
turmoil, strikes in urban areas, the closure of factories and a fall in
production. Indira, on the advice of her economic experts, made every
effort to control prices. Government expenditure was cut drastically,
a limit on company dividends was imposed, a compulsory deposit
scheme on all salaries and incomes was levied, a major drive was
directed against smugglers. With the tough measures taken by government, vested interests in the country went all out to oppose the Prime
Minister. She would have succeeded in convincing the people of India
of her right intentions but, unfortunately, rumours of increasing
corruption around her, and her arrogance, alienated many of her
admirers. Traits within her which had been dormant surfaced. 'She
had always listened to gossip, but now she kept people uncertain,
intimidated them. Her difficulty was she could not communicate with
people,'[7] said N.K. Seshan in an interview with the author. Her
assistants who had worked with her over the years found her imperious. 'She would brook no criticism, nor was she prepared to be

questioned. She never trusted anyone completely—now she grew secretive, never divulged her mind, never changed it whether she was right or wrong. She would keep people guessing, wanted people to ask favours of her—it was one way of expressing her power. Sometimes I feel that she lost her balance after Bangladesh. Sanjay was in complete control. She would have been a great Prime Minister had Sanjay not been there.'[8]

One of her chief political opponents, Atal Behari Vajpayee, then President of the Jana Sangh, an extreme right-wing party, commented: 'She was unable to take criticism, saw in every Opposition move a foreign hand. She felt everyone whispering against her—something going on behind the bush, on the other side of the wall.'[9]

I met her one evening during the period when Sanjay and his Maruti company were under serious attack. I found her angry and distressed. She felt that the Opposition was trying to destroy her through Sanjay and it was not fair. The young man should have a chance. Suddenly, she spoke of the time when, immediately after marriage, she had gone with her father to Kulu. At the home of the Roerichs she had met a Cossack priest, an adventurer Father Constantine. He later built a plane in two garages in Bombay, and would take up his friends for a joy ride. She said, 'If he could build a plane, why can't Sanjay build a car?'[10]

SIX

Prabha, the wife of Jayaprakash Narayan, died in 1973, leaving her husband bereft and adrift. Convinced that parliamentary democracy had failed, Jayaprakash Narayan launched his movement, "Youth for Democracy", appealing to the youth in the country to come forward and restructure the political system. His ideology was ambiguous, his postulates never clearly defined, but he was a legend, a personification of hope, and his rhetoric attracted a large number of young and idealistic men and women to the movement. Simultaneously, in Gujarat, an agitation was started by students which escalated into the Navnirman (regeneration) movement against the corruption and misdeeds of Chief Minister Chimanbhai Patel and his government. Prime Minister Indira Gandhi, busy solving the grave economic crisis that faced the country, did not pay attention to Gujarat and expected the students' movement to be controlled by the Chief Minister. Students were her constituency and even when she grew aware of the possibility of growing chaos, she hesitated to take tough action. Jayaprakash Narayan's support of the Gujarat students' movement changed the situation dramatically and the focus of attack turned on her.

As the movement escalated, power passed from the students to anti-social elements. The agitation grew violent, law and order collapsed, shops were looted and burnt. The leaders of the movement demanded the dismissal of the Chief Minister, the dissolution of the Legislative Assembly and fresh elections. Threats of kidnapping legislators' children forced the legislators to sign letters of resignation from the local Assembly. Money was being extracted from the MLAs to ensure their safety. 'Before the dust finally settled, 103 people had been killed, 300 injured and more than 8,000 arrested.'[1] For some reason, Indira still refrained from interfering or taking massive action. As the intensity of the campaign grew, Indira appeared paralysed. The movement challenged the very basis of Indira's leadership and finally forced Indira to accept Chimanbhai Patel's resignation, dissolve the Assembly and impose President's rule on the state.

Morarji Desai went on a fast unto death in Delhi demanding fresh polls in Gujarat. At first Indira refused to intervene but the aged leader refused to relent. Finally, Indira's advisers convinced her that to let Morarji Desai die would make him a martyr and the political repercussions against her would be very serious. The State Assembly elections in Gujarat were announced and Morarji Desai gave up his fast.

In May 1974, taking advantage of the growing unrest in the country, George Fernandes, then President of the Railway Workers' Union, served notice on the government that railway workers would go on an indefinite strike unless their demands were met. Negotiations had little effect.

A railway strike and the stoppage of movement of essential commodities would have led to chaos within the country. There could have been starvation deaths and the collapse of all industrial and commercial activity. It was a grim situation and as the strike went into effect, Indira Gandhi's government struck back with fury. Railway workers were arrested, their families thrown out of their government allotted houses, the army called in. Fernandes and thousands of his workers were jailed. Indira was at her most ruthless. The strike collapsed, but an undercurrent of confusion and unrest began to make itself felt in most parts of the country.

*

At 8.05 a.m. on 18 May, the Atomic Energy Commission successfully carried out an underground nuclear explosion at Pokhran in the deserts of Rajasthan. For the moment, the country forgot its troubles and responded to India's entry into the nuclear age with wild enthusiasm. The Prime Minister thanked the scientists responsible for the great achievement and insisted that the nuclear energy would be used solely for peaceful purposes and that India had no intention of making the nuclear bomb. The Western powers were intensely distressed by the explosion of the nuclear device, as to them it was another example of India's intransigence, an attitude that had its origins in India's refusal to sign the nuclear Non-Proliferation Treaty (NPT), an agreement it regarded as discriminatory. Indira insisted that the Pokhran experiment was part of her government's research and development work with the aim of harnessing atomic energy for peaceful purposes.

Addressing a jubilant Lok Sabha on 22 July 1974, Indira ended her speech: 'No technology is evil in itself. It is the use that nations make which determines its character. India does not accept the principle of apartheid in any matter and technology is no exception.'

Indira was exhausted and went for a short holiday to Simla, accompanied by her family. After many years she went riding, fell off the horse and cracked her finger.

Upon hearing about the incident, Siddhartha Shankar Ray, then Chief Minister of West Bengal, wrote:

> I was distressed to hear about your accident, but relieved to know that it was only a finger that got cracked. How did you manage to fall on your finger when there were so many other comfortable "places" to fall on?
>
> As usual, I went back to Alice and remembered what she said to the Knight—"I'm afraid you've not had much practice in riding." This she had to say for whenever the horse stopped (which it did very often) the Knight fell off in front; and, whenever it went on again (which it generally did rather suddenly), he fell off behind. Otherwise, he kept on pretty well, except that he had a habit of now and then falling off sideways; and, as he generally did this on the side on which Alice was walking, she soon found that it was the best plan not to walk quite close to the horse.
>
> The Knight was, however, very offended when Alice talked about lack of practice, and he asked, "What makes you say that?" as he scrambled back into the saddle, keeping hold of Alice's hair with one hand, to save himself from falling over on the other side. (Horror of horrors— where was Sonia when you fell?) "Because," said Alice "people do not fall off quite so often, when they've had much practice."
>
> "I've had plenty of practice," the Knight said very gravely: "plenty of practice!"
>
> "The great art of riding is to keep—." Here the sentence ended as suddenly as it had begun, as the Knight fell heavily on top of his head exactly in the path where Alice was walking.

Enough of Alice. Please look after yourself and have that finger put right quickly.[2]

She was amused by the letter and, three days later, wrote back from Delhi:

It should be obvious to anyone, even Alice, that had I fallen, I could not have avoided hurt in the more padded sections. Had I fallen off a horse on the rocky path, I would have cracked many bones. It follows therefore that if only the third finger of the left hand is cracked, one has not fallen at all. However Alice would have been quite right in saying that I have not had any riding practice for a considerable period. I had mounted the horse quite accidentally without being properly clad or shod for a ride. As a result, I got two big bruises on my thighs where they rubbed against the saddle and decided to get off the horse. As I was getting off, the horse decided to bolt. Had I got on proper shoes, nothing would have happened. I had swung my right leg around, but the left foot remained stuck in the stirrup because of my crepe soles and when I yanked it, my foot came out but the shoe remained in the stirrup! As I was holding the reins and the saddle with my left hand when the horse jerked forward, the brunt of it was on my third finger which cracked. I did not fall or even sit down on the ground. Hence only the finger injury plus the bruises previously acquired. Anyhow, it was much ado about nothing. There has never been any pain and fortunately I find that the third finger on the left hand is not as useful as it would appear to be. Having it immobilised does not interfere with any activity. But in order to prevent congestion of blood, I am supposed to keep my hand up in the Buddha pose of blessing the multitude.[3]

*

With mounting food shortages, rising oil prices, diesel and kerosene in short supply, the cessation of US economic aid, the threat of sabotage and drought and the seething unrest, it was inevitable that Jayaprakash Narayan drew large crowds as he travelled through the length and breadth of the country. In Bihar, a students' agitation under the leadership of Jayaprakash Narayan had commenced along with the revolt in Gujarat. He wrote an article in which he said that the people of the country themselves must fight, in peaceful ways, of course, for deliverance from the corrupt system under which they were suffering. Apart from corruption, they must also fight hunger, unemployment, inflation and economic injustice of many kinds.

Unlike in Gujarat, Indira Gandhi struck back at the Bihar movement. Lathi charges and tear gas were resorted to by the police to quell the agitators. Jayaprakash Narayan was in the thick of one of the processions and would have been seriously hurt if his followers had not surrounded him and protected him.

On 5 June 1974, at a meeting held in Patna, Jayaprakash Narayan demanded the dismissal of the Bihar Ministry on grounds of corruption and the dissolution of the Assembly. He called for a total revolution.

Gravely concerned with the situation in the country, some of Jayaprakash Narayan's friends attempted to bring about a *rapprochement* between JP and the Prime Minister. Achyut Patwardhan, a close colleague of Jayaprakash Narayan and a hero of the freedom struggle, had abandoned politics after India attained independence. Deeply moved by J. Krishnamurti, he had gone to live and work in a village in Varanasi. He came to Delhi and asked me, as an old friend, to arrange a meeting between him and the Prime Minister. I was present at the meeting and Patwardhan suggested several possibilities to Indira Gandhi. Earlier, Achyut Patwardhan had held discussions with Jayaprakash Narayan. It was suggested that JP could make a conciliatory statement to which Indira would respond, following which the two could jointly draw up a programme for the return of a moral tone to government and the country. Indira listened to Patwardhan and Achyut came away with the feeling that she would cooperate in the search for a solution.

On 11 October 1974, I received a letter from the Prime Minister:

It would certainly be most welcome if JP were to make a statement along the lines suggested. But I am afraid that

the idea of establishing a non-party government in consultation with him would mean the death knell of
democratic functioning. Is it possible to find other ways of
"moral" co-operation with JP, such as cleansing the election process?[4]

I sent the letter to Achyut Patwardhan who was expected to meet
Jayaprakash Narayan at Patna. Unfortunately, Achyut did not go, but
asked Sugata Dasgupta, the then Director of the Gandhian Institute
at Varanasi, and a close associate of JP's to take the message to Patna.
Later, Achyut was to comment that it was a grave mistake on his part,
for Sugata Dasgupta deliberately distorted the message and no clear
commitment from Jayaprakash reached Achyut. Dasgupta had
hedged, asked Achyut to work out consequential steps of the meeting
before JP would issue any statement or agree to meet the Prime
Minister. Anxious to open lines of communication to resolve the crisis.
without rigid commitments on either side, Achyut suggested that
practical steps should be discussed at a meeting between three
nominees of the Prime Minister and three from Jayaprakash Narayan.
This was a compromise solution and was not the basis of the discussion
which had taken place earlier between the Prime Minister and Achyut
Patwardhan. I sent the letter to the Prime Minister.

On 16 October 1974, the Prime Minister wrote:

I have given thought to the matter. Apart from getting a
great deal of publicity, I wonder whether a meeting between three nominees of either side to thrash out alternative proposals can be useful or fruitful. Because of the
publicity, there may be a certain amount of posturing. I
wonder whether it is not possible for Achyut himself to
have a discussion in depth with whosoever (he is) in touch
with on JP's side. If this person knows JP's mind and can
speak authentically and can also be depended upon, that
would give some basis for further discussions. Of course,
we must be sure that such a person is conveying JP's ideas
and not projecting his own bias.[5]

Attempts continued to bring about a meeting between JP and the

Prime Minister, although many of JP's colleagues, viewing the growing economic chaos, felt that Jayaprakash Narayan should not yield but take full advantage of the situation. A meeting was finally arranged in November 1974, but advisers on both sides were determined to see that the confrontation should continue. Jayaprakash Narayan came to meet the Prime Minister, expecting to find her alone. To his dismay he found her flanked by Jagjivan Ram and Y.B. Chavan. Jayaprakash Narayan was insistent that the Bihar government, which was very corrupt, should be dismissed. Indira felt that it was an elected government, chosen democratically and she had no authority to dismiss it. Charges and counter-charges were made and the meeting ended on an acrimonious note.

Indira's problems were mounting. In a comment to a friend she said: 'There are no normal days for a Prime Minister of India. On a good day there are perhaps two or three very urgent problems. On a bad day there could be a dozen. After a while you learn to live with this although you never quite get used to it. If you get used to it, I think it is time to leave your office. A Prime Minister must always be a little upset, never, unbalanced.'

Immediately after Indira's election victory, her defeated opponent, Raj Narain, had filed an appeal in the Allahabad High Court against the election result claiming that widespread corrupt practices were responsible for Indira's victory and that the election should be set aside. His friends had scoffed at him, told him not to be foolish. Indira had won with a very big margin and there was no way Raj Narain could succeed in unseating her. But this dogged wrestler from Varanasi had persisted, spent days in Rae Bareilly gathering snippets of information to prove his charge. The hearings had dragged on, at least two judges had retired before 1974. Indira Gandhi, the first Prime Minister to appear as a defendant in any court, was in the dock for five-and-a-half hours to face a tough cross-examination. Her demeanour was dignified and there was no trace of fear. Rumours were current that the case was not going too well for her. In the midst of the fury of Gujarat and Bihar, the case rarely came to public notice.

PART VI

1975–1977

I shall seize fate by the throat.
It shall never wholly overcome me.

–Beethoven when he was going blind[1]

You do not know the limits of your
strength, you do not know what you do.
You do not know who you are.

–The Bacchae[2]

ONE

In early June 1975, I met Indira Gandhi in the evening, in her book-lined study at 1, Safdarjung Road. I could see from her relaxed posture that she wanted to talk at length. I spoke of my approaching visit to France, England and the United States, and of the people I was to meet. I enquired whether she had any messages.

Indira was scheduled to be in Mexico by the end of June to attend a world conference on women, where she was to be the main speaker. She asked me whether I had any suggestions for her Mexican speech. We conversed, an easy flow, where the ear was tuned, where there were pauses, punctuations in the mind—we could be silent and the dialogue would continue. We spoke of the role of woman in a society where tradition was breaking down and new challenges were shattering women's responses to the inner and outer environment. It was a topic which we had discussed on several earlier occasions.

'You know I am not a feminist in the accepted sense of the word,' she said. 'Till I was 12 years old I hardly knew the difference between being a boy or a girl. I was brought up amongst boy cousins, climbed trees with them, flew kites and played marbles.' But, she said, 'That is not the normal experience of girls in our country. Women in India, perhaps in most of the world, are so dominated and discriminated against. There is so much unnecessary cruelty and humiliation.'

Indira had drawn a notebook to her and had started taking notes. She was critical of the West where the emancipation of women was equated with an imitation of men and a fierce determination to acquire their behaviour patterns.

'To be liberated,' she said, 'a woman should be free to be herself. Rivalry between women and men is unnecessary, in fact is destructive and itself a bondage.'

We discussed the freedom struggle and the support the Mahatma and Jawaharlal Nehru gave to women. Their support brought women to the forefront without a major struggle. There were few obstacles in India to a woman reaching the highest position. In villages a woman still lived in an epic flow of time: myth and mystery were re-enacted within her and renewed energy. A peasant woman had little need to be other than what she was—this gave her a rootedness and dignity.

She could age without losing grace—hold sorrow or joy, death or birth, immense cruelty or affection with the strength that is in the ageless earth. We spoke of women amongst the land-owning aristocracy and certain sections of the middle-class where the woman was rudderless, treated as a possession passed from father to husband to son. Her bondage was real, society was relentless and no enactment of laws could ensure her freedom. It was education, the capacity to be economically independent and an energy that could erase her conditioning, that alone could free her from her fears and the bondage of centuries.

We spoke of the women of Madhubani in Bihar. For centuries they had been bound to an archaic tradition, with little freedom to be themselves. The discovery amongst these women of a live, imagination, rich in colour, symbol and myth, coupled with inherited skills which enabled them to be recognized as powerful painters, transformed their lives and social relationships. They emerged as wage-earners supporting the household. Freed from centuries of bondage, they retained an immense dignity and rootedness. For Indira they were symbols of a strong conditioning ending without struggle.

She wanted to probe deeper—I spoke of the insights arising in my own mind, the feeling that there were creative springs, a subterranean river of energy within, that was available to a woman. This river waxed or waned, depending upon a woman's ability to touch it and drink of its waters.

'That is what I mean when I speak of a woman being herself,' she said.

I could see that she was listening with great intensity.

'But ignorance, tradition and a growing materialism obstruct this,' I said. 'The immediacy of direct perception is disappearing. We seek through concepts and so rarely drink of the waters.'

'Why is it,' she asked 'that in seeking to be free there is this demand to deny the essence of being a woman? Why do we compare?' She paused, 'My mother was fragile but could stand alone.' Suddenly she turned to me, 'Do you feel dependent?'

I paused and looked into myself for a feeling of dependence. The question opened up bylanes of consciousness. 'One has to be challenged at depth to know how one would respond. Fear is elusive, so all-pervading, it lingers in inaccessible crevices of the mind. But no, I don't feel I need a wall behind myself. Dependence is not my problem.'

'I have taken my own decisions throughout my life, I can stand alone,' she said. 'But there is so much possessiveness. One needs space to be alone with oneself. The question really is, can a woman be a wife, share companionship with a husband, be a mother and yet be herself, live a life of the mind or a life of action—political, social, cultural?'

'Does our present culture and society permit this?' I asked. 'The Indian male is so inordinately spoilt by tradition and society. His ego needs continual attention, nourishment—otherwise he feels neglected and is at times destructive.'

She chuckled. An attendant brought in a slip and I knew it was time for me to go. I said 'Perhaps we shall meet at the end of the month at Mexico.' Suddenly she became serious, hesitated and said 'It depends on what happens on the 12th.'

'What is to happen on the 12th?' I asked.

'The Allahabad judgement,' she responded.

I had not followed the case that had arisen out of her 1971 election, which she had won with over 100,000 votes. There was an election petition. Raj Narain, the defeated candidate, had filed an appeal challenging the election result on grounds of unfair practices. The grounds were trivial. They related to a delay in the official notification of a government servant's resignation—he was to work for her in the election—a technical mistake for which the Prime Minister's Secretariat was responsible. No one held that the delay was mala fide. The thought of a Prime Minister being unseated on minor technicalities just did not arise.

'You can't be serious,' I said.

'I am very serious, Pupul. I have a feeling that all is not well.'

It disturbed me and I left feeling that her nervousness was similar to the lurking anxiety all of us go through when we wait for an examination result.

I left for Paris. On 12 June late in the morning—by then I had forgotten that it was the date when the judgement was to be delivered—someone called and quite casually said, 'The judgement has gone against Indira Gandhi and she has been unseated. The judge has debarred her from holding office for six years.' I could not believe I had heard right and asked him to repeat what he had said. Later, I tried to telephone Indira, but found it impossible.

I was in London, staying with Brij Kumar Nehru, the Indian High Commissioner. We talked late into the night. The British papers were full of the judgement. The London *Times* commented that it was like a British Prime Minister being debarred from holding office on a parking offence. Everyone, including B.K. Nehru, expected her to resign. I was not sure. I tried to telephone her from London, but could not reach her.

I arrived in New York on 25 June. Early on the morning of the 26th, Dorothy Norman, a mutual friend at whose home I was staying, woke me to tell me that she had just heard that Indira had arrested a vast number of Opposition leaders, including Jayaprakash Narayan, Morarji Desai and others.

People started telephoning to ask whether a civil war had broken out in India. There was no news and friends of India were anxious and disturbed. I dressed hurriedly and went to the office of Rikhye Jaipal, the Head of the Permanent Mission of India in New York. He was sitting by the telephone waiting for instructions. I phoned India's Ambassador in Washington; he too had no information. So I decided to phone Indira. I was told that it would be impossible to reach her, but to my surprise, in five minutes, she was on the line. I asked her what had happened. I also told her of the rumours and the reports of civil war. She could feel from the tone of my voice that I was greatly disturbed, and said 'Don't be anxious, Pupul, no civil war has been declared. It is true I have imposed Emergency and a number of Opposition leaders have been arrested, including Jayaprakash Narayan and Morarji Desai. Jayaprakash addressed a meeting at Ram Lila grounds where he appealed to the army and police not to obey the orders of Government.' I could sense from her voice that she was very tense. She said 'No Government can tolerate this.' I told her of the atmosphere in New York. I did not know then that censorship was total. She said she would immediately dictate a note and send it to me so that I could reply to any queries made to me. By the next day a note reached me under the signature of N.K. Seshan, her Private Secretary 'as dictated for Pupul Jayakar by Prime Minister.'

Message from Prime Minister:

• Atmosphere of violence was increasing. Opposition parties had planned a programme of disruption, bandhs, gherao, etc. from 29th of this month. Jayaprakash especially once again strongly incited industrial workers, police and armed forces not to obey orders. RSS had plans to disrupt communications and transport and tamper with municipal services. In preparation some RSS and other extremists had gone underground. I doubt if any government would have tolerated such movements to grow to the extent which we have. Campaign of hate and calumny had become hysterical and the objective of the Opposition was to bring the Central Government to a standstill and to create anarchy. As you know, the newspapers were deliberately provocative, encouraging such elements. It became necessary to prevent disruptive activities. Therefore Emergency has been declared under the provision of our Constitution.

- The number of persons arrested is about 900. About, two-thirds of them are anti-social elements and one-third are political, most of them are left or right extremists whose ideology is violence and who, although not believing in democracy, are taking advantage of democratic freedom for their own purposes. Political leaders are not in jail but kept under detention, comfortably in houses.

- General public reaction is good; most people saying that such measures should have been taken earlier. There is tranquillity all over the country. Attempts at hartals and bandhs completely failed except in four towns in Gujarat where they were sponsored by Janata Front Government, and even here were only partially successful.

- You know what has been happening in Parliament and outside. Freedom was being misinterpreted as licence by a majority and democracy was being derailed. Our measures are intended to enable a return to normal democratic functioning.

- Delay in giving news is due to suddenness of events and to necessity of legal and administrative arrangements. Although this has caused some confusion it has also contributed to the peaceful atmosphere.

- Information about the situation in India is available both with our

Embassy in Washington and also with our Permanent Representative in New York. In case you want more information, please
contact Rikhye Jaipal.

The above message was dictated by P.M. for Mrs. Jayakar.

Sd/-
N.K.Seshan
28/6/75
Private Secretary to the Prime Minister
Tele: 382160 (P.H.) 372312 (S.B.)

*

It is instructive to reconstruct the events of the days that preceded
the imposing of the Emergency. On the morning of 12 June, Indira
awoke to the news that D.P. Dhar, a friend and close associate, was
dead. He was a former Minister in her Cabinet, Chairman of the
Planning Commission, and Ambassador to the Soviet Union. Dhar
was a man of wit, audacity and courage, as also a man of deep
commitment to the country. He had been Indira's trusted friend and
adviser. Indira dressed hurriedly and arrived at Dhar's house early in
the morning to mourn with the family.

She returned to 1, Safdarjung Road, her residence, sombre and
distraught. Her son Rajiv Gandhi found her in her study, gazing out
on to her tiny enclosed garden of evergreens. He told her that the
judgement had gone against her; Justice Sinha had declared her
election invalid. A few minutes later another message came through
that the judge had debarred her from taking part in any electoral
processes for the next six years. She received the news with a stoic
calm. A few days earlier news had percolated to her that forces
inimical to her were operative and that the judgement would go
against her. Vengal Rao, then Chief Minister of Andhra Pradesh, had
intercepted a message from Jayaprakash Narayan to Sanjiva Reddy.
Jayaprakash told Reddy that he had definite information that the
judgement was going against Indira. 'She will be disqualified for six
years. This is the time for us to attack. I want your support.'[3]
Jayaprakash told Reddy that he had contacted K. Kamaraj in Tamil
Nadu but that Kamaraj was hesitant.

Secret reports of the activity of underground religious societies (the Anand Margis, a tantric sect in West Bengal, claimed their share in the court decision) had also reached her. Uma Shankar Dikshit, then Information Minister, was approached by an officer of the Income Tax department who told him, 'Mrs. Gandhi's election will be declared invalid. Changes will take place in the country. You are one of the people we have chosen.'

'Who are you?' Dikshit asked him.

'We are religious people and we are running this country. There is a spirit behind us which moves us.'

Dikshit, a member of her Cabinet, suspected the man was a spy and had repeated the conversation to Indira. He was convinced that there was a conspiracy against the Prime Minister. What the Opposition could not accomplish through the polls, they were attempting to manipulate through a court verdict. Memories of these events flowed through Indira's mind when she heard of the adverse judgement. Her first remark to R.N. Kao, then chief of the Research and Analysis Wing (RAW) when he saw her that day was 'Do you remember what I told you?'[4]

Siddhartha Shankar Ray, at this time Chief Minister of West Bengal, was in Delhi on that fateful day. Within minutes of hearing the news, Ray was at Indira's home, along with H.R. Gokhale, the then Union Law Minister. On seeing them, Indira said, 'It has been a terrible day. D.P. Dhar is dead.'

Her instinctive response to the judgement was, 'I must resign immediately.' Siddhartha Shankar Ray argued with her. 'Let us think it over. You should not take a decision in a hurry.' But she was adamant.

Uma Shankar Dikshit, Jagjivan Ram, the then Minister for Agriculture and Irrigation and D.K. Barooah, President of the Congress, reached her home a few minutes after Siddhartha. It was an oppressive, dust-filled day. The heat was fierce, the atmosphere murky. It was difficult to breathe. Gossip, ambition and double-talk distorted the situation. Every politician present swore loyalty to Indira, yet everyone of them was aware that the incredible had happened, the prime minister's post was within their reach.

As the leaders gathered, some turned to Indira, others went into huddles in small groups, weighing the odds, assessing the strengths of individual leaders. The bargaining had commenced; the proposals and counter-proposals.

Sanjay Gandhi, who was away in his car factory, came home at lunch-time. Unaware of what had happened, once he was told he was quick to gauge the situation. He took his mother to her room and told her angrily that he would not let her resign. He was particularly outraged to learn of Barooah's suggestion that she should take over the Congress Presidentship from him, while he took over as Prime Minister, for a short period, till her appeal was heard by the Supreme Court. Sanjay pointed out that once Barooah had taken over as Prime Minister he would not vacate the post for her. Behind their facade of loyalty, he was sure her colleagues were driven by personal ambitions. They all sought power. She should not resign under any circumstances.

Now came news over the teleprinter that the court had issued a stay order for twenty days. This would enable Indira Gandhi to appeal to the Supreme Court. The tension within the house eased; no immediate action was necessary. As the politicians sensed that Indira Gandhi was not to resign immediately, their attitude changed. They were quick to swear their unwavering loyalty to her. A statement was drafted. 'Mrs. Gandhi continues to be Prime Minister. It is our firm and considered view that for the integrity, stability and progress of the country her dynamic leadership is indispensable.' Cabinet ministers signed, chief ministers and Members of Parliament rushed to Delhi to affirm their loyalty. As the news spread, vast crowds gathered before her house, some arriving spontaneously, others brought there by Sanjay's comrades in trucks from Uttar Pradesh, Haryana and as far away as Madhya Pradesh. Men and women shouted slogans that Indira should remain Prime Minister. Fiery speeches were made. The issue was out on the streets.

Indira came out again and again from the house. She stood on a ladder to address the crowds. She was passionate, emotional, careful not to attack the judge or the judgement; she lashed out at the Opposition for using the judgement to destroy stability in the country. Nani A. Palkhivala, a well-known constitutional lawyer from Bombay, was approached by her legal advisers to fight her appeal in the Supreme Court. He agreed. The court was in session but the vacation judge, Justice Krishna Iyer, was to hear the interim appeal on the stay order. Palkhivala assured Indira that she had a strong case and that her affairs had been badly handled during the original hearing. Indira realized that the period before the appeal would be used by her opponents to create crisis conditions to force her resignation. Her political managers went into action. Huge meetings and rallies were held in Delhi and in other parts of the country in support of Indira. The Congress decided to organize a vast meeting to be addressed by Indira the day before the case came up before the vacation judge.

D.K. Barooah, sensed that his proposal to be acting prime minister had not found favour in Indira's eyes, so he was the most vociferous of everyone. He was quoted as having said, 'Indira is India, India is Indira, the two are inseparable.'

The greater the pressure mounted by the Opposition on her position as Prime Minister, the more defensive and abrasive were her speeches to the crowd. She spoke of plots against her, of anti-national forces wanting to destabilize the country, of the hand of foreign governments. She thanked the people of India who continued to have faith in her; she promised to work towards the eradication of poverty and the transformation of society.

Even the Opposition could see that she enjoyed enormous popularity among the men and women of the country. But they were adamant that Indira Gandhi should resign, pending the Supreme Court's final disposal of her appeal. To force the issue they sat before President Fakhruddin Ali Ahmed's house refusing to move before he had accepted their demands. It was only after the President asked them to await the Supreme Court judgement that they left. Justice Iyer delivered his judgement on Monday, 22 June. Granting a partial stay order, he pronounced that Indira could continue as Prime Minister till the appeal was disposed of by the full bench of the Supreme Court; she could attend the Lok Sabha, take part in its deliberations but she had no right to vote nor could she draw any emoluments during the interim period before her appeal to the Supreme Court was finally heard.

On 24 June, Siddhartha Shankar Ray was in Delhi. He found a message from the Prime Minister's House awaiting him: he was to come to see her at her office as early as possible. He found a tense Prime Minister sitting at her desk with a sheaf of papers before her. He suspected that they were secret information reports. She read out paragraphs to him.

Information had reached the Prime Minister that Jayaprakash Narayan was to hold a mammoth rally on the Ram Lila grounds in Delhi on 25 June at which 'he was going to ask the armed forces and the police to revolt and disobey orders which they did not consider lawful.'

'Siddhartha, we cannot allow this,' said a tense Prime Minister. 'I want something done. I feel that India is like a baby and just as one should sometimes take a child and shake it, I feel we have to shake India.'[5]

Siddhartha Shankar Ray went home to consult his constitutional law books. He found that under the Constitution, internal Emergency could be declared when there was a threat to the internal stability of the country. Ray said he was convinced that what had taken place in Gujarat was a derailment of democracy. 'You remember, in Gujarat, Congress M.L.A.'s were forced to resign. Their houses were burnt. They were attacked and there was serious trouble. And now the same thing (trouble) had already started in Bihar. The Bihar legislature is in danger of being dissolved. If this were to happen in both Gujarat and Bihar, there is no way to stop it spreading.'[6]

Ray also found references in his law journals of decisions of the Supreme Court of the US.

'According to this you don't wait for the actual revolt. If you wait for actual revolution, then it might be too late. So you should take steps before (it happens) if you feel that there is a threat to the stability of the country. So I went into it and came to the conclusion that Emergency should be declared. As a lawyer I was satisfied that a situation had arisen as envisaged by the framers of the Constitution for the imposition of Emergency laws.'[7]

He went back to 1, Safdarjung Road the same day to advise Indira accordingly. While they were discussing the comprehensive powers available to government, her Special Assistant, R.K. Dhawan, came in with the news that Jayaprakash Narayan had castigated Indira at the Ram Lila grounds meeting for not resigning and had appealed to the armed forces and police to disobey those orders of government which they considered unlawful. 'Total Revolution is our slogan, future history belongs to us,' was JP's cry.

During his speech Jayaprakash Narayan announced his decision to set up the "Lok Sangarsh Samiti", a committee to organize a people's struggle with Morarji Desai as its Chairman and Nanaji Deshmukh of the Rashtriya Swayamsevak Sangh (RSS) as its Secretary. Morarji Desai, Nanaji Deshmukh and other senior leaders were to surround the Prime Minister's House and refuse to allow anyone to enter or leave and so paralyse the functioning of government. The committee was to call on their followers to squat on railway lines to see that trains did not move, and to prevent courts and government offices from functioning. Morarji Desai and Deshmukh were expected to start agitations against the Congress party all over the country and so create enormous pressure to force Indira Gandhi to resign. The Prime Minister and Ray realized that unless immediate action was taken to stop this, there would be chaos in the country.

According to most of her friends Indira would not have supported Emergency measures if she had retained her independence; she would have fought the Opposition in the open, on the political battlefield. By now, however, she was hemmed in, surrounded by a growing hysteria; she felt trapped, convinced that plots were being hatched to destroy her and so she invested her future in her son, Sanjay.

On Siddhartha Shankar Ray's advice, a decision was taken by Indira Gandhi to promulgate Emergency laws under Article 352 of the Constitution. By 8 o'clock that night, Indira Gandhi and Siddhartha Shankar Ray were with the President, Fakhruddin-Ali Ahmed. Ray explained the sections of the Constitution under which a state of Emergency could be promulgated. The President's signature was necessary before the decision became operative. Fakhruddin Ali Ahmed, a lawyer by profession, was quick to comprehend the Emergency provisions. He agreed and asked for the order to be sent to him for signature. This was to be accompanied by a letter from the Prime Minister advising the President to promulgate a state of Emergency. On their return, she asked Siddhartha Shankar Ray whether she could declare a state of Emergency without a meeting of the Cabinet and what should be the form of the Emergency declaration. P.N. Dhar, the head of her Secretariat, was called in to provide copies of earlier external Emergency orders promulgated in 1962 and again in 1971 when India was at war. Siddhartha Shankar Ray and D.K. Barooah who were present advised her to declare a state of Emergency immediately, for later ratification by the Cabinet. The four-line declaration of Emergency was drafted. It read:

Proclamation of Emergency

In exercise of the powers conferred by Clause 1 of Article 352 of the Constitution, I, Fakhruddin Ali Ahmed, President of India, by this proclamation declare that a grave emergency exists whereby the security of India is threatened by internal disturbances.

New Delhi, 25th June, 1975   PRESIDENT

With these few words the Government of India was authorized to arrest people without warrant, to suspend civil rights and liberties, to limit the rights of courts to interfere, to impose press censorship. The draft, with a letter from the Prime Minister was taken by R.K. Dhawan, her Special Assistant, for the signatures of the President:

Prime Minister
India

New Delhi, June 25, 1975.

Dear Rashtrapatiji,

As already explained to you a little while ago, information has reached us which indicates that there is imminent danger to the security of India being threatened by internal disturbances. The matter is extremely urgent. I would have liked to have taken this to Cabinet but unfortunately this is not possible tonight. I am, therefore, condoning or permitting a departure from the Government of India (Transfer of Business) Rule, 1961, as amended up to date by virtue of my powers under Rule 12 thereof. I shall mention the matter to the Cabinet first thing tomorrow morning. In the circumstances and in case you are satisfied, a requisite Proclamation under Article 352(1) has become necessary. I am enclosing a copy of the draft Proclamation for your consideration. As you are aware, under Article 352(3) even when there is imminent danger of such a threat, as mentioned by me, the Proclamation under article 352(1) can be issued.

I recommend that such a Proclamation should be issued tonight, however late it may be and all arrangements will be made to make it public as early as possible thereafter.

With kind regards,

Yours sincerely,
(Sd. Indira Gandhi)

Dhawan returned with the order signed by the President a few minutes before midnight of 25 June.

The decision taken, Indira regained her composure and began to draft the speech she was to deliver to the country on television next morning. The full implications of the Emergency laws were never discussed nor was the follow up action that was inevitable. Barooah and Siddhartha Shankar Ray were present while she was drafting her speech. She would write parts of it, read it out and they would make suggestions which were incorporated into the speech. The speech was to be as unambiguous as possible, so that the people could understand in simple language the reasons for the Emergency.

While Siddhartha Shankar Ray and Barooah were with the Prime Minister finalizing her draft speech, Sanjay—aware of the developments—had gathered senior bureaucrats in an adjoining room to consider the draconian measures to be imposed before the next morning. Brahmananda Reddy, the senior Home Minister, was kept in the dark, but Om Mehta, the Minister of State for Home Affairs was with Sanjay, as was Kishan Chand, Lieutenant Governor of Delhi. For advice, Sanjay turned to Bansi Lal, Chief Minister of Haryana, a tough, ruthless Jat peasant leader. Names were drawn up of Opposition leaders to be arrested. Chief ministers were contacted and orders sent out in the name of the Prime Minister to them. Late night arrests took place. Jayaprakash Narayan and Morarji Desai were arrested late at night and taken to the Sona Dak Bungalow, very near Delhi. They were both taken by complete surprise. It was inconceivable to them that Indira Gandhi could take such drastic action. They were housed in separate rooms, so no communication between them was possible.

Maneka, Sanjay's young wife, was sent away to Srinagar so that she was not in the house; she was a curious, intelligent girl, who talked readily and it was feared that this might be inimical to the secrecy that shrouded the entire operation. It was 3 o' clock in the morning before Indira finalized the draft of her speech and went to her room. Siddhartha Shankar Ray found a greatly agitated Om Mehta in the corridor. He told Ray that electricity to newspaper offices was to be cut to ensure that there would be no newspapers the next morning. Siddhartha Shankar Ray was shocked and said this was not the Prime Minister's intention, the whole thing was absurd.

Om Mehta confirmed that it was happening and went on to say that 'tomorrow all the high courts will be closed, the doors locked.'

Siddhartha Shankar Ray was horrified and asked to see Indira again. Her aides informed him that she had gone to her room and could not be disturbed. Ray insisted. As they waited for Indira, Sanjay came out and spoke to Siddhartha. 'You people do not know how to run the country.' Before his mother arrived, he left. Agitatedly Siddhartha Shankar Ray told Indira of Om Mehta's information. She was taken aback, asked Siddhartha Shankar Ray to wait till she found out what was happening. She was away for about twenty minutes; when she returned Siddhartha noticed that her eyes were red and that she had been weeping. 'Something very hard has happened.'[8]

She told him, 'Siddhartha, the electricity to the newspapers will not be cut and the high courts will remain open.'

The next morning, the high courts remained open, but the electricity to most of the newspapers was out. Only the *Statesman* and the *Hindustan Times* were able to publish that day, due to an oversight.

The lists of names for arrest were drawn up in the Prime Minister's Office, and although Sanjay was present, Indira was still very much in control of the situation. That she approved of the list of people to be arrested, can be presumed from the names omitted from the list. Members of the Opposition critical of her and her government, who were her friends and for whom she had deep respect, were kept off the list—Kamaraj from Tamil Nadu, Ganga Saran Sinha, a socialist leader from Bihar and one of Jayaprakash's close friends, S.M. Joshi, an eminent socialist from Poona, and several others did not figure in the list.

Inder Gujral, a suave, soft-spoken politician, was Minister of State for Information and Broadcasting. He was woken up at 2 a.m. on the morning of 26 June by the Cabinet Secretary, who informed him that a Cabinet meeting had been called for 6 a.m. at 1, Akbar Road, Indira Gandhi's personal office. He found K.C. Pant, then the Energy Minister and Swaran Singh, the Defence Minister walking on the lawns. They were unaware of what was happening and felt that the Emergency meeting had been called to announce Indira's decision to resign as Prime Minister. The news of Jayaprakash Narayan's address to the huge rally on Ram Lila grounds the previous evening and his call to the army and the police, to disobey orders, had reached them. They were greatly concerned over these developments and with the decision of the Opposition to 'gherao' the Prime Minister's house and so paralyse her functioning as head of the government. Most of the ministers present were still unaware of the arrests of Jayaprakash Narayan, Morarji Desai and six hundred other Opposition leaders all over the country. The news of the declaration of a state of Emergency had also not reached them.

Indira Gandhi was a little late in entering the Cabinet room. She was accompanied by Om Mehta. They sat down, she turned to her Cabinet colleagues and said: 'Gentlemen, Emergency has been declared and Jayaprakash Narayan and Morarjibhai and other leaders have been arrested.'[9] The statement, in its brevity, stunned the members of her Cabinet. The secret had been very well kept. R.N. Kao, the chief of the organization responsible for external security, the Research and Analysis Wing (RAW), was unaware of the gravity and the all- pervasive nature of the action she contemplated. For a time they were unable to comprehend the dimensions of the new laws and their effect on the country. The only minister to ask questions was Swaran Singh. He enquired why the Emergency was necessary, when an external emergency already existed. Indira informed him that the earlier state of Emergency did not deal with the national situation. The silence in the room was oppressive. They were living a nightmare, midnight arrests, total censorship, proclamation of draconian ordinances denying fundamental rights could not happen, not in India, was the thought in the minds of most of the ministers who had gathered around the Cabinet table. Freedom and democracy were sacred words. They could not be so savagely wiped out; not in India.

But the unbelievable had taken place. I.K. Gujral was astonished that although censorship had been discussed no ordinance had been issued. This was done later in the day by the Political Affairs Committee (PAC) of the Cabinet. As Gujral came out of the Cabinet room he found Sanjay standing in the outer room. His entire demeanour was 'as if he had taken over.' He asked Nurul Hasan, the Education Minister, who was with Gujral, for lists of the lecturers with RSS sympathies in the universities. Sanjay then turned to Gujral and said: 'I want to see the news bulletins before they are broadcast.' Gujral replied that this was not possible. The bulletins were secret and it could not be done. Indira Gandhi was nearby and heard him. 'What is the matter?' she asked. Gujral explained that till the news bulletins were broadcast they were secret documents. She understood, but suggested that a man might be specially posted to bring the bulletins to the house of the Prime Minister. Gujral returned home, determined to resign.[10]

He was soon called back to the Prime Minister's residence. Sanjay was there. The Prime Minister had left for her office. Sanjay was rude, and said the Prime Minister's morning broadcast had not been on all the wave lengths. Gujral lost his temper.

He told Sanjay 'If you want to talk to me, you will learn to be courteous. You are younger than my son and I owe you no explanation.'[11] He went home more determined than ever to submit his resignation, but he was pre-empted by Indira Gandhi who called him and transferred him to another ministry. V.C. Shukla (now Minister for Water Resources) took over the Ministry of Information and Broadcasting. Tough censorship laws were promulgated; one by one, representatives of the foreign press were asked to leave the country.

Indira spoke on television on the morning of 26 June. The country listened with shock and bewilderment. The Prime Minister's voice was unnaturally calm. She did not stress any event. The lack of passion to express the undercurrent of strong emotions that underlay this momentous moment, was in itself symptomatic of her mind. She was informing the people of India that a large number of political leaders, some of them comrades of her father, patriots and freedom fighters had been arrested during the night and imprisoned. The word "Emergency" which figured in her speech did not convey the awesome powers which she had taken to herself.

For the first few days after the declaration of Emergency Indira was very apprehensive. She did not know what repercussions the state of Emergency and the arrests would have on the country. But the swiftness of the action, the secrecy that surrounded it, the speed with which follow-up action was organized, the absence of news, destroyed any possible protest. The Congress party, the Opposition parties, traders, hoarders, smugglers, trade movement leaders were all caught unawares. Rural India did not awake. People in the cities, unable to turn to newspapers for information, huddled together in the homes of friends. Voices dropped to whispers, fear, the dread of the tomorrow, raised its head like a coiled serpent. 'I had no idea with what speed this fear would catch up with us. The day censorship was imposed it seemed as if every one had lost his voice.'[12]

K. Kamaraj, the highly respected leader from the south, who as former Congress President had been the individual most responsible for Indira's election as Prime Minister, was shattered. Speaking at Sholingar in Tamil Nadu on 27 June, Kamaraj said:

> I am shocked to hear that leaders have been arrested throughout the country. This state of affairs is not good for the nation. . . .What happens in Delhi we are not able to know. The radio does not give correct news, newspapers are also not giving correct news. . . . Such an event has no parallel even under British rule.[13]

A day later Kamaraj told students at Tiruvellore: 'I feel as though I have been left in a jungle blindfolded. I cannot visualise the consequences of the Emergency. Could anyone have imagined that such an Emergency would be proclaimed.'[14]

This was the thought uppermost in the minds of most thinking people in the country.

*

As happens in all countries where authoritarian rule takes over, order descended on the cities; corruption was controlled; crimes against women decreased; communal riots did not take place; prices were brought down; railway platforms were clean; the trains ran on time; garbage was less visible on the streets; beggars were not to be seen; clerks appeared to work in offices, smugglers were jailed. Rites, rituals, feasts, festivals, births, marriages, funerals were carried on as usual. The clubs and hotels were full. In city streets and in villages there were few signs to indicate that an ordinance had been enacted which had destroyed the freedom of the country.

On 1 July 1975, four days after the declaration of the state of Emergency, aware that bringing discipline and order to a country lapsing into lethargy would have to be followed by a clear economic and social policy, Indira announced her 20-Point Programme for the social and economic regeneration of India. She realized that the esoteric language planners and economists had little direct impact on people. Few understood the implications of the various Five-Year Plans which had been projected since independence. Her 20-Point Programme was a document transparent in its clarity. It stressed areas of concern that affected the day to day life of Indians throughout the country. The programme consisted of:

- Scaling down prices of essential commodities and streamlining their production and distribution.
- Economizing on government expenditure.
- Compilation of land records, implementing the law on agricultural land ceilings and speeding up distribution of surplus land.
- Stepping up house-site availability to the landless and weaker sections.
- Declaring bonded labour illegal.
- Planning for the liquidation of rural indebtedness, and a moratorium on recovery of debts from the landless, labourers, small farmers and artisans.
- Reviewing laws on minimum agricultural wages.
- Bringing five million more hectares under irrigation, and preparing a national programme for the use of underground water.
- Increasing power production.
- Developing the handloom sector and improving the quality and supply of people's cloth.
- Effecting the "socialization" of urban and urbanizable land and placing a ceiling on ownership and possession of vacant land.
- Special squads for a valuation of conspicuous consumption and the prevention of tax evasion. Summary trials and deterrent punishment for economic offenders.

- Special legislation for the confiscation of smugglers' properties.
- Liberalizing investment procedures and taking action against misuse of import licences.
- New schemes for workers' associations, in industry.
- National permit schemes for road transport.
- Income tax relief for the middle class—exemption limit placed at Rs 8,000.
- Essential commodities at controlled prices to students in hostels.
- Books and stationery at controlled prices.
- A new apprenticeship scheme to enlarge employment and training, specially for the weaker sections.

This was her economic pledge to the nation. She called on chief ministers, Cabinet ministers and state Congress chiefs to follow its provisions and thereby ease the burdens of the poor. She also initiated action to ensure that the programmes announced by her were made operative. The general economic condition of the country improved and for the first six months there was little to suggest that the general public was apprehensive of Emergency and its promulgation.

Secularism was to her a precious inheritance, central to all democratic functioning; to strengthen its roots she banned the parties she considered fundamentalist, extreme rightist or accepting violence as necessary for transforming society. They were the RSS, a militant Hindu revivalist body; the Jamaat-e-Islamia-e-Hind, a Muslim religious organization; the Anand Marg, a sect of Hindu fanatics; and the Naxalites (extreme leftists), accused of murder and violence aimed at the destruction of the social and economic order through violent action.

A session of Parliament was convened on 21 July 1975. A resolution seeking Parliament's approval for the proclamation of Emergency was introduced. With the enormous majority enjoyed by Indira's Congress, it was passed. A few members of the Opposition expressed a passionate concern about the new laws and their consequences to the nation.

Jayaprakash Narayan, shattered by his pre-dawn arrest, fell ill and was taken to the All-India Institute of Medical Sciences (AIIMS) in Delhi. It was here that he started to write his diary. In an entry, dated 21 July he writes: 'My world lies in a shambles around me. I am afraid

I shall not see it put together again in my lifetime. What went wrong?' he asked himself. He too felt there were plots. The arrest of the Opposition leaders and the promulgation of the Emergency was, for him, a plan to replace the existing democracy with a totalitarian regime. He was certain that it was a Soviet plot; he saw two plans instead of one. In one plan, he wrote:

> To which Indiraji is privy and is made to believe that it is her plan, Indira was to remain supreme till her death. The other plan hatched by the Soviets was to take effect at the point of transition from social democracy to Communist dictatorship, at which point Indira was to be replaced by a Soviet stooge.[15]

A few days before my return to India, Bhimsen Sachar, an elder citizen, eighty-five years of age, with a fine record of service to the country, together with seven respected citizens of Delhi, had written an open letter to the Prime Minister:

> . . . .none of us belong to any political party and have no political axe to grind nor are we interested in any political office or power. Our chief interest is in upholding the freedom and dignity of the individual. We regard Pandit Jawaharlal Nehru as one of the principal architects of Indian democracy. He used to say, "No one, however great he may be, should be above criticism." It was he who had said about the freedom of the press, "To my mind, the freedom of the press is not just a slogan from the larger point of view but it is an essential attribute of the democratic process. . . .It is wrong to interfere with the freedom of the press. By imposing restrictions you do not change anything; you merely suppress the public manifestations of certain things thereby causing the idea and thought underlying them to spread further. Therefore, I would rather have a completely free press with all the dangers involved with the wrong use of that freedom than a suppressed or regulated press.". . . .It was he who gave us that memorable slogan "freedom is in peril, defend it with all your might. . . ."

They expressed their anguish at the atmosphere of fear and political repression that prevailed in the country and at the sight of politically conscious citizens choosing to observe a discreet silence, afraid of a midnight knock on their door. . . .

'Must the monster of fear devour us again?' they asked. In view of the seriousness of the situation they proposed to advocate openly the right of public speech and association and freedom of the press. On 25 July, all eight signatories to the letter were arrested and sent to the Central Jail in Ambala, to be released only on 30 August, on a writ petition filed by Bhimsen Sachar in the High Court of Delhi challenging his detention.

I returned to India in July to face the darkness and tensions which had descended on the cities of India. Headlines in the Western press and media had reported the Emergency, the arrests and total censorship. Close friends of India at the forefront of support in her struggle for independence were stunned and vocal in their criticism. The absence of any letters from my friends or close relations while I was abroad, had conveyed to me the atmosphere of fear that now prevailed in India.

I found Delhi a city of outrage, seething with rumours of arrests, hunger strikes, deaths in jail. Angry friends, aware of my friendship with Indira, came to the house to ask me bluntly what I felt about it all.

It was with trepidation and sorrow that I went to see the Prime Minister at her office in Parliament House. The Lok Sabha was in session. She embraced me but the easy, relaxed poise of the past was missing. Her body had slimmed down; there was an aridity in her eyes which made me aware of her isolation and her conflicts. I could not help reaching out to her. For a moment we sat quiet, hesitating to speak of what was uppermost in both our minds. It was I who broke the silence. I kept my voice very low, allowed for pauses. I knew that to reach her, she should not feel threatened. 'I have just returned,' I said. 'The city is full of fear. How can you, the daughter of Jawaharlal Nehru, permit this?' She was taken aback. I could see my words were a shock; perhaps few people had spoken to her so directly. She did not answer me for a time. I could sense the turbulence within her.

'You do not know the gravity of what was happening,' she said. 'You do not know of the plots against me. Jayaprakash and Morarjibhai have always hated me. They were determined to see that I was destroyed and government functioning paralysed. How could I permit this?' She perhaps sensed that though my words were harsh, I spoke out of my concern for her. Her eyes suddenly grew moist with unshed tears. 'Jayaprakash's wife Prabha was very close to my mother but with her death relationships have altered. Jayaprakash has always resented my being Prime Minister.' Again she was silent. 'He has never discovered his true role. Does he want to be a saint or a martyr? Why does he refuse to accept that he has never ceased to be a politician and desires to be the Prime Minister?'[16]

I listened to what she said. No comments were necessary. I asked her again, 'Could you not have dealt with the situation without the arrests of so many people? Why are people so afraid?' I told her how destructive censorship could become. All kinds of rumours were rampant, some true, some false. There was no way for an ordinary human being to know what was happening. Emergency provisions and censorship were fertile soil for fear to germinate and take root.

She listened without interrupting. One could touch the undercurrent of her enormous conflicts. Hardly twenty-eight years ago, at midnight on 14 August 1947, she had placed her hands on the free, ageless soil of India and watered it with her tears. Could she erase that memory from her mind? Could she destroy freedom, with its vast hinterland of struggle, sorrow, pain and death, with a declaration of four lines?

I knew her sufficiently well to be aware that the thought of her friends in India and abroad seeing her as an authoritarian dictator hurt her very deeply. Dorothy Norman in the US, John Grigg in London and Helmut Kreisky in Vienna, had been very critical of her decision and had organized meetings to protest against the proclamation of Emergency, the arrests and the censorship. Democracy in India was like a great jewel luminous with light. Could Indira so easily accept that she had clouded that light? To accept it would be, for her, a betrayal of her patrimony.

I noticed that she had developed a twitch in her eye, a sign of taut emotions rigidly held under control. 'It will not last long,' she said. 'Already the country is returning to normal.'[17] I did not push her further. What I had said was enough for the moment.

We talked about my trip, the mutual friends I had met. Slowly her body relaxed, her eyes softened and she could smile when I left her.

During the weeks that followed I saw her at her home once every ten days. She was always alone and there was little to indicate that 1, Safdarjung Road was the centre of a vast intricate apparatus through which the country was ruled. Security around her house had been reinforced although few guns were visible. She rarely spoke to me of the Emergency or what was happening in the country. I referred to it only when some specific matter had to be brought to her notice. There was a growing sycophancy around her and I could sense her immense isolation.

There was a deep awareness in me that I should not meet her with a tinted mind; should not confront her or force her to view me as a threat. It was also impossible for me to support her. The only way to help was to be silent, to listen, so that she could unburden herself without having to defend herself and her actions; to talk without the wariness which by now had become her habitual response. I could see that she was restless, not at peace with herself. The fear in the country had touched and invaded her. Her ability to retreat into herself, to be free to observe—her most precious gift, and a craft that had matured within her over half-a-century—had dimmed.

Around the first week of August she asked me for some suggestions for her Independence Day speech at the Red Fort. I did not know what to say. There was only one suggestion—the ending of the state of Emergency—but I instinctively knew that to suggest it would block any currents which were converging towards any such action. She sensed my reticence and respected it. I had heard that Sanjay and his entourage were firmly against any display of weakness on her part. She had to face them down if right action was to emerge. The last time I saw her before 15 August, she asked me whether I was going to the Red Fort on Independence Day. I said, 'Yes,' though in previous years I had rarely gone. By now I was convinced that she intended to announce the lifting of the state of Emergency though certain measures might continue to ensure that the turmoil of the past was avoided.

TWO

From 1947 on, the Red Fort from where Jawaharlal Nehru unfurled the national flag, was the symbol of free India's pride. Indira Gandhi was aware of this when she stood on its ramparts. She was addressing not only the crowds that had gathered there that August morning, but vast numbers of men and women who listened to her over television and radio. Though it was the monsoon season there were no rains.

I sensed that something was wrong the moment Indira started to speak. The timbre of her voice was strained as if she was suppressing powerful emotions. The speech was rambling. Her capacity to reach out, to touch the hearts of people, to draw them close to her so that communication reached beyond the word, that voice had deserted her.

She grew emotional about the national flag. She spoke of freedom, linked it with courage and the determination to take hard decisions. Freedom, she said, did not mean breaking institutions but raising the under-privileged to fight against poverty. For this, self-discipline was necessary.

'I have not acted with a happy heart. One has to at times take a hard step, to drink bitter medicine.' She emphasized the need for the country to become healthy; she stressed cleanliness, beauty and newness. She spoke of the need for sacrifice and service. 'Freedom is in danger. If it is to be saved, a sense of duty is essential. I speak to lakhs of people,' she said, 'people from all over the world. I hear all kinds of things but I cannot hear everything.'

She emphasized her stand on democracy. 'We take a pledge to build a new country where tradition and the new come together. The greatest weapon we have is courage. Have faith in yourself. The way is full of thorns but we are making history.'

She had not said a word about the ending of the Emergency. Something had happened. What? On reaching home, I telephoned the Prime Minister's residence to find that she had gone out immediately after her return from the Red Fort. Some time later a telephone call from a friend gave me news of the assassination of Sheikh Mujib-ur Rehman, President of Bangladesh, and his family by rebellious troops at dawn on the morning of 15 August. Mujib, his wife, his three sons, his two daughters-in-law and his two nephews had been killed. The nine-year-old son of Mujib named Russell after Bertrand Russell, was shot dead as he ran to the veranda on hearing the sound of gunfire. I could guess what effect this news would have had on Indira.

R.N. Kao, chief of the Research and Analysis Wing (RAW) had information from 1974 onwards about plots against Mujib-ur Rehman. Underground reports had reached him that revolt was brewing in the Bangladeshi Defence Services. He had personally briefed Indira Gandhi on this. She had sent him to Dhaka to inform Mujib about the plot. 'We were walking in the garden. I told Mujib that we had information about a plot against him, but he was in a state of euphoria. "Nothing can happen to me," he said. "They are my people." This was even though I gave him details of the definite information we had received.'[1] It was in March 1975 that further information reached Kao that the plot against Mujib was being organized within the Artillery. Indira was quick to inform Mujib, but he refused to believe; he was the *Banga Bandhu,* the Founder Father of Bangladesh, he could not be assassinated by his own people. Reports were also current in 1974 that the plot had been masterminded by forces outside the country.[2]

I went to her house on the evening of 15 August 1975, to find that a great fear had taken her over. The threshold of her insecurity had dropped precipitously. She had heard of the murders, as she was about to leave for the Red Fort, she delivered the speech she had so carefully prepared, but the announcement she was to make was erased from her mind.

She told me that the assassination of Mujib was the first event in a plot that would submerge the sub-continent. Mujib was the first to go. The next target, she was convinced, would be herself. The news of the murder of Mujib's young son annihilated all clear thinking. All manner of primal fears had been aroused. 'I have disregarded intelligence reports, but I cannot do so any longer,' she said. She felt suspicious of everything and everyone; every shadow held an enemy. 'Whom can I trust?' she asked me. 'Rahul (Rajiv's son) is about the same age as Mujib's son. It could be him tomorrow. They would like to destroy me and my family.

'Mrs. Gandhi was the target of attack, not by agents of foreign powers but by Indian recruits who were likely to act as stooges of foreign powers and she was quite right in her suspicion,'[4] said R.N. Kao when he met me. Definite information had been reported, by Intelligence agencies, of plots against her and sabotage to strike terror amongst the people and destabilize government functioning. The Anand Margis with their army of *avadhoots,* had percolated most government departments.

Smarting under the ruthless suppression of the railway strike in 1974, George Fernandes, a trade unionist and former member of Parliament, went underground to avoid arrest. Dressed at times as a sadhu, at other times as a Sikh, he constantly shifted residence, travelling from city to city, now in Madras, now in Bangalore, in Baroda, in Delhi, in Calcutta. He was determined to gather together a group which would support him in his determination to strike at Indira through sabotage. Its simple objective was a one-point programme: "Remove that woman". C.G.K. Reddy, one of the con-spirators, in an extraordinary book, *The Baroda Dynamite Case,* published after Indira Gandhi's defeat at the polls in 1977, gives details of the plot and of the various measures contemplated. The assassination of Indira Gandhi was definitely considered a possibility.

> Assassination is simple and direct. It has been employed
> or attempted in every dictatorial regime—a determined
> group organising itself could have removed Mrs. Gandhi
> physically and with her also those who were close to her
> and whose removal was necessary to end the regime.[5]

According to Reddy, they gave up the decision to assassinate the Prime Minister and decided on sabotage instead. A conspiracy was hatched in Baroda, dynamite procured and arrangements made to dispatch it to Varanasi. A few miles from Varanasi was Moghul Sarai, a major junction of railway traffic for North India. This was the target during the railway strike, it remained the most critical point for attack. Its destruction would have paralysed the country. Though the plotters failed in many of their objectives, explosions and sabotage did take place in Bombay, Bihar and Karnataka. Indira Gandhi received secret reports of George Fernandes' plot. 'Fernandes intended to blow me up at a public meeting in Benares,' she wrote to Fori Nehru. The dynamite plot was discovered and the first arrests made in May 1976. George Fernandes was traced and arrested in Calcutta on 10 June and a case of conspiracy was filed against him and his associates. The news of the arrests and details of the plot to dynamite railway junctions and bridges confirmed Indira Gandhi's fears.

From 15 August 1975 it became difficult to enter into a dialogue with Indira. She continued to meet me but her eyes were shadowed and she was wary of what she said. I could sense, at times even touch, her storm-swept mind and the nature of her conflicts. But she was not prepared to face herself or acknowledge a heritage that had straightened her spine, given her resilience and an inviolable dignity. She was on the defensive, there was a fierce refusal to probe. No one, including Indira, looked on Sanjay Gandhi as little more than a child. Yet her need for support from someone she could trust totally made her turn to Sanjay on all matters for advice and sustenance.

During this period there was little contact between Indira and Rajiv, her elder son, who had strongly opposed the Emergency. He came to know of Indira's decisions and travel plans through the newspapers. He and his close friends were critical of the provisions of Emergency and spoke against it, at times openly.

In times of darkness and stress, the astrologer or soothsayer who observes the configuration of stars and foretells the future is sought for by men and women in India. Those who accept karmic laws, the arrow of time, consider the future as preordained. Today's action entangles tomorrow, that is karma's law. Very few in India ignore the mysterious power of the astrologer, even when it anticipates sorrow and generates anxiety. Rites, rituals and austerities are prescribed by the soothsayer to change or deflect the flight of the arrow: causation, according to these magician soothsayers, can be changed. A vast number of astrologers, tantrics, palmists, readers of the *Bhrigu Samhita* converged on the capital. Their one ambition was to reach and influence the Prime Minister.

P.M. Dhumal of Nagpur, a famous astrologer, an Ayurvedic *vaid* and a devotee of Indira, anxious to be of help, informed Nirmala Deshpande, a disciple of Vinoba Bhave, that Sanjay's stars were such that if Indira and her younger son continued to stay under the same roof, Sanjay would destroy his mother or if she survived, Sanjay would be destroyed. Together the stars foretold their doom.[6] He begged

Nirmala to convey this to Indira. According to the astrologer, Sanjay should be sent as far away as possible; mother and son should not continue to live under the same roof.

Nirmala tried to inform Indira in as subtle a way as possible, but Indira was not prepared to listen. The Prime Minister told R.N. Kao, a man she trusted implicitly. 'I am not in very good health, I sleep in my room and Sanjay is next door to me. If something happens to my health, Sanjay will be within call.'[7] The doorway which connected her room through a tiny enclosed passage to Sanjay's room, was kept open after the assassination of Mujib-ur Rehman.

Indira was fifty-seven years old, a precarious age for a woman. The tides of her body were arhythmic. She suffered from a severe hor-monic imbalance which made it difficult for her to come to terms with the body's new emanations.

Throughout her life whenever challenged, her back to the wall, she had let go, stepped back, let her mind lie fallow. Action had followed; clear, precise, uncluttered. Like the tree that learns to bend before a storm and so is seldom uprooted, was the way she had faced crisis. This had given her an agility of mind, the skill to see into situations and people. It had made possible her capacity for unexpected action. It had also given her courage and an intuitive sense of timing. She could take her opponents by surprise and so triumph. But now, confronted with a moment which called for the convergence of every resource within her, she lost her agility, the capacity to be three steps ahead of her opponents. Her mind was tossed hither and thither; the doorways to her inner reserves closed. There was no space for her to step back. Her capacity to listen and observe, to enter into situations, was at its lowest ebb.

She turned to her favoured son, Sanjay, and drew energy from the youth. She saw him tall, lithe of body, arrogant, strong in behaviour, decisive in action, quick in his love for her; a son she could trust, who stood by her side and took over her burdens. Sanjay became her ears and eyes.

For the first time she faltered and let decisions be taken by another. 'She wrapped Sanjay around herself like a blanket to keep out the cold. It was as if she had the shivers.'[8]

THREE

Sanjay Gandhi, Indira Gandhi's second son, was twenty-nine years of age at the time of the declaration of the Emergency.

He grew to manhood a graceful youth, with sensuous curling lips and insolent eyes. He was frugal in his habits, ate sparingly, had few personal possessions. He had grace of manner, was soft-spoken; his intense arrogance and discourtesy were deliberate. Like his mother he could freeze people with his silence. Unlike her, he could also be frank and brutal when the occasion demanded it.

'He was a silent person, very silent. The closest I can describe him in literature is to Howard Roark in Ayn Rand's *The Fountainhead,*[1] said Maneka Gandhi, Sanjay's widow.

From Indira, Sanjay inherited a natural secularism, and Indira's fabled courage, her refusal to accept defeat, her tenacious spirit, her energy and love of adventure. From her he also inherited an ability to perceive essentials swiftly, as also her capacity for decisive action.

From his father he had received an interest in technology and an understanding of its workings; he also had Feroze Gandhi's grit and determination, his ability to draw people to him, his sensuality and his love of life. Sanjay adored his father who saw him sparingly, but who spoilt him, when he did. Feroze's death left Sanjay bereft and resentful of his mother whom he held responsible for the neglect and death of his father.

On the sixth day after Sanjay's birth, when his future was written in invisible letters in the sky, from some unknown ancestor he inherited an incapacity to discriminate between right and wrong. Ends and achievements were important to him, means had little significance.

'It was not that he did not care about means, but he was so young he did not know how. He had very little knowledge of form. Now that I am older, I realize that in India form is as important as content. It was as if Sanjay knew he had very little time. So he decided to deal with content and leave form to be dealt with later. And that came as a cultural shock to a country that is so concerned with form. It doesn't matter if you don't do anything so long as you are known as a good guy, noble or something,' said Maneka to me in an interview.

Indira's upbringing of her sons, from all accounts, was strict. She was careful to see that as a Prime Minister's grandchildren they were not showered with toys. A vast number of pet animals, tiger cubs, pandas, dogs, horses, formed part of their surroundings and both Rajiv and Sanjay grew to love animals. While in kindergarten and junior school, Rajiv and Sanjay attended a private school run by Elizabeth Gauba. She spoke to me many years later of the vast difference between the two children—Rajiv was courteous, well-behaved, a fair student; Sanjay was rebellious, destructive, uninterested in all school activities, rude to his teachers and altogether unmanageable. He grew up a wild, wayward youth, often in scrapes, fiddling with cars, attracting questionable friends.

Sanjay was a dropout from the Doon School in Uttar Pradesh. His mother in despair sent him abroad soon after as an apprentice in the Rolls-Royce Company. He left the company after three years, for he told his mother there was nothing more they could teach him. He returned to India after Indira became Prime Minister. 'From that day Indira could not control him.'[2]

Sanjay never knew deprivation. Born into the home of prime ministers, surrounded by the pomp and splendour of a prime minister's entourage, observing the adulation of the people for Jawaharlal Nehru, and later for Indira Gandhi, perhaps Sanjay came to regard India and its people as the family's personal fief.

He did not inherit from his mother and grandfather their immense empathy for the people of India, their compassion for the poor and unprivileged. He had never seen the lean, gaunt faces of grandmothers wailing for their dead, never looked at the faces of farmers gazing at their drought-stricken fields, never heard the silent yet piercing fear-laden cry for protection that has echoed down the centuries in rural India.

Unlike his mother and grandfather, he had never suffered, never felt helpless, never known isolation or total despair. He did not inherit from Indira and Jawaharlal the maturity which led them to doubt or question. He was a rebel against tradition and custom, impatient of rules and procedures. He had little interest in books or in the cultivation of the mind, nor did he understand the potency of symbol in a mythic society. He had no access to that inwardness which led Jawaharlal and Indira to explore the primal wisdom of India, into millennia of heritage.

Sanjay's ears, eyes and heart were closed to India's underground rivers.

*

The Komagata Maru session of the Congress party was held in Chandigarh on 30 December 1975. It was on the platform of the Youth Congress, an organization Sanjay had built and strengthened over the previous six months, that Indira's son came out from the shadow of his mother, as a leader in his own right. 'You have stolen my thunder,' she said proudly as he stood by her side. She had acknowledged her gratitude to the Youth Congress and to Sanjay for their support at a time when the onslaughts of the Opposition threatened to destroy her.

From January 1976, the tempo of the Emergency quickened. Sanjay launched his Five-Point Programme. With an uncanny skill he identified social and cultural problems, the solution of which would revolutionize India: family planning, tree planting, a ban on dowry, 'Each One Teach One', and the end of casteism.

Indira saw in Sanjay a dynamism and a determination that would enable him to act with strength. She knew he was young, immature, impetuous, but she felt he would learn and that she would be able to control him. But she misjudged her own capabilities; the country was vast, complex, her son self-willed and arrogant. In giving him the freedom to advise and initiate action, she released a destructive energy that became uncontrollable.

From a small motor workshop where he and his mechanic friends worked on welding a people's car, Sanjay with no official position but encouraged by sycophants, members of the Youth Congress, chief ministers and other politicians, virtually became responsible for all development plans in North India. He determined the policies to be pursued, laid down priorities, advised on the fixing of targets, issued instructions, all with a naïveté which had no parallel. 'He started with an inborn arrogance that if I say so, it will be done. It was not a disregard of means; it was just that he did not know the means. He was so young that he had no way of knowing how things work. The mistake was the feeling that the shortest route was the best or that if he said so, things would work out. He felt that if the intentions were totally pure, the way would automatically be found. His intentions were totally pure, crystal clear as Mahatma Gandhi's. The intention was to leave a better India behind,'[3] said Maneka.

Sanjay carefully selected his colleagues in the Youth Congress. His 'flower children' were drawn from the cities and had little knowledge of the villages of India. Yet they toured the countryside and ministers and bureaucrats received and fawned upon them. They travelled not to learn or to serve but to issue orders on behalf of their leader. The politicians and bureaucrats listened, for orders were that Sanjay's wishes had to be carried out. These young ambassadors were supported by experienced chief ministers who, so long as they enjoyed Sanjay's pleasure, were prepared to remain silent. Sanjay's shadow was long and it covered the North Indian countryside. 'Why were people so afraid of Sanjay?' I asked Maneka. 'Why is there always fear of somebody who is a saint?'[4] was Maneka's response.

As the excesses of the Emergency grew, a few people did bring matters to Indira's notice. N.K. Seshan, her Private Secretary, who had worked with her father and was a man known for his integrity, spoke to her of certain wrong actions. 'She would brush me aside or would behave as if she had not heard me.' He believed this was because her advisers and the Intelligence agencies were sending her reports based on what they thought she would like to hear. They were afraid to speak the truth.[5]

In India between the idea and action lie rivers of twilight, within which orders on files are lost, deflected or misinterpreted. Sanjay's ruthless yet simplistic view of statecraft made the Emergency disasters inevitable. The art of governance in India had developed over the millennia. If the ruler awoke to paeans of praise sung by his bards, he had as adviser the *Rajrishi*—the King's Guru—who held him to the straight and narrow path. 2,200 years ago, Kautilya in his *Arthashastra,* a treatise on statecraft, written in the reign of Chandragupta Maurya, laid down several principles for the sophisticated management of a country. These were amongst the earliest influences on the administrative culture of India. The success of the ruler rested on the subtlety with which his ear was tuned to the changing moods of the people. To achieve the desired ends, all means were available to the administrator. Central to all this was the need to understand the psyche of individual men and women, to determine their weak-nesses—coercion, intrigue, bribery were some of the tools available to the monarch to rule effectively. But simultaneous with this stream was the doctrine of dharma: governance based on rhythms that were righteous and moral values that emphasized means to determine ends. Chandragupta's grandson, the Emperor Ashoka, victorious in battle, adopted the Buddhist creed and directed that sandstone pillars be erected on which edicts based on dharma were engraved.

With these memories fused the formal and sophisticated ad-ministrative structures of the Mughal courts. It was during Mughal rule in the time of Akbar, that Todarmal introduced a secular ad-ministration, and so cut governance away from religious mores. But the ethos of sycophancy, intrigue and manipulation continued at the Mughal courts. In the more recent past, these memories underwent further transformation with the Indian Civil Service under British rule. A secular service primarily concerned with maintaining law and order and with extracting the maximum benefits for the British rulers, the ICS assumed the role of servant and master. It was a system which was to produce men of privilege, ruthless rulers, scholars, builders. With independence the service continued. As the nature of relation-ships between the political hierarchy and the administrative machinery underwent change, as development was added to the administrators' numerous functions and as their role became more complex, as pressures mounted, a vast expansion in the administrative structure was witnessed. A stratified hierarchy came into existence with deep roots and enormous vested interests. With increasing pressure, the service was politicized. Threats of transfer, suspension or investigation became the instruments the political leadership used to control the bureaucracy. Yet, under attack, the bureaucracy came together. A vast network, an unstated brotherhood held them in indivisible bonds.

Beginning with the Emergency, according to a senior bureaucrat, only three centres of power and control counted in India. The PM, the CM and the DM—the Prime Minister, the Chief Minister and the District Magistrate. The last, a cog in the hierarchy of power, was the most important, for it was through him that policies and programmes were transmitted to individuals. The DM exercised his powers through petty officials—the tehsildar, the patwari and the station police officer. They carried out orders, took decisions or neglected to take them, depending on their attitude and concerns. They were ruthless or compassionate, made things happen or distorted orders to see that the blame for non-doing fell on the political hierarchy. Whatever pressures the political system forced on them, by 1976 they were cynical of policies and politicians. Sycophancy increased in direct proportion to the increasing immaturity of the rulers. There were attempts by the politicians to create a committed bureaucracy; the commitment was rarely to the people, it was to individual political leadership. Yet there was little the Central or state governments could do to motivate or to inspire the confidence of the bureaucrat. Sanjay did not know that the men he tried to manipulate, had through the centuries developed the instinct to survive and to rule.

A decade later, another group of bureaucrats said to me that Sanjay was able to achieve a performance from the bureaucracy that remains unsurpassed. The message given regarding objectives was definite and clear; the Five-Point Programme had no ambiguities. It gave a sense of direction and purpose, motivated an entire system, brought discipline to a naturally chaotic country. Inflation fell from over twenty-five per cent in 1974–75 to three per cent in, 1975–76. More was done for family planning during this period than at anytime since independence. The largest and most ambitious resettlement programme was implemented under Sanjay's directions during the Emergency.

Two crash programmes became operative during the Emergency. In urban areas, the thrust was on the demolition of encroachments, cleanliness, beautification and tree planting; in rural areas a major programme of family planning was launched.

Indira's monumental error was the imposition of censorship. The new Ministry for Information and Broadcasting manipulated the censorship laws to tyrannical effect. On the slightest pretext, newspapermen accredited to important newspapers and magazines abroad were asked to leave the country. With the departure of Mark Tully, the British Broadcasting Corporation (BBC) stopped functioning from India. The reporters of the *Guardian* and the *Baltimore Sun,* amongst others, were asked to leave the country. With few left from the foreign media to report events, distorted news was smuggled out of India to appear as headlines in the international press. A few eminent Indian columnists were arrested and imprisoned under the Maintenance of Internal Security Act (MISA). By December 1975, mandatory pre-censorship was imposed on parliamentary proceedings; newspapers were not allowed to keep editorial spaces blank as a mark of protest. In some cases quotes from Mahatma Gandhi, Rabindranath Tagore and even the Bhagavad Gita were blacked out by junior clerks in the censorship offices. Many newspapers and magazines were asked to submit to pre-censorship, which led some magazines to close down in protest while others continued to report non-controversial events, such as visits by the Prime Minister and her Cabinet colleagues to inaugurate various functions.

Since independence, India had been proud of her free and independent press; vernacular newspapers reached distant villages, where farmers and artisans gathered in the evenings in village squares to have the news read out to them. As newspapers stopped reporting the real news, people turned to rumours to satisfy their curiosity. Efforts to limit criticism of Emergency measures, to eliminate dissent and to prevent news from reaching government critics, led to disaster. By December 1975, a situation arose in which people did not know what was happening a few miles from where they lived. It also resulted in the Prime Minister being cut off from news of the countryside. The culture of censorship ensured that even Indira received from her information bureau only such reports as were palatable to her. Visitors to the Prime Minister were carefully screened so that all flow of news was controlled. Indira was totally isolated from the protests, disturbances and firings in the country. The darkness of the Emergency hemmed her in.

The Emergency, government felt, provided an appropriate atmosphere for tackling the family planning problem, the most crucial challenge faced by the Indian polity. In her speech to the 31st Joint Conference of the Association of Physicians of India, Indira stressed the size of the population problem.

> We must now act decisively and bring down the birth rate speedily to prevent the doubling of our population in a mere 28 years. We should not hesitate to take steps which might be described as drastic. Some personal rights have

to be kept in abeyance, for the human rights of the nation,
the right to live, the right to progress. . . .[6]

In normal circumstances a massive drive for family planning would have been hailed in India by most of those who cared about the country, for it was recognized that the rising population was India's most critical problem.

Dr Karan Singh was the Health and Family Planning Minister during the Emergency. Unfortunately, the Central Government and his Ministry and the implementing agencies at the state level were not overly concerned with the manner of implementation of the family planning programmes. The concentration was on vasectomy. But the nature of the operation was such as made it inevitable that simple village folk saw in it a threat to their virility and so they came to equate sterilization with impotence. The absence of social service personnel to prepare the ground, to educate people, to alleviate primal fears and heal psychological wounds, was traumatic. There was a mindlessness, a secrecy and absence of a human presence behind the family planning drive which led people to feel that a machine had taken over, concerned only with numbers.

By the middle of 1976, the family planning drive reached a peak; the targets for sterilization were laid down for every state and district. As the figures for sterilization were reviewed they were continually revised upwards and impossible targets set, with little consideration or concern for the facilities and medical personnel available for such an escalation in numbers. The Central and state government agencies went berserk. A target of 175,000 sterilizations for the year 1975–76 in Uttar Pradesh was raised to 1.5 million in 1976–77. Out of this 837,000 vasectomies were actually achieved. In Madhya Pradesh, the figure for 1975–76 was 163,000; this was revised upwards to 700,000 in 1976–77 and the achievement was one million vasectomies. In Haryana, a target of 45,000 for 1975–76 was raised by the state government to 200,000 in 1976–77 and the achievement was 222,000.[7]

There was constant pressure from the Central Government to improve performance. The state governments were left free to introduce their own incentives and disincentives. Incentives included the preferential allotment of houses, lands, educational facilities etc. In certain states, the salaries of teachers were withheld if they could not fulfil the quota allotted to them for motivating citizens to undergo sterilization. Many of the teachers were widows, who found it impossible to approach men to ask them to undergo sterilization. To refuse salaries to these vulnerable women caused massive resentment.

In Delhi the family planning drive came under the direct supervision of Sanjay Gandhi. Programmes for sterilization were associated in the minds of the people with the massive demolitions that took place in the city. No distinction was made on grounds of religion or caste. Turkman Gate in Old Delhi, an area with a majority of Muslim population, became a symbol of the nature of Emergency operations. The people's anger led to violence—lathi charges, arrests and police firings followed. The suddenness and the ruthlessness of the operation took the people by surprise; it was as if an earthquake had struck; people cowered in fear.

In Uttar Pradesh, Madhya Pradesh and Haryana as family planning targets were raised and the officers in charge found it impossible to fulfil their quotas, some young men were taken off buses and forcibly sterilized. In other areas opposition to the family planning drive led to rioting, violence, shootings and deaths. It was only in South India, that family planning did not unleash a backlash.

The achievements in family planning during this time were, by any standard, remarkable. From 26,24,755 cases of sterilization reported in 1975–76 for the whole country, the figures rose to 81,32,209 in 1976–77—an increase of over 300 per cent. In the two years of the Emergency the number of sterilizations reported was 1,07,56,964.[8]

The Shah Commission has inquired in depth into the deaths and excesses due to the over ten million sterilizations reported for the two years from 1975 to 1977. The figure, which includes wrongful sterilizations and deaths due to the operation or from firing against demonstrators, is 2,322, a figure which would have remained unnoticed in a drive of this order, planned and executed in normal circumstances.[9]

It was towards the autumn of 1976 that Indira began to sense and was profoundly disturbed by news that percolated to her of forcible sterilizations, uprisings, shooting and deaths. A feeling grew in her that the situation was out of control. She was swift to act, but it was already too late. Orders were issued by the Central Government in November 1976, asking the state governments to withdraw all coercive measures in the family planning drive. These orders were ignored or never issued, for some of the worst excesses took place around Delhi in the last two months of 1976.

Meanwhile wild rumours swept through North India, of massive forcible sterilizations and deaths. The rumours invoked mythic fears, emptied whole villages, and made able-bodied men seek refuge in sugarcane fields at the sight of a government vehicle. Injections at immunization centres were refused on the grounds that they would lead to sterilization.

The living oral traditions of this country travel via the voice of the story-teller, wandering mendicant, soothsayer; these travellers of the long roads, take their oral tales to village squares. Born of rumours and secrecy, events become distorted. They grow to epic proportions, heroes and villains loom large on the canvas. With total censorship, Indira was projected to the rural dweller, perhaps deliberately in some instances by her opponents or by forces inimical to her, as an elemental female energy, unleashed, and relentless in her pursuit.

The factor of gender was invoked with catastrophic effect.

FOUR

By the summer of 1976, disturbing rumours were current that the government had decided to beautify Old Delhi. The gardens that surrounded the monuments from before the Partition had been taken over by refugees to build huts. These huts were now to be demolished, the refugees evicted and fresh gardens laid out on the sites. Alternative accommodation was built to house the people evicted from these areas. But the demolitions coincided with the monsoons, causing endless hardship and despair. The new houses built in far-flung colonies, still lacked the minimum needs of water, drainage and light. The occupants of the huts to be razed had to move and force had to be used to evict them.

Ami Crishna, Indira Gandhi's Personal Secretary and a friend, spoke to the Prime Minister of the demolitions in Delhi. 'They are turning refugees out of colonies and every one is very concerned. It has rained on and on, why can't they wait another week? They know that the rains have flooded everything. What is the hurry?' Indira sent for Sanjay Gandhi and spoke to him. She told Sanjay that Ami Crishna was very unhappy, she had heard that water was entering the alternative houses in the colonies built for the dispossessed. She asked Sanjay to ascertain the facts and let her know. He came back to her. 'Rubbish!' he said, 'We have provided alternative accommodation.'

'She believed him, but I knew that the roofs were not up.'[1]

A telex message sent by the Resident Commissioner, Government of Uttar Pradesh, from Delhi to the Commissioner and Secretary, Lucknow, stated:

> As desired by the Chief Minister, I called upon Shri Sanjay Gandhi and showed him the various plans for urban development of Agra. Shri Gandhi appreciated the programme and expressed the view that with immediate effect the State Government should endeavour to remove cattle from the streets, unauthorised structures and beggars. This programme was to be extended to Varanasi.

The beautifying of Agra and Varanasi was to be completed within six months so that by winter, which was the tourist season, the two cities would present a clean appearance.

I was to visit Varanasi in August and went to see Indira to ask if there was anything I could do. I found her agitated, reports had reached her of attempts to beautify Varanasi. 'The city needs cleaning up,' she said, 'but to beautify Varanasi has ominous overtones.' She asked me to speak to the Commissioner and attempt to discover what was happening to the city.

I stayed at Rajghat in Varanasi, in a cottage at the edge of the river, where I could see dawn in the flowing waters of the Ganga. I had spent my childhood in the city and was familiar with its lanes, its wayside shrines, its temples and its myths. Varanasi is one of the oldest living cities in the world. A legend of the city tells this story: the Sun at the first dawn, visited Varanasi as a pilgrim; loathe to leave, he swore never to forsake the city, and so became Varanasi's oldest citizen.

On my arrival, angry visitors came to me with tales so horrendous that I felt they must be exaggerated. The Commissioner and the Chairman of the Mahapalika (Municipal Corporation) came to Rajghat and drove me to Vishwanath Gali, the lane in the heart of the city that leads to the main Vishwanath shrine where the primordial *linga* of all beginnings is enshrined. It is a stark symbol of the creation and is considered the holiest shrine in the world by the Hindu faithful. On the way, the Commissioner spoke of various efforts being made to remove encroachments, to plant trees and to give the city a new clean look.

For centuries, Vishwanath Gali had remained unchanged. The lane was narrow, winding, cool, for sunshine never entered its pathways, paved with ancient river stones smoothed by river water and bearing the patina of the feet of pilgrim and mendicant. It was flanked by houses built in the seventeenth and eighteenth centuries, with narrow frontages and balconies and terraces open to the sky. Pigeons flew in flocks from ateliers to rooftops; paper kites filled the sky. The oldest families of Varanasi lived in these houses; landowners, businessmen, the rich and the impoverished aristocracy. From the roofs of their homes they saw the city born of dawn and the Ganga, eternal yet inconstant in her flow. They understood the subtlety of the city, its extreme contradictions, its gods, its myths, its mysteries, its legends, its vernacular.

As in all ancient cities of pilgrimage, the arts flourished in Varanasi. The sacred and the profane existed side by side, for it was through the lavish gifts of the world that the pilgrim approached the shrine with its primordial symbol of creation. Austerity and abundance were part of the same stream. Along the lane walked the holy sanyasis with matted hair. Bulls had right of way. Along Vishwanath Gali also walked young peasants with their brides, grandmothers and bent old men who came to touch the soil of the city, to see the sun captured in flowing waters and so to die on the river banks without struggle. Varanasi is a city of light and life, a city of death and darkness. It is a city of ecstasy and a city of horror. It defies time and judgement, as it had defied the invaders who tried to destroy it. It is ancient beyond the most extended horizon of human memory.

As we walked along the lane, the Commissioner said casually that the Governor desired to drive by car to Vishwanathji. I expressed surprise.

'You cannot take a car through this lane,' I said.

'We are broadening the lane,' he said.

'How?'

He said, 'We will break down the walls of some of these houses and pave the road so that a car can go through.'

'How can you break down seventeenth-eighteenth century buildings?' I enquired in horror. 'These stones are many centuries old.'[2]

He was silent, but I saw that he was not convinced. As we walked on we came to the shrines of Hanuman, Devi, Ganesh and other minor gods, the guardians to the main temple. I asked him what he would do with the godlings. He said they would be removed and put into a nice concrete structure.

'But they are the guardians of the city, you cannot change their location,' I said.

Again he did not choose to understand and said, 'Sanjayji wants the city made beautiful.'

'But you cannot play with Varanasi,' I said. 'This is the holiest of holies and several thousand years old.' By now I knew that it was hopeless talking to him. I was numb, unable to accept the fact that centuries could be destroyed with such ease.

We drove to Kamacha, the road which was being "beautified." Kamacha looked as if a bomb had fallen on it. A bulldozer stood to one side, with two eyes painted on the front.

It had finished its task of beautification. It had bulldozed, cut through the front of houses leaving sitting-rooms with half the floor space cut away; rooms were open to the road, verandas smashed. Any impediment that came in the way of broadening the road had been removed. The map used to determine what was an encroachment was dated 1920. In the eyes of the authorities, in a city of exploding population, no fresh housing was needed or had been authorized after 1920 and every house built after that was an encroachment.

I was aware that many of the houses which had had their frontages destroyed had been built long before independence. I found it difficult to speak and asked the Commissioner, 'Was this necessary?' He shrugged his shoulders and said, 'We had instructions to remove all encroachments and the front of these buildings encroached.' I asked him whether he would agree not to destroy anything further till after my return to Delhi. He had received word from the Chief Secretary that the Prime Minister had asked me to see what was taking place, and, therefore, readily agreed.

By now the furious owners of the buildings surrounded me and insisted on giving me photographs of the site, to show the Prime Minister. I was shaken and on my return to Delhi went immediately to see Indira Gandhi. I told her of what I had seen, what the Commissioner had told me and handed over the photographs. She hit the ceiling. I had never seen her so angry; she picked up the telephone and asked her Special Assistant, R.K. Dhawan, to put her through to Narayan Dutt Tiwari, then Chief Minister of Uttar Pradesh. She exploded when she spoke to him. Did he know what was happening in Varanasi? She said she had seen the photographs and would he come immediately to Delhi to see her. She put down the phone, put her hands to her face and said, 'What is happening in this country? No one seems to tell me.' There was utter despair and sorrow in her voice. 'Do you think they would have really broken down Vishwanath Gali?[3] She was aware of the gravity and the consequences of such an act.

The next day I went to see Narayan Dutt Tiwari. He was in a state of panic, asked me what should be done; he had no idea that the demolitions were taking place on the basis of a 1920 map. When he understood what the city officials intended to do with Vishwanath Gali, he froze. He had no knowledge of what was happening. No one was clear as to who had given the orders. Who was responsible? There was a mindlessness behind the whole operation that was terrifying.

It is difficult to assess the exact role Sanjay played. He rarely spoke publicly, gave few interviews, made little effort to establish any rapport with people. His signature never appeared on official files. He remained a figure obscured by the darkness of the Emergency.

'Sanjay was the face of the Emergency,' commented his young widow. 'Even if a leaf dropped, people said Sanjay must have done it.'[4]

FIVE

By the autumn of 1976 Indira Gandhi ruled supreme. The country was peaceful to all intents and purposes. A vast number of smugglers and black-marketeers had been arrested, prices had been controlled, foreign exchange reserves were at an all-time high. The underground conspiracies and plots were smashed, most voices of revolt quenched, the conspirators behind bars. Jayaprakash Narayan was released in November 1975, his health shattered; in anguish, he questioned himself on where he had gone wrong. He had supported, in late 1976, the initiative of M. Karunanidhi, former Chief Minister of Tamil Nadu, to initiate a dialogue between the government and Opposition leaders languishing in jail. A document was issued from jail by the Opposition titled, "This we believe" emphasizing their stand on non-violence, secularism and democracy. A much-published letter was written by Biju Patnaik of Orissa while in jail to Om Mehta, the Minister of State for Home, suggesting points for discussion to save face, yet find a way out for the jailed Opposition.

B.K. Nehru, then High Commissioner of India in Great Britain, on a visit to India, spoke bluntly to Indira of the impact of the Emergency on the British public and the Western world. Indian democracy had been regarded as a beacon of light amidst the surrounding dictatorships of Asia. India's image was now smudged. B.K. Nehru urged Indira to lift the Emergency and restore democracy to the country. P.N. Dhar, a well-known economist and Indira's Principal Secretary, joined B.K. Nehru in urging Indira to withdraw the Emergency and call for elections. Under his directions a report was prepared by the Institute of Policy Research which indicated that in the event of an election Indira Gandhi would win with a comfortable majority. It suggested that the situation in the country be normalized and elections called. She listened to both of them but took no action.

The news of Zulfikar Ali Bhutto's call for elections in Pakistan triggered an enquiry in Indira. 'Could the image of India be that of a dictatorship while Pakistan became a democracy?' Michael Foot and Jennie Lee visited India on her invitation. They had expressed their dismay at Jayaprakash's call to the army and navy to disobey government orders, but Indira was aware of an uneasiness in her relationship with them. She felt a total isolation. She visited Anand Mai Ma and wept before her; doubts were arising within her, there was no one she could trust.

While under attack from abroad and from her opponents within the country, people who were prepared to use violent means to destroy her, she was tough, ruthless and one-pointed in her intentions, but as her position grew unassailable the miasma that clouded her started to dissolve. Her superb instincts came alive, intuitions arose within her that all was not well in the country. The atmosphere was oppressive. She sensed a growing anger amongst the people; she started to listen and to doubt her advisers.

Voices from her friends in India and abroad came through to her. 'We would not have expected Indu to act so.' It was growing difficult for Indira to face herself or justify continued repressive measures. The title of a benevolent dictator was difficult for her to accept.

In August 1976, I spoke to her of the advisability of J. Krishnamurti— a teacher of supreme wisdom, to visit and lecture in various cities in India. She had known him for years, had met him at my home in the Sixties and Seventies. Attracted by his luminous presence, and his teaching based on self-knowledge, she had discussed the teacher with me on several occasions but had fought shy of actually meeting him alone or in an extended dialogue. He did not come to India in the winter of 1975. His response to the Emergency was one of deep sorrow. He felt that authoritarian rule should not have been imposed in India. He wrote to me in 1976 asking for news; his friends abroad were certain that dictatorship in India had come to stay and that India would lapse into the same authoritarian pattern of government as other Asian countries. He was told that no dictator was known to give up power except through a counter-revolution. He questioned me in his letters over and over again. His teaching was centred on freedom, the seeing of "what is", the liberation of the mind, and action arising out of freedom. Would he be permitted to speak in the prevailing atmosphere, he asked? I spoke to Indira, told her what he felt, asked her whether he could speak freely. She said, 'He is most welcome.' I warned her that he would speak of freedom with all its implications. She repeated. 'He is most welcome.' I asked her whether I could speak to the chief ministers of states where Krishnaji was scheduled to speak, and inform them that she had endorsed his visit. She told me to do so.

In Indian epics, at a critical moment when immense doubts and conflicts arise in the mind of the Hero, there is a crucial encounter with a Sage, a coming face to face with the outsider and so with oneself. Indira's meeting with Krishnamurti may be compared with a moment of such mythical intensity. Krishnamurti had nothing to ask of Indira, nothing to give her, save the word that triggers the journey of self-knowledge; out of this direct perception of the self there arises action that is independent of the Sage and of the will of the seeker.

Krishnamurti arrived in Delhi on 24 October. He was my guest and I invited Indira to dinner to meet Krishnaji. She came to the house dressed in an old rose pink sari, one of her favourites. Shyly she told Krishnaji, who awaited her, that it was her birthday by the Indian calendar. He greeted her with affection. He had sensed her tortured and emotionally disturbed mind. He took her hand, held it and they sat for some time in silence. 'Madam, you are very disturbed,' he said. She was startled. She was accustomed to people looking up to her and now this fragile, straight-backed eighty-year-old sage looked her in the eye and beyond.

'Yes. The situation has become very dangerous. What shall I do?' She tried to explain to him what had happened in the country in the last eighteen months. Krishnamurti interrupted. 'I would not understand,' he said.

Her left eye was twitching badly. Krishnaji offered to help her with it. In his childhood, he said, his mother had told him that his hands could heal. Indira did not reply for a minute, nor did he pursue the matter. Suddenly she said, 'Yes, would you help me?' Krishnaji put his hands on her eyes and she grew very quiet. As they got up she asked him whether she could see him again.

'Any time,' he responded.

It was 9 o'clock when they came out of the room. At dinner, sitting between Krishnamurti and Achyut Patwardhan, she was very silent. The food was good but she ate sparingly. Krishnaji did not draw her into the conversation nor did he look towards her or talk to her throughout dinner. He sensed she was vulnerable and he did not wish to intrude. To ease the tension Krishnamurti started a conversation with L.K. Jha, who was a good friend. They related anecdotes and later Indira joined in the laughter. Towards the end of dinner Indira had recovered her composure enough to tell a story of two Soviet cosmonauts who, on their return from outer space, went to visit Nikita Khrushchev, and were asked by him in secret, 'When you were up in the heavens, did you see mysterious lights, strange beings? Did you see a great, mysterious, white-bearded figure surrounded by light?' 'Yes, comrade, we did,' the cosmonauts responded. 'I was afraid so,' said Khrushchev. Then he warned them, 'This is between ourselves, don't tell a soul.' Later, the cosmonauts travelled round the world. They visited the Pope at the Vatican. After their devotional formalities were over, the Pope took them aside and said, 'My sons, when you were up there, did you see lights or come upon a vast figure with a white beard?' 'No, Father,' they replied, 'we saw no lights nor did we see a bearded figure.' And the Pope said, Ah, my sons, I thought so. But on your soul don't tell this to anyone.' Everyone at the table laughed.

When we were alone Krishnamurti spoke to me of his meeting with the Prime Minister. He appeared deeply moved. He said 'There is something very fine about Mrs. Gandhi but she is greatly troubled.'

On 28 November I received a letter from her suggesting another meeting. She had a very busy schedule that day; there was a Cabinet meeting, Parliament was in session and the matter of the prolongation of the life of the Lok Sabha for another year was under discussion. I telephoned N.K. Seshan, her Private Secretary, to suggest a time. He said he would enquire and let me know. Indira came unexpectedly at 11 o'clock, unaccompanied by her security guards and went immediately to see Krishnamurti. They were together for more than an hour. She came out of the room with tears streaming down her face. Aditi, my grandniece, was reading in the sitting-room; Indira quickly controlled herself, smiled at Aditi and asked her what she was reading. I took her to the car. By then her security staff had arrived and awaited her.

Krishnamurti did not speak to me of his meeting with Indira except to say that she was very disturbed and that he sensed great violence around her. For months after the meeting Krishnamurti held Indira in his consciousness. He kept asking about her and about her early life. He was deeply touched by her ability to listen, and by her refusal to defend her actions. 'She is possibly the only person in her position who can be open, who can listen without reacting. There is courage in her and she will face adversity without being destroyed,' he said.

Years later, when alone with Indira, I asked her whether she cried easily. She said, 'I did not weep at Sanjay's death. Sorrow does not bring tears, but when I am deeply moved, specially by great beauty, I weep.' After her father's death, a white flower placed in a vase by her bedside shattered her and she had wept.

She spoke of her meeting with Krishnamurti in 1976. 'I sobbed and could not stop my tears. I have not cried like that for years.' She told me of what happened during the second meeting. She had described to Krishnamurti the events in India over the last year. 'I am riding on the back of a tiger,' she had told him. 'I do not mind the tiger killing me, but I do not know how to get off its back.' He had listened intensely, said if she were intelligent and unafraid she would know how to deal with the tiger. 'What should I do?' she had asked. He had refused to advise her but suggested she should take everything, her own life, all the conflicts, the sorrows, the attacks on her, her actions, the wrongs, and look at them as if they were one problem and then act without motive or fear of consequences. 'Right action is necessary, it does not matter what the result will be.' She had asked him, 'How?' He told her not to ask 'How?' but to look without letting thought operate in the looking. They had sat quietly after that. As she got up to leave, he had said 'Do you realize that if you act rightly you will have to face the consequences? They will try to destroy you.' She had left with the feeling of having been soaked in compassion.[1]

It was on 28 October that a frail movement arose in Indira to end the Emergency and call for elections whatever the consequences. She had considered the possibility of defeat; she realized that the future was unknown, the possibility of great travail lay in the months ahead but for her there had to be an expiation. There was no alternative. The debt had to be repaid.

Momentous happenings are often born of innocence, compassion and silence. The meeting with Krishnamurti had triggered a movement in Indira's unconscious. The voice of the sage had sunk deep. She started to dream; dreams beyond recall, but she awoke to her father's voice resonant within her. His presence lingered, urging her to formulate the decision that lay at the edge of consciousness. Indira kept her counsel.

By 5 November, the life of the Lok Sabha was extended by another year. The elections were now scheduled to be held in early 1978. Indira did not reveal her mind at the Congress session held in Guwahati towards the middle of December. Sanjay Gandhi was the hero at the meetings of the Congress conclave. Indira reaffirmed her faith in the Youth Congress, D. K. Barooah, the Congress President eulogized Sanjay, called him a Vivekananda.

It was to R.N. Kao, chief of the Research and Analysis Wing (RAW), that Indira spoke of her decision to release the Opposition members held in prison under the Maintenance of Internal Security Act (MISA) and to call for immediate elections. Kao was surprised but promised her a report on the political situation in the country. Indira's decision was a shock to her family. Sanjay was dead against it, and so were Bansi Lal, then Chief Minister of Haryana, R.K. Dhawan and other supporters of Sanjay. According to Maneka Gandhi, Indira had asked the Intelligence Bureau (IB) to assess the results of an early election. The IB reported back that Indira's Congress would lose. 'Indira stormed into Sanjay's room one morning, saying the IB was infiltrated by the RSS and she could no longer trust them. By now she had erased the IB report from her mind, mentally torn it up.'[2] R.N. Kao came back to the Prime Minister with an assessment that there was some danger in immediate elections. He advised her to release the Opposition, allow for a cooling off period, and call elections in six months.[3]

Indira was adamant in her decision to hold immediate elections. Sanjay tried to argue with her, to persuade her to change her mind. 'They could not understand her determination.' Sanjay went to her and said, 'You are committing a most horrible mistake.' She listened. 'There was no drama, no scenes, nothing.'[4] The next day Sanjay told her, 'Look, it is not that we are against elections but I would strongly advise you to call off the Emergency immediately, release the Opposition, wait one year to undo the damage, to quench rumours. Release every one, stop all the programmes, take a break and next year hold elections.' 'But for the first time he found her immovable.'[5] She consulted the chief ministers, who were reluctant to oppose her wishes.

On 18 January 1977, Indira announced her decision to hold elections. The country would go to the polls on 19 March. On the same day she released the leaders of the Opposition. Later, others detained under MISA were freed. She did not however lift the Emergency laws. If the imposition of the Emergency was a shock and a total surprise to the Opposition, the calling for elections and the release of Opposition leaders held under MISA left them anxious and bewildered. They were extremely suspicious of Indira's reasons, were wary of her, were certain that it was a trap.

Ganga Saran Sinha, a socialist and a close friend of Jayaprakash Narayan, as he was of Jawaharlal Nehru and Indira, was with JP when news of the elections reached them. They found the news unbelievable, particularly after the life of the Lok Sabha had been extended in November. 'Indira has shown much courage. It is a great step for her to take,'[6] Jayaprakash commented.

The Emergency had ended but it had left an indelible imprint on the Indian psyche. The peoples of India had lost trust. Since independence the country had faced famine, turmoil and war, but the villager and the urban-dweller had felt that the government that ruled was their government and the police and the law enforcing machinery were there to protect them. This attitude vanished. The government and its police became alien, factors of fear to be fought and outwitted. People started to feel that injustices could only be remedied by street violence, revolt or sycophancy.

During the Emergency the ear of government closed to people's complaints; this had inevitably led to the closing of the ear of the people to government appeals. It was not the enormity or savagery of what happened during the Emergency but the terror it invoked and the insecurity it generated that drove a wedge between the ruler and the ruled.

I was in Bombay, Krishnamurti was about to leave for Europe when we heard the news of the coming elections. I felt deliriously happy. Krishnamurti shared my joy and spoke to me at length about Indira. He was prepared to go to Delhi to see her, but I dissuaded him, knowing that she would be greatly preoccupied with the coming campaign.

The day before he was to leave, he asked me to keep him informed. Then suddenly he asked, 'What happens if she loses?'[7]

Newspaper editors and columnists, political leaders and intellectuals were puzzled: Indira had not called the elections from a weak position. 'Why had she done so?' they asked. 'Would it be a fair election?' They were certain that she could not afford to lose. The consequences for her were too serious.

I returned to Delhi on 20 January to find an invitation to dinner from the Prime Minister awaiting me. She was radiant when I met her, her defensive look had disappeared. Madame Barre, the wife of the then French Prime Minister, Raymond Barre, was at dinner with her son. The table was laid with elegance, with Indira's favourite orchids placed at the centre of the table. The menu was specially ordered by her. There were five of us for dinner, the two French guests, Indira, Sanjay and I. Right through dinner, Indira spoke in French to Madame Barre. She joked and laughed and looked as if she did not have a care in the world. Sanjay was very glum, ate poached eggs and hardly spoke to the young Frenchman. We savoured caviare and other delicacies. During dinner we discussed everything but the elections; poetry, theatre, fashion, Indian culture and the West.

After dinner I lingered. Indira spoke awhile on her dramatic decision to hold elections and I expressed my admiration. Her look was quizzical. 'Am I leaping into an abyss?' she asked. 'At the moment you look as if you could leap into a pit that extends to the netherworld and emerge triumphant,' I replied. We laughed and I went home.

A few days later I met her at the Rashtrapati Bhavan "At Home" on Republic Day. The sun shone, it was cold, the women were dressed in all their finery, the diplomatic corps was present, the generals were in uniform, the lawns were green, carefully tended, the roses were blooming. It was a brilliant occasion, with Indira mingling with the guests, listening, talking, laughing, at peace with herself. She was a gracious Prime Minister at the height of her glory and power.

The Opposition was in disarray. At their first meeting Jayaprakash was despondent, convinced that the Congress would win. The Opposition felt that there was not enough time for them to get together or to plan a common programme. Confused messages were reaching them of the people's reactions.

Hope was kindled at a massive rally held on 30 January in New Delhi and addressed by all the important Opposition leaders. Vast crowds gathered to greet Jayaprakash, Morarji Desai, Charan Singh and other prominent members of the Opposition. The crowds were seeing them for the first time after eighteen months; they were emotional and cheered wildly.

The Congress Working Committee (CWC) was to meet on 2 February. A day earlier Jagjivan Ram, then the Minister of Agriculture and Irrigation, went to Indira's house and spent exactly five minutes there, from the time he came out of the car and went back to it. He said, 'If you lift the Emergency, it will add to your stature.'

Indira said, 'This matter was examined by the Home Ministry and many provisions of the Emergency have already been relaxed by it. The time has not come for fully lifting the Emergency.'

Jagjivan Ram: 'You should be able to deal with whatever situation that might arise with existing powers.'

Indira Gandhi: 'I will take this up with the Home Ministry again.'

When they gathered that February morning at Congress head-quarters, they found Jagjivan Ram's seat empty. Indira respected Jagjivan Ram's political acumen and his seasoned understanding of the Indian situation. She was a little concerned when he continued to be late for the meeting and was about to ask R.K. Dhawan, her Special Assistant, to enquire when the Minister was expected, when suddenly Dhawan brought in a note and handed it to her. She read it, turned to her colleagues and said, 'Gentlemen, Babu Jagjivan Ram has resigned from the Congress:' There was panic. Indira remained out-wardly unmoved. She instinctively realized that Jagjivan Ram's defection would totally change the election scenario. Later in the day she heard that Jagjivan Ram, H.N. Bahuguna and Nandini Satpathi had resigned from the Congress and organized themselves into a party called "Congress for Democracy".

Jagjivan Ram's defection electrified the country and the electoral scene. He had been a stalwart of the Congress party and undisputed leader of the Harijan community. The trickle of support for the Opposition became a rushing wall of water that swept the North Indian states.

In the first week of February I heard that Indira was ill. She had herpes and was resting. She had draped a scarf over part of her face and was in pain when I met her. We spoke of homeopathic remedies. She was to start her election campaign very soon, so she needed a quick cure. Allopathy was the only answer. She was greatly concerned that the illness would leave marks on her face, and wanted to be sure that this did not happen.

A few days later I got a call from her house. Indira had come from

Indira Gandhi being sworn in as Prime Minister by President S. Radhakrishnan, January 1966

Indira Gandhi with the army on the Kashmir front during the Indo-Pakistan war, September 1965

Indira Gandhi with her sons Rajiv and Sanjay strolling near the Eiffel Tower, Paris, 1966

At the marriage of Rajiv Gandhi with Sonia Maino in the Prime Minister's House, 1, Safdarjung Road, on 25 February 1968

t the marriage of Sanjay Gandhi with Maneka Anand

Portrait of Prime Minister Gandhi's family; sitting (from L to R): Sanjay, Indira Gandhi, Sonia; standing: Rajiv Gandhi and Maneka; front: Rahul and Priyanka, the children of Rajiv and Sonia

Indira Gandhi at the cremation of
Sanjay Gandhi, Shantivana, June 24
1980

The sorrow of Indira Gandhi, 1980

Rajiv and Indira at the funeral of Sanjay Gandhi

Prime Minister Indira Gandhi walking amongst the hills in Rishi Valley with J. Krishnamurti, December 1980

Indira Gandhi, J. Krishnamurti and Pupul Jayakar, Rishi Valley, December 1980

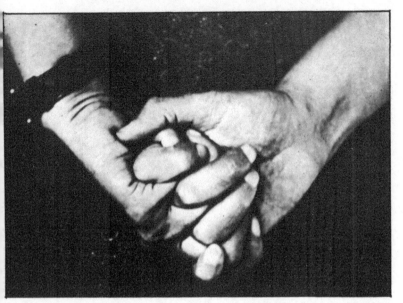

A determined Prime Minister: tightly locked hands of Indira Gandhi at the time of the Bangladesh war, 1970

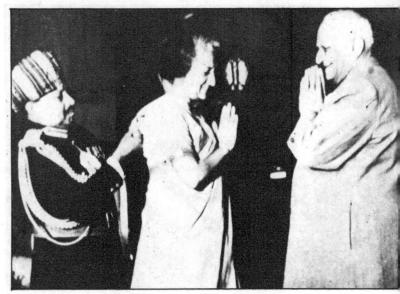

Prime Minister Indira Gandhi receiving the Bharat Ratna award at Rashtrapati Bhavan, New Delhi, from President V.V. Giri, 1971

Prime Minister Indira Gandhi in Dhaka with President Mujib-ur Rehman and his family, 1971

Prime Minister Indira Gandhi rides to her office in a horse carriage to economize on the consumption of petrol in 1973. Security men escort her in cars

Indira Gandhi in her garden at the Teen Murti House with grandson Rahul and grand-daughter Priyanka

Prime Minister Indira Gandhi at the AICC meeting in New Delhi, 1973

Indira Gandhi with Vinoba Bhave at Patunar Ashram after her defeat at the polls in 1977

Indira Gandhi with Anand Mai
Ma at the mother's Ashram
in Hardwar

Indira Gandhi smiles as she rides the
elephant Moti to Belchi, Bihar 1977

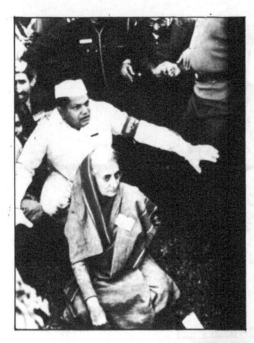

Indira Gandhi protests against government harassment, 1978

Indira Gandhi listens to the woes of an elderly man in Chikmaglur, where she was fighting a by-election to return to the Lok Sabha. 1978

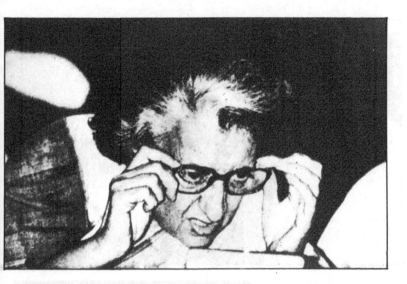

Indira Gandhi at the AICC meeting held in New Delhi in 1979. Attacks against her son Sanjay led by Devraj Urs and Tarkeshwari Sinha had mounted. Indira's face expresses her emotional involvement in the issues raised

Indira Gandhi in the lawns of her home 12, Wellingdon Crescent, receiving the bouquets and greetings from the crowds that rushed to meet her after her party's victory

Sanjay Gandhi and Prime-Minister-elect Indira Gandhi after Sanjay's victory at Amethi, 1980

Indira Gandhi garlanded after her election as leader of her victorious party and Prime-Minister-elect

A portrait of Prime Minister Indira Gandhi 1983

esiding over the NAM summit in New Delhi, 1983

a meeting of the Parliamentary Board, finalizing the list of candidates for Uttar Pradesh. The moment I saw her I sensed that she was very disturbed. She told me that D.K. Barooah was stabbing her in the back. He wanted to select a hundred of his men as candidates. She was angry. 'I will fight this election and then resign. I am fed up. There is no one I can trust.' Towards the end of the conversation she expressed her growing concern with political trends in the country. 'This election is going to be very tough. I do not know whether all these people who come here for tickets realize this.'

Her first election meeting was at the Boat Club in Delhi. I went and sat in my car to hear her speak. The crowd was vast but there were few voices raised to hail her; the slogans shouted were in a low key. She was apologetic, on the defensive, her voice had lost its power; the words she used did not touch the heart or carry any conviction. I could see that while there were few demonstrations against her, people at the edge of the crowd were fading away. It was an ominous portent.

She toured the country relentlessly, sleeping for less than three hours every night, travelling by road, by helicopter, by car, stopping at villages, speaking to the old and the very young. Even though reports of Opposition triumphs appeared on the front pages of the media there was apprehension amongst the Opposition parties. The Emergency had still not been lifted, rumours were afloat that Indira would cancel the election, re-impose the Emergency or rig the ballot. Stories were also current that if she lost, the army would be called out, that she would leave the country, that she would . . . they did not know what, but they were sure that she would do everything to see that the Opposition did not come to power.

Pratima Singh, a Member of Parliament, and friend of the Prime Minister, toured Bihar with her and was present when Indira Gandhi addressed election meetings. It was evident that the usual rapport between Indira and the crowd was missing. Greatly disturbed, seeing the eyes of the women turn away from her, Indira moved into the crowd. She spoke to an old grandmother, 'Are you happy?' There was no response. 'What is wrong?'[8] she asked in desperation, only to be met with silence.

Wherever they went, they found the villagers polite. They offered them tea and fruit but were silent when asked for their vote. In one village a ten-year-old boy spoke to Pratima Singh:

'This village will not give you the vote.'

'Why? Look, Indiraji is so beautiful, so good.'

'Yes, she is, we have listened to her.'

'So you will vote for us.'

'No *masi* (aunt), we will only vote for the farmer's symbol. We have decided to defeat the Congress. We will give a chance to older people.'

'Look, son, you children should change that.'

'Oh no. We children are going to say everywhere, "the Congress is going to lose."'[9]

Pratima Singh travelled from village to village, spoke to women, reminded them of the Prime Minister's concern for women and their welfare. On one occasion a woman spoke up: 'That's all right, but sister, what about the *nasbandi* (vasectomy)? Our men have become weak, we women have become weak.' In their wisdom, they sensed in the virility of the man and his seed, strength and nourishment.

In Haryana a tough Jat woman, an agriculturist, when approached for her vote, spoke of vasectomy, and commented in a strong earthy idiom, 'What is the use of a river without fish?'

The message was clear and unambiguous. The disillusionment with Indira and the Congress leadership had permeated the rural mind; it was impossible to shake their decision and desire for change.

As election day drew near, R.N. Kao went to see the Prime Minister. He spoke of the possibility of her losing and the aftermath. He knew she had no intention of rigging the polls and that the will of the people would prevail. He said to her, 'I have many armed paramilitary forces and I would like to bring them to Delhi, just in case there is any violence. It would not be beyond these people (the Opposition) to organize a march to your house. The crowds could get out of control—the police would say they were helpless. If anything happened (to you) they would say what could we do? Crowds could enter your house, rough you up.' She understood the threat. 'I suggested to her that to avoid such a situation there had to be a fall back position, which was that these forces should guard her against such a contingency.' She refused to consider such a solution. She told Kao not to worry about her, she asked him to look after her children.[10]

SIX

When the last day of electioneering was over I went to Indira Gandhi's residence. She looked ten years older, the attack of herpes had taken its toll. Her hair was ungroomed and she looked malnourished and thin. She had travelled incessantly for five weeks, addressing over twenty meetings a day. She had been shouted down, had heard angry voices raised against her. She had seen the thinning of crowds, people walking away from her meetings. There were few cries of "*Zindabad*". Tears arose in her eyes as she described what had happened. 'I cannot bear it any more. They have kept me a prisoner within these four walls.' Stories of family planning excesses, of torture, of wrongful arrests had started to pour in. She was bewildered by the reports, did not know whether they were true or false, but realized the extent to which she had lost contact with the people of the country. I could almost touch her terrible isolation.

There were grave forebodings within her of the disaster facing the party, but she did not appear concerned about her own personal defeat. Though her exhaustion was absolute, yet her mind was clear, her body flexible. There was sorrow in her for things done or not done; but all that evening at no time did she say that she had made a mistake in calling the elections, nor did she hint of any measures to suppress the Opposition, or thwart the disaster that loomed ahead.

I was at home till late in the afternoon of 20 March 1977. I listened to the radio's election bulletins, but they were non-committal. At around 5 o' clock, my cousin, Kisan Mehta, phoned. His voice was very excited. 'Have you heard that Indira is trailing. Raj Narain leading?' I could not believe it and told him so. Raj Narain was a freak on the political canvas. A huge, heavy-shouldered man, a wrestler in his early years, he had emerged from the *akharas* of Varanasi, to political notoriety. He was regarded by some as a buffoon or court jester; by others as a shrewd man of the soil, who understood the vernacular rhythms of the farmer and the artisan and was familiar with the songs, the legends, the loves and hates that charged their hearts. A devotee of the gods and goddesses, traditional in his views, earthy in his image, he likened himself to Hanuman, the monkey servitor of Rama, the Hero King. In the India of 1977, Charan Singh,

319

the tough Jat leader from Uttar Pradesh, embodied Rama to Raj Narain's Hanuman.

The news that Raj Narain, a character born of some archaic vernacular story-teller, could defeat Indira Gandhi seemed impossible. It could only happen in the theatre of the absurd. But I was disturbed, and telephoned P.N. Dhar, Indira Gandhi's Principal Secretary to enquire whether the news was true. His reply was casual. 'Don't believe in rumours, Pupul,' he told me. 'It is not true. The counting was delayed.' I was restless and took the car to a newspaper office, before whose facade the election results were being flashed. The trends from the south were trickling in. Indira and her party were in the lead; stray reports from the northern zone were disturbing. But no final results were yet in. It was at the home of a friend that I learnt that it was on the ticker that Indira was trailing. I was at her residence within a few minutes.

As I drove into the gate, I found that an ominous silence had descended. There was no bustle of people, no familiar sounds, no cars parked outside. The children were nowhere to be seen. A grim-faced secretary took me straight to Indira who sat alone in her oatmeal and green-leaf sitting-room. She rose as she saw me and said, 'Pupul, I have lost.' I was stunned and could find nothing to say. We sat together in that non-verbal communion we had shared on occasions through the years. There was an inevitability about the event, the unravelling of a karmic law that rarely falters. It was as if she had anticipated her defeat. Indira sat, her spine straight, her face stoic; a tightening of the lines accentuated its beauty and austerity. She was a woman of heroic descent; in her defeat she was endowed with grace.

I asked after Rajiv Gandhi and Sonia; they were in their room, Sanjay Gandhi was away in Amethi. He was due after midnight. A friend of the family came in to sit with us. At 10.30, Indira rang the bell, asked for dinner and sent for Rajiv and Sonia. They came after a long time. Sonia was crying quietly, Rajiv was grim, tight-lipped. Dinner was served, Sonia and Rajiv ate some fruit, Indira her cutlets, salad and vegetables. No one spoke during dinner. R.K. Dhawan, her Special Assistant, came in and said the news was on the ticker that Raj Narain's 10,000 lead had become 20,000. There were no comments. After dinner I sat with her again in the living-room along with Rajiv, Sonia and Mohammad Yunus, an old friend. No one spoke.

There were no further interruptions, no further news. I was there till 12 o' clock.

As I was leaving I was alone with Rajiv. He said, 'I will never forgive Sanjay for having brought Mummy to this position. He is responsible.' He paused. 'I had spoken to her about Sanjay and what people were saying on several occasions, but she refused to believe.' I said, 'There were rumours in the city that if the Congress had won Sanjay would have been Home Minister, and people were very afraid.' Rajiv said, 'Even that is possible. He would certainly have tried.' There were tears in his eyes.

I left and went to P.N. Dhar's house. After midnight, Dhar was outside with Om Mehta, G. Parthasarathi and one or two other people I could not recognize in the dark. Some of them were on their way to the Cabinet meeting at the Prime Minister's House. The first matter before the Cabinet was the repealing of the Emergency law. Very few spoke, most of the members present had lost their seats. It was the worst debacle the party had ever faced. As the Cabinet meeting ended and the cars sped away, Indira went to Rajiv's room. The warnings of R.N. Kao were in her mind. Her children and grandchildren had to be protected. She asked Rajiv and Sonia to take Rahul and Priyanka and spend the night with friends. She wanted them away from the house till the atmosphere in the city had settled down. Sanjay arrived from Lucknow at 4 o' clock in the morning to find Indira alone.

PART VII
1977–1980

While running in haste, the hoofs of the deer are not seen.

–Baudha Gana O Doha[1]

At times it seemed they were running not so much against a diminutive 62 year old political candidate but a myth, a legend in a sari and dusty sandals.

–Newsweek[2]

ONE

In the haze of her defeat and the grace and dignity with which she accepted it, few people have acknowledged the nature of Indira Gandhi's action. No authoritarian ruler in supreme control had ever given up power or submitted to possible political extinction with such integrity. Her action brought strength to the democratic roots of the country and gave its vast electorate a never-to-be-forgotten understanding of the power of the vote. Perhaps her action was the most significant of any action since India's independence.

Throughout the night of 20 March 1977, the citizens of North India remained awake. It was a night of wild rejoicing. Drums beat, people danced and sang songs of triumph. Sweets were distributed free. Fireworks illumined the sky in celebration of Indira's defeat. As the returns came in, the tempo of rejoicing increased. The defeat suffered by the Congress was cataclysmic: in the whole northern belt of Uttar Pradesh, Madhya Pradesh, Bihar and Haryana, Indira's Congress had won only a single seat; a cyclone had hit and destroyed the monolithic structure of the Congress, a party that had held power for over thirty years.

I was at Indira's house the next morning. Habits die hard—ashen-faced Congressmen and women and Indira's friends continued to address her as Prime Minister. The enormity of the Congress' collapse was beyond the grasp of either the victor or the vanquished. Indira had accepted her personal defeat with a stoic silence, but the disaster that had struck her party left her numb. In the southern states, Indira's Congress had emerged victorious but the southern victory could not compensate for the northern defeat. Indira was aware that power had passed on to the Janata Party. Her loss was absolute.

For over seventeen years with her father and for eleven years as Prime Minister, Indira had held power and lived a life of complete security. Now, suddenly, she had nothing. India had yet to develop a culture where with the loss of power a prime minister could return to lead a private life; N.K. Seshan, Indira's Private Secretary, had handled her personal affairs and accounts from 1947. According to him, at the time of her defeat, Indira had very little money of her own. She was aware of the difficult days that lay ahead.

Indira Gandhi resigned as Prime Minister on 22 March 1977. In a statement issued by her later, she extended her good wishes to the new Janata government:

> I hope that the secular, socialist and democratic foundations of India will be reinforced. The Congress Party and I are ready to give constructive cooperation in the common tasks that face our nation.
>
> Elections are part of the democratic process to which we are deeply committed. I have always said, and I do believe, that the winning or losing of an election is less important than the strengthening of our country and ensuring a better life for our people.
>
> We are proud of our great country. As I take leave of you as Prime Minister, I should like to express my deep gratitude to my colleagues, to my party and to the millions of men, women and children who have given me their trust, cooperation and even affection over the years. My love and concern for the welfare of every section of the people remain unchanged. Since childhood my aim has been to serve the people to the limit of my endurance. This I shall continue to do. My good wishes to you now and always.

The resignation was accepted by the acting President, B.D. Jatti. She was asked to continue in office till the Janata government took over. Newspapers and media around the world carried headlines on her defeat. Its extent was mind-boggling; no one had expected the unprecedented reverses, including Indira Gandhi's personal defeat. Observers from abroad were certain that Indira Gandhi's political career was at an end. Senator Patrick Moynihan, former US Ambassador to India, in a statement to the *New York Times,* said that only rarely in history did people have the opportunity to change political parties that governed them by voting their preferences. 'India has now done so in an extraordinary assertion that democracy is not a luxury belonging to the rich.' Soviet analysts attributed Indira Gandhi's election defeat to mistakes and excesses committed after the imposition of the Emergency. Raj Narain addressing a mammoth rally in Agra, told the crowd that he had let loose a mantra which led Indira to blindly enter a trap, so that she did something (called the elections) against her own judgement and wishes. The world and India saw the moment as an inspiration to all democracies. It was a historical moment that was to reverberate through many lands, yet no one was prepared to give Indira her due.

Morarji Desai, selected leader of the Opposition parties by Jayaprakash Narayan in a move for a consensus Prime Minister, was called upon to form the new government. From the day of its inception, seeds of disintegration and strife were sown, jealousies and ambitions were at the forefront. Charan Singh and Jagjivan Ram felt that they had a greater claim to the prime ministership than Morarjibhai. Under the Janata umbrella, vastly disparate elements had come together. The Cabinet's inability to evolve a cohesive ethos which would enable it to function, made its collapse inevitable.

As the days passed, uncertainties ravaged the atmosphere in Indira's home. The hatred and fierce anger of the new political leadership towards her, especially of those of them jailed during the Emergency, was palpable. Rumours were on the increase, all manner of accusations against Indira and Sanjay Gandhi were current. The little men who came alive at the periphery of political activity were busy. They travelled from Indira to Morarji Desai, to Charan Singh and to Jagjivan Ram, carrying stories of Indira's decision to declare Martial Law on the night of her defeat, about the refusal of the army chiefs to carry out her orders; about Sanjay flying out of the country. Indira was to retire, they said; at another moment they claimed that she was taking over the Congress presidentship and was gathering support to stand for the presidentship of India, the election for which was due shortly. Stories of torture, murder and the forcible sterilization of millions during the period of Emergency rule were widely discussed. Everything was possible, everything had happened.

News was quick to reach Indira that the Janata political leadership was geared to destroy her and Sanjay. Charan Singh made a statement in Parliament that there had been some thinking on the part of Indira of shooting Opposition leaders in jail during the Emergency. She reacted strongly, refuting the statement. In the drawing-rooms of the intelligentsia, in coffee-houses, in the vast conference rooms of officials and ministers and in the haunts of Indira's colleagues and party persons, strategies to isolate and destroy Indira and her son were planned. It was clear that the Janata leadership sought revenge, her own party leadership, an alibi. At first by sheer habit her political comrades had rallied around her, 'The country needs you.' Her first post-defeat announcement was, 'The collective judgement of the people must be respected.'

She told me and a number of her friends that a great burden had been lifted from her shoulders. She expressed her intention to retire to some sylvan spot in the Himalayas—Dr Karan Singh offered her a cottage in the interior of the Jammu hills—but the mother in her waited to see what action the new government would take against her son. She had taken control of the situation, asked Sanjay to keep a low profile, to seek anonymity till the situation stabilized. Sanjay announced that he was quitting politics. 'I am all the more sorry if what I did in my personal capacity had recoiled on my mother.'

As days passed, the official perquisites that surrounded the Prime Minister's residence were removed from 1, Safdarjung Road—the secret telephones, the secretarial staff, numerous air-conditioners, the official servants, the gardeners and guards all vanished. Indira had long forgotten how to set up or run a house. The last occasion she had done so was in 1942, immediately after her marriage. Now with her house stripped of furniture and kitchenware, Indira was left to set up house with what she could salvage from Anand Bhawan; the rest of the household requirements, a refrigerator, air-conditioner, heaters, pots and pans and kitchenware had to be purchased or borrowed. Much of this burden fell on her elder daughter-in-law, Sonia Gandhi.

The first act of the new government, a fortnight after taking over, was to announce, on 7 April, the establishment, under Section 3 of the Commission of Inquiry Act 1952, of a Commission headed by Justice J.C. Shah, a former Chief Justice of the Supreme Court, to inquire into all complaints of excesses during the Emergency 'be it by the highest political authority or the lowest government functionary.' The Shah Commission was to submit its report within six months. Its setting up pointed to the new government's determination to take action against the former Prime Minister, a woman who had arrested, jailed and so humiliated them.

I visited Varanasi in early April. On my return, I wrote to B.K. Nehru, then High Commissioner of India in England:

> I have just returned from Varanasi and what has happened in the Gangetic plain is staggering. It is not the Emergency which has defeated her but family planning and the word of mouth communication which spread like wildfire through the whole area, exaggerating, distorting excesses of every nature. The muzzling of the Press and later calling for elections, and what then happened, appear now, in retrospect, inevitable. Authority if it is to be used has to be absolute, but if there is a dichotomy in the mind of the person who is exercising it, the result is obvious.

> There are various problems that have arisen regarding her house; where she is going to stay; what she is going to do; which only she will be able to answer after some time has elapsed. But she needs people around her who have warmth and real friendship for her and a certain healing which can only come through her own deeper investigations into her motivations and aspirations. I feel confident that she will heal herself and emerge again as a major force in this country. For the present, one can only give her affection and support.[3]

It was approximately at the same time that Indira also wrote to B.K. Nehru's wife, Fori:

> The voting was a "coup" by the bureaucrats at all levels. The people, many sections, were angry and we may well have lost anyway, but not in this manner. That is an old story. The attitude of the government is one of vindictiveness and harassment. So our own people are turning against me to save their own skins. The wildest stories are being circulated about Sanjay—that he was a member of a dacoit gang, is one of them. I am accused of causing (the) deaths of all kinds of people. Because of surveillance people are hesitant to come, because of phone tapping the phone has become virtually useless. Those who voted for

us rather conspicuously are being harassed, especially the poor. Debts which had been cancelled from the very poor and the landless or tribals—are being reclaimed with compound interest.

Do I sound grouchy? I am deeply worried though I realize that the warfare is psychological and I must keep my chin up.[4]

A press that had wilted under severe censorship and an intelligentsia that was mute during the Emergency came to vigorous life, as they recovered from the shock of the Janata victory. Unaware of the parameters of the excesses, malpractices and abuse of authority during the Emergency, the government, the people, Indira and her party, were at first prepared to accept that the wrong-doings were far-reaching. It was clear that Indira had not envisaged the brutalities of the Emergency before she promulgated it, nor, once she had declared it, could she control the excesses that it spawned. At the first meeting of the Congress Working Committee (CWC), held shortly after her defeat, a letter was sent by her to D.K. Barooah, the Congress President, in which she accepted total responsibility for all that went wrong during the Emergency. 'I am not interested in shielding anyone. I have no caucus to defend or group to fight.'

She was absent from the meeting of the CWC held three days after the Janata victory, to review the election disaster. The Congress leadership remained in awe of her. They hesitated to conduct the meeting in her absence. D.K. Barooah, Y.B. Chavan and Kamalapati Tripathi went to her house to escort her to the meeting. Indira was grim-faced as she entered the Congress headquarters, to be greeted by slogans of praise and the sound of bugles. She was too shrewd a woman not to sense the undercurrents and the seething rebellion amongst those present, leaders who had held high positions during the Emergency. She was right in her surmise, for after she left, Barooah, Siddhartha Shankar Ray and other senior Congress members openly attacked Sanjay, while Kamalapati Tripathi and Y.B. Chavan sat silent as they listened to criticism ascribing the Congress defeat to the mother and the son. News of this reached her at her house. She knew she could face them, outmanoeuvre them, leave them by the wayside, but Sanjay was her Achilles heel; he was vulnerable. Like a tigress at bay she stood between him and her enemies.

By the middle of April, D.K. Barooah, under pressure from the party, resigned from the presidentship of the Congress. Now Indira's superb political skills came alive. She listened as senior politicians advised her to stay at home and not to leave the house under any circumstances; others advised her to undertake a pilgrimage on foot from the southernmost point of India to the Himalayas, staying in village huts, re-establishing her contacts with the village women and men of the country. Her friends warned her of the danger to her life; they were fearful that she would be molested if she went out of the city. Indira listened, but kept her options open.

The Congress Presidential election was fixed for 6 May. Indira was now an ordinary member of the Congress, but the candidates knew that Indira's support was critical for them to win the election. Brahmananda Reddy from Andhra Pradesh and S.S. Ray from West Bengal were the two main candidates. Dr Karan Singh, who would have been the Maharaja of Kashmir if the princely states had survived, announced his candidature the night before the election in response to what he called an "inner voice". He sought Indira's support. She told him he should not contest, for he would lose. But Karan Singh was adamant. Indira was proved correct. Brahmananda Reddy won with an overwhelming majority.

*

Every morning and evening I saw Indira at her house. There were visitors in the mornings, but in the evenings I would find her alone, sitting in the veranda in the summer heat, without a fan, looking out into the garden, to the pale gold of a dust-filled sky. With sunset, shadows lengthened to obscure the trees, the grass and the lily-filled pool. There was little to say, but I could sense that my presence helped. We would watch Sanjay, dressed in white, handspun cotton, his great Irish wolfhound by his side, walk alone, back and forth in the twilight. He never approached us, was silent and inaccessible. Indira's eyes followed him, observing his every movement. 'He is so young,' she said to me.

The Janata Party was determined that Indira leave 1, Safdarjung

Road. It was a small house, but to the Janata it was a symbol of power and Prime Minister Desai was determined to use it as his official residence. For a time the Prime Minister was ambivalent and under advice from Jayaprakash Narayan did not actually ask Indira to vacate but his government demanded from her a very high rent. When she refused, they grudgingly agreed to give her alternative accommodation at 12, Willingdon Crescent. They insisted on charging her the market rent. For thirty years Indira had had little time for her personal affairs. The house was crowded with piles of books, papers, gifts, luggage, clothes. She was reluctant to destroy anything; every book, every gift and paper held a memory.

The atmosphere at 1, Safdarjung Road grew turgid; seeking solitude Indira would come unannounced to my house. On her first visit she said, 'I have come, Pupul, to sit quietly,' and I left her to herself. The house held silence and I could sense her need to be in an atmosphere free from fear and tension. As May approached and it grew hot, I suggested that she sit in an air-conditioned room but she refused. It was only on one occasion that I saw her with a desperate look. 'I have definite information that they will put Sanjay in jail and torture him.' I did not know what to say.

On 21 April I was to attend an evening reception hosted by the British High Commissioner to celebrate the birthday of Queen Elizabeth. Indira telephoned to enquire whether I was going and suggested that I take her with me. We drove together in my car to No.2, King George's Avenue—the British High Commissioner's residence. As we entered, I noticed that Sir John Thomson, the British High Commissioner, was agitated. He had not expected Indira to attend the reception. There were hurried whispers down the receiving line and a minister of the High Commission stepped forward to escort us into the garden. For a while, she and I stood together alone. People did not know how to respond to Indira, they were hesitant and curious. Slowly some people came forward to surround her and talk to her. She smiled and shyly responded. By then, Prime Minister Morarji Desai had arrived and Sir John Thomson had escorted him on to the lawn. People encircled them, and those around Indira started to melt away, to move towards the Prime Minister. Indira appeared not to notice those who went, but she was registering every face. She knew people were watching to see how she would react. She continued to talk with ease to the few people who lingered. We stayed for over an hour before returning home. I was told by Indira some months later that instructions had been sent out by the Ministry of External Affairs to the Ambassadors and High Commissioners in New Delhi that invitations should not be sent to her, as it would cause embarrassment to both the host and to the new government.

Soon after Indira's defeat, I resigned from various assignments I held with the government. Indira was dismayed. 'You are not in politics, you are an honorary worker, Pupul . . .' she told me. 'Never resign. Let them throw you out and so put themselves in the wrong.'

'It is difficult for me to work with people who don't trust me,' I said.

I had known Morarji Desai for long years, but ceased to visit him when he made it clear that I could not be a friend of both Indira and him.

Prime Minister Desai agreed to meet me on receiving my letter of resignation. A few days before my appointment with him, I was with Indira. She handed a note to me, from which I gathered that she was anxious that I convey her mind and her future plans to Morarjibhai, to assure him that she posed no threat:

> Pupul,
> The stories appearing about me and Sanjay or the rest of the family are incorrect. I am gradually disengaging myself from the politics. It was not possible to do so immediately. I am not in the running for any post. (There were strong rumours current that she would take over as Congress President as also stand for the presidentship of the country.)
>
> My special interests have always been children, welfare, environment, wild life, etc. I shall try and take up some such work. Articles have appeared saying that I have no intention of giving up the political battle, hence the above explanation. Also I am not an aspirant for the Presidentship either of the Congress or of India, but those who predict a political comeback for me are perhaps deliberately doing so to alarm both the government and the Congress. As you know, I truly have no desire to remain in any sort of politics.[5]

Prime Minister Desai was courteous but cold when we met. He enquired after my sister, my daughter and the rest of my family. As soon as I mentioned Indira's name, he grew wary; when I proceeded to tell him of her future plans, he froze. I was familiar with his attitudes and so I continued to speak of Indira's problems regarding her future accommodation in Delhi. By now he was stern and, in a tone well-known to me, started a homily. I left soon after and drove straight to Indira's house to tell her of my meeting with the Prime Minister.

Indira was to see Morarji Desai a few days later. Her first meeting with him was stiff and formal and she felt an intense hostility. 'I got a terrible allergy while we were talking. My insides got swollen. I did not have enough handkerchiefs; my nose was running,'[6] she said. A few days later she also saw Charan Singh, then the Home Minister. Here, too, she sensed antagonism and a fierce desire for revenge.

On 30 April 1977 she wrote to B.K. Nehru:

> A lot of political people come every day, but there is absolutely no one for me to turn to. Pupul is a brick, the only one who has taken any trouble, but neither she nor GP (G. Parthasarathy) who was helpful as regards the house, can advise on the day-to-day problems which are cropping up, or the long-term ones . . .. The financial position as regards the lawyer's fee is a nightmare. It seems that the best way for anyone with the present government is to cast stones at us. . . .We are the victims of a monstrous propaganda campaign opening in the Press in the shape of the most fantastic even vulgar rumours. Some group in the RSS or an outside agency is working very systematically and clothing us with every possible vice. Frank Anthony said to me the other day, "How can there be a question of a fair trial when people's and judge's minds are being conditioned and influenced by the atmosphere created by the media."[7]

As the days passed and the Congress leadership insisted that she remain secluded in the house, Indira Gandhi's name disappeared from the front page of the newspapers. She was becoming irrelevant. James Cameron, a journalist who had known India and the Nehru family for long years, in an interview for the *Guardian* found Indira Gandhi the loneliest and most apprehensive woman in the world. She had aged many years since her defeat. He wrote:

> She is resigned and wary. Like a broken boxer hoping for a miracle. There will be no miracle for her. . . .So there they were—the young and defeated Indira Gandhi, drawn and muted, and the sprightly old man Morarji Desai sitting confidently and at long last on the right side, right hand of his old friend, God.[8]

By the middle of May, Indira moved to 12, Willingdon Crescent. The house was small and cramped. Indira had one room of her own. It was overcrowded with trunks on which were stacked files, magazines, newspapers; books were piled on the floor; her favourite easy-chair was the only piece of furniture in the room apart from the bed. An upholstered backrest on the bed served as a support as she wrote her notes and letters. She had no stenographer. She met her friends either in the veranda, in the dining-room or in her own bedroom. She met politicians and her lawyers in a small room at the entrance of the house. Nirmala Deshpande, one of Vinoba Bhave's closest aides, was sent by him to Indira to travel with her, to meet the stream of visitors who continued to see her in the mornings and to provide general secretarial assistance.

I had dinner with Indira very often; I knew she did not like to eat alone. Her family members were rarely present. Rajiv Gandhi and Sonia were with their friends, Sanjay with his lawyers. The dining-room was crowded, a sideboard from Anand Bhawan was cluttered with jars, bottles, plates, tumblers and fresh fruit. When her old cook, a retainer from Anand Bhawan, was killed in a car accident, she found it difficult to find a replacement. There was always the fear that a man would be planted to spy on her or that she could be poisoned.

Yet, despite the circumstances she found herself in, Indira continued to offer me dinner with the same èlan as she had when she was the Prime Minister, even though, at times, we dined on a boiled egg, a boiled potato and a mango. Occasionally I carried food from my house and we picnicked together. Sonia, when at home, cooked delicious Italian pasta meals. Sometimes Nirmala put together simple Maharashtrian food.

One early June morning, I read in the newspapers that Maneka's father, a Colonel in the Army, was found shot dead in an open field. The body had been carefully laid out on a newspaper, a pistol by his side. I hurried to Indira's house to find her on the porch waiting for a car to take her to the bereaved family. I accompanied her to Maneka's house. No one was sure whether it was murder or suicide. A new horror had entered the already shattered household. The astrologers forecast that hostile stars warred with each other; portents of death and disaster hovered over the family.

The interrogation of Sanjay by the Central Bureau of Investigation (CBI) had gathered momentum. The investigating team had searched their criminal records to find evidence to connect Sanjay with some heinous crimes. Unable to do so, they charged him and V.C. Shukla with destroying a satirical film on Indira's political manoeuvres. The film was titled *kissa Kursi Ka* (The Story of the Chair). It was a criminal charge and although of little interest to the public who imagined Sanjay guilty of far more vicious crimes, the criminal case came under a section of the penal code which carried a maximum sentence of life imprisonment. Hemmed in on all sides, it was growing clear to Indira that there was no space in the country to which she could retire. To survive she had to fight.

J. Krishnamurti learnt of Indira's defeat when he was in California. In a letter to me, dated 22 March, he wrote: 'She is out of the political world now and I wonder what she is going to do. When you see her, please give my love to her, will you?' On 31 March he wrote again: 'I have received your letter after the election. I am glad you were with her when the news came. I feel somewhat responsible in this event, as I told you in Bombay, she may be defeated. Anyhow, please give her my love.' In the letters that followed, he continued to enquire about her.

I left New Delhi by the middle of June. I could see that Indira was upset at my leaving Delhi, but there was nowhere I could stay nor did I have the money to rent a flat in the city. On 21 June, Indira wrote to J. Krishnamurti:

> I want to write but I don't know what. I thought I had acquired a measure of quiet within myself but it is obviously not sufficient for the sort of pressures that I am ex-

periencing. I have smiled through the long-standing campaign of calumny against me and my family. This continues. In addition, we were constantly watched, followed and harassed.

Sanjay, my son, is having to face numerous cases in different States on matters with which he is not concerned. They are trying to involve him even in murder cases. One concerns Sundar, a notorious murderer and dacoit who died in custody. It is said the police killed him. This may be so, for these people are difficult to handle and such cases have occurred in this and other countries. But the government is now trying to make the police report that it was done at Sanjay's behest. Needless to say Sanjay knows nothing about it. Businessmen, government employees and others are threatened with dire action if they do not speak or sign affidavits against us. Some are resisting to their cost.

Sanjay may have made mistakes regarding his car factory. It is difficult not to in Indian conditions and the complicated rules and regulations. But so far as I know, and have been able to gather from lawyers and businessmen, there has been no wilful wrong-doing. The irony of it is that this concentrated attack on what is supposed to be our corruption comes at a time when known smugglers and others who have been responsible for damaging the national economy are set free and allowed to function as they please. There are ministers of the Cabinet who are known to be corrupt—at least five have had cases against them.

Sanjay himself, though subjected to such hardship and humiliation—raids on his premises, CBI questioning, and the actual cases, is behaving with dignity and equanimity.[9]

It was in this atmosphere that she received a message from Vinoba Bhave to visit him in his ashram at Paunar. It was the break she desperately needed. The leadership of the Congress party had started to attack her directly and were not prepared to provide funds for her journey. She was informed by the Home Ministry that security would not be available for her outside Delhi. Afraid of what would happen to Indira, Vasant Sathe, one of the few Congressmen who remained constant to her, decided to accompany her to Paunar. As the aeroplane was about to land in Nagpur, Nirmala Deshpande and Sathe saw a vast crowd gathered to meet them at the airport. For seconds they were afraid. They did not know whether the crowd was friendly or was there to savage Indira. Instinctively Indira knew that it was not a hostile crowd. She landed to welcome cries, 'Indira move forward, we the people are with you.'

A large number of women, part of the crowd, performed *arti* to welcome her. Red *kumkum* was applied to her forehead and she was garlanded by vast numbers of people. She moved through the crowd as if she was part of them. For those moments she was free of all tension.

Indira stayed in Vinoba Bhave's ashram for two days. The ancient anchorite was observing silence when she went to him, but he broke it and in his cryptic language said, 'Move forward, move forward.'[10]

People from all over the area had travelled by train, truck, bullock cart and on foot to see Indira. On the first night she awoke to find that two busloads of girl students had come from a distance of over a hundred miles to greet her. She was out of bed in an instant. On returning to her room after meeting the girls, she told Nirmala, 'Never stop anyone from meeting me. It is from these simple people that I gain my strength.'[11]

The press had gathered at Vinoba's ashram. Indira was asked questions on the Emergency, on her defeat, on Sanjay's role and on her future. David Frost of the British Broadcasting Corporation (BBC) interviewed her. While answering questions about her son Sanjay and the excesses of sterilization, Indira grew excited and said that the attack against Sanjay was an attack against her. The issue of sterilization had been whipped up deliberately. When asked whether she was upset by her party's defeat, she replied that life was not pleasant; she had no idea whether the Janata government would take her to court. Was she worried? Frost asked. 'Nobody likes it,' she said. 'But if one has to face something, one faces it.' Asked whether the thought of prison frightened her, she commented, 'No, not at all. I have been to prison—but it is not something one likes.'[12]

Indira returned from Wardha to Delhi to face even more harassment from the Janata government.

TWO

Early in July 1977 terror struck Belchi, a tiny, inaccessible village in Bihar, surrounded by paddy fields, mountains and waterfalls. The landowning community attacked this village of landless Harijans, massacred families and threw their bodies into a raging fire; amongst the dead were two tiny children. News of the killings was slow to travel and it was three days before the massacre hit the headlines of national newspapers. The government machinery was slow to act. Before the Congress leaders could react or respond, even as Y.B. Chavan, leader of the Opposition decided to visit Belchi, Indira left for the remote village to extend her support to the terror-stricken, under-privileged people of the area.

In 1977, Indira's Congress had lost every seat to the Lok Sabha in Bihar. Her friends were apprehensive about her personal safety, the local people were against her, violent men and dacoits roamed the countryside; with no security there was danger. Indira was determined to go. At Patna a crowd awaited her. Amongst them were some of her faithful followers, Pratibha Singh and Bhishma Narain Singh, the Whip of the defeated Congress party. They started for Biharsharif *en route* to Belchi. It was raining heavily; at Biharsharif she was warned not to proceed further as the river was in flood and all pathways to Belchi washed away. She refused the advice, refused lunch and travelled by jeep; the vehicle later had to be towed by a tractor. She hoped to reach Belchi before sunset. The rain became torrential, the tractor stuck in the mud and slush and it appeared impossible to proceed further. Indira said she would walk to the river bank. Reluctantly, some of her followers accompanied her. As they reached the river, stormy winds made the crossing on foot impossible. Boats were not available, nor were the boatmen prepared to take any passenger across. Villagers who had to come out of their huts to join her procession begged her not to proceed further. After a while, realizing that Indira was determined to cross and that nothing would stop her, they brought an elephant, owned by a temple in a nearby village, for her to mount and cross the river. Moti, the elephant, had no howdah, but a blanket covered its back. With the help of her companions Indira mounted the elephant's back. A terrified Pratibha Singh sat behind

Indira, holding on to her sari. Out of the 500 Congressmen who had begun the journey with her at Biharsharif, only two were left at the time they came to the river bank.

The river waters were in spate, the currents strong. It was difficult for Indira and Pratibha to keep their balance as the elephant waded through mud, and chest-deep water. It was late evening by the time they reached the outskirts of Belchi, the site where the bodies of Harijans had been thrown on to a common pyre and burnt. The terrorized children and women of the massacred village had taken shelter in a double-storeyed building. It was dark by the time Indira reached them. Torches were lit, and it was in this light that wrinkled old men and women, young widows, tiny children threw themselves at Indira's feet. They saw Indira as their only hope. Indira listened intently to their tales of terror. She drew them close, comforted them. They knew Indira cared, had braved dangers to listen to them.

The grief and horror that had struck these landless people who lived at the edge of starvation, brought home to Indira the reality of her defeat. For twenty-eight years she could have demanded redress and action; she could have protected them, brought the murderers to trial. Now there was little she could do but give of herself, mourn with them, extend her hand in friendship. Indira's presence and her concern for them helped to assuage their grief. The horror and fear still surrounded them. Sinister forces lurked in nearby villages and in the ravines; it was only a sense of the inevitability of life and events, of an unravelling karmic law that helped them to survive.

It was night before Indira left Belchi. The rain had stopped but the sky was overcast with thunder and heavy clouds. A boat was available to ferry them across the river, but as it reached the other bank, the load being too heavy, it sank. Indira waded through the river on the last part of the journey and it was 10.30 at night before, drenched by rain and river water, she reached the main road where cars and jeeps awaited. Out of the darkness she heard the sound of drums and women's voices calling out to her. 'We voted against you, we betrayed you. Forgive us.' The women sang songs in Indira's praise, garlanded her with flowers, brought *puris* and *halwa* for her to eat and sought her blessings. The men of the village carried lanterns or flaming torches to light her way. Time had come full circle, the anger that had made these people vote against her had been quenched.

340

The elephant-ride had left a sixty-year-old Indira bruised and sore. The only food she had eaten on the journey upto now was an apple which one of her comrades had carried for her. She spent the night in Patna at Sadaqat Ashram. The next day she called on an ailing Jayaprakash Narayan. He was very friendly and they both grew emotional; she spent an hour with him discussing the massacre at Belchi and the plight of the Harijans. When they both came out together, he wished her well. They smiled at each other as she left for the airport.

I was in Delhi in September. Indira had just returned from a trip to Hardwar where she had met Anand Mai Ma, the woman saint who had been close to her mother. Anand Mai Ma gave her a rosary of 108 *rudraksha* berries to wear.

Indira had addressed large crowds at Hardwar, lashed out at the Janata government, challenged them to arrest her. 'Why is the Janata afraid of a frail woman like me?' The crowd roared in approval. She accused the Janata Party of betraying Harijans, called on them to fight fiercely—yet she admitted to her mistakes during the Emergency, apologized to the people for what had happened.

She spent time with me in Delhi, told me of the prevailing situation. She described her triumphant visit to Belchi and the large crowds that gathered to hail her wherever she went. 'But,' she said, 'this does not mean that the Janata government will fall. In spite of the growing discontent amongst people, the Janata will rule for five years. Power is a tremendous force for keeping politicians together.' She said she had secret reports that the Janata government had promised not to pursue any of the cases against her former ministers if they agreed to blame Sanjay for all the lapses during the Emergency. She knew that they would betray her. She was totally alone, deeply hurt, did not quite know what the future held for her and her son. In the time left for her before her inevitable arrest, she decided to travel extensively to re-establish her presence, to contact men and women in distant parts of the country.

A few days later Indira went to Agra by train from Delhi. There was a stampede at the station and people got hurt. At the mammoth meeting she addressed later, she was critical of the policies of the Janata Party—prices were rising, black-marketeering was on the increase. At every meeting she admitted and expressed regret for the steps taken during the Emergency that had hurt some people. Never-theless, she said, the time of the Emergency had brought economic stability to the country, checked the rise in prices, increased foreign exchange resources and ended smuggling. She pointed out that it was she who had called for elections, and when defeated had accepted the people's verdict.

Indira's reception at Agra confirmed the growing fear in the Janata Party that she was gaining public sympathy. Charan Singh, from a rest-house in Bhatkal, issued a statement saying that people con-sidered the Janata government impotent for letting six months pass without having jailed Indira. What was needed was a Nuremberg form of trial for her crimes during the Emergency. Rumours of the im-minence of her arrest reached Indira by the middle of September. She warned Nirmala Deshpande that the arrest would take place either on 2 October, the Mahatma's birthday, or the next day. So it did not come as a surprise when, on the evening of 3 October, the Central Bureau of Investigation (CBI) sent their officers to her house at 5 o'clock. Sanjay and Maneka were playing badminton on the lawn; Indira was meeting her lawyers on the stand to be taken before the Shah Commission. A nervous N.K. Singh, a senior officer of the CBI, asked to see Indira Gandhi, the former Prime Minister. She kept the CBI contingent waiting for an hour before she came out with her lawyers, to be informed by Singh that he had orders to arrest her and release her immediately on bail, on execution of a personal bond. A copy of the First Information Report (FIR) was missing and Indira Gandhi refused to move before she had seen the warrant for her arrest. She was determined to build the situation to a critical point and then to create an atmosphere of sympathy, even martyrdom; towards this end she demanded that she be handcuffed, and refused to move unless the officers did so. N.K. Singh stood nonplussed, at which point she went back to her room.

The telephones at the house had been cut, but not before a huge crowd had gathered. These were the stalwarts of her party, newspaper reporters, members of Sanjay's Youth Congress, excited lawyers and Congressmen and women. They raised slogans against Charan Singh and Morarji Desai, hailed Indira, 'Move forward, Indira, we will die together.' It was 8 o'clock when Indira came out, calm, immaculately groomed, in a white sari with a green border, to be garlanded and showered with rose-petals. She decided to hold a press conference from the roof of the police car. She was due to visit tribal Gujarat the next day and she asked the press to convey her apologies to the people of Gujarat for her inability to be with them. 'I have tried to serve our people and our country to the best of my ability. No matter what charge or charges are made against me, this arrest is a political one.'

Nirmala had prevailed on Indira to allow her to accompany her. She knew the police would object, but in the confusion, Nirmala stepped into the police car unnoticed and refused to move till Indira joined her. From Indira Gandhi's house the police car, preceded by a jeep, followed by cars with her two sons, their wives, lawyers and Congress supporters, drove towards the outskirts of Delhi. The destination was not clear; there was speculation and doubt, till they turned off the main national highway to the road leading to the Bhatkal Lake in Haryana. As they reached a railway crossing, the cars came to a stop. Two mail trains were due, which meant a wait for over half an hour. Indira was permitted to leave the car, to sit on a parapet, to get some fresh air. She walked to a culvert and sat down, surrounded by her lawyers. They advised her, excitedly, that without a warrant from a court, she should not agree to cross the city line of Delhi. Her lawyers were vocal, the police insistent. There were fierce arguments. Indira refused to move. The excitement mounted. The police officers were bewildered, did not know what to do or where to take her. There was confusion as no one had thought of this eventuality.

Ultimately, the CBI officials agreed not to take her out of the city, so Indira re-entered the car and the CBI drove around Ring Road for two hours while a decision on her destination was being taken. It was well after ten o'clock before they arrived at the Gazetted Officers' Mess at the New Police Lines at Kingsway Camp. She entered her "prison" with composure, said goodbye to Rajiv, Sonia, Sanjay and Maneka, was saluted by the policemen on duty and went into the guest-house with her head held high. She was offered food which she refused.

By now Nirmala Deshpande was in tears. Indira diverted her, started to tell stories; soon Nirmala relaxed and even smiled. Indira slept soundly. Nirmala was awake most of the night, but dozed after 3 o'clock. She awoke at dawn to find Indira already bathed, exercised and ready.

Rajiv had arrived by 9 o'clock in the morning, along with Indira's lawyer and a friend. The news of her arrest had spread in the city and crowds gathered outside the lock-up, The police refused to tell her which court she would appear in. Rumours spread that she was to be arraigned in the Tis Hazari court and the members of the Youth Congress gathered outside the building. In order to avoid them, the CBI brought her to the Magistrate's court on Parliament Street. The Janata Party had arranged a demonstration and hostile crowds shouting 'Hang Indira' greeted her on her arrival. A few voices cheered her as she pushed her way through the crowd to enter the court. Tempers flared, tear-gas and lathi charges were used by the police to disperse members of the Youth Congress who had now gathered in large numbers outside the court building. Produced before the Magistrate, Indira refused a chair, and stood for eighty minutes while the charges against her were being argued. They pertained to the use of jeeps during her elections and an illegal contract given by her government to a French oil company. Though the charges were made, there was no documentary support. The Magistrate held, 'Even according to the CBI, there are no grounds for believing that the accusation is well founded.' The Magistrate ordered Indira Gandhi's unconditional release. Sanjay ran out of the court to cry out, 'Dismissed, dismissed.' The news was greeted by her supporters with wild euphoria, slogans were shouted; the police used tear-gas on the crowd, and the gas entered the courtroom to irritate Indira's eyes. Her nose was blocked, her eyes red as she emerged from the courtroom. A wildly excited Rajiv is reported to have told a foreign correspondent, 'Even Mummy could not have thought out a better scenario.'

Driving back to her Willingdon Crescent bungalow, Indira's car was stoned by the supporters of the Janata and crowds tried to force their way into her car. Her supporters were convinced that the Janata government would go to any length to end Indira's political career.

The foreign press was very critical of the arrest. The *Guardian* saw it as a perilous decision. The precedent established in a democracy to hold a predecessor to account was a trap which from beginning to end was fraught with political danger. World opinion was critical of the Janata Party for having done nothing to tackle urgent economic problems. 'There is a distinction between justice and revenge,' said the *Financial Times*. *Le Monde* of Paris pointed out that political prisoners of the world over were regarded as martyrs and that Indira Gandhi would be more a problem to the Janata government in prison that at liberty.

By this one act of wrongful arrest, the Janata leadership brought Indira Gandhi back on to the front page of newspapers in India and abroad.

The suddenness of her arrest and the swiftness of her release came as a major blow to the credibility of the Janata government. Ramakrishna Hegde, then General Secretary of the Janata Party, rushed to the former Prime Minister to express his anguish at what he termed a disaster. 'It was done clumsily and came as a shock to many of us.' Morarji Desai told Hegde that he had approved of the action because Charan Singh, Home Minister, had assured him that there was a cast iron case against Indira. Hegde replied that valid or invalid, fair or unfair, the arrest was unnecessary. He felt the people had already punished Indira and there could not be any greater punishment. The same stand was taken by Atal Behari Vajpayee of the Bharatiya Janata Party (BJP).

'The arrest and trial led to Mrs. Gandhi's resurrection. It created a sympathy wave. People began to say they gave the Janata party a mandate to undo Mrs. Gandhi's undemocratic measures, to re-establish rule of law, not a mandate to undo Mrs. Gandhi herself. It was certainly the greatest mistake.'[1]

Indira was quick to sense the potency of the moment; she decided to keep her rendezvous with the tribal people of Gujarat and took off for Bombay, *en route* to Surat. At Bombay airport, Indira was greeted by vast crowds. People were eager to reach her, to touch her hand. Speaking from an open car she told the gathering of her arrest and the desire of the Janata leadership to destroy her.

She was to tour the tribal belt of Gujarat for three days. The tribals adored her. Little platforms were set up every few miles, from which she addressed the gathered men and women. She spoke in villages, in small towns, in district headquarters. She ate with the tribals in their homes, off their thorn-sewn leaf plates; found their simple food delicious; spoke to them in Gujarati; communed with them on their problems : the harvest, education, culture; viewed their paintings and artifacts with empathy and respect. It was a triumphant journey.

Driving late at night through a forest in Surat district, she suddenly asked the car to stop as she had heard, indistinctly, the sound of a voice. A few minutes later, a tribal appeared from the forest holding a flower garland. For ten years, he said, he had waited to see her. He spoke in Adivasi Gujarati and called her 'mother'. 'It is you who have given us the right to live an honorable life. I have collected these flowers and made this garland with a heart full of love.'[2]

Women came out of their homes to hold her hand as if she belonged to them. She stood in homage before their divinities, their Pithora paintings of horses and riders.

At first the Congress party had not come forward to welcome Indira in Gujarat, but seeing the massive response her visit generated, they sought her out. At one of the district headquarters the Opposition had organized some stone-throwing and anti-Indira sloganeering. The police officer in charge of the district expressed his deep devotion for Indira, insisted on travelling with her by train to see the crowds did not molest her. It was a slow train and crowds had gathered at every wayside station. Vasant Sathe, the loyal Congressman who had accompanied her from Delhi was horrified, felt Indira would be trampled under, as she insisted on getting down from the train to mingle with the crowd. 'Don't be concerned about my safety,' she said, 'I will find protection from the people.' She moved through the crowd with ease, they gave way for her, created space, welcomed her, shouted slogans hailing her. The police officer Chauhan, who accompanied the party to the borders of Gujarat, told them that every policeman in Gujarat would give his life for Indira.

The people saw her as a lone, fragile woman, straight-backed, her head unbowed, standing up to tough men who were intent on destroying her. The female of the species is never hunted in India. She knew the attempts being made to destroy her would evoke an image that touched the psyche of the Indian people. The Janata had defeated her but for the people she was their daughter, their sister, their mother, and they would not let anyone destroy her. On the train journey back to Delhi she told Vasant Sathe that clouds were gathering on the horizon. She knew that few of the senior Congress party men were with her. She would need trusted Congress workers around her and the backing of a party organization if she and the party were to survive.

Plans for her future tours in the country were drawn up hurriedly. Sanjay did not accompany her on her travels but had emerged from the shadows to advise and plan every step of her future strategy. With Indira's image blocked out on television and radio, and the newspapers intent on their attack against her, the only way to make her presence felt was to travel relentlessly, to appear before people, to speak to them directly. She was to visit Madurai; now the Opposition was determined to take revenge for her Gujarat triumph. At Madurai airport, with Margatham Chandra Shekhar and Prabha Rao on either side of her, Indira travelled in an open car to the meeting where crowds awaited her. Fortunately, Prabha Rao had insisted on carrying two pillows with them; perhaps some rumours of the hostility of the crowds had reached her. As the car turned a corner, a short way from the airport, a mob that had gathered with lathis and stones, attacked the car. Indira was pushed to the floor, and a pillow was placed over her to protect her head; the two women used the other pillow to protect themselves. The crowds surged onto the car with their lathis, stones hit the car, Indira was grazed on her back and thigh. Prabha Rao was injured. The Congressmen who followed Indira in another car suffered head injuries. The demonstrators shouted 'Death to Indira,' 'Down with the queen of corruption' and waved black flags tied to stout bamboo-sticks. The police burst tear-gas shells and resorted to a lathi charge to disperse the crowd. Some demonstrators were taken into custody.

Indira drove to a rest-house. Her companions were shaken. When newsmen tried to contact her, Indira sent a message saying she did not want to be disturbed.

Yet, Indira Gandhi addressed the meeting she had come for and drove from Madurai to Tiruchi where another meeting was scheduled. At Tiruchi the crowds again turned violent, the traffic was paralysed and stones littered the route she was to travel. As the crowds surged menacingly towards the venue of the Congress meeting on Promenade Road, where a crowd of 30,000 waited to hear Indira Gandhi, a pitched battle between the demonstrators and the police took place. It appeared impossible for Indira Gandhi to find her way to the meeting but she refused to postpone it and appeared on the platform at 11.30 at night and spoke for a few minutes. The crowd went wild.

Indira was scheduled to travel by rail to Madras. She missed her train because of the violent incidents which delayed her meeting. Expecting her to be on the train, miscreants boarded it and set it on fire. Indira and her companions boarded a slow train later that night to Madras. For safety, they crowded into one compartment and put up the metal shutters, locked the doors and sat up all night. By now the news that she was on the slow train had reached her enemies. Huge stones hit the shutters as the train stopped at local stations. The roar of the crowds demanding the death of Indira could be clearly heard in the compartment.

On the morning of 31 October, on her return to Madras from Tiruchi, a concerted attempt was made to kill Indira. The Opposition party in Tamil Nadu that was inimical to her organized a demonstration of black flags to obstruct her on her journey to Kanchipuram where she was to meet the Shankaracharya of the Kamakoti Math. The anchorite is head of the most ancient and best-known orders of Hinduism in India and is a deeply religious and learned monk. The demonstrators waiting for Indira's car turned violent, erected barricades, burnt buses, set fire to two trains and attacked the police. The police fired in self-defence and two people were killed and a vast number injured. The fury of the mob resulted in all traffic from the heart of the city to the outskirts being blocked for hours. Meanwhile, Indira and her party travelled by another circuitous route to Kanchipuram. As they reached the monastery, they found that the Shankaracharya was observing silence. Indira's detractors maintained that he had done so deliberately to avoid a discussion with her. The Shankaracharya and Indira sat in the courtyard with a well separating them, and it was across the waters of the well that Indira spoke to the Shankaracharya of her predicament and asked him what she should do; should she retire if it were possible for her to do so, or should she fight the injustice. The Shankaracharya continued his silence. After an hour as she arose with folded hands to leave, he spoke. 'Follow your Dharma,' he said, and lifted the palm of his hand in a gesture of blessing. She made her obeisance and left.[3] In time, the openpalm of benediction would become, with the split in the Congress party, her party's symbol.

*

Though the Emergency was over, the psychological trauma it had

348

evoked was too deeply embedded to be erased. Fear and a resultant sychophancy tainted most political and social actions in the succeeding decades.

Indira's sixtieth birthday fell on 19 November. In normal circumstances flowers and sweets, gifts from her friends and relations would have filled her home, and crowds would have appeared on the lawns of her house, for, at sixty, one enters the last phase of life; surrounded by children and grandchildren, friends and relations, soaked in the affection of an extended family, one faces the future with equanimity. Instead, Indira's sixtieth birthday passed unnoticed. The media ignored the day and remained silent. There was one exception, the *Illustrated Weekly of India* where Khushwant Singh, its editor, in defiance of the Janata government's anger, published articles on Indira, authored by Yehudi Menuhin, Jennie Lee and this writer. While the rich and influential forgot her, craftsmen and villagers, women from town and rural communities continued to see her every morning. In a postcard to me in November she wrote:

> The Madhubani ladies were here for an exhibition at the Agricultural Expo. Every time they saw me, they clung to me and wept. I had them over for tea one afternoon. We spoke of you. With all good wishes for 1978.[4]

> Indu

THREE

The Shah Commission commenced its sittings at Patiala House, New Delhi, on 30 September 1977. Conducted in the full glare of publicity, the commission developed an atmosphere of a people's court. The proceedings were tape-recorded and microphones were used to relay them to those who waited outside the courtroom. Two hundred chairs were provided for lawyers, the press and the public within the chamber; crowds gathered outside the building. There were fights between the Janata activists and Sanjay Gandhi's Youth Congress; slogans were shouted demanding Indira Gandhi's conviction and death, counter-slogans hailed Indira as their leader. People jostled to get into the courtroom and on one occasion there were fist fights in front of the Bench.

Former ministers of Indira Gandhi's Cabinet, bureaucrats and politicians made statements before the commission. Indira was correct in her surmise that many of her former colleagues would betray her. 'Politicians with flexible consciences and new-found courage have turned crusaders for truth.'[1] Justice J.C. Shah sat on the Bench, his eyes gazed straight at the witnesses, his questions were sarcastic, and were repeated over and over again in his cross-examination. The former ministers and bureaucrats wilted before his onslaught. They admitted to their wrong-doings but stated that they had been pressured by the culture of the Emergency and by the fear psychosis that gripped them. They blamed Indira Gandhi for their predicament. 'Our tongues were tied,' they said. The statements were punctuated by cheers and jeers from the people present in court.

In the preliminary investigations conducted by the Central Bureau of Investigation (CBI) it became evident that the wild rumours current after the Emergency, linking Indira Gandhi and her son Sanjay Gandhi with many of the reported excesses, when translated into First Information Reports (FIRs) and chargesheets, contained little that was cognizable and could be directly attributed to the former Prime Minister or her son. The main thrust of the legal proceedings, therefore, attempted to establish that the Emergency itself was illegal and that the state of the country was not such as could warrant its promulgation. Therefore, the arrests, the censorship and the actions arising from the Emergency ordinance were illegal and Indira was culpable.

In November 1977, the Shah Commission requested Indira Gandhi to appear before it to help them with their deliberations. The request was couched in polite language, but the message was full of menace. The former Prime Minister was asked to make statements on matters pertaining to the legality of the Emergency and to answer charges arising out of statements made by her former ministers in their appearance before the Shah Commission. In a written statement she challenged the commission on the manner of its functioning. She referred to the way people were encouraged to make statements, pressure was exercised, subtle hints thrown and promises made in advance, allurements offered to persons whose statements were recorded in secrecy by the investigating agencies. These statements were made the basis of the cases against her and her son. Justice Shah had ruled that there would be no cross-examination of witnesses. This enabled them, Indira said, 'to make reckless statements with impunity, without fear.' Any conclusions, according to her, reached by the commission on the basis of these statements would be 'one-sided, illegal and contrary to the principles of natural justice.' She was on firm ground when she told the commission that the advice of the Prime Minister to the President could not be a subject of inquiry by the commission as the Constitution held that it was the prerogative of Parliament. 'It must be borne in mind that it would be impossible for a democratically elected government to function effectively if it is to live under fear of politically inspired inquisitorial proceedings against its policies and decisions by the subsequent government.' She referred to the oath of secrecy incumbent on a minister taking office and said: 'It is neither the Central Government's privilege nor the privilege of the Minister of Law, it is an obligation which is necessary for the effective functioning of government.' She told the commission that she was not prepared to do what she was forbidden to do under the oath of secrecy.

A massive attack against Indira had been launched by the media. Indira Gandhi drew the attention of the commission to the atmosphere that prevailed in the country and the attempts being made to destroy her reputation. The issues before the commission were prejudged by newspapers. Pakistani newspapers compared Zulfikar Ali

Bhutto's trail in Pakistan with that of Indira Gandhi in New Delhi.

The judicial atmosphere necessary in a court was vitiated by the loudspeakers, the remarks of the public within the courtroom and the free fist fights. A lack of gravity distorted the proceedings. In this atmosphere Indira Gandhi felt that justice would not prevail and so refused to appear before the commission. Determined to force her presence, Justice Shah asked the commission to issue a summons, demanding her appearance before it on 9 January 1978.

Throughout her political life Indira rarely forgot that she was living and creating history; it was a sense her father had transmitted to her. It was to determine her words and her attitudes in the tumultuous years that lay ahead. Her back to the wall, Indira now planned her defence with meticulous care. She sat for hours with her lawyers, weighed each phrase, sought alternative words to ensure elegance of language, consulted her friends, found historical allusions, selected them with a finely tuned ear. The Janata leadership failed to realize that in their decision to force Indira to appear before the Shah Commission, they had provided Indira with a stage. She was adept at political theatre and now fighting for the survival of her son and herself, she assumed the role of a Joan of Arc on trial, refusing to recant or retrace a step.

Indira Gandhi appeared before the Shah Commission as scheduled on 9 January 1978. As Justice Shah commenced the proceedings, Indira remained seated beside her lawyer, Frank Anthony. At first, Justice Shah asked her lawyer if Indira Gandhi was willing to make a statement as required of her or would give evidence on oath. 'What does your client propose to say?' Frank Anthony replied that his client was not legally bound to make a statement on oath. Justice Shah then turned from her lawyer to repeat the question to Indira Gandhi, asking her more than once to come to the witness chair and answer questions. She refused to budge. Justice Shah asked her again, 'Are you willing to make a statement or not?' She replied, 'Sir, I have said I am declining because I am not legally bound.' She was again asked if she had any statements on the facts recorded by the commission in the eleven cases with which she was connected. Indira Gandhi replied that she was not legally bound to do so, since complying with the commission's request would go against the oath of secrecy she had taken as Prime Minister.

An angry Justice Shah held that a *prima facie* case had been established by her refusing to answer questions put by a public servant and thereby she had committed an offence under Section 179 of the Indian Penal Code (IPC). Indira Gandhi interrupted, 'Milord, I do not permit my statements to be edited by the court. I said I am not legally bound to make a statement.'[2] Justice Shah directed the Secretary of the commission to file a formal complaint against her in the court of a Magistrate on the basis of what Indira Gandhi had said. Later he maintained that Indira Gandhi and her counsel were playing with the commission. He would not permit it to become a farce.

Indira Gandhi was recalled by the Shah Commission on 15 January. It was clear to Indira that she was to be pilloried, humiliated, destroyed psychologically and later physically. She entered the commission room defiant and angry, her tiny figure drawn up to its full height, her head unbending. There was an impregnable dignity about her as she faced Justice Shah. After the preliminary proceedings were over, the Presiding Officer pointed to the witness chair and said to Indira Gandhi:

'Will you please come to this chair?'

She did not move.

'Will you please come to this chair?' Justice Shah repeated the question.

'No, Sir. I have already stated my position that I am not bound to make a statement.'

'Will you come to this chair, please?'

'No, Sir.'

'Are you willing to make a statement on oath?'

'I shall not answer any further questions.'[3]

Indira Gandhi was defiant, her dignity unflawed, her replies clear and unambiguous. An outraged Justice Shah began to dictate an order that Indira Gandhi be prosecuted in a Delhi Magistrate's court for her conduct before the commission.

As soon as he finished his dictation, Indira Gandhi, her lawyers and her family left the courtroom.

FOUR

With the appearance of her former ministers before the Shah Commission, and their plea that they had been forced to act wrongfully because of the pressure brought to bear by the Prime Minister, Indira Gandhi, a split in the party became inevitable.

Indira Gandhi resigned from the Congress Working Committee (CWC) on 18 December. In a letter to the Congress President, Brahmananda Reddy, she wrote: 'There are moments in an individual's life when the inexorable logic of events leaves no option other than the one which may appear extreme. For some weeks I have had the feeling that one such decisive moment has arrived in my life.' On 21 December, Indira Gandhi's supporters announced that they would hold a rival Congress session on 31 December and 1 January. It was described as 'a Convention of Congressmen to discuss the broad and basic issues confronting the country and the Congress.' The reaction of the CWC presided over by Brahmananda Reddy was sharp and immediate. Indira Gandhi was expelled from the Congress party.

On 3 January 1978, the Congress party split. This was the second time that the Congress party had split after Indira Gandhi took over as Prime Minister. Indira became President of the Congress (I) and the open palm of benediction became her party's symbol. The message to follow her Dharma, for Indira, was a sign to fight her persecutors who she felt were determined to destroy her and to destabilize the country. Senior Congressmen with an all-India reputation, convinced that Indira was a spent force, refused to join her. Vasant Sathe asked Y.B. Chavan, the Minister of External Affairs in Indira's former government, the reason for his negative attitude. 'Vasant,' he said, 'you do not know history. A person rejected the way Indira has been rejected by the people cannot stage a come-back. I have sympathy for her. She is Jawaharlal's daughter, but at present even to be seen in her shadow is destructive.'[1]

With the formation of the Congress (I), the tempo of political activity at 12, Willingdon Crescent increased. It was open house; visitors crowded to see Indira; her party members, with anxious faces were in and out of the house, gathering to hold secret meetings, to plan future strategies. Lawyers were frequent visitors with advice for

Indira and Sanjay Gandhi on the stands they should take before the various commissions of inquiry set up against them. The Central Bureau of Investigation (CBI) intruded to interrogate Indira in the cases launched against her.

Indira met visitors on the lawns, under the awning of tents, in the ante-room, which at times resembled the platform of a railway station. The only room where she could relax was her bedroom and, at times, the dining-room. Indira took the lack of privacy, the reverberating house, the continuous stream of visitors, in her stride. This was the atmosphere in which she had grown up as a child. Memories of the 1930s and her days in Anand Bhawan arose in her mind. Sanjay was a political animal and was quick to adapt to the changing atmosphere. By now he was working with Indira on determining her future strategies. Whenever he was free of lawyers and courts, he was closeted with members of his Youth Congress to plan action to disrupt the functioning of the Janata government. Maneka lived on her nerves: the excitement and the adventure, the secret meetings and the hush-hush atmosphere, was, for her, like participating in an adventure novel. For Rajiv Gandhi and Sonia, the lack of privacy was intolerable. The constant threats, the grim scenario, the uncertain future, frayed their nerves. Their friends could not visit them. Sonia, unused to the atmosphere, was anxious for the safety of the children, concerned with the effect the tensions and chaos within the house would have on them. As there were few servants, Sonia was often called upon to cook and do the marketing; it is remarkable that in those chaotic conditions she could attend to the household chores without a break-down.

Tensions had built up between the sisters-in-law, Sonia and Maneka. They rarely met or spoke to each other. The brothers went their separate ways. Rajiv was a pilot, a government servant; Sanjay, his mother's main confidant, was at the centre of the political battle.

The dogs were everywhere. Sanjay had two Irish wolf-hounds and Bruno, a bull mastiff, a ferocious dog who was a threat to every visitor and could only be controlled by Maneka and her husband. Rajiv and Sonia had a daschund, Reshma, and an Afghan hound, Zabul. The dogs fought, to the horror of Sonia. Maneka was unperturbed.

While Indira took the dangers that surrounded her with grim defiance, the tensions at home tore her apart. A culture unique to the household arose. The "combatants" rarely confronted each other, rarely met, but addressed curt notes to one another to express their hurt and anger. This led to many misunderstandings.

With her truncated yet closely-knit party Indira fought and won the State Assembly elections held in February in Andhra Pradesh and Karnataka. These were crucial victories. Aware of her growing strength, she told the Australian Broadcasting Corporation (ABC): 'I am the only opposition.' Her party was also able to form a government along with the breakaway Congress (S) in Maharashtra. The by-election to the Lok Sabha from Azamgarh in Uttar Pradesh, Indira's home state, became the next battlefield. It was May, one of the hottest months of the year in the Gangetic plain. The river had shrunk, the fields lay arid, fiery winds of dust and grit lashed the countryside; few braved the mid-day sun in the afternoons of May. The Janata government had watched Indira's re-emergence with a sense of foreboding. Azamgarh was Home Minister Charan Singh's stronghold and any Indira victory in the heartland of India would be a disaster. The Janata candidate was Ram Bachan Yadav, a local politician with a strong caste following. He also had the money and power of the Janata to support him. The heroes jailed during the Emergency were requisitioned to canvass against Indira. Atal Behari Vajpayee and Chandra Shekhar spoke eloquently of the excesses that had brought the countryside to near revolt. George Fernandes, then Minister for Industry, with his dislike of Indira, and Raj Narain, Minister for Health and Family Welfare, the hero and victor against Indira, travelled from village to village to re-awaken the terrors of the dark years and to persuade the people that their future was secure in the hands of the Janata Party.

Indira personally chose her party's candidate. She was Mohsina Kidwai, a woman and a Muslim from one of the old Congress families of Uttar Pradesh. On her behalf Indira, dressed in a handspun cotton sari with a coarse long-sleeved blouse, her head modestly covered, fought a relentless campaign. During the last phase of the battle, with Mohsina Kidwai by her side, she travelled in a cavalcade of open jeeps with a group of strapping Sikhs, armed with kirpans, acting as her bodyguards.

> She covered about 24 meetings in less than 30 hours,
> when only 14 were listed on her programme. Travelling

at lightning speed she pressed on for about 10 to 12 hours every day, halting in remote dak bungalows at night. She would eat a frugal meal with her entourage, sleep in a stifling room for barely four hours, wake at dawn and after a cold bath and exercises continue her journey to re-discover the people of her country.[2]

Along the way she halted to address groups of peasants gathered by the roadside; women, Harijans and landless peasants crowded her meetings. Though illiterate, the peasants of India through the centuries had gathered a wisdom through listening deeply and through direct and close observation. For them it was a wondrous thing that after fourteen hours on the road, travelling through dust and heat, Indira's sari remained unwrinkled. What would appear trivial to the urban-dweller, for the villager was perhaps the most significant. She would arrive to address them, her head covered; her fragility and the feeling of empathy that glowed from her, touched them. It was not what Indira said, most politicians said the same thing, but what they saw in her lean, haggard face—the marks of her defeat—that moved them. She had aged. They had heard by word of mouth of her daring journey, fording rivers in spate, to visit Belchi. They were aware of the relentless manner in which she was being hunted. She belonged to Uttar Pradesh. Their fathers had listened in rapt attention to her father. She was a daughter of this land of rivers. In this heartland there were no myths to sustain the hunt or sacrifice of a woman, and a mother. Her people could not stand by and allow her to be destroyed. The quick anger that had swept the countryside during the last Lok Sabha elections was quenched.

At the end of her campaign, she drove to Varanasi to bathe in the sacred Ganga. It was a symbolic gesture, for in the waters of the holy river, all impurities are washed away.

On election day, the Harijans and the under-privileged landless labourers dared the anger of wealthy landlords to come to the polling booths. Women, irrespective of religion, caste or creed, in revolt, went against the advice of their menfolk, to vote for Indira's candidate.

A cynical reporter covering the campaign remarked:

So intensive, far-reaching and dramatic was the election

campaign of Azamgarh that even the local whores of Kaliganj soliciting customers in their doorways shot out their hands, palm outwards, to indicate that they supported the Indira Congress.[3]

Mohsina Kidwai was declared elected by a large majority and Indira Gandhi's political calculations were proved correct. She had obtained the bulk of Harijan and Muslim votes as well as the votes of the landless; there had been an unprecedented rise in the number of women who went to the polls.

Indira Gandhi was in Delhi when the results came in. She told her family and those who had gathered to greet her that there should be no celebration of the victory. She understood how mortal a blow her Azamgarh victory was to the Janata leadership; she did not want to aggravate their humiliation. A frustrated and angry Janata government, in panic, hit back. They cancelled the bail of Sanjay in the case of *Kissa Kursi Ka,* in which he was charged with destroying a film against Indira, during the Emergency. He was arrested and taken to Tihar jail in New Delhi:

Indira telephoned late in April, inviting me to Karnataka for a holiday in the middle of May. I was at the airport on 19 May. The corridors and lounges of the terminal were crowded with people waiting to see her. The news of the Janata government's intention to arrest her on 17 May had reached her two days earlier, while she was in Jaipur. Messages had gone out to her party members to keep themselves in readiness for such an eventuality. She was staying with her aunt in Jaipur and her companions kept a vigil the whole night to be available in case of her arrest. At the last minute the Janata leadership changed its mind. Indira was convinced however that it was only a brief respite; with the victory of her party in Azamgarh, her continued forays into the countryside and the growing crowds that welcomed her, the Janata government could not afford to keep her free for very long.

The moment she entered the plane, she put a cloth over her eyes and went to sleep. I was amazed at her capacity to relax and told her so. She said she rarely had difficulty in sleeping; she slept in cars, trains, planes and could also wake up on the instant. Karnataka Chief Minister, Devraj Urs, with his Cabinet colleagues, awaited us on arrival at Bangalore. Indira did not linger at the airport, but drove with Urs, in a cavalcade of cars, straight to Arkavati Niwas, a rest-house built on an artificial lake situated amidst green and hilly country, some miles out of Bangalore. Later that evening, she walked with me in the garden. It was rocky country, heavily planted with plumeria and gulmohar, both in full bloom; the pale oyster of the plumeria and the scarlet of the gulmohar transformed the landscape of verdant undulating country. She climbed a rock and sat on it while I remained at the base. We watched the sun-born colours explode on the horizon, tinting the clouds, the flowering trees, the hills with a transparent luminosity. We watched with wonder colours bloom and fade before we dialogued together. She was to write a long introduction to a volume of photographs on India, to be published in France. We spoke of her book and the cultural streams that went to build the robust Indian mind. She expressed her concern at the increasing vulgarity and noise that were assaults on India's ancient insights and wisdom.

In the midst of our discussion, her attention wandered. She was apprehensive, had booked a call to Delhi to enquire about Sanjay in jail. Sonia had agreed to take a meal for him every morning. Indira was grateful but anxious. At the very mention of Sanjay's name, her heart tripped. I have often wondered whether in Sanjay's birth-chart there was a conjunction of stars which predicted an early and violent death for her younger son. It is difficult otherwise to understand the dark anxieties that swamped this otherwise courageous woman.

We were to spend a week in Karnataka visiting Mysore, the Nagarhole game sanctuary, the Vaishnav religious centre at Dharmas-thal and finally Mercara in Coorg, a small town nestling among tea and coffee estates; we stayed in Mercara for three days, in an old circuit house with high ceilings and gabled roof.

On the journey we stopped at wayside shrines, visited the main temples. At the outskirts of villages or towns, Indira would step down from her car and with Devraj Urs climb on to an open jeep. For Indira her journey through Karnataka, besides being a holiday, was also a journey of exploration. It was after many years that she was free to linger; she could explore local myth and legend; she did not have to look at her watch to keep her next appointment; she was free of what, for her, was an oppressive security. Long before we entered a village, cries of "Indiramma" would reach us. In the main square, children, old and young women and men would surge towards her jeep. Many women would hold their babies out to her for her blessings; they would hand over petitions, garland her with sweet-smelling jasmine and brilliant marigolds. She would get down from her jeep and move into the crowd. I would watch her closely, see her interlock her eyes with individual women and children, establish contact with them; a transmission was made possible without word or concept. I could see the faces of the people soften. Through these simple people, Indira felt close to the earth, to fields, to trees and to the myths that permeated and gave strength to the life of village India. The dignity, affection and simple wisdom of these people of the earth touched her deeply. At each encounter Indira appeared renewed.

The night before our departure for Mercara, Devraj Urs suggested that we visit a very well-known temple consecrated to Subramaniam, the God of Eternal Youth. It meant a detour and it would be several hours before we reached Mercara. Indira was hesitant. Urs then told a story. A king, he said, had to fight a major war. Before embarking on the battle, he vowed to visit a hundred places of pilgrimage. After ninety-nine journeys, news reached him that the enemy had invaded the country. He forgot the hundredth pilgrimage and rushed back to battle. Inevitably he lost and was killed. Indira looked peeved. I commented that after listening to the story she had no option save to visit the temple. So we started before dawn to visit the Subramaniam temple; there, we met the presiding abbot who, from his privileged position, chided Indira on her Emergency rule. Indira was angry. Her mouth grew taut, her spine straight and the veins on her neck grew prominent. Before the abbot finished his sermon, she rose, folded her hands and left the room much to the consternation of the believers.[4]

We reached Mercara late in the evening. She had planned her time-table meticulously. On reaching a rest-house, she would tidy her room, make her bed, straighten a photograph on the wall. It was only then that she would relax or sleep without turmoil. Order soothed her.

We were four days in Mercara. She devoted her time to the essay she was to write. I had warned her that to deal with the vast canvas of India, its religious, cultural, social, economic past and present, was a monumental task and to compress it into an essay that would convey the living sense of India, without recourse to books or references, would be very arduous. And in three days! But she was determined to go ahead.

She would be up at dawn, work on her manuscript, exercise, have a bath and appear at the breakfast table by 8 o' clock sharp. After breakfast she would dictate sections of the essay to a stenographer provided by Devraj Urs. I had taken with me three or four books on culture, religion, customs and rituals, and at times she would turn to me or to Nirmala Deshpande and seek help. At the end of four days, a rough draft was ready.

While we were in Mercara, she would spend some time alone with me in the evenings. She needed to relax, to speak freely, to have someone near her who was concerned about her, who could listen. The hatred and vicious attacks had bruised her and she desperately needed affection and a gesture of closeness. In these four evenings she often went back to her childhood and her young adolescence. She recreated the past, re-living moments of anguish and pain but also the joy and the ecstasy. At times her anxieties for her son expressed themselves. She spoke of her mother with ease, with deep love and sorrow. As an adolescent, Indira felt that she had failed Kamala; she had misjudged her mother's frailty and her incapacity to stand up to Jawaharlal Nehru and his formidable family.

But she rarely spoke of the two men she loved with a passion—her father and her younger son. It was as if she was so tuned to their minds and feelings that she could not think of them as separate to herself.

On our way back she took a detour to the Nandi hills where she was met by her two chief ministers, those of Andhra Pradesh and Karnataka. It was at this meeting that the possibility of her return to Parliament was discussed. Proposals for Indira entering the Rajya Sabha from Karnataka had been suggested. She had registered her name at a local ashram, for she had to claim residence before she could seek entry into the Upper House of Parliament; but her request was turned down by the presiding Magistrate, and the Janata Party launched cases against her for false declaration of residence. Meanwhile Devraj Urs had persuaded D.B. Chandre Gowda, the incumbent Member of the Lok Sabha from Chikmaglur, to resign so that a vacancy could be created from where Indira could contest a Lok Sabha seat.

On her return to Delhi, Indira was quick to write me a letter: 'How can I thank you? . . . Just having you there was a comfort. Situations bring out different emotions in people. Since the defeat, I have sensed a special tenderness and protectiveness.'[5]

*

It had become clear to Indira Gandhi that she should seek re-election as early as possible. Information had reached her that the Janata Party was considering disenfranchising her. Sri Lanka had introduced legislation imposing civic penalties on politicians for crimes against the people. Indira's entry into Parliament would ensure that such action could not take place. If she won, Indira would emerge as the leader of the Opposition in Parliament and would be entitled to privileges given to members of the Cabinet. The choice of the constituency had already been made at the Nandi hills in May 1978.

Chikmaglur is a small district situated in a hilly area amidst the Western Ghats. The tallest peak in the area is called Baba Badun, According to historical records, 'a Muslim saint Baba Badun arrived from Mecca about the 17th Century bringing with him some coffee berries. He built his hut and planted the seeds in his compound. This was the beginning of coffee cultivation in India.'[6] Chikmaglur coffee is regarded as one of the best in the world.

Legends of the epic *Ramayana* are to be found all over Chikmaglur. It was from amongst these heavily cultivated hills that Hanuman, the monkey-faced God, lifted Sanjivini, the life-giving mountain of herbs, to fly to the shores of Lanka, to save the life of the mortally wounded Lakshmana, Rama's younger brother.[7]

The constituency was ideally suited for Indira Gandhi. About fifty per cent of the electorate, of almost 600,000, were women. About forty-five per cent belonged to the Scheduled Castes[8], the backward classes and other minorities. A little over forty per cent of the population lived below the poverty line.

Indira knew that the by-election would be fiercely contested. She was not an ordinary candidate nor was the election an ordinary parliamentary by-election. Her victory would enable her to reach across the boundaries of her constituency to the peoples of India and beyond the oceans to the media of the world. Her defeat would resonate over India, destroy her credibility and make it impossible for her to defend herself. It would be a final rejection of her by the people of her country.

She visited Chikmaglur before she finally made up her mind to contest. She was enchanted by the landscape of lush green vegetation, the little villages nestling amongst the hills. The leaders of the plantation workers and the chiefs of the Gram Panchayats met her and expressed their fervent hope that she would agree to stand and represent them in the Lok Sabha. Devraj Urs, Chief Minister of Karnataka, had strongly supported the proposal.

Indira finally agreed to contest. But shortly before she had to file her election papers, Urs' enemies convinced her that it would be a trap as Urs was inimical to her and would betray her. She decided to contest anyway. Chikmaglur means 'the abode of the little daughter'. Legends in the area connected the name with King Rukmangada who gave away the verdant area as a dowry to his younger daughter; to his elder daughter he gave another village nearby which is known as Hiremaglur, town of the elder daughter.

Indira Gandhi filed her nomination papers at 12.30 on 6 October, a time declared auspicious by astrologers. Her campaign commenced on 19 October. Morarji Desai, the Prime Minister, was not quite sure how to deal with Indira and the Chikmaglur election. He refused to campaign against her as he felt that the Prime Minister should not be involved in by-elections. The Janata Party took its time about finding a suitable candidate to oppose Indira. But George Fernandes, then Union Minister of Industry, who, aware of the enormous implications of Indira's victory, confronted the Prime Minister and warned him that if he did not wake up to find a suitable candidate to oppose Indira, Fernandes would resign his ministership and contest against Indira in Chikmaglur. Karnataka was his home territory, he spoke Kannada, could approach the electorate as a son of the soil. Ultimately, Veerendra Patil, a former Chief Minister of Karnataka and a man known for his integrity was selected to battle against Indira Gandhi.

Patil's campaign was leisurely and it was left to a fiery George Fernandes to enter the arena 'like a wounded lion, pawing the ground at every step.'[9] If Fernandes was the lion, Indira was the strong-winged bird that braves the tempest. In the midst of a small cavalcade of cars, Indira travelled the hill roads of her constituency, addressing crowds at larger villages, visiting the coffee estates to speak to coffee pickers and their families, entering tribal huts, always listening to the bent old women and men who came and gathered around her. The rainfall was heavy. Far from the major cities, the people were simple, self-contented, isolated from the political ferment of the rest of the country. The news of Indira's defeat had not reached the poor in the interior areas of the district. 'Yelemma—a toothless coffee picker— did not even know that Indira had ceased to be the Prime Minister, She broke down when told that her leader may be jailed if charges against her were proved. "What charges?" she asked as if to say that kings and queens do no wrong.'[10]

Indira's fair skin, her fragility, her dignity, captured the hearts of the local people. They had never seen anyone quite like her. Photographs of Indira were distributed widely and pinned on the walls of village huts. She was travelling eighteen hours a day at the height of her campaign, rarely stopping for lunch, eating peanuts and fruit in the car, addressing eight to ten meetings a day, continuously for fourteen days. She was visiting temples, churches and Muslim shrines. Careful of every move, anxious not to step on any delicate terrain, she would pause at her meetings and wait for the muezzin's call to the faithful reminding them that the hour of prayer had come. She joined processions of the boar-faced divinity at isolated hamlets; she performed rituals at orthodox shrines.

George Fernandes followed her trail and addressed her audiences immediately after she had left. She spoke of spiralling prices, shortages and increasing poverty; he of the Emergency and its tortures and the issue of democracy against dictatorship. The leaders of the Janata Party, Chandra Shekhar, Jagjivan Ram, Raj Narain and other party stalwarts addressed a number of meetings all over the constituency. Unfortunately they could not speak the local language. The Indian press and the foreign media crowded the hotels. The people of Chikmaglur, the tiny hoteliers, the coffee-shops, the wayside stalls selling garlands, found themselves surrounded by pressmen from all over the world, by leaders, ministers, artists—the money they poured into this district during the three weeks of campaigning that preceded the campaign could support them for months.

A major poster war was launched. Indira's posters read in the local language, "Give your vote to your little daughter". Intellectuals, artists and students gathered in Bangalore to prepare anti-Indira posters for the Janata campaign. The posters appeared on trees along the roadside where Indira was to address a meeting; Indira was portrayed as a double-faced witch, a murderess surrounded by skulls. It was at this time that, unconcerned with the power of symbols, Fernandes committed a major blunder. In this isolated district, the Emergency was a non-issue. Addressing a major public meeting he had put up an enormous poster on which Indira was depicted as a king cobra. The legend read: 'Beware, through this election a powerful cobra is going to raise its hood.'[11] Perhaps he was ignorant or ignored the fact that in Karnataka a crested cobra was worshipped as a protector of the earth. Another poster nearby showed Janata arrows destroying the cobra; to kill a cobra was regarded as most inauspicious in Chikmaglur.

The campaign was peaceful until 1 November, four days before the election. Then tensions increased. At Ujire, Gayatri, a sixteen-year-old college girl, died of shock when she was wounded by a ricocheting tear-gas shell. The event led to violence, processions and increased tension.

By now it was clear that the election result would be in Indira's favour. She was to address a major public meeting at Chikmaglur on 3 November, the last day of the political campaign. Her election managers were concerned that the meeting would be disrupted by stone-throwing and hooliganism. There would be firing, which could lead to a situation in which the Election Commissioner could intervene and order the postponement of the by-election. On 2 November, while driving in her cavalcade to their next halt, news reached Urs that Fernandes had set up a road block further along the road with the intention of a confrontation; the road was to become a battleground. Plans were immediately drawn up to ensure that no confrontation took place between Indira and Fernandes. Indira changed cars to enter an old rather ramshackle car. She was disguised to resemble a nun, and the car slipped away unnoticed along one of the curving roads of the green countryside, to a friendly coffee estate some distance away from Chikmaglur town. Meanwhile the main cavalcade drove on, bypassing the road block.

Indira spent the evening and the next morning talking to the coffee plantation workers and some women tribals. The women fell at her feet, treated her as their benefactor. They saw in her eyes an under-standing of what it was to be woman, to carry the burdens of child-birth, hunger and death. They said that before Indiramma came to power, they had been so poor that they could not afford to eat rice, but had survived on wild grain collected from the hillsides. They had no clothes to wear and sometimes covered themselves with leaves. Now, because of various programmes of her government, they were able to eat rice for the first time.

With the disappearance of Indira, efforts were made by the Op-position to trace her whereabouts. It was too late to plan any alternate strategies. On the morning of 3 November, as the time drew near for Indira's scheduled meeting at Chikmaglur, she grew restless. She kept looking at her watch, told Nirmala Deshpande and Vasant Sathe who were with her, that it was getting late for her final meeting. They, in turn, were determined to keep her away from the political battlefield. News had reached them that the Central Reserve Police (CRP) had been called in to deal with possible incidents of violence. They also knew that Indira would never agree to stay away from the meeting if she grew aware that they were trying to protect her person. There was no sign of a car and an angry Indira decided to go for a walk alone through the hills. It was raining, she was seen in the rain under a leaf umbrella, surrounded by coffee pickers with baskets on their heads to ward off the rain. She lingered, spoke to them, asked after the coffee crop. On her return she found that the car was still missing. By now it was clear to her that her friends had deliberately kept her from keeping her appointment in Chikmaglur. She was angry but, soon realized that they had acted against a genuine threat.[12]

On 4 November, Indira addressed a major news conference at Aldur, twenty-one kilometres from Chikmaglur. The press was relentless in its questions, she was skilful in answering. The reporters asked her why she had fought shy of addressing her last election meeting. She told them that she had heard that there was going to be planned violence and she did not want to be responsible for it.

It poured on 5 November, polling day. In spite of the rain, seventy-six per cent of the voters exercised their franchise. A vast number of women were seen waiting in long queues before the polling started. Immediately after polling day, Indira went to Ramana Ashram, nestled against the sacred mountain, Arunachal, unaccompanied by any of her companions. She had asked those who ran the ashram to avoid giving her any special treatment.

Ramana Maharishi was regarded by people all over the country as amongst the most illumined sages of the century. He had died of cancer in the late Forties. During his lifetime he had erected within the ashram, samadhis—burial sites—to a cow, to a deer and to a crow. All the three animals were inmates of the ashram and when they fell ill, Ramana had nursed them himself before their death. Indira lingered before the samadhi for the crow. By now journalists had arrived and they crowded around her to ask why she stood before the shrine for the crow. She remained quiet for some time, then said:

> Almost all Hindus are cremated, except for the saints. Samadhis are erected only for enlightened men; that Ramana Maharishi should have erected a samadhi for a cow I could understand. I could also understand it being built for a deer, an animal associated with the Ashram, but I was puzzled by the samadhi for a crow. It is only now that I grew aware of the nature of Ramana's compassion. For him all life was sacred.

She ate her meals with the inmates of the ashram, listened to their stories of the saint. Before she left, she sat quietly for over an hour in the room where Ramana had lived and slept. After the tense atmosphere of Chikmaglur, she needed silence.

On her return to Delhi on 7 November, as she was leaving for the Soviet Embassy to attend their National Day celebrations, she was informed that she had won the Chikmaglur seat by a margin of 70,000 votes. The news had reached the Soviet Embassy and the ambassadors present there drank to her victory.

The Chikmaglur victory had historic overtones. In two years Indira Gandhi, a Prime Minister defeated ruthlessly at the polls, was back in Parliament. She had battled against the full might of the Janata Party with all its power and prestige, and against the strategies of the intellectuals, writers, artists and academics of Karnataka. Her victory had a profound impact on the political situation in India.

FIVE

1978 was an year of escalating violence against Indira Gandhi. Every month witnessed the launching of new commissions of inquiry; every day saw a new threat of visitations by the law. The assaults converged from all sides—the network of criminal cases launched against Indira ranged from the grim to the absurd. The intention was to grip and bind her in an intricate *nagabandha,* a serpent hold, so that she would be at the mercy of the Janata Party.

A commission of inquiry was initiated into the death of Nagarwala, a particularly inept embezzler, and his subsequent death in judicial custody. Although the crime took place long before the Emergency was declared, sinister attempts were made to link Indira to his death. It was October 1978 before Justice Chinnappa Reddy of the Supreme Court finally held that Nagarwala died due to natural causes. Immediately afterwards there was another commission of inquiry into the 1975 assassination of one of Indira's former ministers—L.N. Mishra—and an attempt was made to link Indira's name, in some way, with the crime. A furious Indira Gandhi lashed out, 'Even if they kill me, they will say I planned it.'[1]

If these commissions were bad news, the Trikha Commission was an act of unparalleled vindictiveness. It charged Indira with stealing four chickens and two eggs. Criminal proceedings were launched, a non-bailable warrant was served against Indira and the sixty-year-old woman had to travel 2,000 miles to answer the charges in a court in Manipur, in the north-east. The case was adjourned on a plea from the prosecution and Indira returned to Delhi.

It was in this vitiated atmosphere that Indira took her seat in the Lok Sabha. On her first day in Parliament, she was met by cries of "shame" and angry shouts from the Treasury Benches and cheers and the thumping of tables from members of her party. Early in 1978, a privilege motion had been moved against her in the Lok Sabha. It concerned her alleged harassment, when she was Prime Minister, of some officers in the Ministry of Industry, who were investigating her son's automobile company, Maruti. After her defeat, the Lok Sabha referred the matter to the Privileges Committee. Its report, finding her guilty, was to be tabled in the House on 21 November. The Janata

Party's Parliamentary Board meeting had already discussed and decided the punishment to be meted out to her, much before she was found guilty by the Lok Sabha.

With the majority enjoyed by the Janata government, there was no way Indira could escape punishment. She was quick to realize that, in spite of her total vulnerability, the Janata feared her. She also grew aware that the various attempts to destroy her through physical violence, commissions of inquiry, arrests and ceaseless interrogations by the Central Bureau of Investigation (CBI) had failed and the privilege motion was to be used as an excuse to humiliate her and destroy her political future. She, therefore, sought to use the occasion to lift the privilege motion from its petty concerns to a universal battlefield.

She was aware that her presence and demeanour in the Lok Sabha would create history, village tale and song. The Janata patriarchs sitting in judgement in the Lok Sabha were archetypal images. They would be transformed in the rural psyche to the mythical time of the epics, to the *Mahabharata,* where at the Kaurava court, the Fitamas (fathers) sat and watched the humiliations of the fragile yet defiant Draupadi.

Indira exercised her right to address the House on 8 December. Her speech had dignity, passion and defiance. She accused the party in power of converting the House into a medieval "Star Chamber" by raising the question of privilege in what was essentially a question of party politics. There was pandemonium, her voice could hardly be heard, amid the interruptions and jeers from the back-benches of the Janata Party. She claimed that as the Janata Parliamentary Board had already pre-judged the issue, her plea of innocence would be futile. 'May I reiterate emphatically and categorically that in point of fact, I have not committed any breach of Privilege of the House.' The interruption continued. She had a bad cold and at every sneeze there were sneers and jeers. 'Sir,' she addressed the Lok Sabha Speaker, 'I have a bad cold and it seems that even clearing my throat is a provocation to the House.'

Cases against her had been filed in the criminal courts of the country on the very matters on which the Lok Sabha was intending to judge her. This would, she emphasized, pre-judge the criminal trial. She claimed that the motive behind the Janata Party's action was prompted by personal vendetta against her. It was a long and well-argued statement. 'Never before in the history of any democratic country has a single individual, who leads the principal political opposition, been subjected to so much calumny, character assassination and political vendetta of the ruling party.' She pointed out that when she was released on 4 October by the magistrate in Delhi, the Prime Minister had publicly declared that the magistrate had committed an impropriety in releasing her. She reminded the House that the Home Minister had stated openly that the members of the Cabinet of the Janata Party were looked upon as a band of impotent men for not having already put her behind bars.

She claimed that her socialist measures, meant to support the cause of secularism and democratic socialism, had led to a tremendous popular upsurge which the Janata Party in their fury could not accept. She maintained, yet again, that for hardships caused during the Emergency she was deeply sorry. 'I have already expressed my regret in many public forums and do so again.' She reiterated the fact that not all actions, (during the Emergency) came to her notice. It was she who decided to call for elections in 1977. She then stretched her slim body to its maximum height and charged the government with creating conditions of civil war and being helpless in the face of organized communal violence in various parts of the country. She charged the government with weakening the secular foundations laid by Mahatma Gandhi, of surrendering the sovereign right of India to use nuclear technology for India's vital interests; with diluting the policy of non-alignment; with denigrating indigenous science and technology; and with inviting in multinationals surreptitiously to control the commanding heights of the Indian economy. Above all, she charged the government with tarnishing her image, of lowering India's prestige in the world.

At every salvo, the shouts of the reigning political party increased. At times there was chaos, but Indira continued to speak.

> We held our head high in international affairs, not imitating, not boasting, not cringing. Just being ourselves—Indians belonging to a very special civilization, self-reliant, self-confident. This was non-alignment.

> I am a small person but I have stood for certain values and objectives. Every insult hurled at me will rebound. Every

punishment inflicted on me will be a source of strength to me.

My voice will not be hushed, for it is not a lone voice. It speaks not for myself, frail woman, and unimportant person. It speaks not for a so-called "total revolution" involving smugglers, dacoits and others such but for the deep and significant changes in society which alone can be the basis for true democracy and a fuller freedom, which alone can ensure justice and help to create a better man.

The atmosphere in this House has been reminiscent of the scene in *Alice in Wonderland,* when all the cards rise up in the air and shout, "Off with her head"; my head is yours. My box has been packed these several months, we have only to put in the winter things.[2]

The discussion on the privilege motion was adjourned, to be taken up again on 18 December. 14 December was Sanjay's birthday. Indira wrote to her son:

Delhi
13-12-1978
for the 14th

Dear Sanjay,

Here is your birthday again and I cannot help thinking to that day, or rather the day before you were born. It was a mad topsy-turvy time, but in a good sense, not the hypocrisy and reversal of values that one finds today.

What can I say? Remember, everything that strengthens, hurts. Some are crushed and crippled, a few become stronger. You have had to face a great deal from a very young age and I am proud of the dignified manner in which you have done so. I wish I could take your burden but, essentially and ultimately, each person is alone even though he be surrounded by loving relatives and friends.

Therefore be strong in mind and body, learn to tolerate and to try and win over rather than reciprocating aggressiveness and dislike. This I say from my own experience, for I used to react as you do and have found that it only increases one's troubles. A smile and friendly word to one's enemy costs nothing and even if it brings nothing, it gives one a certain satisfaction. It makes one a better person. Never, never do anything mean.

What can I wish you? Only that these dreadful days slide into the past, that you emerge unscathed in your innocence, your honest intentions proved and that people recognize your worth and quality. God bless you and with all my love.[3]

Mummie
(Indira Gandhi)

*

J. Krishnamurti was in residence in Rishi Valley in December 1978. Indira had earlier suggested that she would like to spend a week at the valley so that she could meet and talk with the sage. With the crisis in the Lok Sabha, I was not surprised to receive a telegram cancelling her proposed visit. I left Rishi Valley for Delhi to be with her for four days. Though I slept in the home of a friend, I was at 12, Willingdon Crescent with Indira and her family for most of the day. I found her sons, their wives and her grandchildren had come together in total support of their mother and grandmother. For dinner the first night Sonia had cooked a delicious pasta, there was guava cheese and *amras* (mango cakes) from Allahabad. To ease the tension, Indira started a word game. Many of us fumbled but Rajiv's daughter, Priyanka, was quick, much to the delight of her grandmother. Maneka prattled away about the Congress party members betraying Indira and the quarrels brewing in the Janata leadership. Indira warned Maneka to keep off Charan Singh in the political gossip magazine *Surya* she was editing at the time. I sensed that something was brewing. Later Indira told me that some intermediaries were trying to mediate in the affair—Devraj Urs, Chief Minister of Karnataka, was sent to Charan Singh that morning. Most of the leaders within the Janata Party were against any severe punishment for Indira, but Morarji Desai and the Janata hawks were adamant; they demanded a tough sentence. The Prime Minister would yield if Indira was prepared to make an abject apology to the House. But he knew that Indira would not be a supplicant.

On the same day that Indira was to face the Privilege issue in Parliament, Zulfikar Ali Bhutto in Pakistan was to appear before the Supreme Court to defend himself against the sentence of death passed by a lower court. The coincidence was ominous. The death sentence for Bhutto cast shadows around Indira and Sanjay. In the atmosphere that prevailed anything was possible. Legislation had been introduced in the Lok Sabha to enact a Special Courts Bill which would short-circuit the judicial procedure and give the Special Courts sweeping powers. There would be no appeal from the Special Court.

I accompanied Indira, in her car, to Parliament House on the morning of 18 December. She was mobbed by waiting MPs from her party and the press as soon as we arrived. From the President's gallery, I watched Indira enter the packed House, flanked by C.M. Stephen and Vasant Sathe. From the back-benches of the Janata Party cries and invective were hurled against her. As soon as the proceedings started and the privilege motion was taken up, there were uproarious scenes. Stephen, leader of the Congress (I) in the House, sprang to his feet. His voice thundered and reverberated through the House as he demanded an end to what he said was a farce—that the Lok Sabha had no moral right to expel Indira Gandhi. C. Subramaniam, her former minister, was reasoned, legal. Indira sat in the front row, her spine straight, observing every gesture, listening to every word. The leader of the House, Prime Minister Morarji Desai, had made the position of his government clear. His resolution demanded 'that Smt. Indira Nehru Gandhi be committed to jail till the prorogation of the House and also be expelled from membership of the House for the serious breach of privilege and contempt of the House committed by her.'

It was impossible to hear what was being said. K.S. Hegde, the Speaker, was bobbing up and down in his seat, trying to bring some order into the proceedings. Various amendments were being tabled. I was unused to the noise, the thumping of tables, the questions and cross-questions, and by 5 o'clock in the evening was exhausted and returned to 12, Willingdon Crescent. Sonia and Rajiv were waiting for Indira's return. She came in an hour later, bone-weary and told us that the proceedings had been postponed to the next day. It was clear that Morarji Desai's resolution would be carried, Indira jailed.

I was to leave for Bombay on 19 December, as Krishnaji was arriving there from Madras and I was his hostess, but I suggested I would postpone my departure. Indira insisted that I go. 'Don't postpone it, Pupul,' she said. 'You cannot come with me where they are taking me.'[4]

The Lok Sabha held Indira guilty of breach of privilege on 19 December and resolved that she be committed to jail till the prorogation of the House and also be expelled from the membership of Lok Sabha for the very serious breach of privilege and contempt of the House. The House went wild—Indira was the centre of excited voices, the Janata Party was triumphant. Indira refused to move till the warrant was served on her. Amidst unprecedented scenes of support and cries of "Long Live Indira", she entered the police car. A line she must have heard in London during the war came to her mind. 'Bid me goodbye with a tear and a smile,' she said to the crowd, before she left for Tihar jail. The next morning she wrote to me on a crumpled and stained piece of paper:

Tihar Jail
20-12-78

Pupul dear,

You looked positively ill the other day and I have been worried about you. You are anxious about me but why? Physically and mentally I am well. My cough and cold are much better. I am e(n)sconced (it sounds a good word but the spelling escapes me for the moment) in a large barracks all by myself with two matrons taking turns to look after me. It is fairly clean but indescribably ugly. The fittings unfunctional and badly made. They have made a bathroom for me and I had hot water in the morning. It is quiet and peaceful. I am reading and if the mood comes, may be able to write. I have brought an odd selection of books—all birthday gifts.[5]

Love
Indu

Indira's room in Tihar jail was the same barracks that had been occupied by George Fernandes. She planned her day with meticulous discipline; she woke up at 5 in the morning, did her morning yogic *asanas* and *pranayam* (yogic breathing) drank cold milk brought to her the previous evening by her daughter-in-law Sonia, and went back to bed till 7 o'clock. She then had a bath, meditated for a while and then read one of the six books she was permitted. She tried to write but there is little evidence of this in her papers. Her meals were cooked at home and brought by Sonia every morning and evening.

Indira was given a wooden bed but there was no mattress, the windows were barred but there were no shutters. It was the end of December, the coldest season in Delhi and the temperature came near to freezing point at night. Indira hung her blankets on the bars of the window to keep the cold out and to ensure some privacy. At night she covered herself with a quilt. The evenings were very long and she went to bed early.

On one occasion Sonia brought her daughter, Priyanka, to the jail; the child was permitted to visit her grandmother only after much argument with the jail authorities. Throughout the period in jail, Indira did not permit herself even a second of self-pity, nor was she melancholy. She received two telegrams while in jail from unknown people. The first said, "Live frugally". Indira had cut her diet to the minimum; the other advised her to count the bars in the window. She counted them and there were twenty-eight.[6]

The words of Beethoven sent to her by her father many years ago when she was deeply depressed and Jawaharlal Nehru was in jail, filled her ears, "I will seize fate by the throat. It shall never wholly overcome me." She would not allow a shadow of self-pity to touch her mind. A week in jail gave her the interval she needed to pause, to take stock, enter into herself and gather in her resources. A bouquet of flowers from Indira reached Charan Singh from Tihar jail with her warm greetings on his birthday.

With three years to go before the next elections, she knew that time was on the side of the Janata Party. Was there a way, she asked herself, to drive a wedge between the increasingly fractious Janata leadership, to fire their ambitions, to topple the Janata government?

A letter from Charan Singh awaited her at 12, Willingdon Crescent, upon her release. He had invited her to his home to celebrate the birth of his grandson. A telephone message followed saying that he expected her. Charan Singh and his wife awaited her in the portico when she reached his home. Indira sat on the sofa with Morarji Desai. The Prime Minister remained uncomfortable and silent throughout. Indira's conversation with Charan Singh and his wife was very cordial. She ate the sweets offered to her and took the new-born babe on her lap, to bless the child.

Soon after the birth celebrations, Indira flew to Madras to fulfil her interrupted engagement with Krishnamurti. I was at the airport to receive her. We reached Vasanta Vihar to find Krishnaji on the porch. He took Indira to a sitting-room on the first floor. I waited in a nearby room. They were together for over an hour. Krishnaji came out and called me in. Indira had distressed eyes, but smiled when she saw me. After a while she said, 'Krishnaji has been asking me to leave politics. I have told him I do not know how. There are twenty-eight criminal cases against me.' She paused, searching for the right words. 'I have told Krishnaji that I have only two alternatives, to fight or to let them destroy me like a sitting duck.'[7]

Late that evening I went to see Indira at the government rest-house. A little over a year before, Madras had greeted her with violent demonstrations; this time huge crowds surrounded the house, were on the stairway and in the corridors, greeting her with wild cheers. It was difficult to force my way through. Indira spoke of a changing tide in her favour amongst the people of the country. People in Tamil Nadu, who had mobbed her, stormed her a year ago, were now hailing her as the "mother". Every act of the Janata Party to destroy her had increased the people's support for her. The Janata Party was fragmented, each group trying to destabilize the other. At a recent national camp held in Ujjain, Prime Minister Morarji Desai was openly challenged by senior members of his party for the wrongdoings of his son Kanti Desai. The Prime Minister had lost his temper. 'You are possessed. You need to be exorcised,' he had told his critics.

'A weak and divided Janata can be very dangerous. The days ahead are very critical. We cannot afford to wait. Time is on the side of the Janata,'[8] Indira said.

I asked her how she planned her strategies. She was silent for a while, then said: 'I watch people's faces, I listen to what people say, I observe nature, I observe events; at times at night I let my mind wander, let it roam freely into the future, however dark; thought has very little to do with it. It is like seeing with the pores of one's skin—at rare moments things fall into place.'

'Is it to extend the mind and senses to the limits of the possible?' I asked. She replied: 'It is to see something that has not yet taken shape.'[9]

SIX

Indira Gandhi had exercised her superb political skills to out-manoeuvre the Janata leadership. She had just been released from jail, but for her there was no respite. By February 1979 she was once again at bay, encircled by her political opponents and the rebellious strongmen in her own party. Frantic telephonic messages reached me in Bombay from Nirmala Deshpande suggesting that I come to Delhi as early as possible. 'Indira,' she said, 'is very tense, has ceased to listen, loses her temper at the slightest excuse. Her party persons feel her nerves are shattered.' The immediate cause for the tension was the *Kissa Kursi Ka* case against Sanjay Gandhi which was due for judgement in the very near future. I flew to Delhi on 24 February and went unannounced to 12, Willingdon Crescent at 11 o'clock in the morning. The gates were closed, a government guard was on duty outside. I went in to find the house deserted; an eerie silence hovered, as if people sought refuge in closed rooms. At last an old Muslim woman freedom-fighter, Bibi Amtul Salaam, came out. I asked for Indu. She said the Central Bureau of Investigation (CBI) was questioning her. I went in by the side-door and sat in Rajiv Gandhi's little sitting-room to await her. Rajiv came in a few minutes later. The pallor of his face was indicative of a troubled mind.

An hour later Indira came in. She had lost weight, the skin of her face was tightly drawn across the bones; the veins of her neck were swollen and prominent. She had spent two hours with the officers of the CBI. I asked her how everything had gone. 'Well,' she said. Rajiv left and Indira brought out her book, *Eternal India,* published in France, and now due for an English edition. She asked me whether I would help her with it. I sat with her for a while, had lunch with the family and came back late in the evening. She took me to her room. For an instant her fear-tossed mind was revealed; she broke down and wept. The judgement in the *Kissa Kursi Ka* case was due the next day and she had heard from, what she said were very reliable sources, that Sanjay would be sentenced to seven-and-a-half years of rigorous imprisonment. She was certain that her son would be misused and mutilated. Her helplessness was devastating her. I held her, she grew quiet and we sat down. I could see that rumours were being circulated deliberately to sap her courage. Under great tension she had once again developed a cough and a bad cold.

Next morning I was at the house by 8.30 to be with Indira when Sanjay left for the magistrate's court where judgement would be passed against him. She was at the breakfast table when I went in. A few minutes later Sanjay came in, went to his mother and in a rare gesture of love put his arms around her, his cheek brushing hers; then without a word he sat down to eat his porridge and boiled eggs. Maneka was covering her nervousness by talking incessantly of the pressures being brought on the judge to enhance the sentence on Sanjay.

Throughout breakfast Sanjay remained quiet and displayed no emotion. As he got up to leave, I asked for some curds and fed Sanjay a teaspoonful. It was a symbolic gesture of blessing. Indira went with him to see him drive off with Maneka in his Matador van. She came back to the room, her face drained of all emotion.

We spent the hours translating her French book into English. She was attentive and dealt with the translation without permitting her anxieties to divert her mind. During the time I was there between 8.30 and noon, no one entered the room—neither friend nor relative.

As 12 o' clock approached, she rang the bell to ask whether any news had come. Finally an aide came in to tell her that Sanjay and V.C. Shukla had been found guilty on all counts. Judgement had been withheld and sentence would be passed the next day. There was nothing to say.

I stayed for lunch. Sanjay came with Kamal Nath (now Minister of State for Forests and Environment) and his other Youth Congress friends. Indira took Sanjay aside to her room for some minutes, then both joined us for lunch that had been ordered from a restaurant. Rajiv and Sonia were not present, though they were in Delhi at the time. Maneka was extremely upset during the meal, she hit out against various members of Indira's party, made wild allegations against others. Indira was quiet, spoke hardly a word. The next day, I was there in the morning. Sanjay left with Maneka in the Matador van, the rest of the family were not to be seen, and again there was a waiting. Indira was unable to concentrate on the translation of the book. Anxiety like a many-branched banyan tree, had taken root. She walked from the tiny sitting-room to the bedroom and back, several times, kept ringing the bell to enquire whether there was any news. It was 12 noon before R.K. Dhawan, her Special Assistant, came in to say that Sanjay and Shukla had both been sentenced to two years' imprisonment, but bail had been granted to them. I observed the dread for her endangered son recede. Sanjay and Shukla would appeal to a higher court—in normal circumstances the legal process in India is a slow affair. Indira knew she had time and many things could happen in between.

I spent the evening of 28 February with her. The Budget was coming in on the television and one of her aides brought in the Budget papers which she gave to me to look over. Dinner was a bizarre feast; Sanjay ate scrambled eggs, Indira and I caviare and toast with a boiled potato. Pointing to the caviare, Indira commented that it was a gift from the Russians to assure her that the coming visit of Morarji Desai to Russia would be a formal one and for all the welcome they gave him, their friendship was with her. She chuckled and Sanjay and I joined in the laughter.

That night she wanted to talk and I stayed with her till well after midnight. For all my friendship, I was not of her world; I posed no threat at any level. I remained an outsider, a mirror. She could unburden herself without threat or backlash. She spoke with complete candour of the problems she faced in the family. She did not know what to do. The house was chaotic, everything had broken down. We spoke of Maneka and her hysterical outbursts, but Indira was compassionate. 'People forget that Maneka is barely 21,' she said. 'Her father was murdered a little over one year ago. Long jail sentences threaten Sanjay. They are trying to involve him in terrible things. Maneka is under great strain. People should understand and forgive her hysteria.'

The papers had reported that unity moves were afoot and discussions were taking place between Indira and the other Congress led by Swaran Singh and Y.B. Chavan. I had learnt that her leadership of the united party was not negotiable. She had insisted on a decision from Chavan's Congress as to whether its leadership would oppose the Special Courts Bill. Her party persons were anxious to achieve unity to enable them to fight the Special Courts Bill due the next month. But when I referred to the bill, she became vague. 'Will Chavan and the others vote against the Bill?' she queried. She was certain that the united Congress would never accept her as a leader.

I was in Varanasi for a few days. It was there that I learnt that the unity talks between the two Congress parties had broken down. The implications of this breakdown were clear; the Special Courts Bill would soon become law. I returned to Delhi and saw Indira the next morning. She lay on her bed while I sat on the only chair in her room. She saw that I was concerned at what had happened. She told me that she didn't think the unity move between the Congress (I) and Chavan's party would work. 'Pupul,' she said, 'the Special Courts Bill has to be faced. By defeating it in the Rajya Sabha we could have postponed matters by six months. Things are not good, now we have two options—either we can go to the people or. . . .'[1] she hesitated. and I did not pursue the matter. She told me she felt encircled, threatened not only by the Janata leaders but also by her own party. She spoke of Devraj Urs and his ambitions. It appeared that Urs had been meeting Rajni Patel and Chandra Shekhar and through them the senior leaders of the Janata Party. Karan Singh had been against her from the day she did not support him in the elections for the presidentship of the party.[2]

She blamed her own party for the weak position in which they found themselves. 'If Urs and the others had not emphasized unity and talked so much about it, the other Congress would have fallen into our laps. They had ceased to be important. A majority of the opposition Congress members were on the point of breaking away. Now with this talk of unity they have gained new strength.' She kept quiet for a while, then said, I am not an intellectual, but I am of the time—I have a contemporary mind. I keep pace with changing events. Nothing is static. This is the weakness of the Janata Party,' she said. 'There is a rigidity of mind, they work in a groove. They are unaware of changing situations and the changing mood of the people. Probably the leadership is too old.' It became clear during our conversation that she could not afford a divided party. She brooded on another break in the party.

The All-India Congress Committee (AICC) (I) met towards the end of April. The Special Courts Bill passed by the Rajya Sabha was soon to become law. Many of the members of the Congress (I) saw in the passing of the bill, Indira's doom. Rumblings of a revolt were felt right from the commencement of the meeting. A former minister commented: 'She (Indira) is now a political irrelevance. She will be summoned, prosecuted and sentenced.'[3] In spite of her Chikmaglur victory, and all that had followed, Indira's image was at a very low ebb. There was a feeling in the minds of the Janata Party members that the Congress (I) was disintegrating and there was little energy left in the party. A sense of doom had penetrated the minds of Indira's own party members.

Indira's main challenger at the AICC meeting, held in New Delhi, was Devraj Urs, the strongman of Karnataka. His speech at the AICC was a direct assault on Sanjay Gandhi. When he sat down, Indira is reported to have said to him, 'I will resign,' to which Urs replied, 'I can also do that. But that is not going to solve our problems.' Tarkeshwari Sinha, the fiery politician from Bihar, who had deserted Morarji Desai, her mentor, during the Emergency to join Indira, was one of the first to attack Indira. She was an orator and her speech was interspersed with Urdu couplets. She accused Indira of letting her son Sanjay encircle her with a Saturn ring. In the Indian lexicon, Saturn is a baleful planet.[4] A whisper campaign had started, accusing Indira of arrogance and a misplaced sense of grandeur. There was a feeling that Indira had lost control of herself and would no longer be able to face the fury of the Opposition onslaught. A photograph of Indira at the AICC meeting shows her besieged and at bay. It was not easy for her to face an open revolt within her party.

The confrontation with Devraj Urs came to boiling point when a month later the Congress Working Committee (CWC) asked him to resign from the Presidentship of the Karnataka Pradesh Congress Committee (KPCC) on the grounds that he was already Chief Minister. Urs reacted sharply, said that KPCC (I) was an elected body, and that he was not prepared to step down unless the new president was selected through the election process. The Congress Parliamentary Board (CPB) met again on 7 June and seeing Urs' recalcitrant attitude issued a show-cause notice on him to explain why disciplinary action should not be taken against him. Urs' letter addressed to Indira Gandhi was outrageous and used very tough and insolent language. It was vicious in tone and content. Urs accused Indira of demolishing and destroying the party. He said that he and his colleagues were facing 'a diabolical onslaught' by the CWC, under her captainship. It was a male chauvinistic letter in which he expressed his contempt for

Indira as a woman. An outraged CWC met, on receiving the letter, and passed a unanimous resolution expelling Urs from the party for six years. On 25 June, Urs announced the formation of the Karnataka Congress. A majority of the Congress (I) MLAs in Karnataka were on his side. The country's political circles noted that for all her strategy, Indira Gandhi walked into Urs' trap like a lamb being led to the slaughter house. The third split in the Congress led to a further depletion in the character and quality of the Congress (I) membership. Urs immediately called old Congress members belonging to many factions to return and said there was need for a consolidated third force without Indira Gandhi. This move for unity was to be cemented at a convention to meet in Bangalore on 4 July. Despite the confidence of the rebel Congress, they misjudged Indira's capacity to manipulate.

*

A masterly sense of timing made Indira retreat after her battle with Urs. She addressed few meetings. Her instincts, which rarely failed her, brought the realization that any move on her part to reveal her growing strength, any threat of her return to power, would immediately bring together the Janata cabals to cement their fragmented position. Deliberately, planning every move, she erased herself from the political scene. During the period from April to July, with Sanjay by her side, she worked on a strategy to break the Janata Party. Like a superb master-craftsman engaged in fine stitching, her senses honed in to observe the weaknesses and strengths of every member of the Opposition. Her memory-bank held a dossier on every important member of the Janata Party, most of whom, in the past, had been members of the undivided Congress. Mother and son worked closely, with one mind, to search for every weakness, every crevice in the Janata edifice. Indira was an adept as a political fighter and now so fine were her actions, so subtle her plans that they left no trace. She could not allow even a whisper of her stratagems to reach Morarji Desai or Charan Singh. The more intricate her design, the greater appeared her outward frailty.

From January onwards she had established channels of communication with Charan Singh. Sanjay had become a close friend of

Raj Narain, the vernacular strong man, who was responsible for some of the Janata's most spectacular victories; he was a shrewd, earthy politician with an enormous ego. Sanjay, in his many meetings with this ex-wrestler-politician, had suggested to him various methods through which Raj Narain's patron, Charan Singh, could become prime minister. Sanjay had promised him the support of the Congress (I).[5] One of Raj Narain's close friends told me that Sanjay had even suggested that Raj Narain himself was the most suited to become the Prime Minister. Raj Narain had swallowed the bait. Nodding his head, he told Indira's son, 'Yes, my son, it is true. I am always there, but for the moment let Chaudhury Sahib (Charan Singh) become the Prime Minister.' Now Raj Narain began attacking Morarji Desai on every occasion. He lashed out at Morarji's son, accused Desai of corruption and nepotism. A strong lobby existed in Charan Singh's party against the Jana Sangh, one of the major constituents of the Janata Party, for its close links to the Rashtriya Swayamsevak Sangh (RSS), an extreme right-wing militant party. The Janata had forgotten Indira; she had ceased to count. And now the fierce resentments, ambitions and personal dislikes that had simmered in the coalition, below the surface, exploded.

While Sanjay held parleys with Raj Narain, Indira opened a channel through which she could contact Hemvati Nandan Bahuguna, the wily politician from Uttar Pradesh who had once been her Chief Minister of Uttar Pradesh, and who had manoeuvred the coup with Jagjivan Ram in 1977. Indira had heard that Bahuguna was totally disillusioned with the functioning of the Janata Party. Bahuguna was an extremely intelligent and ambitious politician; Indira felt that he could provide the lever to detach the socialists from the Janata front. Secret meetings were arranged between Indira Gandhi and Bahuguna in a neutral house on Barakhamba Road.[6]

The stage was set.

*

The world was in ferment, thunder clouds reverberated over India's neighbours. Zulfikar Ali Bhutto had been sentenced to death.[7] Indira had telegraphed President Zia-ul-Haq on behalf of the former Prime Minister. She had also sent messages to various heads of government, asking them to intervene. The world's leaders had responded, clemency appeals were issued, but Zia was adamant and Bhutto was hanged in Rawalpindi on 4 April 1979. In Sri Lanka, Sirimavo Bandaranaike had been disenfranchised.

President Neelam Sanjiva Reddy gave his assent to the Special Courts Bill on 17 May. The Special Courts were established and were to begin functioning on 14 June. News reached Indira, through friends in the Intelligence agencies, that summons were to be issued against her by the Special Court. She left immediately, with her daughter-in-law Maneka, for Darjeeling for a week's holiday. Sanjay made his presence felt in Calcutta—organized processions, shouted slogans, was lathi-charged, received minor injuries and then went up to Darjeeling to spend three days with his mother and wife. The Special Court summons for the first hearing were served on Indira in Darjeeling. She came down to Calcutta and filed an appeal in the Calcutta High Court for a stay order against the Special Court summons. The presiding High Court judge admitted the appeal and issued a stay order. Indira, Maneka and Sanjay left for Delhi with a copy of the court order which was presented to the Supreme Court next morning. This was to ensure that no further proceedings could take place in the Special Court unless the stay order was vacated by the Calcutta High Court.[8]

The interlude in Darjeeling had seen another happier development. According to Maneka, it was during this period, when Indira went for long walks and Maneka and Sanjay could be alone together in peace, that she conceived her baby. On her return to Delhi, as soon as it became evident that Maneka was pregnant, she and Sanjay wondered whether it was right to give birth to a child in the midst of the terrible uncertainties that lay ahead. When Indira came to know that she was to be a grandmother afresh, she was overjoyed. She forgot all her problems, fussed over Maneka and ran to tell Sonia the good news.

*

Prime Minister Morarji Desai, basking in the glory of the welcome he had received in the Soviet Union, was totally unaware of the state of the nation. The scene in India was abysmal—the monsoons had failed, prices were spiralling upwards at an unprecedented rate, the Central Reserve Police Force (CRPF) had mutinied for the first time, crimes against women had gone up, dowry deaths were reported in the newspapers, a large number of public sector undertakings were on strike, communal riots had flared up in Aligarh, electricity break-downs and shortages had led to the closing down of several industrial units in the country. The eighty-three-year-old Prime Minister was unmoved. He appeared to have lost all contact with reality, in fact had never had any real contact with the people of the country. He refused to listen to his main supporters when they told him of the dangers imminent in the situation. The Monsoon Session of the Lok Sabha commenced in early July. Morarji Desai told newsmen, 'Even if the Skylab* falls here, I will remain unruffled.'[9]

Unaware of the explosive situation in the Janata Party, Y.B. Chavan, leader of the Opposition, moved a no confidence mo-tion against the government on 11 July. This was the first time that such a move was made since the Janata Party came to power. The Lok Sabha was totally unprepared for the aftermath. The motion triggered discontent that had been simmering in the Janata Party over the last few months. On Friday, 13 July, the Prime Minister suddenly woke up to the fact that none of the senior members of his Cabinet was prepared to intervene in the debate to defend his government. In spite of Raj Narain's efforts, Charan Singh had hesitated to quit the Deputy Prime Ministership of the government. It was during these critical days that Charan Singh's favourite astrologer informed him that the stars were propitious for his achieving the highest position in the country. It was with this assurance that he finally resigned.

Frenzied scenes were witnessed in the lobbies of Parliament. No Member of Parliament, save for the Congress (I), wanted mid-term elections and yet, 'Desai was slowly cornered and his government virtually pushed over the precipice.'[10]

On 14 July, Morarji Desai was formally requested to step down as leader of the House by the Janata Parliamentary Board. The Prime Minister refused to do so. Charan Singh did not attend the

---

* The Skylab (a space programme, of the US, that launched its first space station, Skylab, on 14 May 1973) broke into the earth's atmosphere on 11 July 1979, the first pieces striking the earth's surface in the Indian Ocean and southwestern Australia.

Parliamentary Board meeting. On Sunday, 15 July, the socialist group within the Janata Party—George Fernandes, Madhu Limaye, Mrinal Gore, Hemvati Nandan Bahuguna—resigned, to be followed by vast number of junior Members of Parliament. Morarji's formidable majority melted away. Unable to prove his majority against the no confidence motion in the Lok Sabha, Morarji Desai resigned as Prime Minister on 15 July.

The focus of attention moved to Rashtrapati Bhavan. Neelam Sanjiva Reddy, President of India, had to decide whether to call for new elections, to ask Jagjivan Ram the new head of the Janata Party to form a government or to turn to Charan Singh and his newly formed Bharatiya Lok Dal. The papers were full of comments on various permutations and combinations that might arise as the parties jock-eyed for power. The only party the pundits refused to grant a chance of victory was the Congress (I).

With Morarji's resignation, and the fall of the Janata government, Indira was flooded with a great relief. She could not refrain from saying, 'The Janata government which came in roaring like a lion has gone away without the squeal of a mouse.'[11]

On 27 July, Charan Singh was invited to Rashtrapati Bhavan to be asked by the President to form a new government with the support of the Congress (S), of which Y.B. Chavan was the leader. To ensure a majority, Charan Singh had solicited the support of Indira's Congress, which had seventy-two members in the Lok Sabha. She had promised him the support so long as her party was consulted on major policy issues. The President made it clear that the new Prime Minister would have to seek a vote of confidence in the Lok Sabha within a month of his taking charge.

Indira watched from the background. Most of the Congress leaders who had been part of her Emergency Cabinet had betrayed her once again. They waited at Charan Singh's doorstep. So eager was their desire to regain power that they forgot that they were now totally at Indira's mercy. A photograph shows Dr Karan Singh at the new Prime Minister's door, stepping out of his car with folded hands; as a backdrop, the windscreen of his car carries a large photograph of the new Prime Minister—Charan Singh. Y.B. Chavan had entered the Cabinet as Deputy Prime Minister, C. Subramaniam, Brahmananda Reddy, H.N. Bahuguna, Karan Singh, T.A. Pai, K.C. Pant, all former members of Indira's Congress, had become senior ministers while deserters from the Janata Party—George Fernandes, Biju Patnaik, S.N. Mishra and others had joined the Cabinet. The Charan Singh government had been brought to power with the support of Indira Gandhi's party. The minority government could only survive with her support. It was clear to Indira that she held the future of Charan Singh's government in the palm of her hand.

A new confidence permeates her letters. In a circular letter to her close friends she writes:

> If you look at external factors—the harassment, threat of jail, attempts at murder and so on—they certainly are a nuisance. But surely not cause for real anxiety. What is important is how one is personally affected. If one's inner core, peace within oneself and with one's fellow creatures remain constant, isn't that much more important ? People ask about power. Desai as Prime Minister was in a position of power, yet his future was as much, if not more, in my hands as his. And it is even more so as regards the present gentleman . . ..

The letter then turns to her contact with the problems of her country:

> All my life I have had welcoming crowds. I have witnessed the adoration they gave my father and the worshipful awe with which they greeted the Mahatma. But love with a protective and very personal quality was something new and very moving. When I am rushing past in an open jeep in the midst of millions of men, women and children, seeing their eyes light up, my own often fill with tears. I feel very humble and can only mutter like Dicken's Scrooge "God bless them all". I know this is very corny and old fashioned but I do feel that nothing one can do will ever be enough to repay them.
>
> Is this not riches and powers beyond compare? And is it not worth the price of hardship? The question is merely one of values.[12]

Charan Singh was euphoric and felt very much a man of destiny, forgetting completely his precarious position. The Congress ministers, overwhelmed at their return to power, forgot that they held office at Indira's pleasure. Charan Singh was certain that he would win the confidence motion in Parliament and that with this there would be fresh defectors from the Janata Party. He also expected some support from the Communist Party of India (CPI) (M). Though never openly expressed in the discussions between the Congress (I) and Charan Singh's Bharatiya Lok Dal, it was clear that Indira Gandhi's support was dependent on the attitude of the Charan Singh government to the Special Courts. During the twenty-three days that Charan Singh was in power, he did little to tackle the horrendous problems that faced the country. Prices continued to escalate. In his public speeches, made arrogant by his position, he continued to refer to the Special Courts and the necessity to bring Indira to trial. Indira was prepared to wait till the last moment before she acted. This was to ensure that Charan Singh did not turn to Jagjivan Ram for support. Meanwhile, a meeting was arranged by Kamal Nath between Sanjay and Jagjivan Ram's son, Suresh; Maneka was present but was kept out of the discussions and watched television instead.

The Lok Sabha was to meet on 20 August. On 19 August Indira Gandhi withdrew her support to the Charan Singh government. Faced with certain defeat in the Lok Sabha, Charan Singh resigned and turned to the President, requesting him to dissolve the Lok Sabha and call for fresh elections. Charan Singh felt confident that he would win a majority at the polls.

Towards the end of August rumours were current in Bombay that plots to assassinate Indira were being hatched in various parts of the country. Astrologers had a field day, prophesying certain days as very dangerous for Indira. A message came to me from the daughter of S.A. Dange, the Communist stalwart, to ensure that Indira did not travel by plane on a particular day. I telephoned Indira and gave her the message. From my voice she must have guessed that I was concerned and she told me on the telephone that Delhi was thick with rumours that she would be bumped off in September. 'If I were to listen to what people tell me, not a single day would be safe for me to travel.'[13] In an interview on the British Broadcasting Corporation (BBC), a decade earlier, Lord Chalfont had questioned her on her response to danger. Her reply was clear. She did not avoid danger, nor did she seek it. 'I do not search for danger, but if it is there, I meet it. Determination is something I seem to have been born with—for that I am very single-minded indeed.'[14]

It was towards the end of December 1978, while she was still in Tihar jail that Indira had planned her future strategy, laid out the chess board, sensed the opposition moves, while she appeared to remain a pawn of no significance. She had journeyed through thick forests, crossed rivers in flood, faced angry mobs and now only one obstacle lay before her. She had to leap across the final stretch and reach what she considered her rightful position. *Alice in Wonderland* and *Alice Through the Looking Glass* were favourite stories of her childhood. On the eve of the elections did the stories surface?

Before the fall of Charan Singh, she took to the road. With practically all the senior Congressmen against her, Indira knew-that she had to rely on the Youth Congress and its organizational capacity to ensure that the vast numbers of people in rural areas who supported her, could reach the polling booths. With the help of Sanjay, Indira examined the map of India, identified the culture of each constituency, decided on the key people who could be persuaded to support her. Her withdrawal from the political scene had enabled her to start her election campaign without the Opposition and the media taking much notice of her movements.

Indira travelled light, by plane, helicopter and car. She was. determined to reach every constituency, to speak to the weaker sections, the economically under-privileged, women and Harijans who were her natural vote bank. To accompany her, Indira took her Personal Assistant, and three security men. Two suitcases held half-a-dozen coarse khadi saris, two large flasks—one for cold milk and the other for boiled water—two pillows, some peanuts, dry fruit, a few apples and an umbrella to shield her against the sun.[15]

In the interior villages, far removed from the noise and gossip of the major cities, surrounded by the poor and defenceless, Indira would move into the crowd; she would drop a word here, a gesture there; smile at an old woman; hand a flower to a child. In her capacity to draw them close, to flow in their rhythms, she conveyed her concerns.

Her message to the electorate was simple. She had discarded all abstractions, did not emphasize ideologies. Her message was "Vote

For a Government That Functions." She concerned herself with the day-to-day problems of the poor—escalating prices, the shortage of kerosene, the breakdown of electricity which stopped the functioning of tubewells, the inadequate organization of drought relief, the increasing crimes against women. The Janata leadership rallied on one major theme for their election campaign—any victory of Indira would mean the re-imposition of the Emergency, and a denial of democracy and freedom. They built up Jagjivan Ram as their leader and were confident that the electorate would not forget or forgive Indira and her party for their actions during the Emergency. This indicates the extent to which they were cut away from the mood of the people.

On 7 October 1979, Jayaprakash Narayan suddenly died in Bombay. He had been seriously ill, a forgotten man, for the two-and-a-half years that the Janata Party was in power. Alone, except for a few close relations and friends, he had spent months in the Jaslok hospital in Bombay.

Indira flew to Patna to attend his funeral. In spite of their differences she had known and liked Jayaprakash from her early childhood on. He was a close friend of her father and his wife Prabha had been Kamala's confidante. She writes:

> Poor old JP! What a confused mind he had, leading to such a frustrated life! He was a sufferer of what I can only call Gandhian hypocrisy. Not that Bapu was hypocritical, but he did not prevent its breeding all around him, by forcing people to take vows which they could not possibly fulfil and standards which they had no intention of living up to. While claiming to be a devout Hindu, his negation of the wholeness and totality of life as envisaged by our seers was more akin to the Christian view of original sin. I suppose you know that when JP and Prabha went to seek Bapu's blessings immediately after their wedding, Bapu made Prabha swear to Brahmcharya (celibacy). This was just too much for J. That and jealousy of my father probably conditioned the rest of his life. It is nonsense to say that he did not want office. One part of him did, very much so . . . '[16]

By November 1979, Indira emerged from the dark; while the Opposition parties were busy with their quarrels and their manoeuvres, they found that she had out-distanced them, was far ahead in the electoral race. *India Today,* reporting in its issue of December 16–31, said:

> For 40 days during the past ten weeks, she travelled over 40,000 kms by plane, helicopter and by car, addressed 350 meetings in 250 of the 542 Lok Sabha constituencies. Her campaign managers are making meticulous plans to ensure that she will cover the remaining constituencies between December 15 and January 4. This will mean that she will have spent 62 days and nights travelling at the rate of 1,000 kms a day addressing 10 meetings. Thus she will have been heard or seen by an estimated 9 crore—90 million—people literally throughout the country, almost one in every four voters.[17]

There were 529 Lok Sabha seats to be contested in the elections. By the end of December, an opinion poll conducted by the Indian Market Research Bureau (IMRB) predicted a marginal victory for Indira, conceding her an overall majority, with 291 seats out of the 529 to be declared. On the eve of the election, Indira wrote out on a slip of paper her expectations. She believed she would win 350 seats; when the election results were declared she had won 351. The extra one was because she had stood for election from two seats—Rae Bareilly, where she was defeated in 1977, and Medak in Andhra Pradesh. She won from both with an overwhelming majority.

Throughout the years she was out of power, Indira kept contact with what was happening in the world, at the frontiers of human thought. She heard of the new concept of the intellect as a resource tool and wrote to Jean-Jacques Servan-Schreiber, a supporter of computer literacy worldwide, inviting him to meet her in Delhi to explore the potential for computers for India. The interview was fixed two days before the election results were to come through. Indira had returned from her last election meeting and her exhaustion after the election campaign gave her an austere beauty that evening. By now she was confident that she would win the elections and resume the role of prime minister. Already her mind had turned away from the elections to the future and the formidable tasks that lay ahead. According to Servan-Schreiber, what disturbed her most was the vast number of young people who would never get an education. 'I think there must be about 250 million children, under 15, who haven't yet learned how to read or write.' The problem was where she should start. If technology meant employment, then it had a major place in India. 'She wanted to know more about a tiny chip with fine, barely visible lines she saw in my hand; a microprocessor.'

'American or Japanese?'

'It doesn't matter, they're all the same,' I answered. 'These machines spread a revolution that has no homeland and knows no borders. They are all made of sand.'

'Sand? Really? What do you mean made of sand?'

'They create work where they are installed. Wherever people understand this, they can replace heavy machinery, and free men from hard labour.'

Indira interrupted. She wanted the opposite. Her people want work. 'How could a little chip, the microprocessor, trigger a revolution that would make the Western notion of industrial progress out-of-date? How could employment no longer depend on the accumulation of factories? Could it really be true that a people's chance for development, regardless of its current level, was no longer industrialization, but this new computerization?' She had listened intently to Schreiber's plan but was not convinced.[18]

The day the election results were due, I was at the airport in Bombay, on my way to Delhi. The flights were delayed by several hours. The airport authorities had arranged to flash the results at the air terminal. The trend was clear within a few hours. Indira's Congress was sweeping the country. Indira was leading in both her constituencies by a very large margin. It was 11 o'clock at night before my flight reached Delhi. By then the election results were clear, her party had won with an overwhelming majority. Early the next morning I drove to 12, Willingdon Crescent. Barriers had already been erected to provide security to Indira Gandhi, the incoming Prime Minister. Vast crowds had gathered outside the gates and were milling around in front of the garden. I recognized editors of newspapers, Congressmen, businessmen and simple people from all walks of life. Flowers were everywhere. I could see and recognize friends with broad smiles on their faces embracing each other, hailing Indira. I found it difficult to push my way through. Ultimately, one of her old retainers recognized me and helped me enter the house. As she turned to me, I said 'What shall I say to you?' 'Don't say,' she replied, carne up to me, put her hand on my shoulder. There were tears in her eyes. I could see that she was deeply moved. Though she had known that the tide was in her favour, the shock of victory had left her numb. Suddenly all her burdens were lifted at a stroke.

She was called into the garden several times during the day where vast crowds awaited her with garlands of marigolds and roses. Her sari covering her head, the *rudraksha mala* given to her by Anand Mai Ma around her neck, she stretched out her arms to the people. There was an enigmatic smile on her lips but her eyes were sombre, questioning herself and the crowd. She had witnessed euphoria before, she had also seen anger and vengeance; did she wonder at what lay in the future? She was once again Prime Minister of India, but her years in the wilderness had left deep scars that were to inhibit her actions. A suspicion of people, a sense of betrayal and a lack of trust were to journey with her for the rest of her life. The immediacy of action and the insights of her early years, that enabled her to react with precision and strength, would be replaced by an approach of hesitancy and caution. In addition, she would, in the future, be fiercely protective of those who had stood by her during her years in the wilderness.

For the rest of the day and the night, 12, Willingdon Crescent was the centre of celebration. Sanjay was by her side, a brilliant orange shawl thrown around his shoulders. Maneka witha broad smile on her face was fluttering around, talking excitedly to mediamen. Rajiv, Sonia and their children were also much in evidence. People danced in the streets.

> Wayside altars display her flower-decked likeness . . . Truckloads of boys cruise the streets yelling adulatory slogans through the loudspeakers. The prices of sugar, kerosene, potatoes and onions have all fallen dramatically. Shopkeepers are afraid that the new government will seek out hoarders and clamp black-marketeers into jail.[19]

Indira was interviewed by French television on the evening of her victory. She asked me to sit inside while the interview was taking place. In the midst of it, her Special Assistant R.K. Dhawan came in. The cameras were switched off as Dhawan whispered in Indira's ear. As she passed me, she whispered, 'That is Jimmy Carter on the telephone. Maggie must have told him he should make friends.' The President of the United States had established a close friendship with the former Prime Minister, Morarji Desai, and the return of Indira would mean building up of a new relationship with her. She came back in fifteen minutes, a smile on her face. Later that evening she told me that President Carter had been very cordial and she had learnt that it was not Prime Minister Margaret Thatcher who had spoken to him but James Callaghan, the former Prime Minister of Britain.

I had to return to Bombay as J. Krishnamurti was to arrive there as my guest. The night before my departure, I went to see Indira. The old èlan had returned; once again her tread was light. She told me the country was in a very difficult economic position. She needed people to help her. She asked me to draw up lists of people who would support her in her various development programmes. She appeared deeply worried about events in Afghanistan, invaded by the Soviet army towards the end of December. The world's eyes were on Indira to see how she would react. 'How could the Russians do it?', she said to me. 'It will be like Vietnam. The Afghans are tough, they know guerrilla warfare. There can be no victory.' Then, a little later, 'This has brought the cold war to our doorstep. The great powers will fight their battles around our frontiers.'[20]

She told me that rumours had already started that she would take revenge on the Opposition, particularly those individuals who had attempted to humiliate her and to destroy Sanjay. 'This whole thing has to be quenched. People feel that I will go after Kanti Desai. I do not want to hurt Morarji Desai in any way.'[21]

I returned to Bombay with a rejoicing heart. Krishnaji was happy to hear of Indira's victory and asked me how she had received the news.

The next morning after breakfast he took me to his room. In a grave voice he said, 'Indira will face great sorrow in the year to come and you should be in Delhi as much as possible.' He was silent for a while. 'It is a strange coincidence that you should be so close to an outsider like me and also be a friend of the Prime Minister. Such situations just do not happen. Be very watchful of yourself. Be deeply aware of every thought and action.' His words penetrated deeply. I grew aware that he had sensed a great darkness overshadowing Indira. He did not speak of it again while he was in India.[22]

PART VIII
1980–1984

She was delicate beautifully made
So small, so unafraid
Till the bullets (bombs) came
Bullets (bombs) are the same, delicate
beautifully made.

–Epitaph by C.S. Louis[1]

At this year's end the boat departs,
Light as a leaf.

–Shih Jun Chang[2]

ONE

Indira Gandhi was elected leader of the victorious Congress (I) on 6 January 1980, and was called upon by President Neelam Sanjiva Reddy to assume the office of Prime Minister. Astrologers and stargazers flocked to her door to warn her that the stars were confused and that the approaching total eclipse of the sun was dangerous for her and her son. Her senior colleagues advised her to take office on 14 January, the day of the solar equinox according to the Hindu calendar. Indira was no longer a rebel against superstition and tradition; in the past she would have defied the stars, but now she was wary, preferred to tread with caution.

This was her fourth swearing-in as Prime Minister. In 1966, she was apprehensive. In 1967, with a reduced majority in the Lok Sabha and the old guard of the Congress determined to obstruct her in every way and to force her out of the prime ministership, she was grim. In 1971, she was filled with a wild euphoria. In 1980, she was sombre, without a trace of her imperious arrogance.

She was sixty-two years old, as President Sanjiva Reddy administered her the oath of office in the resplendent Ashoka Hall of Rashtrapati Bhavan. Immaculately groomed, surrounded by her family, friends, Cabinet ministers, Members of Parliament, her voice was tremulous as that of a young adolescent as she took the oath; 'I, Indira Gandhi, swear in the *name of God* that I will bear true faith and allegiance to the Constitution of India . . .. I will do right to all manner of people in accordance with the Constitution and the law, without fear or favour, affection or ill-will.' Indira Gandhi had been out of office for thirty-four months.

If in 1966 she had sworn on the Constitution of India, in 1980 God found place in her pledge. She permitted little rejoicing after the swearing in, but immediately went to her office in the west wing of South Block and, with her advisers and secretaries, faced the formidable agenda placed before her. In the days of waiting to take the oath, she had cogitated on the choice of her future Cabinet ministers. Most of the senior figures who were her colleagues, and had advised her over the years, were no longer with her. She had to choose her Cabinet from an inexperienced assortment of parliamentarians, over twenty per cent drawn from her son's Youth Congress, with little administrative experience or understanding of parliamentary strategies and procedures. Surprisingly, her final choice did not include many of the familiar faces from the Emergency days, nor did she provide, as expected, a ministership for her son, Sanjay Gandhi. In the aftermath of the Emergency she needed Sanjay but wanted him unobtrusively by her side, to mature under her watchful, maternal eye. She felt confident that, with his youth and drive, he could revitalize the Congress party and ensure that development projects in the countryside were implemented. With an inexperienced Cabinet, she was aware that her burdens would increase; so, right from the start, she decided to draw in, at various levels, advisers of merit to help her in the tasks that lay ahead.

She was facing a breakdown of law and order in the country, rising inflation, a scarcity of essential commodities; the aftermath of the severe drought of 1979 had brought the grain stocks of the country to an all-time low. The problem of refugees from Bangladesh, settled for years in Assam, had suddenly flared up. The Assamese, claiming to be sons of the soil, were not prepared to permit their neighbours from across the borders, a homeland within their State. The agitation came at a particularly inopportune time for oil prices were at their peak; the trouble in Assam led to the stoppage of oil from the oil fields located in the North-East.

To gear up India's internal resources, to bring down prices, to seek alternate energy resources and to conserve the environment was, for her way of thinking, impossible so long as a vast number of states remained under the rule of the Janata Party. She knew that the writ of the Central Government could not work in those states and a strained Centre-state relationship would make any attempt on her part to solve economic or environmental problems impossible.

She had already taken the decision to dissolve the state assemblies headed by Janata governments, impose President's rule and call for fresh State Assembly elections. On her defeat in 1977 the Janata government had done likewise and so established a precedent. Reports of a massacre by the police in Gorakhpur district of Uttar Pradesh provided her with the opportunity to put this part of her plan into action. She was amidst the victims within days of its taking place, promised them relief and assured them that punishment would be meted out to the policemen responsible. She also spoke on the incapacity of the state government to control the law and order situation. President's rule and fresh elections appeared imminent. A press correspondent in Gorakhpur asked her, 'Are you stooping to the level of your opponents?' She replied, 'There is no question of level because I do not stoop, I stand straight, I walk straight and my policy is straight.'

Indira took full advantage of the disarray in the Opposition to impose President's rule and call for nine State Assembly elections in May 1980. The Rajya Sabha elections were due in June; it was the membership of the state assemblies that would determine the new membership of the Upper House in Parliament.

A new generation had come of age; to transform and build a new society, a younger membership was necessary in the state assemblies. Indira encouraged Sanjay to plan the election strategy and to select the new candidates.

Sweeping aside the advice and tactics suggested by the elders in the party, and supported by his mother, he handpicked his band of determined youth to stand as Congress (I) candidates for the assembly elections.

The *Times of India* called the generational change 'India's cultural revolution.'

*

Within days of her taking over as Prime Minister, an unprecedented number of dignitaries visited India—President Giscard d'Estaing of France, President Zia-ur Rahman of Bangladesh, President Sese Seke Mobutu of Zaire, Kenneth Kaunda of Zambia, Yasser Arafat, Andrei Gromyko, Foreign Minister of Russia, a Special Emissary of President Jimmy Carter and a senior minister from Japan—all came to meet and assess the mind of the new Prime Minister. The world leaders were aware that, with Indira Gandhi as Prime Minister, a formidable new presence had appeared in one of the most critical areas of the world. Indira Gandhi was quick to assess the situation; the power equations had changed on India's northern borders with the Soviet invasion of Afghanistan; the United States' move to strengthen its presence in the Indian Ocean was inevitable. India's special relationship with the Soviet Union gave it a key position to negotiate between the two superpowers. She realized the essential need to steer clear of a very dangerous international crisis. In a private meeting with Gromyko she expressed sorrow and anxiety at the Soviet invasion, but promised not to be overtly critical. To the representatives of the United States she was wary in her responses, tentative, ambiguous. She acknowledged that the Soviet move had made India and Pakistan frontline States. She hoped that the US would adopt a cautious approach. She queried them on their decision to re-arm Pakistan and to strengthen their nuclear presence in Diego Garcia. To Bruno Kreisky, the former Chancellor of Austria, who, during the Emergency, had backed the Socialist International in their stern criticism of Indira's government, and who had come to India to make amends, she said: 'We feel the reverberations and hear the clash of rival powers around us.'

The international press had descended on her. She told a correspondent of *Newsweek:* 'We do not want to see America weak, but on the other hand we do not want them to do anything that will increase tension near us.' She said the Western world was very pro-Janata Party, but she acknowledged, at the same time, that the 'Soviets would like India to be weaker so that I would be more dependent on the so-called Leftists here.' She had noticed in the Western media a superior, cynical, almost colonial attitude which she deeply resented. So far she had refused to hold a press conference or meet Indian journalists and editors.

I returned to Delhi on 13 February. By then the state assemblies under Janata rule were dissolved and President's rule had been imposed. As Indira Gandhi was acting exactly as the Janata government had done in 1977, they could hardly protest. I went over to dinner at the Prime Minister's House. An air of elegance had entered the rooms of 12, Willingdon Crescent, replacing the stark utilitarian atmosphere of the past. The house was full of servants, familiar faces were back, there were cascading flowers everywhere. Sonia Gandhi had taken special care over the menu; there was soup, delicious pasta, fresh crisp golden lettuce, cheese, fruit and chocolate.

Before Indira took the oath of office, she had visited 1, Safdarjung Road as she intended to go back to her old house. She found the conch-white paint she favoured on the walls replaced by the Central

Works' Ministry's favourite tones of pastel pinks and blues—colours which shrank spaces and which she was not prepared to live with. The rooms of her old house were now crowded with heavy furniture. She decided to stay on in 12, Willingdon Crescent till 1, Safdarjung Road had been repainted in tones of white and the furniture she had used earlier as Prime Minister, brought back from the store-house of government.

On 16 February there was to be a total solar eclipse. It was to occur in India after eighty-four years. The newspapers were full of sombre predictions, astrologers foretold earthquakes and other primeval disasters. In an archaic myth the headless planet *rahu* devoured the sun and people stayed at home, fasted, performed puja and recited mantras to free the sun from its cosmic danger. No schoolroom explanation could erase the primordial sense of doom that spread over the country.

Indira had invited me to the house to watch the solar eclipse on television. We had an early lunch and, as the hour of the eclipse approached, Maneka in her ninth month of pregnancy was sent to her room, for the eclipse was regarded as a direct threat to the unborn child, no pregnant mother was allowed to expose herself to its baleful influence. Rajiv Gandhi was in the garden where he had set up a telescope and ensured a sufficient number of dark glasses through which the eclipse could be watched; Rahul and Priyanka were excited and helped Rajiv in the garden. Sanjay pottered around. We sat in Indira's bedroom watching Thomas Hardy's *Far From the Madding Crowd* on the video. The eclipse commenced at 2.30 p.m.

From Delhi the total eclipse was not visible, a tiny sliver of the sun remained undimmed. The stars did not come out in the sky, nor did darkness descend, but as the moon engulfed the sun, a mysterious blue light spread over the garden and shadows were erased. The moment the moon's presence shadowed the sun, Indira got up, went to her room and stayed by herself till the eclipse ended. This was not the robust Indira of the pre-Emergency days. I was surprised to see how influenced she was by ritual and superstition. The deathly fears that stalked her from the days of the Emergency lingered. What was she afraid of? What shadow, what darkness walked beside her? Though puzzled, no trace of prophecy arose in my mind that we were approaching the end of the doom-swept story of mother and son.

At dinner one night Swami Dhirendra Brahmachari came in, followed by R.K. Dhawan, Indira Gandhi's Special Assistant. I gathered that the familiarity and ease of access was due to the casual atmosphere that prevailed during Indira's years out of power. Those around her at the time took her a little for granted. The yogi folded his hands and sat down. Rajiv gave him some cheese and chocolate which he ate with relish. The Brahmachari spoke of some appointment Indira had made in the Education Ministry. He was vehemently opposed to what she had done. At first Indira was offended with him, said he knew nothing about it, that she knew the man was competent and knew his job. Brahmachari kept on protesting, became strident, even aggressive.

Suddenly Indira flared up and in chaste Hindi chastized him, 'Don't think I do not know what has been going on around me all these years,' she said. 'I know what was happening and how Sanjay's name was used by people to cover up. I will see to it that this ends. I will not permit corruption around me. I will not tolerate it under any circumstances.' The Brahmachari was upset, 'You have said a great deal.' Indira thumped the table. 'I will say much more. All this will stop.' The Brahmachari was silent, then rose and walked out. R.K. Dhawan who had stood all through the conversation, mumbled some words and left. There was dead silence at the table. Rajiv made an innocuous remark and we discussed food. Indira was quiet for the rest of the dinner.

A few days later at dinner again at 1, Safdarjung Road, I saw the Brahmachari enter and sit at the table. He ate his chocolate and cheese. There was peace and calm as he discussed the Prime Minister's coming visit to the Vaishno Devi temple in the high ranges near Jammu.

The presence and access of Dhirendra Brahmachari to Prime Minister Indira Gandhi's home and table has never been explained. It was in the mid-1950s that a Hath Yogi from Mithila was introduced to the then Prime Minister Jawaharlal Nehru by Jayaprakash Narayan.[3] Jawaharlal was self-taught in Yoga. He, in turn, had taught his daughter, but there were many mistakes in his practice which needed correction. The father and daughter found the new teacher excellent and his methods of teaching *asanas and pranayams* benefited both of them. Certainly the system helped Indira. For years she was frail-bodied and constantly ill; her pleurisy had left her susceptible to colds and coughs, but by the time she became Prime Minister, her constitution had changed. Her body, though very frail to look at, was tough and resilient; she could bear hardships and an enormous energy sustained her. In a letter to Dorothy Norman, Indira wrote:

> I get up early these days to do a special set of exercises. It is a system (part of Yoga) that was taught to us by an excellent, good-looking Yogi. In fact it was his looks, especially his magnificent body, which attracted everyone to his system which is easy and practical. He is however exasperating to talk to—so full of superstition.[4]

In the early Seventies Dhirendra Brahmachari visited the house without being overtly visible; certainly there was little easy access to Indira's dinner table. This changed during the Emergency. It was during these years that talk of the Brahmachari came to the forefront. He had reportedly started to use Prime Minister Indira Gandhi's name to pressurize officials and businessmen. A sizeable plot of land was made available to him by the Himachal Pradesh government to set up a luxurious Yoga Centre. Another luxury Yoga Centre was presided over by him in Delhi. He owned a private plane and shuttled between his two estates. After Indira's defeat, news of a gun factory owned by the Brahmachari came to light and the Janata government launched proceedings against the yogi on various grounds. Indira's victory in 1980 brought the yogi back to power and the easy access to the house, permitted during her years out of power, continued.

Indira, when questioned by a friend of the family on the role of the Brahmachari in the household, at first did not answer, but when pressed, said, 'There must be a reason for him,' but then refused to elucidate further.

The Brahmachari came from Mithila, one of the major centres of tantric learning and ritual practice. An adept of this esoteric knowledge of power, he was one of the main people around Indira who brought her rumours of dark tantric rites, enacted in secret shrines, by her ill-wishers to destroy Sanjay and her. It is likely that the Brahmachari spoke of the equally powerful rites and mantras of protection that could be used against these destructive forces. In her anxiety to protect her son, Indira possibly agreed to counter-rituals being performed to destroy the magical weapons of destruction released against her family.

With Sanjay's death, the Brahmachari's place in the house started to wane. Rajiv and Sonia had never hidden their dislike for this holy man. By 1983 the Brahmachari was no longer visible at the Prime Minister's House.

*

From Bombay I had sent Indira notes she had asked for on matters that needed her urgent attention, and names of people who could be inducted in areas of development and culture. Soon I was to receive a message from her to say that I had not included what I wished to do. 'Anything you want,' was the phrase communicated to me. The suggestion from the Prime Minister was that I join her Cabinet to take charge of culture, handlooms, crafts and social welfare. For a moment I was tempted. It would enable me to re-structure many areas for which I had the skills and which needed attention. I sent an answer that, as I was dining with her two days later, I would discuss the matter with her. She was in a joyous mood at dinner, played word games with the children and later took me to her room to bring out the book *Eternal India* on which she continued to work, translating the French into English, a task for which she needed my help. Suddenly she laid the book aside, turned to me to ask whether I had received her message. 'Yes,' I replied. I hesitated and said, 'Could I take a day or two to decide?' She was surprised at my answer, but said 'Yes.'

I went home in a turbulent state of mind. Could I refuse her? I asked myself. And yet the thought of being in her Cabinet, with all its limitations and restrictions on my own freedom of life and expression, was distasteful to me. I was aware of the adulation, sycophancy, the arrogance of power around a Cabinet minister. Had I a place in such a situation? The next morning I awoke with a lucid mind and I wrote to her hoping she would understand that what I sought in life was freedom, a search to discover myself, to probe, to dialogue, and to question. I said that to accept her offer would limit this freedom. It would be like being put into a cage and my mind and senses would shrivel. I assured her of help in any way needed, even suggested that I could be her adviser.

The next evening I was again at 12, Willingdon Crescent.

Indira came in and I could sense that my letter had come as a shock; as Prime Minister, she was not used to refusal. She was very much the Prime Minister as she stepped back, established a distance, the warmth leaving her voice. Later as I was leaving, she spoke, 'I got your letter. What are the alternatives?' I suggested once again that I could be her adviser and head any special committee. She nodded her head, 'It will have to be worked out.' I did not push my presence but remained away. Within a week I received a message that she expected me for dinner. I went back and found her warm, generous and affectionate—a friend. She asked me to accept the Chairmanship of the Advisory Committee for the Festival of India in Great Britain due in 1982. My acceptance was immediate. It was a challenge and I promised to work out my ideas and get back to her. Many months later she said to me, 'I think you were wise to refuse what I suggested. Perhaps you will have greater freedom to function now.'

*

In May 1980, Indira returned from the funeral of Marshal Josip Broz Tito, full of grave concerns. She met the ageing Leonid Brezhnev, after an absence of four years. Her meeting with Hua of China was her first with the political leadership of China after the late Sixties. Margaret Thatcher was the new Prime Minister of Great Britain; the American Presidential elections were due in a few months. At Belgrade she had felt the state of insecurity that pervaded international relations. With Ayatollah Khomeini's return to Iran, a new Islamic fundamentalism was surfacing. The non-aligned forces were taking sides in the cold war and so were unable to act from a position of strength. The oil crisis weighed heavily on the resources of the developing countries and their leaders were preoccupied with themselves. In an interview she remarked:

> The civilisations of the West have reached a crisis point. The known systems have become outdated. They no longer operate efficiently or answer all the questions, and in this I include both Capitalism and Communism as they are understood in classical terms.[5]

She was musing out aloud.

It was clear to her that the major powers did not want to comprehend the truth that inter-dependence was essential for survival.

> The challenge of the 80s will have to be met. The great powers are still bound in the straitjacket of concepts such as balance of power, inter-block rivalries and spheres of influence—the world has become much more complicated and the gap between the rich and the poor widens every day. A country like India does not fall into their (great powers') schedule.[6]

*

In March Indira presided over the World Conservation Strategy meeting in New Delhi. During her election tour she had travelled by car over the length and breadth of India, noticed the ravaged landscape, the rapid growth of the desert, the deforestation of the Himalayas. The trees she had loved from childhood were disappearing. Man's relationship to the tree based on an understanding of nature as life-giving, had yielded to a growing exploitation of nature. She understood the importance of evolving national strategies to ensure that the principles of conservation pervaded development planning and that the reckless exploitation of nature ended. She spoke of the need for city forests; Delhi was doing pioneering work. 'We must have trees to shade our roads and act as shelter holds in coastal cities.' She had a warning for the developed nations who, in their search for affluence, were the worse ravagers of the environment.

One of her first acts as Prime Minister was to stop any further work on the Silent Valley dam project in Kerala, the last major rain forests in India. All work on the dam was now stopped. The clearance of forest and cutting down of trees ended and she asked her experts to re-examine the whole project. She was aware of the problems she faced in India where "centuries co-exist". The complexity and diversity of the country, the exploding population and the pressure on land were posing enormous problems of conserving the environment yet ensuring development. Environment and energy were high priority issues on her agenda for the future. She wrote to the chief ministers suggesting a drive to plant "a tree for every child" and emphasizing the vital importance of developing a new attitude of respect towards old, culturally-accepted, energy-saving technologies, along with the right use of the new technologies available.

She was wary of multinationals and their marketing strategies for technologies which India could not afford or support. She was suspicious of multinationals controlling the levers of economic power and so imposing another form of bondage on India and the Indian people. She had no answers to the contradictions but one central issue was clear: India had to be self-reliant and Indira's main concern was national interest. She was unwavering in her commitment to an independent India. 'The great powers had to understand'; she said that 'they are true friends only when we are not satellites.'[7]

In the third week of March, Indira reached me in Bombay on the telephone. 'I have become a grandmother again. Sanjay has a son.' I rejoiced with her.

I was in Delhi again in May, with my family, *en route* to Srinagar where I was to spend a month on holiday. The result of the State Assembly elections had just come in. Indira's party had swept the polls in all the states except Tamil Nadu. Mother and son were jubilant.

With victory, Sanjay was to emerge as a national leader in his own right. He was no longer the arrogant, inexperienced youth of 1975. The years out of power had given depth to his understanding of people and situations. He had learnt from his mother the skill of planning strategies, winning over people and emerging triumphant in elections. He would never again be considered politically irrelevant. Without challenging his mother's authority, he was determined to free himself from her shadow, to establish his own independent roots in the body politic and to ensure that those elected held allegiance to him. His campaign discarded all radical rhetoric, all ideological appeals to the electorate. He projected himself as a pragmatist, interested only in getting things done. The people of India were weary of slogans; they wanted a government that would provide them jobs and ensure their basic needs at reasonable prices.

Whispers had started in the capital even before the results of the State Assembly elections were declared, that within a year Sanjay would emerge as the Prime Minister of India. It did not come as a surprise, therefore, when the Uttar Pradesh Congress Legislative

Party in their first meeting elected Sanjay as their leader and appealed to Indira to appoint him as the Chief Minister of Uttar Pradesh, the largest State in India.

Politicians and friends flocked to Sanjay to congratulate and felicitate him on his appointment. Indira however thought otherwise. She refused her son the role of Chief Minister of Uttar Pradesh. She told his well-wishers that Sanjay had to learn a great deal before he could take on such an onerous responsibility. Vishwanath Pratap Singh (later to be Prime Minister from 1989–1990) was appointed Chief Minister and Sanjay was inducted into the All-India Congress Committee (AICC) as its Secretary. For a short while Sanjay rebelled, but finally calmed down.

While I was in Delhi I went to the house for lunch. Sanjay came in with a garland of *rudraksha* beads, 108 Gauri Shankars, the rarest of all *rudraksha* rosaries, in his hands. He asked me what I thought of it. I gasped in surprise at the extraordinary quality of the necklace, normally worn only by Shankaracharyas.

He smiled and tried to put it on. Indira immediately stopped him, 'You are too young.' That was the last time I saw Sanjay alive.

TWO

23 June 1980 was a hot, angry day. Indira Gandhi was in her study when Sanjay Gandhi came to her room early in the morning as he normally did to discuss this and that, smiling, confident, direct and full of fun as usual. A little while later he had left for the flying club. During the past few days Indira had noticed that Sanjay was very restless. He had flown recklessly in a light two-seater Pitts S-2A plane, taking up into the air his wife, R.K. Dhawan, Indira Gandhi's Special Assistant and other close friends. They complained to Indira of the grave danger of an accident. She chided Sanjay, but he was wildly excited with the plane and refused to see reason.

On the morning of 23 June he reached the flying club a little early, did not wait for Madhavrao Scindia (now Union Minister for Civil Aviation and Tourism), who was to be his fellow-passenger, but invited Captain Subhash Saxena, former Chief Instructor at the Delhi Flying Club, to go up with him. He flew for twelve minutes over 1, Safdarjung Road and Rashtrapati Bhavan. According to an eye-witness, the aircraft dived perhaps to perform a loop, failed to pull out of the dive and crashed into a drain in the capital's Diplomatic Enclave. The crash was within a mile of 12, Willingdon Crescent, Indira's home during the years out of power.

Indira was informed of the crash at 8.20 a.m. Vishwanath Pratap Singh, then Chief Minister of Uttar Pradesh was waiting to see the Prime Minister early that June morning. He was on his feet as he saw her rush past him, her hair dishevelled, a wild vacant look filling her eyes. Her Personal Assistant rushed behind her to join her in the car which was waiting outside. Sensing that something ominous had happened, V.P. Singh followed the Prime Minister's car, to arrive at the scene of accident, seconds after Indira. The plane was a total wreck, the bodies of the two occupants crushed and mutilated. Before Indira's arrival the fire brigade had extricated the bodies and an ambulance was waiting to take them to hospital. She saw the crushed face of her son. A mother's cry broke from her.

Even now long past when the deer remember it.
They drop the grass from their mouth.[1]

Indira was back in control of herself in an instant, took charge, ordered Sanjay's and the co-pilot's bodies to be put into an ambulance, got in herself and stood holding the overhead rack, till they reached the Ram Manohar Lohia Hospital where the doctors in attendance declared both crash victims dead. Within minutes the news spread through the capital and political leaders from all the parties rushed to the hospital. Amongst them were Atal Behari Vajpayee and Chandra Shekhar. Indira wore dark glasses to shield her eyes and emotions. Seeing her standing alone, Vajpayee inexpressibly disturbed, blurted out 'Indiraji in this moment of great travail you will have to show great courage.' She did not reply, he said, but looked through him, as if to say what was he talking about? He was taken aback and asked himself if he had made a great mistake. She then turned to Chandra Shekhar, took him to one side, and said 'I have for some time been wanting to speak to you about Assam. The situation is very grim.' 'We will speak of it later,' he said. But she was insistent. 'No, no. This matter is very important.' A baffled Chandra Shekhar could not understand how a mother could speak of Assam when her young son's dead body lay in the next room. In the evening, when Atal Behari Vajpayee, Chandra Shekhar and Hemvati Nandan Bahugana met, Vajpayee commented 'Either Indiraji had transcended sorrow or she is a woman of stone. Or is it that she wants to prove that even at this moment, in the midst of this mortal blow, her concern is with Assam and India's problems?' 'Perhaps,' he said, 'this was the impression she wished to create. An attitude such as this was very much part of her personality.'[2]

Coming face to face with Vishwanath Pratap Singh in the hospital, Indira Gandhi asked him to return to Lucknow urgently, as there were many important issues that he had to deal with.

The reason of his visit to Delhi to see her was forgotten.

Throughout the time the doctors were stitching together Sanjay's mutilated body Indira stood in the room. Maneka Gandhi was informed of the accident some time after the body was brought to the hospital. She was beside herself with anguish and insisted on entering the room where the doctors were still busy with her husband's body. Indira who had come out of the room, to comfort Maneka, prevailed on her to wait in another room till the doctors had finished "treating the emergency". Indira consoled the wife and mother of Captain

Saxena and enquired frequently about them throughout the time she was in the hospital.

It took the doctors around three hours to prepare Sanjay's body. When they had finished, Indira asked them to leave her alone with her son for a few minutes. They hesitated, but she told them firmly to go out. Within four minutes she came out of the room, the dark glasses hiding her eyes and what they held. She then went to the room where Maneka sat, to tell her that Sanjay was dead. Large crowds had gathered, many of those present, including Sanjay's close friends, weeping.

I was at breakfast at the Government House at Srinagar with L.K. Jha, the then Governor and my family, when I was called to the telephone. Mrs Vasant Sathe, wife of the then Information and Broadcasting Minister, was on the line. She was hysterical, said Sanjay's plane had crashed and asked whether I could take the next flight to Delhi. She did not know of Sanjay's condition. There was a flight in the next ninety minutes and I caught it.

It was difficult to register the news immediately. It was on the plane that I was told that Sanjay was dead. On my arrival at Delhi airport I drove straight to Indira's residence. I found the aides and servants in a state of shock. Rajiv and Sonia Gandhi were abroad with their children. There was no one at 1, Safdarjung Road to take charge. I was told that the adjoining bungalow—1, Akbar Road which Indira used as an office—had been prepared to receive the body, which was due to arrive shortly. Huge blocks of ice had been placed in a trough and covered with a white sheet; in the main room Brahmins had gathered and were chanting from the Bhagavad Gita. The news had spread and large crowds were outside the house and in the garden. I stood waiting in a corner of the room. There was a sudden bustle at the door, the crowds were pushed aside and Indira came in, her head covered. She wore a long-sleeved blouse. She looked around her but did not seem to take in anything. Immediately behind her was the bier. The body was laid on a platform, the face was exposed, one eye and the head were badly damaged, the nose smashed. I winced involuntarily.

Maneka came in. There was a total absence of coordination in her movements. She sat down next to me on the sheet spread next to the body for relatives and close friends. 'Not Sanjay, not Sanjay, anyone but Sanjay.' She was speaking to herself, blind to the crowds and those seated beside her.

By now some order was established and the crowds started filing past the body. There were ministers, friends, strangers. Some of them came up to Indira, weeping. She consoled them; sat amongst the mourners, silent and unmoving. After about an hour she went out, came back, took Maneka by the hand and walked away with her.

At around 4.00, exhausted I walked over to 1, Safdarjung Road and sat in the dining-room. Rajiv was expected back that night and Indira appeared anxious about his journey. She was walking backwards and forwards between the two houses without purpose, without direction. At around 5.00 she came and sat with me. For a minute we were alone. She said, 'Where do I go from here, Pupul?'[3] With both her hands she held her stomach close, a gesture I had witnessed amongst peasant women mourning their dead. The death of a child is a spasm of the womb; it is the womb that cries out; filled with the weight of death, the crucible cracks.

*

Fori Nehru, Rajan Nehru (wife of Ratan Nehru, an ex-Foreign Secretary) and I decided to spend the night in the house. Indira learnt about it, insisted on making arrangements, arranged for mattresses to be placed on the floor, ordered tea and toast to be brought to us. It was a long, endless night. Indira did not sleep. She was anxious about Rajiv's return, concerned whether the plane would be on time. She would go to her room, return to the room where Sanjay's body lay, come to the room where we slept to check if we were comfortable, go back to her room; she was endlessly on the move. Rajiv arrived at three in the morning. Mother and son and his family were alone together for a brief while. Then they went to the room where Sanjay's body lay.

It was decided, before Rajiv's arrival, that Sanjay would be cremated at Shantivana, in the garden that surrounded the memorial to his grandfather. Rajiv was concerned at the site chosen, hesitated to speak to his mother, but finally did so. She listened, said it was the chief ministers and Kashmir's Sheikh Abdullah who had suggested it.

Silent crowds lined the roadside the next afternoon as Sanjay's body was carried on an open truck, covered with wreaths and garlands to the cremation site, Indira sat on the ground nearby, holding Maneka's hand all through the funeral rites. There was rather beautiful Vedic chanting, the atmosphere one of great dignity. As Rajiv circumambulated the body before lighting the pyre, and the chanting of the priests rose to a crescendo, Indira suddenly noticed that the Congress flag that had covered the body during the journey was still there and that it would be burnt with the body. She intervened. The logs were lifted and the flag removed before the cremation finally took place.

On 25 June the ashes were brought back in copper urns by Rajiv and placed under a tree in the garden of 1, Akbar Road. Indira broke down and Rajiv put his arm around her and held her. When I went to her house next morning, the *Ramayana* was being chanted in the room where Sanjay's body had lain, and white jasmine flowers surrounded by green leaves outlined the absent bier. The room looked cool and pure. Indira sat during the morning with Maneka and Sonia to mourn with friends and relatives in the customary ceremony.

Rajiv and Sonia, with a vast number of Sanjay's close associates and members of the Youth Congress, travelled to Allahabad to immerse Sanjay's ashes in the Sangam. Indira did not accompany them. The next day she was back at her office in South Block.

I went to see her that evening. The first question she asked me was when I would join her. I knew that with Sanjay's death her need for friends would increase. My reply was instantaneous. I would return to Delhi whenever she wanted and would do whatever she asked me to do. She spoke of her deep concern about Maneka and hoped that she would not remain idle. According to Indira, Amteshwar Anand, Maneka's mother was very ambitious and wanted Sanjay's place for her daughter. 'Unfortunately,' Indira said, 'no one wants to work, everyone wants to be a leader.'[4] Already, Sanjay's death had effected a transformation in Maneka's position at 1, Safdarjung Road. Her relationship with Indira was very insecure. She had always feared Indira, taken refuge behind Sanjay when she had to deal with her mother-in-law. But now she had to come face to face with this formidable woman.

Her baby, Feroze Varun, was the only real bridge. All the grandchildren, including little Varun, now slept in the same room as

Indira. 'After many years,' Indira said, 'I have the children all to myself.' I could see that the baby's cries would not disturb her. In every gesture of the child she saw Sanjay.

On 28 June, five days after Sanjay's death, Khushwant Singh, then editor of the *Hindustan Times* and a close friend of Sanjay and Maneka, deeply moved by the stricken figure of Maneka, wrote a signed column in his newspaper.

'The only possible inheritor of the Sanjay cult figure is Maneka. She is like her late husband, utterly fearless when aroused, the very reincarnation of Durga astride a tiger.'[5] This article was to have far-reaching consequences and create grave misunderstandings between Maneka and Indira.

Indira took me to her room that evening. She Spoke to Maneka haltingly. She had heard, she said, that some talk had started of Maneka leaving the house. But her mother Amteshwar Anand was against it. According to Indira, it was she who was behind Khushwant Singh's article. She asked me whether I had read it? I could see that it had hurt and disturbed Indira. I realized that the symbolism of Durga riding a tiger, was most unfortunate. There could not be two Durgas riding tigers under one roof.

I returned to Delhi in July to find tensions mounting in Indira's house. At first Indira understood Maneka's despair. She was anxious to find something that would occupy Maneka's time and in a surge of compassion for the young widow suggested that Maneka become her secretary and travel with her. This upset Sonia. Letters were exchanged between Sonia and Indira and, Indira realizing her need for Rajiv and his family, withdrew her offer to Maneka. In any other circumstances Indira would have given solace to the stricken young girl and helped to assuage her pain. But her own sorrow had blinded her to another's grief. Isolated and anxious, the twenty-three-year-old started to work on a photographic book on Sanjay. Indira was to write the foreword.

Rajiv's friends gathered to discuss his future. Sonia was vehemently opposed to her husband joining politics. She threatened to leave him if he did so.[6] But his friends intervened, spoke of Indira Gandhi's isolation and her need for support. Rajiv had hesitated to approach Indira with an offer of help. His relationship to his mother was entirely different from Sanjay's. It was based on a deep affection, but clothed with a formality which rarely permitted close and intimate encounters. He felt that she should make the first move. Her pride and ambivalence made this difficult. In her conversations with me she spoke of Sanjay in a special tender way. 'No one can take Sanjay's place. He was my son, but was like an elder brother in his support.'[7] Sanjay's loss was a physical one. She appeared a little hesitant about Rajiv, was not sure how he would take the brutalities and ruthlessness of politics. 'Rajiv lacks Sanjay's dynamism and his concerns, yet he could be a great help to me. But so long as he is a government servant it will be difficult for him to help me. If he gives up the job how will he support himself?' 'Sanjay,' she said, 'was very frugal, but Rajiv and his wife need certain comforts.'[8]

She was growing aware of how entangled her life had been with that of her younger son. Without him there was a vacuum surrounding her. Who would fill it, she was asking herself. Apart from needing someone whom she could trust totally, who would act strongly and swiftly, and keep the windows to the outer world open for her, she needed physical closeness and support. To fill this need, she turned to Sonia. From the autumn of 1980, Sonia's relationship to Indira changed dramatically from that of a daughter-in-law to the role of a daughter. And for comfort, she gathered her three grandchildren close to her.

To the press and her political colleagues Indira was sphinx-like in her silence on Rajiv's future. 'I am not going to talk about it. It is for Rajiv to decide.' But it soon became clear that Rajiv would be persuaded to enter politics and a vast number of MPs and newspapermen started to visit him.

By July, according to reports,

> verbal instructions went out to all party headquarters that the "induct Maneka" campaign should be aborted. The instructions also contained the message that Maneka should not be invited for an official function without the express permission of Mrs. Gandhi. The result was electric. Suddenly Maneka's supporters were singing a different tune.[9]

By now a decision had been taken by Rajiv to resign from Indian

Airlines and join the Congress party.

I was dining most nights with the family. Rajiv was very apprehensive of the growing influence on Indira of astrologers and rituals. It appears that a Gujarati newspaper had predicted Sanjay's death in June and now she was receiving innumerable letters warning her of dangers to Rajiv. Indira wanted Rajiv to give up flying. The newspapers were full of astrological forecasts of dangers to the family in the days ahead. One night, after dinner, while Rajiv and Sonia were still at the table, I spoke to Indira about the destructive atmosphere in the house, with all this talk of astrology and superstitions. It was obvious that her enemies were intent on creating an atmosphere of fear to weaken and destroy her pyschologically. The only response for her should be to have nothing to do with it, to gather all the letters and astrological forecasts and throw them out of the window. 'That's just it,' she said. 'It is because we did nothing and ignored what they said, that this happened to Sanjay. They had foretold the actual date.' There was a wildness in her face, a dark despair. I said she should not let her mind dwell on danger. If there was evil, there were also good forces protecting her.

'What use are they? Could they protect Sanjay? If I had died it would have been right. I am over 60, I have lived a full life, but Sanjay was so young.' Rajiv was grim, did not say a word. We were quiet for five minutes, but it was a quietness in which powerful emotions were awake and shattered the silence.

Then Indira started to speak of something else. In a few minutes she got up and said she would go back to work; she had three hours' work ahead of her. I could not help myself but went up to her, placed my hands on her shoulders and said. 'You are exhausted and should rest.'

'Who will do this work? If I don't do it now, I will have to wake up at 4.00 in the morning.'[10]

She walked to her room, her body stooped, her step heavy.

On 25 August she wrote to her cousin, B.K. Nehru, sent him a *rakhi,* a silk-twined bracelet of protection sent by a sister to a brother on the coconut festival which falls in August: 'Suddenly I feel the need of a brother,' she wrote. 'Also, this is to remind you of your promise to give some guidance in revamping the administration. When do we start? Love.'[11]

B.K. Nehru's response was warm and affectionate. He placed himself at her disposal.

As the pressure of work increased and she had to deal with mounting internal problems within the party and face the avalanche of mediamen from all parts of the world who sought interviews, she found she desperately needed her old energy and determination. In reply to a letter from Fori Nehru, B.K. Nehru's wife, she wrote: 'Yes, I need rest, but I have needed it and not got it for most of my life. And right now, rest is very much a mental condition. All the tears I did not shed in June and July are welling up within me and even beauty has no meaning.'[12]

*

A new economic thrust was expected from the Prime Minister; a growing unrest in the country needed all her skills. Indira had hoped that with Sanjay by her side she would leave internal affairs in the country to her son, only interfering when problems threatened to get out of hand. She expected that with his youth, energy and drive, he would inspire the young people of the country to revitalize and give a new dynamism to her development plans. She was aware of the dangers of programmes remaining on paper without implementation. She had, from the first day of victory, commenced a search for skilled bureaucrats who could handle the administrative machinery and make the bureaucracy work. She had meanwhile determined her own role; she aimed to free herself of day to day administrative problems, to deal with major policies within the country and to see that India's voice was heard, and its presence felt in the capitals of the world. With Sanjay's death the agenda she had prepared with such care, was in a shambles.

Like a wounded bird heals itself, draws close its body and folds its wings, Indira drew herself close. By September she could again stretch her wings and take hesitant flight. At the inaugural function of the National Centre for Performing Arts in Bombay, Indira appeared in an oyster-coloured sari, her hair groomed, elegant and beautiful. She had regained grace.

I was to return with her to Delhi. I could see that Indira's relationship to Maneka was hemmed in by suspicion. Maneka was twenty-three years old at the time of her husband's death, the same age as Indira when she rebelled against her father to marry Feroze Gandhi in 1941. But, forty-one years after her rebellion, Indira was not prepared to understand Maneka's revolt, nor was she prepared to accept the ambiguity of Maneka's position in the household. The girl was young, spirited, ambitious. Since her marriage, she had lived in the midst of political excitement. The high profile of her husband gave her an illusion of power. She was not prepared to withdraw into anonymity, which was inevitable if she were to stay in her mother-in-law's house. From the early days of her marriage she had watched her mother-in-law's behaviour and her skills and, as she was to tell the press two years later, Sanjay had taught her to plan strategies four steps ahead; so she too planned her future.

There were difficulties now over the foreword Indira was to write for Maneka's book on Sanjay. Indira's stand was that she would have done so immediately after Sanjay's death. She had had the time then, but Maneka had not consulted her. Maneka had spoken to Khushwant Singh to do the text and wanted Khushwant to interview Indira on Sanjay. Indira was not prepared to accept this. Maneka was isolated and desperately unhappy; Indira asked me whether I would intervene and speak to her. I took the young girl out to a South Indian meal. I could see that she was deeply insecure. She told me she was very afraid of Indira, was tongue-tied before her, had always been afraid and sought shelter behind Sanjay. Indira's refusal to write the foreword had shattered Maneka. She threatened never to speak to her mother-in-law if she did not write the foreword. I saw the dummy of the book, the photographs of Sanjay had been chosen with great sensitivity; as a baby, Sanjay had had the face of an angel. That night Maneka took the dummy and left it in Indira's room. Indira was emotionally very upset to see the photographs. The past with all its memories: images of Sanjay's childhood pranks, his crashing cars, playing truant, turning to his mother for alibis, haunted her throughout the night.

Sitting in her room, every knock at the door, invoked Sanjay's presence, angry, protective—all of it so easily erased and with so little reason. She told me the next day that she could not sleep all night, and that the book had been very well conceived, but she was determined not to write the foreword. She had erased Maneka from her cherished ones; she saw her now as an outsider, but Feroze Varun was of her blood. The ruthlessness was back in Indira.

I noticed that the door that led from her bedroom to Sanjay's room had closed and the door leading to Rajiv's room had opened. It was symbolic. One period of Indira's life was over, another was to begin.

I was in Delhi for Jawaharlal Nehru's and Indira's birthdays and accompanied Indira on the afternoon of 14 November, Jawaharlal's birthday, to Shantivana where Indira, Rajiv, Sonia, Varun, Rahul and Priyanka planted trees on the site of Sanjay's cremation. Maneka was away in Bombay. No one mentioned her during the planting of trees. Indira was in complete control of herself. As crowds gathered around the car for the return journey I saw her face light up and there was a glow in her eyes as she returned the greetings of the people. Later we went to the Trade Fair and sat in the children's train. Little Varun sat on his grandmother's lap. I could see that he was infinitely precious to her.

On 19 November, her birthday, I found Indira performing puja, early in the morning, before a lithograph of Rama, to the chant of purohits. It was astonishing to see the hold orthodox religion had gained on her. She was embarrassed to see me and said that she was doing the puja for the sake of her aunt. Later that evening she discussed a speech she had to give on values. We had talked of the shadow that falls between the word as idea and action which often is the source of the distortion of values.

We tried to recollect T.S. Eliot's phrase, but could not recall the exact words.

Indira must have spent an hour looking at T.S. Eliot's poems for, by the next day, I received a slip of paper in her own handwriting:

Pupul—The following are Eliot's words in different verses:

1. Between the motion and the act.
2. Between the conception and the creation.
3. Between the emotion and the response.
Falls the shadow.

*

Invitations for the release of Maneka's book on Sanjay were sent out for early December. When the first copy reached the Prime Minister she was very angry. It appears that Maneka had not shown her the final proof and some of the remarks in the text and captions were damaging and, according to Indira, distorted. The release of the book, scheduled to take place in Vigyan Bhavan, was postponed, and the publishers were contacted to alter the captions. Indira was very tense and angry and her relationship with Maneka was at its lowest ebb. She called Maneka and told her that things could not continue the way they were. If she wanted to leave the house it was for her to decide, as also whether their relationship in the future should be that of total strangers or whether they could remain friends. Maneka hesitated, but retreated. The situation, for the time being, was defused. The captions in the book were altered, the book released.

I was in Rishi Valley when Indira came along with Rajiv, Sonia, Rahul, Priyanka and some of their friends to the valley to visit J. Krishnamurti. The Prime Minister had issued instructions that she did not want party men or ministers to crowd the campus. She had also instructed the Chief Minister to see that under no circumstances was security staff to enter the campus. In despair the police authorities had approached us and it was decided that security staff should be so located, as to become invisible. 'It became a game of finding a suitable bush behind which to hide—one stout police inspector even tried to hide behind a slender eucalyptus tree.'[13] Indira was there for eighteen hours—she had breakfast, lunch and dinner with Krishnaji; addressed the students and the staff; planted a *Ficus Benjamina* tree, walked with the sage cross-country towards Rishi Konda. Indira was used to walking fast and easily kept pace with Krishnaji's long Strides. Krishnaji spoke to her on the walk of the many dimensions of sorrow. The valley was green with plants, bushes and tall trees. Sensitive, awake, Indira could participate in the master's dialogue, turn to nature, draw from the atmosphere, the essences that healed her.

She returned to Delhi with the silences of the valley, and filled with the presence of the compassionate sage. The wound of her son's death would sink deep, her face would carry the intensity and altogetherness of sorrow, but the earlier blight would be erased. She had regained a new and vulnerable look. Her step was light and her spine straight.

I took Morris Grave, the American painter of wondrous birds, to see her. She was in a wistful mood. She spoke of the US being in some ways like Russia. She found that people were trapped in both places—

in Russia by the system, in the US by consumerism. The difference lay in that in the US people could break free. They discussed gurus and the movement of young people who had become wanderers in the world. She expressed her sorrow that the manifestation of a sensitive young movement however chaotic had ended. 'Whither are the young going in the United States?' she asked.

A few days later I went with her to see the film *Black Stallion*. The early part of the film was concerned with a boy and a wild black horse ship-wrecked on a coral reef, the relationship of the child and the animal, their encounters against a landscape of gnarled rock and roaring ocean. The child and the horse were rescued, the horse tamed and harnessed, to end on a race track. The film depressed Indira deeply. She had closed her eyes, she said, when she saw the horse harnessed. To her, it evoked the memories and longings of her youth. 'To be a Prime Minister, is to be tamed and harnessed.'

THREE

On 23 June 1981, Indira Gandhi's year of mourning for Sanjay Gandhi ended. Through the year she wore white, ivory or black saris. Immediately the year ended, colour re-entered her wardrobe. The palette had changed to sun-drenched colours of saffron and honey, madder reds and faded pinks, shades of ripe mango and the green of meadow grass. With colour, her sensibilities awoke and with it an energy that enabled her to act with confidence and clarity. Visiting her one evening, I found her dressed in a sari the colour of ripe wheat; she was light in spirit, her mind full of fun and story. As I was leaving, I commented that she had drawn on all her inner resources to overcome sorrow. She suddenly grew serious but did not reply. The next day a letter written in her own hand reached me:

> Pupul,
>
> You let fall a phrase about my overcoming sorrow. One can overcome hate, envy, greed and other such negative and self-destroying emotions. But sorrow is something else. It can be neither forgotten nor overcome. One has to learn to live with it, to absorb it with one's being as a part of life.
>
> Sd. I.G.[1]

Indira met J. Krishnamurti at her house shortly after her return to India from a visit to Cancun in Mexico to attend a Conference of the International Cooperation for Global Progress, called at the initiative of Chancellor Bruno Kreisky of Austria and the President of Mexico. She spoke of the closed minds of the world leaders and their inability to respond to the enormous challenges that faced humankind. Indira's first meeting with President Ronald Reagan at Cancun was warm and friendly. She told Krishnamurti she had enquired of the recent assassination attempt on the President. It appears that when he was shot and rushed to the hospital, by chance all the best surgeons and doctors were present: this saved his life. He would not have survived, he said, if the surgeons had to be called from a distance. He had told Indira that it was a coincidence and only meant that God wanted him to live and govern the United States.

Krishnamurti intervened to ask whether her own security was efficient and could protect her. She replied: 'There are a vast number of guards, but very few of them would risk their lives to protect me.'

Krishnamurti sensed great tension in the house, currents of hatred and anger. He asked Indira whether there was anything wrong. Her reply was, 'The usual quarrels as in all families.' Towards the end of the meeting she asked him whether he found her changed since he first met her. He hesitated, then replied that she had become a little harder. She was taken aback for a moment, then said the hardness was only on the surface. She had developed it as an armour to protect herself. 'When I was young, I was soft and vulnerable and easily hurt.' She spoke of a wall she had built around her. 'I have now broken the wall.' Krishnamurti came back to my house with a feeling of profound compassion for Indira. He was deeply disturbed by the atmosphere of 1, Safdarjung Road. He felt that Indira was completely isolated.

FOUR

Prime Minister Indira Gandhi's first official visit abroad was to Paris in November 1981, on an invitation from the newly-elected President of France, Francois Mitterrand. Briefed on his dynamism, his passion and his intelligence, she was also warned of the depth of his understanding of international politics. She knew that the Emergency had eroded her image in the West. She was viewed by the intelligentsia as an authoritarian ruler with courage, audacity and determination, but amoral in her approach to power. Yet, she knew, that she must win people over, set their doubts at rest and occupy her rightful place as a senior world statesperson, with concerns that extended beyond India's national boundaries, to a world threatened by ecological and nuclear disaster.

During her stay in Paris she was to receive the degree of Doctor of Letters honoris causa from the Sorbonne University. She had asked J. Krishnamurti, at their last meeting, what she should speak about at the Sorbonne University. He said, 'Speak of the place of knowledge in the liberation of man. Knowledge is essential, but has it any place in the ending of sorrow, loneliness, the sense of the void within us?'

Indira spent a month on her acceptance speech. Her Information Adviser, H.Y. Sharada Prasad, prepared a skeleton draft based on her brief: to mirror India's spiritual yet robust heritage against the background of a changing world. She hoped that her words would reach a world audience, and reveal Indira Gandhi in her new incarnation as a reflective woman, a Prime Minister intensely concerned with the future of the earth, with nature, and with the mind of humankind.

From the time she was first elected Prime Minister in 1966, her method of preparing an important speech remained unchanged. She was ignorant of computers, data banks and retrieval systems. Her approach to an important speech was to stretch her mind to its limits, to seek fresh insights. She would turn to friends and advisers, scientists, philosophers and artists, people who she felt had transcended the East-West divide, to seek lateral inputs in the form of information, ideas, quotations.

One afternoon she called me in. I found her sitting on her bed

426

surrounded by drafts, slips of paper, *aides-mémoire,* books, dictionaries; with a pair of scissors and pins, she was cutting and pinning together paragraphs and passages to prepare a first draft. She then sent it to one of her aides to type out. The draft returned, the typing was careless, the paper cheap and flimsy. Her earlier years with Mahatma Gandhi had taught her a frugality in her use of paper. Nothing was wasted. She read out the draft to me. I too, along with many other friends, had sent ideas and written out paragraphs. She would pick a phrase here, a paragraph there, turn to the dictionary to find an appropriate word, a quotation from her father, Rabindranath Tagore or a verse from the Upanishads. She drafted and redrafted the speech, searching for a word or phrase that would reach deep and far. The final draft, the juxtaposition of paragraphs and the wholeness of the speech was always her own. She would work on her speech till the night before she was to deliver it.

Before leaving India for Paris, she had carefully read President Mitterrand's memoirs in French. A maturity of approach and a commonality of interests in literature and nature made communion easy between the two leaders.

Prime Minister Indira Gandhi addressed a distinguished audience of writers, philosophers and academics at the Sorbonne University, in French, and so established an immediate rapport. Her speech covered a vast canvas: 'Ancient Indians had explored vast fields of knowledge; doubt and debate lay at the foundation of their inquiry. It was able to transcend yet hold the material world of the outer and the religious world of the inner.' She asked the wise people of the Western world to see that the traditional concepts of East and West were obsolete. The young in the West turned East for spiritual light, the young of India turned West dazzled by material wealth and scientific knowledge. She stressed the need for a new individual who could relate to matters global—an earth citizen capable of transcending differences without denying provenance or heritage. She further said:

The major crisis was not so much clash of culture as what to do with violence, not only that which is stored in nuclear arsenals but the growing nihilism and callousness of ordinary people. Yet the sense of wholeness, of cosmic totality evades human beings, so does the insight that man is a tiny element in the cosmos and that all life and nature are inter-related and no element can isolate itself.

The challenge lay in seeing,

whether a person moves inward into the divided self or outward into the divided world, the nightmare of a vast entangled structure closes in, causing alienation and in-coherence. There is no sanctity towards life or relation with nature. Goodness is not assumed as a state that is untainted, the flowering of which determines the texture of a culture or a civilization. The wholeness of the earth can come about only with the wholeness of human beings.[1]

She was to stay in Paris for six days. Her meetings with writers, architects, philosophers, social scientists were arranged at the Centre Pompidou—the complex yet dazzling tribute of the technological age to the arts and humanism. Her two daughters-in-law, Sonia and Maneka, had accompanied her on the visit. Indira had insisted that I meet her in Paris. I was present at the Sorbonne University and at the banquets and receptions, and went shopping with her and the family to Printemps. We walked the streets of Paris, visited the Cardin boutique. I listened while Indira met the media. Her last afternoon was free and she invited me to lunch. Sonia and Maneka had their own engagements and Indira decided that she and I would have lunch together at one of Paris' famous restaurants. She intended to shake off her security escorts but that was impossible. I watched Indira very closely as she entered the dining-room. She knew she would be noticed. Her spine straight, her head held high, she did not interrupt her conversation with me as she was taken by the *maitre d' hotel* to the most elegant table in the room, overlooking the Bois. She bowed and gave her most ravishing smile as guests at other tables recognized her and rose to their feet to clap. She ordered her meal in French, displaying her sophisticated understanding of French cuisine. Her entourage was seated at a distant table. During the hour we spent in the dining-room she was in a joyful mood. She spoke of her Sorbonne speech which had been very well received. She had been complimerited by academics and cultural personalities. She had a deep interest in the cultural ethos of France and we discussed people and personalities. Glancing towards her personal staff, she commented, 'They appear to have ordered the whole menu.' She had conquered Paris and was at peace with herself.

President Mitterrand, to express his warmth and admiration for the Prime Minister, broke all rules of protocol when he was present at the airport to bid her farewell. His return visit to India in the winter of 1982 strengthened their friendship. Together they worked on a common agenda for the future of humankind.

*

Surya, the political gossip magazine edited by Maneka and owned by Amteshwar Anand, Maneka's mother, was sold in early 1982 by the mother and daughter to a Rashtriya Swayamsevak Sangh (RSS) sympathizer, without the knowledge of Indira Gandhi. When the news reached Indira, she reacted strongly. The RSS, an extreme right-wing Hindu party, was, for her, the greatest menace for India. She was convinced that unless the party was kept under control, it would devastate and destroy the country. In the sale of *Surya* all her latent suspicions surfaced. Indira grew secretive. I tried to reason with her, but she was obsessed with what she thought was a plot against her.

It was obvious that Maneka could no longer stay with her mother-in-law. Indira told me of a mini-revolt brewing against her in Lucknow, headed by Akbar Ahmed, a member of the Youth Congress and a close associate of Sanjay's. Maneka, through an intermediary, had sent word to her mother-in-law that she would go to Lucknow to address the meeting and that she controlled the loyalty of at least a hundred Uttar Pradesh MLAs who were beholden to Sanjay. Indira Gandhi's response was immediate. A message was sent back to her daughter-in-law that if she went to Lucknow she should not return to 1, Safdarjung Road. Maneka apologized, backed down, but a show-down appeared inevitable.

In normal circumstances Indira would have dealt with the Maneka affair with skill and waited for the right moment to act, but the thought of a possible separation from her grandson, Feroze Varun, clouded her reason. She was deeply depressed when I met her. It was distressing for me to see how rumour and suspicion were playing havoc with Indira's mind. She said she felt worn out, sapped of energy. The situation in the country for the moment was quiet and I told her so.

'My feelings have nothing to do with the situation in the country,' she said. 'I am just fed up with it all.'

On all such occasions, when dark moods beseiged her, a sliver of intelligence provided a door for her to reach out, to enquire and search for clarity. She had time that evening. We sat quiet for a while. She turned to me suddenly and asked whether we could discuss self-knowledge. 'How do you enquire? With what do you probe?' It was a question she had put to me over and over again through the years but every time she asked it was a new beginning. In the quietness there was a slow abeyance of the strong emotive forces that had filled her when we started the dialogue. I said to her, self-knowledge must imply the knowing of what actually is. Could she observe anger, fear, suspicion, hatred pass through her mind without fighting any of these emotions, without suppressing them, without seeking to change them? Could she let whatever "is" come close? I enquired whether she could listen to the outer world of action and the inner world of thought without condemnation or justification. In that state, attention alone was operative and it was that which probed, it was that which revealed. She listened with an intensity, though it was difficult to see what she understood. As I finished speaking, she said, 'Thought plays very little part in my perceptions. It is as if I feel with the pores of my skin.' She spoke of her vulnerability to nature, to the earth, to children and to village people.

A few days later I saw her again. There was a yearning in her to find a religious base. She described her meeting with Maharishi Mahesh Yogi, during the period she was out of power. He had asked her to repeat a mantra, told her she could be another Anand Mai Ma, asked her to leave politics. She had not gone back but the thought of her being a deeply religious person with a potential for the otherwhere, lingered. She asked me whether I thought her religious. She said she did not accept faith or dogma and the other traditional religious beliefs, though she sometimes performed rituals because people expected it of her. She persisted in her question. Did I think she was religious? I did not quite know how to reply, but told her that her very need at times of crisis to be silent, to enquire, to probe, did indicate a strong religious sense.

We started to speak of the religious attitudes and the various religious forces operative in India and of meditation. At a recent meeting with Acharya Tulsi, head of the white-robed Jain sect, and his main disciple, Yuvacharya Pragnya, I had discussed ways of perception. The Yuvacharya spoke of *dhrishti* or direct seeing as central to Jain meditation. He said it came near to what J. Krishnamurti said, but added that for the Jain seeker the transformation of the brain lay in *dhrishti* or total attention on the thymus and thyroid, the two *chakras* or centres of immense power, one between the eyebrows and the other in the throat. I saw a sudden awakening in Indira. She said, 'Don't the Jains start meditation with watching breath?'

'But to watch thought in the instant of its arising slows down breath,' I replied. 'Breath and thought are interlinked.'

The Yuvacharya, as if to test the level of investigation, spoke to me of *tratak,* an esoteric practice which involved the drawing back of the faculty of sight so that the senses changed direction. It was a backward flowing movement. To my amazement Indira was familiar with the word. I could not help asking, did she ever practice *tratak*? Did she create an impregnable distance between her and her opponent through this skill? She laughed but did not answer my query.[2]

It was a matter of continuing wonder to me that a Prime Minister could find time to discuss subtle aspects of meditation and its practice; to discuss self-knowledge, the *chakras* and *tratak* with relative ease in the midst of her enormous day-to-day problems. I said politics did not lend itself to such pursuits. She did not agree. She said politics for her involved the whole of life. 'One does not need a special place to be silent.' I asked her about the pressures in her day-to-day existence? 'I do not see them as pressures.' She had only felt pressure when she first became Prime Minister; during her father's prime ministership, she said, T.T. Krishnamachari had spoken to her of the problems faced by a prime minister. Yet, when it became a reality, the feeling was entirely different. As far as possible she did not permit strong emotions to enter her study. 'It is my ashram.' She spoke shyly and slanted her head to look at and watch my response.

She had started to visit art exhibitions. Her interest in books, music and the cinema was still alive. She sought the company of writers and artists; was in contact with fine craftsmen; met the women painters of

Mithila with a special affection. The hours that she spent with creative people during that month, when she turned away from the affairs of state and the petty quarrels and hurts within her home, renewed her. They brought an edge to her mind, washed it clean of political and domestic trivialities. She was to leave for London soon after to inaugurate the six-month long Festival of India. She looked forward to the visit.

FIVE

Indira Gandhi saw the Festival of India in Great Britain as the commencement of a major people-to-people dialogue. At the many discussions we had together in 1981, she spoke of the closing in of the minds of world leaders. In such a situation it was necessary to stretch out the hand of friendship, to reach beyond the leaders and touch the minds of people. 'In the final analysis it is they who are history's moving force.'

The Festival was a germination and a new beginning, the coming together of young creative minds from India and Great Britain to dialogue through mutual concerns: through music, dance and theatre, exhibitions of ancient art and contemporary artifact, through living creators of heritage. It was an attempt to discover the authentic face of India—an ancient people with young minds, capable of answering the challenges of science and technology, of social change and democracy.

On 22 March 1982, at 8.00 p.m., the Festival of India in Great Britain was inaugurated at a concert held at the Royal Festival Hall in London in the presence of His Royal Highness, The Prince of Wales and of the Joint Patrons of the Festival, the Rt. Hon. Margaret Thatcher, MP, Prime Minister of Great Britain and Northern Ireland, and Indira Gandhi, Prime Minister of the Republic of India. A vast audience of politicians from both countries, scientists, cultural personalities, nobility and the press witnessed the inaugural function. The curtain rose to the beat of the Ranjit drum and to the Indian Presidential Bodyguard sounding a fanfare of trumpets. M.S. Subbulakshmi sang Sanskrit, Telugu and Hindi bhajans, followed by a Ragmala concert composed and performed by Ravi Shankar on the sitar with Zubin Mehta conducting the London Philharmonic Orchestra. It was a historic moment when Zubin Mehta concluded the events of the evening with the national anthems of the United Kingdom and India and the audience rose to its feet. It was the first time in the history of Indo-British relations that the Indian national anthem was played in London, in the presence of royalty. The Prince of Wales flanked by the two Prime Ministers stood at attention as the maestro paid his homage to the country of his birth. I glanced at Indira to see tears fill her eyes, in the Royal Festival Hall.

I noticed a large contingent of policemen surrounding the entrance to the Festival Hall. On enquiry, I was told that groups of Indian agitators were shouting slogans against Indira, a few amongst them demanding Khalistan. I had read of the Sikh demand, but till the spring of 1982 it did not weigh heavily on the Indian mind.

At a formal lunch hosted by the British Prime Minister, the two Prime Ministers spoke of the Festival as the harbinger of a new beginning between the two countries; a formal reception by the Mayor of London was followed by lunch; a banquet was hosted by the Indo-British Association. Prime Minister Gandhi and Prime Minister Thatcher attended the preview of the exhibition of classical Indian art at the Hayward Gallery, a magnificent thematic display of stone sculptures, bronzes and paintings selected to illustrate the Image of Man.

At the Science Museum, an Indian exhibition of science and technology was inaugurated by Indira Gandhi in the presence of Prime Minister Margaret Thatcher. Science in India, from the earliest years of its civilization to contemporary applications of science and technological artifacts, were on display. Indira visited Selfridges where a special sale of Indian products was organized, lunched at the Buckingham Palace with the Queen and Princess Margaret and was at her most skilful at the press conference that she addressed.

She did all the right things—gave a private dinner at Claridges where she was staying, was exquisitely groomed and radiant as she acknowledged the discreet greetings of the guests at other tables. She gave a reception for a few eminent writers, painters, film-makers, scientists and philosophers, went shopping to Harrods; was present at a performance of *Cats,* a musical based on T.S. Eliot's celebrated poems, and ended that day with a candlelit supper at the Savoy Grill. The Prime Minister was at her most gracious.

It was difficult to believe that any problem disturbed her mind. But, in between her various engagements, I could see a rage gathering. She was restless, suspicious, anxious to talk; telephone messages from India reported Maneka Gandhi's preparations to leave the house. Reports of packed suitcases being sent out of 1, Safdarjung Road, were communicated to Indira and there were whispers that Maneka had decided to take a stand and defy her mother-in-law. As a first step in the confrontation she had decided to address a rally called by Congress dissidents at Lucknow. Indira fumed. The news from India disturbed her greatly. She was concerned about Rajiv Gandhi's safety. She spoke to me of plots and intrigues and Maneka's ambitions. Her entourage was encouraging her in her suspicions, adding gossip and snippets of news to an already suspicious mind. I found it impossible to reach her inwardly and was apprehensive of what would occur on her arrival in Delhi.

She returned to India girded for battle, and discovered that Maneka had been away in Lucknow. It was the day of the Rajya Sabha elections. However, by the time Indira returned home, Maneka was back at 1, Safdarjung Road with her two-year-old son Varun, after having taken part in the rally at Lucknow. An astute Maneka, aware of her mother-in-law's likely reactions, had prepared the stage and the situation. Indira, despite her supreme political skills, fell, into the trap. The rectitude and calm Indira had cultivated through many years deserted her. She was like one possessed and lost control of herself. Various versions of what took place are reported. Maneka claimed that her telephone was disconnected, her mother and brother not allowed to enter the house and efforts made to keep her son Varun away from her. A furious Indira, her latent Brahmanic pride surfacing, wrote a very unwise letter to her daughter-in-law, accusing her of rudeness and impertinence from the time of her marriage. She made an unfortunate reference to the difference in their background and culture, suggesting that Maneka was intriguing against the family and ordering her to leave the home and return to her mother unless she was prepared to behave in the future. A defiant Maneka, vehemently denied all the charges against her and voiced her outrage against her mother-in-law for having written the letter for posterity and the press.

In a letter to Indira Gandhi, published in the *Indian Express* on 31 March 1982, Maneka wrote:

> As soon as Sanjay died you started literally torturing me in every conceivable way. I have borne it for a long time because of Sanjay and because I am your bahu. If I had wanted to be against you, I would not have fought so bitterly for you in the Janata years—a fact you seem to have conveniently forgotten—when the rest of your family

was packed and ready to go abroad. I repeat what I have said earlier—I am not political and have no wish to be—but please let me live my life decently without shouting and abusing me all the time. Today you have ordered me to leave the house in front of two witnesses, insulted me in front of the servants, ordered my luggage searched, confiscated my son and told me I cannot take him, abused me in public, called my family names and sacked my servants. For what? I went to the convention as a guest. I spoke and will always speak for you—the rest is upto you.

As the confrontation continued, other voices were raised. A particularly unseemly episode was reported to have taken place between Maneka's sister, Ambika, and Indira Gandhi.

Dr P.C. Alexander, the Prime Minister's Principal Secretary, was called in when tensions were at their peak. 'I had never seen her so distraught, so worried, so anxious, so tense as on that evening. Her face was anguished. The possibility of a separation from baby Varun brought into focus the sorrows and tribulations she had faced throughout her life. The death of her son lingered as a raw wound; the thought of separation from her grandson broke her. Alexander felt helpless. He said, 'Madam, you have faced so many crises during life, you have faced such political turmoil, the death of your son. Why should you feel so upset?' She replied, 'Alexander, this girl wants to take Varun away from me. You know my relationship to Sanjay's son. He is my grandson. He is being taken away.'[1]

On the night of 29 March, Maneka left the house with her son and her maid. She had decided not to return to her mother, but took a room at a guest-house in Golf Links. The next morning, the press, kept closely informed by Maneka, had a field day. Arun Shourie, then editor of the *Indian Express,* one of Indira's most vocal critics, wrote a four-column article on what he called the Prime Minister's efforts at swatting a bee with an axe. Indira was bruised and knew it.[2]

I could see that Indira was very depressed when I returned to Delhi. 'You know Maneka and Varun have left the house.' I said I knew and was sorry. Suddenly she turned to me and said, 'My earliest memories—I must have been a baby—were of my thinking "Why am I here?" and a feeling of bewilderment. And lately I have started to feel that I have been here long enough.' Was this a cry of a desperate grandmother or had she drawn the reference from the Puranic legends where a semi-divine spirit in heaven, because of the anger and curse of a sage, is banished to be born on the earth?

For a time Indira withdrew. She had been wounded and found it difficult to reconcile herself to separation from Varun. Once again Indira found her way to her inner resources to renew herself. There was a sudden remarkable recovery, her poise was back, so was her determination.

She was concerned that at the end of the Festival in England, the presence of India would end; many projects were suggested and discussed. While in England I had met the senior representatives of the National Trust in London and discussed the possibilities of establishing an all-India society concerned with heritage and its preservation. Apart from the Archaeological Society of India, which had its hands full protecting ancient sites, there was no major all-India body to concern itself with identifying, listing and conserving manmade and natural heritage. Indira was enthused with the suggestion. In spite of all manner of obstacles, the Indian National Trust for Art and Cultural Heritage (INTACH) was registered in early 1984 with Indira Gandhi as its patron, Rajiv its first Chairman. The first project of the new Trust was the cleaning of the Ganga as it entered Varanasi at Assighat to the point where it departed from the city at Rajghat.

SIX

Indira Gandhi's official visit to the United States was due in late July 1982, eleven years after she had last visited. In her interview to the American press, she spoke of her earnest wish to reveal to the American people the reality of India—'that it is a country of enormous problems. That it is a country committed to democracy, to peace and non-alignment. It is equally important,' she said, 'for my country to understand US policies.' Questioned by the media on India's dependence on the Soviets brought an immediate reply reiterating India's fierce independence. 'I still belong to a generation whose whole life was spent fighting for freedom. I cannot conceive India shadowed by another power.' The woman whom Henry Kissinger had described to Richard Nixon as 'cold-blooded and tough' was anxious to reveal to the American government and people another face.

She was anxious to make new friends in the United States, to contact young minds at the frontiers. 'I must meet non-governmental people. How, when and where, and above all who?'[1] The Emergency had broken close relationships; eager to meet her old friends she renewed her friendship with Dorothy Norman. They visited the theatre together, saw *Amadeus* and rekindled their old friendship.

I was to receive an ecstatic letter from Dorothy describing the ease with which Indira and she had come together; all conflicts were erased.

Indira Gandhi's first visit on this US trip was to the Metropolitan Museum of Arts in New York where she met the major cultural figures of the city. She spoke to them of the possibility of a Festival of India in the United States and of the tremendous success of the Festival in the United Kingdom. There was need, she said, of a new atmosphere 'that would create bridges of understanding and friendship amongst ordinary citizens.'

There was a warmth in her meetings with President Ronald Reagan, but it was difficult for her to dialogue or communicate with him. With all the goodwill present, their one-to-one meeting lasted barely fifteen minutes. She was to comment on her return to India that she found the President unable to concentrate in depth on issues of vital importance: the nuclear danger and the urgent need for disarmament. The President's attention span was limited and, when anything serious arose, he would switch the conversation to inconsequential matters.

It was soon clear that, with all the warmth and friendship generated by her visit, the State Department's attitude to the sub-continent would hardly change. Their tilt towards Pakistan would continue.

Her meetings with the press were tough, they were relentless in their questions on India's attitude to Afghanistan, but the questions were without malice, the atmosphere warm and friendly. She was skilful in her replies, conciliatory in her approach, but refused to equate the Soviet presence in Afghanistan with the US presence in Vietnam. It was clear to newspapermen that Indira was no country's stooge. Asked, 'Does India tilt?' 'Which way?', she responded, 'I think we stand upright.'

Before she left the United States, in her official communique, it was announced that the US would host a year-long Festival of India in the United States in the summer of 1985. It had been a cordial visit. She had been at her most radiant, the President very friendly, but underneath it all Indira was gravely troubled.

Indira's visit to the United States was followed in September by a visit to the Soviet Union. Leonid Brezhnev was in the years of his physical decline, a very sick man. Indira found it difficult to keep up a meaningful conversation with him. To Andrei Gromyko, she spoke of the clouds that hung over the globe and of issues which were dividing people from people, of nuclear warheads which, she felt, were sown like dragon's teeth over vast stretches. She spoke of South Africa where the Pretoria regime flaunted its arrogance, of West Asia where the Palestinians suffered and wandered homeless as a result of Israel's continued aggression. She was aware that her words would anger the United States but she was determined to reflect what she considered the independent voice of India.

It was in August, in the middle of the monsoons, that I met Indira on her return from her trip abroad. She was in her study, had shut off her air-conditioners and opened the windows to let in her garden of verdant green foliage, each leaf iridescent with falling rain.

For a while she spoke of her meetings with President Reagan and Prime Minister Brezhnev. The future of the human race was in the hands of two old men, frozen in their positions, without the flexibility of mind and courage necessary to cast aside their rigidity, to keep the doors open and enter into dialogue.

Indira was deeply troubled. Her eye had started to twitch and I could see that there was a much deeper depression within her. I asked her whether she was troubled about something.

'For the last month,' she said, 'I have not slept. I feel a great uneasiness, a sense of foreboding between two and three in the morning. Night after night I dream of a venomous old woman, full of hatred, reaching out to destroy me. I lie paralysed, unable to move. But a beautiful human being with a beard protects me and will not let the old woman near.'

'Can you go back to sleep?' I asked.

'The moment I close my eyes, the woman is there. I have been receiving secret reports of tantric rituals and black magic rites being performed to destroy me and my sanity.'

I let her speak, did not interrupt. When she was quiet, I went and sat next to her.

'Over the years you have suffered great sorrow. From your childhood you have pushed all your hurts, your angers, your sorrows into crevices within you, covering them over, never letting them come into the open. Can the surfacing of these dark presences be mindborn, moving out from within to return in the form of dream and dread?'

'Do you accept that there are malignant forces that can be released through tantric rites?'

'Possibly. Even if true, why do you react? You only strengthen these dark forces.'

'Do I disregard all the reports I receive every day? What do I do?' There was a touch of desperation in her voice.

'All that has happened has made you very vulnerable. Is it possible for you to be so alert, so aware, that the awareness builds an impregnable wall which no evil intention can penetrate? Can your ear be so open to intimations, even of evil, without letting them touch you or leave a scar? Then evil loses power, for there is no energy of reaction to sustain it.'

I quoted J. Krishnamurti: 'Can you watch fear as a cat watches a hole in which a mouse has taken refuge?'

I came away from 1, Safdarjung Road, with a sense of helplessness.[2]

Krishnamurti's annual visit to Delhi in November 1982 provided an opportunity for Indira to speak to him of her terrors and the stories of plots and black magic rituals that were being performed against her. He listened and asked her to sit quietly with him and let silence pervade her.

A few days later they met again at her home. He found that the atmosphere within the house had grown quiet. I was present at the meeting when she told him that the uneasiness she felt at night had disappeared and that she was sleeping soundly. She no longer dreamt of evil beings attempting to destroy her. She felt a quietness within her.[3]

Indira's inner enquiry that had been dormant for years was awake and she wrote to Krishnamurti, while he was in Madras, on the nature of Truth and Reality. He wrote back immediately. I do not know whether the correspondence continued, but the dreadful fears that had invaded Indira in the autumn of 1982 do not appear to have threatened her again.

In my view, it is about this time that she wrote what was to be called her last will, found amongst her papers after her death:

> I have never felt less like dying and that calm and peace of mind is what prompts me to write what is in the nature of a will.

> If I die a violent death as some fear and a few are plotting, I know the violence will be in the thought and the action of the assassin, not in my dying—for no hate is dark enough to overshadow the extent of my love for my people and my country; no force is strong enough to divert me from my purpose and my endeavour to take this country forward.

> A poet has written of his love "How can I feel humble with the wealth of you beside me!" I can say the same of India. I cannot understand how anyone can be an Indian and not be proud—the richness and infinite variety of our composite heritage, the magnificence of the people's spirit, equal to any burden or disaster, firm

in their faith, gay spontaneously even in poverty and hardship.[4]

*

In November 1982 Indira's attention turned to Shakti, the primordial female principle as energy, which creates, sustains and destroys. In our meetings we spoke of the earliest manifestations of sacral energy as symbol and icon.

The further you push back the frontiers of pre-history, the further recedes the presence of the sacral feminine, with her links to nature, to the earth, to the elements, to forest shrub and seed, to water, to air and sound.

In its earliest form this elemental energy appears as hieroglyph— the triangle and the circle. With the entry of sound as the *Bij Akshara* (the seed form) into the heart of the hieroglyph, there is a quickening and a capacity for transformation. She moves to enter the plant world and her body is now formed of leaves and buds; her abode shifts to trees; she is potent with the power to transform, to heal and to protect. She next enters the animal world, to manifest with a human body, but with the head of a tiger, a wolf, a bird or a serpent. Finally, she arises in human form and now she draws into herself all her previous incarnations. Her hieroglyph she places over her heart or on her generative organs; the plants she holds in her two hands, the animals become her vehicle. And now as a composite of plant, animal and human, she is supreme, incandescent with power and mystery, for she holds all forms of creation within her.

During our discussions Indira had asked me whether I had heard the *Sapta Sati* (the song in glory of the Goddess) chanted. I had not. 'It is like thunder; it fills the ears, the heart; it pervades.'

The discussions on Shakti must have lingered, for, in December 1982, while on a visit to Agartala in Tripura, Indira Gandhi had what she referred to as a rather extraordinary experience.

> You know how much I prefer the small primitive temples to the rather ostentatious and more commercialised ones. This afternoon the Maharani took me to Tripu Sundari in her constituency in Udaipur. I went reluctantly as I wasn't

sure what she was up to. As I entered (the temple), I felt a close affinity, as if I were with a living person, an old friend. I wanted to sit and talk! But, of course, there were the priest and the Maharani, Maharaja and Rajendra Bajpai and we had only a few moments to spare. But the presence of these others didn't bother me or affect the atmosphere. I felt like telling this to you.

PS. In flight to Vishakapatnam—23-12-82:

I got a strong allergy during the night. Is it superstitious to think that it had something to do with the visit?[5]

SEVEN

There was a restlessness in the villages and cities of India. Strong winds of change were sweeping the country. A changing landscape bore witness to the pressures generated by the burgeoning population and its impact on land, forests, water and employment. An awareness of the potency of the vote and the access to political power had released divisive forces in the countryside. New power groups based on caste in rural communities, were flexing their muscles, the son-of-the-soil theory gaining ascendancy. Divisions based on language, custom, religion, caste were tearing the country apart. The immense contradictions present in the country were surfacing. A growing religious fundamentalism had strengthened the communal divide. Violence was on the increase. Barbarism had revealed its ravaged face.

The generation born after freedom was coming of age, free of the burdens of the past, of memories of the freedom struggle. There was a fresh churning of the cultural mind of India. Writers, artists, dancers, film-makers, theatre people were seeking clues to India's ancient civilization. They were also awake to the pulse beat of the new. Film stars had evolved their own lexicon, new icons and myths were in the making. An exodus of the poor from rural societies to burgeoning city slums, and achieving a certain level of affluence had created tensions in village and city. Women were awakening to their potential and hesitantly seeking their own measure. They were finding their way into new professions, emerging as politicians, doctors, social scientists and communicators.

The Eighties saw the rise of a new middle-class and with it, inevitably, a growing consumerism. Transistor, radio and television had become status symbols. The noise of loudspeakers and a growing vulgarity and ostentation was visible in festivals and marriage ceremonies, replacing an old world of restraint and dignity. A material culture could result only in material sensibilities. And yet from within this culture, a few young people were breaking through to seek alternatives; the germ of a hesitant, listening, probing, creative mind, added a new dimension to an otherwise arid landscape.

Instinctively Indira Gandhi was aware of the nature of these vast movements. Indira's presence, her stamina, her strength, her refusal to get caught in the battle of caste and religion, her unflinching stand on secularism, her genuine concern for the poor and depressed—the tribal and the landless, and a living contact and support for the cultural scene, acted as a centrifugal force. She was not prepared to accept fragmentation. She endeavoured to hold the country together however powerful the forces that confronted her. But Indira was restless and deeply worried. How long could these vast contradictions continue to co-exist in India? She saw herself as Sisyphus constantly toiling.

She wrote to J. Krishnamurti:

This is a depressing time. Has the world come to dead end?

More and more poeple are realising what is wrong and what can be done. Yet we drift in the opposite direction. A handful of people have the power to affect the lives of all other millions who inhabit this earth. The few are wrapped up in themselves and what they consider their immediate interests in terms of place and time, and the many are willing to be pushed along in the illusion that they are free and guiding their own lives. The world needs your spirit of compassion and direction to look within themselves and the courage to act accordingly.[1]

The State Assembly elections for Andhra Pradesh and Karnataka were due in January 1983. They were the first major elections to be held after Indira's sweeping victory in 1980. The results would have a significant effect on the Indian political scene and would determine to some extent the Parliamentary elections due in 1985. Both the States were Congress (I)'s strongholds. They had voted for her party from the time of their inception. Not a trace of anxiety shadowed Indira's mind as she asked her son, Rajiv Gandhi, elected to the Lok Sabha in May 1981, and Arun Nehru, a distant cousin and a member of the Lower House of Parliament, to take charge of the election strategy in these two Congress-dominated States. 'They will make mistakes, they will learn. Why are we so afraid of making mistakes?' she told a friend.

With the death of Sanjay Gandhi, the uncanny sense of timing political action, an instinct that enabled Indira to act with precision and power, had diminished. She was a woman who, in the past, would listen intently to her advisers and political comrades, but acted on her own instinct; an intuitive skill had enabled her to feel into a political situation and plan her electoral strategy with a formidable strength. Her opponents over the years had learnt to fear her. Her decision to entrust the elections to inexperienced young men, instead of mature, seasoned politicians of the states who knew the divisions based on caste, religion and local politics; to permit them to choose the candidates, to determine the strength of the Opposition, perhaps indicated that Indira did not consider the challenge of these elections sufficiently grave. In place of an aggressive, down-to-earth campaign with an understanding of local factors of heritage, caste, creed, dominant life patterns and ground level problems, as also an understanding of the psyche of women and the under-privileged, Rajiv Gandhi and his comrades introduced into the Congress culture a new style of functioning where maprooms were set up to determine 'very safe, safe, borderline and unsafe constituencies' and a high rhetoric replaced ground realities. Rajiv's former career was that of a pilot with Indian Airlines and Arun Nehru's that of a President of a medium-size industrial house, Jenson and Nicholson. They had little expertise, skill or instinct appropriate to the electoral battlefield. Prem Bhatia, senior editor and diplomat, in one of his columns, was to remark of them in another context: 'They were political illiterates who imagined that power is mathematics, computers or word-processors, qualities that counted little in the battle ahead.'

In Andhra Pradesh the Congress (I) came face to face with N.T. Rama Rao (popularly known as NTR), a film-actor-turned-politician, who, during his years as a film-actor, established for himself a formidable presence. In thirty-three years he acted in 300 films, playing the role of gods and divine sages, of heroes and wise men, potent symbols in a South Indian State where sixty per cent of the rural population were devotees of the cinema. When N.T. Rama Rao first appeared on the political scene, Indira Gandhi refused to view his emergence as a threat and referred to the phenomenon as a political joke. But during the last year, Rama Rao had organized a strong regional party, named it Telugu Desam, the party born of the

Telugu people. He saw himself as a warrior on the battlefield, a son of the soil, protecting a three-thousand-year-old heritage in danger of being destroyed by the rulers from North India. His claim was that the Central Government had taken Andhra for granted, had humiliated its leaders; he particularly referred to Rajiv Gandhi's public rebuke of Chief Minister T. Anjiah in the previous year. Huge cutouts of the actor-politician dressed in dazzling robes worn by the gods and garlanded with coloured electric bulbs were erected all over the State; from one upraised hand a cornucopia of grain fell to the earth, to be recycled back, from the other yards and yards of cloth swept the ground around him. Food and cloth were his promises to the people of the State. Large cutouts of Indira Gandhi appeared to counter-balance N.T. Rama Rao. Indira appeared in the role of a mother claiming the allegiance of her children, while cutouts of a smiling Rajiv under the caption "Hope of the Nation" appeared in many places. In the tumult of electioneering few people noticed that the women of rural Andhra secretly left flower offerings and lit oil lamps before N.T. Rama Rao's portraits. However much they loved Arama (Indira), Anna or elder brother (NTR) was their hero, born to guide them to their new destiny.

For the Congress (I), the Karnataka elections were never in doubt; the electioneering was low-key.

Prime Minister Indira Gandhi, on the eve of her election campaign in Andhra and Karnataka, had delivered the Besant lecture at the Theosophical Society in Adyar, Madras, and had spoken on values. Later, she had lunched with J. Krishnamurti and spent time in serious dialogue with him. From discussions on truth, self- knowledge and the nature of religion, to switch to the ethos of political campaigning proved a disaster. Indira as usual travelled from district to district in the two States of Andhra Pradesh and Karnataka, appearing before vast crowds, appealing to them to vote for her party.

When the election results were declared, to the bewilderment and horror of the Congress (I), they had lost in both states. They found that unknown to them a whirlwind had swept them away in Andhra, while in Karnataka they lost by a narrow margin. The elders of the Congress party blamed the young leadership and their computer strategies for the debacle and launched a campaign against Rajiv. Indira was furious. Maneka Gandhi out in the cold made snide remarks about her brother-in-law's political innocence and lack of those qualities that make for political leadership. An incensed Indira lashed back: 'The marriage of Maneka with Sanjay was the result of a conspiracy of certain forces who wanted to infiltrate into my home.'[2]

Reacting to a feeling that Indira Gandhi after Sanjay's death was losing her fabled capacity to win elections, her credibility in question, she told the Congress in Delhi, 'Let it be clear to all that Indira Gandhi has never been overpowered by grief. I was born in a family in which one's sense of duty has always superseded one's sentiment for the kin.' Within herself a new question had arisen: 'Was she losing dexterity?'

In December 1982, a scurrilous campaign was launched against Maneka and her mother by people around the Prime Minister, with the result that Maneka stopped sending Feroze Varun to visit his grandmother, the Prime Minister.

In a letter to Krishnamurti, Indira expressed her anguish:

> These days I am worried about the situation.
>
> Winning and losing are part of democracy and one takes them in one's stride. But in India there is a bitterness and vindictiveness.
>
> Like a shallow stream, people overflow or dry up. The defeat in the South has given courage to all forces who are narrow, divisive and destructive. The West and especially the USA seems determined to destabilize our sub-continent. They are fully supporting Zia, not realising his precarious and unpopular position within Pakistan. British commentators have also started writing about the "basic" instability and disunity of India. Within our country, I do not get sincere support from our own party and I am attacked on every side by all other parties, most of whom have not taken the trouble to analyse problems and international pressures. Even thinking people who may sympathise do not speak up. So only a one-sided picture is projected to the public.
>
> How will India hold together?
>
> How could we convince the USA that we are not at all

against them and that our friendship can have value only
if we are strong and stable in ourselves. The US Administration does not seem to have learnt anything from
their experience with the countries which blindly accepted
their guidance.

I am sorry to burden you with some of my troubles.[3]

The elections to the Assam Assembly were scheduled for
February The State was in ferment; grim warnings had reached Indira
from her Intelligence officers, of an undercurrent of seething violence
in the State. In a dark and bitter mood, shattered by her defeat in
Andhra Pradesh and Karnataka, deeply wounded at her inability to
see her grandson, Indira, as if driven by the furies, refused to accept
the advice of her Intelligence officers as well as her colleagues and
insisted that elections in Assam be held in February 1983. The
leadership in Assam refused to co-operate in the election process
unless electoral rolls were revised to exclude those refugees from as
far back as the Fifties and Sixties who had fled Bangladesh and spent
generations in building a new life in Assam. The cut-off date was
disputed between the Assam leadership and the Centre. The State
was sharply divided, the indigenous Assamese people of the lowlands
and the Luhang tribals were anti-election, while the Muslim and
Hindu refugees and Bodo tribals favoured the holding of elections.
A fierce confrontation was inevitable. The polls commenced on 14
February. The Assam leadership refused to take part and the Congress, with no opposition to fight, won the elections with ease.
Violence erupted on an unprecedented scale. It was a triangular
war—the Assamese peasants massacred the Muslims and the tribals,
the Bodo tribals killed the Muslims and Assamese peasants, the
Muslims struck back in revenge. This culminated in a massacre of
unprecedented proportions on 18 February, the last day of polling, at
the village of Nellie, where over a thousand women and children were
hacked to death by Luhang tribals. The men of Nellie village were
absent, they too were on a raid to kill Assamese in settlements across
the river. It took ten days for the news from this inland village to reach
Delhi. Indira flew immediately to Assam and listened grim-faced
when the survivors from Nellie pointed to the few silent, desolate huts
that still remained standing. The stench of corruption and death was

everywhere. Mobs of tribal people armed with spears, *daos,* crying *Jai Ai Ahom* which means "Long Live Mother Assam", had surrounded the village and hacked to death mothers clutching babies to their breasts, little girls and boys. The survivors spoke of an entire generation being destroyed so that no new births could take place. The total absence of children's cries, which is part of the rhythm of a village settlement, devastated Indira. A darkness overtook her. She thought she would faint, had to hold herself together and blank out her mind as she heard fathers and the few women mourners. Indira issued orders for immediate relief measures.

Indira returned to Delhi and, with that ruthless capacity that was part of her personality, cut away the horrors of Nellie, and turned to her new agenda, to host the Non-Aligned meet on 7 March 1983. The agenda was finalized, Vigyan Bhavan, where the meeting was to be held, was redecorated, hotels spruced up and entertainment—banquets, music and dance performances—arranged.

Indira was elected Chairman of the Non-Aligned Movement (NAM) and took over from former Chairman Fidel Castro of Cuba. The NAM had, in the last decade, lost its vigour and its solidarity; a sharp cleavage in ideologies amongst member-nations was further accentuated by the role of the two superpowers exercising their influence. Indira realized that, if NAM were to exert any influence on the international situation, unity was essential. With extraordinary skill she steered clear of all ideological divides and brought the membership together on a commonality of interests.

In her speeches in NAM and in her meetings with Heads of State, she emphasized that the Non-Aligned Movement could gain strength only if they stood together and spoke with one voice. Once again in her opening and closing address she spoke of the dangers of a confrontation between great powers and the annihilation of the human species through the use of nuclear weapons and the clear moral obligation of those who possessed these weapons to ensure that they were never used. She reiterated NAM's call for a new international economic order and the launching of global negotiations. She reaffirmed her solidarity with liberation movements and opposition to all forms of interference and intervention.

For her the NAM was not a mere or casual collection of individual states, it was a vital historical process, a commingling of many historical, spiritual and cultural streams; an expression of the aspirations of the long-deprived and the newly free. 'It is an assertion of humankind's will to survive despite oppression, despite the growing arms race and ideological division.'[4]

She wrote to Dr Erna Sailer, a friend and former Austrian Ambassador to India on 13 March 1983:

> The conference of the Non-Aligned was indeed a success. From the beginning, the atmosphere was of utmost friendship and co-operation. Perhaps I have an advantage as many of the leaders of the developing countries regard me more as a sister than a Prime Minister or Head of Government. Everyone was most helpful. We had a spot of bother over Iran and Iraq, but finally some words which I suggested for our statement on this issue were accepted by both. Almost every day the meeting lasted till 3 or 4 a.m. and I usually had to be back in the Hall by 8.45 a.m.; but it was not at all tiring.[5]

On 8 June 1983, Indira delivered the Raul Prebisch lecture at Belgrade. Her theme was peace and development. 'On this small planet of ours, there is no room for permanent enmities and irreversible alienations. We have to live side by side.' She quoted Buckminster Fuller, 'Either war is obsolete or man is.'

Her theme remained constant—the inter-relation of security, development and environment—nuclear and chemical weaponry was genocidal and ecocidal.

She further said:

> I am a soul in agony. As one who feels passionately about freedom, I cannot but be alarmed at the continuing, pushing domination, the new methods and forms of colonialism. This is all the more pernicious because it is less obvious and recognizable. I am asked if non-violence will work in today's world. Nothing ever works ideally. Non-violence is neither cowardice nor resignation. On the contrary, an unarmed crusader needs far more determination, discipline and daring.[6]

Hiren Mukherji, the erudite member of the Marxist Communist Party, had in the past battled against Indira on the floor of the Lok Sabha. Reminiscing on her, five years after her death, he referred to this speech. 'Karl Marx,' he said, 'would have liked her reference to the developing countries as "the step-children of the Industrial Revolution".' He recalled his letter to her in early 1984 when the Punjab problem had reached a boiling point and Indira was moving towards a full-fledged confrontation. Hiren Mukherji wrote to give her a pat on the back for being a good girl. Her reply quoted by Mukherji:

> Thank you also for your "pat on the back" though I wonder if my hand can reach my back in the midst of the present consistent shower of brickbats—people ignore the difficulties of today's world and the great care and determination needed to fight the forces of neo-imperialism, which are fast gaining ground all around us and I am afraid within our country too.

(Feb 9, 1984)[7]

EIGHT

As Chairperson of the Non-Aligned Movement (NAM), Indira Gandhi travelled abroad incessantly during the latter part of 1983. She met leaders of small countries in West Asia and Europe, made her presence felt, absorbed cultures, shared views, made friends, emphasized the important role smaller nations played in determining the future of the world. In her new role, Indira's concerns and responsibilities once again extended beyond the horizons of India: by now Indira had emerged in the comity of nations as one of its undisputed leaders. This made massive demands on her time and energy. Her body at sixty-five was lithe and trim; her face, as she appeared on the TV screens as Chairman of NAM, addressing the United Nations, was austere, the cheek bones prominent, two silver streaks of hair like frozen flames swung back from her forehead, the effect one of a rare distinction. Her voice was low-key—there were no histrionics. She emphasized the fact that survival did not rest in ideologies, on cultures that were materialistic, whether Capitalist or Marxist. With words that go far beyond the contours of national or international politics, she touched the petals of a perennial wisdom.

> All that begins must end. And the seeds of the ending are present in the beginning.

> We must create a new international order of humanity where power is tempered with compassion, where knowledge and capability are at the service of all humanity.

While she was in New York she visited the Metropolitan Opera to listen to Puccini's "La Bohème"; hosted a dinner where she met intellectuals—the guest list included Wassily Leontief, Nancy Wilson Roos and several other authors and academics; she walked on Fifth Avenue to visit Scribner's where she bought Italo Calvino's *Italian Folk Tales,* Ken Follett's *On the Wings of Eagles* and *Impressions of Italy* by Goethe. During her visit she inaugurated an exhibition of photographs of Jawaharlal Nehru. The images of her father evoked his presence.

It is not easy for me to speak about him. Because he was—any human being is difficult to know—a sensitive and deep human being is even more difficult to know—and being a daughter doesn't help. Of course, to me he was not just a father, he was a teacher, sometimes, a remote teacher since he was in prison.

One of the ways I learnt the most from him was not by what he said or what he did but what he made me do. I was always stretched by what I thought was beyond my capacity. Looking back, what I thought was my parents being rather harsh on me was a boon that helped me a great deal in later life.[1]

*

The Commonwealth Heads of Government Meeting (CHOGM) was hosted by India in New Delhi on 23 November 1983. Queen Elizabeth, II, of Great Britain, as the Head of the Commonwealth, was present along with the Duke of Edinburgh. Indira was aware of the sharp differences of views that existed amongst various members of the Commonwealth. Once again, with immense skill, she kept out the divisive factional confrontations. She spoke of the various trouble-spots in the world; the gathering storm in West Asia, the explosive situation in Lebanon, the Iran-Iraq war, a tense Central America, the fight for independence of the Namibian people.

The Commonwealth brought together a third of the member states of the United Nations. Speaking on the occasion, Indira Gandhi said:

It is a genuinely eclectic grouping of nations, comprising many races, religions and diverse geographical regions. No constitution, act or treaty limits the ambit of its concerns. It is a North-South forum, encompassing a representative range of developing countries and some of the developed. It is also a forum where non-aligned countries meet those who belong to military alliances.

Divergent views were expressed during the closed door meetings. At the concluding session Prime Minister Indira Gandhi appealed for a dialogue in an age of vast changes. 'The inter-relationship between problems and events is not merely more widely recognised but is actually tightening in ways that suck us into their vortex and close our options.'

For people of her generation George Orwell's book *1984* had acquired prophetic meaning.

> We find that big brothers have minds that could intrude into our very lives and do intrude in various ways on the earth and from the skies. Every human institution today is on trial—all of us here carry responsibilities for our people. Many of us are products of freedom struggles for long periods—freedom has come to most of us but it has to be made real for all people, freedom from want for many in our countries and freedom from fear for all continents. The struggle continues.[2]

I remember her aglow with pride at the banquet she hosted at the end of CHOGM. The dinner was perfect; the menu ordered by Indira superb. After dinner Birju Maharaj, India's foremost Kathak dancer, performed with his disciples, Saswati, Durga and Aditi. It was a brilliant occasion as, surrounded by Presidents and Prime Ministers, the Prime Minister of India and Chairperson of NAM rejoiced and received the congratulations of the dignitaries. This was the last great gathering she was to host. India and Indira Gandhi were at the threshold of 1984.

The glow was quick to fade. December found Indira Gandhi full of apprehensions. Punjab was afire. From Kashmir, Assam, and Sri Lanka, voices of a growing unrest reached her. The Opposition and the media demanded strong action. She knew that in the next few months she would be called upon to take some of the hardest decisions of her life.

Indira had not seen her grandson, Feroze Varun, for nearly a year and the sorrow of the reparation ravaged her. She was wounded but retained her stoic demeanour. I commented on her calmness. 'At times the sea has no ripples but deep within are mighty movements,'[3] she replied.

The extent of Indira's despair is expressed in a letter to

J. Krishnamurti dated 26 December:

> I don't know what to write because I am so full of anguish.
> I have the feeling that I have strayed on to an unknown
> planet. Avarice and the desire to dominate have been with
> us since the world began, or rather since the human race
> began, but never on this scale and at such peril. Yet how
> many care for anything but the immediate and they do not
> even try to understand that.

> I had meant only to let you know that I had received your
> message and how much your thoughts mean to me. I'm
> sorry I've rambled on—at the same time there are few
> people to whom one can talk and with you one does not
> need to talk.

> I treasure our brief meetings.[4]

NINE

1984 was ushered in by a visit to India and to Indira Gandhi of Philip Morrison, the physicist from the Massachusetts Institute of Technology (MIT), who carried a message of grave portent.

> Our meeting was on a work-day afternoon at the place and time she met with petitioners in general. A Secretary was present. Above all we were impressed by the intensity and directness with which she listened. She grasped at once what was our concern. Then she told us of the indifference with which Reagan had met her personal appeal on the test-ban issue when she was in New York at a UN session. We felt that she would ponder how best to gain the ends we all shared, and that her experience at the centre of power gave her understanding we could not have.[1]

Later, Morrison sent Indira a paper: "Bystanders at Risk: Will the Paddy Freeze?", in which he referred to the consequences of a nuclear attack:

> . . . .Nuclear strategic attacks would lead to fires on unprecedented scale: whole cities aflame; gas and oil wells, storage tanks, and refineries burning freely; vast fires raging widespread over forest and field. . . .

> The consequences could be apocalyptic: everywhere darkness at noon. The unprecedented quantity of black smoke spread in the winds from many hundreds of simultaneous conflagrations would form a curtain over much of the northern hemisphere in a matter of weeks. The warming rays of the sun by day could not reach the ground, but the infra-red radiation from the surface of the earth could take out the surface heat into space by day and by night.

> The outcome of unrelieved twilight day after day, perhaps

broken now and again by brief spells of clearing, might be sudden winter within a few weeks. It would be a bizarre displaced season, carrying spells of freezing weather even where a winter never comes. By some estimates ice would form south, to the flooded paddy fields near the equator. The open sea holds too much heat to cool so rapidly, and the temperature contrast could drive chains of howling rainstorms, freezing and warm by turns, across the tropical coastlines.

India would be one of the countries gravely imperilled. Powerless to change the scenario, Morrison's words affected Prime Minister Indira Gandhi deeply. She wrote and spoke about the possibility of the nuclear winter to her colleagues and friends. It was her theme at the 71st session of the Indian Science Congress she addressed at Ranchi:

Human survival overshadows all achievements to better human conditions. The nuclear winter would bring an irreversible ecological and genetic change whose nature and limits cannot be predicted—should this accumulating knowledge not disturb us, should we not feel concerned by the perversity of the theory of limited and winnable nuclear war?

Memories of the death of a young son filter through her speech as she quotes from Rupert Brooke: 'Life to be sure is nothing much to lose but young men think it is and we are very young.'

She further said:

We who may or may not be young but are human, cannot but have the same feeling about the continuance of the human race, not as automatons but with a fullness of humanity. The human mind has to be mobilised against the nuclear menace and everything that lessens our humaneness. In this, scientists should recall the spirit of the 1954 Einstein-Russell manifesto which declared:

> We are speaking not as members of this or that nation,
> continent or creed, but as human beings, members of the
> species Man, whose continued existence is in doubt. . . .
> There lies before us, if we choose, continued progress in
> happiness, knowledge and wisdom. Shall we, instead,
> choose death?[2]

She was deeply depressed, felt isolated. By April, as she had
confessed to her father over forty-five years earlier, she was 'filled
with dark moods, as one possessed and all this with disastrous results.'
There was menace in Punjab; communal riots in Maharashtra;
trouble in Sri Lanka; yet it was to Kashmir that she turned her ruthless
eye. Advised by hawks within her circle, she was bent on action. Dr
Farooq Abdullah, warm-hearted, generous but ineffective as Chief
Minister of Kashmir was in trouble. Rumours of plots to destabilize
Kashmir, of the infiltration of spies to spread insurrection in the valley
were conveyed to the Prime Minister. The then Governor of Jammu
and Kashmir was her second cousin B.K. Nehru. The Prime Minister,
in numerous meetings and messages, urged him to act and dismiss the
Farooq Abdullah government. He refused. A battle was waged between these two scions of one family, both tough, both with mighty
egos, both determined not to yield. Finally, Prime Minister Indira
Gandhi used her authority to transfer Nehru as Governor from
Kashmir to Gujarat. He was furious but proceeded to Gujarat.
Jagmohan, then Lieutenant Governor of Delhi, was appointed the
new Governor of Jammu and Kashmir. On 2 July, exactly one month
after Operation Bluestar in Punjab, Governor Jagmohan held a
meeting of the dissident members of the Assembly at three o'clock in
the morning; Dr Farooq Abdullah was woken up at 6.00 a.m. to be
informed that his government had fallen and a new government,
headed by his brother-in-law, G.M. Shah was being installed.

On 15 August 1984, Independence Day, Indira Gandhi addressed
the nation once again from the ramparts of the Red Fort. Her voice
was sombre, she spoke as a leader of the nation and not as the head
of a political party. She warned the country of dangers ahead and
appealed to the nation to remain united.

On the same day as she addressed the country, a grave situation
emerged in Andhra Pradesh. Indira had never forgotten the euphoria

generated by the victory of N.T. Rama Rao against her in early 1983.
N.T. Rama Rao suffered a heart attack in the summer of 1984 and
went abroad for a bypass surgery. In his absence Indira's supporters
sought to overthrow NTR's government. They engineered a revolt
amongst members of the State Legislative Assembly who belonged to
NTR's Telugu Desam party. Large sums of money were rumoured to
have reached some dissidents. As Rama Rao returned home in a
wheel chair, he found, to his dismay, that his government had fallen
and that Governor Ram Lal had dismissed him and called upon
Bhaskar Rao to head a new government. In spite of his frail health,
N.T. Rama Rao refused to accept what he considered an intrigue of
the Central Government. He called together his advisers, marshalled
his followers and widespread demonstrations occurred throughout
Andhra Pradesh. The nation was shocked, the newspapers angry.

The Economist of London indicted Prime Minister Indira Gandhi
in the strongest language. An editorial carried a caricature of the
Indian Prime Minister, depicting her as a long-nosed, dancing goddess, wielding a sword in one hand, the other hand holding a bag of
money.

> Mrs. Gandhi, now in her 15th year as India's Prime Min-
> ister, has always viewed India's opposition as an unneces-
> sary evil. . . . But, with a general election in India only
> months away, even a fragmented opposition evidently
> posed an unacceptable risk. So, like the warrior goddess
> Kali, she set out to smite all centres of opposition power,
> starting in the tiny ex-kingdom of Sikkim, moving on to
> terror-ridden Punjab, and then to the opposition-ruled
> States of Kashmir and Andhra Pradesh.[3]

TEN

The partition of India in 1947 divided Punjab into two States—western Punjab became part of Pakistan and the eastern district remained in India. The population of this new State was fifty-two per cent Sikh and forty-eight Hindu. For over 400 years the culture and lifestyle of the Hindus and the Sikhs in Punjab was so closely interwoven that in many families one son took to the Sikh religion and another to the Hindu; inter-marriages were common. The Hindus worshipped at Sikh gurudwaras and the Sikhs participated in Hindu festivals. Harmony and a capacity for hard work brought Punjab prosperity. 'The minute man's lot improves at all, and they have their eyes opened, then they learn anger. Self-awareness leads to self-assertion, mingled with religion, it's a very explosive mixture—possibly suicidal.'[1] Divisive tendencies surfaced with independence. The Sikhs sought a separate identity.

Indira Gandhi became Prime Minister of India in 1966. Trouble had begun in Punjab from the years of her father's prime ministership but it was she who had decided to divide Punjab into Haryana and Punjab. During Jawaharlal Nehru's prime ministership, the Bhakra dam, a hydro-electric project, which ranked among the major dams in the world, was built as a "temple of free India" to harness the rivers that flow through Punjab. Regarded as one of the best-administered States in the country, Punjab prospered. The Green Revolution was made possible with adequate supplies of water, fertilizers and improved varieties of seed; this transformed the landscape of Punjab. A massive growth of small-scale industries brought wealth and prosperity to the countryside.

In addition to their industriousness, the Sikhs were considered a martial race. Though they formed only two per cent of the population of India, their presence in the armed forces of the country was considerable. They were regarded as a tough, brave, courageous people.

It is rumoured that in 1979, Giani Zail Singh, with the active support of Sanjay Gandhi, decided to meet and abort the challenges of the Akali Dal—a moderate political party allied to the Janata Party and in power in Punjab—by building up an alternate leadership under Jarnail Singh Bhindranwale a thirty-seven-year-old, unknown and insignificant village preacher.

In the vast crowds that had gathered around Indira to hail her victory in 1980, a number of Sikhs with turbaned heads formed part of the rejoicing crowd. The euphoria that swept Indira and the Congress (I) to power in 1980 led to the defeat of the Akali government in Punjab and the Congress (I) won the elections. Giani Zail Singh was appointed Home Minister in the Central Government, and Darbara Singh, Giani Zail Singh's sworn enemy, was elected Chief Minister of Punjab. This arrangement was Sanjay's strategy to hold the balance between the two warring factions. With Sanjay's death the strategy collapsed. Enmity, petty jealousies, intrigues and manoeuvres took over Punjab politics.

Indira had not met Bhindranwale face to face. In her earlier years as Prime Minister,' her uncanny instinct to see into people, would have enabled her to go beyond the outer facade of this tall, bearded preacher, to identify the fierce passions and the seeds of fanaticism that lurked behind his shadowed eyes. He would never agree to be an insignificant pawn, and could not be manipulated to suit the Congress.

By the late autumn of 1980, Indira had to confront the complexities of the new situation in Punjab. The Akalis, deprived of power by the 1980 elections, staked their claim for Chandigarh, a city planned by Le Corbusier as the capital for an undivided Punjab. They now demanded Chandigarh as their exclusive capital. Haryana, the new-born State, claimed in lieu of Chandigarh the Hindi-speaking areas of Abohar and Fazilka. The Akalis were also demanding a major share of the river waters of the Ravi and Beas, to be shared between Punjab, Haryana and Rajasthan.

Bhindranwale was arrested in 1981 for the murder of a senior editor of a vernacular daily, but was released on bail shortly thereafter under direct instructions from the Prime Minister. No reasons for this release are available. At this time, Bhindranwale, surrounded by gun-toting stalwarts, stalked freely through the streets of Delhi and was also seen in Bombay. By 1982, Bhindranwale had broken free of the Congress (I) and had emerged as the voice of the militant protest against Congress rule and a cry for Khalistan, a separate Sikh state, became his battle cry. He was supported in his demand by Sikhs within the country and without—in Canada, the United States, Great Britain, Germany.

In 1982, Giani Zail Singh became the President of India and
P.C. Sethi was appointed Home Minister. The President, the Chief
Minister, the Akalis and the militants under Bhindranwale, pulled in
different directions. Bhindranwale was openly preaching secession.
Vast sums of money and arms entered Punjab and the Golden Temple
from Sikhs who had settled abroad. Negotiations between the Prime
Minister, a weak Home Minister and several other negotiators acting
on behalf of the Prime Minister and the Akalis commenced from 1981.
Between the years 1982 and 1983 contradictory reports exist as to
what took place, but ultimately all the negotiations failed. In April
1983, violence erupted in Punjab. Bomb blasts, murders and looting
became a daily routine. Ultimatums were issued by even the
moderates. Sant Harchand Singh Longowal announced that,

> our patience is getting exhausted. She (Indira) should stop
> playing with fire. This is not Assam. We will die like
> soldiers at the hands of the police—we will tolerate no
> further ruse till she (Indira Gandhi) stops playing *Holi*
> with our blood.[2]

The violence and terror in Punjab continued to escalate at an
alarming pace. Indira Gandhi, a woman capable of swift, unexpected,
ruthless action, hesitated and sought advice from the Opposition,
academics and even involved them in the negotiations with the Akali
leadership. Never in her rule as Prime Minister had she appeared so
vulnerable. It was not that she was afraid for herself, but some instinct,
some insight into the psyche of Punjab made her hold back. Was it an
instant of extended vision, a capacity to see beyond the immediate?
Or did her admiration for the valour of the Punjabi people, their
sturdiness and passion inhibit action? Or is it that she hoped that by
some miracle a solution would be forthcoming?

Prem Bhatia, editor of the *Tribune,* in a front-page editorial wrote: 'The
scope for talks will become even more limited if initiative in the matter is
further delayed. What is needed now is political wisdom and courage.'[3]

*

A.S. Atwal, Deputy Inspector General (DIG) of Police, was shot dead on 25 April 1983 as he came out of the Golden Temple after offering prayers at the shrine. On 5 October 1983, a massacre took place of Hindu bus-passengers who were dragged out of their bus and shot. Their assailants escaped. A red alert was sounded in Delhi and special guards were provided to political leaders and those on the hit-lists of the Punjab terrorists. By now, Bhindranwale along with his followers, had entered the Golden Temple complex and his arrest would only be possible through a direct confrontation between government forces and the terrorists within the shrine. Bhindranwale had emerged as a formidable force; from within the Akal Takht he issued hit-lists and *firmans* (official orders) and gave interviews to the press. He warned Indira Gandhi: Peace and violence are from the same root. We are like a match-stick, that is made of wood and is cold. But when you strike, it flames.'[4]

It was rumoured that police or military action was imminent but Indira continued to hesitate. Highly sophisticated arms hidden under cartons of milk and foodgrains were smuggled into the Golden Temple in 1984. She feared that the Sikhs would feel outraged if the Golden Temple complex was made the target of attack.

Her Intelligence agencies reported a major plot hatched by Sikh non-resident Indians (NRIs) living in Canada, the United States and England, with Bhindranwale to massacre the Hindus in Punjab and drive them out of the State; to instigate Sikh and Hindu riots in the rest of India so that, while the Hindus fled from Punjab, the Sikhs from other parts of India would seek refuge in their Punjab homeland.

By April–May 1984, a number of bodies, including one of a woman mutilated and tortured to death, were discovered in the drains outside the Golden Temple complex. The decision for a major military confrontation was finally taken sometime in May 1984. By this time Prime Minister Indira Gandhi's relationship with President Zail Singh had deteriorated very rapidly.

Dr P.C. Alexander, former Principal Secretary to Indira Gandhi, in a conversation with the author, said: 'Indira Gandhi was convinced that the strategy of the Akalis was to use Bhindranwale for getting their demands accepted. They would tell her that, although they were prepared to accept what she offered, it would be unacceptable to the extremists. She was aware that no solution was possible which would be acceptable to the militant fringe of the agitation, and at the same time take care of the moderate and other communities. She was adamant that the settlement in Punjab should not in any way affect the unity and solidarity of the country. Any suggestion to buy peace by giving in to the demands of the militants was totally unacceptable to her. This is where the break came.'[5]

When Dr Alexander was asked as to who was responsible for the decision to mount Operation Bluestar, in which a strong contingent of military forces surrounded and later entered the Golden Temple on 5 June 1984, he declined to answer. He said, 'I can't talk about that. There is a big secret about it. There are some facts which should come out, but I can only speak about it after I get Rajiv's (who was Prime Minister at the time) permission.'[6] He hinted that the secret he was unable to divulge was directly linked to the breakdown of relations between the President and the Prime Minister.

On the evening of 2 June, Prime Minister Indira Gandhi made a broadcast to the nation. The gravity of her words and the anguish on her face left me with no illusions. She spoke of her heart being heavy with sorrow, each day's tragedies adding to the anguish. Dialogue on Punjab had failed. She told the nation that agitation had passed from leaders who were willing to negotiate into the hands of a few who had scant regard for the unity and the integrity of the country:

> Innocent people, Sikhs and Hindus, have been killed. There is arson, looting and sabotage. Holy shrines have been turned into shelters for criminals and murderers. A systematic campaign is spreading bitterness and hatred between Hindus and Sikhs. And worst of all, the unity and integrity of our motherland is being openly challenged by a few who find refuge in holy shrines. . . .This is not the time for anger. Too much blood has been shed. Violence leads to counter-violence and some misguided Hindus seem to think that this is the heroic way to meet terrorism. There can be nothing more senseless and dangerous than such thoughts and actions. We have to recognise anew our responsibility to the future—a future of which all can be proud.

Towards the end of her speech she appealed to the Akali leaders to call off their threatened agitation and accept the framework of a peaceful settlement which had been offered. 'Let us join together to heal the wounds.' Hearing her on television, I was convinced that the next few days would be tragic for her and for the nation. I decided to cancel an impending visit to Greece and did not leave on the morning of 3 June as planned.

R.K. Dhawan, the Prime Minister's Special Assistant, phoned to say that the Prime Minister wanted to know why I had not gone. I said that after hearing her on television, I realized that great dangers faced the country and I could not leave. Two hours later he telephoned to say that the Prime Minister felt that I should go, she had a letter for the Greek President which she wanted me to give him with her greetings. I told Dhawan I would see the Prime Minister that evening.

Indira was at peace with herself when I saw her. I felt that the critical decision, whatever it was, had been taken and having taken it, she had stepped back, for the future was no longer within her control. I told her that it was impossible for me to go to Greece while the situation in the country was so grave. 'You and the country will go through fire.'

'Everything is under control, Pupul,' she said. 'Go.' She asked me to meet her on the evening of the fifth; she did not mention Punjab but gave me the letter to the President of Greece.

We discussed Greece and my forthcoming visit to Crete on 5 June. She had been to Greece in 1983 and had been deeply moved by the warmth and spontaneity of the people. 'Creativity is alive there and you must have noticed that luminosity of light that is unique to Greece.' We spoke of Greek theatre and its capacity to capture the tragic moment. Later I had dinner with the family. We played word games. There was nothing in her demeanour to indicate any anxiety. It was only later that I came to know that, while she was speaking to me that evening, she already knew that the army, called out on 1 June, had found the Golden Temple a fortress manned by young men with sophisticated weapons; the army's call to the armed personnel within the Temple to surrender, had failed. She was also aware that a vast number of people had gathered spontaneously at the site on hearing the news of the siege of the Temple. They intended to defend the Temple and anything, even civil war, was possible. It was only on the next day, when I reached Rome on my way to Greece, that an official

from the Indian Embassy met me at the airport and informed me that
the troops had entered the Golden Temple.

Andrew Neil, editor of *The Sunday Times,* London, interviewed
Prime Minister Indira Gandhi on the morning of 6 June:

> It was only 8 a.m. but already the temperature was heading
> towards 100°F. Mrs. Gandhi, a small figure in a simple
> green sari, walked among the 1,000-odd people who came
> in orderly groups into the garden. The only security was
> one guard with a rifle at the gate; the phalanx of guards
> which most world leaders now find essential was nowhere
> to be seen. . . .As we spoke, Mrs. Gandhi showed no strain
> or anxiety about what was happening in Amritsar.

> Losing control is not something that happens easily to
> Mrs. Gandhi. This tough little woman has presided over
> a subcontinent of 700 million people—one sixth of
> mankind—for the past 18 years, with a brief interlude
> when she lost the 1977 elections.[7]

Despite Neil's observation, the strain of the last few days had taken
its toll on Indira. She had not slept through the night of 5 June. She spoke
to Andrew Neil of the forces that were attempting to destabilize Punjab,
of outside elements who were creating trouble, and she accused Sikh
extremists of terrorizing the moderates so that no compromise was
possible. It was a disjointed interview. Indira Gandhi meandered, spoke
of fundamentalism still not being a problem in India, but said she was
concerned about regionalism, language, caste and, in some areas,
religion. Questioned on whether she felt powerless to deal with corruption, she referred to the previous government who made allegations
against her and of the smugglers and the corrupt who were arrested by
her, but became heroes overnight when the Janata Party came to power.
Asked when she would hold the elections (which were due in January
1985) she responded, 'You will hear when they are announced.' Andrew
Neil questioned her as to what would happen to India after she was gone.
The Prime Minister replied: 'India has lived a long, long time—thousands
of years—and my 66 years hardly count. India will survive and India will
always find its feet. It has been through tremendous vicissitudes in its long
history and it has come through.'[8]

There was little news in Greece about happenings in India and it was only on my return after a fortnight that I came to know of the battle that had raged for twenty-four hours within the Golden Temple before the troops controlled the situation. The Akali leaders who had taken shelter in Guru Nanak Nivas were rescued, but Bhindranwale and his close associates were found dead in the basement of the Akal Takht, killed in the firing. The casualties were very heavy.

What remains unexplained is that the date of the attack coincided with the martyrdom day of the fifth Guru Arjun Dev. Pilgrims had gathered to participate in the celebrations from all over Punjab. Though attempts were made to provide them safe passage out of the Golden Temple precincts, many were caught in the crossfire and killed.

Immediately after Operation Bluestar, when troops entered and took possession of the Golden Temple and its surrounding areas in Amritsar, it was decided by the senior officers of Indira's government to remove all Sikh guards from amongst those in charge of the Prime Minister's security. But, rather than act on their own, they had forwarded the proposal to the Prime Minister for approval. Indira had refused, said that she was Prime Minister of a secular country and any attempt to exclude the Sikh guards from their positions would only add to their feeling of humiliation and inward hurt. The compromise decision taken to post a non-Sikh with every Sikh officer was for some unknown reason never implemented.

I saw Indira a few days after my return. She had aged. There were lines on her forehead and a supreme gravity in her eyes. She did not wish to speak of Punjab and I asked no questions. We discussed my visit to Delphi, my meeting with the President and Melina Mercouri, who was Cultural Minister of Greece. I told her that the amphitheatre at Delphi—closed for several hundred years—had opened and *Oedipus Rex* performed while I was there. As I was leaving she walked with me to the door and pointed to a lawn beside the house where she intended to plant a grove of *kadam* trees. To her it was a gesture of new life.

On 2 July Indira wrote to Dr Erna Sailer:

> Actually the danger (to India) is far from over. I think we
> have realized only the tip of it. The tentacles are spread

deep in our society and it will be a difficult and long task to create the realisation of this danger which can only be faced by a united people.

Our action in Amritsar was in no way directed against the Sikh community, the Golden Temple or other Sikh temples, or even against the Akali Dal Party. Our action was purely against those whom we call terrorists, for want of a better word. Different types of people were involved but together they were causing terror and insecurity in the Punjab besides endangering the country's unity and integrity.[9]

Years later Indira would be criticized for Operation Bluestar, yet at the time, the Army operation at the Golden Temple had received support in India from the Opposition, from the media and from the man-in-the-street. Nikhil Chakravartty, a senior journalist, a year later commented:

. . . .The Akali leadership had surrendered to extremists in its camp who were openly clamouring for secession; the sanctum sanctorum of the Sikh community, the Golden Temple at Amritsar, was virtually handed over to the fanatic gang amassing arms with impunity and indulging in terrorism all over Punjab and beyond. No political option was left before the government to deal with this menace, which had no precedent. It was a testimony to Indira Gandhi's courage and commitment to the unity and integrity of the nation that she ordered the launching of Operation Bluestar by which the army smoked out the terrorists from the sacred precincts of the Golden Temple.[10]

ELEVEN

I have attempted to trace as in a river, Indira Gandhi's life from its source; to identify the forces that lurked in her unconscious, that determined and at times distorted her moods and actions. As a river vanishes from view when it enters impenetrable gorges, it becomes arduous to discover its stormy flow, its whirlpools and its waterfalls. So in Indira too, there were periods when dark moods overwhelmed her, she disappeared into herself, became secretive and it was no longer possible to contact her or come close.

In 1979 the threat to Sanjay Gandhi's life and liberty tore Indira apart. Unlike her mother she was never a devotee, could not surrender herself to god or man. Krishna as a divinity played no role in her life. I do not remember an image or icon of this playful god in her room or her house. Indira, advised by her senior colleagues, agreed to perform *Lakshachandi Path,* a ritual where a hundred thousand verses were recited to invoke the primordial power and energy of Chandi, the all encompassing mother. These rituals were held in the Kali temple at Jhansi. The *yagna,* the oblations to fire, and the recitation of the verses were conducted in secret from 1979 to 1983. It was a period when I saw her often, a period when she spoke freely of her problems, but never during our many many meetings and conversations did she reveal her contact with living rituals connected with elemental female energy. While she sought protection and power for her son in the sanctuaries of Chandi, in secret rituals of shamans and tantrics, she was also in contact with J. Krishnamurti, Lakshman-joo, one of the last exponents of Kashmir Shaivism and sought the presence of Anand Mai Ma. This raises imponderable questions. At what impenetrable level of her unconscious did she hold these contradictory, explosive energies? The one, the path of the seer, the way of negation of power, of compassion, of liberation, likened to walking the edge of a sword and the other, the way of Chandi, of primordial female energy, wielding the sword of power. Could these two cosmic forces be held in one consciousness? And yet outwardly, meticulously in word and deed, she trod the secular path, never losing step, refusing to mingle her role of Jawaharlal Nehru's daughter, the inheritor of a rational, scientific temper, her responsibilities as Prime Minister with her own inner necessities.

The rituals to Chandi held at Jhansi ended in 1983. Her contact with Krishnamurti and Lakshmanjoo continued, and as Indira in 1984 turned towards the last year of her life, forces released by the very contradictions within her, built her future and drove her to her inevitable destiny.

*

October in India is a mellow, dulcet month, the skies washed clean by the late monsoon rains, the trees and plants vigorous with young life. It is a season when the first intimations of cold enter and colour the pale morning breeze.

Indira too felt that her days were drawing to a close. This feeling seemed to permeate everything she did that last month of her life. Like a secular pilgrim, she reached out to the four quarters, of the country, travelled to various parts of the Indian subcontinent. The interviews she gave to newspapermen, the insistence with which she sought out people to talk about herself, and her pilgrimage to places sacred to her race, had the quality of a final testament; she was trying to give meaning to her life; telling her people how she wished to be remembered; speaking wise words of warning.

The global crisis was at its peak. Late in December 1983 a South Korean airliner was shot down over Soviet territory. The aircraft had strayed from its route and crossed over sensitive Soviet sites; in spite of repeated ground warnings, the aircraft had given wrong signals and was shot down. The world held its breath as the two superpowers flexed their muscles and war hovered on the horizon. A growing mistrust made every word suspect. On 4 October, at a dinner in honour of the visiting Prime Minister of New Zealand, Robert Muldoon, she had referred to India's efforts to bring the East, West, North and South close. 'The words "developed" and "developing" as currently used, confuse information with wisdom, and accumulation of material goods with happiness. This is as perilous to the future as the equation of military strength with security. True security could only come with understanding, friendship and co-operation amongst nations.'

The same evening, speaking at the Ram Lila grounds on Dussehra day, she stressed the path of courage and pointed out that the major problem that faced the country was the threat to unity from forces of sectionalism, casteism and religious groupings. Her dialogue with the people of India stretched back two generations.

In an interview with Stein Viksveen of *Stavanger Aftenblad* on 6 October 1984 she recalled that long involvement: 'Our family has, in many ways, more problems than other Indian families—miracles are expected of us.' She added a remark about her son: 'I don't know what Rajiv will be doing later, at the moment it is (Congress) party work.' Questioned about her own political future, she disarmed the questioner by her remark: 'I will live and continue in Indian politics as long as I can laugh and smile. The more I work, the more energy I get. Although we from time to time have serious backlashes, we still haven't forgotten to laugh.'[1]

Inaugurating the international conference on the Buddha in Delhi on 10 October, she referred to the war clouds looming high on the horizon and to nuclear weapons that ringed India's oceans and posed a new threat that called for greater vigilance and preparedness; but, she said, ultimately it was the Buddha's teachings that were valid, 'victory only left a trail of sorrow and bred hatred.'

That evening she went to a concert of Japanese religious music. She had felt offended that religious music should be treated as entertainment, and expected to be bored. 'I had a strange experience, I had heard Japanese music . . . some of it I liked, some I didn't understand. So when it began, I thought it was very slow and was going to be terribly boring.' But she lost herself in the music. 'I really went into a state of meditation, and it was quite a shock when it ended, and the people were all applauding. I don't consciously meditate at any time; I don't have a meditation hour. But I do have these kinds of experiences.'[2]

I was entertaining some delegates to the Buddhist conference at my home when Indira unexpectedly joined the party to listen to the scholars' subtle discussions. She came without her usual security staff. That the Prime Minister should be so free of the visible trappings of office, amazed the scholars from South-East Asia. They crowded around her; she listened as they answered her questions as to how the Buddhists were aiming to face the global challenges, the increase of violence, the growth of materialism.

I spent the 12th evening with her. She met me with a transparency.

Her defences were down, all the aridness had disappeared. In the autumn of her life, she was summing up her thoughts. There was a testamentary quality about her words. She appeared to have come to terms with her experiences, with sorrow and esctasy. 'I have felt ecstasy, but I have also known the darkest possible sorrow. One has to live with ecstasy and sorrow because, for me, they do not go away. Either you go under, you lose your mind or you die, but if you want to go on living, you just absorb them as if they are part of you. There has to be freedom to live and learn.'

There was a constant shifting of subject and mood, a flow of thoughts that were not monitored. 'In the last year,' she said, 'when I travel in the countryside, I get a sense of the antiquity of the land and the people but I also sense a new explosive movement. Rural India is awake.'

'The pace has changed, so has the rural sense of time,' I commented.

'One notices it in the environment,' said Indira. 'I feel it is also happening in the rural psyche. I have started to wonder what lies ahead.'

'And yet this change, this churning is creating a future in which we all are inextricably involved. There is a churning which is also creation.'

'Yes. From it emerge both the elixir and the poison.[3] But who will discriminate? There are so many contradictions, so many forces in operation. The Indian capacity to receive and absorb the alien is at an ebb. We copy and imitate.'

'At times I feel that in India the contradictions are so tightly interwoven, so closely inter-connected, that it is difficult to pull out a strand and examine it. It is this tightness of weave that gives strength to the fabric. Is it this that gives stability?'

'Perhaps, but when an ancient country is catapulted into a new technological culture, what happens to the rural mind? Will the world of materialism take it over? In what direction are we moving? Can mystery and sacredness survive? Something from deep within me tells me that India will survive, it must survive with its wisdom intact. It is the responsibility of all of us to see that nothing happens to threaten its survival.'

As the shadows lengthened, I remembered an archaic legend, evidence of the sophistication and depth of the peasant mind. In

Kerala, at certain sanctuaries of Bhadrakali, the female divinity as energy, there is no icon of the mother but a bronze mirror; the work of local craftsmen, shaped in the form of a *yoni,* a woman's generative organ, it replaces the icon in her shrine. The mirror reflects "an image of Herself" and in her reflection is the image of her devotee—turning back the worshipper to journey within.

'Can a symbol as potent as this be erased?' I asked. She was quick to respond. 'Symbols are important but so are living experiences.' She started speaking of a day in her life when she felt an overwhelming surge of joy. It had no cause, but the explosion was of such intensity that she felt the earth would open and swallow her up. The ecstasy had transformed her face, and people commented that she looked radiant. When she felt that she would disappear into the earth, it was not a death wish. She said she had never been afraid of dying at any age. 'I have felt it as a natural process, a part of life. One lives a certain number of years, and then one dies.'

I could see that she was deeply vulnerable and said: 'You have asked me several times to write your biography and I have always refused. Maybe, a time has come when I should write the biography.' 'Yes, yes,' she said, 'we must start tomorrow.' I was hesitant, said I would need some preparation, but there was a definite urgency about her this time. She picked up the phone and asked R.K. Dhawan, her Special Assistant, to arrange a meeting for the morning of 13 October and another meeting for 15 October. As I was leaving, she commented in a very matter-of-fact manner, 'Whatever happens to me—I feel I have paid all my debts.'[4]

I went home to stay awake till late at night thinking of Indira. A woman so closely tuned to the country and its people; so complex, so skilful, so far-seeing, so concerned, so capable of an insightful listening, so moved by beauty; and yet, at times, so primeval, so obsessive, so brittle, even trivial—a woman who refused to be measured, who laid her own ground rules.

I wondered to what extent her childhood and adolescence had moulded her life. Certainly the betrayals, the insecurity and the massive burdens that had been thrust on her, some of which she had taken on herself, had contributed to her incapacity to communicate with ease. It had left her secretive and suspicious; incapable of trusting people fully. At a tender age she had learnt the power of silence; it kept her opponents guessing—while it gave her time.

She was no democrat but she loved her country with passion and tenderness. Like a tigress guarding her cubs, her antennae would awake at the slightest threat. She never ceased to regard herself as a guardian of India and its frontiers.

Her courage was epic. She dared, refused to be intimidated whatever the odds. She made grave mistakes; the intelligentsia never forgave her for the Emergency. In essence they never forgave themselves for their silence and the fear that enveloped them; for their incapacity to act—except for a handful of people—to fight her with the same degree of courage and fearlessness. But if she sinned, 'she sinned bravely.'

As a woman Prime Minister, she had little advantage. At first her colleagues tried to manipulate her, refused to take her seriously, till she had proved her mastery over the political process and defeated them on their own ground. After that they lost contact with her and relationships were broken.

She had a special rapport with artists, authors, poets and philosophers. She could get deeply involved with scientists and was fascinated by their new discoveries; she was like a child when she witnessed man's landing on the moon. This was equally so when she met ecologists and environmentalists. There was passion when she spoke of the degradation of the environment and the need to nurture and conserve.

Her love for the cultures and peoples of tribal India, for the peasant, the artisan, the weaver, her contact with the creative and sensitive elements in the country, gave her strength.

She was open, accessible, and drew energy from them. Her concern for the poor and deprived went far beyond political strategy. She could reach out, touch them and draw them close.

The feudal landlord, the wildly rich, the trading community and the new middle class, brought to the surface her supreme arrogance. She froze in their presence, distanced herself from them. They feared her and waited for an opportunity to strike back.

She was ambivalent about bureaucrats; she respected their experience and intelligence, but was suspicious of their knowledge of government procedures and ways of circumventing them. She also could sense their insidious capacity to block what she felt was the will of the people.

In international affairs she played a major role in giving strength to the non-aligned. Her poise and dignity, her refusal to treat with the great powers, except on terms of equality, gave her and this country a pride and confidence. Her voice was heard with gravity in the international forums of the world. She had one basic concern—to build an India that was free of both blocs—an India that was respected and took its rightful place in the comity of nations.

In the first few years of her prime ministership, Indira could act with courage and defiance and had the driving force to see that her plans took root in the country. The stronger the opposition, the more supple the sinews of her body and the swifter her insights for political action. It was a period when she was at her most creative. The years that followed, the period of the Emergency and her defeat at the polls demanded great resilience in her to survive. Back to power in the Eighties, there was an edge to her mind in spite of her growing age, and a determination to fulfil many unfinished tasks. She was firmly entrenched in the belief that she and the lineage from which she came were the instruments for the transformation of India. No doubts on this score disturbed her mind. In Sanjay Gandhi, Indira had identified the driving force, the person and the energy to act out her vision for the future.

Indira was an Indian mother, passionate, possessive and protective. To Sanjay she gave of her love abundantly. At times, seeing the mother and son together, an image from the archaic past of India came to mind, of the hollow-eyed, long-limbed, narrow-hipped figurine from Mehrgarh (2700 BC) where the primal woman cradles a baby to her breasts; no consort appears, nor does he seem necessary. In an epic age, Indira could have been Gandhari of the *Mahabharata,* for, with her clear, penetrating sight and her capacity to see through people, she turned away her face, chose to be blind, like Gandhari, to the arrogance and wilfulness of her son, and so awakened the lurking furies, those tempestuous Karmic energies that pursued the family and destroyed Sanjay. (Indira Gandhi's assassination and the savage killing of her elder son, Rajiv Gandhi, lay in the years ahead.)

Sanjay's death left Indira shrivelled. It severed an invisible umbilical cord that had bound them close.

She was aware of the divisive forces that were active in the country, the rising expectations, the pressure on land, jobs and environment.

Major movements were taking place in rural India, violence was on the increase. Yet, she hesitated, was ambivalent; every step she took was after long cogitation. When she did act, it often led to disaster. There was an ebb to her extra-sensory perception for political action. I had asked her once in early 1984, when I found her weighed down with her problems, whether, it was not all too much for her. At first she did not respond, but after a while she said: 'There is no way out for me; it is my responsibility.' I wondered what lay ahead.

TWELVE

I went to see Indira Gandhi on 13 and 15 October. I arrived with a tape recorder; now she was not speaking to me alone, but to history. I was to be her ambassador, representing her to an unknown future. She spoke at length of her childhood and her growing up. Towards the end of that morning I asked her what she considered the basic problem of this country. Her response was immediate. 'The basic problem is poverty. If that is solved, nothing else matters.' Again she stressed that in the process of improving the level of living, that special quality which gave the Indian people an inner strength should not be lost. I commented that with development, in most countries, there was an end to serenity. Did she think it would happen to India?

'I don't really know, but we have to try and preserve it. However carefully we try to separate what is really worthwhile and eternal in our values from the many superstitions which have gathered around them, we cannot always succeed. Most people see religion not as a basic philosophy or the essence of life but as the mantras that they may have learnt to utter at a given time. That is why my father spoke up so strongly about the scientific temper and against astrology. People must go back to the very roots, to the source of faith. Our philosophy says that the divine is in each one; there is light and strength in each one of us. We have to find a way of discovering the energy that is within us. I was asked when I went to our nuclear installation in Bombay: "Where do you get your energy from?" I said, "It is nuclear energy. You have it outside and all of us have it inside. You must learn to use what is inside you."'[1]

'What do you feel will give this country sustaining strength?' I asked.

'Perspective, first of all. It looks as though everybody is all the time thinking of the now—what we could get now for ourselves, whether it is the individual or a group or a caste or a religion. This is taking us away from what is good for us even for the present.'[2]

'Any approach to India has to be tentative; people must turn to the roots, to the source for light.'

Towards the end of our meeting Indira started ruminating about the future. She saw two strains: 'There is this strain of confrontation, the build-up of nuclear weapons, the use of space for purposes of confrontation. All this is going on on one side. It has grown enormously in this last year. This poses a threat to all of us. But along with it, I think, a feeling is growing that something else is needed in life. Those in power, and those who have the knowledge, are thinking along the old ruts. They think of a problem in fragments and pieces: "This is my problem", "this is the other country's problem", "this is environment", and "this is industry", whereas all of them are so closely interlinked. If you have the holistic view and you recognise that the whole of humankind is in danger, in trouble or in crisis, then you will realise that it is only by everybody being together that we can solve it.'[3]

Later, when we were alone, we spoke of her marriage to Feroze Gandhi. I asked her 'When you were 16 or 17 years old, didn't you feel the desire to be admired?' 'Pupul, I was so sure that I had nothing in me to be admired.' She then recalled that the first time she had been openly admired was at Shantiniketan, and how she responded in anger, feeling that she was being made fun of. 'Even with Feroze, it was not at all sex. I tried to explain to him that I wanted children and companionship.'

In the Sixties, when Indira was living in her father's house, or even later, stories had circulated in the gossip circles of Delhi, that she had relationships with other men. I myself had heard these stories, some spread by her close relatives. I knew Indira well, saw her frequently and felt that these rumours had no basis in fact. She delighted in being admired, liked to be surrounded by good-looking, witty, intelligent men, but the sexual side of her was underdeveloped. She appeared to confirm this that autumn afternoon.

'A part of the problem is,' she said, 'that I do not behave like a woman. The lack of sex in me partly accounts for this. When I think of how other women behave, I realise that it is a lack of sex and with it a lack of woman's wiles, on which most men base their views of me.'[4]

She did not think she could have married anybody except Feroze, even though they fought "like wildcats" and he had asked her for a divorce. She recalled the occasion—how she had been very upset at the time, had resisted and wept so that her face was swollen. 'Finally I said to Feroze that if "it (divorce) is what you want, all right." He turned and said: "Do you mean to say that you will let me go like that?" Then I lost my temper and said, "This is the limit. I say—we have our differences, but there are the children; all you say is—separation. When I say—all right, you blame me." Feroze was very attached to me, but he listened to what other people said. You know Pupul, I have never carried on with anybody. But they would spread all kinds of stories and Feroze would believe them. I said to him, "How can I ever prove anything? I hardly go out except with my father and you, and when I am touring I always have someone with me."'

I asked her whether Feroze was upset when she came to live with her father. 'It was Feroze's idea. My father asked me to set up his house. I discussed it with Feroze and he said go. But by then he already had an eye on somebody.' After 1950 Feroze was a Member of Parliament and lived in Delhi. The situation seemed to have become more complicated. Feroze had made her feel very possessive. 'He said to me, "Don't strangle me with your love." It was very difficult,' she said, 'to strike a balance in our relationship.'[5]

We were to meet again to continue the oral story of Indira Nehru Gandhi, but no date was fixed.

On the evening of 26 October, I was at the Prime Minister's House with some urgent papers relating to the future of handloom weavers. Indira had taken special interest in their development and this made it easy for me to explain the grave implications of the file that I carried with me. She made some notes on her memo-pad which was always with her, put it aside and turned to me. I could see that she had laid aside all her problems. There was an openness, a mellowness in her as she watched from her study the leaves on the bushes respond to changing light of the setting sun. Suddenly she turned to me to say that she had decided to fly to Srinagar the next morning. Governor Jagmohan was reluctant and unhappy over her visit. He spoke of unrest in Srinagar and of unruly crowds wandering through the city. He was perplexed by her persistence but she was determined to undertake the trip to see Srinagar in autumn when the chinar leaves explode in colour: from a deep vermilion through tones of burnt sienna to pale amber. 'Have you visited the Valley in November?' she asked me. I said yes and suggested that she visit Gandharbal to see the great grove of chinar trees turn autumnal red. She said she wanted to sit under the trees, to drink in the colours, to watch the chinar leaf reach its maturity and drop from its stem. Her two grandchildren, Rahul and Priyanka, with their friend Devyani, were to accompany her. She was to lunch with me a week later, on 3 November, to meet J. Krishnamurti and the Dalai Lama. I asked her whether she remembered the engagement. 'It will be a historic occasion and I look forward to it,' she replied.

She had half-an-hour before her next visitor was due. I was startled to see her eyes awake to intimations, and reach beyond the little room in which we sat. The evening cries of migrating birds from the vast deserts of Siberia came into the room. She too heard the bird cries and a listening delight brought youth to her face; with the birds her mind took wing. She spoke again and again of her visit to Kashmir and her desire to see leaves maturing to full glory.

Observing her over these years I suddenly saw that Indira too had reached a maturity. It had been an infinitely slow process like the ripening of madder dye—a fabric dyed in myrobalan at first appeared drab-hued, but when repeatedly washed and dried in the sun, it ripened, trapping sunlight. At its maturity it was red, not a surface pigment but penetrating warp, thread and woof; a colour which as it faded would undergo a graceful process that retained beauty.

'You remember, Pupul,' she asked me, 'that ancient chinar tree in Bij Bihara? I have just heard that it had died.' She spoke as if she was referring to an old friend.

'Once again,' she said, 'a feeling is arising in me, Why am I here? And now I feel I have been here long enough.' I had rarely seen her in such a mood, her thoughts entangled with death. 'Papu used to love rivers, but I am a daughter of the mountains and my heart is free of care. I have told my sons,'—for an instant she appeared to forget that Sanjay was dead—'that when I die, to scatter my ashes over the Himalayas.' It was a strange remark, strangely made. 'Why do you speak of death?', I asked. 'Isn't it inevitable?', she replied. Just then P.V. Narasimha Rao the then Home Minister (now Prime Minister) came in and I got up to leave.

As I was at the door, I heard her call out my name and I turned. 'Remember what I told you, Pupul. Remember.'[6] She reached Srinagar early next morning, travelled by helicopter from the airport to the Chashma Shahi guest-house, that overlooked the lakes, mountains and the life-giving, green paddy fields.

In the autumn of 1988 I travelled to Srinagar to follow in Indira's footsteps and retrace her day. She saw very few people, attended to no official business, sat on the lawns in the sun, looked at tree and water; watched the earth glow fragrant with falling leaves. The laughter of her grandchildren filled her ears. Later that afternoon she sent a message to Kunti Sahni, a woman she did not know well. She spoke to Kunti of her fruit orchard and the craft workshop she had organized with local women. Kunti had never been asked to meet her before and she could not understand the reason. Later, in the evening, disregarding the advice of the Governor and his aides that she should not visit the city, she had motored down to Dalgate, got down from her car to speak to people who crowded around her. She had always felt safe in crowds, never felt their menace. To her Principal Secretary, Dr P.C. Alexander, she said on her return, 'The people of the valley love me.' That night in Srinagar, she played word games with the children over dinner and slept early.

The next morning at dawn she climbed Shankaracharya, a sacred hill nearby, walked to the top to visit the temple, had breakfast with the children and then left to meet Lakshmanjoo, who had his ashram at the corner of the Nishat gardens. Lakshmanjoo was expecting her.

On my visit to Srinagar in 1988 I too met the sage. To reach his ashram I had to travel along Gupkar Road, the path which Abhinav Gupta[7] travelled with his dancing university in the tenth century, to visit his guru who lived miles along the road at Dachigam—now a game sanctuary. Surrounded by yogis, wise men, musicians and dancers, Abhinav Gupta rested every few miles to discourse and dialogue on tantra, aesthetics, and the nature of the self. The master, surrounded by savants, by beautiful women playing musical instruments, sat in the *vira asana* pose, sipping wine and savouring beauty. 'He plays on his resonating lute with the tips of the quivering fingers of his lotus-like left hand, while his eye-lids trembled in ecstasy.'[8]

Abhinav says: 'If one meditates even for a moment, on one's real nature, that is pure rest; then the heart becomes a great bird and flies into the sky to find a woman to make love to.' The beauty, essence and flavour of the great sage lingered.

As I came to the ashram, I found the gate open and walked in. The place appeared deserted, but some movement in a hut nearby attracted me. The hut was open on all sides and the sage was lying down, but sat up cross-legged immediately he saw me. I had met him several times earlier and I remembered his high cheekbones, his aristocratic face, straight nose, slightly flared nostrils, short cropped hair, com-passionate mouth and young eyes; he was nearly seventy years old. He had grown older since I last met him, but his gaze was still direct, his presence filled the hut.

We spoke together of our earlier meetings. He remembered and smiled. I asked him of Indira's last meeting with him. 'Why do you ask?' he said. I told him I was writing a book on her. He nodded his head. 'She came early in the morning and sat there,' he pointed to a space. 'She spoke of death. She felt that her time was over and death was near.' I asked him if he felt this was so. 'Yes,' he replied. 'I too felt death was very close to her.'

They sat together for some time without speaking. He later pointed to a small building nearby. 'I asked her if she would inaugurate it.' She said, 'I will come if I am alive.' His eyes were limpid as he spoke. 'She had a premonition that her life was coming to an end.'

I asked him whether she had intended to visit the Sharika temple after she left him. He said, 'Yes.' Sharika was the patron Goddess of the Kashmiri Brahmin community of the valley.

Indira had spoken of the shrine to Lakshmanjoo. On an earlier visit to the anchorite, she had shared a *parantha* with a mynah bird. 'The bird sat there,' Lakshmanjoo pointed to the window sill. As we spoke a gust of wind, elemental in its power, swept through the hut. The leaves broke into sound and we into laughter. It was a freak of nature and the wind stopped as suddenly as it had started. As I was leaving, I said, 'Look after yourself.' 'As God wills,' was Lakshmanjoo's response.

On 28 October Indira visited the dargah of Hazrat Sultanu Ar-a-Sin, the tomb of a Sufi saint at the base of Hariparvat. As she came down the steps, she slipped but was unhurt. From there she went as a pilgrim to a sacred place of her ancestors, the temple of Sharika—a vast aniconic stone that rose to the skies. For centuries powdered *sindoor*, a potent orange red, a symbol of energy awake, was applied to the rock to give it awesome power. Indira surrounded by the priests of the temple performed the puja and heard *Chandi Path* chanted; she received fruit as offering and the vermilion *tilak* of the sun as the mark of the Goddess touched her forehead.

She returned to Delhi soon after. Early next morning, on 28 October, she travelled to Bhubaneshwar from where she flew across the State by helicopter to meetings where she was surrounded by crowds of children, women and men. She spoke with them, shared their misfortunes, questioned them on their problems. Her programme was badly planned. The helicopter criss-crossed the State needlessly. On the night of 29 October the Chief Minister brought her a collection of handwoven "tie and dye" saris for her to see. She was known to respond with delight to these masterpieces of the handloom weaver. But when Wajahat Habibullah, one of her aides, knocked at her door, he found her in her dressing-gown, desperately tired. She told him that she was exhausted and could not sleep It was very hot at the last meeting she addressed on 30 October. Seeing the ocean of people before her, sensing their hopes, their concerns, their joys and their sorrows, a moment of prophecy entered her:

> I do not care whether I live or not. I have had a long life and if I am proud of anything it is that I spent the whole of my life in service. I am proud only of this and nothing else. And as long as there is breath in me so long will I continue to serve, and when my life goes I can say that every drop of blood that is in me will give life to India and strengthen it.[9]

And then she was to look into the eyes of the people she had loved so passionately and say to them words that have gone unheeded: 'I hope that our young people, our women, everyone, will think of this and take the responsibility upon their shoulders, and not look up to anyone as a leader. Leaders come and go.'[10]

In that instant she spoke in the fullness of her maturity.

On the morning of 30 October, the day she was in Orissa, the escort jeep that travelled with her grandchildren to school in Delhi met with an accident; a car rushing in from a side lane hit the jeep, no one was hurt but the children's car under orders sped back to the house. Indira was told of this accident in the evening on her return from Orissa. Dr P.C. Alexander, her Principal Secretary, saw her at night. She still wore the red sari in which she had made her speech in Orissa. She looked exhausted. 'She had an obsessive fear of her grandchildren being harmed, either abducted or hurt. From June she had lived with that dreadful thought. She kept on repeating that it was a plot to kidnap the children. Nothing I said could allay her fears.'[11] Alexander was to be away in Bombay the next morning to attend a meeting of the Atomic Energy Commission. Indira decided she would rest the next day, sent for R.K. Dhawan, her Special Assistant, and asked him to cancel her appointment except for her meeting with Peter Ustinov who was to interview her. That night she could not sleep. Sonia Gandhi saw her light on and went into the bathroom to find her looking for some pills. She found them and went back to bed.

*

Indira Gandhi's bedroom and study faced south. The morning of 31 October dawned a fiery gold; it was half-an-hour before light reached and touched her garden. In spite of the earlier fatigue, she performed her *asanas,* bathed and selected a tussar silk sari in tones of muted saffron. She had a sparse breakfast, spent an hour on her official papers; Rahul, her grandson, came in to chat with his grandmother as he normally did before she left for her morning appointments. She was ready by 8.30, but was surprised and a little impatient to learn that her television interview with Peter Ustinov had been postponed to after 9.00 o'clock. R.K. Dhawan came in a little later to say that the team was waiting with the Principal Information Adviser, H.Y. Sharada Prasad, at 1, Akbar Road. She walked through her dining-room and the little ante-room which contained the old maps of India collected by her on her travels, on to the paved path bordered by shrubs and evergreens, passed the champa tree with its last flowers of autumn, towards the gate which separated her residence from her personal office at 1, Akbar Road.

As Indira approached, Sub-Inspector Beant Singh, a Sikh member of her security guard for over nine years, came forward to open the gate. She smiled and folded her hands in greeting, as she saw him lift his hand as if to salute her; but the hand held a revolver and he shot her in the abdomen from a distance of three feet. An instant later Constable Satwant Singh suddenly appeared from the other side of the gate to fire twenty-five bullets with his sten-gun into her body. The time was sixteen minutes past nine. Her security guard and personal staff scattered.

She fell to the ageless earth and with her forehead "touched yonder sky."[12] Her eyes were open. The time was 16 minutes past 9. The telephone rang at my home at a few minutes to 10 and I heard a voice say: "Indira Gandhi has been shot"—a reality difficult to grasp. It was too immediate, too close, too dark to accept. For moments I was disorientated. Seconds later I took control of myself and sought the driver of my car, who was not available, and so it was my nephew, Asit Chandmal, who drove me to the Prime Minister's residence, situated ten houses away from where I lived.

As I approached 1, Safdarjung Road, the Prime Minister's residence, my heart tripped as I saw barriers being erected. A shroud of silence enveloped the house. A few security guards had gathered at the gate and on the pathways within the compound, whispering amongst themselves. They recognised me and let me in. I got out of the car and walked to the opening in the hedge which led to Rajiv and Sonia's rooms. To the other side lay the path Indira, earlier that morning, must have walked to reach the gate of 1, Akbar Road, her private offices, where she was shot.

Before entering the house I asked my nephew to wait, little realizing that I was placing him in imminent danger, for Chandmal's was an unknown face and the security guards were in no mood that morning to see strange faces within the Prime Minister's compound.

It was possibly shortly before this time that the assassins—Beant Singh, a senior security officer who had accompanied Indira on several of her trips abroad, and Satwant Singh, a junior recruit—were arrested. It was reported that immediately after the shooting Beant Singh and Satwant Singh threw down their arms and Beant Singh said: " I have done my duty. It is now for you to do yours." Little is known about what happened subsequently, but, taken to the barracks of the security guards, Beant Singh was shot dead presumably while trying to escape and Satwant Singh was grievously wounded.

In a secret meeting held at the Prime Minister's office a few days after the Blue Star Operation in June, it was decided not to post any Sikh guards at the Prime Minister's house or office. When the top secret file reached the Prime Minister, she had refused it and sent the file back with a query: 'Aren't we secular?' The officers responsible had no answer.

I entered Rajiv's sitting room to find a shattered Nina Singh, wife of Arun Singh, an intimate friend of Sonia's trying to calm the two frightened and hysterical children—Rahul and Priyanka. Seeing me they cried out: 'What has happened to Dadi, Pupulji? Where is she? Where have they taken her?' I had no answer, but I stayed with them for a few minutes and then walked to the room of Dhawan, the Prime Minister's Personal Assistant, to find Sharda Prasad, her Secretary, Information, weeping. 'They have killed her,' he said. 'The security guards have shot her.' He too was in no state to explain what had happened, but arranged for an official car and an outrider to take me to the All India Medical Institute where a shattered Sonia had accompanied the dying Prime Minister. I left Dhawan's room and walked very slowly back to where my nephew stood. By now I was aware of how foolish I had been to leave my nephew alone. I walked with him to the gate, told him what had happened and asked him to go home.

I drove in the official car to the hospital. The news had not spread. The movements on the road were normal. I entered the hospital by a side entrance and was allowed up to the ante room next to the operation theatre, to find Sonia alone. She was in a state of extreme shock. Terrified for her children, memories of the massacre of Mujib and his family including Russel, Mujib's son, a boy of Rahul's age, might have arisen within her. I gave her news of the children. She had started to tremble, could hardly speak and I did not want to ask any questions.

I knew that Rajiv was away in West Bengal. I was later to learn that Dr. P.C. Alexander, Principal Secretary to Indira, along with the Cabinet Secretary, had gone to Bombay to attend a meeting of the Atomic Energy Commission and that the President was on a visit abroad. In the next hour some of Indira Gandhi's close relations and a few friends gathered. Tension was mounting. The extreme gravity of the situation was evident. Senior members of the Cabinet and leaders of the opposition parties could be seen huddled together, talking in whispers. The Vice President of India, R. Venkataraman, was in a conference room on the lower floor with senior officials of the Central Government.

At 2 o'clock the doctors came out of the operation theatre with the news that the Prime Minister was no more. There was an enormous silence. Indira's presence had spread over the land providing strength and stability to her admirers as to her critics, providing solace to the tribal and the poorest peasant.

Sonia was anxious to see her children. She asked me whether I would accompany her home to bring back fresh clothes to dress the Prime Minister. Driving through the streets, one could see that the news of Indira's death had still not reached the city. Everything continued to be normal.

Sonia broke down when she saw her children at 1, Safdarjung Road. They clung to her and asked after their grandmother. We were at the house for an hour. I helped Sonia choose Indira's favourite old rose saree and blouse and a 'Rudraksha Mala'—a gift from Anand Mai Ma. Priyanka and Rahul refused to be left behind and accompanied us back to the hospital. By then the atmosphere on the road had completely changed. Shops were closing down. We could see men with anxious faces hurrying home on their bicycles. Crowds had started to gather and move towards the All India Medical Institute. Its gates had closed and a strong contingent of police were in place.

Rajiv Gandhi, touring in West Bengal with Pranab Mukherjee, had heard the news on BBC. Special arrangements had been made for an Air Force plane to fly him from Calcutta to New Delhi. It was 3.30 before the plane landed and he drove straight to the hospital. Rajiv's close friends from the Doon School years, later to function as his aides, had gathered at the airport and travelled back with him. As he entered the ante room, his tender face was devastated. Sonia was sobbing. His children were desperately afraid. I felt I needed to leave them alone and walked into the passage. Finding a chair, I sat down. I did not know how long I stayed there, but suddenly I found Rajiv and Pranab Mukherjee enter. I rose to go back, but Rajiv beckoned to me and said: 'They want me to agree to be Prime Minister. They say the country will go up in flames if I do not agree.' My reply was that they were right.

President Zail Singh arrived by 5 p.m., having rushed back from his tour abroad, on hearing the news. The relationship between the President and Indira Gandhi was strained; it had deteriorated from the time of the Blue Star Operation and rumours were rampant of the intrigues within the President's residence. It was the President's prerogative to name the new leader and swear him in as Prime Minister. Arun Nehru had gone to the Airport to receive President Zail Singh and drove back with him. During the drive it is rumoured that he made it clear that the President had no potions and that Rajiv Gandhi would be the new Prime Minister.

Rajiv Gandhi was sworn in late in the evening as Prime Minister at a grim and solemn ceremony at Rashtrapati Bhavan. Later that night they brought the former 'Pradhan Mantri's' body home.

Delhi did not sleep that night. The news of the assassination of Indira Gandhi had swept the city and the distant colonies; it had travelled across lands and oceans. As night fell, crowds gathered in narrow crooked lanes.

There was a growling density of hatred and terror that darkened and thickened the night. Blood lust awakened, a deathly essence long suppressed entered the arteries, destroyed oxygen, shrivelled the heart. The hunted took shelter away from the light, seeking long shadows. Women crouched in terror as they peeped from darkened rooms. They heard the baying for blood and saw flames leap from human torches. They closed their shutters, curled into themselves, drew their children close. Some found shelter in neighbours' homes. For others there was nowhere to turn.

I was out of bed before dawn and reached Teen Murti House by 8 a.m., where a side entrance opened on to the room facing the porch where the body of Indira Gandhi lay, her spine shattered, yet straight in death. An unarmed crusader, her battles were over. She would tread an unknown path, listening, watching, running nimbly to her tryst with her ancestors. Would it be the path of the sun or the path of the moon? But Indira Priyadarshini would not be satisfied with the oft trodden path, the grass worn thin by many feet.

A vast crowd had gathered at the locked gates of Teen Murti House. It was a turgid crowd waiting to voice the agony and grief as also its anger. At 9 o'clock the gates opened and, like a deluge, the crowds poured in. Visceral howls of revenge had started: '*Khoon ka badla, khoon se layenge*—Blood has been shed, we seek the vengeance of blood.' Those who sat around the body drew in their breaths. The security guards were uneasy. The odour of hatred and blood polluted the air.

I saw Rajiv come forward and reach out to the shrieking crowd that passed before his mother's shattered body. His face was tender, stricken. The courage of Indira and Jawaharlal flowed through him as he faced the crowd that was drunk and insane. Seeing Rajiv, the cries rose in a crescendo.

For three hours I sat and the shock and terror of yesterday and the savage epiphany of the crowds filled me with horror and unease. My heart tripped and I started to tremble as reality engulfed me. After a few moments I slipped away through a side entrance to find Rajiv in the corridor talking to H.K.L. Bhagat. 'Pupulji,' I could hear Rajiv's voice and turned to him. 'Go and rest,' he said. 'I have asked Bhagatji to go immediately to the colonies across the Jamuna and see that violence does not escalate.' I nodded my head and left the building.

At home my secretary, Jose, was waiting on the doorstep. The telephones had been ringing. People had been calling. Delhi was in flames. They wanted me to do something. I picked up the phone. It was Rami Chabra, a journalist and dedicated family planning activist. She was tense and frightened. 'Gurudwaras are being burnt down. The crowds are dragging Sikhs by their hair out of their homes and making bonfires of them before our eyes. The police are turning away their faces. Law and order has broken down. Do something.'

I hesitated, not knowing what to do. Her voice continued: 'There is chaos everywhere; no one listens.' I asked Jose to take down the locations where the worst arson and bloodshed was taking place. I knew I had to act. Till yesterday I would have telephoned the Prime Minister's personal office and some action would have followed. But today there was nowhere to turn.

I decided to contact Home Minister Narasimha Rao and phoned his office. He was not there, but they asked me to try the P.M.'s house. I phoned and his secretary told me that the Home Minister was with the Prime Minister. I asked to be put through. Narasimha Rao came on the line. I repeated the phone messages, the news of the monstrous rape and killings, the growing arson and looting, the horror of it all. 'Speak to the Prime Minister,' he said and gave the phone to Rajiv. I repeated what I had heard. It was difficult as yet to address Rajiv as the Prime Minister, difficult to comprehend that the power and massive authority wielded by Indira now vested in him. 'Can you come over?' he asked. 'I am sending my car so that you are admitted to the house without any problems.' I went to 1, Safdarjung Road, to the room where the new Prime Minister sat with Narasimha Rao. For a moment I forgot where I was. I spoke of the frenzy and the growing terror, the killings and the brutality.

Rajiv and Narasimha Rao were listening intently. Rajiv seemed helpless, bewildered, He turned to the Home Minister and asked: 'What shall we do?' Narasimha Rao did not respond. Rajiv then turned to me and said: 'What should I do, Pupulji?' By now I was in control of myself and said: 'It is not for me to say what the Prime Minister should do, but let me say what I think your mother would have done. She would have called out the army and seen that law and order was maintained at any cost, that innocent people were not butchered and that looting and arson were brought under control. She would have come on television and with all the prestige, power and strength of the Prime Minister of India and with all the love she had for the people of this country, warned the people that it was right to grieve but not to seek revenge, and that she as the Prime Minister would under no circumstances permit the butchery.'

Rajiv had listened, but I could see that he still sought guidance. He asked me whether I would send him a draft of what I had said. I hesitated. He started a discussion with the Home Minister on the need for calling out the army. The dialogue between them was not my business and so I got up to leave. Rajiv came with me to the door and repeated his request for the draft note. He said it was urgent.

Back at 11, Safdarjung Road, I found Jose waiting. The telephone had been ringing incessantly. I sat down and dictated a note for the Prime Minister. In unambiguous terms, in words that held strength, authority and power, in words that would heal and in words that would warn, I tried to express the P.M.'s message to the people of India to remember that his government existed and would take stern action if violence and the killings continued. I sent Jose with the note to 1, Safdarjung Road, while I sat quietly with myself. The growl of the city started to reach Safdarjung Road.

Around 6 o'clock a special urgent bulletin was telecast on Door Darshan. I waited expecting to see Rajiv's face fill the screen, but it was Narasimha Rao, the Home Minister, who appeared. The strong breath needed to face the cyclone was not evident. The speech had neither the anguish of the son nor the massive authority of the Prime Minister. The army was not called out that night, and the terror and barbarity continued. The seed was sown and suddenly the bleak and terrifying tomorrow started to unfold.

On the night of 2nd November, groups of Sikhs determined to stand up to the holocaust scattered and entered back lanes of the bungalows of New Delhi. Law and order had so completely broken down that they approached within half a furlong of the Prime Minister's residence.

Two muffled Sikhs entered my house—11, Safdarjung Road—by the gate opening on to the back lane. The room of the dhobi was open and the old rogue was absent, possibly joining in the rioting. They approached his wife and said: '*Din tumara hai, Rat hamari hai*—The day is yours, the night is ours'—and vanished into the darkness to visit other homes on Safdarjung Road. The dhobin collapsed in terror. She covered her head with a sheet and lay trembling till her husband returned the next morning. The law and order officers visited my house and insisted that I post security guards, but I refused for I felt it was safer to be anonymous.

The killings, burnings and raping lasted three days. At last the army was called out and an uneasy peace descended on the city. The wounds inflicted did not heal. Enquiry Commissions were established, but hardly anyone was brought to account. The immense cauldron of revenge remained red hot. When you mortally wound a nation, who is to make atonement?

Indira was cremated on the land next to Shantivana, the cremation sites of Jawaharlal Nehru and Sanjay Gandhi, on 3 November. Rajiv Gandhi, sworn in as Prime Minister on the evening of 31 October 1984, performed Indira's last rites on a brick platform heaped with fragrant logs of sandalwood. There were no blue flames in the fire that leapt towards the setting sun; red, saffron and gold were her colours and saffron and gold were the flames.

Those essences that, at the moment of death, enter the cave of the heart, departed to their natural habitat; speech entered fire, the breath entered into air, the eye into the sun, the mind into the moon, listening into the quarters, the self entered the ether, her hair into herbs and trees and the blood into water.

Indira Nehru Gandhi, the conservationist, would have approved.

Today undulating grass meadows, reminiscent of the park lands of Indira's ancestral home, Kashmir, surround her cremation site Shaktisthal—the abode of energy. Groves of trees, interspersed with boulders collected from every state in the country, appear on mounds and along the pathways. On the site where Indira was cremated, a weathered rock of jasper with veins of iron ore rises over fifteen feet into the sky. In India, crude iron ore is the symbol of Shakti, an energy without end. Jasper, blood red when polished, is a rock harder than granite; iron ore, when smelted, is fluid fire.

EPILOGUE

When violence had remade the bed of men on the earth,
A very old tree, barren of leaves, resumed the thread of its maxims . . . and another tree of high degree was already rising from the great subterranean India,
with its magnetic leaf and its burden of newfruit.

−"Winds"[1]

Epilogue
MAGH MELA 1985

The doomswept story of Indira Gandhi and her two sons ended on 21 May 1991. Rajiv Gandhi, Indira Gandhi's elder son, former Prime Minister and leader of the Opposition in the Lok Sabha, was brutally assassinated at an election meetion to be addressed by him at Sriperumbudur, a temple town and the birthplace of the Vaishnava saint, Ramanujacharya, forty miles away from Madras. He was on the last lap of the election meetings held after the resignation of Prime Minister Chandra Shekhar. The election forecasts had hailed Rajiv Gandhi as the future prime minister and the Congress party as the favourite in the battle of the polls.

The forty-six-year-old Rajiv Gandhi had had a gruelling day, addressing a number of election meetings all over the country and had arrived in Madras to be met by a vast crowd who hailed him as the future prime minister of the country. The cries of welcome had brought a glow to Rajiv's tired face. He had decided not to go to Sriperumbudur but to stay the night at Madras. He was however persuaded by Congress workers that the crowds which would have gathered at the meeting site would wait for him till late at night. Ultimately he left for his last election meeting by car. For almost all his other election tours his wife, Sonia Gandhi, had accompanied him, but, exhausted by the heat and constant travelling, she had decided to stay over in Delhi.

The cavalcade of cars reached the site a few minutes after ten. Rajiv Gandhi approached his mother's statue painted in brilliant silver oil colours, to garland it before walking to the rostrum. Security was lax. In the milling crowd few people noticed Dhanu, a young dark-complexioned, buck-toothed woman, holding a garland of sandalwood in her hands. As Rajiv Gandhi approached the few steps that led up to the rostrum, Dhanu came forward and bent as if to touch his feet. This triggered the lethal belt of explosives tied around her waist and hidden by the folds of her salwar. It was a powerful bomb and, as it exploded, it shattered Rajiv Gandhi's body and the bodies of the Congress workers and the entourage who stood around him.

Rajiv's death was savage and immediate. The body of the young woman, later identified as a member of the Liberation Tigers of Tamil Eelam (LTTE), the terrorist group of Sri Lanka, was cut in two and her limbs scattered. The one-eyed leader of the group, Shivarasan, who was present near the rostrum till the last moment, slipped away seconds before the explosion. It was by sheer chance that the camera and film of a photographer, Haribabu, who had been snapping pictures of Rajiv Gandhi at the site, remained intact, although the photographer died, shattered by the bomb blast. When the film was developed, the face of the assassin and that of Shivarasan emerged, making it possible for the Special Investigating Team (SIT) to find its first clues. A vast and meticulously planned plot to assassinate the former Prime Minister was ultimately revealed. It was rumoured that the manner of the killing was inspired by novels and films from the West.

No one is quite sure as to what happened subsequent to the explosion. It was only after a lapse of some time that the security officers manning the site came in search of the former Prime Minister. Immediate telephone calls to Madras and Delhi informed the family and the world of the news of the assassination. The country was stunned. Rajiv Gandhi's body, accompanied by his wife Sonia, and his daughter Priyanka, was brought to Delhi on the morning of 22 May to lie in state at Teen Murti House.

Rajiv Gandhi was cremated on 23 May, with full state honours, his son Rahul lighting the funeral pyre at a site close to Shaktisthal.

I was revising the last pages of Indira Gandhi's biography when the telephone rang with the news of the assassination. For days and months after the tragedy, the implications of the savage deaths of Indira and her immediate family left me with an anguish and with a major query. What play of the stars determined the end? Where were the seeds sown? What karma was generated to converge and destroy? The question remains unanswered.

The story of Indira Gandhi which started as a playful tale on 19 November 1917, had, over the years, grown into a vast and complex story of betrayal, violence, tragedy, war and death. Epic winds had lifted the story and created a myth of the twentieth century.

*

Prayag's story of pilgrimage never ends. Sacred season and sacred site continue to draw pilgrims from the four cardinal points of India. Vast numbers of people, grown manifold from 1917, travel the pilgrim's path to meet and mingle and continue their ever present rendezvous with the sun. Bullock carts and horse carriages give way to over-crowded trains and buses—to tractors; millions travel.

The river Ganga has shrunk and grown shallow. It attains its glory only when the monsoon waters enter and overflow its banks. Jamuna, the smoky blue river of Prayag, has lost its playfulness. It is now a trickle, has grown turgid, pollution-dark. The sand banks have spread. The vast banyan and peepal trees, symbols of constant renewal and wisdom, whose spreading branches provided leaf cover and gave shelter and shade, have been cut down, leaving the sand banks naked to the wind and rain.

The underground Saraswati, the lost river of insight and the arts, flows. Is there an ear open to share in her intimations?

To the south-east, Vindhya Vasini Durga retains her power and her devotees. But where are her sacred groves? Where are the wild grasses and the seed scattered by birds that gave potency to the soil? Where is the hibiscus bush and where is the lush vegetation which was her habitat?

At the Mela site hundreds of bamboo stalls are erected to sell souvenirs to the pilgrims, but the brass and bell metal utensils polished into golden objects of beauty, have disappeared, and now there are vessels of aluminium and plastics. The bangle-seller sells plastic bangles—at places plastic flowers appear. Huge posters, garish in colour, portray the gods as film heroes. Today's icons, they create new myths. The oral storytellers are dwindling away. The Nautanki players are rarely seen; the monkeyman and the man with the bear gather no crowds. The astrologers sit in their usual places; the uncertainty of tomorrow is good for their business. Here great abbots of religious sects establish themselves in clearly demarcated spaces. The philosopher and wise man are present. Abandoned bulls and cows still wander at will.

Sounds of chants, evening songs, the bhajans, weightless as they float along the river banks, filtered through the fragant smoke from fires lit against the freezing winter nights, are shattered by loudspeakers and transmitters raised to a pitch (that distort pure sound and resonance.) The story loses power; magic and mystery cannot survive neon lights. Yet faith remains untouched.

Notes

Prologue

1. *Aiteraya Brahmana,* 7.15.
2. Indira Gandhi in conversation with the author (from the author's notebooks).

PART I

1. Jawaharlal Nehru to Indira Nehru, in *Selected Works of Jawaharlal Nehru,* Delhi: Orient Longman Limited, 1984, Vol. 11 pp 594, 595 & 596.

Chapter One

2. M.J. Akbar, *Nehru: The Making of India,* Harmondsworth: Penguin Books, 1988, p. 10.
3. ibid.
4. B.K. Nehru in an interview with the author (on tape).
5. ibid.
6. Vijayalakshmi Pandit, *A Scope of Happiness: A Personal Memoir,* Delhi: Vikas Publishing House Limited, 1979, p. 57.

Chapter Two

1. J.B. Kripalani, *Gandhi: His Life and Thought,* New Delhi: Publications Division, Government of India, 1978, p. 81 [originally published in Hindi as, *Mahatma Gandhi: Jeewan aur Chintan*].
2. Jawaharlal Nehru, *An Autobiography,* Delhi: Oxford University Press [henceforth OUP], 1982, p. 41.
3. B.R. Nanda, *The Nehrus: Motilal and Jawaharlal,* New York: John Day, 1963, p. 203.

4. Ganga Saran Sinha in an interview with the author (on tape).

Chapter Three

1. Siddhartha Shankar Ray in an interview with the author (on tape).
2. *What I Am: Indira Gandhi in Conversation with Pupul Jayakar,* Delhi: Indira Gandhi Memorial Trust, 1986, p. 31.
3. ibid.
4. Jawaharlal Nehru, *An Autobiography,* Delhi: OUP, 1982, pp. 203–04.
5. *What I Am,* Delhi: Indira Gandhi Memorial Trust, 1986, p. 9.
6. ibid., p. 7.
7. ibid.

Chapter Four

1. *What I Am,* Delhi: Indira Gandhi Memorial Trust, 1986, p. 10.
2. Indira Gandhi in an interview with Lord Chalfont for the BBC, 26 October 1971.
3. B.K. Nehru in an interview with the author (on tape).
4. Indira Gandhi in an interview with Lord Chalfont, 26 October 1971.
5. Indira Gandhi to Emanuel Pouchpadass, in *My Truth,* Delhi: Vision Books, 1981, p. 22.

Chapter Five

1. *Collected Works of Mahatma Gandhi,* New Delhi: Publications Division, Government of India.
2. ibid.
3. ibid.
4. "At Dandi on the shores of the ocean—Mohan (Krishna) plays at making salt."
5. Mahatma Gandhi to Abbas Tyabji, 16 March 1930, in *Collected Works of Mahatma Gandhi,* New Delhi: Publications Division, Government of India, Vol. 43, p. 86.
6. *Selected Works of Jawaharlal Nehru,* Delhi: Orient Longman Ltd., 1984, Vol. 12, p. 646.

7. *Young India,* 10 April 1930, in *Collected Works of Mahatma Gandhi,* New Delhi: Publications Division, Government of India, Vol. 43, p. 204.

8. *Collected Works of Mahatma Gandhi,* New Delhi: Publications Division, Government of India, Vol. 45, p. 221.

9. ibid., p. 428 (see Appendix III).

10. Indira Gandhi in an interview with Lord Chalfont for the BBC.

11. *Selected Works of Jawaharlal Nehru,* Delhi: Orient Longman Ltd., 1984, Vol. 4, p. 358.

12. A page from a notebook of Indira Nehru on the work of the Vanar Sena (Monkey Brigade), Delhi: Indira Gandhi Memorial Trust.

13. *Selected Works of Jawaharlal Nehru,* Delhi: Orient Longman Ltd., 1984, Vol. 12, p. 666.

14. ibid., p. 668.

15. ibid., p. 657.

16. Indira Gandhi in an interview with Nimai Sadhan Bose, *Sunday.* 16–24 November 1984.

17. *Freedom's Daughter: Letters Between Indira Gandhi and Jawaharlal Nehru 1922–1939,* ed. Sonia Gandhi, London: Hodder and Stoughton, 1989, p. 44.

18. *Selected Works of Jawaharlal Nehru,* Delhi: Orient Longman Ltd., 1984, Vol. 12, p. 419.

19. Promila Kalhan, *Kamala Nehru: An Intimate Biography* Delhi: Vikas Publishing House Ltd., 1973, p. 47

20. ibid., p. 67.

Chapter Six

1. Jawaharlal Nehru, *An Autobiography,* Delhi: OUP, 1982, p. 246.

2. Krishna Hutheesing, *We Nehrus,* Bombay: Pearl Books, 1968.

3. Indira Gandhi in an interview with Lord Chalfont for the BBC.

4. Indira Gandhi in a conversation with the author in Mercara (from the author's notebooks).

5. Erik Erikson, *Gandhi's Truth: On the Origins of Militant Nonviolence,* London: Faber and Faber Limited, pp. 447–48.

6. *What I Am,* Delhi: Indira Gandhi Memorial Trust, 1986, p. 30.

Chapter Seven

1. Promila Kalhan, *Kamala Nehru: An Intimate Biography,* Delhi: Vikas Publishing House Ltd., 1973, p. 66.
2. *Freedom's Daughter,* ed. Sonia Gandhi, London: Hodder and Stoughton, 1989, p. 56.
3. Shanta Gandhi in an interview with the author (on tape).
4. *Remembered Moments: Some Autobiographical Writings of Indira Gandhi,* Delhi: Indira Gandhi Memorial Trust, 1987, p. 53.
5. *Selected Works of Jawaharlal Nehru, Delhi:* Orient Longman Ltd., 1984, Vol. 5, p. 408.
6. *Freedom's Daughter,* ed. Sonia Gandhi, London: Hodder and Stoughton, 1989, p. 68.
7. Kamala Nehru to Prabha, wife of Jayaprakash Narayan, 19 June 1933, the Jawaharlal Nehru Memorial Trust archives.
8. ibid.
9. ibid.
10. *Selected Works of Jawaharlal Nehru,* Delhi: Orient Longman Ltd., 1984, Vol. 6, p. 505.
11. ibid., p. 509.

Chapter Eight

1. *Selected Works of Jawaharlal Nehru: Prison Diary,* Delhi: Orient Longman Ltd., 1984, Vol. 6, p. 312.
2. Kamala Nehru to Prabha, 17 September 1933.
3. Promila Kalhan, *Kamala Nehru: An Intimate Biography,* Delhi: Vikas Publishing House Ltd., 1973, p. 137.
4. *Selected Works of Jawaharlal Nehru, Delhi:* Orient Longman Ltd., 1984, Vol. 6, p. 227.
5. *What I Am,* Delhi: Indira Gandhi Memorial Trust, 1986, p. 13.
6. *Selected Works of Jawaharlal Nehru,* Delhi: Orient Longman Ltd., 1984, Vol. 6, p. 263.

Chapter Nine

1. Edward Thompson, *Tagore, Sage, Poet and Dramatist,* London:

OUP, 1948, p. 189.

2. *Remembered Moments,* Delhi: Indira Gandhi Memorial Trust, 1987, p. 17.

3. *Freedom's Daughter,* ed. Sonia Gandhi, London: Hodder and Stoughton, 1989, p. 98.

4. *Remembered Moments,* Delhi: Indira Gandhi Memorial Trust, 1987, p. 17.

5. *What I Am,* Delhi: Indira Gandhi Memorial Trust, 1986.

6. Indira Gandhi in conversation with the author (from the author's notebooks).

7. *Freedom's Daughter,* ed. Sonia Gandhi, London: Hodder and Stoughton, 1989, p. 124.

8. Indira Gandhi in conversation with the author (from the author's notebooks).

PART II

1. Simon Bolivar to his tutor, Simon Rodrigues, 19 January 1824, in Gabriel García Márquez, *The General in His Labyrinth,* London: Jonathan Cape, 1990.

Chapter One

2. *Selected Works of Jawaharlal Nehru: Prison Diary with Letters,* Delhi: Orient Longman Ltd., 1984, Vol. 6, p. 311.

3. ibid., p. 307.

4. Kamala Nehru to Prabha, 29 March 1935, the Jawaharlal Nehru Memorial Trust archives.

5. Kamala Nehru to Prabha, 15 April 1935.

6. *Freedom's Daughter,* ed. Sonia Gandhi, London: Hodder and Stoughton, 1989, p. 158.

7. ibid., pp. 158–361.

8. ibid.

9. Nayantara Sahgal, *Indira Gandhi: Her Road to Power,* London: MacDonald & Company, 1978, p. 29.

10. *Selected Works of Jawaharlal Nehru,* Delhi: Orient Longman Ltd., 1984, Vol. 12, p. 690.

11. ibid., Vol. 6, p. 389.
12. ibid., Vol. 12, p. 685.
13. Zareer Masani, *Indira Gandhi: A Biography,* Delhi: OUP, 1975.
14. ibid., p. 45.

Chapter Two

1. Jawaharlal Nehru to Ghosiben Captain, 28 December 1935.
2. *Selected Works of Jawaharlal Nehru,* Delhi: Orient Longman Ltd., 1984, Vol. 13, p. 690.
3. *Freedom's Daughter,* ed. Sonia Gandhi, London: Hodder and Stoughton, 1989, p. 235.
4. Indira Nehru to Jawaharlal Nehru, 11 February 1936, ibid.
5. ibid., p. 185.
6. ibid., p. 253.
7. Mahatma Gandhi to Indira Nehru, 30 March 1936, ibid.
8. ibid., p. 404.
9. ibid., pp. 282–33.
10. ibid., p. 281.
11. Indira Nehru to Jawaharlal Nehru, 21 October 1936, ibid., p. 287.
12. Iris Murdoch, "Indira at School and After", in *Indira Gandhi: Statesmen, Scholars, Scientists and Friends Remember,* Delhi: Indira Gandhi Memorial Trust, 1985, p. 308.
13. *Freedom's Daughter,* ed. Sonia Gandhi, London: Hodder and Stoughton, 1989, p. 295.
14. Indira Nehru to Frank Oberdorf, 24 October 1936.

Chapter Three

1. *Selected Works of Jawaharlal Nehru,* Delhi: Orient Longman Ltd., 1984, Vol. 13, p. 645.
2. ibid., p. 671.
3. Vijayalakshmi Pandit in an interview with the author (on tape).
4. Indira Gandhi to Dorothy Norman, 21 September 1960, in *Letters to an American Friend 1950–1984,* New York: Harcourt Brace Publishers, 1985, p. 78.
5. Sarvepalli Gopal, *Jawaharlal Nehru: A Biography,* Cambridge: Harvard University Press, Vol. I, 1976, p. 232.

6. *Selected Works of Jawaharlal Nehru,* Delhi: Orient Longman Ltd, 1984, Vol. 13, p. 702.

7. *Freedom's Daughter,* ed. Sonia Gandhi, London: Hodder and Stoughton, 1989, p. 389.

8. Sarvepalli Gopal, *Jawaharlal Nehru: A Biography,* Cambridge: Harvard University Press, Vol. I, 1976, p. 236.

Chapter Four

1. *Freedom's Daughter,* ed. Sonia Gandhi, London: Hodder and Stoughton, 1989, p. 405.

2. Indira Gandhi in conversation with the author (from the author's notebooks).

3. *Freedom's Daughter,* ed. Sonia Gandhi, London: Hodder and Stoughton, 1989, p. 408.

4. Indira Nehru to Jawaharlal Nehru, 1 May 1939, ibid., 410–11

5. ibid., p. 416.

6. Indira Nehru to Jawaharlal Nehru, 15 July 1939, ibid., p. 421.

7. Jawaharlal Nehru to Agatha Harrison, 4 May 1940, in *Selected Works of Jawaharlal Nehru,* Delhi: Orient Longman Ltd, 1984. Vol. 11, p. 390.

8. Jawaharlal Nehru to Indira Nehru, 11 March 1940, ibid., p. 446.

9. Jawaharlal Nehru to Indira Nehru, 10 April 1940, ibid., p. 457.

10. Jawaharlal Nehru to Indira Nehru, 23–24 May 1940, ibid., p. 471.

11. Jawaharlal Nehru to Indira Nehru, 11 May 1940, ibid., pp. 465–66.

Chapter Five

1. Jawaharlal Nehru to Indira Nehru, 23 May 1940, in *Selected Works of Jawaharlal Nehru,* Delhi: Orient Longman Ltd., 1984, Vol. 11, p. 470.

2. *Remembered Moments,* Delhi: Indira Gandhi Memorial Trust 1987, p. 62.

3. Jawaharlal Nehru to Indira Nehru, 15 May 1941, in *Selected Works of Jawaharlal Nehru,* Delhi: Orient Longman Ltd., 1984, Vol. 11, p. 594. The letter, while he was in prison, was never sent.

4. ibid., p. 581.

5. Jawaharlal Nehru to Indira Nehru, 4 May 1941, ibid., p. 589.

6. *What I Am,* Delhi: Indira Gandhi Memorial Trust, 1986, p. 18.
7. *Selected Works of Jawaharlal Nehru,* Delhi: Orient Longman Ltd., 1984, Vol. 11, p. 601.
8. ibid., p. 646.
9. Jawaharlal Nehru to Indira Nehru, 9 July 1941, ibid., p. 644.
10. ibid., p. 646.
11. From the author's notebooks.

Chapter Six

1. Pages from a prison diary, 24 July 1941, in *Selected Works of Jawaharlal Nehru,* Delhi: Orient Longman Ltd., 1984, Vol. 11, p. 655.
2. Hansa Mehta in conversation with the author (from the author's notebooks).

Chapter Seven

1. *Selected Works of Jawaharlal Nehru,* Delhi: Orient Longman Ltd., 1984, Vol. 11, p. 739.
2. *What I Am,* Delhi: Indira Gandhi Memorial Trust, 1986, p. 22.
3. ibid., p. 25.
4. Indira Gandhi in an interview with the author (on tape).
5. Krishna Hutheesing, *Dear to Behold,* Bombay: India Book House, 1969, p. 92.
6. Eve Curie, *Journey Amongst Warriors,* London: William Heinemann Limited, 1943, p. 432.

Chapter Eight

1. Mahatma Gandhi's speech at the AICC meeting, 8 August 1942, in *Collected Works of Mahatma Gandhi,* New Delhi: Publications Division, Government of India, Vol. 76, p. 392.
2. ibid., p. 389.
3. Bipan Chandra *et al, India's Struggle for Independence,* Delhi: Penguin Books India (P) Ltd., 1988, p. 462.
4. *Remembered Moments,* Delhi: Indira Gandhi Memorial Trust, 1987, pp. 29–30.

5. *Selected Works of Jawaharlal Nehru: Prison Diary with Letters,* 7 April 1943, Delhi: Orient Longman Ltd., 1984, Vol. 13, p. 101.
6. ibid., 14 June 1943, p. 165.
7. Indira Gandhi in an interview with Lord Chalfont for the BBC.
8. Jawaharlal Nehru to Indira Gandhi, 26 June 1943, in *Selected Works of Jawaharlal Nehru,* Delhi: Orient Longman Ltd., 1984, Vol. 13, p. 172.
9. ibid., *Prison Diary with Letters,* 14 July 1943, Vol. 13, p. 186.
10. ibid., p. 220.
11. Jawaharlal Nehru to Indira Gandhi, 16 August 1943, ibid., p. 260.
12. ibid., *Prison Diary with Letters,* 27 February 1944, Vol. 13, p. 361.
13. Jawaharlal Nehru to Indira Gandhi, 24 February 1944, ibid., p. 564.
14. Jawaharlal Nehru to Mahatma Gandhi, 30 July 1945.

PART III

1. Indira Gandhi in an interview with Nimai Sadhan Bose, *Sunday* 16–24 November 1984.

Chapter One

2. Jawaharlal Nehru to Feroze Gandhi, 4 April 1946, J.N. Papers, Nehru Memorial Museum and Library [henceforth NMML], pp. 588–89.
3. Indira Gandhi to Frank Oberdorf, 6 August 1946.
4. Ram Nath Goenka to Ganga Saran Sinha.
5. Nikhil Chakravartti in an interview with the author (on tape).
6. Indira Gandhi in an interview with Lord Chalfont for the BBC.
7. *What I Am,* Delhi: Indira Gandhi Memorial Trust, 1986.
8. ibid.
9. ibid., p. 27.
10. ibid., p. 29.
11. ibid., p. 28.
12. Indira Gandhi in an interview with Lord Chalfont for the BBC.
13. *The Years of Challenge: Selected Speeches of Indira Gandhi 1966–1969,* New Delhi: Publications Division, Government of India, 1971, p. 300.

Chapter Two

1. Indira Gandhi in conversation with the author (from the author's notebooks).
2. *The Complete Greek Tragedies: The Bacchae,* trans. William Arrowsmith, Chicago: The University of Chicago Press, 1958, p. 551.
3. Sanjay Gandhi in an interview with *Surya,* July 1979, p. 25.
4. Zareer Masani, *Indira Gandhi: A Biography,* Delhi: OUP, 1975, p. 103.
5. Indira Gandhi in conversation with the author (from the author's notebooks).

Chapter Three

1. Indira Gandhi in conversation with the author (from the author's notebooks).
2. Indira Gandhi to Dorothy Norman, 26 May 1969, in *Letters to an American Friend,* New York: Harcourt Brace Publishers, 1985, p. 121.

Chapter Four

1. A page from Indira Gandhi's notebook.

Chapter Five

1. Inder Malhotra, *Indira Gandhi: A Personal and Political Biography,* London: Hodder and Stoughton, 1989, pp. 61–62.
2. Zareer Masani, *Indira Gandhi: A Biography,* Delhi: OUP, 1975, p. 106.
3. ibid.
4. Indira Gandhi in conversation with the author (from the author's notebooks).
5. Indira Gandhi to Dorothy Norman, in *Letters to an American Friend,* New York: Harcourt Brace Publishers, 1985, p. 57.
6. ibid., 24 September 1959.
7. ibid.
8. ibid.
9. ibid.

Chapter Six

1. Indira Gandhi to Dorothy Norman, December 1959, in *Letters to an American Friend,* New York: Harcourt Brace Publishers, 1985.
2. Welles Hengen, *After Nehru Who?,* London: Rupert Hart Davis, 1963, p. 160.
3. Michael Brecher, *Succession in India,* London: OUP, 1966, p. 7.
4. Indira Gandhi in conversation with the author (from the author's notebooks).
5. ibid.

Chapter Seven

1. Indira Gandhi in conversation with the author (from the author's notebooks).
2. ibid.
3. Indira Gandhi to B.K. Nehru, 17 May 1964.
4. Michael Brecher, *Succession in India,* London: OUP, 1966, p. 31.
5. Krishna Hutheesing to A.C.M. Nambiar, 6 July 1964.
6. Indira Gandhi to Dorothy Norman, 11 June 1964, in *Letters to an American Friend,* New York: Harcourt Brace Publishers, 1985, p. 104.
7. Inder Malhotra, *Indira Gandhi,* London: Hodder and Stoughton, 1989, p. 84.
8. Indira Gandhi to the author, 11 October 1964.

Chapter Eight

1. Romesh Thapar in conversation with the author (from the author's notebooks).
2. Former President R. Venkataraman in conversation with the author (from the author's notebooks).
3. Indira Gandhi in conversation with the author (from the author's notebooks).
4. ibid.
5. Vijayalakshmi Pandit in a statement to the press.
6. J. Anthony Lukas in "She Stands Remarkably Alone", the *New York Times,* 17 March 1966, p. 133.

PART IV

1. *The Peacock's Egg: Love Poems from Ancient India,* trans. W.S. Merwin and J. Moussaieff Massan, San Francisco: North Point Press, 1981, p. 35.

Chapter One

2. ibid.

3. J. Anthony Lukas in "She Stands Remarkably Alone", the *New York Times,* 17 March 1966.

4. Indira Gandhi in conversation with the author (from the author's notebooks).

5. Zareer Masani, *Indira Gandhi: A Biography,* Delhi: OUP, 1975, p. 153.

6. Indira Gandhi in reply to a debate in the Lok Sabha, 7 November 1966, in *The Years of Challenge,* New Delhi: Publications Division, Government of India, 1971, p. 16.

7. L.K. Jha in an interview with the author (on tape).

8. ibid.

9. Indira Gandhi in conversation with the author (from the author's notebooks).

10. L.K. Jha in conversation with the author (from the author's notebooks).

11. André Malraux, *Fallen Oaks: Conversation with President de Gaulle,* London: Hamish Hamilton, p. 550.

12. *Time,* 1 April 1966, p. 30.

13. B.K. Nehru in "Jawaharlal Nehru, Memories of a Special Magic", the *Telegraph,* 8 July 1988.

14. *Time,* 8 April 1966.

15. ibid., 1 April 1966.

16. L.K. Jha in an interview with the author (on tape).

17. ibid.

18. *Time,* 8 April 1966.

19. H.Y. Sharada Prasad in conversation with the author (from the author's notebooks).

Chapter Two

1. Former Prime Minister of the erstwhile Soviet Union, Aleksei Kosygin to Indira Gandhi, as told by Dr I.G. Patel to the author (on tape).
2. ibid.
3. Indira Gandhi in conversation with the author (from the author's notebooks). Years later I discovered that Ambassador John Galbraith had interviewed Prime Minister Indira Gandhi in New York for Channel 13 on 3 April 1966.
4. *Time,* 6 May 1966.
5. "Person to Person", broadcast over AIR, 12 June 1966.
6. Indira Gandhi in conversation with the author (from the author's notebooks).
7. Indira Gandhi in a speech to Congress workers at Pune.
8. *Time,* 2 June 1966.
9. "Person to Person", broadcast over AIR, 12 June 1966.
10. C. Subramaniam in an interview with the author (on tape).

Chapter Three

1. Indira Gandhi in conversation with the author (from the author's notebooks).
2. Dr I.G. Patel in an interview with the author (on tape).
3. ibid.
4. *The Years of Challenge,* New Delhi: Publications Division, Government of India, p. 1971, 22.
5. Indira Gandhi in conversation with the author (from the author's notebooks).
6. Sarvepalli Gopal, *Radhakrishnan: A Biography,* Delhi: OUP, 1989, p. 345.
7. Indira Gandhi in conversation with the author (from the author's notebooks).
8. Indira Gandhi in a speech to the Lok Sabha, 6 June 1966.
9. A senior member of the IFS who was present when the conversation took place, but wishes to remain anonymous.
10. Vijayalakshmi Pandit in an interview with the author (on tape).

Chapter Four

1. Indira Gandhi in conversation with the author (from the author's notebooks).
2. Romesh Thapar in the *Economic and Political Weekly.*
3. ibid.
4. Dr I.G. Patel in an interview with the author (on tape).

Chapter Five

1. Indira Gandhi in conversation with the author (from the author's notebooks).
2. ibid.

Chapter Six

1. Martand Singh, of Kapurthala, in conversation with the author (from the author's notebooks).
2. Field Marshal S.F.H.J. Manekshaw in an interview with the author (on tape).

PART V

1. Diane Wolkstein and Samuel Noah Kramer, *Inanna: Queen of Heaven and Earth, Her Stories and Hymns from Sumer,* Harper and Row, 1983.
2. *The Complete Greek Tragedies: The Bacchae,* trans. William Arrowsmith, Chicago: University of Chicago Press, 1958.

Chapter One

3. *The Years of Endeavour: Selected Speeches of Indira Gandhi August 1969–August 1972,* New Delhi: Publications Division, Government of India, 1975, pp. 749–750.
4. Field Marshal Sam Manekshaw in an interview with the author (on tape).

5. ibid.

6. Dr I.G. Patel in an interview with the author (on tape).

7. *The Years of Endeavour,* New Delhi: Publications Division, Government of India, 1975, p. 526.

8. L.K. Jha in an interview with the author (on tape).

9. Allen Ginsberg "September on Jessore Road", in *Collected Poems 1917–1980,* New York: Harper and Row, 1984, p. 571.

10. Ganga Saran Sinha in conversation with the author (from the author's notebooks).

11. ibid.

12. L.K. Jha in an interview with the author (on tape).

13. Gita Mehta in an interview with the author (on tape).

14. Vice-Admiral M.K. Roy in an interview with the author (on tape).

15. Indira Gandhi in an interview with Jonathan Power, the *Washington Post,* 13 January 1980.

16. Indira Gandhi in an interview with Michael Charleston for the BBC, 1 November 1971, in *The Years of Endeavour,* New Delhi: Publications Division, Government of India, 1975, p. 541.

17. Indira Gandhi in reply to the welcome speech of President Nixon, in Seymour M. Hersh, *The Price of Power,* New York: Summit Books, 1983, p. 456.

18. Indira Gandhi in conversation with the author at Mercara, May 1988 (from the author's notebooks).

Chapter Two

1. Field Marshal Sam Manekshaw in an interview with the author (on tape).

2. Indira Gandhi in a speech to the Lok Sabha, 6 December 1971.

3. L.K. Jha in an interview with the author (on tape).

4. ibid.

5. From the author's notebooks.

6. ibid.

7. Indira Gandhi to Richard Nixon, 15 December 1971, in *The Years of Endeavour,* New Delhi: Publications Division, Government of India, 1975, p. 611.

Chapter Three

1. Indira Gandhi in a statement to the Lok Sabha, 16 December 1971.
2. Indira Gandhi to the author (from the author's notebooks).
3. H.Y. Sharada Prasad in conversation with the author (from the author's notebooks).
4. Indira Gandhi in a speech to the Lok Sabha, 17 December 1971.

Chapter Four

1. Indira Gandhi in conversation with the author (from the author's notebooks).
2. ibid.
3. *Artharva Veda Samhita: Hymn to the Earth,* trans. William Dwight Whitney, Delhi: Motilal Banarsidass, 1962, 12.1.11.

Chapter Five

1. Benazir Bhutto, *Daughter of the East: An Autobiography,* London: Hamish Hamilton, 1988, p. 54.
2. Indira Gandhi in reply to an attack by members of the Opposition in the Lok Sabha, December 1971.
3. Indira Gandhi in a debate on bilateral relations in the Lok Sabha, 31 July 1972, in *The Years of Endeavour,* New Delhi: Publications Division, Government of India, 1975, p. 656.
4. N.K. Seshan in an interview with the author (on tape).
5. ibid.
6. C. Subramaniam in an interview with the author (on tape).
7. N.K. Seshan in an interview with the author (on tape).
8. ibid.
9. Atal Behari Vajpayee in an interview with the author (on tape).
10. Indira Gandhi in conversation with the author (from the author's notebooks).

Chapter Six

1. Inder Malhotra, *Indira Gandhi,* London: Hodder and Stoughton, 1989.

2. Siddhartha Shankar Ray to Indira Gandhi, May 1974.

3. Indira Gandhi to Siddhartha Shankar Ray, May 1974.

4. Indira Gandhi to the author, 11 October 1974.

5. Ralph Buultjen in "Indira Gandhi, Crisis Management and Political Survival", *Darshan,* March 1987, Vol. 4, p. 3.

PART VI

1. Jawaharlal Nehru to Indira Gandhi, 14 August 1943, in *Selected Works of Jawaharlal Nehru,* Delhi: Orient Longman Ltd., 1984, Vol. 13.

2. *The Complete Greek Tragedies: The Bacchae,* trans. William Arrowsmith, Chicago: University of Chicago Press, 1958, p. 565.

Chapter One

3. Uma Shankar Dikshit in an interview with the author (on tape).

4. R.N. Kao in an interview with the author (on tape).

5. Siddhartha Shankar Ray in an interview with the author (on tape).

6. ibid.

7. ibid.

8. ibid.

9. Inder Kumar Gujral in an interview with the author (on tape).

10. ibid.

11. ibid.

12. Raj Thapar in "Images of the Emergency—Just to Remember", *Seminar,* March 1977, p. 32.

13. Nayantara Sahgal, *Indira Gandhi: Her Road to Power,* London: MacDonald & Co., 1978.

14. ibid.

15. *Jayaprakash Narayan: Prison Diary,* ed. A.B. Shah, Bombay: Popular Prakashan, 1975. p. 5.

16. Indira Gandhi in conversation with the author (from the author's notebooks).

17. ibid.

Chapter Two

1. R.N. Kao in an interview with the author (on tape).
2. ibid.
3. Indira Gandhi in conversation with the author (from the author's notebooks).
4. R.N. Kao in an interview with the author (on tape).
5. C.G.K. Reddy, *Baroda Dynamite Conspiracy: The Right to Rebel,* Delhi: Vision Books, 1977, p. 26.
6. Nirmala Deshpande in an interview with the author (on tape).
7. R.N. Kao in an interview with the author (on tape).
8. ibid.

Chapter Three

1. Maneka Gandhi in an interview with the author (on tape).
2. Amie Crishna in an interview with the author (on tape).
3. Maneka Gandhi in an interview with the author (on tape).
4. ibid.
5. N.K. Seshan in an interview with the author (on tape).
6. The "Shah Commission of Enquiry—Third & Final Report", Chapter XXX, p. 154.
7. ibid., Chapter XXI, pp. 153–207.
8. ibid., Chapter XXX.
9. ibid.

Chapter Four

1. Amie Crishna in an interview with the author (on tape).
2. From the author's notebooks.
3. Indira Gandhi in conversation with the author (from the author's notebooks).
4. Maneka Gandhi in an interview with the author (on tape).

Chapter Five

1. Indira Gandhi in conversation with the author (from the author's

notebooks).

2. Maneka Gandhi in an interview with the author (on tape).

3. R.N. Kao in an interview with the author (on tape).

4. Maneka Gandhi in an interview with the author (on tape).

5. ibid.

6. Ganga Saran Sinha in an interview with the author (on tape).

7. J. Krishnamurti in conversation with the author (from the author's notebooks).

8. Pratima Singh to Helen Ciaoux, notes sent to the author from the latter.

9. ibid.

10. R.N. Kao in an interview with the author (on tape).

PART VII

1. *Baudha Gana O Doha,* one of the earliest vernacular masterpieces from Bengal.

2. *Newsweek,* 31 January 1980.

Chapter One

3. Author to B.K. Nehru, 16 April 1977.

4. Indira Gandhi to Fori Nehru, 17 April 1977.

5. Indira Gandhi to the author in a letter (undated, from the author's notebooks).

6. Indira Gandhi in conversation with the author (from the author's notebooks).

7. Indira Gandhi to B.K. Nehru, 30 April 1977.

8. James Cameron in "The Most Apprehensive Woman in the World", the *Guardian* (reproduced in the *Statesman),* 21 September 1977.

9. Indira Gandhi to J. Krishnamurti, 21 June 1977.

10. Vasant Sathe in an interview with the author (on tape).

11. Nirmala Deshpande in an interview with the author (on tape).

12. Indira Gandhi in an interview with David Frost for the BBC.

Chapter Two

1. Atal Behari Vajpayee in an interview with the author (on tape).
2. Vasant Sathe in an interview with the author (on tape).
3. R. Venkataraman in conversation with the author (from the author's notebooks).
4. Indira Gandhi to the author, November 1977.

Chapter Three

1. Indira Gandhi's written reply to the Shah Commission's request for her to appear before it and answer queries.
2. Indira Gandhi in reply to a question posed by Justice J.C. Shah, the *Statesman,* 10 January 1978.
3. ibid.

Chapter Four

1. Vasant Sathe in an interview with the author (on tape).
2. *India Today,* 16–31 May 1978.
3. ibid.
4. From the author's notebooks.
5. Indira Gandhi to the author, 28 May 1978.
6. *India Backgrounder,* 18 November 1978, Vol. 3, No. 33(137), p. 1442.
7. ibid., 13 November 1978, p. 1441.
8. *India Today,* 16–30 November 1978.
9. ibid.
10. ibid.
11. ibid.
12. Vasant Sathe in an interview with the author (on tape).

Chapter Five

1. From the author's notebooks.
2. Indira Gandhi in a debate on privileges in the Lok Sabha, 12–18 December 1978.

3. *Sanjay Gandhi,* ed. Maneka Gandhi, Bombay: Vakil, Feffer & Simons Limited, 1980.

4. Indira Gandhi in conversation with the author (from the author's notebooks).

5. Indira Gandhi to the author, 20 December 1978.

6. From the author's notebooks.

7. Indira Gandhi in conversation with the author (from the author's notebooks).

8. ibid.

9. ibid.

Chapter Six

1. Indira Gandhi in conversation with the author (from the author's notebooks.).

2. ibid.

3. *India Today,* 1–15 May 1979.

4. Pandit Jagannath Upadhyaya in conversation with the author (from the author's notebooks).

5. From the author's notebooks.

6. ibid.

7. Benazir Bhutto, *Daughter of the East: An Autobiography,* London: Hamish Hamilton, 1988, p. 3.

8. Kamal Nath in an interview with the author (on tape).

9. *India Today,* 16–31 July 1979.

10. ibid.

11. From the author's notebooks.

12. Extract from a circular letter from Indira Gandhi.

13. From the author's notebooks (an extract from Indira Gandhi's letter to Fori Nehru).

14. Indira Gandhi in an interview with Lord Chalfont for the BBC.

15. *India Today,* 16–31 December 1979.

16. Indira Gandhi to Fori Nehru, 9 October 1979.

17. *India Today,* 16–31 December 1979.

18. Jean-Jacques Servan-Sehreiber in "The Knowledge Revolution".

19. *Statesman.*

20. Indira Gandhi in conversation with the author (from the author's notebooks).

21. ibid.
22. ibid.

PART VIII

1. Jawaharlal Nehru to Indira Gandhi, Ahmednagar Jail, 11 September 1943.
2. Shih Jun Chang, *The Penguin Book of Chinese Verse,* Harmondsworth: Penguin Books, 1962, p. 62.

Chapter One

3. Ganga Saran Sinha in an interview with the author (on tape).
4. Indira Gandhi to Dorothy Norman, 17 April 1958, in *Letters to an American Friend,* New York: Harcourt Brace Publishers, 1985, p. 48.
5. *Business India,* 11 June 1980.
6. ibid.
7. Indira Gandhi in an interview with Raman Luis Acuna, March 1980.

Chapter Two

1. *The Peacock's Egg: Love Poems from Ancient India,* trans. W.S. Merwin and J. Moussaieff Masson, San Francisco: North Point Press, 1981, p. 17.
2. Atal Behari Vajpayee in an interview with the author (on tape).
3. Indira Gandhi in conversation with the author (from the author's notebooks).
4. ibid.
5. The *Hindustan Times,* 28 June 1980.
6. From the author's notebooks.
7. Indira Gandhi to the author (from the author's notebooks).
8. ibid.
9. *India Today,* 16–31 August 1980.
10. Indira Gandhi in conversation with the author (from the author's notebooks).
11. Indira Gandhi to B.K. Nehru, 25 August 1980.

12. Indira Gandhi to Fori Nehru, 30 September 1980.
13. From the author's notebooks.

Chapter Three

1. Indira Gandhi to the author, 7 July 1981.

Chapter Four

1. Indira Gandhi's address to the Sorbonne University, 12 November 1981.
2. From the author's notebooks.

Chapter Five

1. Dr P.C. Alexander in an interview with the author (on tape).
2. Arun Shourie in "Swatting a Bee with an Axe", the *Indian Express,* 6 April 1982.

Chapter Six

1. Indira Gandhi to the author (from the author's notebooks).
2. ibid.
3. ibid.
4. *Remembered Moments,* Delhi: Indira Gandhi Memorial Trust, 1987, p. 79.
5. Indira Gandhi to the author, 22 December 1982.

Chapter Seven

1. Indira Gandhi to J. Krishnamurti, 1 July 1982.
2. *India Today,* 30 April 1984.
3. Indira Gandhi to J. Krishnamurti, 20 January 1983.
4. Indira Gandhi in a speech at the seventh NAM, in "The New Delhi Message", p. 150
5. Indira Gandhi to Dr Erna Sailer, 13 March 1983.

6. Indira Gandhi in a lecture titled "Peace and Development", at the Raul Prebisch Lecture, Belgrade, 8 June 1983.
7. Indira Gandhi to Hiren Mukherji, 9 February 1984, quoted in "In Remembering Indira Gandhi", 1989.

Chapter Eight

1. Indira Gandhi at the inauguration of the Nehru Exhibition, New York, 27 September 1983.
2. Indira Gandhi at the inaugural speech of CHOGM, 23 November 1983.
3. Indira Gandhi in conversation with the author (from the author's notebooks).
4. Indira Gandhi to J. Krishnamurti, 26 December 1983.

Chapter Nine

1. Philip Morrison, 1984.
2. Indira Gandhi in a speech at the 71st session of the Indian Science Congress, Ranchi.
3. The *Economist,* 25 August 1984.

Chapter Ten

1. V.S. Naipaul in "India After Indira Gandhi", the *New York Times,* 3 November 1984.
2. *India Today,* 4 April 1983.
3. Prem Bhatia in an editorial, the *Tribune.*
4. Richard Weintraub, the *Washington Post,* 2 November 1983.
5. Dr P.C. Alexander in an interview with the author (on tape).
6. ibid.
7. Indira Gandhi in an interview with Andrew Neil in "India After Indira", the *Sunday Times,* 6 June 1984.
8. ibid.
9. Indira Gandhi to Erna Sailer, 2 July 1984.
10. Nikhil Chakravartty in a comment on Operation Bluestar, 1984.

Chapter Eleven

1. Indira Gandhi in an interview with Stein Viksveen, *Stavanger Aftenblad,* 6 October 1984.
2. *What I Am,* Delhi: Indira Gandhi Memorial Trust, 1986, p.33.
3. In the Indian myth of Creation, the oceans are churned by the gods and the demons. The mythical mountain, Meru, is the stick used for churning and the rope is the great serpent, Vasuki, on whose coiled head the earth rests. Out of this churning emerges all manifestation. From it arises, a pot of poison and a crucible of nectar of immortality. The pot of poison, if allowed to float freely, will destroy all living things. In order to save Creation, Mahadeva (or Shiva), God of Gods, appears and drinks the poison holding the blue fire in his throat. His name changes to Neelakantha, He of the blue throat, and the earth is saved.
5. Indira Gandhi in conversation with the author (from the author's notebooks).

Chapter Twelve

1. *What I Am,* Delhi: Indira Gandhi Memorial Trust, 1986, p. 16.
2. ibid., pp. 18–19.
3. ibid., p. 35.
4. Indira Gandhi in an interview with the author (on tape).
5. ibid.
6. From the author's notebooks.
7. Abhinav Gupta, a great religious teacher of the tenth century, was the founder of the Kashmir school of Shaivism and a major school of aesthetics. He was also the author of an early treatise on Tantra.
8. An extract from the *Dhanya Shloka,* four verses written by a disciple of Abhinav Gupta, tenth century.
9. *Remembered Moments,* Delhi: Indira Gandhi Memorial Trust, 1987, p.78.
10. ibid.
11. Dr P.C. Alexander in an interview with the author (on tape).
12. The *Rigveda,* Book 10, verse 125, hymn to Vach as the deity Shakti, the power behind the universe.
13. Peter Ustinov, the *New York Times,* 2 November 1984.

13. The *Brhadaranyaka Upnishad,* 3.2.13.

Epilogue

1. Perse St. John, "Winds", New York: Bollingen Foundation Inc., 1953 [reprinted by permission, Princeton University Press.]

Index